THE BOYS

BOOKS BY MARTIN GILBERT

THE CHURCHILL BIOGRAPHY

Volume III: 1914–1916
Document Volume III: (in two parts)
Volume IV: 1917–1922
Document Volume IV: (in two parts)
Volume V: 1922–1939
Document Volume V: 'The Exchequer Years' 1922–1929
Document Volume V: 'The Wilderness Years' 1929–1935
Document Volume V: 'The Coming of War' 1936–1939
Volume VI: 'Finest Hour' 1939–1941
Document Volume VI: 'At the Admiralty' 1939–1940
Document Volume VI: 'Never Surrender' May–December 1940
Volume VII: 'Road to Victory' 1941–1945
Volume VIII: 'Never Despair' 1945–1965

Churchill: A Photographic Portrait
Churchill: A Life

OTHER BOOKS

The Appeasers (with Richard Gott)
The European Powers 1900–1945
The Roots of Appeasement
Children's Illustrated Bible Atlas
Atlas of British Charities
Atlas of American History
Atlas of the Arab-Israeli Conflict
Atlas of British History
Atlas of the First World War
Atlas of the Holocaust
The Holocaust: Maps and Photographs
Atlas of Jewish History
Atlas of Recent History (in preparation)
Atlas of Russian History
The Jews of Arab Lands: Their History in Maps
The Jews of Russia: Their History in Maps
Jerusalem Illustrated History Atlas
Sir Horace Rumbold: Portrait of a Diplomat
Jerusalem: Rebirth of a City
Jerusalem in the Twentieth Century
Exile and Return: The Struggle for Jewish Statehood
Auschwitz and the Allies
The Jews of Hope: The Plight of Soviet Jewry Today
Shcharansky: Hero of Our Time
The Holocaust: The Jewish Tragedy
First World War
Second World War
The Day the War Ended
In Search of Churchill

EDITIONS OF DOCUMENTS

Britain and Germany Between the Wars
Plough My Own Furrow: The Life of Lord Allen of Hurtwood
Servant of India: Diaries of the Viceroy's Private Secretary 1905–1910

THE
BOYS

TRIUMPH OVER ADVERSITY

Martin Gilbert

Douglas & McIntyre

VANCOUVER/TORONTO

96 97 98 99 00 5 4 3 2 1

Douglas & McIntyre
1615 Venables Street
Vancouver, British Columbia
V5L 2H1

Published simultaneously in Great Britain by Weidenfeld & Nicholson,
The Orion Publishing Group, London

Canadian Cataloguing in Publication Data

Gilbert, Martin, 1936-
The boys

ISBN 1-55054-540-X

1. Holocaust, Jewish (1939-1945)—Personal narratives. 2. Holocaust
survivors—Biography. 3. World War, 1939-1945—Concentration camps—
Europe, Eastern. 4. World War, 1939-1945—Children—Europe, Eastern. 5.
Jewish children—Europe, Eastern—History—20th century. I. Title.
D804.195.G54 1996   940.53í18í0922   C96-910462-6

Jacket design by Joseph Mills
Typeset in Great Britain by
Selwood Systems, Midsomer Norton
Printed and bound in Great Britain by
Butler & Tanner Ltd., Frome and London
Printed on acid-free paper

The publisher gratefully acknowledges the assistance
of the Canada Council and of the British Columbia Ministry of
Tourism, Small Business and Culture.

To 'The Boys'
with admiration, affection and gratitude

CONTENTS

ILLUSTRATIONS

Section one

Section two

MAPS

ACKNOWLEDGEMENTS

I AM GRATEFUL FIRST and foremost to Ben Helfgott, who urged me to write this book, and who has helped me at every stage, and over several years, with historical material and guidance. It was his determination that this story should be told that sustained my efforts. I am also grateful to several of the boys whose friendship, even before I started work, has meant a great deal to me; and to all the boys – and girls – who contributed to this account. At the end of these acknowledgements I have listed the names of those who sent me their stories.

I am also grateful, for personal recollections, to Naomi Gryn, and for help with various queries to Rachelle Gryn. Others who have helped me in the preparation of this book are Nadia Abisch, Robert Craig, Ruby Dreihorn, Jean Ettinger, Joseph Finkelstone, Annie Fox, John Freund, Paula Goodman, John Harris, Marilyn Herman, Dr Michael Katz, Bobby Lenzner, Nathan Lewin, Marylyn Light, Ann Lipman, Stanley Medicks, Sarah Meron, Jo-Anne Parker, J. Ramsay Homa, David Turner, Phyllis Vegh and Dr Harold Woolfson.

The Imperial War Museum Sound Archives made available to me the recollections of Aron Zylberszac. Herbert Krosney let me use several of the filmed interviews he made at the boys' fifty-first reunion dinner, and also made valuable textual comments, as did Elsbeth Lindner, who saw the book through its various stages from manuscript to publication. Kay Thomson not only transcribed many of the testimonies but also offered many valuable suggestions with regard to form and content. Tim Aspden turned my rough drafts into maps of the highest quality. Rickie Burman and Carol Segal, of the Jewish Museum, London, ensured that many battered and faded photographs could be reproduced in book form The typescript was read to good effect by Jane Birkett and Jenny Overton. I was assisted in preparing the index by my sons David and Joshua.

My wife Susie has been a constant source of encouragement. She was determined that the story of these 732 men and women, now mostly in their mid-sixties, should be told through their own words, and as a contribution both to the history of the Holocaust, and to the human capacity for hope and renewal.

The following provided me with recollections which I have used in this book. I am grateful to all those who set them down for me. I have made reference by name to every one of those – more than a hundred – who set down their stories for me, and who answered my questions. I have added their place and year of birth.

'Polish boys':

Jack Aizenberg (Staszow) 1928
Chaim Ajzen (Bialobrzegi) 1929
Harry Balsam (Gorlice) 1929
Mayer Bomsztyk (Staszow) 1927
Howard Chandler (Wierzbnik) 1928
Mayer Cornell (Kielce) 1927
Arieh Czeret (Budzanow) 1929
Zvi Dagan (Piotrkow) 1930
Max Dessau (Piotrkow) 1925
Sam Dresner (Warsaw) 1928
Michael Etkind (Lodz) 1925
Stanley Faull (Warsaw) 1929
Sidney Finkel (Piotrkow) 1931
Rose Fogel (Lodz) 1927
John Fox (Tuszyn) 1928
Sam Freiman (Jeziorna) 1926
Morris Frenkel (Lodz) 1925
Simon Gilbert (Rymanow) 1926
Moniek Goldberg (Glowaczow) 1928
Jan Goldberger (Bielsko-Biala) 1927
Henry Golde (Plock) 1929
Rose Goldman (Lodz) 1929
Avraham Goldstein (Miedzyrzec) 1928
Witold Gutt (Przemysl) 1928
Pinchas Gutter (Lodz) 1931/2
Roman Halter (Chodecz) 1927
Ben Helfgott (Piotrkow) 1929
Arek Hersh (Sieradz) 1928
Mayer Hersh (Sieradz) 1926
Jerzy Herszberg (Poznan) 1929
Manfred Heyman (Stettin) 1929
David Hirszfeld (Bobowa) 1929
Abram Huberman (Pulawy) 1926
Chill Igielman (Bialobrzegi) 1928
Solly Irving (Ryki) 1930

Arthur Isaaksohn (Richnow) 1929
Ray Jackson (Lodz) 1927
Minia Jay (Warta) 1927
Sala Kaye (Wolanow) 1927
Kopel Kendall (Bialobzegi) 1928
Kurt Klappholz (Bielsko) 1927
Shimon Klin (Zdunska Wola) 1927
Pinkus Kurnedz (Piotrkow) 1928
Sam Laskier (Warsaw) 1927
Izzie Light (Lodz) 1930
Chaim Liss (Lodz) 1931
Sala Newton-Katz (Lodz) 1929
Michael Novice (Warsaw) 1927
Moshe Nurtman (Warka) 1929
Chaim Olmer (Sosnowiec) 1927
Salek Orenstein (Opatow) 1928
Michael Perlmutter (Opatow) 1928
Arthur Poznanski (Praszka) 1927
Icchak Raizman (Lodz) 1929
Joseph Ribo (Cecylowka) 1932
Bob Roberts (Ozorkow) 1927
Moshe Rosenberg (Cracow) 1927
Sam Rosenblat (Radomsko) 1922
Chaskiel Rosenblum (Konskie) 1928
Naftali Rosenzweig (Ksiaz Wielki) 1929
Jack Rubinfeld (Bircza) 1928
Zisha Schwimmer (Gorlice) 1928
Joshua Segal (Lodz) 1926
Menachem Silberstein (Lodz) 1927
Anna Smith (Lodz) 1930
Harry Spiro (Piotrkow) 1929
Lipa Tepper (Dukla) 1926
Mala Tribich (Piotrkow) 1930
Hersz Wajchendler (Wierzbnik) 1927
Menachem Waksztok (Klodawa) 1927
Alec Ward (Laskarzew) 1927

Sam Weizenbluth (Warsaw) 1926
Krulik Wilder (Piotrkow) 1928
Salamon Winogrodzki (Piotrkow) 1929
Abraham Zwirek (Plock) 1925
Esther Zylberberg (Lodz) 1928
Perec Zylberberg (Lodz) 1924
Aron Zylberszac (Lodz) 1927

'Hungarian boys':
Henry Abisch (Rakhov) 1928
Wilem Frischmann (Uzhgorod) 1931
Victor Greenberg (Majdan) 1929
Alex Gross (Polana) 1928
Roza Gross (Polana) 1930
Hugo Gryn (Beregszasz) 1930
Jacob Hecht (Ruskova)1929
David Herman (Mukacevo) 1931
Steven Kanitz (Kispest) 1927
Steven Pearl (Cuhea) 1928
William Rosenberg (Mukacevo) 1929
Meir Stern (Svalava) 1929
Betty Weiss (Rakhov) 1929
Israel Taub (Mukacevo) 1929
Hershel Taub (Mukacevo) 1927
Maurice Vegh (Rahkov) 1930

Other members of the '45 Aid Society
who have written to me:
Margaret Acher (Warsaw) 1928
Toby Biber (Cracow) 1925
Morris Frenkel (Lodz) 1925
Mark Goldfinger (Rabka Zdroj) 1928
Bronka Gordon (Warsaw) 1928
Michael Honey (Novy Jicin) 1929
Lucy Hyman (Lodz) 1933
Jack Kagan (Novogrudek) 1929
Henry Kaye (Konin) 1927
Rudy Kennedy (Rosenberg) 1927
Joseph Kiersz (Uniejow) 1926
Michael Lee (Lodz) 1924
Joe Perl (Bochkov) 1930
Sam Pivnik (Bedzin) 1926
Lili Pohlmann (Cracow) 1930
Ken Roman (Gorlice) 1926
Zigi Shipper (Lodz) 1930
Edyta Smith (Warsaw) 1929
Barbara Stimmler (Alexandrow
   Kujawski) 1927
Rena Zabielak (Warsaw) 1924

I am grateful to more than fifty other boys whose stories I have been able to tell from articles and recollections which they have published in their Journal and elsewhere. My thanks also go to those helped the boys after their arrival in Britain, and who sent me their recollections: Helen Bamber, Barbara Barnett, Bianca Gordon, Carmel Gradenwitz, Denzil Jacobs, George Lawrence, Maureen Livingstone, Julie Mahrer, Thelma Marcus, Yogi Mayer, Susan Medas, Clinton Silver, Dr Manuel Silver, Joan Stiebel, Reuma Weizman and Arnold Wesker.

INTRODUCTION

FEWER THAN 100,000 JEWS survived the death camps, slave labour camps and death marches of Hitler's Reich. This book is about 732 of those survivors; most of them boys, about eighty of them girls. What these particular 732 have in common, apart from their wartime experiences, is the journey they made together, after liberation, from Europe to Britain. They travelled under the auspices of the Central British Fund, a Jewish organisation which had been active in helping refugees since the rise of Hitler in 1933.

The first group of the 732 youngsters were flown from Prague to Carlisle in August 1945, the second from Munich to Southampton. A third group was flown some months later from Prague to various places in Britain. Later, all three groups were sent to residential hostels throughout Britain.

Most of those who were brought to Britain under this scheme were in their middle to late teens. All but a dozen of them had lost their parents, as well as brothers and sisters, murdered between 1939 and 1945, usually in circumstances of the utmost savagery. Almost all the youngsters had been trapped by the war from the very first days of the German invasion of Poland on 1 September 1939. 'I was eleven years old when the war broke out and the nightmare began,' Henry Golde later wrote. 'I always say that at the age of eleven I became an adult, and five years later I became an old man. That is what I and countless others like me have seen and were forced to live through. Most people will never experience what we did, even if they live to a very old age.'[1]

All of the 732 'boys', as they call themselves – and this includes the girls among them – had seen death at close quarters. Many of them had seen their parents, or brothers and sisters, killed before their eyes, or taken away to a death camp at the time of the deportations from the ghettos. Today, these 'boys', whom I shall refer to in this book without quotation marks, form a group of friends whose companionship is deeply rooted in appalling common memories. A few of them were friends from their pre-war childhood. Some had first met in the ghettos and slave labour camps. Most became friends after their arrival in Britain. Today

---

[1] H. Golde, 'It seems like only yesterday', *Journal of the '45 Aid Society*, No. 18, December 1994.

they are banded together under the auspices of their own charitable organisation, the '45 Aid Society, named after the year in which the first of them came to Britain. Other survivors, who came to Britain later, were drawn to the society for the comradeship which it provided.

The reason there were so few girls among the youngsters brought from Prague is that it was much harder for girls to survive. At each deportation from the ghettos, a few boys under sixteen were selected for slave labour; almost all the girls of a similar age were sent with their parents to the death camps, where all the deportees were murdered. Girls under sixteen who did survive were mostly those who had managed to go into hiding, and were not betrayed. In Poland, this meant hiding for two or three years.

Each year the boys meet for various events, the highlight being their annual reunion to commemorate their liberation; to celebrate their rebirth after their almost inconceivable ordeals. At their reunions, while rejoicing in their daily life, they also recall old times: the years before the war when they enjoyed childhood, the war years when both their childhood and their family life were violently interrupted and destroyed, and their rehabilitation in Britain. This book tells their story, as recounted to me in letters and conversations, or in articles published since 1976 in their journal, *Journal of the '45 Aid Society*. The book begins with their early memories of towns and villages where Jewish life had evolved a pattern, over several hundred years, of family life, worship, and the intensity of a self-contained Jewish environment, surrounded by a mostly alien and often hostile world.

This is in part a gruelling story, which those who lived through it often found painful to set down, as it is painful to read. It is also a story of courage, bravery, survival and renewal, of triumph over adversity. When the Germans invaded Poland in 1939, most of those whose story is told in this book were only nine or ten years old. As youngsters, they were the horrified eyewitnesses of the disintegration of civilised behaviour, and of the carrying out of a monstrous pattern of destruction, the imposition of tyranny and barbarism in the worst form imaginable, and the negation of civilised values. Together with their parents, brothers and sisters, they were prisoners for four years and more in the wartime ghettos, slave labour camps and concentration camps. Today they are among the fewer and fewer remaining witnesses to the cruelties practised in those ghettos and camps. As the Second World War drew to a close, almost all of them were on death marches, some of which lasted for many weeks, and during which many of the marchers either died of exhaustion or starvation, or were shot for being unable to continue. Of those who were sent on the death trains, they were the fortunate ones who survived.

After liberation came the slow, hard process of adjusting to freedom, first in Europe and then in Britain. Their new lives reflect their tenacity. The strength of the bonds that have held them together is mirrored in the close friendships made after the war which have lasted for more than five decades.

I have a personal reason for writing this book. It is twenty-two years since I first met Rabbi Hugo Gryn, a survivor of Auschwitz, and one of those whose story is told in this book. Not only did he encourage me to devote time to recording the fate of the Jews during the Second World War, he also introduced me to the members of the '45 Aid Society, of which he was, and is, a part.

The boys have an incredibly strong sense of comradeship, born of common wartime adversity, and nurtured during their early years together in Britain. At each of their annual reunions, which I have attended over the last eighteen years, and during many talks with them at other times, I was struck by their experiences, and encouraged them to record them. Three years ago one of their most active members, Ben Helfgott, suggested to them that they send me their recollections, and urged me to write an account of their lives. This book is the result. Ben Helfgott, who represented Great Britain in two Olympic Games, as a weightlifter, was able, as chairman of their society, to exhort, cajole and encourage more than a hundred and fifty of his fellow-boys to send me their stories. Some of their accounts were four or five pages long, most ran to twenty or thirty pages, and several filled more than a hundred pages. There is no doubt that every story could have been extended to form a short (or even a long) book on its own. Every account which I received contained aspects of the Holocaust that are not to be found elsewhere: episodes, attitudes and reflections.

Almost all the boys in this book had only three or four years of formal education before the outbreak of war. After that they knew only camps and death, at a time when other children of their age, even in Nazi-dominated Europe, were able to study. In the very years when I was learning the alphabet at school in Toronto, those whose stories are told in this book were in ghettos and slave labour camps. Each one who wrote to me made enormous efforts, both emotionally and physically, to set down a comprehensive account. Some had already felt a need to record their experiences. 'My children always wanted to know my story,' Krulik Wilder wrote on the fiftieth anniversary of his liberation. 'I always found it very difficult to sit down with them and tell them my story, but after fifty years I feel the time is now right to put pen to paper and try to tell them what happened to me and my family and the Jewish people.'[2]

Martin Gilbert
Merton College, Oxford

12 May 1996

---

[2] Israel (Krulik) Wilder, 'Krulik's Story', manuscript, sent to the author, 1 January 1995.

CHAPTER 1

Pre-war Years

EACH OF THE boys has vivid recollections of his or her childhood before the storm. The world in which they lived was, for most of them, the vibrant, bustling, sometimes poor but often thriving world of inter-war Poland. Depending on the part of Poland in which they lived, their parents had been subjects of the Russian Tsar, the Austro-Hungarian Emperor or the German Kaiser. A majority of the boys themselves had been born the citizens of independent Poland, a State created after the First World War, at the dawn of what so many people believed would be a new era of peace, prosperity and liberty. The Jewish minorities of the new sovereign states of Eastern and Central Europe had been promised rights and representation that had been denied them under the earlier imperial regimes. The Jews aspired, some of them fervently, to become integral members of the new societies, and to participate fully in the social and cultural life of the country.

The boys whose story is told in this book came from towns and villages whose Jewish communities played a significant part in the daily life of the region. Every one of these communities was destroyed during the Second World War. The memories which the boys guard are among the last living testimonies to the Jewish world of those towns, fifty-five years after that world was destroyed forever. Sometimes they are the sole remaining witnesses to the pre-war life of their town. 'We, the "Boys" who went through it all,' Menachem Waksztok has written, 'came from the communities of Europe where Jewish life had a form, a culture, a pattern and a light.' His own pre-war community was a small town in Poland, Klodawa. In this 'small one-eyed town', he later wrote, the two thousand Jews were the majority. 'Most of the shops, tailoring concerns, watchmakers, bakers and timber merchants, also the dentist and doctor practices were in their hands. The men went to the synagogue for morning and evening prayers – in fact the one synagogue and *shtiebl*[1] were their meeting-places – centres of their lives.

'We children, from the age of four, received our education in the

---

[1] A house of prayer; often a small room in a house or an apartment block.

cheder.[2] One went there as a matter of course, to learn to read and write, by stages progressing to the learning of Chumash, Rashi, and so on.[3] Illiteracy was unknown, and no matter how poor or limited physical and day-to-day life was, life of the mind and spirit was very rich indeed.'[4]

'We celebrated all the Jewish holidays,' recalled Joshua Segal, born Jehoszua Cygelfarb in the industrial city of Lodz on 24 December 1926, 'and every Friday night my mother lit the candles, and the whole family and guests would be there for dinner. Our house was an open house, with visitors and relatives coming from out of town, showing up all the time.'[5]

In the town of Bydgoszcz, Sam Rosenblat, five years older than Joshua Segal, had begun to play violin solos with the town orchestra from the age of nine. 'The composers were Schubert, Mendelssohn etc.,' he wrote. 'I also performed at Jewish gatherings, accompanied by my older sister at the piano. As a payment, I would receive a cake.

'At the age of seventeen, when I was in my last class, my parents started to plan for me to continue my studies in Paris, where my uncles lived. Unfortunately the war broke out and all plans for any musical future were abandoned. After the war, when I was in England, I picked up a violin, attempted to play it, and realised that with my damaged fingers (a result of labour in the camps) and five years of interruption, I could no longer think about a career as a violinist.'[6]

'I have very fond memories of my childhood,' Rose Fogel, from Lodz, recollected. 'My father had great compassion for humanity, was active in many organisations. He had a wonderful sense of humour, which helped us in the worst of times. We all went to a private Yiddish school. My father loved to read. He introduced us to classical literature when we were very young.'[7]

Another girl among the boys, Rose Kalman, was from a poor family in Lodz. Her father Yitzhak had been a prisoner of war in Russia from 1914 to 1919, 'not a strong character or strong in health', she recalled. It was her mother, a wigmaker, who was the breadwinner in the family. There were six children. 'We were often hungry, and I wore very old clothes which were second-hand, my shoes also. Our flat consisted of a

---

[2] Religious classes for children.

[3] Chumash: the five books of Moses (from the Hebrew word *chamesh*: five); Rashi: born in France in 1040, died 1105 (his name is an acronym of Rabbi Solomon ben Isaac) wrote a commentary that clarified the biblical text. It remains one of the most influential and comprehensive works of biblical exegesis.

[4] Menachem Waksztok, 'Letter from Israel', *Journal of the '45 Aid Society*, No. 3, April 1977.

[5] Joshua Segal (Jehoszua Cygelfarb), letter to the author, 17 February 1995.

[6] Sam Rosenblat, 'My Other Life in Another Time', manuscript, sent to the author, 24 January 1995.

[7] Rose Fogel (Dajch), letter to the author, 18 January 1995.

room which was a bedroom and sitting-room, and a kitchen where part of it was a bedroom. The older ones usually slept in the kitchen and the rest slept with my parents in the same bed. My father loved to sing, and I remember one memorable morning when my mother was already up – he was sitting up in bed with us at the other end and sang to us. It was a magical moment. He had such a beautiful voice.' Yitzhak Kalman enjoyed a game of cards, but, his daughter recalled, 'his luck was often down. My mother would be angry with him and there were many rows.'

Rose Kalman remembered her first 'real and serious experience' in Lodz. She was on her way home, having taken some food to her sister Hinda, a dressmaker. 'On the way back I stopped to admire a lovely hat shop. As I was gazing at the merchandise, a young Polish woman also stopped and stood next to me. She pushed me and then called me a dirty Jew ("Parszywa Zydowka"). Defiantly I called her a dirty Pole ("Polska Hamka"). I ran off and she followed me. I ran into an apartment building up to the third floor. It was so dark with just a few doors. I knocked on one, and as luck would have it, it turned out to be a Jewish lady. I could hear footsteps coming up behind me. I told her I was being chased and she hid me. A few minutes later my pursuer also knocked on the same door asking if the lady had seen me. She denied having seen me and my pursuer left the building. I was very frightened to leave this safe house, but when I did, fortunately my pursuer had left the building.'[8]

Like Rose Kalman, many boys have recollections of the darker side of life in Poland when they were young. Recalling his home town, Klodawa, Menachem Waksztok reflected more than half a century later: 'It was a very anti-Semitic area before the war.'[9]

Pinchas Gutter was born in Lodz in 1931 or 1932; he cannot remember the year, and none of his documents from childhood survived the war. An orthodox boy, who wore Hassidic sidecurls, he later recalled how, 'walking the streets of Lodz with my mother could be anxiety-provoking, as she would often be accosted by strange non-Jewish men who must have assumed that she was a Polish Christian because of her looks. We often used to cross from one side of the street to the other to avoid confrontations. I clearly recall a specific instance when a well-dressed Pole challenged my mother angrily, saying, "How can a beautiful Polish woman like you serve rotten Jews!"'[10]

Kurt Klappholz was born in the Polish town of Bielsko-Biala, only fifteen miles from the Czech-Polish border. 'Around the mid-1930s', he

[8] Rose Kalman (Goldman), letter to the author, July 1995.
[9] Menachem Waksztok, in conversation with the author, 30 December 1994.
[10] Pinchas Gutter, recollections, letter to the author, 23 March 1996.

recalled, 'I remember being very puzzled that my father was not President of Poland – he seemed to me a well-educated man, and I thought that was a position to which he would have been ideally suited. It will not surprise you that I found it hard to account for the fact that he did not occupy that position. I attributed it to anti-Semitism, which was widespread in Poland.'[11]

Sam Dresner was born in Warsaw. The city's 350,000 Jews – a third of the population of the Polish capital – made it the second largest Jewish community in the world, after New York. 'We were living in great poverty in a basement in one room,' Sam Dresner later wrote. 'I had a younger sister. My father, who was a carpenter, also had his working bench in the same room. Despite that I never felt deprived of anything, probably due to my mother's care. We lived in Ulica Prosta, 105. It was a mixed district of Poles and Jews living in the same tenement houses almost in equal proportions. In spite of occasional beatings I received from Polish boys, I seem to remember being quite proud of Poland and being Polish.'[12]

Salek Falinower was also born in Warsaw. His father had inherited a metal foundry and engineering business which had been owned and operated by his family for seven generations. 'I lived in Twarda Street, Warsaw, with my parents, Naftali and Rachel Falinower (née Frydman) and one brother (Gerald – Chiel Zalman Falinower) and one sister (Henia Falinower),' Stanley Faull, as he became, later wrote. 'I started school at the age of five, at the same school as my elder brother. He was five years older than me, and my sister about seven years older than me. In 1937, after my brother's thirteenth birthday, he was invited by my mother's family in Brighton, England, to come to England for educational purposes, to study the metal foundry and engineering industry. It was planned that he would return to Warsaw after obtaining suitable qualifications, and he duly left for England.

'The existing business was more than 150 years old and very antiquated. It was my father's wish that I too should go to England to be educated when I was thirteen (in 1943) so that in the future my brother and I would be able to improve and modernise the business and run it together, with the benefit of whatever up-to-date technology was available.'[13] When war broke out, Salek Falinower was nine years old. His journey to Britain, and reunion with his brother, was to come only after five and a half years of torment.

A third Warsaw boy was Meir Sosnowicz. When he was ten years

[11] Kurt Klappholz, 'Testimony', transcribed tape, 1995.
[12] Sam Dresner, letter to the author, 28 January 1995.
[13] Stanley Faull (Salek Falinower), letter to the author, 12 October 1995.

old, 'I was rushed to the hospital,' he recalled, 'with what turned out to be a ruptured appendix. It nearly cost me my life. While the doctors were doing their part to help me, my mother went to the *rebbe*[14] to ask what else could be done for me. The rebbe told her to give me an additional name, Alter (meaning Old One), and he would say prayers for me. Later, when I had recovered, my father took me to the rebbe so that I could give him some *tz'doko* (charity) money myself in thankfulness for my recovery. The extra name was now a subject for teasing by my brother David, who called me "Alter Mayer" which is a pun for "old carrot" in Yiddish. My family called me Moniek. To celebrate my recovery, my parents gave me a violin.'[15]

Berek Obuchowski (now Bob Roberts) was born on 28 January 1927 in the town of Ozorkow. About twenty per cent of the town's population were Jews. He was sent to the local State school, and three times a week would go to cheder after school. Polish was the language spoken at school, Yiddish at home. 'I lived with my parents, grandfather (maternal) and my two sisters and a brother,' he later wrote. 'I was the youngest. Our house was on one level, with an orchard at the back with apple and pear trees, and gooseberry and redcurrant bushes. We had a couple of horses and carts which my father owned, and hired out as transport with two drivers. We had a shop attached at the side, where my father sold groceries and hardware. We also owned some further accommodation at the side of our house which was let to four families, each of them renting one large room. In the summer season, we had a kiosk – seven kilometres away in a summer resort between Ozorkow and Zgierz where my mother and older sister would go to sell provisions by the roadside – I would go there in my summer holiday from school to help out.

'On Saturdays, the men in our family, including myself, would go to services at a shtiebl, which was in the same road where we lived. We used to make a *succah*[16] each year in one of the sheds attached to our home. We were moderately religious, and my mother would make her own *challas* and *lokshen* for Shabbas.[17]

---

[14] A learned man: the *rebbe* (who was also an ordained rabbi) was a teacher and mentor within the community, and in many *shtetls* the ultimate legislator on local Jewish religious issues.

[15] Michael Novice (Meir Sosnowicz), recollections, manuscript, sent to the author, June 1995.

[16] A specially-constructed booth, built next to a home, or on a balcony, made of branches, leaves and fruits, in which Jews eat and sleep during the festival of Succoth (Succot), the harvest festival.

[17] Challas: the woven bread over which a special prayer is said on Friday night (the Hebrew, as opposed to Yiddish, plural is *challot*; the singular, *challa*). Lokshen: noodles; especially popular on Friday night – when they can be served in three separate forms: first in chicken soup, then with the main chicken dish, and finally as a sweet pudding. Shabbas (also Shabbes): the Sabbath, the period

'At school I remember one incident when I intervened in a fight between a couple of bullies punching a Jewish boy, and I dragged one of the bullies into the River Bzura and held him there with his feet in the freezing ice. I was quite tough as a youngster, and from that time at school, I was never bullied, although the mother of the non-Jewish boy came the next day and abused me verbally.'[18]

Sam Freiman, from the town of Konstancin-Jeziorna, near Warsaw, later wrote: 'I remember one day in summer I wanted to make extra money, so I set up a table outside our shop with bottles of soda water with juice and sold it in glasses. At the same time my uncle was sitting on the shop stairs and a Christian boy went by and hit my uncle on the head. He bit his tongue and screamed. My father ran out from the shop with a hammer in his hand. When the boy ran away he threw the hammer. We heard the boy shouting "Jesus". The boy's brother was a policeman. He came round and told my father that it served him right.'[19]

Alec Ward was born in the town of Laskarzew. 'When I was liberated from slave labour and concentration camps,' he wrote, 'I did not remember my date of birth. After arriving in England in 1945, the Red Cross traced my records from Buchenwald concentration camp, which stated I was born on 1 March 1927.' While he was still an infant, Alec Ward's mother died in childbirth. His father, Szmul Mosze Warszaw, was a glazier, going from street to street seeking out broken windows to repair, carrying his glass in a frame on his back. When his father remarried, Alec Ward's stepmother, Sara Bronstein, looked after him and his sister Lea. 'When I was a young boy,' he recalled, 'I sang in the synagogue. My parents were very proud of my singing voice. One day when I sang in our cellar, my stepmother called our neighbours to hear my rendition of a synagogue service. I was extremely embarrassed when I came up from the cellar and saw our neighbours clapping.'

Szmul Mosze Warszaw moved several times, in search of a living, first to Laskarzew, then to Parysow, and finally to Magnuszew. Looking back, Alec Ward recalled the pattern of religious life in his youth: 'The synagogue in Parysow was very beautiful, with a dome and a stone floor. The cantor's voice reverberated round the synagogue which is still very vivid in my memory. On Friday afternoon the Jewish town crier proclaimed the coming of the Sabbath and announced it was time to go to the synagogue. On Saturday afternoon the whole Jewish community seemed to walk in the streets (*spatzerin*). On Purim people were criss-

---

from Friday sunset to Saturday sunset when all work ceases, and when the family is together at home and in synagogue; also Shabbat (the Hebrew as opposed to the Yiddish form).

[18] Bob Roberts (Berek Obuchowski), recollections, manuscript, February 1996, sent to the author, 4 March 1996.

[19] Sam Freiman, recollections, sent to the author, June 1995.

crossing the streets with presents, consisting of freshly baked cakes and biscuits. On Yom Kippur in the ladies' part of the synagogue one could hear a great amount of crying. On Simchat Torah, there was great rejoicing by the whole community, and on Pessach, in our new clothes, of which we were so very proud.'[20]

Alec Ward also recalled life in Magnuszew in his childhood. 'Although there was a certain amount of poverty in Magnuszew,' he later wrote, 'there was also a great amount of laughter and happiness. I remember many Jewish weddings which lasted for two days with beautiful Klezmer music, and Brit Milahs[21] which we as children, were very happy to attend as we received sweets and cakes.'[22]

Every boy has memories of the years before 1939. 'I remember, as a small boy,' Menachem Silberstein recollected, 'being taken by my father to the Mikva,[23] where all the bearded and serious-looking men came to submerge themselves in the steamy hot well. As soon as they undressed they began behaving like little boys, fooling about, making jokes and singing Yiddish songs.'[24]

The town of Klodawa, Menachem Waksztok recalled, was typical of the many shtetls in Poland 'where the Jews felt themselves to be Jews without any doubt. In fact, we did not think of ourselves as being in the Diaspora. We were in Klodawa, and it was the *goyim* – the non-Jews – who were the outsiders.'[25]

Abraham Zwirek was born in the town of Plock on 18 December 1925. His father and one of his uncles were partners in a small workshop which produced hardware and galvanised roofing for farmhouses. 'I would often go to the workshop, which was in the same street in which we lived,' he recalled, 'and watch my father at work. This experience helped to save me in the camps during the war, as I would pretend that I was a skilled worker in hardware and roofing.' My first recollection,' Zwirek continued, 'was at the age of four years when my father and I waved goodbye to my aunt and her baby daughter on the banks of the River Vistula. They were emigrating to England to join my uncle who

---

[20] Alec Ward, 'My Story', manuscript, sent to the author, 31 May 1995. Purim: the festival recalling the triumph of Mordechai and Esther over Haman, the Persian ruler who sought to exterminate the Jews. Yom Kippur: the day of fasting and repentance. Simchat Torah: the festival of the Rejoicing in the Law. Pessach: Passover, celebrating the Exodus from Egypt.

[21] Circumcisions.

[22] Alec Ward, 'My Story', manuscript, sent to the author, 31 May 1995.

[23] A ritual bath (also, in its Yiddish form, Mikveh).

[24] Menachem (Mendel) Silberstein, 'Here and Now', *Journal of the '45 Aid Society*, No. 3, April 1977, page 21.

[25] Menachem Waksztok, 'Letter from Israel', *Journal of the '45 Aid Society*, No. 3, April 1977, page 7.

had emigrated a year earlier to escape poverty and anti-Semitism in the hope of a brighter future.' The baby daughter, Ida, was only a year old: hers, in the light of hindsight, was a journey to life.

Of Jewish life in Plock, Zwirek wrote: 'On Saturday afternoons many of the Jewish men and women would walk by the banks of the River Vistula with their families, and the mothers of young babies would often sit on the benches breast-feeding them. I attended the local Jewish school from Monday to Friday mornings – all the lessons taken from Polish textbooks – and in the afternoons I would go to Hebrew classes and learn about Judaism for three hours per day. At our home the conversation was always in the Yiddish language; my mother and grandfather were very religious. My father was not very orthodox. He was a councillor on the local borough council, and also a representative of the Jewish community regarding welfare and trade. On the outskirts of Plock there were two barracks housing two battalions of the Polish Army, the 4th Cavalry and the 8th Artillery. Among these soldiers were two hundred Jewish men. My father would negotiate with the military authorities each year before Passover to allow these men to have leave so that they might have their meals for eight days in the local Jewish Community Hall. On the second Seder night[26] I would go along with my father to join in, and then I would go each day on my own. I was the only child there, and I thoroughly enjoyed myself with the soldiers.

'I would play each day after classes with my Jewish and non-Jewish friends who lived nearby, either in the yard or street outside our apartment, or football by the banks of the river about ten minutes away. Not far from my school was a Catholic school. Very often on my way home, the boys from that school would abuse us verbally and shout out, "Dirty Jews go to Palestine". They would either throw stones at us – if we were in the minority – when we would run home or back to the safe area of our own school, or, if we walked home and there were quite a few of us, the Catholic boys would lie in wait in groups. We would try to defend ourselves by fighting it out. We were most often the losers, as there were many of them. The average age at that time would be between nine and thirteen years old. When I came home, cut and bruised, my father would be upset, but encouraged me to come home in a large group with my friends, and to stand and defend ourselves. If this was not possible he would sometimes come to meet me. Up until 1939 our family got on quite well with our non-Jewish neighbours and they respected us. After the war began I cannot truthfully say that this was always the case.'[27]

[26] The second night of Passover.
[27] Abraham Zwirek, letter to the author, 12 December 1994.

Many boys remember the cry 'Go to Palestine!' being hurled at them with various offensive epithets. Almost every Jewish family in Poland knew someone who had made the journey, and the commitment, to live in the Jewish National Home.[28] The Tarbut schools, with Hebrew as their main language of instruction, were a strong stimulus to thoughts of emigration. So too were the Zionist youth movements, which made emigration to Palestine their goal. The Arab riots of 1936, in which dozens of Jews were killed, including several recent immigrants from Poland, cast a pall of apprehension over the Zionist zeal. The boys, most of them aged eight or nine at the time, were too young to have become part of an active Zionist group, but they were aware nevertheless of the ferment around them. 'The two things that were preoccupying my parents,' Ben Helfgott, living in Piotrkow, recalled, 'were the persecution of the Jews in Germany, and the killings that were taking place in Palestine.'[29]

Ben Helfgott's parents, at the instigation of his strongly Zionist mother, obtained permits to emigrate to Palestine. His father was about to sell his share in their flour mill when his mother – Ben's grandmother – dissuaded him from leaving. 'It seemed inconceivable to her,' Ben later recalled, 'that he should want to leave Poland with his wife and children for a distant land where riots and disturbances were commonplace and where the future was uncertain. My grandmother was more persuasive than my mother. The arrangements were unmade and the tickets were never bought.' Relations between mother and mother-in-law became severely strained. Later, during the war, Ben's mother blamed his grandmother for their plight. 'When we sat around at home during the long curfews,' he later wrote, 'I pieced together the truth of what had happened.'[30]

During the carefree years, Ben Helfgott made his mark among the young boys of Piotrkow. His sister Mala recalled, almost sixty years later: 'Ben was very popular with his friends and always a leader. I remember one day, in Piotrkow before the war, coming across a group of boys and one of them saying, "Don't start with her, she is Ben Helfgott's sister".'[31]

Pinkus Kurnedz, also from Piotrkow, remembered his parents being 'very Zionistically minded'. His father 'used to spend a lot of time helping people to emigrate to Palestine'.[32] Amongst the Jews of Poland, Perec

[28] A phrase, and a concept, given legal authority by the British Government's Balfour Declaration, issued in 1917 and confirmed by the League of Nations in 1922. Jews from Poland made up the largest single group of immigrants to Palestine between 1922 and 1939.

[29] Ben Helfgott, in conversation with the author, 14 November 1995.

[30] Ben Helfgott, 'Memories of Poland', *In Face of Adversity*, Frank Cass, London, 1991, page 146.

[31] Mala Tribich (née Helfgott), recollections, letter to the author, 24 March 1996.

[32] Pinkus Kurnedz, letter to the author, 8 December 1994.

Zylberberg from nearby Lodz, recalled, 'the idea of a national home in Palestine was being trumpeted louder than ever'.[33] Shimon Klin, from Zdunska Wola, remembered his stepmother's sister, who lived in Jerusalem, sending his father a much-prized Palestine Certificate, enabling the family to emigrate. 'Because of the Arab riots,' he recalled, 'my father was advised to wait until the country was more peaceful.'[34]

Moishe Nurtman also remembered the Palestine dimension, in the context of local anti-Jewish actions, and of rabbinical hostility to Zionism. His home town was Warka, on the River Pilica, sixty kilometres south of Warsaw. 'Non-Jews in Warka had an accepted resentment towards us, which I could not absorb as a child,' he wrote. 'I could not understand why. As a child I remember we had a shop. There were Poles whom we called Fascists; they would stand outside our shop and not let the Poles buy from us. I used to watch this and could not understand it. It was a boycott against Jews. The police let it happen and my family were unable to prevent it. The customers – some kept away, others didn't. The Fascists didn't appear to use violence, but their presence was enough, by starting arguments. They did not wear uniforms. But they were known people – two or three of them outside the shop. The boycott went on until war broke out. My parents didn't have to mention this because it was something you felt. They believed the Lord would put things right. We were a religious family.

'Father read papers on politics. At one time we were going to emigrate to Australia, so he faced a difficult decision whether to leave Poland or stay, considering there were so many of us. Emigrating to Palestine; it was a dream. Father was religious, and at the time the rabbis were not too keen on emigration to Palestine, and would not advise it, so I believe this would have put a terrible strain on my father. At the time their philosophy was: rule yourselves according to the Bible. They believed, according to the Bible, that when the Messiah came the dead would rise, and all the Jews would roll themselves to the Holy Land.[35] So it was thought that it was not practical to leave for Palestine at that time, as the rabbis talked of such a journey in terms of the coming of the Messiah.'[36]

Jona Fuks, from the small town of Tuszyn, near Lodz, was born on 2 February 1928. He has vivid recollections of his schooldays, of life in

[33] Perec Zylberberg, recollections, diary entry for 23 July 1993.

[34] Shimon Klin, letter to the author, 16 January 1995.

[35] Jewish belief includes the concept that when the Messiah comes there will be a physical resurrection of the dead, and the gathering together in Jerusalem of all the Jewish dead from all over the world. According to one tradition, the bodies of the dead will roll themselves to Jerusalem. Many pious Jews wish to be buried in the Jewish cemetery on the Mount of Olives, so that they will not have so far to roll, and will reach the Temple Mount, across the Valley of Jehoshaphat, all the sooner.

[36] Moishe Nurtman, letter to the author, March 1995.

the town, and of the political debates among his elders. Recalling this time, John Fox (as he became) wrote: 'I was in a class with forty-three children. Three of us were Jewish. When the teacher walked out of the classroom the Poles would throw things at us, curse and spit on us. When the teacher returned she would pretend that nothing had happened. We wouldn't complain because nothing would be done about it, and the other children would beat us up if we squealed on them. Many days I would come home from school with a bloody nose or a swollen lip from getting beaten up in school. Every morning when the school prayer was offered everybody knelt down except the Jewish children. I would not kneel down, of course, and I would get hit from the back and from the front. The teachers would see me getting beaten but they would not interfere.

'These beatings went on in school almost every day. I would come home and cry and complain and say that I didn't want to go to school any more. But my father would insist that I had to go to the Polish school. He would say that if I didn't know how to read and write when I grew up I wouldn't get anywhere in life. He insisted that the only way I would get an education, apart from our religion, was in the Polish schools.

'Most of my extended family was involved in the tailoring business. They had their own workshops. Sometimes they worked together and other times they had separate ventures. Most of the clothing enterprises were made up of the members of one family and two or three – or up to a dozen – workers who would work for that family. My father had pressers, tailors, and buttonhole makers working for him. The work was strictly seasonal. For the winter my father and his brothers manufactured men's coats with inner linings and wadding made of sheepskin. In the summer they made suits and light wear.

'In the season I worked on a sewing machine. We had treadle machines in those days. I helped my father. As soon as a child could walk they started helping. My entire family, my mother, my brother and sister helped. My father was the mechanic for all the machinery that we had. We had to cannibalise all the machines to keep things working. We never threw anything away.

'Because there were seasons in the clothing business we worked three months and we were off three months. In the summer-time my father had a grocery store in the woods where people came from Lodz for two months to spend their vacation. There were small houses in the woods, which was like a resort. The grocery store that we had was like a general store. You could buy anything there from a pencil to butter and fish. I would go to market with my father and help him buy the things that he sold in the store.

'My father worked very hard. All of the Jewish men worked very hard. In those days you had to be very competitive. We went to the markets in our town and in neighbouring towns to sell our wares. My father made a living, but it was a very hard life. If he was finished with tailoring because the season was over he had to do other things to make a living. He even brought fish to town in barrels and sold them. Every Tuesday there was a market and farmers would bring in their products and we would buy things from them and they would buy things from us. If we didn't make sales on Tuesday we suffered the rest of the week.

'My father would go to other markets to sell his wares. He would go in with other people and they would rent a wagon and two horses and go to markets in towns that were ten or fifteen miles away. We sold mostly topcoats and heavy overcoats for drivers who drove carts at night. The material was about a half an inch thick, because it was very cold in Poland in the winter-time. I remember that my father had to use a hammer to turn the lapels because the material was so thick.

'Life for the workers that my father hired was very difficult. They made a living when they worked but when the season was over they had to borrow money from my father. When they came back to work they earned much less because they had to give my father some of the money to pay off their debt. They were poor. Everybody was poor. Life was a constant struggle. But no matter how poor you were there was always food for everyone. There were kosher butchers and grocery stores where people could buy on credit. Very seldom did anyone pay with cash in one of these stores. At the end of the month you went in and settled your bill. Everyone waited until the end of the month to get paid. If you didn't get paid from this person then the next person didn't get paid and so on.

'Life for my mother and the other women was very hard. She took care of the cash, and the laundry, and she cooked all day. We had a stove that was heated with wood and coal which had the dual purpose of heating the house and being used for cooking. We had a heater with tiles that you could put coals in, to keep it hot the whole night. The women did everything. They were the movers and the shakers behind the men. The men worked, but the women had control of the incoming and outgoing money.

'Women played a significant role in the community, too. It was up to the women, including my mother, to help families that were in need of food and clothing. If someone died in a poor family it was the duty of the women to see that the children were taken care of. Especially in the winter when these families didn't have any heat, the women in the community would be sure that their needs were met.

'Grandfathers and grandmothers didn't go to live in an old people's home. We didn't discard them. They stayed with us until the end. But if the grandparents had too many children there could be a problem. The family had to get together and decide when they were going to take the grandparents into their homes.

'Before the war my father had a lot of Polish friends. We had a certain kinship with the Poles. Even the Polish police would come into our home and sit around and talk with us. My father also had quite a few German friends before the war. At Christmas-time the Poles were busy engaging in holiday festivities and they left the Jews alone. It was only at Easter when we would be affected. My father would tell us not to walk too far outside the city because when the Poles came out of church they were looking to start fights with Jews. They were told in the Gospel in church that Jews had killed Christ. They would shout that we "Filthy Jews" should get the hell out of Poland and go to Palestine. They told us that we did not belong in Poland.

'Those were very trying times for Jews in Poland, especially for the Jews who had Polish neighbours. The Polish children would throw stones, and even though their fathers might tell them not to do so, they didn't break their arms, they didn't stop them, if you know what I mean. But we had a Polish maid whose name was Veronica. From the day I was born we had a Polish maid who lived in our house. I remember the day that she got married, in 1938. We went to her wedding and my family gave her furniture and other gifts as presents. She spoke Yiddish like a Jewish person and she was a part of our family.

'Jews were organised in Poland at the time. We had our own civil guard which we paid taxes to support. We were taught to carry a stick and to pretend that it was a gun. Some of us belonged to Zionist organisations. My father believed in Jabotinsky, the leader of the Zionist Revisionists at the time. We all had uniforms which we wore on certain occasions. I belonged to the Revisionist youth organisation called Betar, which believed that the only way Jews could survive was through force. We believed at the time that the only way we could get Palestine for the Jews was through force. We felt that we could not get a homeland for Jews in Palestine through political action. My father was one of the leaders of the Zionist organisation in our town. My uncle was also a councillor. Jews were allowed to have one or two men on the town council. We were constantly talking about going to Palestine. Zionists were going to Palestine all the time, but we could not all go.

'Throughout the 1920s and the 1930s Jewish youth was changing. We were beginning to move away from the strictly religious point of view and we were becoming more practical. All of the Jews that we knew were involved in discussions, and were listening to speakers and readers, because they were hungry for information and understanding.

People knew what was going on in the world even though they were only working people. They made it their business not to be ignorant. Even though many people were not educated, they were well versed in history. They knew about the rebellions against the Tsar and other important events in history.

'Jews would get together, on Saturday or Sunday or in the evenings, in Zionist clubs, which had speakers nearly every week. We came with our fathers and we listened and when we got home we would ask questions. Everybody was hungry for education. I think that European Jews were the most knowledgeable people on earth, because they wanted to know about the world around them.

'Those early years of my life were good times for me. I knew everybody by their first name and everybody knew me. We had a good feeling toward one another. It was our domain. There was time for everything. Life was good. I felt very comfortable being Jewish in those days. I was very proud of being a Jew. We felt that God was hovering over us and taking care of us, and that he would protect us. I absolutely believed this to be the case. We truly felt that God would protect us, and we did not believe in violence. We were so indoctrinated with our religion and our beliefs that I think that it hurt us when the war came.'[37]

Leopold Tepper, known as Lipa, was born in Dukla, a small town in southern Poland only fourteen kilometres from the Slovak border, on 30 November 1926. There he lived with his father and mother, Zelig and Eva Tepper, and his elder sister Chana. 'There also lived in Dukla my mother's four sisters and their families,' he wrote. 'One other sister and her family lived in Stropkov in Slovakia. Of all these families only one other person remains alive today, my cousin Shimon who lives in Israel.'

Today, Lipa Tepper lives in London. His earliest recollection of childhood in Poland was when his father took him to religious school when he was three, 'and I sat on his shoulders and he carried me all through the town and into cheder. I distinctly remember my first teacher in cheder whose name was Chaim Mordechai Malumed and he taught me the *aleph-bet*[38] and to read Hebrew in the *siddur*.[39] Subsequent to that I went to very many different teachers as far as my Hebrew education was concerned.

'At the age of seven I attended school, secular school, and it was intended that I would go to that school from the age of seven to fourteen. I got up in the morning and went to school at 8 o'clock, returning home just after 1.00 p.m. and after lunch I would then go to cheder and

---

[37] John Fox (Jona Fuks), recollections, Gala Recognition Dinner brochure, Hilton Hotel, Philadelphia, 8 September 1993.

[38] The ABC (in Yiddish, Alef-Beis).

[39] The prayer book.

return home at approximately 6.30 to 7.00 in the evening. My father and my mother always impressed on me that I was not a child, and kept reminding me that a Jewish boy does not play with stupid things and does not do things which all other boys do because he is Jewish and therefore he has got duties to perform and things to do which are unlike anybody else's.'

The problems at the secular school in Dukla were common throughout inter-war Poland. The predominance of orthodox Jews was likewise commonplace. So too was the stress among Jewish parents on a devout and thorough religious education. As Lipa Tepper recalled: 'Attending school was a pretty hard thing because we always used to get called names and we kept being told by the little Christian boys and girls with whom we attended school that we killed their God – something which I could never understand, but since it was told to me, it must have been true. I never actually learned Jewish history as such. I learned first of all to pray, then Chumash and Rashi and from then on I went on to Gemara[40] and things pertaining to that but I never actually went through the Tanach[41] as such and I have a scant knowledge of Jewish history.

'My education at school was not of a very high calibre in view of the fact that, on recollection, I had no motivation for it. I dare say if I had been motivated I would have done better. I wore the traditional garb of a religious Jewish boy, i.e. a dark grey long frock coat and a black velvet peaked cap. I had side curls, or *peyot*.

'My father and my mother considered themselves enlightened Jews. My mother was the survivor of a cholera epidemic at the age of seventeen in the First World War. Incidentally this cholera epidemic killed her mother and father and two of her sisters. It claimed a lot of people in the Dukla area, and my mother, as a girl of seventeen, was evacuated to Vienna, where she stayed in a girls' home. Later, she went out to work and was forced to look after her three younger sisters and send them to school, etc.

'She became absolutely fluent in German and she always used to tell me that her teacher commented that the worst person to teach German was a person who spoke Yiddish. He must have been a Jewish teacher, because he said that they could not divide the two languages and always interspersed one with the other.

'My father was a corporal in the Austrian army and he was taken prisoner of war. I remember him talking about Bosnia-Herzegovina and

---

[40] A record of the rabbinical discussions, compiled from 200 BC to AD 600, examining pertinent issues of Jewish law, both religious and civil, and recording the ongoing debate among the rabbinical sages on the nature and meaning of the oral tradition.

[41] The Bible, consisting of three sections which form the acronym of the word Tanach: Torah, the five books of Moses; Nevi'im, Prophets; and Ketuvim, writings).

Sarajevo and things like that and I dare say it must have been in that area that he was taken prisoner. He spent five years in Siberia. He therefore spoke Russian in addition to fluent German, Polish, Yiddish and suchlike.

'My parents seemed to have lost the shtetl outlook, in that they felt that certain things which people in the town did were not so much uncivilised, as unnecessary from a religious point of view. They used to talk politics which I obviously did not understand but I got snatches of things that remain with me to this day. For instance, I heard the names of Nelson and Lady Hamilton mentioned in our house. I also heard the names of Karl Liebknecht and Rosa Luxemburg mentioned. I did not know in what connection or what they were supposed to mean but I recollect today those were things that my parents often talked about.

'Although my parents were devoutly religious, they had what I would term today an egalitarian point of view, in that they believed that the suffering of the masses should be alleviated. I do not know if they had socialist ideals. I could not define in those days what that meant but their ideals were definitely egalitarian – without doubt.

'My father worked in a peculiar job. There was a sawmill in our town belonging to a Jewish company called Handler, and my father was periodically engaged to go to a village, buy a small forest, engage the staff, fell the timber, and ship it into the town for the sawmill and he used to do that at regular intervals. My mother was a dressmaker who had several girls employed in the house and they would make dresses for ladies throughout the town and so on.

'My sister attended the Bet Yakov, which was the girls' school, similar in a way to the boys' cheder.[42] And she attended secular school like I did in the morning.

'The town itself seemed to be all Jewish, i.e. ninety per cent or thereabouts of the shops were Jewish. There were only about three or four non-Jewish shops in the town and they were primarily the non-Jewish butcher, the post office, a non-Jewish grocer and so on. We did not in any case frequent these places, they were of no concern to us. We just passed them in the street and that was all. I don't imagine that there would have been one Jew in this town who ate treife[43] food or did not attend the synagogue at least sometimes. There was, however, one

---

[42] The Bet Yakov (House of Jacob) school system was established in Cracow in 1917 by Sara Schnirer, for orthodox Jewish girls. It combined traditional Jewish studies with industrial training. By 1929 there were 147 Bet Yakov schools in Poland (and twenty more in Lithuania, Latvia and Austria). Bet Yakov teachers' training institutes began in 1931. The schools were reopened after the war in England, France, Belgium, Switzerland, Uruguay, Argentina, the United States and Israel.

[43] Unkosher.

person I remember who did not attend synagogue on Yom Kippur. He was called a "communist" and everybody knew him.

'I knew everybody in the little town and everybody knew me. That is to say, I could not go to any street and not be able to find my way home without somebody saying, "Oh, you're Zelig Tepper's son, come, I will take you home".

'We were not rich but on the other hand we never lacked anything. We owned the building that we lived in which was a bungalow. Normally it would have been a timber structure because, timber being so cheap in that area, all the houses were constructed of wood, unless they were very tall houses and then they would have been brick-built.

'I lacked motivation at school because I never recall my father or my mother asking me what had I learned there. On the other hand, I recall on very many occasions my father asking me what I learned in cheder and so I excelled in that. In the later years I remember my father quoting passages from the Scriptures, and expecting me to understand them in Hebrew, which I actually did. For instance, when I complained about having to get up at six o'clock in the morning to go to cheder because the days in the winter were short, not allowing sufficient time to go to cheder after school, my father said to me, quoting the Ethics of the Fathers, "Heyey az kanamer, kal kanesher, ratz ka-tzvi, vegibor ka-ari, la-asot retzon avicha shebashamyim", the translation of which is, "Be as strong as a leopard, as light as an eagle, run like the deer and be as mighty as the lion to do the bidding of your Father in heaven". I understood it perfectly well and never complained again.

'If ever I had time, such occasions as Sunday afternoon or Saturday afternoon, or sometimes in the evening, I used to be friendly with several kids in town and we used to walk round and talk. I don't ever remember having toys or anything like that. I was always told that Jewish boys did not play with stupid things like that, and therefore I did not need toys. On Saturday afternoons, in the summer, I used to attend cheder to learn Pirkey Avot – the Ethics of the Fathers.'

Lipa Tepper recalled how, as he continued with his Hebrew education, 'I learned what was to be learned in one cheder and then advanced to a cheder of a higher calibre. That is to say, when I learned to pray and I could pray properly, I then went to a Chumash and Rashi cheder where I learned to read and translate Chumash and Rashi's commentary and I spent quite some time in that cheder learning the portion of the Scripture that was due to be read that week, and to translate it and to understand it as well.

'From a Jewish point of view, the town was a completely self-contained unit; for example, there was a Jewish town council, called the "Kahal", with a man in charge who was called the "Rosh Kahal". Unfortunately

I do not remember any of their names. I don't think in those days I took any interest in who was what. There were various committees. There was a committee called "Hachnasat Cala" which, in the case of any girl whose parents could not afford to give her a wedding, took over, and arranged such a wedding. There was a committee called "Bikur Cholim" which meant, just as it suggests, visiting the sick. There was an "Hachnasat Orchim" which again did exactly as it implied, it took care of wayfarers. However, wayfarers were normally taken care of in the synagogue, that is to say that if a stranger came into town our people would have an argument over the privilege of taking him home to dinner. There was a committee called the "Chevra Kaddisha", which took care of dead people, doing all the things necessary up to and including the burial of the person.

'So to all intents and purposes the town did everything for itself. We had a Beth Din,[44] and an Av Beth Din who was in charge of the Beth Din, which took care of all civil or religious disputes. That is to say, any two people in dispute would ordinarily go to the Beth Din first and have their dispute sorted out, before ever contemplating going to the civil authorities. And so life went on in a completely normal way until the outbreak of war.'[45]

Roman Halter was born on 7 July 1927 in the small village of Chodecz – called by the Jews, in Yiddish, Hotz. Eight hundred Jews lived in the village. Only four survived the war, Roman and the three Pinczewski sisters. One of them, Nadzia Pinczewski, who has been living in Australia since the end of the war, met Roman in London in 1995. It was their first meeting in more than fifty years. 'Nadzia and I remembered our childhood in Hotz,' Roman wrote, 'the times we spent by the lake where in summer we swam and in the winter we ice-skated. We reminisced about the walks through the hills covered in pine trees and about the places where in June we picked wild strawberries, and in August and September collected baskets full of mushrooms. Hotz was a lovely place for us; it was our world, as we didn't know any other.'

Stimulated by his talk with his childhood friend, Roman recalled many aspects of daily life in Chodecz, where his family and Nadzia's were among the more prosperous inhabitants. 'We had food every day,' he commented, 'but we had no running water in the house. The water was brought daily in buckets from a well and two metal containers were filled – one was for washing and washing-up and the other for drinking

[44] The Beth Din (also, Bet Din), a Jewish Court of Law: literally, a House of Judgement. It is headed by a man of particular erudition. Av Beth Din; the 'father' of the Jewish Court of Law.

[45] Lipa Tepper, letter to the author, 30 January 1996.

and cooking. We had no proper toilet in the house; the wooden structure with a pit below was a sort of "thunder-box", and it was situated at some distance from the house. We could only use it when it was not too cold. Thus in winter in a tiny room in the house stood a sort of bucket with a wooden seat which was emptied a number of times a day.

'In our bathroom we had no bath but a number of large flat metal bowls. Water was heated on a coal- and wood-fired stove, which was mainly used for cooking and baking. In the winter it also heated part of the house. Grandfather, father, mother and the grown-up members of the family would wash individually by placing the large flat metal bowl on the floor and standing in it and pouring clean water over themselves with a container resembling a watering-can. I took it for granted that this was how grown-ups washed.

'When I needed a wash at the age of six or seven or eight my mother would place me in the middle of our wooden tub, which was mainly used for laundry, and in it I would sit like in a kayak to be soaped and scrubbed by my mother. This bathroom served once a week as a laundry room when a woman would come on a Monday, heat the water in a cauldron and hand-wash the clothes and linen.'

Roman Halter also remembered, as Menachem Silberstein had done, the weekly ritual bath. 'The grown-ups went to the Mikveh once a week,' he wrote. 'There they were soaped or scrubbed or massaged or flogged with birch twigs. After having been massaged or flogged, the men would begin dressing, and while they dressed they would either sing dirty Jewish ditties or tell jokes. My father and grandfather didn't consider the Yiddish jokes and songs suitable for my young ears, and I would be ordered to sit and wait in the small lobby by the entrance door where I could only hear peals of laughter. I was sorry to miss the fun, the songs and the dirty jokes. I promised myself that when I became Bar Mitzvah I would persuade my father and grandfather to let me hear the songs and jokes. Somehow though, in my heart I didn't think that my father would be persuaded.'[46]

By the time Roman was thirteen years old the Germans were in Chodecz, and the time of communal baths and jokes was over.

Arthur Poznanski was born on 7 November 1927 in Praszka, a small town in western Poland only a few miles from the German border with Poland. His father Wladislaw was the headmaster of the local State-run school for Jewish children. Having spent two years studying medicine at the Sorbonne, Wladislaw Poznanski had been forced to return to Poland on the death of his father, to earn a living to support his family. His wife

---

[46] Roman Halter, recollections, 19 February 1996, sent to the author, 26 February 1996.

Perla was a teacher who specialised in arts and crafts. They met when she came to teach at the Praszka school, fell in love and married. 'In Praszka,' Arthur Poznanski recalled, 'we occupied a spacious apartment that took up the whole first floor of a house that used to belong to a Polish nobleman. We had a live-in female servant and at times also a nanny. However, Praszka was a very small town with very few amenities and my parents wished to settle in a bigger town with more and better facilities.

'On my father's application for a transfer, he was offered the position of senior schoolmaster in a school for both Polish and Jewish children in Wielun, a much larger town with a population of about fourteen to fifteen thousand, with a hospital, cinemas, and better amenities. My mother was offered a teaching position in the same school. We moved to Wielun where we lived in an apartment in one of the main streets in the centre of the town until the outbreak of the war. Here we also had room for a live-in maid. And we had electric lighting, something new for us, as Praszka had no electricity supply.

'Most of our month-long annual summer vacations we spent in Rabka Zdroj, a spa in the Carpathian mountains. There we could play with other children in the forest or climb the hills and wade through mountain streams; a veritable paradise for children and a restful retreat for adults.

'In spite of some minor annoyances from the local anti-Semitic youths who used to attack Jewish children on the way to school, we enjoyed a fairly comfortable existence. My parents were respected and liked by most of our Polish and Jewish neighbours and colleagues. We had a kosher household but my parents were not overly religious. We only spoke Polish at home and had more Polish than Jewish friends.'[47]

In Bielsko-Biala, a town within sight of the mountains that form the Polish-Czech border, Jan Goldberger, who was just twelve when war broke out, recalled his earliest memories of anti-Semitism in the streets. 'Jew, a pig is following you', and 'Disbelieving, scabby Jew', the boys at the neighbouring school would call out. They would also throw stones at the Jewish boys. 'Whenever I came home and told my mother, she would tell me to avoid them and run away. As you can see, it was a way of life that had become accepted over the years. There were fights virtually every day at school between the non-Jewish and Jewish children, as the two schools were across the road from each other. It was therefore arranged that the two schools would come out at different times.'[48]

In Sieradz, on the Warta River, Mayer Hersh witnessed a young Catholic priest 'boycotting the open market where most of the stallholders

---

[47] Arthur Poznanski, recollections, letter to the author, 24 January 1995.
[48] Jan Goldberger, 'Jan Goldberger's Story', manuscript, sent to the author, 14 August 1995.

were Jewish. In minutes, all potential non-Jewish customers had disappeared'. He also remembered the non-Jewish caretaker of the building where he lived who volunteered to work on German farms in 1938. 'On his return, he said with a smirk on his face, "When Hitler comes over here he will cut all your Jewish heads off".'[49]

David Hirszfeld, from the village of Bobowa, was just ten years old when the war broke out. He recalled, just before the war, 'being chased by Polish children who threw stones at the wheels of my bicycle, which led to a fall, and I almost ended up with a broken nose.'[50]

In Przemysl, a town that had been part of the Austro-Hungarian Empire before 1919, and then became part of Poland, Witold Gutt was sent to a Polish not a Hebrew school. He was, he explained, 'being brought up as a Polish patriot. However, I was told to strike out if anyone at my school abused me as a Jew. This I did from the outset, and established a situation where Jews in my class were not molested.' A favourite term of abuse, hurled at Jewish boys on their way home from school, was 'Ty parszywy Zyd' ('You scabby – or mangy – Jew'). 'A few wise families,' Gutt reflected, 'had left for Palestine'. Nevertheless, Jewish life flourished. 'There was a lively cultural club in the Jewish community, and there were sports clubs and an active social life for the younger people. Excellent Jewish bread and pastries were available!'[51]

Fifteen miles from Przemysl is the small town of Bircza. Israel (Srulek) Rubinfeld was born there on 3 December 1928. At the age of four he began his Jewish studies: the Hebrew alphabet, reading, writing, the Torah and the Tanach. The small classroom was the rabbi's kitchen. At the age of seven he entered the local school, while continuing his Jewish studies for four hours each day once school was over. Relations between Christians and Jews were 'decent' at school, he recalled. 'We were only subject to Jew-baiting and name-calling on Wednesday afternoons, after the priest taught the Catholic children their catechism classes. Then, we were called "Christ-killers" and "Judas, dirty Jew", and told, "Jews, go to Palestine". Physically and mentally we held our own. We stuck together and felt pretty confident. In the classroom and at sports we got along well.'[52]

Kopel Kandelcukier was born in the Polish town of Bialobrzegi, south of Warsaw, on 7 March 1928. Of the 9,000 people in the town, 2,500 were Jews. Kopel's father was an ironmonger. The local Catholic school

[49] Mayer Hersh (Herszkowicz), letter to the author, 12 December 1994.

[50] David Hirszfeld (Hirschfeld), 'The David Hirschfeld Story', manuscript, sent to the author, 9 February 1996.

[51] Witold Gutt, letter to the author, 7 December 1994.

[52] Jack (Israel) Rubinfeld, 'Jack Rubinfeld', manuscript, sent to the author, undated (1995).

which he attended held classes on Saturday. Jewish children were exempt from these, and a Christian friend, the son of the local magistrate, helped him catch up with the classes he missed, including maths, chemistry and Polish. After school, which ended on weekdays at two o'clock, he went on to cheder. 'On a Saturday my father was very proud of me when I recited the weekly *parasha*[53] by heart with the musical notes. My father was a Hassid and spent a lot of time studying the Talmud, and of course expected me to at least become a rabbi.'

The Jewish community of Bialobrzegi had a good cantor. Choir practice was held in Kopel's home, 'as we could accommodate them all'. Kopel himself was in the choir from the age of ten.

'In the late 1930s,' Kopel Kendall recalled, 'I noticed young Poles with black armbands in the town, with placards saying "Don't buy from Jews". Around Christmas and Easter was the worst time for us Jewish people. The Christians walked the streets in procession, following the Cross, and we had to stay indoors to avoid unnecessary trouble. Although there was some friction between Christians and Jews, we held our own.'[54]

Michael Perlmutter was born in the Polish town of Opatow on 21 April 1928, the youngest of three children. 'We had a comfortable and spacious home. My parents owned and operated a sweet and chocolate factory, it was successful and provided an above-average lifestyle.

'We were always wary of the anti-Semitism around us, and did not wander into forbidden territory where we could, and usually did, get brutally assaulted by the roving bands of Poles. I had my first such experience when I was into my third month of the first year of public school, at the age of seven. I was leaving school at the end of the day, when I was suddenly surrounded by the Polish pupils yelling at me, "You dirty Jew, we will get you clean!" and they proceeded to dunk me in a barrel of freezing rainwater. I was eventually released, and by the time I got home – it was a half-mile walk – I was totally encased in ice. I spent that whole winter in bed with pneumonia.'

The seven-year-old boy's parents enrolled him in the Hebrew-language Tarbut school in Opatow 'which luckily had just opened. It was sheer delight being amongst civilised school mates, and life was beautiful!'[55]

Also born in Opatow, within six months of Michael Perlmutter, was Salek Orenstein. Nearly half a century later he recalled the life of a young Orthodox boy in that bustling Jewish community. His education had begun at an early age, 'when I would be brought to cheder by the

[53] The weekly portion of the Five Books of Moses, read in synagogue every Saturday.
[54] Kopel Kendall (Kandelcukier), recollections, letter to the author, 2 September 1995.
[55] Michael Perlmutter, letter to the author, 4 March 1995.

"Belfer", a type of Pied Piper figure, who went about the Jewish houses collecting all the tiny children. I remember him shouting, "I'll come and fetch you at nine o'clock", which strikes me now as rather ridiculous because I am quite certain that he never had a watch. At cheder I sat on a little bench, about twelve inches high, in front of a large board on which was written the Alef-Beis: the ABC. Our *melamed*[56] was a comical character chiefly because he had no teeth; when he opened his mouth to speak we could all see that it was completely empty. It was an early start to my Jewish education but it paid off; by the age of five I was quite experienced in Chumash and Rashi.

'I loved cheder. I especially looked forward to going there on a day when my mother had given me pocket money to buy myself a little treat. Outside the cheder sat an old, old lady with a face full of wrinkles. She was called Yentel Beila and her head was covered in a *cupke* – a headscarf – studded all over with glass and coloured stones. There she sat, on an old brown stool on a straw-packed cushion, swathed in heavy shawls and cloaks to keep in the warmth. In front of her stood a pot full of glowing charcoals, a sort of portable stove I suppose, over which she roasted a rack of steaming beans. Her sleeves, her shawl and even her chin were blackened by the fire which she tended all day long. For five *groszy*,[57] I could buy myself a measure of beans wrapped in newspaper. I was very pleased indeed. With the beans in my hand I made a right royal entrance into the cheder classroom, all the little cheder boys begging and pleading for a taste and promising me something special in return.

'As I grew older, cheder occupied the afternoons, while every morning was spent at secular school. There were two schools in Opatow, a Jewish school established by a Zionist named Weissblum – a Tarbut school where the language of instruction was Hebrew – which I attended for just a short while before the war. There was also a local Catholic junior school and that was where I was sent. I believe that the Orthodox Jews of Opatow took the view that it was preferable for their sons and daughters to be educated in the Catholic school rather than – *chas ve'challilah*[58] – learn a distorted version of the Bible.

'I shall never forget the torment of the Jewish children in the Catholic school. I remember arriving in school one morning and somebody greeting me by pushing *chazer*[59] into my mouth – for a laugh. The teachers, also non-Jews, did not intervene in any way. You can imagine

[56] Teacher.
[57] One grosz was a hundredth of a zloty; 25 zloties were £1 sterling. In the money values of 1996, the beans cost about a penny.
[58] 'Heaven forbid': literally, 'Spare me, may it be far from me'.
[59] Non-kosher meat, including pork.

the sort of education we received there. We were frequently attacked as we left school to make our way home. They threw stones at us and they pushed us around. That was our preparation for what was to come.

'There were eleven Jewish children in my class, six girls and five boys, I think, and once a week a Jewish teacher would come in and give us some religious instruction. The rest of the time, we had to remove our caps and stand up together with the non-Jewish children while they said their prayers and crossed themselves. The truth was that the Jewish children were brighter and achieved better results than their non-Jewish students and on account of it, they hated our guts even more.'

As well as school, there were the Jewish communal activities into which every Jewish child was drawn. 'As a little boy I also had my duties,' Salek Orenstein wrote of himself as a seven- and eight-year-old. 'Each week I was entrusted with taking the chickens to the *shochet*.[60] The live chickens were put into a little basket with their heads sticking out of the bottom. I was given two groszy or three or five – I can't quite remember which – to hand over to the shochet with the chickens. He slaughtered them in the ritual way, and after having extracted the blood, he put the chickens back into the basket – again with the heads sticking out – so that by the end of the journey there was no longer any visible trace of blood.

'The slaughterhouse was not very far from our home, just four or five minutes away, but then, of course, you could cross the whole town in ten minutes! Another of my chores was to bring the *chulent*[61] pot to the baker on Friday afternoon. Our pot had a special ribbon tied around it, in blue and red. My mother had put it there so that when I picked it up the following day on Shabbes morning, I would be able to recognise our pot immediately and not bring back somebody else's food!' This mistake was not uncommon.

'There was no water supply in our flat,' Salek Orenstein continued, 'no tap, no toilet, no bath. All water for the daily needs of the home was stored in a big barrel that stood in the kitchen and the Jewish water-carriers – men and women alike – used to come up and refill it once or twice a day. At the same time, the water-carriers used to exploit the service by asking my mother to give them a little bit of hot water (with a dash of tea) if they could see the kettle standing on the stove. "Gib mir a bissale heiss wasser" ("Give me a little hot water"), I remember them begging.

'Our regular water-carrier was a chap named Zisskind and I always

---

[60] The shochet (also spelt *shoichet*) was the ritual slaughterer, who prepared (or 'koshered') the chickens and other meat according to the rules of Kashrut.

[61] Also spelt *cholent*: a traditional Saturday dish, of meat, potatoes, beans and onions; it would be prepared on Friday and taken to be cooked at the communal bakery oven.

gave him hot water to drink. But before I did so, I used to ask, "Zisskind! Tehillim Perek Heh, Pasuk Lamed-Alef – Psalms, fifth chapter, line thirty-one – tell me how does it start?" He could tell you any reference that you cared to give him, all by heart, and he always got it right first time. You could check a thousand times and it was always correct. He must have been learning Torah all his life.

'One day, this fellow Zisskind called with our delivery and said, "I must inform you, your water barrel is lined with dirt". There was no filter of any description. The water often came up from the well with some fine deposits that had accumulated gradually, settling at the bottom of the storage barrel. That day he refused to fill the barrel until it had been thoroughly cleaned out first and he used this as a bargaining tool. "If you give me a glass of tea," he said, "I will take the barrel downstairs, wash it out and you will have nice, pure water."

'I must have been seven or eight years old at the time, but I was clever enough to know that clean water is better than dirty water, and we made a deal. When he saw me puffing and blowing out my cheeks to ignite the flame for his hot water, he suggested I add a bit of paraffin to it. In his eagerness, he spilled the paraffin and singed his beard, but he got his drink and I never mentioned this adventure to my mother.

'I will never forget Zisskind as he left our flat with his empty pails. Each time he did so his lips were moving, reciting Psalms. He never stopped. I could bump into him three or four times in one day around the town delivering water to his regular customers, and whenever I saw him he was always *davening*[62] and all his conversation was punctuated with a standard exclamation: "Baruch Hashem" ("Blessed be the Lord").'

Salek Orenstein also recalled the characters who were part and parcel of Jewish life in Opatow when he was a young boy. 'On Fridays, I remember, a little man, known as Reb Moishe, came to our house bringing with him a small bottle full of wine which he carried secretively inside his *kapoteh*.[63] The reason that the wine was kept hidden inside his kapoteh, I discovered, was that he did not want to expose it to non-Jewish eyes. I was fascinated by this and asked him, "Why do you hold it like that in the lining of your coat?" To which he replied, "So that the goyim – the non-Jews – should not see it." If a goy saw the wine – still less touched it – the wine would not be fit to use for Kiddush.[64]

'From his right-hand pocket he produced a little cup and poured out four or five measures of wine, raisin wine which he had made himself, and transferred them into our own household container. I watched him

[62] Praying.
[63] A long black coat.
[64] The prayer over wine, recited in every Jewish household on Friday night and during festivals.

closely as he did this and often challenged his accuracy by commenting: "It was not a full cup! You didn't give us the correct measure!" "Reb Moishe," I used to say, "you should see the milkman Reb Favel's measuring cup, it is much bigger than yours!" To which he answered: "Oy! Red nicht kein narischkeiten! Er hot sore milch, ich hob gutten wein!" ("Oh! Don't tell me such nonsense! He has sour milk, I have good wine!")

'Every morning, summer and winter, Favel, the old milkman, went from house to house, carrying two large buckets of milk. The only other item of equipment was the zinc measuring cup which was suspended by a small chain from the side of one of these buckets, rattling and thumping as he walked around the town making his deliveries. He was a small man with broad shoulders, and a long, wide, red beard which practically covered his entire face. He wore a sackcloth apron tied around his belly with a length of rope, front to back. A piece of red material – for wiping his beard – hung down from the rope. It had two knots in it; one for the coins which he was saving to buy food for *Shabbes*,[65] the other knot containing change to give the *balebustas*.[66] Whenever he was late with his delivery, he had one standard excuse: "I went first to the ladies who have just given birth to babies. Azoi shteit geschriben" ("That is how it is written – ordained").'[67]

Moniek Goldberg was born in the small town of Glowaczow on 5 May 1928. His father manufactured shirts and underwear, travelling from town to town to sell their goods. 'My parents worked very hard,' he recalled. 'They went to the markets in neighbouring towns. So, it was Monday in one town, Tuesday the market was in Glowaczow, then Wednesday and Thursday out of town. They left early when it was still dark and returned home late, past dark. It was especially hard for them in winter. I remember my sister and I used to get into their beds to warm them for their return home. To run our house my cousin Esther was there ever since I can remember, until just before the war when she got married.

'I don't remember when I started cheder but I must have been very young as in cheder I was always ahead of boys my age. At age seven I started secular school and to this day I remember the names from the roster listed before my name. We must have been about forty children. From the Jewish children in my class I am the only one who survived. The routine was as follows: I got up, washed, recited prayers, ate

---

[65] The Sabbath.
[66] Women in charge of the household.
[67] Salek Orenstein, 'Beyond Belief, A Survivor's Story', manuscript, sent to the author, 1995.

breakfast and went to school from 8 a.m. until noon. From school I went directly to cheder where Esther was waiting for me to make certain that I ate lunch. I didn't get home until about five in the evening.

'There was very little anti-Semitism. Actually, as a young boy, I experienced none. I played with boys both Jewish and Gentile whose fathers had played with my father. To the best of my recollection the teachers in the school were fair.'

When Moniek Goldberg was nine years old his parents moved to the nearby town of Kozienice, where 'for the first time I came face to face with anti-Semitism. There were fights in school. Every day I had to go home the long way round so as to walk with Jewish boys for safety's sake. The teachers were blatantly unfair. A Jew had to be excellent just to get a passing grade. After a fight, the Jewish boys would always end up getting punished. For a boy of nine years who had never experienced such treatment it was very hard to take. My parents also started talking about the dangers of going to the markets. There had been a pogrom in Przytyk.[68]

'"Don't buy from the Jews" became a national slogan being openly preached in the churches. The "picketniks" would stand in front of Jewish stalls and harangue the Poles not to patronise them. It was not unusual for Polish hooligans to break windows or turn over Jewish stalls in the markets, knowing that we had no legal redress. So, my parents, as indeed all Jews, lived with grave forebodings about the future. Life had to go on. There was really no way out for them. Looking at it now, as a man sixty-seven years of age, I see that they had very few options and had to make the best of it. And so life went on.'

Moniek Goldberg joined the Kozienice *yeshiva*.[69] His older sister was considering going to Palestine, and was worried whether their parents would let her go. Every Friday evening, life was transformed by the coming of the Sabbath. 'After the candles were lit, everything seemed to slow down. When we walked to synagogue for services, the best way that I can describe my father is that he walked like an aristocrat, somehow taller and straighter. I can still see my mother's face when I made Kiddush for myself the first time. After we ate, we sang *zemirot*.[70] There are survivors from Kozienice who remind me now that they used to sit on our porch and listen to us sing.'

Reflecting on those pre-war days, Moniek Goldberg wrote: 'That world is gone. Of my father's nine brothers and sisters, only one sister survived, in Russia, and lived to reach Israel, where she passed away in 1978. Of

---

[68] A small town forty-five miles south of Warsaw in which two Jews were murdered during a pogrom in March 1936.

[69] A school, often residential, for the study of orthodox Judaism.

[70] Songs: of prayer and sabbath rejoicing.

my mother's family – she had three brothers and five sisters – only one
brother survived, as he had emigrated to Canada in 1912. I had eighty-
two first cousins that I knew, and can recall by name. Only five of us
survived – not counting four in Canada.'[71]

Arek Hersh – like Mayer Hersh (but no relation of his) – was born in
the town of Sieradz on 13 September 1928. He had three sisters, Mania,
Itka and Dvora, and a brother, Tovia. Sieradz was a town of about
twenty thousand Christians and five thousand Jews, 'set in rural surroundings', Arek later recalled, 'with forests on the horizon and fields of
rape-seed shining like gold in the summer'. It was also a garrison town,
and his father Szmuel Jona, a bootmaker by trade, 'was kept busy making
officers' boots – so busy sometimes, in fact, that he had to employ two
people to help him'. Theirs was an Orthodox family, 'faithfully following
all the Jewish laws and traditions. Each week my father took Tovia and
me to synagogue.'

The religious orthodoxy of Arek Hersh's parents was typical of the
modern orthodoxy that had developed in many Polish Jewish families at
that time. 'Both my father and mother were very modern in outlook,'
he recalled. 'They loved dancing and won several competitions. My
father was a great believer in socialist ideals, and was very interested in
world politics, history and psychology. Though he was kind and had a
good sense of humour (a trait inherited by Tovia), he was also a great
disciplinarian. I remember once he caught me playing cards with some
friends, and he took me home and lectured me on the evils of gambling.
He never had to resort to violence to make us obey his word, but
nevertheless obey we did, both out of respect for his viewpoint and out
of fear of his disapproval.

'My mother, Bluma (which in Hebrew is *Shoshana*, which means Rose),
was a very beautiful and gentle woman. She was slim with high
cheekbones and dark hair drawn back into a bun. She put great store
in the value of education, and used to tell me that when I grew up she
would ensure I received the best possible chance for higher education in
order to learn a profession. Her ancestors were Spanish, as could be seen
from her looks, and my father's were Russian. My father's family had
come to Poland from Russia one hundred and fifty years before; my
mother's family could be traced back to the Spanish Inquisition.'

On market day, Arek Hersh recollected, peasants from the surrounding
villages came to Sieradz 'in national costume, clattering through the
cobbled streets in their clogs, to sell butter, eggs and fruit'; and in their

[71] Joseph (Moniek) Goldberg, 'Biographical Sketch', manuscript, July 1995, sent to the author, 14
August 1995.

turn bought clothing and other necessities, such as sugar, salt and flour, from Jewish shopkeepers. Arek Hersh also recalled 'columns of soldiers, some on horseback, all carrying guns', who passed by on their way to manoeuvres. 'My friends and I used to march behind these columns, carrying pieces of wood on our shoulders in place of guns, and we used to watch the ceremony of swearing allegiance to Poland which was held in the market square.'

One of Arek Hersh's earliest memories was of the death of his sister Dvora from whooping cough. She was only three years old. At the funeral, he remembered his parents 'supporting one another in their grief. My sisters walked either side of my parents, whilst Tovia and I walked behind. I remember the mourners clearly, the men in their black coats and hats, the women in their fox collars, some with shawls over their heads. I remember, also, two beggars walking beside us, all the time rattling their tins, pleading for money.

'The funeral procession slowly passed by the park where Dvora and I used to play. It was autumn, so the trees and the ground were covered in golden leaves, the birches swaying to and fro in the breeze. We arrived at the cemetery gates, then passed through them to little Dvora's newly-dug grave. The path was narrow, the tombstones on both sides written in Yiddish, Hebrew and Polish. As the Rabbi gave a eulogy prayer, committing Dvora's body to the ground, I stood and wept, broken-hearted.'

In 1935 Marshal Pilsudski died. He had been the father of Poland's inter-war independence, a distinguished soldier and a benevolent dictator. Arek Hersh was then six years old. Shortly after Pilsudski's death, Arek's sister Mania took him to the cinema. Part of the programme that day was a newsreel showing Pilsudski's funeral. 'Mania and I, sitting in the front row, had to look up at the screen,' he later recalled, 'and I remember being engrossed in what I was watching. Suddenly, however, there came a shot of the cavalry charging straight at the screen, and of horses' hooves and underbellies as they leapt over what was presumably a cameraman sitting in a ditch. Being so young, I was absolutely terrified; it had seemed as though the horses were charging straight at me. I felt very ill and couldn't stop shaking, and Mania had to take me home where I was immediately put to bed.

'My mother called the doctor, who examined me, and, though he admitted he was puzzled as to what was actually wrong with me, prescribed me some medicine. Tovia fetched the medicine from the apothecary. It looked and tasted awful and had not the slightest effect on my condition. I lay in bed, crying and shaking with fear, my body racked with sharp pains. I remember my mother trying to comfort me, whispering soothingly in Yiddish, "Sha mein kind" ("Be still, my child"), and singing a lullaby, "Shluf mein kinderle, shluf" ("Sleep, my little child, sleep"). She was very worried about me, but eventually I drifted into sleep.

'I awoke later with the sound of wind driving the rain against the windows. My lips were dry and I felt as though I was burning up. I cried out for my mother, who burst into the room together with my grandmother, Flora Natal, and my father. My mother held me to her body and stroked my face gently. She said to Flora, "What can it be? Even the doctor doesn't know." For a few moments the room was silent, my father running his fingers through his hair, my grandmother staring at me intently. Then suddenly my grandmother announced that she was going to see a medium called Golda to ask if she could help. Without another word, she left the house.

'Half an hour later my grandmother returned, accompanied by an old Jewish lady with a long, bony face, a shawl protecting her head against the rain, and piercing eyes which regarded me intently. The Jewish lady asked my mother if she could have a pan and either some wax or candles. These items were provided for her, and she placed the wax in the pan, then began to melt it over the fire. As she was doing this, she placed a hand on my head and began to pray. This went on for quite a while, until finally the old lady removed the pan from the fire and displayed its contents for us to see. To our astonishment the wax in the pan had formed into the shape of a horse. By the next morning I was feeling much, much better.

'I leave open to your judgement the explanation for this strange occurrence. Personally I believe the medium, Golda, performed some sort of exorcism over me, ridding me of the terrible fear that had taken a hold. Certainly from that point on I began to recuperate very quickly, and a few days later I was up and about again and playing with my friends.'

While he was still young, Arek Hersh's family moved to the town of Konin. There, while on the way to school, he encountered one of the town's characters. 'He was an old man dressed in a fur hat, a Russian-type caftan and high boots with his trousers tucked into them. He had a beard and a large handlebar moustache, and he earned his living by selling edible oils. He owned a horse that he blindfolded with a sack, and which would plod round and round, pulling a wheel which ground the sunflower seeds that produced the oil. We used to watch this process, fascinated. The old man used to stop us and talk to us as we passed by his premises. He would ask us to pull his finger, and as we did he would fart. We were absolutely intrigued by this behaviour, but very soon we got used to him and refused to do his bidding. Instead we used to watch other children fall into the trap, and as they did we would fall about with laughter. The old man never seemed to run out of wind and could always oblige.'

Returning after a few years to Sieradz, Arek Hersh had warm memories of the journey to school. 'It was a beautiful walk, especially in the summer, cutting through a large park and also along a path with an apple orchard on one side and a pear orchard on the other. There were also strawberry patches, and in the summer, when the strawberries were ripe, we used to pick and eat them. The school itself was an old building, and round the back there was a pond where I would spend many happy hours watching the frogs leaping in and out of the water. I used to love watching the animals and birds, and often on the way home I would stop in the park to see the antics of the squirrels or the storks beside the River Warta bringing food for their chicks.'

The school in Sieradz was a Hebrew school, where Arek Hersh learned the Bible and the Five Books of Moses, translating from Hebrew into Yiddish. He remembered his teacher, Godlewicz, a man with a small beard and spectacles who walked with a stoop. There were ten boys in the class, and the teacher 'would make us repeat a sentence over and over again until I grew bored and began speaking to the boy sitting next to me. When this happened, Godlewicz would hit me with the ruler the same amount of times as he had told us to repeat the sentence.'

Arek Hersh had particularly fond recollections of the winter months. 'When the river froze over we used to go down and ice-skate on it. Often I used to go home with my head covered in bumps where I had fallen over, which my father would press with a silver coin to reduce the swelling. As well as ice-skating I also loved sledging, and had my own sledge which I had made from wood and iron bands which were used to bind packing cases. I used to lie flat on my stomach and launch myself down the steep slopes, guiding myself along with the toecaps of my shoes.

'We used to watch as horses and carts delivered large chunks of ice that had been cut out of the River Warta. This ice would be sprinkled with sawdust and stacked in a large ice house where it would stay until summer, when it would be used for such things as making ice-cream and in hospitals. However, though the winters were severe, this did not prevent the peasants from coming into Sieradz on market days. The peasants would appear on sleighs pulled by horses with bells round their necks. It was a lovely sight. Often we used to hang on to the backs of sleighs and be pulled along until the driver spotted us. Then he would lash out with his whip, and we of course would let go quickly.

'Another trick of mine was to tie the rope of my sledge on to the back of a horse-drawn sleigh when the driver was not looking. This way I used to travel many kilometres without the driver being aware of me.'

In September 1938 Arek Hersh celebrated his tenth birthday. 'I was still doing all the mischievous things that boys of my age do – climbing trees for conkers or walnuts or fruit, and being chased by the park keeper, playing games such as *palant*, which is played with a bat and a piece of wood that is pointed at both ends (the idea being to hit one of the points with the bat, which would then fly into the air, then to hit it again: whoever hit it furthest would be deemed the winner) and generally just having fun. We were little aware of the impending world situation, and even less aware of its implications.

'I think the first indications that all was not well among the Jewish population came when German Jews began to be sent across the border to Poland. As Sieradz was only fifty miles from the border, many of these Jews came into our town, full of stories about the inhumanity of the Nazis and about how badly Jews were being treated in Germany. However, although these people were being forcibly expelled from the country and allowed to take only a few possessions with them, they were well-fed and smartly-dressed and seemed to be of the general opinion that things in Germany would soon improve and they would be able to return home. A committee was set up in Sieradz to help these people, and they were absorbed into the Jewish community. Though we personally couldn't take anyone as we had no room, my father helped organise homes for all those who had been sent across the border.

'Another indication of the growing strength of Nazism at this time was the higher degree of anti-Semitism among the Volksdeutsche (Ethnic Germans) living in and around Sieradz.[72] I remember one market day I went into a Jewish-owned shop in the market square, and as I entered, two Christian Poles stopped a couple behind me, a peasant and his wife, with the words, "Don't go into this shop. It is owned by Jews."

'Even among the children anti-Semitism began to increase. On many occasions we would come out of school to be apprehended by Christian boys shouting, "Dirty Jew, go back to Palestine". As a child I did not realise the deep meaning behind all these actions, but the blind senseless hatred I felt will be ingrained in my mind for as long as I live. I did not understand why we were suddenly being treated as second-class citizens: Jews in Poland did their military service, they fought for their country; my father himself was a case in point. However, it must be stressed that this mindless racism did not extend to everybody. We still had many non-Jewish Polish friends who were really wonderful to us. In the

---

[72] German-speaking families whose forebears had lived in Poland (and also in other parts of Central and Eastern Europe) for several centuries.

cinemas the newsreels began to show how Poland was preparing for war.

'My father and his friends would stand outside the synagogue with their prayer books in their hands, and one would say, "There will be an invasion", while another would argue that there would not.'[73]

Like Arek Hersh, Abram Huberman, from the town of Pulawy, remembered the death of Marshal Pilsudski in 1935. 'There are two things I remember from my school (apart from the constant battles we had with the non-Jewish pupils on the way to and from school)', he later wrote. 'One was the parade we took part in when Marshal Pilsudski died. All the children wore black armbands, and very solemn music was played. The other was when my class was asked to write a letter to a school in Czechoslovakia, welcoming them to Poland. This happened at the end of October 1938, when Germany occupied Czechoslovakia, and gave a small part of it to Poland. It was that part to which we wrote. The idea was that whoever wrote the neatest letter, that was the one to be sent. I had the doubtful honour of having my letter chosen.'[74]

Israel Wilder, known to his friends as Krulik, was born on 3 December 1928 in Piotrkow Tribunalski.[75] There were 55,000 people in his town, of whom 15,000 were Jews. 'Outside our apartment in the square where we lived,' he later wrote, 'there was always activity and excitement, droshkis (horse and carriage) were parked outside. There was also a pub next door, people sitting and drinking beer, discussing politics of the day and often engaged in financial transactions.

'We lived in a small apartment, my mother – my beautiful mother Chaja – my gifted older sister Basia, and my father Lajb. The apartment consisted of two rooms, no running water, no toilet, no luxuries, but nevertheless I only remember the happy life. The toilets were outside at the back of the yard, it was dreadful to go down there in winter, people made a mess all over the place.

'As a small boy I remember my school, there were mostly Jewish children. I remember I was a very poor student. My sister who went to the same school as me, and was four years older, always got top marks in every subject, whereas I got dreadful marks. Whenever I brought home a report from school, my parents always shouted at me, and said, "Look at your sister's marks, why can't you get marks like that, don't you like school?" I liked playing at school but did not like schoolwork.

'However my favourite pastime was when we went home and we

---

[73] Arek Hersh (Herszlikowicz), 'My Childhood', manuscript, sent to the author, 17 October 1994.
[74] Abram (Alfred) Huberman, recollections, letter to the author, 7 May 1996.
[75] One of the largest cities in western Poland. There was also a Piotrkow Kujawski a hundred miles to the north, and a tiny village of Piotrkow fifteen miles south of Lublin.

used to fight with the kids from other schools. I also remember well, cheder, where my grandfather was a melamed (teacher). Again I did not like cheder either. Like all the boys, all I wanted to do was play, after all, I was only seven or eight years old.

'Before the war my father had a stall in the market selling hosiery. When I did not attend school my favourite time was when I went to help him in the market. When he was not working in the market he was very active and involved in the Bund movement, a Jewish socialist movement with a Jewish cultural identity.[76] The great event was in May, when it seemed like the whole town was marching on Labour Day. We kids used to run about following the marchers; this event took place every year. I also enjoyed very much the winters in Poland because we could skate in the streets. In our square there were numerous boys and girls snowballing and skating, and I have many memories of those days.'[77]

Ben Helfgott, whose grandmother had persuaded his father to give up his desire to go to Palestine, recalled the Jewish poverty even in Piotrkow, a prosperous city. 'I will always remember,' he later wrote, 'little boys, shoeless, dressed in tatters, going round begging with the hope of nothing more than a crust of bread. I recall on one occasion a boy about my age knocking at our door. I turned him away. My mother called me, and severely reprimanded me, saying, "You should be grateful that you are not in that position yourself" – and she ensured that I gave the boy more than his crust of bread.

'I realised my mistake immediately and have not forgotten its lesson. The incident with the beggar had a profound influence on many of my actions since then. From a warm home like ours, a flat in an apartment block which to the beggars of the town must have seemed like paradise, the life of the poor was so distant, yet it was part of our everyday existence.'[78]

Salamon Rafael Winogrodzki, like Krulik Wilder and Ben Helfgott a boy from Piotrkow, was born on 17 March 1929. 'Trying to remember as a child of ten years old,' he recalled, 'the town seemed to be quite big. We did not live in what was known as the Jewish Quarter. We lived in an apartment (my family owned the whole block of these apartments) on a street called Pilsudskiego which was named after President Pilsudski. It was the main street of the town.'

The members of young Salamon's family were his father Chaim, his

[76] Founded in 1897, the Bund was the largest populist Jewish political organisation in the Tsarist Empire (of which Piotrkow was a part). The word BUND is an acronym for the Russian General Union of Jewish Workers in Russia and Poland.

[77] Israel (Krulik) Wilder, 'Krulik's Story', manuscript, sent to the author, 1 January 1995.

[78] Ben Helfgott, 'Memories of Poland', *In Face of Adversity*, Frank Cass, London, 1990, page 148.

mother, Hanna, and his two sisters, Esther and Ruth. He was the eldest of the three children. 'My father was a French-polisher and he had his own business, in which he employed other people. Also our immediate family owned a sawmill in Piotrkow, which gave employment to a lot of people in the town. We were a middle-class family. We had a very comfortable lifestyle; as children we never wanted for anything. I remember going on holidays to the lakes many times with my family.

'I went to a school which was mixed Jews and Christians. I remember I did enjoy my schooldays, and I must have done reasonably well as my family never complained or showed any disappointment in my school-work. I did enjoy football in the summer and tobogganing in the winter. As far as anti-Semitism at school was concerned, I did not have too much trouble as I was friendly with Jewish and Christian boys. And the only reason why I think they did not bully or fight with me was because my father and the immediate family gave work to nearly all the boys' fathers. All this came to an abrupt end at the beginning of September 1939.'[79]

Another of those whose home was in Piotrkow was Sevek Finkelstein (now Sidney Finkel). Born on 19 December 1931, he was among the youngest of the boys brought to England in August 1945. 'My first real experience of the hatred of Jews by Poles,' he recalled, 'was when I was seven or eight and walked to my school. On the other side of the street there would always be a gathering of young kids who would call out "Ugly Jews", and they would throw stones and things at us. I just could not understand why they were doing that to me. I did not know them and they certainly did not know me. In a sense, if anyone was going to throw stones it was supposed to be me. The idea of throwing things at others had a certain appeal to me. I soon thought it out as being normal behaviour. They were throwing stones at me, not because of who I was as an individual, but because I was born into a Jewish family. Being Jewish was to be inferior and deserving of punishment. I did not like it that they threw stones because I was Jewish, so I used to cover my face with my hand so that they would not know I was Jewish.'[80]

Yosek Rotbaum (now Joseph Ribo) was born in Glowaczow in 1932, but spent part of his childhood in a village, Cecylowka, which consisted, he recalled, 'of two rows of wooden houses with thatched roofs, and a dusty road dividing the two sides of the village'. His father sold timber, animal skins and fruit. In the early spring, long before the fruit had

---

[79] Salamon Winogrodzki, letter to the author, 20 March 1995.

[80] Sidney Finkel (Sevek Finkelstein), 'My Story', manuscript, sent to the author, 12 September 1995.

ripened, he would buy in advance the fruit crop of entire orchards from some of the villagers, and then he would take up residence in the village where the fruit was to be harvested. In the summer of 1939, Joseph Ribo recalled, 'there was no empty house available for rent, so Father put up a tent-like shack in one of the orchards, and had it thatched with straw. Mother arranged the interior. The sleeping quarters were at one end of the shack and the living quarters at the entrance.

'And so we lived in the midst of nature, my father Israel – called Srul by the Poles, mother Rikle (Regina), eleven-year-old Nahman, nine-year-old sister Rivka; five-year-old sister Kraindle and myself – seven-year-old Yossale, called Yosek by the Poles. We kids loved the summers in the village. The transition from the dreary and dusty *shtetl*[81] of Glowaczow, where we lived for most of the year, into the evergreen and more open surroundings of the village, was exhilarating, especially Cecylowka, whose pasture fields bordered on a brook; and beyond the brook was the forest, full of wonders and fright.

'We used to join the Polish kids who took their family's livestock for pasture. There we would play together, splash around and try to catch fish in the shallow brook, and, very cautiously creep into the forest. There were plenty of tales circulating about the dangers of the forest. There was always a kid who would swear that his grandma saw the dwarfs sleeping underneath the shrubs and that we should be careful not to make a noise and wake them up.

'By the time we filled our bellies full of raspberries and blackberries, we would start to move towards the village, dirty, wet and full of scratches, but happy. The scolding by mother was inevitable.'[82]

Twice a week Yosek Rotbaum's parents would bring a tutor – a melamed – to the village to teach their children to read the Jewish prayer book. 'All of us children resented having to stay at home,' he recalled, 'instead of being out in nature and playing with other Polish boys and girls.' He also remembered the many guests who came to stay in their village house. 'Every Jew who happened to pass in the vicinity,' he recalled, 'or get stranded for one reason or another, would knock on our door. They were always welcome, and a hot meal and a straw mattress were always provided. Some people even took advantage of my parents' hospitality!'[83]

Shloime Zalman Judensznajder (now Solly Irving) was born in the small Polish town of Ryki on 12 August 1930. About 2,500 Jews lived there.

---

[81] Shtetl: a predominantly Jewish town or village in Eastern Europe.

[82] Joseph Ribo (Yosek Rotbaum), 'Yosek, My Adventures During the Second World War', manuscript, sent to the author, 18 April 1995.

[83] Joseph Ribo (Yosek Rotbaum), letter to the author, 14 March 1996.

'I was attacked and beaten up many times on the way home from school,' he recalled. 'One particular incident is still fresh in my mind. I was set upon by a few boys, and after a good beating they stuffed my mouth with bacon. My parents were furious and took me to the headmaster. The next day at assembly, the headmaster called me out in front of the school, to show him who the culprits were. He was quite a big man, and I was a very small eight-year-old. He pulled me round the playground, not by my hand but by my ear, and to this day I suffer pain in my left ear.'

The eight-year-old Shloime could not remember 'having time for play'. After school, his oldest sister Rivka would meet him outside their home with some lunch, and take him straight on to cheder. Then, 'after coming home for supper, I would go on to a different Rebbe for some other lesson. I remember the Friday evenings when my father would test me on what I had learned during the week on the Torah, and I was full of nerves. I would then go round to the Rebbe of the town for the same test. I remember the dark winter evenings when I went to the Rebbe with a lantern, which I had made from a bottle with a candle in it. It was also fun at times skating in my shoes, and rolling down a little hill on my bottom, and getting a good spanking for doing so.'[84]

Another childhood recollection was that of Howard Chandler, born Chaim Wajchendler in December 1928 in Wierzbnik, on the outskirts of Starachowice, a hundred miles south of Warsaw. 'There were four children in our family,' he recalled, 'the oldest a girl, and three boys of whom I was the middle one. We owned a two-storey, twelve-room house that my maternal grandfather built. We occupied four of the rooms and the rest were rented out.

'My father at one time had studied law and was very knowledgeable. He counted among his friends all in the legal profession, including all the judges, in town. He was very much in demand in the Jewish community for free legal advice and at times intervened on behalf of litigants so that trials involving Jews would not be held on Jewish holidays.'

All the boys testify, as Howard Chandler does, to the importance of the Jewish holidays in their pre-war lives. In the hundreds of large and self-contained Jewish communities in Poland, these holidays were celebrated, not as a minority in a predominantly Christian atmosphere, but with all the centrality, joy and satisfaction of a totally secure Jewish environment. The all-encompassing Jewishness of the Jewish sections of each town was their most notable, and their most comforting aspect. By

---

[84] Solly Irving (Shloime Zalman Judensznajder), 'Memories of a Past', manuscript, pages 2–3, sent to the author, 5 April 1995.

1945 that Jewishness, together with the Jews who had sustained it, had been totally destroyed.

Other aspects of the Jewish town life are mentioned by all the boys. 'My family operated a general store where we all participated, including my mother and grandfather,' Howard Chandler wrote. 'My grandfather died just two weeks before the war broke out. My other grandfather, whom I never knew, was a shoichet.[85] He was strictly orthodox. He had a long beard, as had my maternal grandfather. Father did not have a beard and we the boys did not have peyot.[86] Father dressed modern during the week and on Sabbath and holidays wore orthodox garb. My sister attended a Bet Yakov school for girls and we attended cheder as well as the Public School which was compulsory. Education in our family was highly valued and we competed for good marks in school.

'We were, I would judge, modern orthodox. All Jewish holidays were strictly observed and our house was strictly kosher. There was one church and one Bais Medrash[87] to which was attached a yeshiva. We had an official rabbi and two or three other rabbis, each with his own followers. There were various Jewish organisations, religious, secular and political, as well as sports clubs. There was also Jewish representation on the local town council. Thursday was market day and most people took part since most Jews were artisans or storekeepers. Therefore this was the most important business day and people converged on the market square, which was almost in front of our house. The economic mainstay however was the government-owned ammunition plant where no Jews were allowed to be employed. Jews even avoided going near the fences of these factories lest they be accused of spying.

'Jews and Catholics lived a tolerable coexistence, provided the priest in the only church was a decent person. But if he happened to be anti-Semitic, the relationship deteriorated, particularly just prior to the outbreak of the war and with the influence of German propaganda.'[88]

Zisha Schwimmer was born in the village of Strozowka, just outside the Polish town of Gorlice, on 5 April 1928. 'We shared a house with my aunt Deborah,' he recalled, 'and with grandfather Joseph, who lived at the front of the house. My aunt owned a grocer's shop in the front of the house. My grandfather was a cattle tradesman and owned a little farm with one cow. We – my father Mayer, my mother Esther Liba, my sister Rachel and my twin brother Chaim – lived in the back of the house. My father owned a shoe workshop in the same house. He made

---

[85] A ritual slaughterer (in its Hebrew form, shochet).
[86] Sidelocks.
[87] House of Prayer (also, in Hebrew, Bet Midrash)
[88] Howard Chandler (Chaim Wajchendler), letter to the author, 23 February 1995.

handmade shoes for Jewish shops in Gorlice. My mother got the orders and delivered the shoes to the shops.' School was until one in the afternoon. 'After an hour's break for a sandwich lunch, we went to cheder in the afternoon. We did not come home until six or seven in the evening. There wasn't much time to play. Toys were unheard of. At school, pupils used to shout at us "Hitler is coming to get you".'[89]

Harry Balsam was born in Gorlice a year after Zisha Schwimmer, on 8 May 1929. He lived there with his father Moses, his mother Adele, his three brothers Danny, Sanek and Joseph, and his sister Gitel. 'My father was very orthodox and was the warden of the synagogue,' he recalled. 'In the morning we used to go to the elementary school and in the afternoon to cheder. We were brought up speaking two languages simultaneously, Polish and Yiddish. We were quite well off by local standards. My father was a miller and we had plenty of flour to bake our own bread. For the Sabbath we used to bake challahs, and if I remember correctly we used to take challahs and give them to our relations living in the same town. I thought we were quite comfortable, but thinking about it today I don't suppose we were quite as comfortable as I really thought.'[90]

South-east of Gorlice, beyond Poland, across the Carpathian Mountains, lay the mountainous region of Ruthenia.[91] Before 1914, like Gorlice, it was part of the Austro-Hungarian Empire. In 1919 it became the most easterly region of the new state of Czechoslovakia. In October 1938, a year before the outbreak of war, at the time of the disintegration of Czechoslovakia, Ruthenia was annexed by Hungary. It was not until March 1944 that German rule led to the imposition of ghettos there, and the rapid deportation of the Jews of the region to Auschwitz. Among those who were to become the 'boys' of this story were more than a hundred from Ruthenia. One of them, Victor Greenberg, recalled his childhood in the village of Majdan, where forty-two Jewish families, and about twice as many Ukrainians, farmed the hilly countryside. 'The picturesque mountains, hills and rivers are breathtaking,' he wrote, in an account which reflects the experience of most of the 'boys' from Ruthenia. 'Life revolved round religion, the rabbis ruled supreme. The festivals were the highlights in life. It was an environment comparable to that of *Fiddler on the Roof.* The Jews and Ukrainians had their separate

---

[89] Jack (Zisha) Schwimmer, letter to the author, 1 January 1995.
[90] Harry Balsam, letter to the author, 8 May 1995.
[91] Predominantly Slav-speaking, from 1772 to 1917 Ruthenia was divided under Russian, Austrian, Hungarian and occasionally Turkish rule. From 1918 to 1938 it was the easternmost province of Czechoslovakia. Annexed by Hungary in 1938, it was incorporated in the Soviet Union in 1945 (Ukraine since 1991).

cultures, they did not really mix socially. The Jewish and Czech children attended Czech secular school. In addition, the Jewish kids had an extensive course of Jewish and religious studies, which began at 6.30 a.m., followed by secular school from 9 to 12.30. After lunch it was back to cheder till evening. A very busy schedule, but we nevertheless found time for recreation and games.

'Overall, the two major communities had a reasonable coexistence, since it suited both parties to trade respectfully, as each was preoccupied with the struggle of feeding and bringing up their families. Until 1939 I had a normal happy childhood, surrounded by a large, loving family and friends. But they were economically hard times for all concerned. No one lived a Life of Riley, or as they say in Yiddish, "Wie Gott in Frankreich" ("Like God in France").'[92]

For the Jews of Poland, there were many intimations of danger as the European crisis intensified during 1938 and early 1939. Perec Zylberberg, living in Lodz, was not quite fifteen when Hitler's armies entered Prague in March 1939. 'The life of a young person aged fifteen is full of wonders, discovery and expectations,' he wrote in a recent diary of his recollections. 'The events that were then unfolding were a culmination of at least a good number of years of my life. As a schoolboy I experienced many instances of overt and covert animosity from Polish boys and adults, sometimes more from children than grown-ups. Sometimes the reverse. The consciousness of its existence was a constant companion.

'My school years, which lasted until 1938, were a period in which we knew about harassment. We, that is the immediate family and relatives, were scattered in many Polish and foreign lands.'

Ben Helfgott and many other boys share the recollections of Perec Zylberberg that 'thoughts of leaving Poland for pleasanter places were often brought up at the dinner table. There was a noisy and pointed attempt by the then Polish government to limit the chances of a useful life for the Jews of Poland. It took various forms. Economic boycott, anti-Jewish legislation, restrictions in admitting Jews to schools of higher learning, as well as a covert action to make Jews feel insecure. Besides the real-life contact with neighbours and other people from the same street and places around us, we also had the news from abroad crowding in on us. The general atmosphere was loaded with apprehension. And yet we were looking forward to better days. We were the proverbial optimists.'[93]

That summer Perec Zylberberg and his sister Esther both went to Jewish

[92] Victor Greenberg, recollections, letter to the author, 8 December 1994.
[93] Perec Zylberberg, recollections, diary entry for 24 June 1993.

summer camps. He was a member of SKiF, the children's organisation of the Jewish Socialist Bund. His sister went to a summer camp run by TOZ, the Polish Jewish agency devoted to the health of the young. 'Oblivious to all around us,' Perec Zylberberg recalled, 'we each had a good summer in this last year of peaceful bliss. Events around were gathering speed. Czechoslovakia was being dismembered, Western Europe was getting the jitters. We were informed as to what went on. And yet we didn't believe it was for real. We didn't think it was the prelude to our own fate. So when I came back from summer camp, just a few days before the end of August 1939, the air in Lodz was charged with electrical currents. It was the same as I had left it, but only in its physical shape. The atmosphere was what one would call ominous.'[94]

Esther Zylberberg also recalled her holiday that summer. 'I was particularly happy and pleased with myself in the summer of 1939,' she wrote. 'I had done well in my examinations, and was enjoying camp life in the countryside near Lodz. There were quite a few children amongst us who hailed from Germany. They and their parents had been expelled from Germany because of their Polish origins. Sad though it was for them, for us children it was added excitement, for we engaged in teaching them Polish. In turn, we learned a smattering of German from them.

'It was there, while we were at summer camp in Wisniowa Gora, that we children were informed, on Thursday, 31 August 1939, that war was imminent, and that the camp was to be disbanded the next day. On Friday, 1 September, we said goodbye to our friends and teachers in the hope of meeting up again at the TOZ camp the following summer.' The memories of 'that last, golden summer', Esther Zylberberg wrote more than fifty years later, 'are still vivid in my mind, and I cherish them as the last carefree days of my childhood'.[95]

Jack Aizenberg was eleven years old in September 1939. 'I went to the Pardess Zionist School in Lodz, at 29 Zawadzka Street,' he recalled. 'Our background, our heritage, and our identity was dominated by our teachings, and I lived in a home of love and care, and basked in a childhood of Jewish consideration. Pardess School was named from the Hebrew word for orchard. We were the saplings of our time. On 1 September 1939, and the invasion of Poland, our orchard was destroyed, and we were cast into a world of emptiness and despair almost beyond belief.'[96]

[94] Perec Zylberberg, recollections, diary entry for 27 June 1993.

[95] Esther Brunstein Zylberberg, 'Childhood memories', *Journal of the '45 Aid Society*, No. 18, December 1994.

[96] Jack Aizenberg, letter of protest against a BBC programme critical of the bombing of Dresden, April 1995, manuscript, sent to the author.

CHAPTER 2

The Coming of War

G ERMAN FORCES ATTACKED Poland before dawn on Friday, 1 September 1939. They crossed the Polish border at many different points in the north, west and south, rapidly advancing deep into Polish territory. In the air, German fighters and bombers struck at Polish troop concentrations and military installations across Poland. Thirty-five million Polish citizens, of whom three and a half million were Jews, watched with helpless trepidation as the strongest mechanised army in Europe breached the border and overran the Polish defences.

Each boy has his own recollections of the day when, as a youngster, he saw the whole focus and pattern of life overturned, as German forces swept through Poland on land and in the sky. 'Early one Friday morning,' Salek Orenstein, from Opatow, recalled, 'we were woken by the ugly noise of the siren being sounded in the middle of the town. It was a primitive, pump-action siren which had to be operated manually by a town council official. I wondered what it was all about. I soon found out. The townspeople gathered in the market square and the news was broadcast: Germany had declared war on Poland. Everyone seemed very perturbed, but many took comfort from the fact that it was bound to take months before the German army actually reached us. There was no enemy in sight, not a single aeroplane to be seen. It was 1 September 1939. Autumn was upon us and Opatow was very cold. I was shivering.

'The siren went off a second time that day, around lunchtime and that was when my family decided that we had all better take shelter. I myself had just noticed two aeroplanes in the sky, flying so low that I could literally see the expressions on the pilots' faces. At first I had no idea whose planes they were, but I soon learned to distinguish the German *hakenkreutz* (the swastika) and understand its meaning.'[1]

'It was a beautiful morning that day,' Joseph Ribo recalled of the tiny village of Cecylowka, 'with clear blue skies dotted with occasional white clouds. There was water in the ditch on the roadside after a night's rain, and I, together with a few other six- to seven-year-old Polish boys and girls, was wading in it. Suddenly a high-pitched whistle cut the quiet air of the village. The villagers, those who were not in the field tending

---

[1] Salek Orenstein, 'Beyond Belief, A Survivor's Story', manuscript, sent to the author, 1995.

to their crops, came running to the road to enquire what the commotion was all about.

'The whistle was becoming louder as it came nearer to us, and sounded urgent. After every two to three whistles, there was some announcement. Soon we recognised a policeman walking alongside his bicycle. The policeman was going from one village to another announcing that the war had broken out and that every able-bodied man must report immediately to the Brzoza police station, about six kilometres away, and register for military service.

'The policeman was a stocky and a heavily built man with a big moustache, flushed red cheeks and sweat running down his forehead. He acted very excitedly and looked disarrayed with his three-cornered hat stuck on the back of his head. He looked a pitiful figure.'[2]

Friday night, the holiest and most homely night of the Jewish week, was spent by the Jews in Opatow, as in so many Polish towns on that first day of war, in a cellar – 'nothing but a deep dirty hole in the ground with an earth floor, crammed with rubbish,' Salek Orenstein recalled. 'A filthy stench filled the air.' Six families were crowded in the cellar together. 'As if that were not enough, rats ran across the unmade floor, their red eyes flashing in the light of our candles. My little sister cried.

'We surfaced at nightfall and blacked out our windows with old blankets. We tried to continue with our Shabbes meal as best we could, but it was a *fershterte* – a disturbed – Shabbes. We had no heating or water prepared and none of us had had the chance to wash that day. Now that my blanket was needed as blackout, I slept with a coat thrown over me. By morning, the whole town seemed to be covered in posters and emergency notices. We still went to *shul*[3] but our minds were troubled by nagging thoughts of how this situation would develop. The one redeeming feature was that we had our chulent, which I collected from the baker as usual, and we tried to convince ourselves that the invaders were many hundreds of miles away. The siren continued to sound all day on and off, and each time it did we ran down to our dismal shelter which seemed to grow worse with each visit. The ceiling was very damp and dirty water dripped down on all our heads.

'On Sunday, I accompanied my father to the stables. Our horses had been neither fed nor watered in two days. When the barn door opened, they charged out furiously, heading straight for the river. Meanwhile we cleaned out their stalls. We also had a few small dogs living at the

---

[2] Joseph Ribo (Yosek Rotbaum), 'Yosek, My Adventures During the Second World War', manuscript, sent to the author, 18 April 1995.

[3] Synagogue.

stables and we gave them whatever bones and leftovers we had from our Shabbes meal. They had not eaten for two days either and they already looked weak.

'From our position, outside the town gate, my father and I could see the Polish soldiers on the march, their rifles tied on with string!'[4]

All over western Poland, that Saturday morning was fraught with new sights and fearful omens. In Bialobrzegi, eleven-year-old Kopel Kandelcukier recalled a caravan of Gypsies passing through the town. 'I will never forget the day the planes machine-gunned the column. There were dead bodies and horses strewn about the road.'[5] Krulik Wilder was not yet ten years old when war broke out. 'The first two days were chaotic,' he recalled of his home town, Piotrkow. 'We were hiding in the cellar when the bombs were falling on the town, especially on Saturday, September 2. It was horrendous, people crying, praying, exclaiming "Shema Israel" ("Hear! O Israel"). At this point my father decided, like many others in the town, that we would all try to escape to the east, but unfortunately, when we got to the town of Radom, just over a hundred kilometres from Piotrkow, the Germans caught up with us. We were bewildered and confused, and, not knowing what to do, my parents decided to return to Piotrkow.'[6]

Twelve-year-old Meir Sosnowicz was in Warsaw when war broke out. 'Within days a bomb fell in our courtyard,' he recollected, 'creating a crack in the wall which remained unrepaired until we left Warsaw. Although I was at home at the time, no further damage was done to our apartment or the people in it. Other houses in our street were completely demolished and people killed, and I remember that the stench of burnt material permeated the air for months afterwards.'[7]

Michael Etkind was fourteen in September 1939. A boy from Lodz, he was on holiday with his family at Wisniowa Gora. 'It was a beautiful late summer's day,' he recalled, 'but the peace was interrupted by the hum of aeroplanes in the cloudless sky, and the stillness was broken by distant explosions that caused the ground to tremble beneath our feet. Somebody suggested that we should build an anti-bomb shelter, and so we started to dig a long trench; if nothing else, it helped to relieve the tension. The radio announced heavy fighting, and claimed that dozens of enemy planes and tanks had been destroyed.'[8]

Ben Helfgott, who was not yet ten years old, was also on holiday on 1 September 1939. 'That day,' he recalled, 'a beautifully warm sunny

[4] Salek Orenstein, 'Beyond Belief, A Survivor's Story', manuscript, sent to the author, 1995.

[5] Kopel Kendall (Kandelcukier), recollections, letter to the author, 2 September 1995.

[6] Israel (Krulik) Wilder, 'Krulik's Story', manuscript, sent to the author, 1 January 1995.

[7] Michael Novice (Meir Sosnowicz), recollections, manuscript, June 1995.

[8] Michael Etkind, '"Youth" Remembered', manuscript, sent to the author, 4 January 1996.

day, we were staying with my mother's father in Sieradz. It was Friday morning and we had to be back in Piotrkow because school was due to begin after the summer holidays on Monday 4 September. Mother wanted to get home early – so that she could prepare for the Shabbat. Fish had to be cooked, the chicken prepared, the table linen and silver just so. The Shabbat is spoken of in Jewish tradition as the bride and it was our duty to welcome her in style.

'That Shabbat would prove to be horribly different. Normally the journey between the two places took about two hours by bus. We would leave at seven o'clock in the morning and my father would be waiting to meet us at nine. No sooner had we got on the bus to begin our journey than there was the sound of aircraft overhead. We knew they were not Polish. Within minutes of hearing the aircraft, there was the more menacing sound of bombs falling. We all left the bus and took what shelter there was in the ditches at the side of the road.

'Fortunately, none of us was hurt. But it took eleven hours for the journey to be completed.'[9]

Ten-year-old Arek Hersh, in Sieradz at the outbreak of war, later wrote: 'I was sitting with my older brother, Tovia, outside our house. We had just got back from the synagogue and everything was calm, when suddenly, from out of nowhere, we heard the sound of a plane. This was immediately followed by a barrage of rifle fire as soldiers began firing at the plane, which swooped low over the houses, then flew away.'

Arek Hersh's father decided that their family should leave Sieradz and seek greater safety further east, out of the line of advance of the German army. They made off, on foot, for the town of Zdunska Wola, fifteen kilometres to the east, reaching the home of Arek's cousins that afternoon. 'While the "grown-ups" were talking,' Arek recalled, 'I ran next door to where my uncle Moshe lived with his two sons, David and Tovia and their sister Mania. They were very pleased to see me. Suddenly we heard a noise in the sky. We all ran out into the street to watch a "dogfight" between German and Polish fighters. No one was shot down, and after a short while they flew away.'

That night passed peacefully. 'The next morning I went into the yard at the back of my cousin's house. At the end of the yard was a fence and then fields, growing maize. Suddenly there came the deafening roar of engines as several planes started dive-bombing. I looked up and saw the German cross on the planes' fuselage. There were no Polish planes in sight and no sound of anti-aircraft guns to be heard. The planes started strafing and dropping bombs all around, and then wave after

[9] Ben Helfgott, 'Memories of Poland', *In Face of Adversity*, Frank Cass, London, 1991, page 149.

wave of other planes came over, filling the sky, their noise deafening. They bombed and strafed everything and everyone in sight, creating panic among the civilian population, as was their objective.

'People were running in all directions. I dashed into the maize fields, not realising what I was doing. Soon another wave of German "Stukas" came swooping down, the noise so appalling that we couldn't tell which direction they were coming from. Two planes dived towards where I was hiding. When I realised that they were coming towards me, I ran back towards my cousin's house. Apparently my parents were out, frantically looking for me. My brother Tovia was calling me, "Arek, where are you?" I called, "Here". Suddenly there were more planes approaching in our direction, bombing and strafing as before.

'I ran towards the railway station, not realising that this was the wrong thing to do. As I ran through the maize field trying to take cover amongst the tall, thick plants, another plane started to dive-bomb towards me. Panic-stricken, I ran towards the road. To my right a horse lay dying, beside which was a man, a woman and three children. They must have been the victims of a direct hit as they were all badly injured, two of them having had their legs blown off in the blast. A terrible fear overcame me. I changed direction, and once again started running towards my cousin's house, when suddenly everything went quiet. The planes' mission was over. We watched as they turned and flew away. By now my parents had spotted me from a distance. How happy I was when I saw them again. I thanked God for delivering us alive from that dreadful nightmare.'

The Hersh family made its way from Zdunska Wola further eastward, keeping to country roads as the main roads were crowded with other civilians fleeing and soldiers making their way to the front. 'We crossed open fields,' Arek Hersh later wrote, 'the sun shining overhead in a blue sky. Some Polish cavalry passed us with horses pulling several artillery guns. A high-ranking Polish officer drove past in a chauffeur-driven car, then came infantry soldiers singing a rude army song. As we approached a railway yard my father decided we should sit and have a rest under a tree. We sat there, looking at a goods train standing on a line with no engine attached to it.

'Suddenly we heard the roar of planes overhead, and quickly ran to a nearby orchard to try and find some cover. As we started to run, the planes appeared and began strafing and bombing the train that was full of ammunition. All hell broke loose as the ammunition exploded, bullets ricocheting in all directions. Everybody in the area began to run for their lives, the Polish units of cavalry and infantrymen scattering in all directions as they were pursued by the German fighter planes, creating havoc and panic. I saw two soldiers on horseback who were pulling a gun carrier behind them, when all at once one of the gun-carrier's wheels hit a tree and sent the two unfortunate soldiers flying through the air.

'The planes flew away, leaving a trail of wounded soldiers and devastation. For a while we were all still too frightened to emerge from the shelter of the trees as ammunition was exploding all around us, but eventually my father ran to see if he could be of any assistance to the two soldiers who had come off their horses. He found, however, that one was already dead and the other couldn't move. My father gave him a drink of water and then ran towards the road, hoping to find some help.

'Ten minutes later he came back with two cavalrymen who had lost their horses in all the commotion. They carried the soldier towards the road, one holding his head, the other his legs, while my father supported his waist. The soldier was in extreme agony. After several minutes my father came back to us, very upset, and told us that we were getting out of this inferno. We collected our things together and started walking.'

In the town of Lask, the Hersh family was given shelter by Moshe Kaminski, a poor Jew who had come up to them in the market square and offered to help. He and his wife lived in a dilapidated house with no electricity. A sewing-machine was their main possession. Moshe Kaminski and his wife slept in a single bed in one of their two bedrooms; their six children shared a double bed in the second bedroom. 'There were just two rooms and a kitchen in the house; no bath, just a toilet in the yard,' Arek Hersh recalled. 'We washed ourselves from a jug and bowl. That night we all slept on the floor, but it was better than the open air.'

Eventually Arek Hersh and his family found shelter with relatives in Lodz, thirty-five kilometres from Lask. 'Mother took all three of us to look around the shops,' he recalled, 'where we saw Jewish people discussing business in Yiddish as if nothing was happening.' That first night, however, the war came to Lodz. 'We were woken from sleep by heavy bombardment. We could hear the familiar, frightening sounds gradually moving nearer and nearer. Everybody started to get out of bed, some naked, some in their nightclothes. People began running out into the street to see what was going on. Neighbours began to arrive from the second and third floors as the building was a tenement. They all congregated in my cousin's flat, asking for advice. Should they go in the direction of Brzeziny, they wanted to know – it was a town on the way to Warsaw. Many made that journey, and many were killed on it, as the German planes strafed them.'[10]

---

[10] Arek Hersh (Herzlikowicz), 'Sieradz, August 1939', manuscript, sent to the author, 1995.

On the morning of Saturday, 2 September 1939, Ben Helfgott was still in Piotrkow. 'All of us were gathered in the basement of a nearby shop,' he later wrote, 'fearing that the town might be bombed. We didn't have to wait long before the explosions occurred. Although I was barely ten years old and my two sisters were younger, we were still old enough to react with horror as a man injured by shrapnel was brought into our ready-made shelter. His wounds were extensive and he was smothered in blood. It was our first experience of the realities of war.

'After the bombing there was panic. The population of the whole town seemed to be moving east away from the invading army. We were no different. My father hired a carriage, a droshki, and we drove out of town, travelling in a pitifully slow procession of humanity. We turned up at Sulejow, a village of five thousand people, about fifteen kilometres away. When we arrived there, it couldn't have looked more peaceful. Certainly you wouldn't imagine that a hideous war had just begun.'[11]

On the following morning, Sunday, 3 September 1939, both Britain and France declared war on Germany. 'There was jubilation,' Michael Etkind, still in the holiday village of Wisniowa Gora, later wrote. 'Now there was nothing to worry about. Hitler would be destroyed in no time.'[12]

Fifteen-year-old Perec Zylberberg, and his younger sister Esther, who had returned from Wisniowa Gora to Lodz on the outbreak of war, also remembered that dramatic moment when news of the British and French declarations of war was announced. 'At last we were not afraid. We thought that this was it. There was hugging and kissing. How long could it take now before Hitler was defeated? The French army was the strongest in Europe, the British ruled the seas.'[13]

'The weather that Sunday was beautiful,' recalled Ben Helfgott, whose family had gone to Sulejow to seek refuge from the bombs. 'People were walking around in the warm sunlight as though life really was as serene as the sun made it seem. I started playing with the local boys. Within minutes I had new friends. A lovely, lovely day – until as the sun began to go down we heard the sound of planes overhead. They swooped down and started dropping incendiary bombs. Seconds later, this pretty little village was a mass of flames. At ten years of age, I had never seen anything like it before. I have also seen nothing like it since – not even Dante's Inferno could have been visualised in this form.

'No one knew where to go, but they were all running in different

---

[11] Ben Helfgott, 'Memories of Poland', *In Face of Adversity*, Frank Cass, London, 1990, pages 149–50.

[12] Michael Etkind, '"Youth" Remembered', manuscript, sent to the author, 4 January 1996.

[13] Esther Brunstein and Perec Zylberberg, in conversation with the author, 10 May 1996.

directions, some with their clothes on fire. Blindly running. Cats, dogs, horses, cows, all of them aflame, too, all running. Madly, pointlessly, agonisingly. Instantly, whole families were consumed by flames. That we managed to escape unhurt was a real miracle. As we ran into the nearby woods, I could see people falling all around us – picked off by machine-guns from the aircraft ahead. There was the terrible sound of screaming. Sometimes just screams. Sometimes names – "Moishe!" "Gittel!" Names that might never be heard again, but which at that moment were being called in other towns and villages all over Poland.

'Then there were those looking for their children, for parents, for grandparents, for brothers, for sisters. About three thousand people were burnt and killed within a very short time, whole families wiped out and many decimated. By a miracle our family of five was saved. Our horse was killed, our carriage destroyed. So my father led us on foot away from the village.'[14]

Thousands of Jews had fled, as had the Helfgotts, from Piotrkow, and from other towns in western Poland, in search of a smaller town or village in which they might find shelter. Scvek Finkelstein was only seven years old. 'My family decided that we would leave Piotrkow and go to the town of Sulejow, eight miles away,' he recalled. 'That day was very festive for me, it was like a national holiday. I was excited because it was like going on a day's outing in the country. I cannot remember whether all my sisters were with me that day, I knew that Issie had been called up to the Polish army and he was somewhere on the front line.

'As soon as we were on the road to Sulejow it seemed to me that the whole town of Piotrkow was on its way to this village. The one-lane dirt road was packed with people, wagons and horses escaping from the town. Dad's brother Bernard lived on the outskirts of the village, and we stopped there first. I remember that he had a factory that glazed ceramics and pottery. He had kilns that were dug into the sides of hills. It was all a lot of fun for me looking over my uncle's place. The next day we continued our journey and soon came into the village.

'The dirt streets of Sulejow were completely jammed with people. There was literally no space to move, it was so crowded. Soon I heard the sound of planes overhead. I was standing and looking at the planes as they dived out of the sky throwing explosives and incendiary bombs. The houses around me collapsed and the people inside were running out to the street and a second wave of fighter planes came streaking down with their machine-guns blazing, shooting the people down as

[14] Ben Helfgott, 'Memories of Poland', *In Face of Adversity*, Frank Cass, London, 1990, pages 149–50.

they were racing for any kind of shelter that they could find.

'The little village was completely on fire. I heard the screams of people and animals, and most of all I remember the horrible smell of flesh burning. I was still standing with my eyes on the planes when I felt my mother throw me down to the ground and cover me completely with her own body. While I lay on the ground I could feel the heat from the burning houses and next to us was a coal yard that was catching fire. I have no idea how long I lay on the ground but some time later I stood up and was completely alone. Mother had gone off and all I saw around me was total chaos and destruction with dead bodies everywhere, and lots of screaming from the wounded.'

Sevek Finkelstein was, he recalled, 'walking around stunned and not knowing what to do and not really understanding what had happened. I had never seen death before and the scenes were awful for me to behold. I came across my father who took me by the hand and we ran as fast as we could into the deep forest. We were really scared that the German planes would come back and indeed they did a second time. It was only after the war that I learned that more than a thousand people had been killed that day, and that entire families were completely annihilated.

'We stayed in the forest for several days, in a constant state of fear. I was not happy staying in the forest, especially having to sleep on the ground. There were many other people there with us. I saw the remnants of the Polish army, very glum and disappointed-looking. I was very hungry and was not shy of complaining about the lack of food. Finally my father knocked on the door of a hut where some older peasants lived. Dad was able to persuade them to serve us some food. The peasant woman served me boiled potato and cabbage and it tasted so delicious that it has remained my favourite food till now.

'Eventually we moved out of the forest and re-entered Sulejow. This village was in a complete shambles. The houses were either burned or had collapsed. They were gathering the corpses and burying them in a mass grave. Father and I went looking amongst the corpses for Mother. We could not find her and eventually, to my father's relief, he was told that someone had seen Mother get on a wagon travelling to Warsaw. We left Sulejow, getting a ride in a horse-wagon back to Piotrkow. The owner of this wagon was a friend of my father and he allowed me to sit up front and hold the reins. That made me feel really proud. When we entered the town and passed our building we were astonished to see that it was bombed, and that our second-floor apartment had collapsed.'[15]

---

[15] Sidney Finkel (Sevek Finkelstein), 'My Story', manuscript, sent to the author, 12 September 1995.

Lodz was also bombed by the Germans that Sunday. One of the boys who recalled that bombing was Perec Zylberberg. He was working as an apprentice in a textile factory around which trenches had been dug throughout the previous two days as a protection against air attack. It was intended to roof over the trenches for greater safety, but there proved to be no time for that. As the first bombing attack on Lodz began, the workers at the factory were, he recalled, 'ushered into the open trench in the garden plot, adjoining the wall of the factory building. Then it happened. The whole world seemed to explode around us. It got dark, although it was only the afternoon. I just remember being thrown about. Without thinking, as I recall now, I darted out into the garden. From there I made my way to the street and continued to run in the direction of the open spaces, which abounded in my neighbourhood. Some people sheltering in a house pulled me inside. They yelled at me not to go in the direction I had been heading. That was the location of anti-aircraft guns. There the bombs kept on coming down constantly.

'Totally shaken, with wounds on my head, I somehow calmed down a bit. My father, who wasn't in the trench with us, because he had been locking up the flat, ran down towards the garden. Finding pandemonium all around, he couldn't spot me anywhere. Some people said that they saw me split seconds before the impact. Others were actually saying that they thought I was under the ruins of the brick wall which had crumbled upon us. Others still thought that they saw me darting away in the direction of the fields. Not being able to find me under the rubble, my father started running in my direction. Of course he found me. What a traumatic experience. That, and subsequent events, gave my psyche an irreversible jolt. No more did the war seem to be exciting. It put the fear of the oncoming apocalypse into sharp relief. So much for the beginning of a long, tragedy-laden period. It abruptly put an end to childhood, laughter and play.'[16]

The factory next door to the one in which Perec Zylberberg worked had also been bombed. 'They had a large basement,' he later remembered. 'As the alarm sounded all the workers, and the inhabitants of the building adjoining the plant, ran for shelter to the basement. Some passers-by also tried to use that shelter. Some managed to get in. The owners of the plant, however, were very vigilant anti-Semites. They refused entry to Jewish passers-by. Those not allowed in ran to other houses. There is no implied justice or otherwise. But the truth is, that those inside perished. What happened to the ones who had to find shelter elsewhere is not known to me. I still hope that they survived.'[17]

[16] Perec Zylberberg, recollections, diary entry for 28 June 1993.
[17] Perec Zylberberg, recollections, diary entry for 30 June 1993.

That Sunday, in the holiday resort of Wisniowa Gora, as streams of Polish civilians moved eastward to try to escape the advancing German army, Michael Etkind's family did not know which way to turn. 'Peasants on horse-drawn vans and carts, with their livestock trailing behind, and families with bundles on their backs, were moving slowly in the direction of Warsaw,' he recalled. 'They looked tired and bewildered and did not answer our questions, but only asked for water. The night sky was lit up in the west, from where a steady rumble could be heard. The stream of civilian refugees was joined by soldiers and officers retreating in disarray, and even some tanks passed slowly along the road. This went on uninterruptedly for almost two days.

'Rumours began to circulate that the Germans were killing all the men, irrespective of whether they wore uniforms or not, and that all men had to go to the capital to defend it. Caught up in the panic, my father, with the other men, departed in the direction of Warsaw. My older brother Jacob was spending the summer in Zakopane, in the mountains, and we did not know whether he managed to return to Lodz.

'When the stream of refugees had passed, an eerie silence fell over the village, and my mother, left with the three of us, my younger sister Henka, my youngest brother Lolek, and myself, decided that we should make our way back to Lodz. For safety's sake we would walk at night; we joined a group of about two hundred women and children making their way back to their homes in Lodz. A lone Polish officer appeared, confiscated my bicycle, and pedalled off in the direction of Warsaw. The sun was setting as we passed the empty railway station, from which we would have normally departed for Lodz.'

The journey from the holiday village continued. 'Suddenly, a German aeroplane came screaming over the treetops at the edge of the road, and with its undercarriage tore all the telegraph wires above the railway track, and then disappeared into the distance. The telegraph wires vibrated and hummed a long low mournful sound. We scrambled out of the ditch at the edge of the road, gathered our belongings, and silently walked on. Slowly the sky darkened, but no lights appeared in the wayside cottages, and their dark shapes were silhouetted against the starlit sky. The silence was only broken by the cries of the younger children.

'As we neared Widzew, on the outskirts of Lodz, we passed a group of men in prison garb who greeted us with catcalls and shouted: "You're going in the wrong direction, the Germans will kill you."

'We entered Lodz before dawn. The town seemed deserted; we thought that all the inhabitants had fled. We rang the bell of our gate. Five minutes later the caretaker's wife let us in.'[18]

---

[18] Michael Etkind, ' "Youth" Remembered', manuscript, sent to the author, 4 January 1996.

On Sunday 3 September 1939 the German army entered the Polish town of Bielsko-Biala, known to most of its Jewish inhabitants by its German name, Bielitz, and with a substantial German minority. Kurt Klappholz was then twelve years old. Together with his father, he went into the centre of town to view the scene. 'We gazed at their columns in amazement,' he later wrote. 'Never before had we seen an army so well equipped. Moreover, the troops were not only trained for fighting – a training which on that occasion proved redundant, they had obviously also had good training in making propaganda. They rose from the benches in their troop-carriers, bench by bench, gave the Hitler salute, and chorused one or another of their well-known slogans – "Ein Volk, ein Reich, ein Führer" ("One People, one Nation, one Leader"), "Wir danken unserem Führer" ("We thank our Leader"), etc. While the day before the town centre had been almost empty, now it was thronged with frenziedly jubilant crowds, most of them the German inhabitants, who not only loudly repeated the soldiers' slogans, but showered their liberators with flowers, cakes and sandwiches. The crowd's jubilant enthusiasm was infectious. I still remember that even my father offered a cigarette to a German soldier. Even so, we did not stay to see the end of the "parade" but returned home, where several of our neighbours were talking excitedly.

'While my father joined in the conversation, I distanced myself from the little group, and started to brood over what I had just seen, and began to cry. My father noticed this and came over to ask why I was crying. I wiped my tears and began to mumble that Poland was lost. Then I paused, looked him in the eyes and said: "Papa, ich glaube, dass wir diesen Krieg nicht überleben werden" ("Father, I fear that we will nor survive this war"). He patted me on the head gently, smiled, and tried to calm my outlandish, childish fears.'[19]

Alfred Huberman recalled the coming of war to Pulawy. 'As we lived near the river, where there was a newly built strategic bridge,' he wrote, 'the German Luftwaffe bombed the town. We then took whatever we could carry and set off for a smaller town, Konskowola, leaving Pulawy via the main road. The whole road was alight. Because of the heat from the flames of burning houses on both sides, crowds of us walked in the middle of the street. We stayed in Konskowola until the Germans marched in; it did not take them too long. The short time we were there, bombs were falling all over the place, there were fires everywhere, and dozens of us were crowded into one room. I remember my grandparents

---

[19] Kurt Klappholz, 'The Day the UK Declared War on Hitler', *Journal of the '45 Aid Society*, No. 7, April 1980.

were with us (my mother's parents) and I really got to know my grandfather for the first time, and I thought him quite sweet, although he had the reputation of being a very strict tyrant. I suppose that is why so many of his children left home, some of them to France, where many more survived than those who remained in Poland.

'We also had my Auntie Tzirl and her family with us. She had four children, the youngest was a baby girl only a few months old. The bombs were falling, the noise was terrific, and the baby girl lay there smiling. That baby kept us going.

'On returning to Pulawy, I remember walking down the street with my father. The street and the surrounding area were in ruins, just the brick chimneys were visible. It probably did not take more than a few incendiary bombs to set alight the whole area, but still I walked towards our house hoping against hope that, by some miracle, ours would be the only one left standing. Alas it was not.

'We then squatted in a building near the law courts for a few weeks. When the ghetto was established, that part of town was out of bounds, so we moved in with my mother's parents who had two small basement rooms.'

Alfred Huberman also learned, within a few weeks of the German conquest of Poland, of the fate of his uncle and older sister, who were living in Warsaw during the German siege of the capital. 'During that battle,' he wrote, 'my sister Rivka, who was one of twins, got killed by a piece of shrapnel. She was living with my Aunt Miriam and Uncle Mordechai. Their flat was hit. My uncle got a direct hit and was killed. My older sister Idessa found my sister Rivka just hours before she died of her injuries in a Warsaw hospital.'[20]

The German army entered Lodz on Friday, 8 September 1939. At that very moment Perec Zylberberg, his mother and sister were on their way to the home of his uncle and aunt and their young son in the city centre. 'We wanted to be together with auntie and the young cousin,' he later recalled. 'It seemed to have been an impulse. Somehow, closely-related people wanted to share their closeness. They were the closest relatives that we had in Lodz. As we came to the city centre, so the first outriders on motorcycles came into view. They almost looked like ordinary men. Only their uniforms were different. What stuck in my memory was the applause that erupted on their arrival. At first nobody could tell exactly who those jubilant people were. It didn't take long, however, to realise that these were the much vaunted Volksdeutsche. Of course we knew of their existence before the war. They were not hiding

[20] Alfred (Abram) Huberman, recollections, letter to the author, 7 May 1996.

their ethnicity. They only made us all believe that they were loyal citizens of the Polish State.

'So, we had a ready-made occupation machine. At the time that we saw the German patrols come in, my mother remarked that they, the Germans, were a tough lot. She remembered them from the First World War. According to Mother, they were strict but reasonably observant of the law and could even be fair at times. Such impressions were held by many people of Mother's generation. It was soothing to hear her talk thus.'[21]

Arek Hersh also witnessed the arrival of German troops in Lodz. Leaving the building in which he was sheltering, 'I noticed people running towards Plac Wolnosci (Freedom Square). I followed the crowd, wanting to know what was going on. After watching for several minutes, I noticed a number of motorcycles with side-cars, travelling very fast. These motorcycles were being driven by German soldiers dressed in long grey leather coats and helmets. This was my first realisation that the Germans had finally arrived. I ran home to my relations and parents to tell them the news.

'The next day I watched the might of the German army marching into Lodz; an incredible sight which lasted hours. There were columns of soldiers with heavy artillery pieces, some drawn by shire horses, some by motors. There was division after division of motorised infantry driving armoured vehicles, and there were planes flying overhead. I was overwhelmed by the weaponry and the discipline of this army, like a huge, well-oiled machine advancing inexorably on Warsaw.

'On the third day I saw German officers catching Jewish men and burning or cutting off their beards. They were laughing delightedly and being photographed in the process of these activities. "Such barbarism," I thought. This was my first taste of German brutality and their attitude to the Jews. After watching such horrific scenes, my father decided to return with our family to Sieradz. Little did we realise there were much worse things to come in all our lives. We took our leave, saying goodbye to our cousins and friends in Lodz. Everybody agreed we would be better off in a small town.

'The journey back was by bus, a journey which took us past Lask and Zdunska Wola. The roads were full of German troops going towards Lodz and then Warsaw. Their column was never-ending. On the sides of the roads, I could see crosses with German helmets on them, hundreds upon hundreds. Not one Polish helmet did I see throughout the journey from Lodz, and I presumed from this that as far as the Germans were concerned, it didn't matter where the Poles were buried.

---

[21] Perec Zylberberg, recollections, diary entry for 2 July 1993.

'At last we arrived back in Sieradz. So much had happened that it seemed we had been gone a year, though it had only been two weeks. We found many of our belongings had been plundered, though the crates of fruit that we had left in the cellar remained intact. My parents quickly went to work, selling it off before it could go bad. It felt now as though our lives were starting to return to normal again. It seemed that nothing else mattered as long as we were all back home and alive. Next day I ran to see if my cousins were all back, and was delighted to find that my uncles Pesach, Natal and Moshe had returned in one piece with their families. Quickly we caught up on one another's news; we each had different stories to relate of the past two weeks.

'Soon after we returned to Sieradz, I was caught in the market square, and together with many other Jewish men was made to dig up bodies of German soldiers killed in the battle around Sieradz and put them into coffins.' Arek Hersh was just eleven years old. His birthday was on September 13: 'I was horrified by what I saw – decomposed bodies, some minus arms or legs which had been blown off by grenades. It was a terrible experience for me, the true horror of war, and it had a lasting effect on my life. From that time I have always believed it is better to talk than to cut each other to pieces in battle. I only wish that the statesmen of this world would think the same way.'

Suddenly the terrors of war had changed. Running away from an advancing army, and being bombed, were replaced by new terrors. 'The Germans were now beginning to round up Jewish men in the streets for work,' Arek Hersh recalled. 'On many occasions I saw these men being beaten up for no apparent reason. I was caught several times and made to unload wagons of coal and briquettes (compressed coal dust). In the first winter, I remember working with French prisoners of war and later on with British. We had problems conversing with each other, as none of the prisoners spoke German, Polish or Yiddish, so we developed a form of sign language. I was sorry for the prisoners of war because they were guarded by German soldiers with guns, whereas we were still free to a certain extent.

'At that time, the Jewish children were deprived of their education as the Germans closed our school. Standing by the main highway one day, very near to our closed school, I watched the German army convoys travelling towards Lodz, probably bound for Warsaw. I was amazed at the size of artillery guns and the large quantities of weapons. The Polish army had nothing to match it, and I thought it was no wonder the German army had taken Poland in such a short time. Our army had never been trained for such a blitzkrieg (lightning war).

'Once again Sieradz became an army garrison town. Newly built barracks had been left intact by the Polish army when they withdrew, and now the Germans were using them for their own training facilities. One day I watched the German army columns marching down our street on their way to manoeuvres, singing "Wir fahren gegen England" ("We are marching against England"). England, which was to become my home in later years, then seemed a foreign faraway place. I reflected, however, that it must have been important for the Germans to feel they had to sing about it.'[22]

From the earliest days of the German occupation, Jews in Sieradz were 'dragged out of their beds at night and shot against a wall,' thirteen-year-old Mayer Hersh (no relation of Arek) recalled. On one occasion the Germans took fifty hostages, Jews and non-Jews, 'who were very well-known personalities, such as priests, doctors, dentists etc.,' and then rounded up Jews in the street to dig a mass grave at the Jewish cemetery. 'Very soon, those fifty victims arrived and were all shot and buried straight away. One of those shot was not quite dead. By chance, he was being buried by a close friend of his. The victim clutched the turn-up of his friend's trousers and said, "How can you bury your friend alive?" His friend suffered a nervous breakdown as a consequence.'[23]

Arek Hersh witnessed another frightening example of German behaviour in Sieradz in those early days of the occupation. His family were at home having lunch. 'Suddenly we heard the sound of jackboots marching in the street, and thinking that the German army were undertaking manoeuvres, I dashed to the door to watch. What I saw chilled me. Soldiers were stopping at every door, four armed men to each house. It was obvious their intentions were hostile. I shouted to my father and my brother, Tovia, to hide, and I myself dashed up to the pigeon loft where I could observe more clearly what was going on. Disturbed pigeons flew everywhere at my panicked entrance, but the loft provided a very good vantage point.

'I saw German soldiers dragging Jewish men from their houses, and kicking and beating them in the street; with horror I noticed that my father was among them. The Jewish men were forced to run towards the market-place, whereupon two rows of armed German soldiers were waiting for them. They then had to run through the German gauntlet where they were savagely kicked and clubbed with rifle butts. My cousin, Idel Natal, only twenty-one years old, was kicked to death in this mêlée.

'All the men were then taken to the army barracks and kept there overnight. The Germans, it transpired, were accusing some Jewish men of firing at a German soldier, and, not knowing who was responsible, were holding all Jewish men as hostages until the culprit owned up.

[22] Arek Hersh (Herszlikowicz), 'Sieradz, August 1939', manuscript.
[23] Mayer Hersh (Herszkowicz), letter to the author, 12 December 1994.

Fortunately, a Polish Christian woman happened to have seen the shooting, and she went to the German police and told them the truth. It eventually came to light that it had been a Polish Christian, and not a Jew at all, who had carried out the shooting in a moment of drunkenness.

'After this incident all the men were released from the barracks, some with broken arms and legs. My father got off lightly with a few bruises. Thus ended a terrible and tragic episode in our town. My cousin was dead and many others had been crippled for life. And all because the Germans couldn't be bothered to find out the true facts.'[24]

In Lodz, Rose Fogel recalled how, during the very early days of the German occupation, the Germans took her brother Shlomo, then aged nineteen, 'to dig ditches, and beat him up badly. He ran away to Russia to save his life. Unfortunately he died in Russia.'[25]

One of Aron Zylberszac's first vivid memories after the Germans occupied Lodz, 'was part of their – I believe – campaign of fear. They took a number of Jews at random, and hung them up in the Baluty Platz by their necks. People were forced to go and look at them, and they hung there for days and days. I saw it. As a child, a twelve-year-old, I thought, "How in the world could this happen?" Their brutality was such that as soon as a German came near us we were paralysed with fear'[26]

In Warsaw, Sam Dresner recalled his first experience of the Germans, soon after the capitulation of the capital. 'They had set up field kitchens to serve the population, who were starved as a result of the siege which had lasted a few weeks. As the queue formed for the soup, the soldiers started shouting "Juden raus" ("Jews out"). As they could not tell who was Jewish they soon found help from the Polish youngsters who went round pointing out who was Jewish. What hurt most was the fact that the boy who pointed at me was the same boy with whom I had worked a few weeks ago building barricades at the top of our street. And my father and uncle were still in the Polish army.'[27]

Near Warsaw, Sam Freiman, who was then eleven years old, recalled the arrival of the Germans in Konstancin-Jeziorna. 'They picked up three young men, who were leaders of the three Jewish organisations, Betar, Poale Zion and the Bund,' he wrote. 'They took them out of town and shot them. Then they ordered the Jewish community to collect the bodies. This was done to terrorise us into submission. We could not believe that such behaviour could happen.' But there was more to come

[24] Arek Hersh (Herszlikowicz), 'Sieradz, August 1939', manuscript, sent to the author, 1995.

[25] Rose Fogel (Dajch), letter to the author, 18 January 1995.

[26] Aron Zylberszac, recollections, transcript, Imperial War Museum Sound Archives.

[27] Sam Dresner, letter to the author, 28 January 1995.

in those early days. Sam Freiman used to take food to a house where a watchmaker and his wife were looking after two people, a widow and a scholar, both of whom were deranged. 'When the Germans came into the village,' Sam Freiman recalled, 'they took them from their home and shot them.'[28]

Howard Chandler (Chaim Wajchendler) recalled the day when the Germans occupied his home town of Wierzbnik. 'When the war started I was almost eleven years old,' he wrote, 'and had just passed from Grade 3 to 4 with good marks, and did not quite understand what it was all about. The first thing I remember after the town was occupied was that when it came time to start school again, the Jewish students were not allowed back to school. That is the only schooling I had – three grades. Even at that age I realised that things were changing fast. Jews were restricted in their freedom and were not able to carry on with regular business or work.

'On the first Yom Kippur in 1939, September 24, the Germans set fire to the synagogue. It was late at night and flames could be seen from far away. Everyone in the area stood outside their homes with some belongings ready to flee lest the fire spread and consume everything in its path. Fortunately, it was contained and no one was inside the synagogue. I still tremble when I recall that event, especially on Yom Kippur.

'As time progressed, things deteriorated. We were ordered to wear armbands to identify us as Jews. Movement was further restricted, and we were ordered to surrender precious metals, jewellery and furs, as well as to give up radios under threat of death. So-called "contributions" had to be paid in order to bribe German officials.'[29]

When the German forces entered Opatow, ten-year-old Salek Orenstein witnessed their arrival. He had gone down to the market-place 'to see what was going on. As I stood there, I heard a continuous loud rattling noise which grew louder and louder with each passing second. Then I saw it. I had no idea what it was at first, I had never seen a tank before. A German soldier wearing a black uniform was standing up in the turret swivelling the huge gun around in all directions. The market-place was utterly deserted.

'I froze to the spot, my hands clasped behind my back. The soldier jumped down and shouted, "Was hast du?" He must have thought that I was holding a weapon. I understood a little German, as my mother's home town of Lodz had once been occupied by them.[30] So a little of the

---

[28] Sam Freiman, recollections, letter to the author, June 1995.

[29] Howard Chandler (Chaim Wajchendler), letter to the author, 23 February 1995.

[30] The Germans had occupied Lodz in the First World War, after a hard-fought siege against the

language had rubbed off on her and consequently on us. This pleased me because anyone speaking German in Opatow was considered a "cut above". As he bent down, I could see the shiny, silver markings decorating his uniform, the skull and the crossbones. "Wo ist der Hauptstadt?" ("Where is the town centre?") he barked at me, but I was too terrified to answer. I ran home as fast as I could and went straight down to the cellar, where my parents were hiding, terribly concerned for my safety. Then I told them about my brush with the Germans.

'That evening was unlike any other. Bright light replaced the usual pitch darkness. The German army had set fire to a whole street of shops and houses to light their way through town. The burnt houses were still smouldering in the morning. The Germans had arrived in force. The first thing I saw when I went down to our stables was the army regiment's field kitchen. My father had heard how the Germans delighted in tearing the beards off Jewish faces, so he took the precaution of trimming his beard back to a much shorter length.

'Once the Germans had settled themselves into two of the local schools they began to issue orders. Apart from the strict curfew that was immediately imposed, we were not allowed to store any food on pain of death. It was quite simple: anyone caught in the streets after eight o'clock at night would be shot. Equally, if you attempted to hide food you would be shot, no questions asked, no chance to bring your case to court. We were made to hand over all our stocks of food and put on yellow armbands.

'Within a week, some of the Poles appeared around town with swastikas on their arms, claiming to be Volksdeutsche of German ancestry, which was laughable because they could not speak a single word of German! They were simply sympathisers. And they gave us hell. They smashed up our shops and looted.'[31]

Arthur Poznanski was not quite twelve years old in September 1939. Shortly before the German invasion of Poland he and his two brothers had left the border town of Wielun with their mother, in order to be with their grandparents in Piotrkow, a city which, being eighty-five kilometres further east, seemed to offer greater safety. He later recalled: 'My father stayed to collect his salary, something he never managed to do as the town was bombed on the first day of the month. He escaped and joined us in Piotrkow where we sheltered in a cellar. We left the town hoping to find shelter from bombardment in the villages, fields, or

Russian defenders. In 1940 the Germans changed the name of the city to Litzmannstadt, in honour of the German General (Litzmann) who had conquered it in 1915.

[31] Salek Orenstein, 'Beyond Belief, A Survivor's Story', manuscript, sent to the author, 1995.

forests but found, however, these had also been bombed and strafed with machine-gun fire from aircraft. So we returned to Piotrkow, which was now occupied by the Germans. My younger brothers were left with our grandparents and I returned with my parents to Wielun, where we found our apartment occupied by Volksdeutsche and all our possessions stolen or confiscated. We found alternative accommodation and bought some essential furniture for it but the frequent round-ups of intellectuals forced my father to escape back to Piotrkow, where he was not well-known.'[32]

Krulik Wilder's family had fled eastward from Piotrkow when the German invasion began, but by the time they had reached Radom the whole of central Poland had been overrun, and they had no option but to return to Piotrkow. 'On our return,' the young Krulik later recalled, 'to our dismay, we found that the Jews were being terrorised. All education and schooling stopped, and on 28 October 1939 the first ghetto was established.'[33]

In Lodz, Michael Etkind recollected, 'the buying of food became an ordeal, even if you had the money. Queues would suddenly form in front of bakeries, but often, after waiting for hours, you would walk away empty-handed. How proud and happy you were when you managed to buy and bring home a loaf of bread.' On one occasion a German soldier and a civilian entered the Etkinds' flat. When they left, they took with them two suitcases filled with valuables, including his mother's wedding ring, which they had made her take off. 'My mother later explained that the civilian was an Ethnic German.'

Michael Etkind also remembered that, as winter approached, 'life was becoming harder and more precarious. We had to wear armbands with the Star of David (this was later changed to two yellow stars with the word "Jude" on them). We had to take our radio set to the police station. Piotrkowska Street, the Oxford Street of Lodz, was renamed Adolf Hitler Strasse, and Jews were not allowed to walk there.[34] Every day another sinister-looking placard in German and Polish would appear in the streets announcing some new restrictions and ending with a warning. We soon learned that the slightest infringement of the rules meant the death sentence.

'In addition to these official orders, Jews were being rounded up, ostensibly for work, but in more cases than not simply to be tormented. The Germans would catch people in the streets, or they would enter

[32] Arthur Poznanski, recollections, letter to the author, 24 January 1995.

[33] Israel (Krulik) Wilder, 'Krulik's Story', manuscript, sent to the author, 1 January 1995.

[34] A year earlier, Berlin's Jews were forbidden to walk along the Unter den Linden.

Jewish dwellings and take away one or more members of a family –
usually the adult males. Some of those taken never came back and no
one knew what happened to them, but more often those caught for
work would come back, beaten, degraded, demoralised.

'The stories of sadism beggar description. Two Jews would be ordered
to push a car, while the German driver would put it into reverse gear.
Public lavatories had to be cleaned with toothbrushes. A friend of mine
was caught, with a number of others, and taken into a school converted
into barracks, where they were surrounded by a group of smiling soldiers.
Two men in white coats, looking like medical orderlies, entered the
room: one of them held a long knife. They ordered one Jewish man to
follow them. Ten minutes later the two Germans returned splattered
with blood and selected another victim. The soldiers were roaring with
laughter. Eventually my friend's turn came: he was led across the yard
into a shed, in the corner of which was a cage with geese. My friend
had to hold a goose, while the German with the knife cut its throat.
After plucking off its feathers, my friend was allowed to go home.

'On the night of 10 November 1939, the eve of Polish Independence
Day, we were awakened by a loud explosion. The following morning we
learned that the monument to Kosciuszko (the Polish national hero) in
Plac Wolnosci had been demolished by the Germans.[35] The equivalent
in London would be the demolition of Nelson's Column in Trafalgar
Square. On that very day, several people were hanged in public and left
hanging for three days as a warning against any possible acts of
resistance to mark November 11. There were none.'[36]

For eleven-year-old Michael Perlmutter, whose life had been 'beautiful'
since the age of seven at his Hebrew-language school in Opatow, the
coming of war 'ripped the life of my family to shreds'. At the outbreak
of war, he recalled, after his parents' sweet and chocolate factory had
been confiscated by the Germans, 'my father was abducted and shot'.[37]

Alec Ward was twelve when war came to Magnuszew. 'We had to
wear yellow stars on our arms. Jewish children were not allow to attend
school. We were not allowed to travel on the railways or slaughter any
animals for Jewish consumption, etc., etc. One night my uncle Mendel
and his partner had a cow slaughtered, and distributed the meat to the

---

[35] Tadeusz Kosciusko (1746–1817), a Polish patriot who fought in the American War of Independence (1776). In 1794 he led a Polish national uprising, defeating the Austrians, but was
wounded and taken prisoner later that same year. He died in exile in Switzerland when his horse fell
over a precipice.

[36] Michael Etkind, ' "Youth" Remembered', manuscript, sent to the author, 4 January 1996.

[37] Michael Perlmutter, letter to the author, 4 March 1995.

Jewish inhabitants. The following morning the Germans shot my uncle's partner and my uncle went into hiding.'[38]

Roman Halter, then aged twelve, recalled the day on which German troops entered Chodecz. Until then, law and order had been kept by the town's chief of police 'who looked like Marshal Pilsudski's double. He also had that huge downturned moustache. He carried a vodka flask to be used on any occasion. He, together with about twenty Polish and Jewish leaders, were rounded up at night and shot.' Those killed that night included the town's two doctors, an elderly Pole and a young Jew.[39]

What did these terrors portend? Might they not be a spasm of violence in the moment of victory, that would pass as quickly as they had arrived? In some towns things seemed less ominous than in others. 'The war infringed on our liberty literally from the start,' Lipa Tepper, who was thirteen years old that November, later wrote of life among the Jews of Dukla, 'but since they were not noticeable as major infringements, nobody took notice of them. For instance we were not permitted to enter restaurants or cafés or things like that. Well, since we never entered these places in the first place, it was not an infringement, or never considered as such. It just said on the outside of the establishment that Jews were not permitted to enter, and we didn't.

'Subsequent to that we were told that we would have to wear a white armband with a blue Star of David on it, and again it wasn't a terrible infringement, we wore it. We did not expect the Germans to be pro-Jewish but on the other hand my parents never ever expected the Germans to be anything but humane and nice people, since they knew them from the First World War and assumed they would be the same.'[40]

It was an assumption difficult to maintain for long. When the Germans entered Przemysl, in southern Poland, on 14 September 1939, they were committed, under the terms of the Nazi-Soviet Pact, to hand the city over to the Soviets, which they did two weeks later. But on September 19, during their brief period of occupation, the German authorities seized forty of the leading Jewish citizens and executed them. Among those murdered that day was engineer Abraham Gutt, whose son Witold was then eleven years old.

Sala Bernholz was also eleven when war broke out. Shortly after the Germans entered her home town of Wolanow, near Radom, 'they raided our house and took away my father. Later we were told that they had

[38] Alec Ward, 'My Story', manuscript, sent to the author, 31 May 1995.

[39] Roman Halter, recollections, sent to the author, 19 February 1996.

[40] Lipa Tepper, letter to the author, 30 January 1996.

rounded up twenty-five Jewish people and shot them in the street. My uncle came, but he did not want to tell us what had happened; he only asked for my father's *taless* (prayer shawl). My father is buried there in the Jewish cemetery.'[41]

Such killings were commonplace throughout Poland that autumn, shattering whatever hopes the Jews might have had in a benign occupation. There was to be no repetition of 1914–18, when the Germans were a relatively civilised occupying power. Instead, the random killings in German-occupied Poland in September and October 1939, in which a hitherto unprecedented number of 16,000 Jews were murdered in less than three weeks, set the tone of future German conduct, and were an ominous pointer to what was yet to come.

[41] Sala Kaye (Bernholz), 'Sala Kaye remembers', *Holocaust Testimony 1*, published by Roman Halter and Michael Etkind, London, 1983.

CHAPTER 3

In the Ghettos

FOR SEVERAL MONTHS after the German conquest of Poland, Jews could, in a move fraught with danger, leave their towns and make their way to other cities in Poland, or try to cross the eastern border into the area occupied by the Soviet Union. As many as a quarter of a million of the two and a quarter million Jews who lived in the German-occupied area made their way eastward, before the new German-Soviet border was closed in November 1939. Many of them survived the war in the comparative safety of Soviet Union. Arek Hersh, who was just ten years old during the first weeks of German rule in Sieradz, remembered those who were making their way eastward.

'Thousands of Jews and Christian Poles made the journey,' Arek Hersh later wrote, 'but my father failed to make a decision quickly enough. I remember a conversation in which he said the Germans weren't that bad in the First World War, but I now realise that that was an illusion that some people kidded themselves with. Perhaps this is why I began to value decisiveness. When an opportunity arises, I believe it should be taken quickly. My father was a good man – he trusted in God, he did his duty towards his religion, his family and his country. Perhaps, in spite of the history of persecution of the Jews, he could not envisage the evil which was to be unleashed. This is one of the many things I was never to have the opportunity to discuss with him. My aunt Hela and uncle Benjamin left for Russia, where we had some relatives, and because of their foresight survived the war.

'I remember people coming to my father for help in hiding their money and valuables when they crossed the border. He used to make a hole in the heel of his boot, fill it with paper money and jewellery, then cover it with leather or rubber. I was hoping that my father would take us on the same road to Russia, but when he did finally decide it was too late: the border was already closed. Our fate was thus sealed. The butchers plundered houses, shot or hanged hostages, and rounded people up in the streets like animals. One had to hide not to be caught. Professional people in high pre-war positions were taken away and shot for no apparent reason.'[1]

[1] Arek Hersh (Herszlikowicz), 'Sieradz, August 1939', manuscript, sent to the author, 1995.

In the first weeks of the German occupation, labour camps were set up throughout Poland. All Poles, including thousands of Jews, were seized on the streets of their towns and sent to forced labour. This might be to clear up the rubble of the September 1939 fighting, to build fortifications on the new German-Soviet border, to drain swamps, to deepen canals or to repair railways. In the town of Opatow – known to the Jews, in Yiddish, as Apt – stonebreaking was a task for which the Jews were summoned from the outset. Within two weeks of the German occupation, the authorities demanded a hundred Jews for work in the local quarry. 'My brother was among the "volunteers",' Salek Orenstein recalled, 'and each day he walked the five kilometres to the quarry while I helped my grandmother in the shop; a limited amount of trading still continued. But after a while, it was decided that my elder brother would be more useful to her and we changed places.

'At the quarry, I was given a large hammer for breaking the bigger stones and a smaller hammer, with a sort of handle, for smashing the little stones into two-inch granules. These were piled up in heaps of a certain height. That was part of the problem; every day we were expected to produce a standard measure. We began in the early morning and by the time evening came the pile of stones had to be one metre high. This was checked by the Volksdeutsche overseers. If they were not satisfied you would stay behind until they were.

'Things were not so harsh for me yet. I soon discovered that little piles of the previous day's stones had been abandoned in heaps around the quarry. So what do you think I did? I went straight to work beside one of these piles and had a good head start! I gave the impression of working very industriously and quickly became known as the best worker in the entire quarry. I certainly developed muscles there, but doctors have since told me that I was much too young for such hard physical labour, and I am paying the price for it now.'[2]

Living in the southern Polish hill town of Dukla, Lipa Tepper recalled: 'I was recruited to work forced labour in one of the local quarries from which the Germans had arranged to get rocks for road-building which they needed for vehicles going to the front. The company I worked for at the time was called Emil Ludwig from Munich in Germany and initially I got full wages, although I cannot remember how much. I worked there twelve hours a day, five days a week and eighteen hours at the weekend which they called "Wechsel Schicht", or changeover shift, which meant that the shift which worked night work would work all night Saturday night and a half a day Sunday, and go home Sunday at lunch-time to return Monday morning. The shift that worked night

---

[2] Salek Orenstein, 'Beyond Belief, A Survivor's Story', manuscript, sent to the author, 1995.

work would commence work on Sunday afternoon and work all night Sunday to return Monday night, and so life went on until the first expulsion.

'The first expulsion took place when German SS men with dogs surrounded the town. They shouted, "Raus, raus, raus" ("Out, out, out") and threw us all out. They then marched us to the nearest town, which was on the River San, the river which divided the newly-occupied German and Russian parts of Poland. We stayed there for a period of three days. The Russians would not allow us into the Russian part, and the Germans would not allow us to return.

'After three days the Germans allowed us to return home. However, on arriving back at home we found that during our absence the Poles had helped themselves to everything that we possessed. We literally arrived to bare floorboards. My mother managed to get her sewing-machine back – I cannot remember how – and a grandfather clock. We slept on the floor, as we had no beds, no bedding, no chairs, no table, no kitchen utensils, literally nothing. Slowly my mother scraped together a home such as she could. An odd chair from here, a bed from somebody else.'[3]

Forced labour was only a prelude to what the Germans had in store for Polish Jewry. At the end of October 1939 they set up the first ghetto, in the town of Piotrkow. In all the ghettos established by the Germans during the subsequent months, hardship was imposed from the outset. Those Jews who lived in the centre of the towns, as so many did, were forced to move out, normally in the course of a few days. In most cases the area of the town which the Germans designated as the ghetto was a poor, cramped, run-down quarter, often without the basic facilities available elsewhere in the town.

Salek Orenstein's family, who had lived in a certain comfort in Opatow, in a home overlooking the market-place, were given two weeks to move out 'into whatever hovels we could find'. 'It was sheer hell,' he recalled. 'There was no flooring at all, just trodden earth on to which my mother sprinkled as much sawdust as she could gather from the yard in an effort to keep the place clean. My mother and father slept on a sort of sleeping shelf made up of planks of wood, no mattresses. My brother and I slept on straw-filled sacks, my elder sister with my grandmother and my little sister slept beside my mother.

'In the morning we removed the sacks and placed them outside in the yard under the shelter of a little porch to create more room to move about inside. Also out in the yard was an earth closet – I would not call it a toilet because you could not sit down – but at least it had a door.

---

[3] Lipa Tepper, letter to the author, 30 January 1996.

Paper was in desperately short supply. It was forbidden for Jews to work in shops and markets outside the ghetto, or to obtain food or other supplies from outside. Rationing was strictly imposed, far harsher for Jews than for Poles.' In Opatow, Salek Orenstein recalled, two Jews who were caught attempting to leave the town were shot, and women found with unauthorised grain 'were killed on the spot'.[4]

In Warsaw, twelve-year-old Meir Sosnowicz recalled the efforts to continue education for Jewish schoolchildren. 'This was also the period when I was ready to move to a higher-level school (gymnasium),' he later wrote, 'but all formal education was stopped for Jews. Illegally, my parents, together with other parents, arranged for some private tuition by a teacher from the school which I should have attended. This teacher taught us German and Latin. In the middle of one of our study sessions the Gestapo broke in and removed the teacher. We heard later that he had been taken to Auschwitz, therefore probably being one of the very first occupants of that infamous institution. We never heard from him again; neither were there any more attempts at further formal schooling for us.'[5]

In Bialobrzegi, Kopel Kandelcukier, who was twelve years old in March 1940, recalled the privations and the dangers of the early months of the ghetto. 'We lost our business and nearly all our home, as we all had to accommodate all the other families whose homes had been taken away. Terrible demands were made on the Jewish people such as money, more jewellery, pots and pans, all to help the German war effort. There was also a curfew from 8 p.m. Food by now was very scarce. Food was on ration, but only for people who worked for the Germans such as in the forest and electric company and State farms run by the Germans. The young strong men in the town were singled out, taken away and never seen again.

'My father disappeared in late 1940. The only way we could survive was to keep selling things to our Polish neighbours for food. The overcrowding and starvation caused sickness and typhus. With lack of medication, many died. There was also a Polish police station where the commandant had two sons who befriended me and lived quite close and helped my family and me to survive. The only way to get food was to creep out of the ghetto and get to the nearest village and barter for food. A few of us young boys risked our lives to do this. Coming back, some Poles would point us out to Germans, that we were Jews, in return for

[4] Salek Orenstein, 'Beyond Belief, A Survivor's Story', manuscript, sent to the author, 1995.

[5] Michael Novice (Meir Sosnowicz), recollections, manuscript, June 1995. From June 1940 until the beginning of 1942, Auschwitz was primarily a punishment camp for Poles. The first Jewish deportations there began in the spring of 1942.

a bottle of whisky and cigarettes. I was always extremely lucky as my appearance was like an Aryan.'[6]

Chill Igielman, who was eleven years old when war broke out, also recalled conditions in the ghetto in Bialobrzegi. 'The only way to get food,' he wrote, 'was to get out of the Jewish area, and to try to get to farmhouses, but if you were caught by the Germans you were shot. We were very cold as we could not get any firewood to heat the house, so we tried to sneak out at night to break up wooden fences, but if you were caught doing this the Germans would shoot you. The Germans knew Jews were managing to escape to neighbouring villages, so they offered a reward of two pounds of sugar to any Pole who would point out a Jew they knew had sneaked out. This meant it was not just Germans we had to be on the lookout for but also Poles, especially young ones.'[7]

In almost every ghetto, all Jewish schools were closed. Those children who were young enough and small enough tried to avoid the rigours imposed upon their parents. Krulik Wilder was not quite eleven when the ghetto was established in Piotrkow. He later recalled: 'My father could no longer go to the market and earn a living. I at the tender age of ten years, managed to get in and out of the ghetto and smuggle in cigarettes which I sold in the streets for a profit. There were quite a few boys engaging in this occupation and I had my own corner in the ghetto selling tobacco and cigarettes.

'One day I was standing on my corner when a Gestapo man with a large Alsatian dog appeared. He grabbed hold of me, took all the cigarettes, and said, "Now run". I was terrified. I was sure he was going to set the dog after me. I started running as fast as I could. He used to delight in descending on the ghetto with his ferocious black dog who wreaked havoc on the helpless and terrified victims. On another occasion six Gestapo men caught me with smuggled cigarettes. I thought they were going to shoot me. Instead they formed a circle around me and proceeded to kick me around like a football.

'In order to avoid being rounded up and sent away, my father got a regular job in early 1941 in the Hortensja glass factory which was situated just outside the town, and received a small wage and extra food. In addition, he worked at home making armbands with the Star of David to eke out a living. All Jews over the age of twelve had to wear armbands.'[8]

[6] Kopel Kendall (Kandelcukier), recollections, letter to the author, 2 September 1995.

[7] Chill Igielman, 'A Record of the Early Life of Hillel Chill Igielman', manuscript, sent to the author, November 1994.

[8] Israel (Krulik) Wilder, 'Krulik's Story', manuscript, sent to the author, 1 January 1995.

Also in the Piotrkow ghetto, nine-year-old Sevek Finkelstein recalled a day when, on a street close to the offices of the Jewish Council, 'the Jewish police rounded up a bunch of kids and brought us to a place where some German trucks needed to be unloaded. I went to work picking up sacks that were handed to me off the lorry on my back. I thought that I was doing well when one of the big kids who was on the truck handing me the sacks, just threw one on my back. It hurt my back and I could not hold on to the sack which fell and split open, emptying flour. I went up to the German officer and told him that it was not my fault because the guy on the truck threw the sack at me, and besides the work was too difficult for me. This German did not make any reply, except to go to his holster to take out his revolver. Then he shouted at me to stand against the wall.

'I did as he said, and everyone around stopped working and was watching. This German stretched out his arm getting ready to shoot me. I just stood there not believing that this was happening to me, but at the same time I felt no fear or any other feelings. I was just indifferent to what was going on. Some man came along and began to talk to this German very quietly and confidentially. Soon the German lowered his arm and put his gun back. The Jewish man shouted to me, "Go home", and I slowly did so.'[9]

Among those also in the Piotrkow ghetto were Ben Helfgott and his younger sisters Mala and Lusia. Their father, who was on good terms with many Christian Poles, managed to persuade a Catholic family in nearby Czestochowa to take in both Mala and her cousin Idzia Klein, both of whom, it was intended, would pass as Christians, and thus be safe from the privations of ghettos and anti-Jewish violence. 'We both missed our parents,' Mala later recalled, 'but Idzia was so homesick that she asked to be taken back, but was told that it was not yet safe to do so. However, when she told them that her parents had very good friends in Piotrkow who were looking after their valuables, and she could go to them, they agreed.

'As far as I was concerned, Idzia was lucky because she was back with her parents and I still had to wait. However, when I was eventually taken back and handed over to my father in the attic of his flour mill, where he was now a worker, my uncle, Joseph Klein, was there too and asked, "Where is my child?" He was told that they had brought her back some time ago and left her with these good friends. He paced up and down repeating, "What have you done with my child?" and we just looked on helplessly. I subsequently learned that they came to these good friends with Idzia, collected a suitcase full of valuables, and

[9] Sidney Finkel (Sevek Finkelstein), 'My Story', manuscript, sent to the author, 12 September 1995.

left. My cousin was never seen again, and the circumstances of her disappearance and probable death remain a mystery to this day.

'I was then smuggled into the ghetto by my father when he returned with the working party, and was relieved and thankful that I found my mother, sister and brother there. My mother comforted me and I could feel her delight at having her children safe and sound home with her. She was, in the true Jewish tradition, a very caring and devoted mother. She and my younger sister Lusia had also been hidden outside the ghetto, as was my father, who soon managed to obtain a work permit.'[10]

Ben Helfgott's recollections of life in the Piotrkow ghetto, when he was eleven years old, are vivid. 'I had around me – strange as it may sound – a belief of invincibility, that nothing could happen to me. There were many times when I was frightened, absolutely terrified; but I had a great belief in my father. He would not allow any situation to get the better of him – so many people collapsed, just didn't know what to do, but my father, somehow, whatever the situation, he always seemed to have presence of mind and courage and resourcefulness. If I wouldn't have had that confidence, and my father's support, I'm absolutely certain I wouldn't be here today.

'I was growing up very quickly; on the one hand I was still a little boy, on the other hand I was very much a grown-up. I lived amongst grown-ups. You see, in the ghetto there was a curfew at eight o'clock, so that's when I would indulge in my world of make-believe, delve into books, or else the neighbours in the building would come and sit and talk and discuss things, play cards and so on – there's hardly a card game I don't know! I used to follow my father – I was the only son, and just my two sisters. I used to sit and listen to them talking politics, and I knew what they were talking about, because I would be on the move outside the ghetto most of the time, and I would often stand by the newspaper kiosks and read the headlines and read as much as I could from the papers. So I was familiar with the names of Chamberlain and Churchill and Halifax and all the political leaders of the time. People were still optimistic, they said, "America will soon join and the war will soon be over, they can't go on like this and they will never win", and so on.

'Radios were forbidden in the ghetto. Anybody caught with a radio would be shot; but there must have been radios in secret, because we usually heard the latest news. I spent a lot of time outside the ghetto at the beginning, I even used to go to the cinema. Of course my life was at stake. But somehow I did not think. When I told my mother about it she gave me a hiding, and she made me swear never to go out again.

---

[10] Mala Tribich (née Helfgott), recollections, letter to the author, 14 March 1996.

But even though I did understand what was involved, I did not want to believe it – I always thought that this won't happen to me.

'Really, when I was outside the ghetto I was not so much afraid of the Germans as I was afraid of the Poles. Because there was no way the Germans would know I wasn't a Polish boy – I didn't conform to the German stereotype of a Jew, I had blond hair, I had a short nose – but I was always afraid that some Pole would denounce me. That was my greatest fear.'[11]

Michael Etkind was fifteen at the time of the establishment, on 1 May 1940, of the ghetto in Lodz. It was an industrial city with more than 200,000 Jewish inhabitants, the third largest Jewish population in the world after New York and Warsaw. Posters had gone up saying that all Jews would have to move from their homes to the designated ghetto area, a run-down part of the city known as Baluty. 'Three days before the final date for leaving for the ghetto,' he wrote, 'there were raids and many Jews living in the vicinity of Piotrkowska Street were shot inside their dwellings. This was designed to stampede the Jewish population into leaving for the "safety" of the ghetto. Needless to say, it succeeded.

'During the next three days, thousands upon thousands of makeshift sleighs could be seen converging on the ghetto area, loaded with bundles of bedding. The ground was frozen and there was a blizzard blowing as I was pulling my sledge loaded with our belongings. My mother, together with Henka my younger sister and my little brother Lolek, were pushing from behind. We made a number of journeys. We were lucky that my uncle, Szolym, already had a room and we moved in with his family for the time being. There were three adults and five children in a room of about 250 square feet.'[12]

Perec Zylberberg was two weeks short of his sixteenth birthday when the Lodz ghetto was established. 'To have been a young Jew in pre-war Poland wasn't always easy nor very benign,' he later wrote. 'There were days of high idealism, full of meaning. There were also heavy days of near despair for the whole family. But to find yourself a prisoner in your own town was so new and such a degrading experience that it left us all gasping for air. For no reason, save the fact that we were Jews, we had to wear special identification badges and walk only on streets designated for us. Even that was hard at times. The German sentries all around the ghetto were in some cases shooting at people walking legitimately close to the wiring around the ghetto. Many people died

[11] Ben Helfgott, in Rosemary Dinnage (editor), *The Ruffian on the Stair*, Viking, London, 1990, pages 272–291.

[12] Michael Etkind, '"Youth" Remembered', manuscript, sent to the author, 4 January 1996.

that way. I remember everybody around me saying that whenever the "redhead" is on duty, there will be victims. So fear for one's life was present, even inside the ghetto compound.

'There were no newspapers, nor was listening to the radio permitted. News of the war and what was going on in other places was very scanty. Sometimes, Germans who were working in the administration of the ghetto, would say something that was repeated. Sometimes, by a fluke, an old newspaper would be salvaged. Of course in those days it was all a novelty. All over the ghetto, former rich and poor alike were wondering what all this was about. A whole large city was divided into separate districts.

'In all this bewilderment, with so many whys and ifs, the only relief was a feeling of being at least among Jews. This feeling came from having endured such nerve-racking months of deportations, random beatings and shootings and continuously being picked off the street under all kinds of pretexts. We still thought, then, that we were dealing with a cultured and civilised society. War and subsequent restrictions were all put down to the temporary deviation from known and established practices. We still harboured the ideas that my mother brought up, upon watching the German entry into Lodz. A harsh people, but very much taken with upholding law and order. There was still a functioning mail service.'[13]

Fifty-five years later, Esther Zylberberg echoed her brother's reflection that, once inside the ghetto, 'at least we were among Jews, at least we weren't afraid.'[14]

From the first months, the situation inside the Lodz ghetto changed continually, and always for the worse. 'Some streets kept on being taken out of the compound,' Perec Zylberberg recalled. 'People left behind in the city were being brought into the ghetto. Some Christians with Jewish ancestry were picked up and also sent into the ghetto. While all this changing was going on the ghetto got used to having a Jewish police force, fire-fighting brigade, gaols, a large administration and distribution network, and almost everything else that makes up a living social organism. The only thing that didn't appear in the new Jewish-only place was the opportunity to make a living. We all lived in a kind of limbo. Without the ability to work, and yet the distribution places still had available various sorts of food. It wouldn't be long before an eruption occurred. Hunger and sickness showed their ugly faces. Overcrowding and the hot summer of 1940 helped to depress very many people.'

[13] Perec Zylberberg, recollections, diary entry for 28 July 1993.
[14] Esther Brunstein (Zylberberg), in conversation with the author, 10 May 1996.

The Germans had appointed Dr Chaim Rumkowski to be the 'Aeltester der Juden' ('Elder of the Jews'), at the head of a Council of Elders known as the 'Beirat'. Before the war Rumkowski had been active in social work. Under his authority, stamps and banknotes were issued, and Jewish police kept order inside the ghetto. The diminishing ration scales were imposed by the Germans. As hunger increased, riots broke out. 'The Jewish police tried to contain the outburst,' Perec Zylberberg, then an active member of the Jewish Socialist Youth Movement – the youth wing of the Bund – continued. 'It only intensified the situation. Policemen got beaten up. They left the streets in panic. Some of them shed their uniforms. Some were only wearing their trousers. They were frightened. The demand of the rioters was for food. Looting was spreading.'

When Rumkowski was told of the riots, Perec Zylberberg later wrote, he 'called without hesitation the German security force. It did not take long for truckloads of armed policemen to arrive in the ghetto. Immediately there were victims. Shots rang out for a long time. When the Germans finally left the ghetto, the calm that descended was one of despair and hopelessness. The only positive thing to emerge was the creation of soup kitchens. Rumkowski called a meeting of party leaders. He pleaded for internal peace. He promised to start efforts to get people to work. The internal life of the ghetto resumed its course. Some of the promises were implemented. As part of the promised deal, two soup kitchens were opened by the Bund.

'The Bund also organised a so-called "tea-hall". Bread and tea could be gotten there. Our activists were put in charge of all this. We even got permission to open a food distribution centre. Although it looked imposing, it was only a cosmetic operation. Hunger and hopelessness still persisted.'[15]

Perec Zylberberg was one of those boys who saw Chaim Rumkowski in action. One the most controversial of all the ghetto elders in German-occupied Poland, Rumkowski provided the work details which the German authorities in Lodz called for, and, in due course, the men, women and children they demanded for deportation. In the Warsaw ghetto, in July 1942, Rumkowski's opposite number, Adam Czerniakow, committed suicide rather than provide the Germans with deportees. Rumkowski believed, however, that by facilitating the repeated deportations, he would enable the remaining inhabitants of the ghetto to survive. Perec Zylberberg recalled, fifty years later, the impression Rumkowski made on him. 'He used to prance around the ghetto streets in a horse-drawn droshki. He would stop at random and deliver a speech as soon as he saw a few people around a particular spot. Usually it was

---

[15] Perec Zylberberg, recollections, diary entry for 29 July 1993.

in front of a soup kitchen or food distribution centre. He didn't tolerate any dissent. He sometimes hit people and other times insulted them.

'He used to claim indirectly the title of King of the Lodz Ghetto. He boasted about his grand designs for making the ghetto tick like a watch. His manner of dress was one of affront to the poor, impoverished ghetto people. He wore long, shiny boots and spotless clothes. He just made the bystanders feel, or he wanted to make them feel, inferior and powerless. In his mannerisms he copied the German style. So did his cronies, crawlers and henchmen. He used to use his name, CHAIM, as an implied conduit to life (the Hebrew word *chaim* means 'life'), that is what the name suggested. He also let it be known that, just as the world-renowned leader of Zionism, Chaim Weizmann, was aiming to lead the Jews into their own land, so would he lead his Jews of the Lodz ghetto to the promised land. In my opinion, based on what I saw and heard through the ghetto period and after, Rumkowski was a power-crazed man, given to theatricals, pomposity and extreme egotism. Having surrounded himself with his own cronies, he acted out his day in court in a manner befitting a crazed aspirant to greatness. His doings were mostly tragic. But sometimes comic, and even benevolent at times.'[16]

As well as hunger, disease impinged more and more upon the Jews in the Lodz ghetto. Towards the end of the summer of 1940 there was an outbreak of typhoid fever. Michael Etkind had reason to remember it. 'My younger brother Lolek, who was twelve, contracted the disease and died three weeks later,' he recalled. 'When my younger sister Henka became ill, she was also taken to my aunt's room where she managed to recover. No sooner did she feel better than my aunt's daughter, Fredka, became ill. She was taken to a hospital where she died a week later. In December, I fell ill. When I recovered we moved to another dwelling in Lagiewnicka Street. By now there was more vacant accommodation in the ghetto.

'With the colder weather the typhoid epidemic came to an end. Tuberculosis of the lungs and starvation became the two major killers. My uncle Szolym together with my aunt Fania would come to see us every afternoon to bring some food. My mother became progressively weaker, and could not go on with the teaching that she had been doing for many years. She would not eat, and seemed to have lost all desire to live.

'After my recovery from typhoid I was constantly hungry and could not comprehend my mother's loss of appetite. A doctor, an old friend of the family, suggested that she should go to the hospital, but she would

---

[16] Perec Zylberberg, recollections, diary entry for 2 August 1993.

not hear of it. She would lie in bed and talk to us about her childhood, and her parents who died before we were born. On one occasion she said that she would die as soon as the weather was a little warmer. She died the day after my sixteenth birthday, 10 March 1941. As it was a Saturday, the funeral took place on the following day.

'My uncle made all the arrangements. There was a long queue at the cemetery. Some people were bringing their deceased on handcarts, as the horse-drawn black vans could not cope. The gravediggers would refuse to dig deep enough pits unless they were given bread by the mourners.'[17]

Also in Lodz was fourteen-year-old Roman Halter, who had been deported to the ghetto there from his home town of Chodecz. 'From 1942 I was alone,' he later wrote. 'My family were dead. I was thin and weak. We called such people "Klapsedras" – after the black-bordered notices that were printed in the newspapers and posted up on walls when someone died. I was a "Klapsedra". And it was not easy for a "Klapsedra" to talk. Talking required energy. It was so much easier to write. So I kept a journal of thoughts and feelings and of some events in the ghetto.' One of the three Pinczewski sisters, who had been deported with Roman Halter from Chodecz, 'was well-read, and she offered constructive criticism of my jottings'.[18]

Rose Kalman's father died in the Lodz ghetto when she was thirteen years old. 'When we had to identify his body,' she wrote, 'I remember there was such a strong smell of chlorine. This smell stayed with me for many years. He died of hunger. My brother Smalech died also some months later.'[19]

Hunger in the ghetto affected even those who were fortunate enough to have found work. Michael Etkind had become 'Postman No. 102' in the Lodz ghetto, an enviable position, for it entitled him to a double bowl of soup every day. Even so, he was constantly hungry. 'The basic food rations were given once a fortnight,' he recalled, 'and those unable to restrain themselves would have nothing left, say, by the middle of the second week. By the time they received their next ration they would be so crazed with hunger that they would eat their loaf of bread and small quantity of butter in one day.' It was, he added, 'easy to recognise those who had only days to live; and they were legion. It was not only their unsteady gait, and their skeletal appearance but most of all that vacant, other-worldly expression in their eyes. They were referred to – as Roman Halter was – as "Klapsedras", goners. Later on, in the camps, they were

---

[17] Michael Etkind, '"Youth" Remembered', manuscript, sent to the author, 4 January 1996.
[18] Roman Halter, recollections, sent to the author, 19 February 1996.
[19] Rose Kalman (Goldman), letter to the author, July 1995.

referred to as "Musulmen". It would be difficult to ascertain whether more people died of tuberculosis of the lungs or of starvation. Winter and summer one would see spittle with blood on the pavements. I developed a slight, but irritating pain in my right lung which persisted for months.'

Michael Etkind went on to ask, in the retrospect of half a century: 'Which was the better time in the ghetto, or the worse, my friend, the winter or the summer? The winter, when the pavements and the roads were frozen solid for over three months, when each step taken in your clog-clad feet was an effort and required the skill of an experienced skater, when the icy wind went right through you and took your breath away, when you tried to wash in the frozen bowl of water in your room, when you squatted on the iced-up seat of the outdoor lavatory; or the summer?'

For Michael Etkind, the summers in the Lodz ghetto 'were worse, the place seemed more drab, people more miserable, more resigned. I would remember the beautiful Polish countryside, the pine forest stretching towards Tomaszow Mazowiecki, and the river. There were no birds in the ghetto; hardly any trees (except in the cemetery). There was nothing to eat for the birds – why should they stay in the ghetto? Even the sparrows, who were so plentiful when the streets were full of horses pulling droshkis, disappeared. No dogs, no cats, no mice; they would not find any crumbs to eat. Remember the potato "cakes" that women would make out of potato peelings they grabbed from the outside of the communal kitchens? Hunger knows no season – in that respect there was no difference between the summer, winter, or spring and autumn.

'But the news was worse in the summer; the Germans were winning.'[20] In the summer of 1940 the Germans conquered Holland, Belgium and France.

The twelve-year-old Arthur Poznanski was in Wielun during the first year of the war. 'My mother organised private classes that I helped her to run,' he later wrote. 'We even taught German, which we both knew very well, to some Volksdeutsche children. Living conditions for Jews were getting rapidly worse. We were relocated to an open ghetto and many Jews were rounded up and deported, allegedly to labour camps, but were not heard of again.'[21] Howard Chandler (Chaim Wajchendler) recalled the creation of a ghetto in his town of Wierzbnik, the rounding up and kidnapping of Jews for forced labour, 'the arrest of Jews and Gentiles never to be seen again,' and the constant search of houses. 'The

---

[20] Michael Etkind, '"Youth" Remembered', manuscript, sent to the author, 4 January 1996.
[21] Arthur Poznanski, recollections, letter to the author, 24 January 1995.

Jewish population of our town was considerably increased,' he wrote, 'by Jews who were expelled from the cities of Lodz and Plock and all Jewish households had to accommodate them and share everything with them on a permanent basis.

'One day a German soldier was shot and another wounded while on patrol on our street. A house was surrounded and some people arrested, and after some days a gallows was erected in the market square which was in the centre of town. The following Sunday, while the people were leaving church, they were halted and made to watch the hanging of about ten people. I was right in front watching as it was right near our house. Among those hung were a young girl, her mother and her grandmother – all Poles. I later found out that the hangmen were Jews conscripted for this task, and bribes had to be paid to the Germans to allow the hangmen to wear masks in order not to be recognised and to avoid acts of revenge by the Poles.

'In our town there were large ammunition factories and it was said that people employed there would receive better food rations and would be exempt from deportations. My father and older brother, among others, secured employment there some time in 1941, and later on obtained work permits for my mother, my sister and myself. These work permits were highly prized and much sought after by all Jews – it was like a permit to life itself. Jews were allowed, even encouraged, to work in the factories after the German occupation.

'For my younger brother, all necessary arrangements were made so that he be hidden and cared for by a Polish family. Although our town expected the same fate as befell all the Jewish communities with regard to expulsions, we were hoping against hope that it wouldn't happen to us because of the great numbers that were employed in the ammunition factories.'[22]

In the Staszow ghetto, Mayer Bomsztyk recalled how, other than the quite inadequate rations, 'there was nothing to be had. There was no wood or coal to burn for heating in the bitter Polish winter. In theory we were supposed to receive a ration of food each day. It was never enough, and many times the ration did not arrive, so we were always very hungry and cold. It was a miserable existence. We never knew what to do for the best. Some people thought if they volunteered to work for the Germans they had the best chance of surviving, so in 1941 my elder brother Jonathan volunteered to work in a munitions factory in Skarzysko-Kamienna. That was the last time we saw him.'[23]

---

[22] Howard Chandler (Chaim Wajchendler), letter to the author, 23 February 1995.
[23] Mayer Bomsztyk, recollections, sent to the author, 6 May 1996.

The Galician town of Gorlice experienced the same hardships as those imposed on all Polish Jews during the early months of German rule, even before the imposition of the ghetto. 'It was impossible to earn money at that time,' ten-year-old Harry Balsam recalled, 'and my youngest brother Joseph and I tried to think how we could make some money. We were approached by people to smuggle goods from one town to another. Not everyone was allowed to go on trains, but as we were under twelve nobody actually said anything to us. We were smuggling saccharin from one town to another, and got paid for doing this. We didn't realise how dangerous it was.

'My oldest brother Danny, and my sister Gitel, couldn't help with the smuggling because they were over twelve years of age, and anyone over twelve had to wear the yellow Star of David, so it was difficult to get out of the town ghetto. Thing were very bad. One day I was walking with Danny in the town. He was seventeen. I am convinced that a Polish pupil from his class recognised him as a Jew, and told the Gestapo that there was a Jew walking in the town. The Gestapo came over to us, put a hand on my brother's shoulder, took out his gun, shot him in front of me, and told me to disappear.

'Well, you can imagine that must have been the worst hour of my life. I didn't know where to turn. I knew I couldn't go home and tell my mother what had happened to her son. So I ran to our cousins' house nearby and told them what had taken place. It was an agonising moment for all of us. Going back fifty years, or rather fifty-five years, it still remains in my mind that this was the first time that I saw the German Gestapo pull out a gun and shoot somebody.

'Up until then I had heard about it, but I had not seen it for myself, and you can't imagine how I felt, especially as it was my brother. The worst was still to come, because we heard that the Gestapo, after shooting someone during the day, didn't want to leave any trace of that particular family, so they used to come at night and take the whole family out and shoot them as well so that there would not be anyone left to bear witness. Actually we were fortunate because a friend of my older brother was working for the Gestapo, as a liaison between them and the Jews, and we managed to persuade the Gestapo to leave us alone. We were very lucky as we would have almost certainly have been massacred.

'The year was 1940, the year that the ghetto was formed in Gorlice. We were forced to move from our house into the ghetto where we had to share one small house with four other families. I was still with my mother, sister and brother Joseph, who was a year younger than I, and I knew that I would now have to be the breadwinner for the family. Whilst in the ghetto they used to round us up, and in the winter we would have to go and clear the snow from the roads. It was very heavy snow, and to shovel it away was very hard work. It was freezing cold and we weren't exactly dressed for that kind of work and weather. We had to clear the roads and the pavements, where there was a pavement, although it was mostly roads.

'We worked for ten to twelve hours a day and everyone had to do it. There were some people with trades and skills and they were used by the Germans to work in factories for the war machine. I never got paid for this work, but I was happy to be working outside the ghetto because I was able to bring back into the ghetto bread, butter or whatever I could get hold of. Life carried on like this for quite some time, until they started the deportations.'[24]

In Dukla, near the Slovak border, Lipa Tepper recalled the time just after the German occupation when he was put to work. He was only fourteen. Forced labour was used in one of the local quarries which the Germans took over to hew out the rocks for road-building. The roads near Dukla were to be needed in the summer of 1941 for vehicles going towards the Russian front. 'I remember one night,' Tepper later wrote, 'coming home from work after a twelve-hour shift and being extremely hungry. I sat at the table and my mother gave me some food and she sat down beside me and proceeded to tell me that a German soldier walked past one of the people in town, a fellow called Chaim Spira, and the German actually took out his gun and fired at the man at point-blank range and killed him.

'My mother was very distraught at that. It was the first time she had ever experienced a German soldier, or any soldier for that matter, shooting an unarmed man in cold blood. As she was telling me that, as I realise now, she was obviously seeking my support. I, however, because of my age, and because I did not think like a grown-up, did not seem to be able to help her in any way, and she just walked away from me distraught. Years later I had cause to regret that.

'There was in our town a garrison of Grentz Shutz Politzei or, as you would call them in English, "Border Police". They lived literally round the corner from where one of our rabbis lived, and they used to see him go out in the yard with his beard and his *koppel*[25] on his head and so on and they could not contain themselves any more. After a while on one Friday afternoon they went into his house and actually murdered him with tables and chairs. They beat him to death and they did not allow any time for *tahara*,[26] or anything, and so we, the people, had to

[24] Harry Balsam, letter to the author, 8 May 1995.

[25] A skullcap (in its Hebrew form, a *kippa*).

[26] The preparation of a dead body for burial, including washing and dressing. Out of respect for the

carry his coffin dripping with blood all through the town to the cemetery. That made a very, very profound impression on me and has, I think, left a void in my heart which remained there for a long time to come. I could not understand it. I could not even understand any of it. I was just smitten by it, literally. However I was to experience a lot worse afterwards.

'Our town was to all intents and purposes what they called a shtetl. That is to say, it had a square, and running off this square were several streets in each direction, fairly long streets but that is all there was to the town. We now found people getting caught in the market-place and beaten up. They then returned bloodied and distraught. You would occasionally see a man who did not shave his beard being caught by two SS men and his beard being cut off in a very rough fashion.'[27]

Alec Ward was just thirteen when the ghetto was established in Magnuszew. This ghetto, he recalled, 'consisted of a very small part of the shtetl near a lake. My family lived in an outhouse in very cramped and inhuman conditions, without any facilities whatsoever. My father had many Christian friends on the Aryan side of the town, and he very often smuggled himself out of the ghetto to carry out some work for them, in return for some food which he smuggled into the ghetto for us.

'One day a group of Hitler Youth arrived in the ghetto and gave us a few hours' notice to be evacuated to the ghetto of Kozienice in the district of Radom. They marched us the fifteen kilometres and we were only allowed to take items which we could carry. My parents could not take anything as they had to carry two small children, one was three and a half years old, and one was a baby.

'The ghetto in Kozienice was much bigger than the previous one. The Germans crammed into it all the Jewish communities from the surrounding shtetls. My father had no possibility of providing even a meagre amount of food for his family. We lived in one room and slept on the bare floor. During our first night there we had a robbery, and my father's only pair of shoes were stolen. He walked about barefoot till I left him. My father realised that we were not going to survive much longer and ordered me to take my younger brother Lajb, who was about nine years old, and try to escape. When the German guard, with his fixed bayonet on his gun, was occupied searching someone, I picked up the barbed wire and my brother was free and then my brother lifted up the barbed wire and I was free.

dead, during the purification ritual those performing it say, 'We hope the way we dealt with you was not offensive.'

[27] Lipa Tepper, letter to the author, 30 January 1996.

'We walked back to Magnuszew and lived in the forest and fields for three months. Our former Christian neighbours gave us some food occasionally, but begged us not to come back again as they were frightened that someone would betray them to the Germans. We avoided sleeping in the same barn or haystack for two nights running in case we were discovered by the farmers and given away to the Germans. This fear was with us constantly while roaming about for three months. I instinctively took a protective role towards my little brother, although I was only young myself. He was a very intelligent boy and co-operated with me one hundred per cent.'[28]

The bond that grew up between the fourteen-year-old Alec and his nine-year-old half-brother was a potent aid to their survival. Like so many such lifelines, however, it was eventually to be shattered. The little Lajb was not to survive the war.

Menachem Silberstein had left Lodz with his parents, and gone to a small village near Kozienice. 'We got a room there from the Judenrat,' he later wrote, 'and started to make a living by trading with the Polish farmers. This place we stayed in was a very quiet place, and we did not see any Germans at all. There was also a German colony next to this place. The people there all knew my father, as he had grown up with them. One of the German farmers suggested to my family that he would let me stay with him as one of his family, as nobody knew me there.

'The name of this family was Sorget – Michael and Olga. They had a daughter named Emma and a son named Reinhold. I stayed with this German family for one and a half years. I was moving around freely as if I was a German boy, and even had German friends without them knowing that I was Jewish. Sometimes I even attended Hitler Youth meetings, and listened to the radio, a thing that was forbidden.

'One day the Poles found out about me staying with this German family. There were some other Jewish boys and girls who were living with other families in this German colony. The Polish police, together with the German Gestapo, came over and started to kill everybody they found. Mr Sorget helped me. He hid me in the barn, and when they came to his farm asking about me, he expressed surprise that I was Jewish and said, "I wondered why he escaped and left me with all the work." He took a big risk by saying that. He also gave the Germans a lot to eat and drink and they left. He came over to my hiding-place and told me I had to leave immediately. He gave me a full sack of food.

'That night I left by foot for Magnuszew, the small village where my family lived, that was already closed off with barbed wire. It was made

---

[28] Alec Ward, 'My Story', manuscript, sent to the author, 31 May 1995.

into a small ghetto. Throughout the time that I had been working at the Germans' farm, I had gone every Sunday by bicycle with a sack of food for my family. It had been given to me by this German farmer.

'The Magnuszew ghetto was guarded by Jewish police and no one was allowed to leave this place. When I arrived there that night everyone was crying, as they were sure that I had been shot. Sixteen other boys and girls were shot that day.

'The Germans started to send out people from Warsaw and the surroundings, to camps like Treblinka and Majdanek. The only thing these people knew was that they were being sent east. By that time, this little Magnuszew had grown from sixty to seventy families to about 600 to 700 families. They lived in the school, the synagogue. It was very crowded: ten to twenty persons in one room. People started to die from starvation, typhoid and other illnesses. My father and I were burying the bodies. This was our work. It was the year 1942.'[29]

In the Sieradz ghetto, Arek Hersh was only eleven years old when his father and elder brother evaded a round-up for slave labour. He was immediately seized in their place and taken for a medical examination to an army barracks on the outskirts of the town. The doctor examining him said he was too small to be sent to the labour camp. But, Arek recalled, a member of the Jewish Council who was present told the doctor 'that my father and brother had escaped and that was the reason why I was present'. The doctor stamped Arek's card as fit for work, 'and from that point my fate was sealed. I resigned myself to the fact that there was no other option open to me. I thought to myself, "Maybe because I'm so small I might have a better chance of survival. They might just give me a lighter job".'[30]

Arek Hersh was taken with several hundred older boys and men to a labour camp near Wrzesnia, on the main Warsaw-Berlin railway line. Its name was Otoczno. From the moment the deportees arrived at the camp they were subjected to great savagery. 'One guard, called Rudi, was in charge,' Arek recalled. 'He came from the Sudetenland, and was particularly brutal. I remember he was blond, of medium build and he wore glasses. He killed prisoners by hacking them to death with a spade. He was indeed one of the worst barbarians in the camp. Our working days lasted for fourteen hours. For many workers life became so bad that they threw themselves under passing trains as they could not take any more. Many others were hanged for the most trivial things, such as

[29] Menachem (Mendel) Silberstein, letter to the author, 29 March 1996.

[30] Arek Hersh (Herszlikowicz), 'The Beginning of the War', manuscript, page 47, sent to the author, 1995.

begging for a potato in the village or walking away from a work column to urinate without asking the guard's permission. The excuse that the guards gave was that they thought the prisoner was trying to escape.

'Starvation was another terrible problem. The workers were given only one small piece of bread, some black coffee and a little watery soup per day. There were ceaseless terrible beatings on the ramp[31] until the person was near death. All this summed up the terrible existence of most of the prisoners in this hell of a camp, but to us in our barrack we had hope because we thought we were going home.'

Arek Hersh remembered that, as there was no running water in the camp at Otoczno, water had to be brought from the village five kilometres away. 'The Germans provided us with a long metal container on four wheels,' he recalled, 'and we were given the job of hauling this water tank to and fro. It was really work for a team of horses, but why use animals when there was an abundance of human beings to do the work? The Germans roped some teenagers together on to the cart and we hauled this contraption several times a day. I was chosen as one of the boys to do this work. We were guarded by the black-uniformed men who had whips in their hands, and who every so often would lash out with them. Every day the guards were changed, but it never made any difference to their savagery. These black-uniformed guards were the worst barbarians I have ever come across.

'However there was one particular guard who would tell me to unrope myself and walk next to him, the reason being that I was the smallest and somehow he must have felt sorry for me. He also asked the other guards, all Ethnic Germans who spoke Polish, to do the same thing. The situation in the camp got a little easier for me, and though the guards were still all very cruel, I became less frightened of them.

'Another job I did was working with many other prisoners on the Poznan-Warsaw railway line, laying lines and sleepers. This work was terrible, back-breaking for even the fittest of men, and the beatings we received were so savage that many actually died from them.

'On occasions the camp commandant would send me on errands, make me clean his room, polish his shoes or bring him water. He was a small man in his sixties, perhaps five feet three inches tall. He had a slight stoop, grey hair, wore glasses and was very cruel. He used to glean a special delight from seeing prisoners being hanged and making the rest of us watch. He never spoke to me directly, simply shouted his orders, and when he wanted to call me he never used my name, but addressed me as "you". In all the time I knew him, I never once saw him smile.

---

[31] A low platform, common in Eastern European railway stations.

'The hangings started to increase, events which, as I said, we all had to watch. Life in the camp started to get worse as the rations of food grew less and less and the work became harder. Some of the prisoners started showing signs of malnutrition and were dying. There was just one medical man for the whole camp, and he did not have any drugs, so there was very little he could do to help his fellow men. In short, life at Otoczno was a living hell.

'Whenever I got the chance, I would visit the boys and older men who were waiting to go home. I was very envious of them and I asked them to give my mother my love and to tell her I was all right and that she should not worry about me. One afternoon as I was walking towards the wash-house I noticed some strange-looking lorries that had arrived at the camp. These vehicles were all enclosed and were manned by soldiers who had their sleeves rolled up and carried sticks in their hands. These soldiers had SS on their collars, and a skull-and-crossbones insignia on their caps. The lorries were driven to the block that housed the boys and men waiting to go home. They stopped, and the SS men ordered the prisoners out of the barrack and told them to undress, but to leave their underpants on. The prisoners obeyed immediately and the backs of the lorries were then opened up. The SS then proceeded to beat the boys and men on to the lorries.

'The screams and panic which broke out at this treatment were just too terrible. Many were bleeding from the blows that had rained down on them. When everybody was inside the lorries, the doors were closed. Days later I found out from the foreman that as the engine started running it began to pump the exhaust fumes into the back of the lorry. As the vehicle was airtight, this meant that all inside were slowly gassed.

'I don't think I will ever be able to erase from my mind the memory of that terrible day, when I unwittingly witnessed the deaths of my friends. I still shudder when I think that if I hadn't been picked out with those other few boys to work, that too would have been my fate. As more and more people were hanged, one of my duties was to help take the corpses down to the little village, which was several kilometres from the camp, where we would help to bury them. I still remember the spot.'

There were terrible scenes in Otoczno, as in every labour camp to which those in the ghettos were sent. These scenes are difficult to read about, yet those who, like Arek Hersh, witnessed them, had then to live with their memory. 'I had a friend in Sieradz called Beniek Hildesheim, who was my age,' he later recalled. 'He had an elder brother, Szymek, who had been caught begging for a potato. We were ordered to watch Szymek being hanged in the wash-house. Twice those brutes hanged him and twice the rope snapped, and each time, in a dreadful state of shock, he begged for his life. However those barbarians succeeded the third time. That typified the bestiality of the Germans and their extermination methods in the beginning. I was heartbroken as I watched this terrible scene, and afterwards I helped to bury him. He was only twenty years of age, a very intelligent person, and one of the nicest young men anybody could wish to know. Here was I, a child of just eleven years, and already I had witnessed some of the most inhuman acts that man had done to man in recent history.'[32]

Arek Hersh was lucky; one day, when he was cleaning the commandant's office, the commandant peered at him over his gold-rimmed spectacles and said: 'You, I'm sending you home.'[33] He was taken back by train to the Sieradz ghetto. Of nine hundred Jews who had been sent to the slave labour camp at Otoczno between 1940 and 1942, only eleven survived. Arek Hersh was an eyewitness to a slave labour camp of which almost nothing is known, even today, beyond his testimony.

In June 1941 the Germans invaded the Soviet Union, and, in the first days of the new war, occupied the Polish province of Eastern Galicia. The small town of Bircza was one of those which had known, since the short-lived entry of the German army in September 1939, almost a year and a half of respite. But German rule brought the same tragedies as in the more westerly areas. 'They took me to a work camp for two months,' one of the boys, Jack Rubinfeld, recalled. 'During that time, my father and fifty other Jews were rounded up by the Gestapo and Ukrainian collaborators. They were shot and buried in a mass grave on a hilltop near my home.'[34]

Russian prisoners of war were also the victims of the new onward march of German power. 'I remember there were thousands and thousands of Russian prisoners who were brought into my home town,' Pinkus Kurnedz, from Piotrkow, recalled, 'and when they died, cartloads of them were taken to a nearby place for burial.'[35] Ben Helfgott also recalled the Russian prisoners of war in Piotrkow. 'We used to watch them as they walked from their camp, past the ghetto, to where they were working. Every day there were fewer. We did not know what happened to them. But there were rumours.'[36] The rumours were true; at the prisoner of war camp in Piotrkow, as in more than fifty other such camps throughout German-occupied Poland, these former soldiers,

---

[32] Arek Hersh (Herszlikowicz), 'My journey to Otoshno death camp', manuscript, pages 52–57. The Polish spelling of the camp is Otoczno.

[33] Arek Hersh (Herszlikowicz), 'My journey to Otoshno death camp', manuscript, pages 58–59.

[34] Jack Rubinfeld (Israel Rubinstein), 'Jack Rubinfeld', manuscript, sent to the author, undated (1995).

[35] Pinkus Kurnedz, recollections, letter to the author, 5 October 1994.

[36] Ben Helfgott, in conversation with the author, 12 March 1996.

vanquished in battle, were starved and beaten to death without respite or chance of escape.

Pinkus Kurnedz and Ben Helfgott were among many of the boys who were eyewitnesses, not only to one, but two human tragedies of the Second World War, which were being perpetrated at the same time: the deliberate murder of six million Jews, and the deliberate murder of more than three million Russian prisoners of war.

In the ghettos, in the desperate search for food, people continued to try to breach the enforced boundaries. Those who did so were mostly children who could pose as non-Jews: boys and girls who were of fair appearance, and who could speak Polish without an accent. Hanka Ziegler was nine years old when the war began. She and her family lived in Lodz, but early in the war her parents and their five children moved to Piotrkow, where the children had a great-aunt. 'One escaped from one place to another,' Hanka recalled. 'One thought one would be safe. We all stayed in one little room, the seven of us. Another fourteen people came to the room at different times. They were all running away – and getting nowhere. I remember sleeping on a chair with one of my brothers, it was awful. My father got caught foraging for food and was put in prison. I never saw my father again. My brother Wolf was working in the Hortensja glass factory. He was later murdered on a death march.

'My brother Zigmund and I were the breadwinners. He was about fourteen. We collected all the food. He and I started selling bread and potatoes. We didn't have anything else to sell. And then we started scavenging and begging from non-Jewish people. Being such small children we could get through any hole. We learned how to steal, how to beg. My mother was unable to do anything. She just couldn't cope. We were very hungry. So we went out of the ghetto. We went backwards and forwards. Then the day came when they sealed the ghetto.'

The Piotrkow ghetto was surrounded by SS troops, the guards on the gates reinforced, and every possible escape route sealed. 'We were two children, freezing cold, begging potatoes. We came to the ghetto and they wouldn't let us in. A German soldier at the barrier shouted at us, "What are you doing, you children? Go home. Tonight we are sending the Jews out of here." He thought we were non-Jewish children going in to get money from the Jews. We had a sack of potatoes and some flour. We were both very blond children. We spoke good Polish.

'I was crying. I knew my mother was hungry. We walked away from the ghetto. We walked and walked and walked. When we tried to get back to Piotrkow the Poles said, "Look at the Jews, they're all going to be killed." I never saw my mother again, or my little brother Herszel –

he was about eighteen months old – or my little sister Leah – she was about seven.

'My brother and I went from village to village. We were just begging. We changed our names to Polish names. We just went from place to place. We made up some idiotic stories, that our parents had been sent to Germany to work, that we were looking for an aunt. Every time we knocked on someone's door we crossed ourselves, and pretended to be Christian children. We were terribly dirty. My hair was absolutely covered in one great big mass of lice. We had only the clothes that we had left the ghetto with. We scratched and scratched. We were covered in sores. Nobody wanted to look at us. They were frightened of us. We were just like lepers.

'About two months passed. It was freezing cold. We had nowhere to live. We were very hungry. Our clothes were falling off. Then we came to a village, and this woman, she took us in for the night. It was Christmas Eve. She said, "Jesus would like to help you". She was very poor. She was on her own. Her husband had been sent to Germany to work. Her daughter was not quite right. We had this little bag of flour. We gave it to her. She was extremely happy about that. She had some ointment. It took away the itch and it took away the pain.

'The next day it was Christmas. "I'm not going to let you go today, of all days", she said. "You can stay another night". The next day we went out and got some food. She let us stay a third night. Because we fed her, she wanted us to stay with her. Saying that we were her sister's children, she took me to the German headquarters in the village. The place was full of Germans, of Gestapo. My brother didn't come. She gave us new names. She said we had come from Kalisz, that her sister lived in Kalisz. I didn't know where that was.

'The Germans gave us papers to say that we were her relations. We came back to her "little dog" of a house. She sold us to farmers, me to one farmer and my brother to another. It was just terrible. *We* worked. *She* got the food. *We* had the papers.' Hanka Ziegler's torment lasted for two years. Then, 'one day my brother said to me, "The war is over, we're going home"...'.[37]

Every boy can recount a story in which ill-luck and evil were combined. Naftali Rosenzweig had been born in the village of Ksiaz Wielki, twenty-five miles from Cracow. He was just ten years old when the Germans invaded Poland. 'My mother, Chana, was taken away in 1942', he

---

[37] Anna Smith (Hanka Ziegler), in conversation with the author, 16 March 1996.

recalled. 'My father, Chaim, was shot by a Volksdeutsche. We had been hidden by a Polish couple on their farm. Their son gave us away. Of my two brothers and two sisters, I was the oldest. I am the only survivor.'[38]

[38] Naftali Rosenzweig, in conversation with the author, 11 May 1996.

CHAPTER 4

The Days of Deportation

THE DEPORTATIONS OF 1942 and 1943 saw the destruction of Polish Jewry: the centuries-old Jewish communities known collectively before the war as the 'Jewish Nation in Poland'. The first death camp in which Polish Jews were systematically murdered was set up near the village of Chelmno. Jews from nearby towns and villages in western Poland were deported there, as Jews were later to be deported to other death camps, on foot, by horse and cart, and in railway trucks, and murdered immediately after their arrival. In Chelmno, the killing was done by the use of exhaust fumes funnelled into ordinary vans specially converted for the purpose.

The first killings at Chelmno were carried out on 8 December 1941, the day after Pearl Harbor. Thereafter the deportations to Chelmno took place every day, from an ever-widening circle of towns. Week by week, other deportations spread systematically through Poland, with each region designated for a different death camp. The Jews of the Wartheland, which included the area around Lodz, were sent to Chelmno; Jews from parts of central and southern Poland to Sobibor; from Warsaw and the region around it to Treblinka; from Eastern and Western Galicia, to Belzec; from the areas annexed by Germany, to Auschwitz. Sometimes a whole Jewish community would be deported and murdered in a single deportation. Sometimes two or even three deportations, or groups of deportations, would be needed before a ghetto was finally 'liquidated' – in the German terminology.

From Lodz there were continual deportations to the death camp at Chelmno, starting in December 1941. First to be deported were all the known and registered Jewish prostitutes; also whole families of Jews who had been brought to the ghetto from Germany and Austria earlier that winter; and several thousand old people, the sick, and young children. Inside the ghetto, the destination of the deportees was unknown. The Germans insisted that it was a labour camp where food was plentiful, conditions were good, and the work was not burdensome. In fact, all the deportees had been sent to Chelmno, a village forty-five miles from Lodz, and had been murdered there within a few hours of reaching the camp.

That something was false about the German assurances gradually penetrated into the ghetto awareness. 'The deportations kept on getting more frequent,' Perec Zylberberg recalled. 'There were already forebodings. People tried by all means available to get themselves exempted from being sent out. Those higher up, who had some access to information or hints, were frantically trying to make sure that they and their family and friends were spared. Such activity did not escape the general public. The vibrations were felt all around. Any animal who is placed in the vicinity of frightfulness senses the implications. We too sensed an ominous air about us. We did not quite know what and how. We carried on working and trying to be registered in one or another workplace. Working meant a passport to staying on. Rules kept on changing, but the psychology of the situation dictated the moves one made to be exempt from being sent out.

'I remember being asked by one of the leaders of the Bund to try and arrange a contact with the director of the plant that produced carpets. The purpose was to get some people on to the plant register. It was becoming a matter of grave concern. I was successful in obtaining a promise and an okay for a visit by the leader of the Bund. At that time I also got my mother and my sister into the plant. As long as they were employed it calmed the psyche. We were more hungry than ever. The thought of eating was forever in our minds. My family started to feel the pinch of undernourishment. Mother was not feeling too well. Esther, my sister, was bravely carrying on, being a great help and companion to Mother. I remember being worried and frightened. There was no time for crying. Instinctively, we felt the need to encourage one another.'[1]

The deportations from the Lodz ghetto were continuous throughout the first five months of 1942, with constant seizures of those to be deported, mostly by the Jewish police, supervised by German guards.

Berek Obuchowski was fourteen when, in April 1942, the Germans surrounded the ghetto in his home town of Ozorkow, and prepared to deport almost all its inhabitants to the death camp at Chelmno. 'The Germans gave the order for all the Jews of Ozorkow to gather in the main school,' he recalled. 'We were all forced to undress completely, and were stamped on our chests, either with the letter A or B. We were very perplexed, not knowing what it meant. Two days later, after being allowed to go home, we had to return to the school, where we were separated into two groups – A and B. Eighty per cent of the people were in B group – young and old (all ages) including my grandfather, parents, and one sister. They were all taken away and I never saw them again.

[1] Perec Zylberberg, recollections, diary entry for 20 August 1993.

My other sister and I were immediately sent to the ghetto in Ozorkow with the people stamped with A. We were there for only a short period – about six weeks I think – when we were transferred to the Lodz ghetto.'[2]

Fear of deportation was everywhere. Rose Kalman recalled how her mother, her two sisters and her surviving brother agreed 'that whatever happened we would stick together – whoever was selected we would fall in with them. The day soon came and we were rounded up. My mother was selected and my younger sister followed her. I also wanted to follow her but I couldn't move my legs, they felt as though they were glued to the ground. My brother and sister also stayed as if rooted to the spot. After the selection we were all allowed back to our rooms. We felt shocked and bewildered and terrified.'[3]

In June 1942 the Jews of Bielsko-Biala (known to the Germans as Bielitz) were rounded up and deported. They were one of the very first Polish Jewish communities to be deported to Auschwitz. Fifteen-year-old Kurt Klappholz was an eyewitness of the events of that day. 'We arrived at the station in Bielitz, which I knew quite well,' he recalled. 'There was a roll-call there, family by family. The younger people who were there, such as I, were asked to go to the left, the older people were asked to go to a courtyard. And after the war, when I met people in Israel who had heard something about this, I was told that those who were asked to go to the courtyard had their valuables taken from them. So I waited with the young, and with us there were also girls of my age and some of the girls were crying, and one asked whether she could go and join her parents. By then there were Jewish militia from Sosnowiec with us, and the girl who was crying asked one of the militiamen whether she could rejoin her parents, and the Jewish militiaman said that she could, but he would not advise her to do so. Well! This was the first time I heard a remark of that kind, which after the war became much clearer to me than it was at the time.

'Then a lorry arrived which we were asked to mount. I was the last one to get on to the lorry. That was the last time I saw my parents. I still remember what I saw. My father stood next to my mother, and my mother, I think she was crying. People with whom we had shared our flat in Bielitz earlier were also there, including Professor Richard Wagner and his wife, and his son, who was my age. Mrs Wagner cried out to her son that he should stick to me. In the event he didn't, and as far as I am aware, he did not survive the war. I have recounted this event more than once, but I still find it difficult to talk about without having to suppress tears in my eyes.'[4]

---

[2] Bob Roberts (Berek Obuchowski), letter to the author, 4 March 1996.
[3] Rose Kalman (Goldman), letter to the author, July 1995.
[4] Kurt Klappholz, 'Testimony', transcript of tape, 1995.

Israel (Jack) Rubinfeld was thirteen years old when the fate of the Jews of the small town of Bircza was decided. 'A large contingent of Gestapo arrived,' he recalled. 'They issued an order to the Jewish community to come up with a very large amount of money, including dollars, gold, diamonds and all wedding rings. This was to happen within forty-eight hours or everyone would be shot. We delivered all of the gold, diamond rings and dollars held by our family.

'Immediately upon our paying this ransom, they ordered the whole Jewish community – men, women, and children – without exception, to report to an assembly place to be evacuated. Anyone caught outside the gathering place after 4 p.m. would be shot. At 4 p.m. sharp, Gestapo squads proceeded from house to house, and anyone unable to make it on time – the disabled, retarded, or elderly – was shot on the spot.'

The Jews of Bircza were kept in the assembly place throughout the night. 'We were approximately two thousand people surrounded by the Gestapo,' Jack Rubinfeld later wrote. 'They crowded us together like sardines, without sanitary conditions. Early the next morning, while darkness still loomed, shots echoed all over. With the fervour of a cattle drive, they prodded us, in a panic, to the road leading to Przemysl. They did not care how many of us they killed. Some horse-drawn wagons were waiting, and the Gestapo herded the elderly, and the women with children on to them. My mother, my sister Runia, and her infant went on a wagon. I marched alongside the wagons with the men and boys. They pressed us without rest all the way to Przemysl – twenty-eight kilometres away. On the way, the Gestapo seized all of the older people from the wagons, and shot them at the side of the road – my mother was among them. Only Runia and her infant arrived in Przemysl ghetto. After a day or two, it happened again. Reinforced Gestapo units were everywhere. As if we were cattle in the Wild West, with gunfire ringing all around, we were driven in a panic, as we were rounded up, and steered into the cattle market. Approximately twenty thousand Jews, including women and children, from all of the surrounding area were there. There I was separated from Runia. About 160 men and boys were sent to an aeroplane engine factory in Rzeszow – I was one of them.'[5]

Sala Bernholz was fourteen at the time of the first deportation of the Jews of Wolanow. 'I remember my two grandmothers packing their eiderdowns and saying that there was going to be a hard winter,' she recalled. 'They were taken away on open lorries.' Sala, her mother and her brother were taken to the nearby village of Strzalkow, where a labour camp had been established, and then to another labour camp at Blizyn. 'When they moved us to Blizyn,' she later wrote, 'they started

---

[5] Jack (Israel) Rubinfeld, 'Jack Rubinfeld', manuscript, sent to the author, undated (1995).

by taking the little children away from their mothers. I will never forget the crying, but what could one do? They took my brother Moishe away at that time and we could do nothing to prevent them. He was four years younger than me.'[6]

When the Jews were deported from the Rymanow ghetto in August 1942, Simon Lecker was fifteen years old. During the years following the German occupation in 1939 an uncle had taught him watchmaking; this later saved his life when the Germans sought those with a necessary skill. At Rymanow he was among those Jewish men chosen to work in road construction. 'My sisters Rifka, Mania and Genia,' he later wrote, 'together with my mother Berta, perished in a concentration camp. Once we were separated, and I was shipped out with the other men, I never saw them again.'[7]

Harry Balsam, living in the ghetto in Gorlice, was just thirteen years old in the second week of August 1942, at the start of the deportations from his home town. 'Early morning we were rounded up and taken to a kiln (a brick factory), where we spent three days,' he later wrote, 'after which the Germans opened the gates and started screaming: "Everybody out". At the same time we heard shooting. I saw it through a little window, I naturally thought that they were killing us all, so I got hold of my mother, sister and brother and pushed us forward, as I couldn't bear to watch the shooting and thought that the sooner it would be over the better.

'Fortunately we weren't being shot. They were only shooting the people who they found in hiding. We were put in groups of one hundred and dragged to the trains, but I was pulled out of the group. I never heard from my mother, sister and brother again. Each group consisted of ninety Jews and ten Gypsies.

'I was then alone in the ghetto. People were being taken away every day and at that time we did not know where they were being taken. Killing and shooting became a normal everyday event. You constantly heard shots being fired, one here, two there, four somewhere else. It is very difficult to say, but that is how it was, and you got used to the idea that killing meant nothing. You just got used to it. Everyone had one thing in mind and that was to survive.

'The reason why I was pulled out of the group together with others was that there were still some Jews left in the town, and many were being shot as they were being taken away either for trying to run away, or for just not moving quickly enough. These people had to be collected

---

[6] Sala Kaye (Bernholz), 'Sala Kaye Remembers', *Holocaust Testimony 1*, published by Roman Halter and Michael Etkind, London, 1983.

[7] Simon Lecker (Gilbert), letter to the author, 2 October 1995.

and buried and we had to dig the graves for them. We knew that although we were digging graves for them we were digging our own graves, but what worried us was who would bury us, as there would be nobody left to do it.

'One morning at six we were rounded up and told to go to the Appel Platz,[8] which was the focal point, and they sorted out three hundred of us and sent us towards the trains. They told us we were going to a labour camp.'[9] Also taken to a labour camp from Gorlice that day were Zisha Schwimmer and his father. 'My mother and sister were among those lining the street to watch us being marched to the railway station', he recalled. 'My mother called me to join her, but the guards did not allow it. Little did we know that we were going to be the lucky ones.'[10] Those taken by train were sent to slave labour at Plaszow. Those remaining in the ghetto were deported soon afterwards to Belzec, and murdered.

At Dukla, forty-three kilometres to the east of Gorlice, Lipa Tepper was fifteen when the deportations began from his ghetto. 'One day,' he later recalled, 'the town was completely surrounded. There were SS men with dogs everywhere. They came along and shouted "raus! raus! raus!" and we were all taken out of our homes, marched into the town square. Those of us who – as I have established since – were to remain alive, were ordered to stand facing the wall. The people who actually stayed alive were those who were employed in two quarries. All the rest of the people were loaded on lorries and taken out of the town and we have not ever seen them since.

'It has been established that they were shot on that day in a village called Tylawa, which was to the north of our town. We were then marched into one area of the town which was surrounded by wooden fences and this was to be our camp whence we marched out to work every morning and returned every night. Initially we received what I have to assume were reasonable rations, i.e. we got bread and soup and coffee and it was not that bad. However, we all mourned the loss of our loved ones, since we knew then that they had not survived. I do not know how we assumed that, but everybody did, and we knew that they had not remained alive.'[11]

David, Abraham and Moniek Hirszfeld, from the village of Bobowa, in southern Poland, were present when all the Jews of the village were forced to congregate in the market-place. 'My two brothers, Abraham

---

[8] Any place where a roll-call was held.

[9] Harry Balsam, letter to the author, 8 May 1995.

[10] Jack (Zisha) Schwimmer, 'The War Memoirs of Z. Schwimmer', manuscript, sent to the author, 6 October 1994.

[11] Lipa Tepper, letter to the author, 30 January 1996.

and Moniek, and I, were sent to Plaszow camp,' David Hirszfeld later wrote, 'and the rest of the family (my mother Rivka, sister Sabina, and the rest of the extended family) remained in Bobowa.'[12]

None of those who remained in Bobowa were ever seen again. The father of the three boys, who had been badly injured fighting in the Austrian army in the First World War, and was disabled throughout the inter-war years, had died some time before the 'selection'.

Chaim Olmer was fourteen when the Jews of Sosnowiec were ordered to assemble on 12 August 1942. 'On that Saturday very early in the morning,' he later recalled, 'the SS moved into town and anybody who was slow-moving was shot on the spot. When we arrived at the assembly point the SS separated the old and the not so old men, put them on carts, and took them away. They ordered me off a cart and into a house where I had to remove a man's body who had been shot. He had only one leg, and the Poles had been willing helpers to the Germans with the round-up. One Pole took the spade he was carrying and chopped the other leg off the dead body.'

The carts set off towards Miechow. 'As we passed a small wood we could hear shooting. We then knew that the people who were separated earlier were being shot. Some women started crying and the SS dragged a woman from the cart and shot her in front of everybody to quieten us down.

'We passed Miechow and, some ten miles further, near Slomniki, the carts turned off on to a field which had been surrounded by barbed wire. Our group was the first to arrive but the Poles were already there and digging ditches. Our immediate thought was that we were going to be killed, but the trenches were being dug as latrines! Then more and more people were being brought on to the field and we were there for four days in the open in the most terrible conditions.'[13]

'On the Wednesday a further selection took place, with the elderly and those men who looked emaciated being taken away in carts. The men knew what awaited them and put on their *talaisim* and *tefilim*[14] as they were driven away to another field to be shot.

'Our field was near a railway line, and on the fourth day wagons were shunted in. The SS then separated all the women and children and marched them to a waiting train.

'Yet another selection then took place amongst the remaining men and youth. Those whose hands had not been roughened by hard work were sent to join the waiting train. The remainder – including my father,

---

[12] David Hirszfeld (Hirschfeld), 'The David Hirschfeld Story', manuscript, sent to the author, 9 February 1996.

[13] Chaim Olmer, recollections, sent to the author, 17 September 1995.

[14] Prayer shawls and phylacteries.

brother, and I – were put onto wagons of a second train which was shunted into a siding after the first train left. We arrived in Plaszow late the same night.'[15]

'Those four days were the most traumatic for me and probably for everyone there.'[16]

More than half a century later, Arek Hersh recalled the day on which the Jews were deported from his home town of Sieradz. It was on 14 August 1942. 'At eight in the morning we all had to go to the Appel Platz. It was on open ground near the unfinished school, five minutes walk from our house. We took with us what few belongings we could carry. All the Jews from Sieradz gathered on this open ground, row after row of us, where we were counted by the German police. I was only thirteen years old, but by this age I had learned to think for myself. I knew that I must always watch and wait and be one step ahead. I knew from experience that the Germans only spared those who were useful – that is to say, those who were fit for work.

'I myself was too small to be chosen for work, but I took comfort in the fact that my brother Tovia, who was then seventeen, and my sister Itka, who was eighteen, were not only older but were also taller. This meant that their chances of being chosen for work were good. I worried somewhat about the fact that Tovia had a stiff knee due to a football accident when he was ten years old, but this knee did not seem to hamper him too much and nor would it readily be seen as something which would stop him from working. My mother, too, was relatively young – only thirty-nine years old – and very healthy. I thought to myself, "Work will be found for her too". These thoughts were a relief to me. It seemed that I was the only one who was at risk.

'We were all marched to the church, which was situated next to the theatre which had a large forecourt. I looked at the theatre, remembering how often I had been there with my parents to see plays and shows and sometimes to attend meetings. Now, however, the building was used as a theatre no more. Like almost everything else in Sieradz, the Germans had closed that down too.

'Sieradz was a small town and most of its men had already been taken away to work in camps. This left a population of about 1,400 Jews, all of whom were crushed into the church, hardly able to move or breathe. I was full of thoughts of survival as I went through the big gates, and when I saw the German policeman for whom I had worked standing on guard, I smiled and tried to talk to him. However he ignored me. Then

[15] Chaim Olmer, recollections, letter to the author, 1 July 1992.
[16] Chaim Olmer, recollections, letter to the author, 17 September 1995.

I noticed that standing next to him were a group of SS, all with the tell-tale insignia on their collars and caps – a skull with crossbones.

'After a long hour in the church, we were told to go outside. As we walked out, two SS officers asked us what our trade was. Knowing that only those chosen for the workforce would survive, I responded immediately, "Schneider", which means tailor. This lie was wasted on the officers who told me to go along with my family. "Well, whatever happens now", I thought to myself, "at least we shall all be together." This thought brought me happiness.

'I looked over at the other side of the courtyard and saw a group of about one hundred and fifty people who were being told to stand in front of the church square. Everyone else was told to go back into the church. Amongst the group outside were many teenagers and fit-looking adults. I had not been right in thinking that my mother and brother and sister would be selected, but I had been right in thinking that I would not. The one hundred and fifty were the ones who might survive. I stood in the Christian church, and although I knew that my own chances of survival were slim, I felt resigned to my fate and my feeling of happiness that I was going to be with my family persisted. There was silence in the church. I kept my thoughts to myself. Then my mother looked at the three of us and said, "Thank God we are together." My uncles, aunts and cousins all remained in the church with us; none of us had been selected for the courtyard with the other group.

'After a time I became very thirsty and I asked my mother if she had something I could drink from. "I'll go and ask the guard for some water," I said. From our possessions she brought out a metal pan and gave it to me. "I'll only be a second," I told her.

'As I approached the gate, I realised that there was some kind of commotion. I could see an SS officer once again calling out to people, asking them their trade. As I approached with the pan, he shouted at me, "What are you?" I answered automatically, "Schneider." This time the response was different. He shouted the word, "raus!" ("out!"). I did as he asked, and was told to join the group of one hundred and fifty people who were standing outside the square. Now I was struck with horror and disbelief at what I had done.

'The SS man's question had taken me by surprise. I was very small for my age. I had never held a needle in my hand and I did not know one stitch from another. As I walked towards the selected workers, I looked back through the gate, praying that I might at least catch a glimpse of my beautiful mother and my sister and brother. As I walked tears poured from my eyes. Sadness such as I had never known filled me. The pan which my mother had given me I still held in my hand.

'Those of us who had been selected were then marched off to a police station. We were held there overnight, three to a cell, cramped and uncomfortable, no mattresses or beds, and only a bucket in which to urinate. We did not know where we would be taken to from there. I was certain that it would be somewhere where there was work; we were in too good a physical condition to be disposed of. I sat on the floor of the cell and wept bitterly, wondering what had happened to my family. My longing for them was intense and I wished that I had stayed with them. Others tried to calm me. "Don't worry," one man kept saying. Everyone else tried to assure me that my family had simply been taken to another camp.

'We waited, and eventually, just when it seemed that night would never end, our own cell door was opened. We had to put any money and jewellery on the table outside the cell. "You will not be needing such things where you are going," we were told. We emptied our pockets; I had six photographs of my family, which I kept, and the metal pan with which I'd gone to fetch water.

'We were marched from the police station to the railway station, where we were each given half a loaf of brown bread, the only food for our journey. We boarded a train bound for Lodz, a trip which took five hours as the train stopped very often. When we reached Lodz we were kept overnight in the wagons.

'Next morning we were taken to the Lodz ghetto, which was fenced in. At the gates were Jewish policemen and outside were German police. All the people I saw in the ghetto were very thin and undernourished. Those of us who had just arrived from Sieradz were taken to a large block of flats and were accommodated around ten to a room. I did not sleep at all that first night. My thoughts were full of my mother, Tovia and Itka. I thought too about my father, who I knew was in a camp in Poznan, and about my other relatives. I worried about what had befallen them all.

'The next day I walked about, dazed and shaken, not knowing what to do or to whom to talk. All the people I had come with seemed to be in a similar state. As the days went by, I watched every transport that arrived at the ghetto from the provinces, searching longingly for someone from my family. I hoped against hope that another batch of people would be brought in from Sieradz, but these hopes were never realised. I learned from other people that a decision had been made that day in Sieradz to increase the number of people chosen to work by thirty. The thirst which had driven me to go to the church gate to ask for water, and the fact that I had said that word, "Schneider", had made me one of those thirty extra people. It had enabled me to survive.'

As with all the boys, and indeed all survivors, survival depended on a whole series of such chance incidents. Given the length of time during which the fate of the Jews depended on the German whim, one stroke of luck was never enough. Each boy can recount a litany of such moments, without which their eventual survival would have been impossible.

'I went on and on looking for my family and telling myself that they must be alive,' Arek Hersh recalled. 'Later I was to discover that those who had been left in the church, including my mother, my sister and my brother, had all been taken to the Chelmno extermination camp and murdered.'[17]

Kopel Kandelcukier was fourteen years old when the day of deportation came in his town of Bialobrzegi. 'Armoured cars and hundreds of Germans surrounded our little town,' he recalled, 'and gave us five minutes to run to the cattle market, shooting indiscriminately into the running Jews. We were stumbling over dead or dying bodies to get to the cattle market. On arriving I was amazed that my mother and sisters were alive. There was pandemonium there, no one knew what was going to happen.

'Suddenly I was hit over the head by a friendly local policeman who knew me, and who pulled me away from my mother and sisters and pushed me into a marching column picked to work. For the next two weeks I worked with a group of about sixty men for the German electricity company, electrifying the power lines. The policeman then came and took me back to our police station where I could work for them. Also in the town were Jewish craftsmen selected to work for the Germans. I was told that my mother and sisters were marched to the nearest station and on to Treblinka (I didn't have the slightest idea then what Treblinka was).'[18]

Chaim Ajzen was also working on the power lines on the day when the Jews of Bialobrzegi, his home town too, were deported. It was the Jewish festival of Simchat Torah, the Rejoicing in the Law. 'On that particular day,' he recalled, 'I was working on the electricity pole when the train passed and I heard the cries of my people as I stood on the pole twenty metres high. I took off the belt that bound me to the pole and threw it down. I worked all day without a belt but did not fall.'[19]

Mayer Kochen was fifteen when the day of deportation came to the Kielce ghetto on the morning of 20 August 1942. As usual he had been

[17] Arek Hersh (Herszlikowicz), 'From Sieradz to the Lodz Ghetto', manuscript, sent to the author, 1995.

[18] Kopel Kendall (Kandelcukier), recollections, letter to the author, 2 September 1995.

[19] Chaim Ajzen, 'Chaim Ajzen's Story', manuscript, sent to the author, 1995.

taken out of the ghetto on the previous evening for forced labour; he was on the twelve-hour night shift digging trenches alongside the railway. 'One night we were informed that the ghetto was surrounded by the SS and that there was a lot of shooting. The liquidation was taking place. We were due to return to the ghetto at six in the morning, but were not allowed to return until the liquidation was completed. We were marched back about midday to an eerie ghost town, not a living soul to be found in the streets, but plenty of corpses on the ground. We were not allowed to return to our homes, but taken to the synagogue. I never saw my parents, brother, sister, or any of my family after that fatal evening when I set out to work.'[20]

Fifteen-year-old Abraham Zwirek had been deported with his family from the ghetto in Plock to another ghetto, in the town of Suchedniow. As was the case with many Jewish communities, especially the smaller ones, having been confined in one ghetto they were then deported to another. In this way they were uprooted twice from their homes, cut off both from their livelihood and their possessions. On 22 September 1942 all those in the ghetto of Suchedniow were ordered to assemble, and were taken off in different directions. 'My mother was taken on a truck somewhere,' Zwirek later wrote, 'and my father and I were sent to Skarzysko-Kamienna as slave labourers. I was forced to work producing bullets for the German war effort.

'In December 1942 a friend who had been taken with my mother had escaped and eventually found us in Skarzysko. He told us that they had been taken to an extermination camp in Treblinka and he was made to work as a Sonderkommando[21] burning the bodies of the Jews who had been gassed. His mother and mine had been murdered in this manner, on 23 September 1942, the day after Yom Kippur.'[22]

For the Jews of the Lodz ghetto, the day after that most holy day in the Jewish calendar, a day of fasting and repentance, was to be a day of agony. Beginning that day, and continuing for seven days without respite, came a deportation larger than any before, in which 16,000 Jews were deported to Chelmno and murdered there.

Michael Etkind recalled that deportation clearly. 'All places of work were closed,' he wrote, 'and a round-the-clock curfew imposed on everybody with the exception of the police, the fire brigade, the post

[20] Mayer Cornell (Kochen), letter to the author, 25 December 1994.

[21] A 'Special Unit', composed entirely of Jews, who were forced at every death camp to burn the bodies of those who had just been murdered.

[22] Abraham Zwirek, letter to the author, 30 September 1994.

office and certain members of the administration who were issued with special passes. At first the task of rounding people up was given to the Jewish police, without the supervision of the Germans, but this did not provide the desired results. The wailing and screaming went on all night.

'In the morning the Germans moved in. A few people were hanged, some shots were fired. Block after block was cordoned off and everybody had to file past a selection committee consisting of a Gestapo officer and one or two men with automatic weapons. The caretaker of each block was responsible for all his tenants being present. Needless to say, parents tried to hide their children but every possible hiding-place was searched, especially attics and cellars. Anybody found hiding was shot on the spot. The door to my room was smashed with an axe, since I was away and had left it padlocked.

'Those "selected" were put on to horse-drawn vans and taken to collection centres. Anybody strong enough could escape relatively easily, since these vans were guarded not by Germans but by the Jewish police. In spite of this the collection centres were filling up fast with small children, the sick and infirm. Enormous cattle trucks would arrive outside these centres to take away all those herded inside and make room for new arrivals. I soon realised that no one knew what my duties were supposed to be, and began to walk from centre to centre looking for my sister, having heard that the orphanages were being evacuated.

'While walking through the ghetto I saw Gestapo man Fuchs standing with his revolver and making people kneel before him for amusement. I saw Biebow[23] and Rumkowski talking and laughing while being driven in a droshki, and Gertler with his driver. I saw "Boxer", a low-ranking Gestapo man who did most of the shooting with his automatic gun, and I saw the "Rollkommando"[24] trucks being loaded with children outside the hospital in Lagiewnicka Street. The children were crying and would not go into the truck. Two shots rang out. There was silence. The truck was quickly filled.

'The two Rollkommando men, with rolled-up sleeves, climbed up to the top of the van and sat astride at the corners of the open-topped truck, their legs dangling above the children's heads. As the truck was pulling away they shut their eyes and turned their tanned faces towards the sun. After the truck had disappeared the nurses took two little bodies from the pavement. A young rabbi was seen later on proclaiming loudly that there was no God.

'I went to another centre, an old people's home near Marysin. Hundreds of elderly, incontinent ladies were lying on rotting straw and

---

[23] The German administrator of the Lodz ghetto.
[24] The unit of heavy trucks in which the Jews of Lodz were deported from the ghetto.

waiting to be taken away. Some of them were trying to give me their wedding rings and asking me to let them go. I would not take anything and told them that as far as I was concerned they were free to go. They were too weak to get up. At night the vans arrived and Jewish policemen began loading them.

'Suddenly the sirens wailed, announcing an air raid. I started to pray for bombs to rain. Nothing happened. The sirens wailed again. One of the horse-drawn vans, while reversing, slipped backwards into a pond discharging half of its human cargo into the water. I escaped and made my way back to the hospital. Only once was I ordered to accompany a policeman on a van loaded with "selected" people. The horse was walking slowly, and while the van was turning a corner a young man jumped out from behind a wall; his wife and a baby were on the van. A fight ensued between him and the policeman, who ordered me to help him. I did nothing. Eventually the young man managed to rescue his wife but not the baby. The policeman was yelling and blaming me for letting her escape. His receipt stated that there were thirty-two people on the van, but there were only thirty-one. A little further on I slipped off the van and disappeared round the corner.

'The "Szpera" – the curfew – lasted seven days and seven nights, and it ended as suddenly as it started. It was lifted after 20,000 people had been evacuated. The streets began to fill again as the last Rollkommando truck was leaving the Baluty market. How quickly life returned to "normal". There was no room for mental anguish, and those who failed to learn this did not survive for long.'[25]

Roman Halter was fourteen years old when the first deportations had taken place from the Lodz ghetto. He had been sent to Lodz from Chodecz after most of his family had been deported to Chelmno. 'I was the seventh child and the youngest in our large family,' he later wrote. 'By the beginning of 1942 there were just two of us left, my mother and I. We were then in the Lodz ghetto. My mother worked in the factory which cleaned and repaired German soldiers' bloodstained, shot-through, soiled and torn uniforms. For eight hours' hard labour each day each worker received a ladle of soup. I too worked. My place of employment was the metal factory inside the ghetto, at 63 Lagiewnicka Street. The one ladle of soup daily mattered greatly. Without it one couldn't live for long. Those who didn't or couldn't work and had to go without the daily soup died quickly. The starvation ration alone – distributed by the Jewish Council – was not enough to keep one alive.

'Even with the one ladle of soup a day, plus our weekly starvation ration, my mother and I looked like living skeletons. Such people were

[25] Michael Etkind, '"Youth" Remembered', manuscript, sent to the author, 4 January 1996.

called Klapsedras or Musulmen – we were both. But my mother's health was worse than mine. She, in addition to being very thin, began to have swellings around her eyes and ankles. It became difficult for her to walk. And going to work and coming back from work she had to cross the Koscielna wooden bridge. By the beginning of 1942 this became an almost impossible task for her. She could only do this with my help, or someone else's.

'After a time the swellings around her ankles became worse and bigger and they started to move up her legs. By the time the selection, the Great "Szpera" (pronounced Shpera), began in our ghetto in the spring of 1942 the swellings were up to her knees and she walked with great difficulty. When, on the day of the selection, we stood before the SS officer, my mother, in perfect German, began to tell him that we both worked in a factory doing useful work and that ... But he didn't let her finish. He ordered us to be put on to the "cart". Being placed on the "cart" meant being taken to some place to be murdered (later I found out that the place was Chelmno).

'In the part of the ghetto where we lived the streets and roads were too narrow for big lorries to enter. So the people who had been selected were taken by narrow carts pulled by horses to that part of the ghetto where the big lorries awaited them. I was on such a cart next to my mother. She pulled me close to her and said: "I cannot walk. You are still able to walk and run. You must save yourself. When I tell you to jump, jump off this cart and run through the archway towards the open ground in the direction of the public toilets. Climb quickly up on it, and from there on to the fire brigade's fence. Get across to the fire brigade side and lie close to the base of the fence. Don't move for ten or fifteen minutes. Run in a zigzag way. Don't stop if they shout halt or even if they shoot. Be brave. Save your life. Take off your wooden clogs now and hold them in your hands. Throw them over the fence when you reach the toilet. Do all as I have just told you. Now stay close to me. I will tell you when to go. Look into my eyes. May God be with you."

'I did as she told me. And when I came back to the room in which my mother and I lived, the eiderdown was still on the bed. This eiderdown had saved our lives during the last two winters, especially during this last winter of 1941–'42 when people froze to death in their beds. The neighbours said that the selection in our area of the ghetto was finished but that other parts were still cordoned off and the curfew was still on. Now, suddenly I felt all alone. I felt empty and very tired, so I covered myself with the eiderdown and slept for very many hours. When I awoke one of the neighbours gave me hot water to drink and a small crust of bread to cat.

'In the metal factory where I worked many were gone. Josef Chimowicz was the managing director. His brother, Leon (Leon's name was Israel but he was called Leon) was my section leader. Directors and section leaders received a bigger and better ration of food and so did their families. This was called the "Bajrat" ration. The Bajrat people – those who worked for the Jewish Council – didn't look starved. Leon Chimowicz liked me and the way I worked. Someone told him that my mother had been taken away. He came to see me to say how sorry he was to hear it. Then he said that he would like to adopt me; that, as his adopted son, I would also be eligible to receive the Bajrat ration. But, he said, he, his wife and their three small children would take for themselves that part of the ration which made up the difference between the standard starvation ration and the special Bajrat ration, and that although I would only be left with the starvation ration I would have (in addition) the security of his "protection".

'He further told me that I would sleep in the kitchen of their flat, get up early each day and clean the flat and do all that his wife told me to do. Then I would come to the metal factory to work. Did I agree with his terms? I had never seen his wife or his three small boys before, for whom I was going to have to work, but my instinct told me that this proposition might help me to live, to stay alive. So I thanked him and said "yes".'[26]

'In retrospect,' Roman Halter reflected, 'I would not have denuded anybody of his rations. They just skimmed it off.'[27]

'The human capacity for endurance is great,' Perec Zylberberg later wrote, recalling those same September days in Lodz. 'Such a calamity as befell the ghetto in those hellish days of the "Szpera" – as that period became known and identifiable to us – would by normal counts have finished us off as functioning human beings. The scenes witnessed, the personal tragedies endured, the realisation that our previously held notions were just wishful thinking, the sense of helplessness and the three years of constant suffering, should have done away with our will to carry on in those terrible times. We were undernourished, disease-ridden, besieged by constant fear of almost everything. People were not capable of thinking in normal terms. Abnormality became the normality of the times. But how does a person transform himself or herself when normality goes hand in hand with madness? Where lies the strength to carry on with ostensibly normal pursuits? What is one aiming at?

'These bitter thoughts and feelings, played out within our beings, made us totally suspicious of everything around. They made us victims of the worst fears. It seemed as if we had reached the very depths of

---

[26] Roman Halter, letter to the author, 1 March 1996.
[27] Roman Halter, in conversation with the author, 22 April 1996.

existence itself. Some people turned away in disgust from all that had been built by the fruit of the human mind. To those people, accustomed to following teachings of moral and ethical values, it became anathema to continue thinking in such terms. To others, the despondency created a desire for an outlet in some form of supernatural entity.

'The very premise on which our culture rested became unhinged. It was a battle of the deepest solitude. We must have a minute amount of hidden spirit of life within us. At that moment when sanity itself was at stake, we slowly began lifting ourselves out of the deadly stupor.'[28]

Yosek Rotbaum had been expelled with his family from the village of Cecylowka to the town and ghetto of Kozienice. There, in conditions of considerable overcrowding and hunger, his father Israel had managed on a number of occasions to leave the ghetto at night and barter food from the villagers around, fruit farmers with whom he had been on good terms before the war. On several such dangerous journeys his young son Yosek accompanied him. One night, while they were away collecting food, the ghetto was surrounded. Not knowing this, Israel Rotbaum returned to the ghetto, leaving Yosek overnight with a friendly villager, in whose barn, after a welcome meal, the young man fell fast asleep. Fifty years later Yosek (then Joseph Ribo) recalled the events of the following morning. 'After walking a couple of hours,' he wrote, ' I noticed people – mainly villagers – walking away from Kozienice, talking excitedly. That looked to me unusual, because at these early hours, people were going into town and not out of it. This immediately put me on the alert. I hid the rucksack I was carrying underneath some shrubs.

'One of the people walking away from the town, was a farmer from the village of Ursynow, whom I knew. When he noticed me, he came over, pulled me down behind some shrubs and told me not to go into town. He said the ghetto was surrounded by the SS and Ukrainian guards and that all the Jews were being evacuated. I heard what the man said, but I didn't grasp the meaning of it for some time. I knew that what he said was very bad. I sat behind the shrubs for quite a long time, not knowing what to do. At some stage I wanted to cry, but the tears wouldn't come. After some time I decided that I must go into town and see what was happening in the ghetto.

'I tried to compose myself, to arrange my clothes and straighten my hair. I left my hat behind in order to expose my blond hair which, together with my blue eyes, made me look like a gentile. At this stage there was an influx of Poles into the town from all directions. They wanted to see the spectacle of expelling the Jews from the ghetto for

---

[28] Perec Zylberberg, recollections, diary entry for 23 August 1993.

themselves. That suited me fine, because it enabled me to intermingle with the crowd and be as inconspicuous as possible.

'The crowds moved along the ghetto walls trying to glimpse into the ghetto through cracks and crevices in the wooden planks, which closed the ghetto streets. The crowds were driven away by the Ukrainian guards, but would return moments later. I, of course, was very anxious to look into the ghetto. I knew the places where the cracks between the wooden planks were bigger, and ran to peep in through them, whenever possible. I saw carts driven by horses laden with bundles and suitcases, saw some small groups of Jews being ordered by SS soldiers to hurry up, to move faster, to load the carts. After the deportation, the Germans had left behind a group of inmates, together with the Jewish policemen, to search the houses and collect anything that looked of any value. These "goods" were hauled on to the carts and driven away as ordered by the Germans.

'I noticed the crowd was moving in the direction of the train station and I followed suit. When I reached the station, there was a large crowd already there, being kept away at a distance by great numbers of German and Ukrainian guards. I managed to squeeze myself into the first line of the crowd. At a distance of about fifty metres from the train, I could see Jews still being pushed into the last two or three wagons. The noise at the station was terrifying. There were screams and shouts from inside the wagons, orders and curses from the SS men, and frightening barking by the dogs. I remember the screeching of the wagon doors and the metallic crack as the doors locked. These noises accompanied me for many years to come.

'Suddenly I got very frightened. Not of the Germans, but from the sudden realisation that I wouldn't see my parents and brethren any more, and that I was all alone. Where would I stay? Who would look after me? At that I wanted to run to the train and try to find and join my family. But the doors of the wagons were already closed and there were hundreds of Germans and Ukrainians and those fierce-looking dogs.

'As I was contemplating what to do, a Polish youngster, standing a few metres from me, pointed at me and shouted, "Jew, he is a Jew". Instinctively I ran up to him, gave him a push and shouted back: "You are a Jew, you should be on the train". People in the crowd hushed us up and separated us. I was glad to have been shoved away from that youngster, and started to walk back to Kozienice. On the way back to town it dawned on me that I might never see my family again and tears were running down my cheeks.'[29]

---

[29] Joseph Ribo (Yosek Rotbaum), 'Yosek, My Adventures during the Second World War', manuscript, sent to the author, 18 April 1995.

It was 27 September 1942. In the battles being fought on the eastern front for the mastery of Europe, Hitler's forces were even then engaged in their titanic struggle against the Russian forces besieged inside the city of Stalingrad. But whatever the situation at the front, and however hard-pressed the German forces might be on the battlefield, the deportation of Polish Jews continued with as much sense of urgency, and zeal, as the military conduct of the war.

Having been encouraged to do so by his father, fourteen-year-old Alec Ward had escaped from the ghetto at Kozienice some time before the deportation. He took with him his nine-year-old brother Lajb. For three months after their escape they managed to live in the forests and fields around his former home town of Magnuszew, whose Jewish population, together with their father, had earlier been deported to Kozienice. The wooded nature of the area provided the two boys with shelter as they wandered from place to place. 'During the daytime we were always on the move,' he recalled, 'in order to find a few potatoes here, or a few beets and some fruit there.

'It was during such a walk in the fields near the village of Chmielow that we came across a group of Jewish prisoners who were irrigating the land for Volksdeutsche farmers. We found out that they lived in a fire station in the village. We decided to join them in order to have companionship and some warmth at night, as it was autumn by then and extremely cold to sleep in the haystacks. The prisoners were wonderful to us. Some of them shared their meagre rations with us. It was soon after joining that group that the SS surrounded the fire station one morning and took us to Magnuszew where we stood for a few hours in the town square.

'The town looked absolutely dead, devoid of any life. Before the war there was a small but vibrant Jewish community, with Jewish shops, Jewish merchants and artisans. There was a synagogue which acted as a house of prayer and a place to meet. Jewish children played in the streets and there was a very good relationship with the non-Jewish population.

'From Magnuszew they took us to the Kozienice ghetto, where we spent the night. We found the ghetto completely empty, with feathers flying in the streets. The feathers were from the bedding which the Nazis ripped open to look for hidden gold. I found out later that all the Jewish people from the three shtetls including my entire family, except for two cousins who live in Israel, and my family from Warsaw, were annihilated by the Nazis in Treblinka extermination camp in Poland. Our next stop was in the town of Radom where I experienced the first "selection" – one of many during my captivity. The Nazis took my little brother and some elderly men whom they considered unfit for slave labour and shot them.

'It was an extremely painful and unforgettable blow to me and was in a way more tragic to me than leaving my dear family. I somehow considered, in my young mind, that parting from my family would be an adventure. My parents' hearts must have been torn to pieces when they decided to send away their two sons, knowing that their chance of survival was so slim. I grew to love my little brother very much indeed during our time in hiding and would have preferred him to survive instead of me.

'Six people from that group miraculously survived the war. They are my friends – Menachem Silberstein who lives in Israel, David Turek, Moishe Nurtman, Alf Kirszberg, and Sam Freiman who live in England, and myself. Alf Kirszberg and I are the only two survivors from the original Jewish community of Magnuszew. We went to cheder together and his brothers were friends of my father.'[30]

Menachem Silberstein lost most of his family at the time of the deportation from Kozienice to Treblinka on 27 September 1942, including his mother Esther, his two sisters, Henia aged nineteen and Luba aged ten, and his grandmother, 'let them rest in peace'. Some time later, one of the deportees escaped from Treblinka; one of no more than eighty people who escaped, in the course of a whole year, out of three quarters of a million Jews who were taken there and murdered. 'He told us all about what was going on there,' Menachem Silberstein recalled. 'What they do to people, that no one stays alive. Many did not believe him. Some even said that he is out of his mind.'[31]

From Radom, Menachem Silberstein, Alec Ward, and those with them were taken to the slave labour camp at Skarzysko-Kamienna, forty-four kilometres to the south.

Also in Magnuszew at the time of the deportation to Kozienice was Sam Dresner, whose father had earlier managed to escape with his family from the Warsaw ghetto to this small Polish town. 'We had to move into a barn which we shared with some other families,' he recalled. 'It was winter and bitter cold, and the Germans kept shooting people they found outside the barbed wire they had thrown around the ghetto. After a few weeks in the ghetto some Germans came in and a call was made for all men between the ages of sixteen and sixty to go to a little square in the middle of the ghetto. My father went. Then they started searching and discovered me in bed where I had been for the last two weeks due

---

[30] Alec Ward, 'My Story', manuscript, sent to the author, 31 May 1995.
[31] Menachem (Mendel) Silberstein, letter to the author, 29 April 1996.

to typhus. I was just recovering. When my mother showed them my birth certificate (I was only fourteen) they just tore up the certificate, saying I was big enough for work. So I found myself kneeling in the square next to my father. I never saw my mother or sister again. Then we had to run while the Germans chased us on bicycles and horses. We finally arrived at a camp at Jedlinsk.'[32]

Chaskiel Rosenblum, from Konskie, was fourteen years old when his older brother Bolek ran away from the ghetto in the second week of October 1942, on what proved to be the eve of the deportation. With a Polish identity card he went to Konskie station, with a view to taking the train to Warsaw, and hiding there. 'But Bolek never got to Warsaw,' his brother recalled. 'At the railway station a Polish fireman recognised him and called out "Jew, Jew". The Germans seized him and started to beat him to death. As we were told by witnesses, he had lost a lot of blood and he cried for water all that night. After asking my father what would happen to us now, he said to me: "At least we are alive. Bolek doesn't exist any more".'

On the day of the deportation from Konskie, a German officer from the slave labour camp at Skarzysko-Kamienna came to the ghetto and made a speech. 'He said he needed one hundred strong Jews to work at Skarzysko,' Chaskiel Rosenblum recalled, 'and promised they would have plenty of food. My father took me by the hand and we jumped into the truck. The German said to me: "No, we don't need children". My father told him: "Then I'm not going either". The German said: "All right, get on the truck". This was my first step to survival. And this was the last time I saw my mother and my three sisters – waving goodbye while the truck started moving. They were sent to Treblinka and died there. None of them survived.'[33]

Shloime Zalman Judensznajder (Solly Irving) was twelve years old when, also in the second week of October 1942, the Gestapo surrounded the Ryki ghetto and prepared to deport all the Jews to Treblinka, and their deaths. 'Everybody had to assemble in the square,' he recalled. 'There were soldiers running round every house and getting people out. My father got hold of me and my sister Leah, and took us to a side street, having bribed the guard to let us through. He told us what village to go to and who we should go to see. I presumed this person would hide us. He told us that we should try to stay alive, and that was the last I saw of him, my mother and my other sisters.

'Leah and I walked through the fields to reach the village, but the

---

[32] Sam Dresner, letter to the author, 28 January 1995.

[33] Chaskiel Rosenblum, 'Testimony', manuscript, sent to the author, April 1995.

farmer's wife told us that we couldn't stay there as her husband was away with other farmers who had been ordered by the Germans to take their horses and carts to Ryki. The Germans needed to transport the Jewish population, especially those who couldn't walk, to the cattle trucks that were awaiting them at the station.

'That evening when the farmer returned, he came looking for us. He told us that he'd seen my father and oldest sister walking together, and my mother with my two other sisters walking in another line. Although he wanted to help us, he advised us to leave his place as his wife would definitely report us to the Germans. He gave us some food, and my sister and I tried to find some other place to hide.

'The next afternoon we saw a large farm, and people from our town working in the fields. They advised us to lie low till dark, when they would try to smuggle us in. The next day I hid whilst the others went to work in the fields. My sister, being bigger than I, went with the others and wasn't noticed.

'Although I was hiding under the bunk beds, someone must have noticed me and reported me, and they came in with a big dog to look for me. I was taken to the squire of the farm, and he took pity on me and allowed me to stay on and help with the chores. It was rumoured that the squire was summoned to the German authorities and told that he must not have any more Jews working on his farm. When I heard that, I didn't wait to find out if it was true or not, and together with my sister managed to escape.

'Eventually we turned up in the nearby town of Deblin. There we found a relation of ours who was a member of the Jewish Council, and he gave us shelter. A few months later I was walking in the street when suddenly I saw people running and realised that the Germans were coming in lorries and were rounding up the people they had missed previously. I ran home and got hold of my sister by the hand, and we each grabbed our rucksacks (which were always ready packed) and we made off through a window at the back of the house. We ran into the fields.

'A few minutes later we could hear somebody chasing us and shouting, "Halt! Halt!" We kept on running, and a man grabbed us. I pulled away from him, but he held on to my sister's dress. I pleaded with him to let us go, but he refused. I had no choice but to keep on running by myself. I remember falling down and shots being fired all around, and hearing the words, "Halt, halt". I don't remember any more after that, except that when I came round it was dark and I found myself in the middle of a forest.

'I walked along a path and eventually met up with others who had also managed to escape. We walked for weeks, occasionally coming across small groups of partisans. Somehow I was left on my own again, and managed to hide out in different places. I found that there was a camp nearby which was known as the Debliner Lager. In the camp was my father's sister, Tsipora, and a cousin, Chaim, as well as many men and women from my home town. The camp wasn't far from Deblin airfield, where most of the men worked. I knew that they would pass a certain road on the way back from work, and one day I managed to join them.

'My aunt hid me in the women's barracks, until one day there was a new registration, and I stood in the rows together with the other children. Now that I was an official member of the camp, I did not have to hide, and even managed to get some work. I used to do quite well for myself, and was accepted as a fully fledged member of the workforce by the men, and slept in their barracks. I worked in the coal heaps on the airfield for some time. I also got myself a spare time job cleaning the room and boots of a German sergeant at the air base.'[34]

On 6 October 1942 the deportation trains came to the southern Polish town of Chmielnik. Among the Jews in the ghetto were many who had been taken there several months earlier from the northern town of Plock, including thirteen-year-old Henry Golde. 'The order came through whereby all of the young men and women were to be sent to work camps,' he recalled. 'I was one of them. As for the elderly and the very young children, they were taken to the extermination camp called Treblinka, where they lost their lives. That was the last time I saw my family.'[35]

Six thousand Jews were deported from Chmielnik that day, and murdered at Treblinka.

Starting on 14 October 1942 the deportation began of 24,000 Jews from the Piotrkow ghetto. The deportation lasted for seven days. When it was over, only 2,000 Jews remained in Piotrkow. The Germans maintained that the destination of the deportees was a labour camp in the east. It was in fact a death camp, Treblinka, where all the deportees were murdered.

Harry Spiro recalled that early on the morning of the first day 'a general curfew was declared, and we knew that the ghetto was going to be deported. An announcement was made that all those who worked in factories outside the ghetto including Hortensja should leave their homes and meet outside the synagogue. I refused to leave my family,

[34] Solly Irving (Shloime Zalman Judensznajder), 'Memories of a Past', manuscript, sent to the author, 5 April 1995.
[35] Henry Golde, letter to the author, 28 December 1994.

but my mother told me to go. I still refused, and then she physically pushed me out of the house.

'Her last words to me were, "At least let one of our family survive". I still can't get over the strength and courage it must have taken for her to push me out, but she obviously had a premonition of what was going to happen. That was the last I ever saw of my mother, father and sister. I walked away with a heavy heart, completely forlorn as not only had I left my family, but the streets were empty and I was convinced I was going to be shot. That, in my mind, was the longest walk I ever took, away from my dearly loved family whom I never saw again.

'My family was taken away by train. My mother threw a letter from the train, that was eventually handed to me, but unfortunately it was taken from me in the camps. The letter once again stated the wish that one of our family should survive, so she obviously knew the fate awaiting her, and I have no photos of any of my family, just my memories – oh how I would love to have something more to remind me of my loved ones.'[36]

For three years, since the age of twelve, Jehoszua Cygelfarb (now Joshua Segal) had been working in the Hortensja glass factory in Piotrkow. 'Everyone had to gather in the square,' he recalled of the day of deportation. 'An SS officer ordered everyone to stand up, and all those who were working in some capacity were to stand to one side. My brother and I moved to where the officer indicated, and others followed. When it appeared that everyone who fitted into this category had moved over to our section, he ordered the soldiers to take us away. I tried to see my father and mother, but they were lost in the crowd, still standing in the square. I never saw my family again.'

Joshua Segal later learned, from one of his fellow workers in the slave labour camp to which he was sent, 'that an officer moved down the line and selected people to move to the left or right. Fathers and people who had work cards with Swastika approval went to the right, the rest of the families went to the left. When he came to my family, he separated my father from my mother and sisters, but my father refused to leave the family and said, "I go with my wife", and proceeded to go left.

'After the German officer had finished dividing the people, the soldiers surrounded the group and marched them away to the railroad station and loaded them into cattle cars without food or water. They were told they were going to a labour camp. The train started down the tracks, going past the glass factory where I was working. I heard the train whistle, and knew without looking up from my lathe what was in that

[36] Harry Spiro, recollections, letter to the author, 21 March 1995.

train. But I did not know that my own family were in the boxcars, and that I would never see them again.

'Not long after the train had passed, one of the workers walked by my lathe and slipped a small, dirty piece of paper into my hand. He whispered that he had found the paper on the tracks when he was ordered to clean the area after the train had left. He quickly walked away. When no one appeared to be looking, I opened the paper and read: "Jehoszua, they took us away. Not to worry about us. Look after yourself and your brother and fight for your lives. Father." I put the paper away quickly and looked around to see if anyone noticed. What was I to do? How was I going to tell my brother?

'Shortly, another worker walked by and he too put a piece of paper into my hand. The note was brief. "Goodbye. Take care of yourself. Aunty." There was no family left. I was fifteen years old and my brother was nineteen and we were alone.'[37]

Arthur (Artek) Poznanski, a few days away from his fifteenth birthday, was also working in the Hortensja glass factory at the time of the deportations, as was his twelve-year-old brother Jerzy (Jerzyk). On returning to the almost deserted ghetto of Piotrkow, which had been reduced to just two and a half streets, surrounded by barbed wire – 'the most derelict and dilapidated streets in the shabbiest part of the town' – he was handed, by a member of the Jewish ghetto police, 'a note hastily scribbled by my mother in pencil on a small scrap of paper. As I opened it and began to read, I was stunned by the realisation that my parents and youngest brother Tadzio had been deported. My legs buckled under me. Collapsing on a large stone which prevented me from falling to the ground, I was overcome by grief which cannot be described. The day seemed to turn into night. Sudden shivers, a constricted gullet and a cold sweat assailed me before all seemed to recede into the distance, a state of shock. It took a long while before I could move or even think with any clarity. Looking with disdain at my few possessions, which included a leather briefcase containing my stamp collection, I thought bitterly: "No parents, no home, no money and a younger brother to look after; what am I going to do?"

'Overcome with grief, and feeling completely helpless and abandoned, I was convulsed by uncontrollable sobs. Not knowing where to turn or what to do I must have been just sitting on that stone for hours, crying. Between sobs and through the mist of tears I read and reread like a sacred and most precious scroll my mother's farewell note: "We are being taken. May God help you; as we cannot do anything more for

---

[37] Josh Segal (Jehoszua Cygelfarb), letter to the author, 17 February 1995.

you. And whatever may happen, look after Jerzyk. He is but a child, and has got no one else."

'I'll try! – I thought – yes, I'll try, but how? I am so helpless myself in this cruel and hostile environment, unable to even take care of myself. How can I protect him? In a vain attempt to regain some self-control I mentally tried to reason with myself: "Crying and grief for what cannot be undone or altered will not solve any problems. Be a man! And a tough one; even tougher than your tormentors if you want to survive. You have to come to terms with a situation you cannot control or influence." At the time I was glad that Jerzyk was still in Hortensja working the next shift.

'Eventually, some hours later my sobs subsided and my tears ran dry. My eyes were very red, but dry. Curiously, after that day my eyes stayed dry for over thirty years, in spite of many painful, harrowing and traumatic experiences. Oh yes, many times I bit my lips till they bled, screamed and writhed in pain and sobbed, but I was unable to shed tears. I do not know why. Maybe all my tears ran dry on that day in October 1942 in the "Little Ghetto" of Piotrkow.'[38]

Jona Fuks, whose family had been deported from the small town of Tuszyn to Piotrkow, also remembered the selection in Piotrkow. 'My father, my brother, a cousin, and I wound up in the separate area with five hundred people who were working and had passes. My mother and my sister wound up in the other group, with all the other members of my family, including my uncles, my aunts, and my cousins. These people were packed into trains and deported to Treblinka. We never saw any of those members of my family again. They all went to the gas chambers in Treblinka.'[39]

Sevek Finkelstein was only ten years old when the deportations took place from Piotrkow. 'My whole family moved from where we lived to the reporting place,' he recalled, 'carrying with us some miserable possessions. I was left standing with Father and Issie, while Mother, Ronia, Lola and Frania were standing with the other women and children. There was a tremendous amount of hustling and moving around. I could hear the children crying while they were being separated from their fathers and loved ones.

'I was warned by Issie that I was to stand behind them and not move. Father and Issie stood shoulder to shoulder while little me was hidden behind them. Issie attracted the attention of a German officer who came over to us. Issie was showing this man their work permits, while reaching

---

[38] Arthur Poznanski, recollections, letter to the author, 17 February 1995.

[39] John Fox (Jona Fuks), recollections, Gala Recognition Dinner brochure, Hilton Hotel, Philadelphia, 8 September 1993.

out with his hand and placing something in the palm of this German officer's hand. He ordered us to fall out and he escorted them, without seeing me, to another line where we were told to report for work. Together with a few others, we made our way to the barrel factory.

'In the meantime a selection of the women was being made. Very few of them were chosen to stay behind to work. Mother was already selected to be deported, but Lola was fortunate, because just then one of the high-ranking officers for whom she worked as a maid, took her and Ronia out of the deportation line – to one that would stay behind and therefore live. Lola later told me that Ronia refused to be separated from her mother. As Lola was trying to hold her back, she let go of her hand and ran over to the other side where her mother was. This German officer was telling Frania to stay where she was. "Your mother is old, it is all right for her to die, and you are young. Stay with your sister."

'When we arrived at the factory, Issie was told that I must be hidden so that the other Polish workers would not see me. The greatest danger for me was that one of the employees would tell the Germans that a little kid was hiding. I was the only youngster in that place. They placed me high in a loft which was dirty, with cobwebs everywhere, and with no light coming in. I hated being put away all day long. At least when evening came and the other employees went home, I was allowed to come out of hiding and be with the others. I know that the only topic of discussion was what was going on in the ghetto.

'Everyone there had wives and children back in the ghetto. They were told by the Poles that the Germans were shipping one trainload a day. The people were forced into cattle cars, as many as a hundred and fifty to one car. Before they were driven into these cars they had to abandon all their possessions. The people were packed into these railroad cars like sardines. Many of the children were crushed to death before the train even left. I believe that we stayed in that little factory for six days and were then allowed to return to the ghetto. We were not permitted to go back to where we had lived before the deportation. They had set up a one-block area, fenced in with barbed wire, where the remaining Jews, the "lucky ones", were housed. Everyone I knew, all the kids I used to play with in our courtyard, were gone.'[40]

Krulik Wilder was nearly fourteen at the time of the Piotrkow deportations. He had been working for just under two months at the Hortensja glass factory, together with his father. 'All the people who had jobs in factories were temporarily safe,' he recalled, 'because the Germans rounded up all other people who had no jobs – men, women and children.' Many people managed to find hiding-places in cellars, lofts

---

[40] Sidney Finkel (Finkelstein), 'My Story', manuscript, letter to the author, 12 September 1995.

and cupboards, including Krulik's mother Chaja and his older sister Basia. 'But unfortunately,' he wrote, 'the Germans, with the help of the Jewish policemen, were very thorough, and soon discovered most of these hiding places.'[41]

A few hundred people were caught, including Chaja and Basia Wilder. All those caught were taken to the synagogue and held under guard. After a few days, they were sent to the nearby town of Tomaszow Mazowiecki, whose Jews had not yet been deported. When the 7,000 Jews of Tomaszow were sent to Treblinka a few days later, on November 3, those Jews who had been brought from Piotrkow were sent with them. All were killed. After that, any Jews still in hiding in the Piotrkow ghetto were killed where they were found. 'I saw one bastard German go into houses with his black dog, and remove some of the hidden people,' Sidney Finkel recalled. 'I saw that one man and woman were brought up out of their hiding-place on to the street. I saw the German laugh while he shot them both, their brains spattering the street.'[42]

In what had been the Piotrkow ghetto, two thousand Jews now worked where 24,000 had lived only a few weeks before. The area in which they were housed was known as 'the Block'. One of the workers living there was the fifteen-year-old Arthur Poznanski, who later wrote of how the whole Block 'was overrun by rats, mice and vermin, but the worst for us were the bedbugs. It took only a few nights in the garret for all four of us to get covered by red itchy spots which bled and turned septic when scratched. Unable to sleep for much longer than an hour at a time, we were getting desperate, and even tried to sleep sitting uncomfortably on the hard chairs. One day after a sleepless night in a chair, Jerzyk fell asleep on the factory floor during a short coffee break. For this he was badly thrashed by an irate Polish foreman. "Please do something," he pleaded with me, "or the bugs will get us even before the Germans will".'[43]

Arthur Poznanski also recalled how the survivors in Piotrkow were 'frequently plagued by search parties for "illegals" (those who had hidden to avoid deportations to the death camps and returned later to merge with the crowd in the "Block", hoping to avoid discovery). The hunted illegals' existence was precarious, and extremely difficult. Unable to register for legitimate safe employment, they could not get ration cards and were forced to buy food at phenomenal prices on the black market. They were also desperate for shelter, as anyone caught harbouring them

[41] Israel (Krulik) Wilder, 'Krulik's Story', manuscript, sent to the author, 1 January 1995.

[42] Sidney Finkel (Sevek Finkelstein), 'My Story', manuscript, sent to the author, 12 September 1995.

[43] Arthur Poznanski, recollections, sent to the author, 17 February 1995, page 10.

faced immediate execution. Only through influence with the chiefs of the administration, and bribery, did a few of them manage to gain legality. Usefulness to the German economy only temporarily "bought" us life, or a semblance of it. In fact we felt like captives in a giant's cave, waiting helplessly to see whom he might devour for his next meal.'[44]

Arthur Poznanski was transferred that winter from the Hortensja glassworks, which mainly produced jars and bottles for the Germans, to the Kara factory, which produced plate glass. He has written: 'Under the supervision of Polish and German sadists only too eager to use their power over the defenceless Jews, most of whom were unused to hard labour, we were chased and prodded to greater effort with whips, punches, kicks, threats and abuse, and treated worse than animals. Our group had so many daily casualties that we compared ourselves to the victims in the arena in ancient Rome and termed the assignment "The Circus".

'I was one of the first casualties. Unable to even lift a *traga* (an oblong wooden box measuring approximately one cubic metre with a long pole on either side for carrying it) filled with mortar, I was literally kicked out of the workforce and pronounced "fit only to be melted down for soap" – a grim allusion to the rumoured by-products of the crematoria in the death camps.[45] The loss of a prestigious employment in the glassworks for which my parents paid so dearly was a bitter blow. It could have sealed my fate.

'By now, however, I did have some influential friends in the administration, who helped to secure for me an alternative work assignment. It turned out to be work at "Befehlstelle" – a Special Orders Group – mainly employed in clearing the houses in the former ghetto of all goods and possessions left behind by Jews deported to the death camps and sorting these goods, as instructed, for eventual despatch to Germany.

'Disposing of the last traces of many thousands of families (who we suspected, though we were not really sure and refused to credit, were no longer alive) was a heartbreaking operation, but the ever-present threat to our lives hardened us against sentimentality. Every day countless books, diaries, photographs, letters and mementoes of a whole community were thrown on bonfires, while we sorted out mountains of bedding, clothing, furniture, utensils, tools and ornaments, and loaded them on lorries for transport to Germany. I never found anything of great value concealed in the unoccupied rooms, but I did manage to "organise" a few small articles of clothing for Jerzyk and myself.

---

[44] Arthur Poznanski, recollections, sent to the author, 17 February 1995, pages 11–12.

[45] Although it was often rumoured that Jewish bodies had been used to make soap, no evidence has yet emerged that this was so.

'Of course we were watched and frequently searched. Anyone caught in possession of an "organised" article was facing immediate public execution. One young woman was shot in front of the whole work group for having a pair of stockings in her coat pocket, and a man was shot for trying to carry a few potatoes in a pillow case through the gate into the Block. Perversely I kept looking for anything useful to "organise" with a firm belief that I had infinitely more right to any of these goods than the Nazis.'[46]

Chaim Wajchendler (Howard Chandler), then not yet fourteen, recalled the day of deportation, 27 October 1942, in his home town of Wierzbnik. 'As I was on the way to work,' he wrote, 'I was stopped by unfamiliar-looking soldiers and ordered to go to the market square where all Jews were to assemble. Instead, I ran home and alerted everyone, and together we left for the market square, still hoping that our work permits would save us from being expelled. My younger brother, who was eleven years old at the time, went in the opposite direction towards the place where he was to be hidden, as pre-arranged.

'The square was filling up with great commotion. People who were slow to follow the orders were being beaten and shot – families were being separated – children and adults were crying – the feeble and invalids being shot in their houses – it was an experience that I still have nightmares about.

'As the day progressed an order went out that all those who were holding work permits should step out and assemble at the edge of the square on the pavement – men and women separated. My father and I were the first to comply, but on the way I was stopped by the chief of employment, a German (Herr Schwertner) and he questioned me about my age. I stood to attention and told him without hesitation that I was sixteen years old, as my work permit indicated, and that I worked at the smelter. He hesitated and called over an official of the Jewish Council (Mr Birencwajg), who happened to be nearby and asked him if what I said was true. He stepped over and asked me in a low voice, "Who are you?" I told him my father's name and that I was sixteen years old and where I worked. He stepped back to the German and said, "Yes, it is true," and that I was a good worker – then he gave me back my card and let me go by. (I wasn't quite fourteen then).

'Many of my friends of my own age who also had work permits were not so lucky. Their permits were taken away by this German and they were not allowed to join us. I was most fortunate to be standing near a gate when I saw the German looking for me, because whenever he came

---

[46] Arthur Poznanski, recollections, manuscript, sent to the author, 17 February 1995.

by, I hid inside the gate so he could not find me. Just as our column was about to be marched off towards the factories, I noticed my younger brother in the market square, and I knew that the people who were to hide him had betrayed him. My older brother was working the night shift and was detained in the factory and, therefore, was safe.

'My mother, my sister, and younger brother, together with all the others assembled in the square (about seven to eight thousand Jews), were marched down to the railway station, packed on to a train and deported. That was the last time I saw my mother, sister and younger brother. Friends, relatives, neighbours, a whole community just wiped off the face of the earth in such a tragic and brutal way, deceived into believing that they were going to be resettled on abandoned farms in the Ukraine. I can still picture some of our neighbours and townspeople – whole families – and not even *one person* survived.'[47]

Manfred Heyman had been born in Germany ten years before the outbreak of war, in the Baltic port of Stettin. In February 1940 the Jews of Stettin had been deported by rail to the Lublin district. 'The Gestapo came in the middle of the night and arrested us,' he recalled. 'We were allowed to take one suitcase per person, everything else had to be left behind.' Their destination was the small town of Belzyce. His grandmother died there after two weeks. 'She was an old lady who could not stand the terrible journey and upheaval.'

The Jewish population of Belzyce were forced to house and feed the newcomers. There was no electric light and no running water: the water had to be carried from a well in buckets. 'Then one day the whole town was surrounded by Ukrainian SS, and most men were forced out of their houses on to lorries. We were told that they were taken to Majdanek. People who tried to escape were shot. We heard of whole towns being evacuated, but no one knew where the people were taken.' A second, more comprehensive deportation was planned. 'On that day my family and I, with some other people, went into hiding in a loft of our house. The whole town was surrounded by Ukrainians, and then all the Jewish people were put on lorries and transported away. A lot of old people, the sick, and small children, were shot. They emptied the hospital and shot all the patients in the street or in their beds. We could hear people crying, and the shooting in the streets. They ransacked houses looking for people. This went on all day. By the evening it was quiet, and we knew the SS had gone. Next day the people that were left had to bury the dead all day.'

Some time later the Belzyce ghetto was again surrounded by Ukrai-

---

[47] Howard Chandler (Chaim Wajchendler), letter to the author, 23 February 1995.

nians. 'The officer in charge selected the people. My family and I were selected to leave the ghetto. The people who were left behind were shot that day.'[48]

Manfred Heyman, who was just fourteen years old, was sent to a slave labour camp at Budzyn, to work in the aircraft factory there. A year later, Budzyn was one of the camps – the others were Poniatowa, Trawniki and Majdanek – from which the Germans took more than forty thousand Jews and murdered them in what they called, derisively, the 'Harvest Festival'. Manfred Heyman was one of the very few survivors of that atrocity.

Jack Aizenberg was thirteen when the Jews of Staszow were evacuated on 6 November 1942. 'These are my memories,' he later wrote, 'and these are my tears, and when Yizkor, the memorial prayer, is recited, in my mind I see forever the look, the dread and fear and the hopelessness of those who gave me life. This was the time when the spiritual reservoir of Jewish people was almost destroyed. In January 1940 our family had left Lodz as there was talk about the ghetto being established. It was my grandfather, who lived in Staszow, who sent a horse and cart for us. He believed that in a small shtetl, which consisted of seven thousand Jews and seven thousand Christians, we would be safer, and he was right. We managed to live a reasonable existence until November 1942, although in the latter part of 1942 things began to happen, which we were fearing.

'Staszow was one of the last places to be evacuated, but myself, an uncle and a cousin, went into hiding. I was separated that day from my parents. My father said to me, "Let us separate, in case something happens, the chances may be better if we are not together", and how right he was. Myself and two girl cousins and their young brother were luckily taken to an ammunition factory in Kielce to work. The factory was called Hasag. I do not know for sure what happened to my parents and younger brother. I can only assume they were shot, or sent to the gas chamber.'[49]

Mayer Bomsztyk also recalled the deportation from Staszow. 'My family had feared something might happen,' he wrote, 'and we had prepared a hiding place in the cellar of our home, where we hid during the evacuation. A week later we were found by the Polish police, and they took us all to prison. That particular week the Germans needed slave labourers, and we were taken to work in the Hasag ammunition factory in Kielce. The conditions in the factory were terrible, and my parents

---

[48] Manfred Heyman, letter to the author, 5 June 1995.
[49] Jack Aizenberg, recollections, manuscript, sent to the author, April 1995.

did not survive. We never saw any of the people who were evacuated from Staszow again.'[50]

The archives of the Polish Historical Institute in Warsaw show that on 7 November 1942 six thousand Jews who had been deported by train from Staszow to Treblinka were murdered there on arrival.

The fate of the Jews remaining in hiding in Piotrkow since the deportations of October 1942, and of those who, after the deportations, were taken each day to work in one of the factories, has been described by Krulik Wilder. 'For the next few weeks many Jews were killed for all kinds of reasons,' he wrote. 'We lived in the small ghetto in a state of shock and terror. Jews who had managed to hide outside the ghetto were slowly returning. They had found their conditions in hiding impossible. In about the third week in November 1942 an announcement was made that all those who had evaded deportation could register and would be allowed to stay in the small ghetto. Two weeks later about five hundred of those who registered were rounded up and taken to the synagogue. Some were shot inside the synagogue itself.

'We were working at the Hortensja factory in three shifts of eight hours. After work we returned to the small ghetto, always stopping at a checkpoint to be counted, to make sure nobody had escaped. One day returning from work we were stopped at this checkpoint and the Germans selected twenty-five of the smallest boys, including me, and took us to the synagogue.

'When my father discovered that I was one of the boys taken to the synagogue he went to see one of the Volksdeutsche directors, Dr Michelfreid, who was a decent man, to plead with him to intervene with the Gestapo and tell them the boys who were taken to the synagogue were skilled workers. I am happy to say that after three days the doors of the synagogue were opened and they called out the twenty-five names of the boys and we returned to the small ghetto. I am delighted that two of them are now living in London and are very close friends of mine, Harry Spiro and Gary Wino (Salamon Winogrodzki).'[51]

Harry Spiro remembered that, as the Germans called out the names of the young boys who were to be released from the synagogue and sent back to the factory, 'a man came forward with a baby in his arms. The SS man said, "You can go, but the baby has to stay". The man pleaded with them, but they refused to let him take the child out. He said he would stay. They said, "Don't be stupid, you know what's going to happen if you stay", but he refused to leave. I was next to this man, I

[50] Mayer Bomsztyk, recollections, letter to the author, 6 May 1996.
[51] Israel (Krulik) Wilder, 'Krulik's Story', manuscript, sent to the author, 1 January 1995.

saw this happen, but I left the synagogue and went on fighting for survival. I think this is what I mean about being lucky not to be older.'[52] Harry Spiro was then thirteen years old.

Another of the boys taken out of the synagogue was Joshua Segal. 'Upon entering the synagogue,' he recalled, 'I found many others had been taken there, and they were sitting on the floor and against the walls. Some were praying and others were crying. Many had not eaten in days, or had any water. I found some space near the window and sat with my back to the wall and hugged my knees. The hours turned into eternity. The realisation that I was going to be shot by the end of the week came home to me like a jolt and I begged God to save me. I was only fifteen years old and did not want to die.

'I don't know how long I sat under the window. The sun had set, but the area around the synagogue was lit up with many fires. I could hear voices outside that were coming from the Ukrainian soldiers stationed around the synagogue. There was a lot of laughter and from the way the soldiers spoke near my window, I felt that they might be drunk. I rose to my feet and turned to look out of the window. It was at that moment that one of the soldiers picked a baby up that he had brought to the fire and with a single swinging motion threw the baby high into the air, watching it turn upside down and drop on to a large pan that he picked up. I couldn't believe what I had just seen.

'Again the Ukrainian soldier tossed the baby into the air and caught it with the large pan. After the third toss the baby stopped crying and was still. All the while the soldier kept laughing at what he had done. I dropped to the floor and buried my face into the wall until it hurt. My eyes overflowed with tears and my body heaved in convulsions. I could not control myself. Exhausted, I fell asleep, thankful for the peace of being unconscious.'[53]

On the following morning Joshua Segal was among those taken out of the synagogue and sent to work. The 520 Jews who remained in the synagogue were driven with repeated, violent blows from whips and rifle butts to the Rakow forest, just over three kilometres out of town on the main road to Warsaw. 'In freezing conditions,' Arthur Poznanski has written, 'terrorised by bayonets and rifle butts, they were forced to undress, were machine-gunned, and then buried in the trenches. In the confusion of the massacre, six or seven individuals, some wounded, managed to escape. Some time later I met one of them in the Bugaj timberworks, a pale, blue-eyed boy, fourteen or fifteen years old. He told me how, only slightly wounded, he managed to manoeuvre himself on

[52] Harry Spiro, recollections, letter to the author, 21 March 1995.
[53] Joshua Segal (Jehoszua Cygelfarb), letter to the author, 17 February 1995.

top of a pile of bleeding corpses. Covered with heaps of leaves and chunks of frozen earth, and barely able to breathe, he remained virtually motionless until nightfall. Then, under the cover of darkness, he crawled out and dragged himself back to the "Block". The President of the Jewish Administration took pity on him and legalised his existence by enrolling him for employment in Bugaj. I noticed him mainly because of one unusual feature; his hair was completely white.'[54]

The first group of those murdered in the Rakow forest was taken there on 19 December 1942. A second group was taken to the forest on the following day. Among those in the second group, taken in batches of fifty, were Sara Helfgott – Ben and Mala Helfgott's mother – and her young daughter Lusia. 'Anyone who tried to escape was shot,' Mala Helfgott later wrote, 'and there they found the newly dug mass graves waiting for them. They had been prepared by the previous day's victims. They were told to undress and stand at the edge of the graves, when they were shot. The wounded were buried with the dead. My mother was thirty-seven and Lusia was eight years old.'[55]

After the Piotrkow deportations and executions came slave labour for those who had been given a respite. 'I remember leaving my parents' house, where my father and my mother, two brothers and sisters, and also my father's mother lived,' Pinkus Kurnedz recalled. 'I can recall their faces very vaguely. At fourteen years old this was very scary, but also leaving home for the first time, and to be on my own, was frightening.' He was sent to the Hortensja glass works 'and became a master blower. I realised that I had to make myself useful in any way possible to survive.'[56]

In the continuing and massive military battles on the eastern front, there was a dramatic setback for Germany on 31 January 1943 when General von Paulus, the commander of the German army that had been surrounded at Stalingrad (and who that very day had been promoted to field marshal by Hitler), surrendered. But still the Germans remained masters of Europe from the Atlantic coast of France to the Pripet marshes of Russia, and from northern Norway to the Black Sea.

In the Warsaw ghetto, repeated deportations to Treblinka had resulted in the murder of 310,000 Jews between July and September 1942. In April 1943 the surviving Jews rose up in revolt. During the uprising, and immediately after it, 56,000 Jews were killed, some in the ghetto,

[54] Arthur Poznanski, recollections, manuscript, sent to the author, 17 February 1995.

[55] Mala Tribich (née Helfgott), letter to the author, 12 March 1996.

[56] Pinkus Kurnedz, recollections, letter to the author, 5 October 1994.

1. Toby Biber's family in Mielec, Poland, before the war. Toby is the girl on the right. Her mother Gitla and father Jacob Isaac, are in the centre of the picture. They, and her four sisters, all perished in the Holocaust. Her two brothers survived.

2. (left) Jack Kagan's parents in Novogrudek before the war. His mother Dvorah (together with his sister and grandmother) was murdered in Novogrudek; his father Jankiel was killed two years later while trying to escape from a slave labour camp.

3. (below)Wolf and Perla Poznanski, from Praszka, Poland, who perished in Treblinka. Their sons Arthur and Jerzy Poznanski survived, and came to Britain.

4. (above) Perec Zylberberg at work on a loom in a factory workshop in the Lodz ghetto. With him is an old weaver, Y. Zylberstajn, teaching him the craft.

5. (below) The Hortensja glass works, Piotrkow, a photograph taken in recent years. It was here that more than twenty of the boys worked as slave labourers, from 1941 and 1942 until 27 November 1944, when they were deported to Czestochowa and Buchenwald.

6. (above) Boys liberated by Czech partisans. Their train had been travelling from Buchenwald for a month. It was liberated at Theresienstadt on the day the war ended. Two photographs of the inside of the wagon, with several corpses, are too horrific to reproduce.

7. (below) Harry Balsam (centre) with Russian soldiers and their Russian boy-soldier mascot. Harry Balsam's father and brother survived the war, having been deported to Siberia by the Russians in 1940 from Russian-occupied eastern Poland.

8. Some of the boys who were on their way to England gather inside Theresienstadt with a Czech flag. Holding the flag is Moniek Goldberg, from Glowaczow in Poland, now living in Miami. The boy with the cap under the sign 'Ausgang' (exit) is Nat Wald, born in Grudziadz, who died in the United States at the age of forty-one. The boy on his left, in short trousers, is John Fox, from Tuszyn, now living in Philadelphia. On Moniek Goldberg's right, partly obscured by the flagpole, is Henry Golde, from Plock, who now lives in Milwaukee. The boy crouching down below the flag is Cy Gilbert, from Rymanow, now living in Florida.

9. (below) Some of the three hundred boys who were to be on the first flight to England in August 1945 gather in front of the Jan Hus statue in Prague, before leaving for the airport. The very young children in front had been sent to Theresienstadt (from Königsberg) in 1944. The buildings in the background were badly damaged during the Prague uprising in the last days of the war.

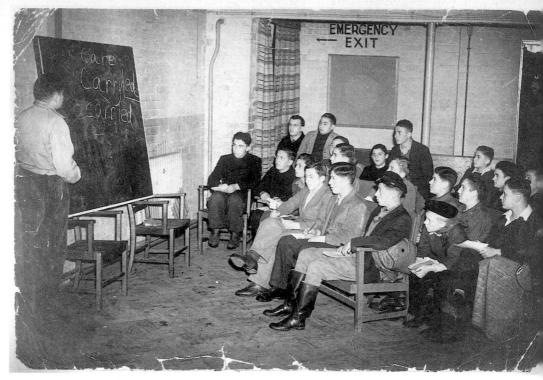

10. (above) An English lesson at Windermere. The boy with his arm on the bench is Jeff Frydman, from Lodz, who now lives in Miami. Next to him (in dark trousers) is Issy Pomeranc, from Gorlice, who died in England some years ago. The small boy underneath the picture frame is Izzie Licht, from Lodz, who now lives in Toronto. The lesson is being given by Heini Goldberg, a pre-war refugee from Germany.

11. (below) An outing at Windermere. The man with the accordion is one of the counsellors, Berish Lerner, a pre-war refugee from Germany, later a counsellor at the hostel in Manchester. The boy immediately below him is Moniek Waksztok, from the small Polish town of Klodawa, who now lives in Israel. The last boy sitting in the front row (right) is Mayer Cornell, from Kielce, who now lives London.

12. (above) Trying on trousers at Windermere. Behind the counter is Alice Goldberger, a pre-war refugee from Germany, who also helped the younger children. The boy on the right, trying on trousers, Sid Baker (Saul Bekierman), from Chmielnik, lives today in Edmonton, Canada.

13. (below) Windermere. Far right is Arek Hersh, born in the Polish town of Sieradz, living today in Leeds. Next to him, in cloth cap, is Harry Wajchendler, from Wierzbnik, who now lives in London. His brother, Howard Chandler (now in Toronto) is the boy sitting in the centre of the picture, in shirt sleeves, hands on his knees. The first boy on the far left without a cap is Moniek Hirszfeld, from the village of Bruznik, who now lives in Brighton. The boy at the back of the picture is Mayer Bomsztyk, from Staszow, who now lives in Manchester.

14. Ben Helfgott, from Piotrkow, who now lives in London, and his friend Nat Wald, from Grudziadz, who died in the United States at the age of forty-one.

15. Minia Munter (now Jay), from Warta, who lives today in London; a photograph taken at Windermere.

16. Salamon Winogrodzki, from Piotrkow, who now lives in London. He gave this picture to George Lawrence, the boys' physical training instructor at Windermere.

others at Treblinka. An estimated 15,000 were still in hiding, in cellars and attics, among them thirteen-year-old Salek Falinower (1943 was the year his father had intended to send him to England to join his brother in studying engineering). 'My sister joined the resistance fighters,' he later wrote, 'and was not heard of again. My parents became separated, I do not remember exactly when. I can remember being with my mother hidden in cellars and bunkers in the ghetto. In the summer of 1943 our bunker was ablaze, we were captured by the Germans and sent to Majdanek. My mother was in the women's section and so we were not able to meet. Up to this point I had always been protected by my parents. Now we were separated and I never saw them again. Having some background of metal engineering, I was selected in the winter of 1943 (aged fourteen) to go to Skarzysko-Kamienna, an ammunition factory supplying the Russian front.'[57]

Pinchas Gutter, the young Hassidic boy from Lodz, had gone with his family for safety to Warsaw. At the time of the ghetto uprising, they had hidden in one of the hundreds of specially-constructed bunkers underneath the apartment blocks. Their bunker, he later recalled, was 'reasonably well-stocked with food and water'. Three or four weeks after the uprising had been crushed, however, 'we were given away by a Jewish informer. Threatened that if we did not evacuate the bunker immediately gas would be pumped in, we crept out to face the Germans who stood waiting for us, armed to the teeth, and shouting "Hande Hoch! Nicht Schiessen!" ("Hands up! Do not shoot!")

'As we emerged, every person was patted down for arms that might be hidden under clothes. It was the end of the day. The sun was going down as we were marched to the Umschlagplatz[58] through the streets of the Warsaw ghetto. Fires burned on both sides of the long column of Jews, a parodic image of the Hebrews leaving Egypt, marching through the divided waters on their way to liberation.

'When we arrived at the Umschlagplatz we were immediately set upon by auxiliary SS of all different nationalities, Ukrainian, Polish and others. We were chased up a stairwell and squashed into rooms packed so tightly there was hardly space to sit. My parents managed to get to a small corner where the four of us could huddle. Water was being sold by the bottle, but only for gold and diamonds. After several days we were loaded on to cattle trucks and taken to Majdanek.

'The journey to Majdanek was horrific. Squeezed into the trucks in such numbers, it was not only difficult to find a place, one had to fight

---

[57] Salek Falinower (Stanley Faull), letter to the author, 12 October 1995.

[58] The railway siding in northern Warsaw, on the edge of the ghetto, which was used as the deportation point for trains to Treblinka and Majdanek.

for every breath of air. It was even more difficult for the children. My parents shielded us as best they could. They had conserved a sock filled with sugar, and from the time we left the bunker until we reached Majdanek my sister and I were fed teaspoons of sugar. My parents did not touch it. As soon as we arrived in Majdanek we were immediately torn apart. My sister looked more like a child than I and my mother would not leave her. They were taken together. I went with the men because I was quite tall. My father told me to say that I was eighteen years old. All the men were chased into a building and stripped naked. We had to throw our clothes, except for our belts, into some kind of wooden contraption in the middle of the room. We then had to run with our belts held high over our heads. We were directed by an SS doctor to go either right or left, one way to immediate death, the other way to a lingering life.'[59]

From Majdanek, Pinchas Gutter was sent to slave labour at Skarzysko-Kamienna.

Very few Jews survived from the hundreds of towns and villages of Eastern Galicia that were overrun by the Germans at the time of their invasion of the Soviet Union in the summer of 1941. Almost all of them were taken by train to the death camp at Belzec and murdered there on arrival, or shot in and around their home towns. Arieh Czeret, who had been born in Budzanow in 1929, was in the Trembowla ghetto during each of the four deportations to Belzec. Around the ghetto, he recalled, 'there was a high fence of barbed wire with only one entrance watched by police. The total population of the ghetto was about seven thousand. Life there was terrible: hunger, typhoid, sickness – and panic at the SS units arriving and collecting people and transporting them to Belzec. At that time we did not know that it was an extermination camp.

'On 5 November 1942 the first round-up took place, and the final destination was Belzec. I ran away from the ghetto to my home town to a farmer I knew, but he did not want to hide me, so I came back to the ghetto and to my family. On 4 March 1943 the Jewish police were looking for young men to be sent to a work camp in a stone quarry at Kamionka. They wanted me to disclose where the men of our building were hiding. I said that I did not know, and although I was too young to be sent for forced labour, they put me in prison awaiting to be sent to camp.

'After a week, the SS authorities came to collect the prisoners. The commander of the camp, by the name of Müller, was receiving the people from the Jewish Police Chief. Noting me, a small boy in shorts,

[59] Pinchas Gutter, recollections, letter to the author, 23 March 1996.

shivering, he asked my age. As I was only thirteen, he started beating me, and shouted at the Police Chief that he required workers and not children. While beating, he shouted at me to disappear.

'On 7 April 1943 there was another round-up, only now the people were taken about three kilometres from the ghetto to near the village of Plebanowka, and were shot on the spot by SS and Ukrainian police. More than a thousand people were killed. The Jewish Council, from the contribution of the ghetto, paid for the bullets. Some people managed to escape, telling the following story on their return: the father of a friend of mine had approached the SS officer at the killing ground, asking him to spare his small daughter. The officer started shouting, "If you have more children bring them here". The father, with rage, attacked the officer, started to strangle him, and bit off his nose. The SS guards ran to save the officer. In the meantime some of the people managed to run away.

'On 5 June 1943 the liquidation of the ghetto took place. Everybody who did not escape was killed, either on the spot, or taken to the same village where the previous killing took place. When the Ukrainian and German police rounded up those in our house, I managed to jump out through the window into a rubbish pit full of feathers. I could hear the shooting and crying of the people. I stayed in the pit until nightfall and managed to get out of the ghostly ghetto and started off towards my home town.

'During the daytime I hid in the fields between the high corn. On my way I stopped at the house of a Polish woman who used to work for my uncle. I stayed with her for about a week, but had to leave, as she was afraid to hide me. Towards evening I left to go towards my home town. On the way three Ukrainian guards got hold of me and started interrogating me. They decided to hand me over to the German police. I managed to break free, and started running in a zigzag as they fired their rifles, but they missed, because it was already dark.

'That night I reached another farmer who used to work for us before the war, transporting goods to our store. I told him that I was the only survivor of my family. He gave me a hiding-place in the barn. I stayed there until the end of June 1943. I asked him for a prayer book and learned all the prayers of the Ukrainian Church by heart. At the farm there was a worker about my age who came from the Carpathian Mountains. I made a deal with him. I gave him my boots and in return he gave me his identity document without a photo. I also asked him particulars about his village and family.'[60]

[60] Arieh Czeret, letter to the author, 22 March 1995.

Arieh Czeret remained in hiding as a Ukrainian until the Red Army liberated the area nine months later.

In Piotrkow, whose pre-war Jewish population had been reduced during October 1942 from more than 24,000 to less than 2,000, Ben Helfgott's sister Mala, who was then twelve years old, remembered how, at the end of July 1943, 'the ghetto was liquidated and only two groups of workers remained. They were to be allocated to the local Hortensja glass factory and the Dietrich and Fischer Bugaj woodwork factory. During this liquidation my cousin Hania and I, as children who were useless for these factories, were lined up outside the barbed wire fence of the ghetto, ready to board the lorries which were to take us to the railway station, for onward transmission to a concentration camp.

'The column was four deep and very long, and we were surrounded by guards with machine guns pointing at us. The woman in front of us, with a baby in her arms, was hit over the head with a rifle. She was in a terrible state, bleeding profusely. I do not know what she had done to warrant this blow. She may just have moved, because her baby was fidgeting. The sight of her in her agony was alone enough to freeze one to the spot. It was certainly very frightening, and we were getting close to boarding the lorry when suddenly I left the line, went up to the SS officer in charge, and asked him if he would allow me to go back inside to my father and brother from whom I had been separated. I must have moved very fast because the guard was obviously not quick enough to shoot. The SS officer looked at me very surprised, probably wondered how I had the courage or the audacity even to speak to him, but smiled and said "Yes".

'He instructed a policeman to take me back, and on the way I said to him, "Just a minute, I have to collect my cousin". He answered that the permission was only for me, and that my cousin would not be allowed to go back with me. I found myself in an impossible situation, my heart was racing and I was terrified at the prospect of leaving Hania or losing the chance of being reunited with my father and brother. I begged and pleaded and said that I could not possibly go back and ask the lieutenant again, and I could not go back into the ghetto without her. He eventually relented.'[61]

Mala and Ben Helfgott, and their father, were among between 1,600 and 1,700 survivors of one of the largest ghetto destructions of the Holocaust. Throughout Poland, the deportations of 1942 and the early months of 1943 had completely destroyed more than three thousand Jewish communities. All that was left of the once vibrant life of Polish

---

[61] Mala Tribich (née Helfgott), recollections 12 March 1996.

Jewry by the summer of 1943 was the much-diminished Lodz ghetto, a few thousand Jews in hiding, and the slave labour camps in which several thousand Jews survived amid savage and relentless brutality.

CHAPTER 5

In the Labour Camps

THE ONLY JEWS who were not deported from the ghettos to the death camps were those who had been selected for slave labour. Mostly this selection was done at the moment of deportation. In some ghettos, it was done shortly before the general deportation. This happened in Bialobrzegi, where Chill Igielman was among those sent to an ammunition factory in Radom. 'The factory had a walled perimeter,' he recalled, 'making it impossible to get out or escape. When we arrived we discovered there was no actual accommodation for us, so we were put in some old disused warehouses. We slept on the cold stone floor, with not even a blanket to keep us warm. We were very hungry as we had had no food since leaving Bialobrzegi twenty-four hours earlier. The following morning we were given a slice of bread and a cup of ersatz coffee. They then allocated people to different parts of the factory for work. However, a hundred of us, myself included, were held in reserve, which meant we had no specific job but were chosen daily to do various jobs. The work we had to do included emptying toilets with a bucket for it to be taken away by horse and cart, and unloading steel, coal and timber from railway wagons. The factory itself produced revolvers, rifles, machine-guns and bicycles.

'On 12 September 1942 – Rosh Hashana, the Jewish New Year – all the Jews were assembled, including those who had arrived in Radom before us, and a high-ranking German officer gave us a lecture on how lazy Jews were, and to prove what would happen to Jews who continued to be lazy, they took out one man and he was shot by a firing squad. Soon after that, the Germans picked out certain Jews to act as police for each working group. The policeman in charge of our group called out four names, and mine was among them. We all thought this meant we also were to be shot, but instead we had to take away the dead man and bury him. After Yom Kippur, we found out through members of the factory's own fire brigade, that all the Jewish people from Bialobrzegi had been taken away but no one knew where. I cried solidly for a week at the loss of my family, and have never shed a tear since.'[1]

---

[1] Chill Igielman, 'A Record of the Early Life of Hillel Chill Igielman', manuscript, sent to the author, November 1994.

Sam Dresner had been taken away from Magnuszew, with his father, before the deportations to the death camps, and sent to a camp at Jedlinsk which until then had been a camp for Russian prisoners of war. 'Most of them seemed to have died from starvation,' Sam Dresner recalled. 'There was only one Russian left, a giant of a man. He was a border guard. He told us that they had been asked to condemn communism and join the Germans. Those who refused were gradually starved. He even showed us where some had been gnawing the floorboards out of hunger. They were all buried in a cemetery behind the barracks. Those who went over were given German uniforms. While we worked we saw them training under German officers. They were all divided into ethnic groups with tabs on their shoulders like "Turkoman", "Georgian", etc.

'The camp was paradise compared to what I was to experience later. We worked under German civilian masters for a German firm. They were building concrete bunkers along a certain line. We were guarded by Wehrmacht soldiers. About six months after we arrived, just before we went to work, an SS man arrived with Ukrainian auxiliaries. We all had to line up; there were just eighty of us. The SS man directed us towards different groups. When my turn came he asked how old I was. I said eighteen, and he put me in the same group as my father. We were split exactly in half; my group of forty people were driven into a barrack while the other forty were taken just outside the camp and machine-gunned.

'Then they came and asked for ten volunteers. Those ten volunteers had to bury the people killed, in a sandy, shallow grave. The surviving forty were put on a lorry and taken to a place called Szydlowiec or Siedlce (I can't remember exactly). It seemed the territory was becoming "Judenrein" ("Jew-free") and they were collecting people from all kinds of places to be sent to Treblinka. A few hours after we arrived there, a lorry arrived and they asked for carpenters and other craftsmen. My father and I volunteered, and that is how we finished up in Skarzysko-Kamienna. I lost my father there. I won't describe what kind of hell that camp was.'[2]

Menachem Silberstein also lost his father – Shlomo – at Skarzysko-Kamienna. 'This was a terrible camp,' he recalled. 'Hard work, very little food. A lot died from typhoid. I myself fell ill and nearly died. My father could not take it any more, and died from starvation and depression.'[3]

In Opatow, Salek Orenstein's father was a member of the Jewish Council.

[2] Sam Dresner, letter to the author, 28 January 1995.
[3] Menachem (Mendel) Silberstein, letter to the author, 29 April 1996.

This had enabled Salek, then aged thirteen, to avoid the first labour camp selection. Several weeks later, however, 'I was walking up from the stores one day,' he recalled, 'when I heard gunshots. The town was surrounded by the Polish Volksdeutsche. There is not a single shred of doubt in my mind that their complicity enabled the SS to carry out their plans. Without them, it would have been a good deal harder to accomplish. There were shouts of "Juden! Austreten!" ("Jews! Out!")

'Shots were fired into the air and people rushed out of their houses at once. In the main street, a dozen open lorries stood waiting and all the young men and boys were ordered to climb in. I was one of them. Old men were hauled off and any individuals who had difficulty climbing up were swiftly eliminated.

'I looked around for my parents and caught sight of my father standing gazing down in horror from the first-floor window of the Jewish Council. His hat was off and both his hands were clasping his face in despair at the sight of his young son being driven away. That was the very last time I saw my father. I did not see my mother again either.

'There were forty or fifty of us crammed into that lorry and it was impossible to sit down. Nobody knew where we were going, but someone said that they thought we would soon be given food. It never came. The lorry drove out through the archway and headed off in the direction of Ostrowiec. I kept looking out for signposts and I did notice one which said "Skarzysko". Throughout the journey, bullets flew over our heads at intervals. Hardly anyone spoke. The only sound was sobbing.

'Four or five hours later we arrived in a wide open area, the entrance to an ammunition factory. We were glad to get out of that lorry as – after five hours – the floor was running in urine. The German drivers had stopped the truck from time to time to relieve themselves, but only themselves. All we could see were some industrial buildings ahead of us. We were brought into the Appel Platz, where we had our first taste of real shouting. "Schnell! Du verfluchte Juden! Wo bist du jetz? In der Synagogue?"[4]

This was the slave labour camp at Skarzysko-Kamienna, an armaments factory in the centre of the Radom district. Divided into three sections, known as Werk A, B and C, it was run throughout the war by a German company based in Leipzig, Hugo Schneider Aktiengesellschaft, known as HASAG. The general manager of the works was an SS colonel. By May 1942 there were five thousand Jewish slave labourers in the factory. After the German defeat at Stalingrad at the end of 1942, the number of Jews sent to the camp increased dramatically, as munitions production became a priority. The treatment of the Jewish slave labourers at

---

[4] 'Hurry! You accursed Jews. Where do you think you are? In synagogue?'

Skarzysko-Kamienna made it one of the most notorious camps of all. The total number of Jews who were sent there has been estimated at between 25,000 and 30,000; the number who died has been estimated at between 18,000 and 23,000 – more than two-thirds of the total inmates – killed by the guards or dying from exhaustion and starvation.

'Men appeared, dressed in white gowns,' Salek Orenstein recalled, 'and inspected us with their penetrating, hate-filled eyes. They divided us into groups, and one batch was marched away to Werk A. I stayed behind until my group was marched to our designated quarters in Werk B, about five kilometres away. We were placed in the control of the Ukrainian Werkschutz,[5] who were no more than taskmasters. They were the Ukrainians: uneducated, ghastly looking, with distorted faces, and even their green uniforms did not fit them properly! Later on we found out that these brutes were actually ex-convicts and murderers, freed from prison by the Germans, who offered them their liberty in exchange for their services. They were totally uncivilised. They wanted nothing more than food, shelter and the opportunity to kill Jews. They all carried guns with fixed bayonets.'[6]

Lipa Tepper was seventeen years old when he reached Skarzysko-Kamienna. There, he later wrote, Jews 'of low moral standard came to the fore. They became kapos[7] and they became policemen etc., and they were ordering people about and issuing punishments and that sort of thing. There was a man I particularly remember, and I dare say anybody who worked in Werk A would remember him, his name was Finger. Finger was a person who assisted the SS in selecting people who were no longer fit for work and they were disposed of. This Finger was a person of very low moral standard and he exerted a lot of authority in Skarzysko-Kamienna.

'I worked there for quite some time. The food was not particularly good, even by camp standards, and I remember particularly on several occasions lining up for my dinner at night and the Jewish kapo putting the ladle into the soup and not going down deep enough to give me anything that would be at all nourishing. When I looked at him he pointedly looked me straight in the face and said, "What's the matter? Why are you looking at me, did I sleep with your sister and fail to pay her?" So these were the types who were in authority then, and I quickly began to realise that not all Jewish people were the same.'[8]

---

[5] Special armed units operating under German SS supervision.

[6] Salek Orenstein, 'Beyond Belief, A Survivor's Story', manuscript, sent to the author, 1995.

[7] Prisoners, usually Jews, who were appointed by the Germans to serve as foremen, to supervise a barrack or a work detail. In return for undertaking these duties, the kapos were given special privileges.

[8] Lipa Tepper, letter to the author, 30 January 1996.

Every slave labour camp had its own panoply of horrors. Many boys have terrible memories of Skarzysko-Kamienna. 'There are many incidents which I remember,' Moishe Nurtman later wrote, 'but the most memorable one was when a German was walking by, and a girl said something, and he just shot her.' Moishe Nurtman also recalled an episode when he was taken outside the camp. 'I remember one time when I went into the town, escorted by Jewish police. We were approached by a Ukrainian, and he said I should not be escorted, because I was not allowed to buy bread, because a Jew had no rights. He took me into another room. There the Ukrainians put two revolvers at my head. They hit me and took my money and bread. And they pulled the trigger, but it was not loaded. It really gave me a tremendous shock. Those Ukrainians were real animals.'[9]

Sam Freiman also recalled the horrors of Skarzysko-Kamienna. 'I remember when I first came to Skarzysko camp,' he wrote, 'I was put on thread machines and lots of oil was spraying on me. All my clothing got soaked with oil, and from that I got sores on my body which festered. After a while I was transferred to a capstan machine and was supposed to produce a hundred rounds of two-centimetre bullets an hour. In one hour at the beginning I could not produce that amount. One of the German overseers, with a kapo, took me into the office, put me over a chair, and the two of them started to beat me. By the time they were finished I could not move. When I walked out of the office I remember I walked like a duck.

'When I was beaten up so much I felt very low in spirit and degraded, and became very ill. Every day the Germans used to pick out some Jews to be taken to the woods and shot. When I was selected to be taken to the woods there was one overseer – his name was Liedig – he used to shoot Jews himself. He used to come out at Appel and boast that he could not eat his breakfast because he had not shot any Jews. But he always used to rescue me. He always shouted to me, "Kleiner, zuruck zu die machine" ("Little one, go back to the machine"). One day two prisoners ran away. The Germans caught them, brought them back to camp, and ordered a roll-call. Everybody was brought out of barracks, and the two escapees were executed. I lost three uncles, my mother's brothers, in that camp. The Germans hanged them. They had taken some leather from the machines.'[10]

Fifty years later, Chaim Olmer, who had been brought to Skarzysko-Kamienna from Plaszow in November 1943, recalled how, on arrival one night, the lights were on in the camp and he and those with him

---

[9] Moishe Nurtman, letter to the author, March 1995.
[10] Sam Freiman, recollections, letter to the author, June 1995.

were 'deposited' on the Appel Platz. 'The sight that greeted us was like something out of hell. Yellow people, dressed in paper sacks, shuffled along as if in a dream. We were told that we were in Skarzysko Werk C. We were allocated to huts and my hut was opposite the washrooms. The smell was unbearable. By the washroom was a big wooden crate. The dead bodies were put into it and it was emptied when it was full.

'The work was horrendous. I was put to work with picric acid (picrine) and it did not take very long before I too was acquiring the yellow skin. We worked twelve-hour shifts on very meagre rations. We were constantly very hungry and were eaten by lice. There were no showers, just taps with cold water. There were continual selections and killings and hangings.

'One winter, when the snow was very deep, we were dragged from the huts and ordered to the storage huts to transport steel shells to the factory for filling with explosives. The skin stuck to the shells, the snow was very deep and it was very hard work to do anything. I really did not think that I would survive the night. It was the worst camp of all.'[11]

Chaskiel Rosenblum also recalled the problems of survival at Skarzysko-Kamienna. 'From time to time there were "selections" during the soup time. The skinnier ones – called "Musulmen", i.e. walking ghosts – were sent on a truck: this meant death by shooting. On one of these occasions I was sent on the truck. My father ran to the Polish foreman and told him: "My son is on the truck". The foreman went to the Germans in charge and said: "I need him, he is in charge of the breaking machine". They let me get off the truck: for them, one Jew or another was the same. They took the truck full of Jews to the forest, made them dig their own graves, and shot them. A few hours later, the truck came back with the clothing and the shoes. We started to fight about who got what. I cannot admit what animals we were. But we were.

'At one Appel, we were standing in the line, and a German said that he needed a Jew who could speak German to be a foreman. They promised he would have a double portion of bread and soup. I pushed my father to step forward, since he spoke German perfectly. But he kicked my ankle, and this kick still aches. I did no more, and, at the barracks, he told me that all those people who were foremen and beat Jews would have to pay for it one day, since they would be accused of collaboration. He preferred not to smoke and not to have an extra piece of bread, he preferred to remain one of the inmates.

'Four months later, my father died. I think he couldn't go on living. He had lost everything, and he hoped that I would make it. He couldn't stand his own misery looking at me, nor his own misery having lost all

---

[11] Chaim Olmer, recollections, letter to the author, 17 September 1995.

his family. Before he passed away, he told me that I would survive and go to Bolivia to meet my uncle. I think he gave up his life, leaving room for me to live.

'Before those who were in charge of taking away the dead came to take my father away, I stripped off his trousers and sold them for a piece of bread. I was hungry. They had made animals out of us: we had no feelings. The day he died, I didn't go to work, and the next day in the factory the Polish foreman asked me: "Did you bury your father?" I think I remember this comment so clearly because I never buried him: he was taken to a common grave.

'Life went on by myself. Two brothers slept above my bunk. They worked outside the factory. They were the rich ones. They had a "general store": bread, cigarettes, rolls. They smuggled all the goods from the town of Skarzysko into the barracks. They were big money movers, and were envied by all the inmates of the barracks, including me. One night I sat on my bunk and put my hand on their bunk. A pair of trousers was hanging there. I put my hands in the pocket and grabbed a handful of money wrapped in paper. I went out of the barrack, dug a hole and hid it. The following morning they woke up shouting that they had been robbed. Of course I kept my mouth shut. From then on, I had an extra portion of bread every day for quite a time. This helped me to survive.'[12]

Kopel Kendall's memories of Skarzysko-Kamienna are similarly vivid after more than half a century. He was fourteen years old, but as he got out of the truck that had brought the surviving Jews of Bialobrzegi to this camp, one of the people milling around 'in peculiar clothing and with shaved heads and KL[13] painted on their backs', told him, with a sense of urgency, 'Say you are sixteen, and a carpenter'. This he did. 'I was billeted in a huge building,' he later wrote, 'with bunk beds at least fourteen tiers high. Thousands of us crowded in without any form of bedding and no sanitation. I noticed straight away that it was better to be on the top bunks, as the lower bunks stank of excrement and urine. The conditions in the camp were intolerable and we were given very little food.

'I was detailed to work in an ammunition factory. The Appel was at six in the morning. We were counted numerous times and marched to work a few kilometres away. We were given soup twice a day with nothing really substantial in it. In the camp we were watched over by kapos who were as bad as the Nazis and sometimes even worse. I then realised that we had all lost our right to life as human beings, and we had nobody to complain to. By winter 1943 the barracks were completed

---

[12] Chasklel Rosenblum, 'Testimony', manuscript, sent to the author, April 1995.
[13] Konzentrationslager (Concentration Camp).

and thousands more came in, some even from the Warsaw ghetto. Conditions even worsened. Then a new commandant took over the running of the camp, Killisman (the hunchback). He was a brutal killer. He had two Alsatian dogs that he let out to kill Jews. He himself would shoot people at very close range with his revolver for no reason.

'We heard rumours in the camp of people being gassed and put in crematoria. I myself could not understand why, or believe it. Every so often there were selections, when we would be lined up, partially clothed, and then have to pass by tables with SS men sitting looking at us. Their finger would point in either direction. I got away with it twice, but the third time my number came up. The following morning when my number was called out I didn't respond. Luckily for me I got away with it. The rest were taken away and never seen again.

'Typhoid was rampant in the camp by now and thousands were dying every day. I contracted it, twelve days' high fever and on the thirteenth day you either lived or died. The lady who looked after the so-called hospital barrack hid me every time they came to take the sick and dead away to be disposed of. I lost all my hair and had to learn to walk again (I feel that in my second life I came back like a gorilla smothered in hair). The longer I stayed in the camp the more streetwise I became. I was promoted to a sweeper, a higher status that gave me time to help deliver the soup and therefore scrounge round the kitchen where I found a few scraps.'[14]

Chaim Ajzen was also taken ill at Skarzysko-Kamienna. 'I was very ill with typhus and went to work with a temperature of 42 degrees,' he later wrote. 'I worked throughout my entire illness. One day I was too weak to go to work and I fainted on the way to the factory. I was taken to the camp hospital where I stayed for a couple of days. The head nurse, whom I had previously met, warned me that on that particular day the SS were coming to take all the sick people in order to kill them. The nurse gave me some clothing to enable me to work outside, so when the SS came I was saved again, but not for long. That same evening I was cold and still very weak and decided to go to the big building where all the policemen and kapos were living. One of them, Mr Teperman, caught me there and gave me a beating. Instead of keeping quiet, I told him that I would kill him for this beating. So he gave me another beating and left me there.'[15]

Alec Ward also recalled, fifty years later, some of the 'outstanding incidents' at Skarzysko-Kamienna, writing of 'the hangings of prisoners, the selections, the dead bodies lying at the barbed-wire fences early in

---

[14] Kopel Kendall (Kandelcukier), recollections, letter to the author, 2 September 1995.
[15] Chaim Ajzen, 'Chaim Ajzen's story', manuscript, sent to the author.

the morning – of Jewish prisoners who had tried desperately to escape during the night and were shot. The painful hunger and malnutrition. The beatings. The man who cried every time he saw me – as I reminded him of his young son who had perished at the hands of the Nazis.'

On one occasion the Germans took Alec Ward and his friend Chaim Ickowicz to the place where prisoners were frequently executed, and made them dig a communal grave. 'They lined up the prisoners taken from the sick-bay and shot them, and they fell into the grave. We were forced to cover the half-dead bodies with earth. In most cases they shot the gravediggers as well. We were very lucky.'

The worst of the work at Skarzysko-Kamienna was making mines. 'The mines were made from picric acid,' Alec Ward recalled, 'and the prisoners only lived for three months doing that work, as the powder affected their lungs. It was a sheer miracle that I survived that length of time there. I put it down to being young, strong and extremely lucky. Before the war, workers carrying out this type of dangerous work drank a large amount of milk and worked short hours. We worked twelve-hourly shifts with half an hour break. There was no milk.

'The hours between two and five in the morning were tortuous. One could not keep one's eyes open, but one had to, otherwise the German overseer would beat you over the head. Our skin turned yellow at that work and it was not until six months after I left the camp that my skin returned to the normal colour. The yellow prisoners and the Musulmen were the pariahs of the camp. I had a very good friend in Werk C who lives in Israel today – Chaim Ickowicz. When one of us was down, in spirit or physically, the other would pick him up. We instinctively helped one another. Chaim and I were together for the rest of the war.'

Alec Ward, who was then fifteen, also recalled the time when he was 'so very weak and despondent, and could not walk up the two steps leading into our hut, and a miracle happened which saved my life. I was queuing up for my ration of soup when a girl asked me who I was. When I told her, she informed me that she was my late Uncle Yidl's lover and that they were planning to marry when my uncle was shot by the invading German troops in Laskarzew where they lived. That angel of a girl – her name was Henia – did some knitting for the Polish Christian women who came into the factories to work as paid workers, and they gave her some food occasionally, some of which she passed on to me. It was not long after meeting Henia that I began to negotiate the two steps into the hut normally. As far as I know, she did not survive the war, but should I ever meet her again I would be prepared to give my all to her for saving my life.'[16]

---

[16] Alec Ward, 'My Story', manuscript, sent to the author, 31 May 1995.

Another of those whose life was saved by kindness at Skarzysko-Kamienna was Salek Falinower. 'The German engineer in charge,' he later wrote, 'ate his meals in his office, and I had the job of clearing up after him. He used to leave food, bread, cheese and other items, all of which were luxuries to me in a very spartan regime. He also left out warm clothing and socks. I am sure that it is only due to this that I survived this very difficult time, when a lot of deaths were occurring all round me due to overwork, cold, starvation and disease.'[17]

Reflecting on the nature of the work at Skarzysko-Kamienna, and on those who supervised it, Alec Ward wrote: 'We had three main German bosses in the mine factory, the director, Schneider, the overseer, Walter, and their senior, a tall, elderly man who walked with a stooped back, whose name I cannot remember. They set us impossible norms to fulfil during every shift and threatened us with punishment should we not achieve their target.

'Schneider never carried out his threats, Walter invariably did so, and their senior was an utter beast of a man who derived great pleasure from his bestiality, especially towards defenceless Jewish women and girls. Had I been asked after the war what punishment they should receive I would have recommended a lenient sentence for Schneider, a long prison sentence for Walter, and that the brute of a beast – the senior – should be hung. I thanked God a thousand times that I came out alive and reasonably well from that deadly hell of a camp.'[18]

Another cruel aspect of that 'deadly hell' at Skarzysko-Kamienna was a call one day for volunteers to go to Palestine. When some men volunteered, hoping against hope that this was one of the much-talked-about exchanges of Jews in German-occupied Poland for German civilians in British-Mandated Palestine, the German overseer picked others, who had not put their hands up, for this miraculous journey. On the following day Salek Orenstein was one of those ordered for a special work duty. 'We had no idea what to expect,' he recalled. 'When we reached the appointed place, we found heaps and heaps of clothing: shoes, underwear, caps, spectacles, anything that you can possibly conceive a man or woman wearing. None of us could understand the meaning of it. But this was not the time to ponder. We were given sacks and told to stuff these items of clothing inside them. Then the whole lot was taken away to a warehouse for searching, in case any precious items had been concealed in the hems of garments or secreted in the heels of shoes. As

[17] Stanley Faull (Salek Falinower), letter to the author, 12 October 1995.
[18] Alec Ward, 'My Story', manuscript, sent to the author, 31 May 1995.

I worked, I could see stains of blood around in blotches on the grass, on the ground. It puzzled me, but I carried on.

'Later that day, the regular Polish machine-operators arrived at the factory. A standard feature of the place was that these workers came in from their nearby villages each day to instruct us on how to operate the machinery. They had been employed by the Polish government before the war. The Germans relied on them to continue its smooth running. The news they brought us that morning was of quite a different nature. "You know what happened to the Jews?" they told us. "They had to undress and they were driven naked to the railway station and packed into cattle wagons." All sorts of different theories began circulating; it was said that the naked people on those trains had been caught trying to escape and were shot dead. I did not know what to make of these conflicting reports.' The Jews who had been told they were going to Palestine had in fact been sent by train to Treblinka, and murdered there on arrival.

'Work on the machinery was hard enough at Skarzysko-Kamienna,' Salek Orenstein continued. But the terrors imposed on those in the camp were horrendous. On one occasion, he recalled, 'everyone was summoned to the Appel Platz, the day shift as well as the night workers. Something must have happened. It emerged in the screaming address of the commanding officer that two people from a transport had disappeared. I knew both of them. They were from Stopnica, a little town not very far away from Opatow. We held our breath. And then we heard the grim verdict. For each missing prisoner, ten would be taken out and shot. They scanned the rows. Twenty feeble people, tottering and on the point of collapse, were taken out. One of them – was me.

'Helena, the Lagerführerin,[19] was watching the scene unfold. She saw that I was one of the unfortunates who had been chosen to die. She spoke up. "No, not this one, he had nothing to do with the escapees, put him back!" and I returned to reclaim my place among the living.

'Beside me stood a little boy, thirteen or fourteen years old. He had come from one of the ghettos and been in the camp for less than a month. He was so new to us that he still wore the neat little blue wool jacket, fastened with a buckle, in which he had arrived. His family had been quite well-to-do. Now he was told to remove his jacket and hand it over to me. So I put it on and he was marched away.

'Later, in our barracks, we heard the shots. The Toteskommander[20] confirmed that before they were murdered, these boys had dug their

[19] The woman camp director.
[20] The 'Death Commander': the inmate in charge of the squad of prisoners who had to remove dead bodies.

own graves. The ground was still solid, it was roughly March, and the graves were so shallow that they could hardly cover them.'[21]

Alfred Huberman later recalled, of Skarzysko-Kamienna: 'One day we were asked, "Does anyone wish to go home?" As I knew that I had no home to go to, I declined. Those who reported to the parade ground joined some others who were being deported to God knows where, never to be seen again.'[22]

Every slave labour camp had its catalogue of horrors. Sam Laskier, who had been born in Warsaw, was one of those who experienced the slave labour camp at Blizyn. He was just fifteen years old. 'We worked in a quarry,' he later wrote. 'The rations were so meagre there was never a moment when we were not hungry – starving. Work was extremely hard, and our Ukrainian guards were very brutal. One day I was pulling a small wagon filled with quarried stone up an incline when a guard accused me of leaning on the wagon, not pulling it. He pulled me into a nearby field and repeatedly ordered me to fall into the mud and get up. I became so exhausted I begged him to shoot me. He just hit me with his rifle butt and forced me back to work.

'One German in Blizyn would pick on well-built Jewish prisoners. He would beat them to death with a leather whip which had a metal tip. Many prisoners, including my cousin Avram Klaiman, died of typhus and they were buried in the nearby forest.'[23]

From the ghetto at Belzyce, German-born Manfred Heyman was deported to the slave labour camp at Budzyn, where an aircraft factory had been set up. 'The SS camp commander was a real sadist,' he recalled. 'He used to shoot people just when he felt like it. He liked German Jews. That is why I passed the selection into the camp.' In November 1943 the Jews from all the camps in the region, including most of the slave labourers at Budzyn, were sent to Majdanek and murdered. Manfred Heyman was among a handful who were taken to another aircraft factory, at Mielec. There, fortune smiled on him. 'I was lucky in this camp; one of the German workers in the factory used to give me, sometimes, a sandwich from his lunchbox.'[24]

After the deportations from Bircza and Przemysl, Jack Rubinfeld was sent with 160 other Jews to work at the aeroplane engine factory at Rzeszow. He stayed there for two years, finishing machine-trimmed screws. 'I was in the custody of the SS,' he recalled. 'Captain Ester was

[21] Salek Orenstein, 'Beyond Belief, A Survivor's Story', manuscript, sent to the author, 1995.

[22] Alfred (Abram) Huberman, recollections, sent to the author, 7 May 1996.

[23] Sam Laskier, manuscript, sent to the author, 19 August 1995.

[24] Manfred Heyman, letter to the author, 5 June 1995.

in charge. He was a very brutal man. He tortured and killed anyone who displeased him.'[25]

As each boy recounts his or her story, elements emerge that are common to all, especially the hunger and the fear. Yet in every story there is also something not seen elsewhere, a unique aspect of the torment of the six million, and of the survival of the hundred thousand. The case of fourteen-year-old Harry Balsam in the slave labour camp at Plaszow, just outside Cracow, is one which stands out in its extraordinary mixture of chance and luck. 'We arrived in Plaszow after a night's journey in cattle trucks,' he recalled. 'When we arrived we had to give up everything we had brought with us. The SS guards were waiting for us and told us to throw any jewellery and money we had on to a pile. They said if anyone was trying to hide anything they would shoot them, but people don't give up their belongings so easily. Most people started throwing their money and jewellery on to the pile when suddenly they took one person and searched him. They found that he still had some money hidden on him and shot him on the spot.

'I happened to be very near and when I saw that, it frightened me and I pulled everything out of my pockets and slung it on the pile and passed by. On that particular day they must have shot seven or eight people. Then we were assembled for roll-call and we were standing in line waiting for the commandant to arrive, he had to decide what to do with us. We stood waiting for about three or four hours, it was fairly cold as I remember, and we were told by the guards that we would have to stand and wait until the commandant came.

'After a while we saw him coming and everybody got scared including the Jewish police who were already in the camp as even they didn't know what their fate would be. When he arrived he looked us up and down. There were three hundred of us. He was marching backwards and forwards and suddenly he realised that there were quite a number of small boys in the group. He started screaming and shouting and said that when he asked for people to be sent to the camp he didn't ask for little boys but for men who could be put to work. He shouted that all the boys must separate from the men. We did this and stood in columns of five.

'Naturally we were all shivering with fear and were shuffling our feet. I was one of the smallest and got pushed to the side where the commandant was standing. I turned round and said, "Can you stop pushing me?" and as I said it he called me out, and I thought, "Oh yes, this is my lot, my luck has run out now, all because I opened my big

[25] Jack Rubinfeld, 'Jack Rubinfeld', manuscript, sent to the author, undated (1995).

mouth." As he called me over, I started begging that I had done nothing and that I had only told them to stand still. He didn't listen and said, "Will you please follow me?" I thought to myself, this is it, I'm about to be shot.

'I followed him into an office where two Jewish prisoners were working, one, a girl, the other a boy. The girl, I can remember now, was a pretty young girl of about eighteen and the boy must have also been eighteen or nineteen. He was dictating something to the girl, who was working on the typewriter. The commandant, Josef Müller, took me into the office and said, "Sit down here." I didn't know what it was all about, but he said that I would become his shoeshine boy.'[26] Through this quirk of fate, Harry Balsam was to survive as Josef Müller's servant and errand boy.

Conditions at Plaszow, a camp through which many of the boys passed, were usually more cruel than this. Jan Goldberger, who had been born in Bielsko-Biala, remembered an incident at Plaszow when two prisoners escaped and were later caught. 'The guards got the whole camp out to watch while the two were hung. They used to put the smallest people at the front, which included me. This was the first hanging that I witnessed.'[27]

After the war, Josef Müller, the commandant who had protected Harry Balsam, was captured by Soviet forces and taken to the Soviet Union. There, he served five years in the Lubyanka Prison in Moscow for war crimes. After his release he was returned to Germany, where he was rearrested and charged again. On 26 April 1961, during his second trial, held at Mosbach in Baden, his wife called out in the courtroom, "Wo is der Balsam?" – "Where is Balsam?" – hoping that Harry Balsam's testimony might help her husband. But no one in the court knew what she was talking about. Müller was sentenced to a further ten years in prison, with five years taken off for the time he had served in Russia.[28]

Like Jan Goldberger, David and Abraham Hirszfeld were among those held at Plaszow who were sent to work on the Cracow-Lvov railway line. They too remembered an incident concerning an escape. 'Every morning we would walk a long distance to work outside the camp, and walk back to the camp at the end of a long and brutal day of work,' David Hirszfeld recalled. 'Since the guards were not very attentive during the entire day, it was possible to escape the working party – with the serious threat of the death penalty if one got captured. My brother

---

[26] Harry Balsam, 'The Harry Balsam Story', manuscript, sent to the author, 14 November 1995.

[27] Jan Goldberger, 'Jan Goldberger's Story', manuscript, sent to the author, 14 August 1995.

[28] Harry Balsam, in conversation with the author, 21 April 1996.

Abraham decided to take the risk, and he ran away one day. Later, I heard that he was caught, and that he died. I never heard any more details about his tragic end. Death was a daily matter in Plaszow camp. Many prisoners died from typhus, and many others died of exhaustion as a result of the hard labour and long marches to and from work. Still others got shot by the guards. Many of those who tried to escape were killed by Polish people.'[29]

Also at Plaszow was Witold Gutt. He had been born in Przemysl. For the first twenty months of the war his town had been occupied by the Soviet Union. When German forces entered it in June 1941 a ghetto was established, as had happened a year and more earlier in the western Polish towns, and labour tasks were imposed which, as elsewhere, were to serve as a protection against deportation. At the age of thirteen, Witold Gutt became an electrician's apprentice working for the German army. On 1 August 1943 the SS officer in charge of the Przemysl ghetto, Schwammberger, collected a group of craftsmen to go to Plaszow concentration camp, to help work on the specially designed interiors of houses being prepared for the SS men there. Gutt was chosen as an electrician. 'My mother pleaded with Schwammberger as the lorry was leaving,' he recalled. 'This was the last time I saw her.'

A month later, on the liquidation of the Przemysl ghetto, Jadwiga Gutt, Witold's mother, was taken to the slave labour camp at Szebnie, and then to Auschwitz, where she died that November. Her son remained at Plaszow where, he later wrote, 'I saw the executions carried out at Hujowa Gorka and was familiar with the sadism of Amon Goeth, whose dogs were set on the leaders of the electricians at one stage.'[30]

Witold Gutt has many painful memories of Plaszow. 'On one particular occasion,' he recalled, 'I was with other electricians and very close to the execution site when suddenly a Gestapo van arrived, and halted near Hujowa Gorka. A short man wearing khaki clothes including a jacket but without any military insignia, emerged from the van; I thought at the time that he was a partisan. The Germans shouted at him, probably "Schnell, schnell". The man ran forward to the execution site followed by shouts from the Germans. When he reached the site he turned, the Germans aimed, fired, and he fell dead.

'This is one of the incidents which remains in my memory and links in my mind with the murder of my father, Abraham Gutt, who was shot under similar circumstances in Przemysl on 19 September 1939.'

---

[29] David Hirszfeld (Hirschfeld), 'The David Hirschfeld Story', manuscript, sent to the author, 9 February 1996.

[30] Witold Gutt, 'Biographical Notes of Dr Witold Henryk Gutt', manuscript, sent to the author, 17 September 1994.

To this day, Gutt added, 'Whenever I meet a man resembling the victim of the Plaszow execution I become anxious'.

Gutt was fortunate that in Plaszow he was befriended by the chief of the Jewish electricians in the camp, a man by the name of Machauf. 'For a time,' he recalled, 'I looked after the motors in the brush-handle factory which was run by the notorious SS man we called "the Mongol" because of his appearance. He had a furious and unpredictable temper, and I saw him beat people nearly to death. He tolerated me for a while, but when he tapped me on the head with a hammer I realised my luck was running out and I asked Machauf to move me before it was too late, which he did. Close to the brush-handle factory there was a second execution site which was not on a hill, but in a dip, and was profanely called "Pizdowa dip" (Pizda = cunt). Frequently we saw the SS execute people who were in the dip. We could see the SS shoot down from above. On one occasion we were asked to carry into the dip the body of a tall, powerfully built Pole who had clearly been beaten to death. While working on cables on the roofs, we saw Poles being severely beaten while working at breaking up stones.'[31]

Also at Plaszow was Moshe Rosenberg, originally from Cracow, who reached his sixteenth birthday in February 1944. He was being whipped one day by guards for daring to take a rest while road-building. After twenty-five lashes the whipping unexpectedly stopped. He looked up and saw the German factory-owner Oscar Schindler. 'I'll take care of this one,' Schindler told the guards, and proceeded to drag the young man to a nearby stable. 'Loud enough for the Germans to hear,' Moshe Rosenberg recalled, 'he shouted, "What's this shit?" Then he threw some food wrapped in paper and walked out. It was his way of smuggling food to the Jews. Without him stepping in, the guards would have beaten me until I was dead.'

A few months later, while he was working in Schindler's factory making grenades, Moshe Rosenberg, exhausted by the night shift and drained by the intense heat of the machines, sat down for a moment. It was already almost morning. At that very moment Schindler came in to the factory, followed by the notorious commandant, Amon Goeth. Schindler saw the young man first, 'raced ahead of Goeth, grabbed my jacket and slapped my face, shouting, "Get back to work!" It was an act. Schindler never hit anyone or raised his voice. If Goeth had found me sitting down he would have shot me on the spot.'[32]

Another of the boys who was saved by Schindler was Naftali Rosen-

---

[31] Witold Gutt, letter to the author, 29 February 1996.

[32] Mike Ridley (Moshe Rosenberg), 'I Was On Schindler's List', *The Sun*, London, 18 February 1994.

zwieg (known to his friends as Tulek). 'It was just my luck,' he later reflected.[33]

Not far from Plaszow were two other camps, Prokocim and Biezanow. Zisha Schwimmer was in both. At Prokocim, he recalled, 'the Germans forced me to sweep the camp. It was a terrible place. Our lives were in danger all the time. If you did your job they left you alone. If you were not well, you had had it. Every morning, after working parties left for work, SS guards arrived to search the barracks. If they found anybody there who had not gone to work, either because of illness, or any other reason, they were simply taken or dragged out of the barracks and shot dead. The sight of this, day in and day out, made me envy my father who did not have to witness all this.' After three months at Prokocim camp, Zisha Schwimmer managed to join his father at Biezanow, where the adults worked in the train locomotive repair works. He was given a job peeling potatoes. 'Working in the kitchen was an advantage, as I managed to get some extra rations for my father, so he did not have to exist on the starvation diet.'

After thirteen months in Biezanow the slave labourers there were moved to a camp that had been built by the SS on the site of a Jewish cemetery in Cracow. It was called Jeruzolimska, the Jerusalem Camp. Compared with Biezanow, Zisha Schwimmer recalled, 'this was hell. Every day the SS rounded up Jews, marched them under guard to a pit, and shot them. We were there for six weeks. It seemed an eternity. We never thought we would come out of this camp alive. The food we received was terrible. Just a starvation diet. Sleeping quarters were also terrible. Then the time came to move yet again. One morning we were all assembled in a field outside the camp. The SS commandant started counting heads. I was the smallest in the camp, and my father and I were afraid that I would be singled out. Luckily I spotted a couple of bricks on the ground, and stood on them, which helped me save my life. After being thoroughly counted by the SS we were all lined up and marched to the railway station. When we got to the station we saw an empty cattle-wagon train standing in the station. We knew the train was for us. We did not know where we were going.

'We were told to get into the wagons, about a hundred people per wagon. The doors of the wagons were shut on us. We could hardly breathe, as there were only two tiny little windows in each wagon. There was hardly any room to sit. If you tried to sit down on the floor you couldn't breathe, so you had to stand up. We did not know where we were going, but were relieved to get out of that hell. Anywhere must be better than that place.

'After a long and terrible journey, that seemed to be eternity itself, we arrived at a railway station. We all felt half dead. Some people never made it. They died on the way. The doors of the wagons were opened and we were ordered by the German guards to get off. The Germans were shouting at us, "Raus, raus" – "Hurry, hurry". We did not know at the time the name of the station. We were assembled and marched along the road to a camp. Czestochowa is a big town. It had four labour camps. The one we were taken to was called Warta.

'Warta was a very big labour camp. It had an ammunition factory attached to it. It was the only labour camp I have been in that had women as well. When we first came there it was small, with only a couple of barracks. More and more barracks were being built, and more and more transports of Jews arrived, including women. There were about three barracks of women. No men were allowed inside the women's barracks, for obvious reasons. In spite of this, there were some women who became pregnant. If any man was found by the Germans inside a women's barrack, he would be taken to the assembly yard in front of the barracks. Everybody was called out on the orders of the commandant to witness his execution by shooting. His body was left in the yard until the next morning as a warning to others.

'The sleeping bunks were stretched from one end of the barracks to the other. With three rows, bottom, middle and top. People just slept next to each other with hardly any room to move. There were no washing facilities. The only way you could wash yourself was by using some of the black tea ration we were given. However, this labour camp was heaven after Jeruzolimska. Although life was bad, and we were not safe, we felt safer than there. We worked in the ammunition factory attached to the camp, assembling bullets into boxes. You had to work fast, but as long as you did your job they did not bother you.'[34]

On the day that the ghetto of Kozienice was liquidated, 27 September 1942, thirteen thousand Jews from the town itself, and from dozens of Jewish communities around it, were deported to Treblinka and murdered. Moniek Goldberg's father and mother, and his three sisters – Rivka, Faigel and Dvoira Raizel (Dreizele) – were among those who were deported that day. Moniek himself had been taken away five months earlier to forced labour at Szyczki, a camp some ten miles away, in an area where military barracks were being built for the Russian soldiers

[34] Jack (Zisha) Schwimmer, 'The War Memoirs of Z. Schwimmer', manuscript, sent to the author, 6 October 1994.

who had defected to the Germans under the Soviet General Vlasov. The task of the Jewish slave labourers, including Moniek and six of his cousins, was to lay the drains, dig the sewers, and fit the pipes and showers.

A few days after the deportation from Kozienice, the Jews working at Szyczki were given permission by their Polish overseer to conduct the Kol Nidrei evening service, with which Yom Kippur – the Day of Atonement – begins. 'As a result,' Moniek Goldberg recalled, 'some people figured that nothing would happen if they didn't report to work the next day. I was still observant at the time and wanted to stay in. There was a man, Moishe Zowoliner, whom my father had known very well, and he had written to him to ask him to look after me. He made me go to work that morning. When we returned to the barracks in the evening the SS from Radom were there. We were all marched to a clearing in the forest nearby. Those who had stayed in were already there. They had dug a ditch and upon our arrival they were all massacred, and we were ordered to fill the ditch with dirt. That was the first massacre I witnessed – on Yom Kippur 1942. I was fourteen years old.

About a week later, a Polish fellow on a bicycle came to the gate and brought the news that the Germans had liquidated the Kozienice ghetto. We didn't know the worst at the time, but I knew I was all alone.'

Moniek Goldberg was taken from Szyczki to a labour camp at Kruszyn, and from there to the munitions factory at Pionki. For the first eight months at Pionki, he recalled, 'I had a terrible time. I was always hungry. My clothes were in tatters. My boots had worn out and I wore wooden clogs. The work was very hard. I worked in a power-generating plant. It was coal-fired, and because there were so few of us we were only four workers to a shift. An eight-hour shift could be sixteen hours depending on the whim of the Polish supervisor. They gave us 1.75 kilos of bread once a week, on Sunday. By Thursday, I had no bread left. Pionki was not a bad camp all things considered, especially when the Ukrainians didn't come inside the camp. They were brutally abusive when they did come in. They would beat anyone just for fun, and violate the women.

'Consider that for almost two years we never saw a German with a gun. The Germans guarded the perimeter but inside it was all Ukrainian guards. All the killings, all the shootings, all the hangings were carried out by Ukrainians – all volunteers. What happened to them? After the war they were declared stateless, political refugees, and permitted entry into Canada, the United States and Australia.

'During my second year at Pionki things improved as I managed to befriend the Pole who was in charge of bringing supplies to the Polish kitchen.'

Every boy recalls at least one episode when he came close to death. This happened to Moniek Goldberg on the day before Christmas 1943. An Ethnic German Volksdeutsche in the camp – 'he must have been drunk – for no reason whatsoever began beating me with a rubber hose. I had been beaten before but this time I reacted. First, I tried to avoid the blows – to no avail. So, I turned round and swung my pail at him, hit his head, and split it open. The supervisor called the guards and they took me to the main gate. I was made to do exercises for hours. The Ukrainians had their amusement.

'Every workplace had a German director. When the director for the generating plant was informed, he came to the guardhouse and struck me across the face with a riding crop. He told me that I was to be hanged as a punishment. As it happened, when one of the cooks heard about my altercation she got in touch with the German lady who was in charge of the kitchen. She was an old lady who walked with a cane. Once the director had declared my sentence she approached him and protested. She said that I belonged to her. Having seen me in the kitchen so often she must have believed this to be the case. She went on to say that I could be punished but not hanged. She must have been well connected to the main director, Brandt, because she won the tussle. I was given twenty-five lashes and lived to tell the story. In retrospect, it was a foolish act taken by an impetuous young boy. I had forfeited my life and was saved by a most improbable fluke.' [35]

To this day, Moniek Goldberg is indignant about the attitude of the Polish civilians who were also being employed by the Germans at labour tasks. 'At Pionki,' he has written, 'we did not get a lot to eat and I had no money. We worked together with the Poles. During the lunch break we would go up to the dining hall, where the Polish workers got soup and bread, to wait to collect their leavings. By far the vast majority would spit, put cigarette ashes, salt, or anything else they could think of to make their leavings inedible. These were Polish workers.'

Recalling these ugly moments led Moniek Goldberg to a wider reflection on the part played by Poles in the Jewish fate. This is a subject on which the boys are often angered, and even in dispute with each other. Ben Helfgott is among those who have worked hard since the war for recognition of the Polish contribution in helping Jews. In 1994 he was awarded a Polish order of chivalry, the Knight's Cross of the Order of Merit, for his part in seeking to enhance Polish-Jewish relations. But

---

[35] Joseph (Moniek) Goldberg, 'Biographical Sketch', manuscript, July 1995, sent to the author, 14 August 1995.

Moniek Goldberg also remembers the other side of the coin. 'In the town where I was born, Glowaczow,' he wrote, 'there was a family called Rosen who had five sons and one daughter. One son married into a family named Starowieszczyk who decided to hide themselves by building a bunker in the forest. They made a deal with a Pole whom they trusted to supply them with food, etc. He was to betray them.

'The entire Rosen family did not manage to get to the village where the bunker was. Mrs Rosen and her daughter and two sons were stranded in the Kozienice ghetto. Mother and daughter were sent to Skarzysko-Kamienna and the sons to Starachowice. In the summer of 1943 the bunker was surrounded and torched by the local Poles with the people inside burned alive, except for the Rosens' son who managed to run out. They chased him, caught him, and locked him up to await the arrival of the SS. He committed suicide. Mrs Rosen, her daughter and two sons survived the war. Afterwards, Moishe Rosen, who was about three years older than me, went back to Poland to see what had become of his family. He was murdered on a train in Poland. These atrocities were committed by Poles and the number of incidents of this nature can by multiplied by the thousands.'[36]

After the selection had been made in Howard Chandler's home town of Wierzbnik, 'our column was marched away under heavy guard to the camp that was made ready for us, about five kilometres away,' he later recalled. 'But first we all stopped at a place where a German officer made a speech and ordered that all money and valuables were to be surrendered and placed in a huge box on the site. All lined up to throw in their valuables. After a few people passed, they were asked if they had fully complied and then they were searched. If they were found to have something hidden, they were shot in front of all of us as an example. This of course put fear into the rest of us and we gave up everything. A few weeks later I found a hundred-zloty note *still* hidden in my jacket that my mother had sewn in. Luckily I was not searched.

'After more were beaten up and shot we were assembled and marched off to the camp under heavy guard. We were assigned barracks, and being almost in shock, I slipped into a bunk where I stayed for three or four days and didn't stop crying. The bunks were so narrow that when you wanted to turn around you had to slip out first, and slip in on the other side.

'Then my father located me and took me to his barracks where things were better – he showed me how to get rid of the lice – he made sure that I ate my soup and reported for work. The work I had to do was very hard and I had to keep up with the grown-ups. But since most people knew me, they didn't complain and helped me when they could. After a while my father arranged for an easier job for me and I worked the day shift. Conditions in the camp varied as time progressed. In winter we were short of warm clothes. The barracks were cold, there was little food, and sometimes we worked double shifts. The distance between the camp and the factories was a long one, and we had to walk.

'The guards were mostly Ukrainians, with German officers in charge. Those who got sick had no hope of getting better, due to lack of medical attention. Although there was a doctor amongst us, there were hardly any medicines. Those prisoners who were assigned to the hospital block just withered away and died or were shot. We had to adapt fast or perish. The food was bad, the barracks were infested with all kinds of bugs and we hardly had any change or replacement of clothing. Sometimes people escaped, and as a result they shot ten people in reprisal. I escaped on two occasions and both times had to smuggle myself back to the factory – fearing that if I was found missing, my father and brother would be shot plus eight others. Neither escape was planned.

'In the summer of 1943 a typhoid epidemic broke out affecting almost all the prisoners – resulting in a great loss of life. In the camp adjoining ours, most of the people who were sick were shot. Jews from other camps were brought in to replace all the victims.

'In the summer of 1944, as the Russian front was nearing, they started to dismantle the factories and we were no longer deemed useful, so we got transferred to a nearby camp. From there people started to cut the wires at night and run away to the forest. This went on for a few days and resulted in many casualties. Then one day in July 1944 we were assembled and packed on a train and shipped off under very heavy guard.'[37] Their destination was another slave labour camp further west.

Like so many of those who survived the ghetto deportations of 1942, Lipa Tepper, from Dukla, was sent during the subsequent two and a half years to several slave labour camps. He can remember to this day the specific attributes of each of them. At Wola Duchacka, not far from Cracow, where he was first put to work laying railway tracks, and then constructing railway repair sheds, he recalled a Jew from the Cracow ghetto. 'His name was Steil. When he first came in to the camp he was an upright young man of the Polish intelligentsia. His bearing was absolutely just so, and he was a very, very strong-looking man. Then

[37] Howard Chandler (Chaim Wajchendler), letter to the author, 23 February 1995.

he caught typhus, and it paralysed him completely. They laid him on the ground, with others who were sick. They were all naked.

'I remember how he pleaded for his life. He knew he was going to be shot. How he pleaded for his life. Years later, when people ever say to me, "I am fed up with life", I look at them and I think of Steil, who really had no life left, and how he begged to remain alive. These people were all shot except for one. The gun jammed and one man ran away naked. Somebody opened a door and this one man ran in. The leader of the camp, Commandant Müller, said, "Okay, he remained alive and he can stay alive", and he was saved.' Steil was among those killed.

From the camp at Wola Duchacka, Lipa Tepper was taken to the nearby camp at Plaszow. 'That was indeed one of the worst hell-holes that it has ever been my misfortune to walk into,' he later wrote. 'People were being shot daily and they were being shot by anybody who carried a gun. There was no mercy, nothing. If you walked out and your face did not fit, you were just dead, it was as simple as that. People were caught all day and every day and taken up the hill and shot arbitrarily. It was done by black-uniformed Russian renegade soldiers, Ukrainians, Germans – anybody. It was indeed a terrible, terrible camp.'[38]

Another of the boys at Plaszow, Jasiek (Yasha) Kurtz, was taken there with his father, a doctor. His father was later shot by the commandant, Amon Goeth, on one of his random, murderous forays into the camp.

Those in the Lodz ghetto who had not been taken away during the many deportations in 1942, culminating in the great deportation that August, survived in the ghetto working in the many enterprises producing material for German military and civilian needs. Some of them were caught up in Germany's slave labour policy, before the final deportations from Lodz in the summer and autumn of 1944. Among those who were deported from Lodz to a labour camp was Michael Etkind, who had survived in the ghetto as Postman No. 102. He was sent to the Czestochowianka ammunition factory in the city of Czestochowa, less than a hundred miles from Lodz. 'At night we could not sleep because of the fleas,' he recalled. 'I would go outside and lie naked in the dry sand. Anything was better than being stung by these jumping beasts that no one could catch.

'Body-lice began to appear. I personally had never seen them in the ghetto. Now we began to itch, and would see those greyish-white creatures half-filled with our blood crawling inside our shirts and trousers. A decision was made to take us to a steam bath. We were ordered to take all our belongings, which by then amounted to little more than

[38] Lipa Tepper, letter to the author, 30 January 1996.

what we were wearing, and were taken to the other side of Czestochowa. We had to walk in the gutter on the road, so as not to hold up any traffic, while our guards walked on the pavements. Czestochowa looked clean and beautiful. The Poles looked well dressed and fed. They either turned away their gaze, or looked sarcastically at us. It was the only time I saw that magnificent cathedral standing at the end of the slowly rising road. There were huge posters depicting Jews as parasites and monsters.

'For a moment I thought, perhaps the Germans are right about us; but is it only the Germans, is it not the whole world? I could not dismiss these thoughts until we got back to the camp from which one could not see the outside world. The way back was even more depressing; all we had to wear was damp and crumpled, and the contrast between us and the passers-by was even greater than on our way to the steam baths. But at least the itching had stopped. The body soon forgets any release and relief from discomfort and concentrates on new problems. The fleas did not disappear, they waited patiently for our return.'

Some of the work at the Czestochowianka slave labour camp was outside the camp perimeter, laying heavy cables along a country road. 'For the first time in years,' Michael Etkind recalled, 'I saw the beautiful Polish countryside. The time was June 1944. Near the road was a small cottage, the window was open and I could hear music; somebody played the gramophone, or was it the radio, I could not be sure. The words were those of the popular pre-war tune, "The whole world is my little blonde girlfriend". A stupid song that brought tears to my eyes; we had heard no music for years.'

The Jewish slave labourers at Czestochowianka worked not far from a camp in which were housed ten thousand Russian prisoners of war. While the murder of the six million Jews has become a well-known fact of Nazi rule, the murder of three million Russian prisoners of war, in cold blood, long after they had surrendered on the battlefield, is far less known. 'We used to see from a distance many Russian prisoners of war,' Michael Etkind recalled, 'but later they disappeared, and the Poles told us what had happened: there were ten thousand Russian prisoners of war in a camp outside Czestochowa. At one point, all of them, with the exception of some twenty of the strongest ones, were fed with soup consisting only of cabbage, which was infested with green caterpillars. (I used to see, before the war, fields of cabbage. After a dry spell, the leaves were eaten up, and one could see dozens of large, green caterpillars crawling on each head of cabbage.)

'The Russian prisoners of war were dying like flies of dysentery. In two weeks' time only the strongest were left who, being fed on normal food, had to bury their comrades. As soon as their task was finished they were shot. Two dozen bullets to kill ten thousand enemy soldiers.'[39]

It was on 4 March 1944 that Perec Zylberberg was deported from the Lodz ghetto to labour camp. 'We left the ghetto in a somewhat subdued but hopeful frame of mind,' he recalled. He was then two months short of his twentieth birthday. 'We were marched off to the Radogoszcz-Marysin railway siding, just outside the ghetto wire. The loading into freight cars and the handing out of bread and marmalade went through in a very efficient way. Some fellow ghetto inmates even sang whilst marching. I could not join them. The songs were spicy and I wasn't accustomed to such hilarity. In such a style and manner I left the ghetto after four and a half years of war and ghetto imprisonment. I was too numb to take in the significance of the event. I suppose I went into a self-protecting shell of nothingness.'[40]

The destination of this labour convoy was Czestochowa, where Perec Zylberberg was sent to the Warta factory, a pre-war textile factory that was being converted to munitions production. 'We were woken up early in the day,' he recalled. 'After being given some kind of a coffee-coloured brew with our daily ration of bread, and now and again some marmalade, we marched off to the nearby factory complex. The work was hard. Very little mechanical help was available. Most of the hauling, carrying of machine parts, and positioning was done with sheer muscle power. We were not overtly mistreated. We were not beaten too often. Now and again someone was kicked or whipped. I don't recall too many instances of being abused. There were also a few occasions when anti-Semitic venom was dished out. I would call the workplace a matter-of-fact slave compound. There were even a friendly few words exchanged sometimes between the German director and some inmates. Some other overseers were dyed-in-the-wool anti-Semites. The bulk of the German staff was an elderly lot of army exemptees. They were thinking very often about their families in Germany.'[41]

The newcomers from Lodz were amazed at the hierarchy in the Warta labour camp, where, under the German commandant and German guards, Jewish foremen, Jewish kapos, Jewish police, and Jewish functionaries were in charge of the daily routine of discipline and production. 'We slowly got accustomed to being ruled by a combination of German masters, Jewish kapos and the administration of the camp life by Jewish barrack elders, the Jewish elder of the camp, and the Jewish camp police,' Perec Zylberberg recalled. 'Each one of those rulers exercised a certain

[39] Michael Etkind, '"Youth" Remembered', manuscript, sent to the author, 4 January 1996. After the war, the corpses of 9,640 Soviet prisoners of war were exhumed from a mass grave at the edge of the Jewish cemetery in Czestochowa.

[40] Perec Zylberberg, recollections, diary entry for 12 September 1993.

[41] Perec Zylberberg, recollections, diary entry for 17 September 1993.

authority in their respective field. The overall authority was vested in the German camp commander. He was a ruthless tyrant. Luckily for us, his fame for bestiality was earned in another camp near Cracow. To us he was brutal, but not as bloodthirsty as he was in the other camp. There was only one execution in the camp. We had to witness the dumping of the corpse of someone who was supposed to have tried to escape. But beatings were very frequent. Almost all those who wielded authority used to carry whips. They used them on many occasions. Jews whipping Jews was a not infrequent occurrence. We, the people from the Lodz ghetto, were told by the others, who were veterans of many camps, that the present regime in the Warta was benign, compared to what they had witnessed before.'[42]

It was possible, then, for there to be a lull in terror, as Jewish slave labourers worked for the increasingly hard-pressed German war machine. But it was only a lull. Russian forces were driving deeper and deeper into central Poland. On 15 January 1945, 'without any prior official notice,' as Perec Zylberberg recalled, 'we were woken up early and given some bread and coffee and told to pack our belongings'.

The prisoners were then marched to the railway station. All five factory camps in Czestochowa were being wound up.[43] Two days later the mass of slave labourers arrived at Buchenwald. On their arrival they were told that Czestochowa had just been liberated by the advancing Russians. 'With a terrible heartache for having so narrowly missed the Russians,' Perec Zylberberg recalled, 'we were counted and assigned to outlying barracks. Although on the verge of freedom, we were once again slaves in German hell.'[44]

During the day of deportation in Opatow, the fourteen-year-old Michael Perlmutter's mother Esther, his sister Hannah and his grandmother Sara had been seized and taken with most of the Jews of the town to Treblinka. He and his older brother Moishe were taken first to the slave labour camp at Skarzysko-Kamienna, and then to the munitions factory in Czestochowa. Of the hunger at the Czestochowianka camp, Perlmutter recalled: 'There were many local Polish labourers – non-inmates – who worked in the factory. They were given a meal ticket for a daily ration of a very substantial soup which was far superior to any we were ever given. The Poles, however, were quite well fed at home, so the soup was no great find for them. Those amongst us, who had some money, watches, or trinkets would buy the meal tickets from the Poles. Once

[42] Perec Zylberberg, recollections, diary entry for 18 September 1993.
[43] These camps were Hasag-Appartenbau, Hasag-Rakow, Hasag-Pelzery, Hasag-Warta and Hasag-Czestochowianka.
[44] Perec Zylberberg, recollections, diary entry for 20 September 1993.

they had the meal tickets, came the problem of standing on the Polish soup-line to collect the soup. Needless to say, it was absolutely forbidden for any Jew to come anywhere near that line. I volunteered to stand on line with two meal tickets, one for the person who had the ticket and one for me; my prize for the risk I took. I had the advantage of being blond and blue-eyed, not typically Jewish looking – and I succeeded for about ten days.

'Then I was betrayed by a Jewish guard exposing me to the SS men, who immediately had me dragged away and taken to the SS guardhouse, where I was brutally and mercilessly beaten until late into the night. I was eventually dumped back into the barracks – a shapeless mass of blood and broken bones. To this day I still remember the inside of that guardhouse. The faces of the torturers are hazy, but the face of the Jewish guard who exposed me is burned into my memory.'[45]

Alec Ward was also among those who, having already spent the second half of 1942 and most of 1943 at the munitions factory at Skarzysko-Kamienna, were sent to the munitions factory at Czestochowa. 'We were eaten alive by woodbugs and other vermin during the night,' he later wrote, 'and although we were very tired after such hard work, we could not sleep. The work was physically considerably harder than in the previous camp but less dangerous to my health. I worked in the iron foundry. When the molten steel was emerging from the furnace I guided it into sand-made forms. Afterwards I cooled the steel with a water hose and when it was semi-cool I threw the steel into wagons which were transported to the ammunition factory. The Polish Christian manager liked the way I was working and occasionally he would give me a corner of his sandwich and some white coffee. The danger of being shot, hung, beaten or selected to die did not prevail in Czestochowa slave labour camp.'[46]

The Lodz ghetto, despite substantial deportations to the death camp at Chelmno in 1942, continued as a working ghetto throughout 1942 and 1943, with innumerable factories within the ghetto providing work for more than seventy thousand Jews. After Arek Hersh's family had been deported from Sieradz to Chelmno in the summer of 1942, and murdered there, he was taken from Sieradz to the Lodz ghetto. He was thirteen years old. For two years he remained in Lodz, surviving on his wits. At one point he was taken in by a Jewish woman who, having said that she wanted to help him, used him as her servant, making his life more miserable than ever. 'All in all,' he later recalled, 'she was careless of

[45] Michael Perlmutter, speech to the Yiddish Club, Toms River, New Jersey, 7 November 1994.
[46] Alec Ward, 'My Story', manuscript, sent to the author, 31 May 1995.

my welfare. Slowly I became thinner and thinner, until eventually my bones protruded so much I resembled a skeleton.' Then, in the summer of 1943, he managed to find a place in the one remaining Jewish orphanage in the ghetto. There he made friends and was, he recalled, 'happy'.

Among Arek Hersh's friends in the orphanage were two older boys who had been deported to Lodz from Czechoslovakia. 'Peter,' he recalled, 'was about fifteen years old and had come from Prague, where his father had been a conductor with a Prague orchestra. Heinz, also from Prague, was the son of a lawyer, and had known Peter before coming to the orphanage. Both boys were very intelligent. The three of us used to walk around the yard of the orphanage, discussing our previous home lives. I learned much about Czechoslovakia from them. Prague was a very cosmopolitan city, and both boys had come from wealthy families. They were used to having servants and spending money on the things they enjoyed. They had been pampered by their parents, taken on holiday to places such as the Sudetenland, Vienna and Budapest. They enlightened me on a life which I never knew existed.

'In Poland the social and economic life was much lower than in Czechoslovakia. We were poor, and had never experienced the grandeur that these two boys had been used to. However, although we had never had much in terms of material wealth, we had had a very happy and stable family life. Peter and Heinz found the life they were now living came as a terrible shock. It went without saying that there was an enormous contrast between Prague and Lodz. They had never seen poverty and starvation, had never been treated as dirt by anyone, and the impact of all this was devastating to them. It was easier for me to come to terms with the situation as I had seen poverty and knew what it was all about.

'Our entertainment in the orphanage consisted of occasionally putting on plays, and of holding little concerts for which some of the children would learn and recite poetry. Sometimes we would sing songs, some of which we had learned in the orphanage and others we had learned at our schools before the war. On occasions we even had outsiders coming in to perform for us, the most memorable of whom was a man called Mr Perkal, a Polish-Jewish writer, who came and gave us some recitations. The one I particularly remember had been written by Julian Tuwim about a locomotive. Myself and the other children sat enraptured by his wonderful performance, watching as he mimed all the actions of the locomotive such as belching out smoke at the station. Evenings such as this – magical evenings – took our minds off our plight, at least for a short while.

'Quieter pursuits in the orphanage included draughts or cards. Some evenings, someone would come and teach us how to draw and paint. As we were forbidden by the Germans to have any schooling, these "lessons" were done in secret. Like the plays and concerts we put on and the performances we watched, the "lessons" kept our minds busy, stopped us from thinking about our empty stomachs and the atrocities outside.

'In the ghetto we were forbidden to practise any part of our religion. We were unable to pray or go to the synagogue. The worst part of this for me was being unable to have my Bar Mitzvah, which is where, at the age of thirteen, a Jewish boy is accepted as a man in the religion, and has the special honour of being called up in the synagogue to read a passage from the Bible. The Bar Mitzvah is considered a great religious step in life. However with no parents, nowhere to practise, and no one to guide me, it was impossible for me to receive this honour, which I so wanted to do.

'My room in the orphanage was on the first floor. From the window I could see the people outside the ghetto, and looking down, could see the spiked wire fence which separated us from the outside. A German policeman guarded the section of fence that I could see, forever patrolling up and down. On the opposite side of the fence I could see Polish Christian boys playing football and hide-and-seek, enjoying the normal, happy life which I longed for. How I yearned to be free like them, to be able to go into the countryside, breathe fresh air, look at flowers and visit rivers and parks as I used to do with my family. My heart ached with loss when I thought of these things.

'One day one of the boys whom I was watching saw me looking at him, and started pulling faces at me and sticking out his tongue. I did the same to him and he laughed. Gradually we began to develop a kind of friendship, silent and distant, using sign language to communicate. This had to be secretly so that the German policeman would not see us. Every day at the same time I went to the window to see the boy waiting outside; he showed me his toys and even wrote his name – Janek Szczepinski – on a blackboard with a piece of chalk. Occasionally he was seen by his father, and was promptly sent into the house, obviously because his father was frightened of the consequences if the German policeman should catch us. This made me very sad, but if we had been caught, the outcome, for me at least, would have been tragic.

'One day, after Janek had been taken inside and I was standing dejected at the window, my friend Szymek came into the room. He asked me what was wrong, and was horrified when I told him of my secret friendship. "Arek!" he said. "Don't you realise what you are doing? If you are found out you will be in serious trouble!" He took me downstairs and introduced me to his sister, Genia, who had just been accepted into the orphanage. Immediately I met her, I knew that I was in love.

'Genia, my first love, made life in the ghetto so much easier to bear. She was a beautiful girl – big brown eyes, black curly hair and a delightful smile. Just seeing her and speaking to her made me feel wonderful. She used to make up stories, write them down and read them to me. Every evening I waited for her to come to supper in the dining-room where we would always sit together and discuss what had happened that day.

'Sometimes Genia and I used to walk through the streets of the ghetto. The buildings were drab and overcrowded, the people poor and hungry, and even the trees, of which there were not many, were thin and undernourished. However, when I was with Genia my surroundings did not seem to matter. We talked and talked, about our families, our past lives and our hopes for the future. Genia's parents had owned a clothing shop in Lodz before the war. They had both died of starvation in the Lodz ghetto in 1943. Other members of her family were dispersed throughout Poland. Some of them had died in the uprising of the Warsaw ghetto a year earlier.

'Whilst in the orphanage, Genia was assigned a job in a leather factory. Sometimes I used to take a circuitous route to work just so that I could walk with her. On the way to the factory we had to pass a bakery, and sometimes we would see men loading up bread for delivery to the other side of the ghetto. The smell which came from the bakery was beautiful, but in our state of ceaseless hunger it was like torture. Nevertheless, we used to stand and watch until the bread was all loaded up, yearning for a piece to fill our grumbling stomachs, but knowing that we would not get one. After passing the bakery we turned a corner where we always parted. Genia would say goodbye, then would walk away, leaving me standing there, watching her until she had disappeared into the distance.

'Often whilst sitting in the orphanage's large hall in the evenings, we would gather into groups and discuss our future plans. We talked a great deal of our home lives and our families and of our ambitions to resume those lives once the war was over. We would, we all said, seek out whoever remained from our families and settle down to a free, comfortable life with them that was full of happiness and where food and warmth were plentiful. We all had a vague idea of how the war was going; we heard rumours, and scraps of news got through to us. From these rumours it seemed apparent that Germany would soon be defeated, that the day of liberation would soon be at hand.

'By June 1944 the rumours of advancing Russian armies ploughing into the German lines became more and more abundant. It seemed that liberation was getting closer and closer. However, ominously, the slow liquidation of the Lodz ghetto was already under way; each day more and more people were being taken out and transported to unknown destinations. The talk within the ghetto was that they were being sent to Germany to do manual work, primarily in the factories and on the farms in order to supplement the rapidly decreasing German man-power.'[47]

These deportations from Lodz were among the last of the war. Of just over 70,000 Jews deported in July and August 1944, some to Chelmno and some to Auschwitz, less than five thousand survived. Arek Hersh was one of the survivors. Genia was not.

---

[47] Arek Hersh (Herszlikowicz), 'The Orphanage', manuscript, sent to the author, 1995.

CHAPTER 6

Auschwitz

THE DEPORTATION OF Jews to Auschwitz took place without interruption throughout the last six months of 1942, the whole of 1943, and the first nine months of 1944. Of the 732 survivors whose collective story is the subject of this book, more than sixty went through that terrible camp. Many of the earliest deportees to Auschwitz were murdered in the first of the gas chambers, built in what became known as Auschwitz Main Camp. But most of the Jewish deportees were killed in four specially built gas chambers at nearby Birkenau, also known as Auschwitz II. Many of those who were not gassed on arrival at Birkenau, but were tattooed and sent to the vast barrack area of that camp, were later transferred to various slave labour camps in the region, including the Buna synthetic rubber and oil factory a few miles to the east, Auschwitz III, and the coal mines at Jawischowitz.

Among the deportees to Auschwitz was Sala Bernholz, originally from the Polish town of Wolanow. Her older sister Towa had been killed in an air raid at the very beginning of the war. Sala was brought to Auschwitz with her mother and her sister Bluma from the slave labour camp at Blizyn. She later recalled how, on reaching Auschwitz, 'two women ordered us to strip, while the German guards stood behind them. Our hair was shaved and our forearms tattooed. I said to a woman: "Please let me keep my photos." She tore my belongings from me, saying: "Be thankful that you are still alive."

'We were issued with long, striped dresses and we looked as if we had suddenly aged, as if we had missed out on our youth and middle years, as if we were ninety years old. We had all passed the first selection. We were taken to block number twenty-two where we slept on triple bunks. Every morning at dawn we were taken to the Appel Platz (Roll-Call Square) to be counted and selected. Dr Mengele was in charge of the selections. He wore a black leather coat, black riding boots and gloves. He had blue eyes. He was tall and slim. He had an evil face and he always carried a whip. One morning at the Appel – we were lined up in threes with my mother behind us – he selected my mother, saying, "Die Alter muss gehen" ("The old one must go"). Just before she was led away, my mother turned to me and my sister, saying, "Let us say goodbye, my children."

'As soon as the Appel was over we ran to the shed where those selected for the gas chambers were kept. There were hundreds of them cooped up in the shed. We called out to Mother, and helped by other inmates we managed to drag her up and out to us through the window. We ran with her quickly, unnoticed by the Germans, back to block twenty-two and gave her some food to calm her. She was shaking like a leaf.

'Sharing one of the bunks near ours was a young woman from Lodz. Before the war she had been a pharmacist. After we had saved my mother from going to the gas chambers, the woman turned to us and said, "Mengele is not going to get me." That very day she ran out to the wires and electrocuted herself. She was burned. Her hands were black. She was hanging on the wires until they took her down. Nobody cried, we were all numb.'[1]

In March 1944 the German army occupied Hungary. Three-quarters of a million Jews, hitherto outside the net of deportation, were suddenly in danger. One of the newly occupied regions was Ruthenia, which between the wars had been part of Czechoslovakia. When war broke out it was under Hungarian rule. With the German occupation the Jews of Ruthenia were forced into ghettos, just as the Jews of Poland had been four years earlier. Then, in May 1944, only two months after the ghettos were established, the deportations began. Their destination was Auschwitz.

Hugo Gryn was among ten thousand Jews who, having been confined in the Beregszasz ghetto in March 1944, were deported to Auschwitz in May. Aged thirteen, he was deported with his mother, his father and his younger brother. He later recalled the arrival of the deportation train at Auschwitz. 'We were exhausted, thoroughly demoralised and frightened,' he recalled, 'and the train stood for some time. We could only hear the shunting of engines, and the crunch of people walking outside. Eventually, well into daylight, the door was pulled open and people were being herded out, an amazing scene. It reminded me of what I imagined a lunatic asylum would be like, because in addition to the SS, who were moving up and down and pushing people around towards the head of the platform, the other people there wore this striped uniform, with a very curious-shaped hat, and they were just moving up and down taking so-called luggage out of the train. One of them, I would say, saved my life, because he went around muttering in Yiddish, "You're eighteen, you have a trade", which I took to be the mutterings of a lunatic,

---

[1] Sala Kaye (Bernholz), 'Sala Kaye Remembers', *Holocaust Testimony 1*, published by Roman Halter and Michael Etkind, London, 1983.

because it was such a curious thing to say – that's all he kept saying to people – particularly to young people.

'My father was there and took it seriously, and by the time we came to the head of this platform where the selection was taking place I had already been rehearsed, so that when the SS man said, "How old are you?" I said I was nineteen; and when he said, "Do you have a trade?" I answered, "Yes, I'm a carpenter and a joiner." My brother, who was there, was younger. He couldn't say he was nineteen, and so he was sent with the old people the wrong way, and my mother went after him. The SS man quite crudely and violently pulled my mother back. She said, "Well, I want to be with my little boy, he's frightened." "Don't worry," he said, "you will meet him later." Well that of course was in fact the last time I saw my brother.'[2] Gaby Gryn was ten years old.

Alex Gross was among the twenty-six thousand Ruthenian Jews deported from the Munkacs ghetto to Auschwitz. He was fifteen years old. He and his brother Sam were taken for slave labour in the nearby Buna synthetic oil factory. Their father was taken straight to the gas chambers and killed. Alex and Sam both survived Buna.[3] Meir Stern, from the small Ruthenian town of Svalava, was just fourteen when the Jews of his town were deported to Auschwitz. His three sisters and his mother survived; his father Zoltan (Bezalel) did not.[4]

Moritz Vegh was deported to Auschwitz from the Ruthenian town of Rakhov, where his father Zev had had a clothing store employing five or six people. 'When we got off the cattle truck, they ordered, "Men, right; women, left". I was a child, I was thirteen years old. I went with my father. My little sister, Esther, she went with my mother. Esther was only eleven. She was holding my mother's hand. When they made a selection of the women, Esther clung to my mother. My mother wouldn't give her up. Had my mother let go of her hand, she would have lived. She wouldn't give her up. They went straight to the gas chamber.

'Then they made a selection of the men. When my father was sent one way, me the other, I just ran after my father. Mengele was there, in charge of the selection. Of course I didn't know who he was at the time. He let me go. He had soldiers there with bayonets who could have got me. He didn't care. He was so busy. There were hundreds of people milling around. One more slave labourer, that was all I was. It saved my life.'[5]

Steven Pearl was deported to Auschwitz from the town of Cuhea, in

[2] Hugo Gryn, in conversation with the author, 1985: Martin Gilbert, *The Holocaust, the Jewish Tragedy*, London, 1986, page 677.

[3] Alex Gross, 'Alex Gross', manuscript, sent to the author, 1994.

[4] Meir Stern, in conversation with the author, 11 May 1996.

[5] Maurice (Moritz) Vegh, in conversation with the author, 4 May 1996.

Northern Transylvania. On arrival at the camp, he recalled, 'all the big, strong-looking men were pulled out of the queue with shepherd-like sticks hooking the men round the neck. When we were separated it was the last time I saw my mother. As I understand it, strong women without children were kept alive to work, and the rest were exterminated by gas. I have been told that my mother was helping another woman by carrying one of her children, and without even being asked it was presumed that the child was hers – and women with young children were automatically exterminated. My younger brother was sent with the women as he was considered to be a child.'[6]

At the beginning of June 1944 Istvan (Steven) Kanitz was taken from his home town of Kispest, not far from Budapest, to a disused brick factory in nearby Monor, where Jews from several surrounding towns were being held. A month later, during the three-day deportation journey to Auschwitz, his mother told him: 'After the war we will all go to Palestine.' In recounting this fifty years later, he commented: 'Alas, too late, much too late! I saw my mother for the last time at the railhead of Birkenau on 12 July 1944, as we were disembarking from the train, not realising that the separation there was to be permanent. My father I saw for the last time a week later. I was unable to say goodbye to either of them.'[7]

Victor Greenberg, known as Kushy, was from the tiny Carpathian village of Majdan. In March 1944, with the German occupation of Hungary, the forty-two Jewish families of the village confronted the unknown. 'We were ordered by the Hungarian gendarme to assemble outside the synagogue,' he recalled. 'We were limited to taking little possessions. We were transported on trucks to a ghetto on the outskirts of the town of Khust. There the Gestapo took charge. Conditions were very cramped, but we were hopeful. Rumours were circulating that we were on the way to settlement in a working place. Some suspected that we were in danger, but no one imagined the outcome.

'In May 1944 we were forced to march to the railway station in Khust, some distance away; the old, the young, the handicapped. We were loaded into cattle trucks under harassing conditions. We were ordered to surrender all the valuables. The wagons were overcrowded and very cramped. There were no sanitary facilities. We travelled three days and nights; by the time we reached the destination of Auschwitz-Birkenau some had died of heat and stench. On arrival, going through the Gestapo selection, when they decided with a flick of a finger who

---

[6] Steven Pearl, letter to the author, 3 February 1996.

[7] Steven (Istvan) Kanitz, 'Recollections by S. Kanitz', manuscript, sent to the author, 19 December 1994.

was to live or die, I was saved by a couple of Jewish inmates who worked on the rail track. They insisted that I said to the selectors that I was eighteen years old, although I was only fourteen. I was directed by the SS to the living section.

'On that day I lost my mother, a twelve-year-old brother David, and a brother, Hershel, ten years of age, many aunts, some uncles with their children, two grandmothers, and friends; all brutally murdered in the gas chambers. I found myself cut off and lonely, in the Gypsy camp in Birkenau. I remained there till autumn 1944. My father, who was in the adjacent section of the camp separated by electric barbed-wire fences, told me unequivocally that it was vital for me to leave with the next selected working transport, or I would be doomed. The Gypsy camp was basically a transit camp, where working party selections took place regularly. It was called the Gypsy camp because it housed the Gypsy people who were considered superior to the Jews. They were in charge of distributing the soup rations. The Gypsies were also, sadly, destroyed when the Soviet army was nearing and the camp was liquidated.

'The selections were carried out during roll-call time. I stood on a stone in the back row of five, in order to appear taller. They were always selecting the strongest looking. It was useless. My hopes were shattered when I was discovered standing on the concrete. They pulled me out and asked me my age, to which I replied that I was eighteen, when in fact I was an undergrown fourteen-year-old. The SS officers' faces showed sneering, sadistic grins, as if to say, "We are going to have some fun here". They did. I provided them with the joke for the day; for entertainment they pushed me around to one another like a ball, asking me at intervals, "How old are you?" I had to maintain that I was eighteen. One of them remarked, "Eighteen, eh? You don't even have hair on your privates!" This remark enlivened and sharpened their game. They punched me about until I was in a state of collapse. I was eventually rejected, and was locked into a barrack full of people who had been selected to be taken to the gas chambers. Realising the consequences, I was determined to escape and managed to climb out at night through a narrow window with a colleague.

'By that time, the people selected to leave had numbers tattooed on their arms. This presented me with a problem. That afternoon the transport was leaving by train. Upon leaving, a number of tables were set up at the gates, where the SS officers checked out the tattooed numbers as the people were going through the gates, on the way to the railway. I stood in the queue almost numb, thinking what to say. I decided to walk up to the oldest of the SS. He asked, "Number?" I stood motionless in fear. He repeated, "Number?" and looked up. I made a gesture with my hands of not having one. He looked, hesitated, and allowed me to pass through the gates.

'My father waited near the fence on the side of the railway path to see if I was leaving. When he saw me and our eyes met he started weeping and walked away, not saying a word. He managed to save my life, but not his. I left him with two of my uncles. None of them survived. How and where they died is not known to me. It must have been soon after I left Birkenau.'[8]

In the summer of 1944 there were still almost 70,000 Jews in the Lodz ghetto. Suddenly their precarious fate as slave labourers in the ghetto was sealed. In June that year 20,000 of them were deported to the death camp at Chelmno and murdered there. In August almost all the remaining 50,000 were sent to Auschwitz. Chaim Rumkowski, the Jewish Elder of the ghetto, was among those deported to Auschwitz in the August deportations, and murdered there together with his family.

Among the Jews deported from Lodz to Auschwitz was fourteen-year-old Izzie Licht. His father Lajb had died of starvation in the Lodz ghetto two years earlier. Shortly after that, his mother Miriam, who had broken her hip in a fall and been sent to the ghetto hospital, was taken away by truck with all the other patients, doctors and nurses, during a sudden raid on the hospital. None of them was ever seen again. With Izzie Licht on the journey to Auschwitz was his handicapped sister Gittele (Gucia), who had been crippled as a result of scarlet fever as a child, and his cousins Frieda, Sonya and Chaim. All four were sent straight to the gas chambers. His sisters Bella and Esther, and his brother Joshua, survived.

While he was in the barracks at Birkenau, Izzie Licht encountered his cousin Babi Gerst, one of many hundreds of young Jews who, although born in Germany before the war (he was born in Leipzig), had been expelled with their Polish-born parents back to Poland in October 1938. 'There was not much left of him,' Izzie Light reflected on his first encounter with his cousin at Auschwitz.[9] It was Babi who pointed out to him one of the chimneys. 'This was the first time I learned about the crematoria,' he recalled. 'Babi did not survive.'[10]

Arek Hersh, from the Lodz ghetto orphanage, was also among the August deportees. One day the order came that the orphanage was to be closed and its children taken out of the ghetto to an undisclosed destination. 'Our shared reaction was one of bitter disappointment, and renewed fear for our future,' Arek Hersh recalled. 'We had all thought

---

[8] Victor Greenberg, recollections, letter to the author, 8 December 1994.

[9] Izzie Light (Licht), in conversation with the author, 11 May 1996.

[10] Izzie Light (Licht), letter to the author, 7 May 1996.

that it would be simply a matter of time before the Russians liberated us, but now we all realised that this had been merely a pipe-dream.'

On the morning after the order had been given that the orphans were to leave, all 185 of them were assembled outside the orphanage. 'We made a pitiful sight,' Arek Hersh later wrote, 'thin, undernourished, frightened and nervous. "Where are the Germans taking us?" was the question everyone was asking, a question to which the *Kierowniczka*[11] could not or would not reply. Some of the younger children were very frightened, and we did our best to comfort them, but in truth there was as much fear in the hearts of us older children too. I think I was more scared than most, as I knew what "resettlement" meant, and I had seen what the Germans did to children who were too young or too feeble to work.

'We set off, carrying what few belongings we possessed. Over my shoulder I had a little blue bag which contained one shirt, one pair of underpants, two handkerchiefs, one pair of socks and a half-finished wooden horse I had been carving. Also in the bag were what I treasured most in the whole world, a number of family photographs. There were one of my brother Tovia and myself standing next to a tree in the park, two of my sisters Mania and Itka, by the River Warta, three of the whole family with my parents sitting in the middle, two of my grandparents, and a few more of my other family. I looked at the photographs of my parents and thought how much I needed their guidance at that moment. I was fifteen years old, a boy trying to be a man. I knew in my heart of hearts that we were marching to certain death, but I did not say anything for fear of spreading panic, and also through some vain, desperate hope that I might be mistaken.

'I saw a boy called Abramek walking in front of me, his face covered in freckles, his red hair like fire in the sunshine. Looking at him, I reflected that we all had tragic stories to tell. Abramek's mother had been ill in one of the ghetto hospitals when, in 1942, the SS had moved in and cleared all five hospitals out, murdering two thousand of the patients, his mother among them. His father had been caught as a hostage and had been forced to dig his own grave with twenty other hostages before being shot into it by the Germans. Thinking of this, I wondered whether we were now all to suffer a similar fate.

'We were marched out of the ghetto and towards the railway station, our clogs clattering on the cobbles. Our Kierowniczka and her husband were at the head of the column. Our other teachers were walking by our side. I remember people opening their windows to look at us as we marched past, their faces solemn, and people bowing their heads as we

---

[11] The woman director of the orphanage.

passed them in the street. This reaction confirmed my worst fears and I
looked around at all my friends, wondering if they realised as much as
I did what "resettlement" really meant.

'The boys walking beside me were my room-mates, Heniek and
Szymek, and another boy called Beniek. Beniek was twelve years old,
intelligent, witty and sensitive. He recited poetry beautifully, was forever
cracking jokes and loved music. In the orphanage he had made a piccolo
for himself from wood, and used to play it in the concerts we occasionally
held in the main hall. Before the war his father had owned a shoe
factory.

'Due to the starvation diet we had received in the ghetto, we were all
very weak and had to stop many times to allow the younger children to
catch up. Two other boys, Krol and Motek, began to walk in front of us,
and Krol turned back to ask if he could sit with me on the train. He
wanted to watch the countryside go by, he said; before the war he had
travelled through the countryside many times by train with his parents
on the way to visit his uncle and aunt in Wielun. All Krol's family were
now dead; his parents had both died of tuberculosis, and his brother and
two sisters had been sent on an earlier transport out of the Lodz ghetto
to meet their deaths in Chelmno. I began to talk to the two boys, though
little Motek, as usual, was silent. He was thirteen years old, very small
and pale, and he had a deformed left hand which meant that he used
to stay behind in the orphanage to do different chores while we went
off to work.

'It was very hot on the march and we were all tired and sweating.
All at once the hopelessness of the situation overwhelmed me. I
thought, "I want to be free to go to school and play with other
children. I don't want to die yet." I burst into tears and my friends,
bewildered, asked me what was wrong. This, to me, showed that
they didn't really know what was happening to us. I told them it
was nothing, that I was just tired from all the marching, and I dried
the tears from my eyes. I thought for the millionth time about my
parents, about Tovia and Itka and Mania and our life in Sieradz. To
stop the tears from coming again, I focused on four men who were
roped together, pulling a truck on rubber wheels that was loaded
down with flour. Their bodies were bowed to the ground with the
weight of the load, and I thought bitterly, "That is all we are to the
Germans, cattle to be worked to death, then slaughtered".

'Waiting in the city square were several lorries. My heart began to
thump as we were told to stop. Our teachers instructed us to climb into
the backs of the lorries, twenty-five children to each one. I made sure I
was with Szymek and Heniek. I looked around for Genia, but she was
well in front of me, helping with the smaller children at the head of the

column. I had a piece of bread hidden in my shirt, left over from my morning ration. On the lorry I was so hungry that I took out the bread and began to eat it, watched by all the other starving children. Unable to contain myself, I ate every last crumb, and afterwards wondered where my next piece of bread would come from. The lorry journey took about half an hour, then the doors were opened and we were ordered out.

'We stepped into bright sunshine to discover we had arrived at the railway station. There were people milling about everywhere, being herded into cattle wagons by SS men with guns. The shouts of the guards – "Schnell! Schnell!" ("Quick! Quick!") – the grinding of shutters as the cattle wagons were filled up and closed, the frightened cries of little children, the moans of the people, all this was very disturbing.

'We were forced to get into line and to shuffle forward as the wagons were filled up. At last our turn came and we were herded into a cattle wagon, packed in like sardines, orphans and strangers alike. The shutters were closed on us, trapping us in humid semi-darkness. "How would we breathe?" I thought. "How would we sleep? What would we eat?" There was only a tiny, narrow window at the top of the wagon, no other light or ventilation.

'Through the crowd I noticed Genia, together with her brother, Szymek, and Heniek, from whom I had become separated. My heart leapt; at least we would be together, I thought. At least there will be somebody to talk to and care for. I made my way over to them as the train began to move.

'As the train progressed, it gradually grew hotter and hotter in the wagon. Little children began to cry, elderly people began to feel faint, and many people started getting desperate to go to the toilet. I was standing on a bucket, looking out of the tiny window, but had to get down when one of the men asked if he could use the bucket for a makeshift toilet. He fenced off a corner of the wagon with a blanket, then put the bucket behind it. That way people could go behind the blanket and thus retain what little dignity they still had left.

'After a while the stench from the bucket became unbearable. However, we had to live with it, as the doors were locked and the window was too high and narrow to empty out the bucket's contents. The heat, too, continued to build, and little children continued to cry. We could not sit down as the wagon was too cramped, and we were all very hungry. Fortunately a few people had brought bottles of water with them which they began to pass round.

'All at once an old woman collapsed, and within minutes was dead. Now, as well as all our other problems, we had a corpse in the wagon with us. I began to pray as never before. "Please God, let us reach our destination soon". My prayers, however, went unheeded; the long day dragged on and on, heading slowly towards night.

'Eventually one reaches a stage where one resigns oneself to a certain situation. During that long, terrible day, I believe that I reached that stage for perhaps the first time since the war had begun. I began to care little about my own fate; I just wished that this horrendous ordeal would end, one way or another. Perhaps the only thing that stopped me from giving up completely was the responsibility I felt towards Genia and her brother.

'Genia was nervous and trembling with fear. She had never been in a camp before and did not know what to expect. I stroked her face and held her hand, the sweat slippery between our palms. I assured her that we would be all right, that I had been in a camp before and I was still alive. She squeezed my hand tightly, and gradually I was able to calm her down a little.

'Every so often I asked Heniek and Szymek to lift me up so that I could look out of the window. When the train curved I could see the guard on the running-board outside our wagon, brandishing his machine-gun. I wondered how close the Russians really were, whether they would ever release us from this ordeal. Most of all I wondered where this train was taking us.

'At last night fell and it began to get cooler, but it also grew steadily darker until it was pitch-black. We slept what little we could, half-standing, leaning against one another, but our sleep was punctuated by the smell of sweat and death and human waste, and by the moans and groans of the people. The darkness, like the heat, seemed to go on and on; a night that lasted a year. When, finally, dawn came it brought very little hope. The train was still speeding on towards its destination, but where that destination was, none of us could say.

'We travelled a little further and then, abruptly, the train began to slow down. Once again I asked Szymek and Heniek to lift me up to the window so that I could see what was going on. The sight that met my eyes was what I had been expecting, yet my spirits plummeted all the same. I saw a camp, barracks, high wire fencing, guards in towers, people walking about in striped suits. The train slowed down gradually and then came to a stop. After a journey that had seemed to go on for ever, we had finally arrived at our destination.

'We waited a further ten minutes, then we heard German voices, the noise of the doors being pulled open. Despite our fear, we were urging them to hurry up, to get to our door. All of us were anxious for that precious moment when we would feel sunlight on our faces again and smell the scent of fresh clean air. At last we heard voices outside our wagon, the rattle of the door being unlocked. I smiled nervously at my friends and gathered my few belongings together, ready to disembark.

'We screwed up our eyes as the brightness of the day hit us, gulped in lungfuls of the wonderful air. However, we did not have much time to appreciate it as the Germans began to shout at us, "Raus! Schnell!" ("Out! Quick!"), and started herding us into lines. All around me was commotion. I heard the shouts of the Germans, the screams of lost, frightened children, the cries of mothers frantically searching for their own sons and daughters. The SS, the same kind of men who had taken my friends away in those closed lorries to their deaths, were very brutal, kicking and beating people into line. There were five thousand people on the platform, which meant there was bound to be some disorder, yet the Germans liked things to be orderly, even when they were taking you to your death.

'There was a long concrete ramp leading from the station into the camp, along which streamed an endless line of people. We had to wait in a queue for our turn to ascend the ramp, all of us nervous, terrified, trying to keep out of the way of the German soldiers. I saw one young mother screaming and clinging to her children as the SS tried to take them away from her. A number of SS waded in and began to thump and kick her, smashing her nose, knocking her to the ground. She lay, screaming horribly with pain, but even then they didn't stop their beating and kicking. I turned away, sickened and shocked, feeling horribly guilty for not going to her aid, but knowing there was nothing I could do, that we simply had to keep quiet and remain unobtrusive, and hope that by some miracle we would survive this nightmare.

'Eventually our line began to move, was herded towards the long concrete ramp. As we got closer I realised that the Germans were separating people into two rows, one row going to the left, the other to the right. I saw that the left-hand row was full of children and old people, and I knew I must avoid that one at all costs. As I neared the two high-ranking SS officers who were dividing the people into these rows, I drew myself up to my full height and tried to give an impression of strength and fitness.

'To my horror the SS men barely glanced at me before indicating that I should join the left-hand row. There was nothing I could do or say; my mind was numb, but racing. I saw that all the children from the orphanage were in this row, shuffling forward, and I joined them, my numbness gradually giving way to an awful sense of terror.

'Suddenly behind us a commotion began, perhaps another small attempt at resistance, accompanied by much scuffling and screaming. With the attention of our guards on this commotion, I instinctively stepped across the dividing line into the right-hand row. I merged in with the people in this row, my heart beating fast, my eyes focused downwards on my shoes. I was certain that I must have been spotted, but no guard appeared to tell me to rejoin the children and the old people. I shuffled in through the gates of the camp, still not fully realising what I had done, still not fully aware that I had just saved myself from certain death in the gas chambers. A man in a striped suit working at the side of the road looked up and said very quietly in Yiddish that we were lucky to be in this group. He informed us that we were in "Birkenau, Auschwitz", which didn't mean very much to me as I had never heard of the place before.

'We carried on walking until we arrived in a small square, surrounded by electric wire fencing and some barracks. We were all men in this group, and we were told to halt and form into rows. We did so, and then simply stood there, waiting for about an hour, facing a door. Suddenly the door opened and a group of women, naked and with their heads shaved, ran out, behind them a number of SS men, herding them along with whips. It was obvious from the reactions of many of the men that they were seeing their wives and daughters among this group. I cannot fully explain how degraded and sickened and ashamed I felt at witnessing this awful spectacle. We simply had to stand there and watch as the SS men whipped and beat the women and screamed at them like pigs.

'The women were driven out of the square and towards the women's camp. The SS men who were guarding us now began to scream at us, "Du Schweinhunde, schnell, schnell!" Feeling angry and disgusted, but unable to protest, we were herded into a large hall.'[12]

At the age of fifteen, Arek Hersh had become one of more than 150,000 slave labourers in the Auschwitz region. Howard Chandler was just sixteen when he was deported to Auschwitz from a slave labour camp near his home town of Wierzbnik. 'We were very crowded,' he wrote of the train journey across Poland, 'had no food, and worse, no water and many people suffocated along the way. After travelling for a few days (but what seemed like an eternity), we arrived in Auschwitz. We were ordered to disembark and were marched off. We arrived at some empty barracks near the crematoria and were ordered to undress. Our clothing was taken away. We were still dazed and shocked from the journey – and we were prepared for the worst.

'We lined up to be showered, believing that this was the end. Luckily we got showered and not gassed. We were given striped clothing and the men were marched off to what was known as the Gypsy Camp where we were lined up in alphabetical order to register and have our

---

[12] Arek Hersh (Herszlikowicz), 'The Orphanage', manuscript.

arms tattooed with a number and then assigned a barrack on one side of the camp. On the other side were housed the Gypsies, whole families together. During that night we heard a lot of commotion and loud noises and when we went outside in the morning, there wasn't a single Gypsy left. During that night the trucks backed up to the barrack gates and all the Gypsies were forced on to the trucks. They were taken to the gas chambers and gassed. In the morning the crematoria were going full blast.

'In early September my brother was sent to another camp. My father and I transferred to the adjoining camp, all within Auschwitz, where we were assigned work. In October, my father was picked to be sent away to another camp – and that was the last time I saw him.

'I stayed in Auschwitz and did all kinds of work – road building, picking up clothes from the storage barracks and sorting them, and I also worked on the receiving ramp where the trains came into the camp. I was there when the Jews from the ghetto of Lodz came in. I was there and watched their selection being made and I watched as they were marched to the gas chambers.

'It was quite common to watch beatings, hangings, people committing suicide by throwing themselves on to the electrified barbed wires that surrounded each camp. I saw people being drowned in the camp pool where water for fire-fighting was stored. There is so much I could tell you about what took place in Auschwitz, but it would be too unbelievable for anyone who wasn't there even to imagine.'[13]

Among the Jews arriving from the Lodz ghetto in September 1944, in one of the last major deportations to Auschwitz, was Rose Kalman. 'We were dressed in many layers of clothes,' she later wrote, 'as we had no idea these would all be taken away from us at the other end of the journey. We were packed to capacity with the foulest smells and urine bowl overflowing. No water or food. When we arrived in Auschwitz my brother and sister and her baby were selected one way – never to be seen again. We were told we would see each other on weekends.

'The butts of the soldiers' guns were sharp and you didn't feel you could argue against them. I had all the baby's things. I wanted to go towards her but knew I couldn't. The baby was so silent I always felt that perhaps she was already dead. I realised I had a bottle of water which was for the baby. We were so thirsty – I went to drink some. Suddenly crowds of people gathered round and tried to pull the bottle out of my hand – I couldn't believe it. I gave my older sister some before I let them have it – you could only drink so much. There was such terror and anxiety. You were in a daze your mind – just in a state of

---

[13] Howard Chandler (Chaim Wajchendler), letter to the author, 23 February 1995.

terror. If they could have taken your brain away they would have done.

'My sister Hinda and I were shaved. We hardly recognised each other. We looked like monkeys. Stripped of everything, we were given clothes and shoes that didn't fit.'[14]

Rose Kalman and her sister Hinda were taken out of Auschwitz on their fourth day there, to a slave labour camp. Her sisters Susan and Hela were sent to the gas chambers, together with Hela's baby.

Aron Zylberszac was also deported from Lodz to Auschwitz in September 1944. 'There were so many people crowded into the cattle trucks,' he later recalled, 'that when we arrived at Auschwitz about twenty-five per cent of the people had died of suffocation. We were jammed in so tight we could hardly breathe. As soon as we arrived they beat us to get us out of the trucks and terrify us into one big barrack room. There was a Jewish fellow, obviously collaborating with the Germans, trying to find out if we had any valuables. Had we gold teeth? Had we swallowed any valuables? We had better own up, because they were going to X-ray us and if they found anything we would be instantly shot. It was a campaign of terror. His threats were so frightening that had I had anything I would have gladly given it up straight away. Another example of the German campaign of fear, and obedience through fear, was how they took German people and put them in charge of Polish people – they took Polish prisoners and put them in charge of German prisoners – they took Hungarian Jews and put them in charge of the Polish Jews, and then they put Polish Jews in charge of Hungarian Jews – and repeatedly played one against the other.

'Being a small child and having lived in Lodz all my life I had never seen any Jews other than Polish Jews. When I saw those Hungarian Jews in Auschwitz and Birkenau I thought that they were Germans – they spoke German and they behaved like Germans – I did not think they were Jewish. I only found out when I ended up with them in another camp. Then I found they were the same as us – Jewish people. It was a very clever campaign by the Germans of setting one against the other.'

On reaching the camp, Aron Zylberszac recalled, 'I was separated from my mother and father. At the time I was just seventeen. I was left with my brother, Isser, who looked after me all the time – it was through him that I survived. My mother was taken from me and my father was taken from me in this place and I never saw them again. One of the Germans to whom I described my parents kept humouring us by saying that he had seen them in this camp or that camp. But after the war we

[14] Rose Goldman (Kalman), letter to the author, July 1995.

found out it was all lies – my father and mother were killed in Birkenau when they arrived.'[15]

David Kutner was also on one of the trains from Lodz. 'On arrival at Auschwitz,' he later wrote, 'I was separated from my mother and sisters. My younger sister was screaming wildly from fear, and her screams will live with me for the rest of my life. This is the last time I saw my mother and my younger sister. I don't, even to this day, know how they died and when. My older sister survived both Auschwitz and Belsen, but died at the age of forty-one in New York.'[16] David Kutner was taken to work in the SS stables at Birkenau, looking after the horses.

Sala Newton-Kaye was deported from Lodz to Auschwitz with her mother and younger brother Rafael. Having contracted tuberculosis of the bone, his foot was in plaster. 'He was pushed to one side, and Mother and I remained on the other. I remember him crying as they took him away, and Mother and I were left standing, unable to help him.' The women were then taken to a bathhouse, stripped and examined. 'It was at this point that my mother was taken away from me, to another side of the bath, and I too was pushed to another place. We neither of us knew what was happening, but I never saw my mother again.'[17]

Rose Dajch, then seventeen, was also deported from Lodz to Auschwitz. 'We were permitted to take one suitcase per person,' she recalled. 'When we got on the cattle car my father opened his suitcase, which was full of books instead of clothes. He took out a book. When everybody around us was crying, my father managed to cheer them up, by reading a book by Sholem Aleichem. That was the last time I heard his voice. When the train came to a stop they took the men to one side, the women to the other. Soon afterwards a German hooked his cane around my mother's neck and pulled her away. When my sisters and I became hysterical, crying, they told us that we "will meet in heaven soon".

'After we were stripped of our belongings, and had our heads shaved, we were marched in the darkness of the night into the barracks of Birkenau. Greeted by a woman in charge with a whip in her hand, we were told to lie down on the cold ground one on top of the other; and to obey, or else we would be taken to the crematorium where the smoke was coming out. After an exhausting trip (three days without food) I fell asleep on top of my sister. I think I must have dreamed it, but when I woke up I was convinced that I had died and gone to hell, because I could not imagine any other place to be like this.

'After the most dreadful three weeks, my sister got sick, and when

[15] Aron Zylberszac, recollections, transcript, Imperial War Museum Sound Archives, February 1991.
[16] David Kutner, 'War Experiences of David Kutner, 1939–1945', manuscript, sent to the author, 9 May 1994.
[17] Sala Newton-Kaye (Hochspiegel), recollections, letter to the author, 10 December 1995.

Mengele conducted the selection he pulled her to the left, my older sister and I to the right. That was when my sister Zisl made the supreme sacrifice. She told me to live and tell the world what had happened there, and she jumped across to my sister Esther, when they were led to the crematorium.'[18]

'How fast it all happened,' Rose Dajch later wrote. 'One minute I was standing in line with my two sisters feeling protected by their presence, then, suddenly, I was all alone. I can still feel the cold dirt floor on which I lay crying, feeling helpless and lonely. When I looked around I saw many others like me crying for their lost loved ones. One particular girl lying next to me looked up with her big brown eyes full of tears and reached her hand out to mine. I was puzzled by her silent gesture. She moved closer and we embraced. Momentarily I felt comforted by someone else sharing the same tragedy.'

The girl's name was Edzia (Esther) Warszawska. 'After Auschwitz we were sent to Oderan, a labour camp,' Rose Dajch recalled. 'We both worked in an ammunition factory. Our friendship became very intense, and we looked out for each other. We spent many hours talking about our lost families; we became more like sisters, bound by the same fate. After the war ended we were liberated in Theresienstadt. We travelled many roads together and promised never to separate.'[19]

Another of those deported to Auschwitz from the Lodz ghetto was Roman Halter. He was just seventeen. 'We, the metalworkers, were put on to the train, which was full of those who had hidden in the ghetto and were found in their hiding-places,' he later recalled. 'The cattle-trucks were packed full with groaning men, women and children. Their doors were then locked and bolted. Those locked inside wanted water. They must have been there for days, by the time we were crammed into the trucks. We could not help them, although their pleadings touched our hearts deeply. When we arrived at Auschwitz-Birkenau we must have been one of the last, if not the last, transport from Lodz ghetto.

'About three-quarters of all those on that train were immediately sent to the gas chambers. Five hundred of us – Jewish men, women and youths – who worked in the ghetto's metal factory and were earmarked for munitions production, were kept together for further transport in Birkenau's "Gypsy blocks". The Gypsies were gassed and cremated just before our arrival in Auschwitz-Birkenau. From Auschwitz, the five hundred of us were taken to Stutthof.'[20]

Minia Munter had also been deported to Auschwitz from the Lodz

---

[18] Rose Fogel (Dajch), letter to the author, 18 January 1995.

[19] Rose Fogel (Dajch), 'A friend in need is a friend indeed', manuscript, sent to the author, 10 November 1994.

[20] Roman Halter, letter to the author, 14 November 1994.

ghetto. Her only surviving sister was with her. 'Shortly after our arrival in Birkenau,' she later wrote, 'Dr Mengele made a selection for work where he separated me from my sister. My sister was sent to a working camp, but I was sent to a cellar with the remaining girls who were not fit for work. After a few hours, they marched us in fives to the gates of Birkenau. We stood in immense heat, without food or drink. It just so happened that on this particular day the crematoriums were not in use – a miracle – so they sent us back into the camp.

'During the following few weeks, they continued selecting people for work. I was rejected three times. Miraculously, the crematoria were not in use. On the third occasion I could see that there was no way out for me. I had this vision that if I did not save myself I would never come out of that hell alive. On that sad occasion, I was together with some cousins whom I found one day in the camp. We decided to stay in the same block, and when the selection came my cousins were selected for work. Again, I was rejected. However I managed to avoid being taken away to die, and soon afterwards I was selected to be sent away from Auschwitz, to Oderan, near Chemnitz.'[21]

Berek Obuchowski was also among those deported from the Lodz ghetto to Birkenau in September 1944, together with his sister and several cousins. 'I was taken with some men and boys,' he recalled, 'behind a tall wire fence on the platform into a field, where we were told to sit down by the Germans. After a few hours they picked out twenty-five young boys like myself. We were taken to a hut and made to undress completely, for inspection to see if we were fit enough for work. I was in a fearful state of terror as the defect I had was in my right buttock, a part of which had decomposed when I was in a coma for six days in the Lodz ghetto, and had been lying in my urine all that time without attention. The flesh had deteriorated and fallen out, leaving a large gap to the bone, which of course was very obvious. The other boys immediately and automatically came to my aid, by standing behind, in front and at the side of me. The moments passed and I am here to tell the tale. From the platform of Birkenau – I never saw my sister again, or my cousins. From Auschwitz I was transferred to Babice, a sub-camp.'[22]

Moniek Goldberg was just sixteen when he was deported from the slave labour camp at Pionki to Birkenau. He was fortunate that after two days in the notorious barracks he was marched off to the nearby Buna synthetic oil factory, also known as Auschwitz III. There, he was doubly

[21] Minia Jay (Munter), 'My Story', manuscript, sent to the author, undated.
[22] Bob Roberts (Berek Obuchowski), recollections, manuscript, February 1996, sent to the author, 4 March 1996.

fortunate: he was befriended by an older man from Kozienice, Abraham Hoffman, who had been a slave labourer at Buna for a long time, and who helped those from his home town; and the kapo in charge of the young persons' work detail was a Czech Jew who, he recalled, 'was a decent man'.

Hoffman would arrange for Moniek Goldberg to wash the soup containers. 'There was always a little left in the pot. Enough to make a big difference.' When the evacuation from Auschwitz came, on 14 January 1945, in open coal trucks, 'we were packed like sardines in a tin. When we arrived at Buchenwald we were huddled together trying to keep warm. A lot of people froze to death. I can ascribe my survival to my youth and my relatively good health and stamina. The fact that I had enough to eat the previous eighteen months helped me.'[23]

For some boys, their stay at Auschwitz was of the briefest duration. Chill Igielman, from Bialobrzegi, was brought there from a slave labour camp at Tomaszow (he had earlier been a slave labourer at Radom). 'We all disembarked, and lined up on the platform,' he recalled. 'There was a band playing music with singers. Then a group of Germans began the selection process. They walked along the platform and pulled out of the line any women or older men, and they were sent to one side and were driven away in trucks. I was asked, by someone I presume was a doctor, what my age was. I replied that I was fifteen years old, although I was only fourteen, but I was not taken away from the platform. The men and boys who were left, myself included, were put back on the train wagons. The train, with us on board, remained stationary all day. We were given a quarter of a loaf of bread, some sausage, and some ersatz coffee. During the day some Jews from Auschwitz came on to the train to clean it. I spoke to them and they told me that it was a terrible place and that we were lucky to be leaving, but nothing else. That evening the train pulled out of Auschwitz.'

Chill Igielman's destination was a slave labour camp at Wiehagen.[24]

Meir Sosnowicz had managed to escape from the Warsaw ghetto before the deportations, and had found shelter with his cousins in Ostrowiec. There, when the time for deportation came in October 1942, and the despatch of almost all the Jews of Ostrowiec to Treblinka, he was working in the nearby Hermann Goering ironworks. He and his cousins remained there until August 1944, when all the factory workers were deported. 'It was only on arrival at Auschwitz that we found out where we were,'

[23] Joseph (Moniek) Goldberg, 'Biographical Sketch', manuscript, July 1995, sent to the author, 14 August 1995.

[24] Chill Igielman, 'A Record of the Early Life of Hillel Chill Igielman', manuscript, sent to the author, November 1994.

he recalled. 'Since we were more or less pre-sorted, i.e. no children, women or old people, our processing progressed much more quickly than with other transports. I do not recall "selection" at this time and the whole group was sent to Birkenau section to be "registered". This registration involved being tattooed with a number in the arm. The number I received was B5247, my cousins were B5245 and B5246. Additionally we were "deloused" by having our hair shorn, taken to the showers with stone-like soap (carbolic?), fitted out with the pyjama-type, striped cotton pants and jacket, and the *Mutze* (cap) shown in many photos of camp inmates. We were probably issued with shoes; the ones with which we came in might have had hiding-places. I cannot remember much about that particular item. Later we were issued with one bowl and spoon for eating our very meagre meals. These were all the possessions we had at the camp. We had no soap, towel, toothbrush.

'We were in Auschwitz for a few days without doing anything productive, which made us feel uncomfortable, because we knew that non-productive people were considered parasites and therefore more likely to be destroyed. One day an SS man came to a group assembled in the street between the barracks (I believe that we were not permitted to be in the barracks during the day). He announced that some professional workers with certain skills were needed at a nearby centre. My cousins and I answered that call. It was announced that they needed *Zimmerleute* (construction workers). None of us had any idea what a Zimmerleute was, we only found that out when we had to repair roofs and erect buildings. The buildings in question turned out to be in Buna-Monowitz, about five kilometres from the main camp, at a factory owned by I. G. Farben. After the war the inmates who survived were compensated for their work. In my case it was about 1,500 marks, a paltry sum![25]

'At Buna we worked daily for the next five months or so, until Auschwitz was liquidated when the Russians were approaching from the east. Details of living and working conditions at Buna are very well described by Elie Wiesel in his book *Night*. Coincidentally, Elie Wiesel was in both Auschwitz and Buchenwald at about the same time as my cousins and I. His description of life there at that time applied to us also. (The difference between his experience and ours was that I already had four years of Nazi experience. Elie Wiesel came fresh from Hungary where his troubles started in the spring of 1944.)

'I want to bear witness that all the experiences described so well by him were experiences that I also had. I, too, experienced the beatings, the starvation, stood through innumerable assemblies in extreme cold, in pyjama-like garments, for hours on end. I saw hangings, had to get

---

[25] Approximately £1,600 ($2,400) in the money values of 1996.

used to seeing the piles of bony corpses and the smell of the crematoria at Birkenau, experienced the "selections" and saw people die in front of me. I shared my bread with those who were still alive. I saw the extra cruelty to the children, both at the camp and at the assembly place when mothers did not want to part with their children. The SS simply snatched the children from their mothers and smashed them against the wall so that their brains spilled out.

'At the whim of the current guard or SS officer we, too, had to do "Mutzen ab, Mutzen auf", ("Caps on, caps off"). There were other sadistic actions by the Germans, too numerous to mention in detail. Almost everything that we did was accompanied by the guards screaming "Schnell! Schnell!" if anyone so much as took a breath slower than the SS had in mind. When we marched out of the camp to work, the Jewish musicians had to play tunes to our marching, while the SS guards counted those leaving. When we re-entered later the musicians had to play again.

'Today I ask myself, "What were my feelings at the time about what was going on?" I really am not sure. I know that we were thinking only of survival, which must be a natural or animal-type instinct. We expected blows, physical or mental, at any time and from anywhere. We did not want to live, it was too much, and we knew that we had no family any more to live for. However, we also did not want to commit suicide, and so we went on going through whatever befell us.

'There was another, very important question: "Where was God?" I prayed to Him to redeem us. I acknowledged His presence. I looked for the miracles of redemption which we had learned about during our Bible studies at home and at school: the Exodus from Egypt, the story of Korah, who was punished immediately for his sins.[26]

'The sins of Pharaoh seemed much less than the sins of the Germans and their cohorts. How long could God allow these obscenities to continue? Where was He? The redemption seemed a long time coming. Would it ever come? This question reminded me, in a very small way, of when, as a child, I hurt myself, and my mother was not around, it seemed for ever until she came. Where was my mother? I was confused. Today we say that God hid himself, turned His face from us, answered "NO" to our request. I know that to this day I cannot understand what He had in mind, to allow all this to happen for so long a time and to so many good and innocent people.

[26] It was during the Israelite sojourn in the wilderness that Korah, and 250 others, rose up against Moses in the desert. 'And the earth opened her mouth, and swallowed them up, and their houses, and all the men that appertained unto Korah, and all their goods. They, and all that appertained to them, went down alive into the pit, and the earth closed upon them: and they perished from among the congregation.' (Numbers, 16:32,33).

'We also had no idea of the progress of the war, whether the Allies were winning or losing, and therefore whether there was any hope for our deliverance. It seemed incomprehensible to us at the time that this mighty power (Germany) could lose the war and that we, the *Häftlinge* (prisoners) who were more like walking corpses, could survive to witness this event.'[27]

Two of the gas chambers at Auschwitz were destroyed in October 1944, during the uprising of those inmates who had been forced to work there disposing of the bodies. All those who had taken part in the uprising were killed. The remaining three gas chambers were dismantled on Himmler's orders in November 1944. Throughout December the Russian forces drew closer. In the first days of the new year the prisoners in the camp could hear the sound of distant artillery. Yet once again the Germans were determined not to allow their prisoners to be liberated. 'In January 1945,' Howard Chandler later wrote, 'as the Russian front was nearing, we were assembled and marched out from Auschwitz. It was bitterly cold and we must have marched for about a week. On the way we were joined by other prisoners of all nationalities.

'It was a most terrible march. Anyone who could not keep up was shot and along the whole route there were bodies lying about. When we reached Breslau (now Wroclaw) we were put on an open freight train half-filled with snow, and whisked off to Buchenwald. Many people froze to death along the way. When the train came into Buchenwald I had to get off the train without my trousers. They had frozen, and stuck to the ice. So I used a piece of blanket for cover.'[28]

---

[27] Michael Novice (Meir Sosnowicz), recollections, manuscript, June 1995.
[28] Howard Chandler (Chaim Wajchendler), letter to the author, 23 February 1995.

CHAPTER 7

Buchenwald

A S THE RUSSIAN army advanced into Poland, the factories in which several hundred thousand Jewish slave labourers had been working for two years and more were dismantled or abandoned. The Jews from these camps were sent by train and truck westward, to other slave labour camps on German soil, and also to the concentration camp at Buchenwald, which served as a collecting centre for Jewish slave labourers brought from all over German-occupied Poland. Buchenwald had been set up in 1937, near the city of Weimar. By 1944 it was largely run, internally, by German Communist prisoners, under the watchful eye of the SS. The stone quarry, where cruel tortures were inflicted on the camp inmates, was run by the SS.

Kopel Kandelcukier was one of several thousand Jewish slave labourers evacuated from Skarzysko-Kamienna to Buchenwald in the summer of 1944. 'Inmates in the know told us that the Germans were losing the war,' he recalled, 'and that really gave me hope of surviving.' He was detailed to work in the nearby quarry. 'I couldn't understand this,' he wrote, 'as there was no end product. Men were lined up against each other carrying rocks up and down, racing against each other and being beaten by kapos and SS men. I was lucky, as I only looked after tools.' A few weeks later he was moved to the Youth Block. 'There life was much better for me, food was better, and we were allowed even to play games such as football.'[1]

Salek Orenstein, from Opatow, was also brought to Buchenwald from Skarzysko-Kamienna. Later he recalled how, before entering Block 66, a barrack in the children's section of the camp, 'our predecessors – quite literally – had to be cleared out. Two men were busy piling up the bodies outside the door. Four across, four down, so that the pile would not topple over. I watched them work. It was nothing new to me. The stench inside the barrack was something terrible. Apparently, the Toteskommander had not been able to clear the barrack promptly; the dead had lain in their own vomit and excrement for some time. This was my new home.'[2]

---

[1] Kopel Kendall (Kandelcukier), recollections, letter to the author, 2 September 1995.
[2] Salek Orenstein, 'Beyond Belief, A Survivor's Story', manuscript, sent to the author, 1995.

Chaim Ajzen, who had likewise come from the slave labour camp at Skarzysko-Kamienna, recalled that aspect of Buchenwald which was unique, when he was called before a committee of the mostly German pre-war Communist prisoners, who were running the internal administration of the camp. 'The first question they asked me was if I knew any kapos or policemen who helped to kill prisoners. I gave them some names, i.e. Teperman, Sczepicki and others. They were all killed in Buchenwald.'[3]

Lipa Tepper was also deported to Buchenwald from Skarzysko-Kamienna. 'What actually happened in Buchenwald,' he later recalled, 'seems to be slightly grotesque to say the least, because when we arrived a man came in and he said to us that in this camp we have a democratic authority as far as is possible and we want to know any people who did you wrong during the years preceding this camp, or who informed on you to the authorities etc., and we will deal with them in our own way.

'Needless to say, during the night there was a lot of noise from people who were now organising themselves and taking out the policemen who had come with us and the kapos who had come with us and they were dealing with them in their own way. The following morning when we went out on Appel we all lined up, and at the end of the line there were several bodies.'[4]

Moishe Nurtman, another of those who had been at Skarzysko-Kamienna, recalled this same aspect of the camp: 'I remember when we arrived at Buchenwald the camp was run by the inmates. The Germans did not interfere. It was mainly political prisoners who were in charge. The first thing they were concerned about was the Jewish policemen who had been cruel to the young children. They would ask us if they were good to us or not, and I remember one instance in Skarzysko-Kamienna, there was a Jewish policeman, he was very cruel. His name was Yarmakow. He hit a girl and broke her jaw. He was very vicious for a small man, and they beat him up. He came crying to me, "Moishe, I was very good to you". I said to him, "You were good to me but you were lousy to other people". And I did not want to know what happened to him. I do not think he survived, because they were killing off all those who were cruel.'[5]

Michael Etkind also witnessed the effect of the trials conducted by prisoners at Buchenwald. One of those who was put on trial was a Pole, against whom a group of Russian prisoners of war in Etkind's barrack had brought an accusation. 'The trial took ten minutes,' he recalled.

---

[3] Chaim Ajzen, 'Chaim Ajzen's Story', manuscript, sent to the author.
[4] Lipa Tepper, letter to the author, 30 January 1996.
[5] Moishe Nurtman, letter to the author, March 1995.

'The Pole was accused of denouncing a number of Russians for taking money, food, or other items, while clearing bombed sites somewhere in Germany. The Russians were invariably hanged for this "crime", while the Pole received more food and other privileges for his services. The Pole was found guilty. Next day, after the six o'clock Appel, four of the biggest Russians grabbed the Pole by his hands and feet and began to throw him up in the air, each time letting him fall on to the hard tarmac. After throwing him up in the air about six times, they carried him back to his bunk which was almost directly underneath mine, fed him and gave him some water. Three days later the Pole looked terrible; his face was completely swollen, his eyes bloodshot and he was blabbing incoherently. At the following day's Appel he tried to approach the SS officer, presumably to complain about his tormentors. But the kapo intercepted him and led him back to the barracks. Immediately after the Appel he was strangled, and his body thrown into the latrine.'[6]

For Jewish slave labourers such as Salek Orenstein, there were several other features of Buchenwald that were unusual for the camps. 'In many respects,' he later wrote, 'Buchenwald seemed to me a "Gan Eden".[7] The cruelty and fear of death that we endured in the other work camps was no longer a constant nightmare dominating our lives. The high-ranking SS with their black leather coats, black ties and swastikas took little part in the day-to-day running of the camp. These duties had been conferred on the political prisoners who wore a different set of uniforms. One of these, quite a nice, stout fellow, took charge of us, laid down the rules and made the announcements.

'Of course there were penalties for those who disobeyed orders, but the atmosphere and the tone was quite different, a definite improvement as far as I was concerned. The distribution of food was much fairer, too. The political prisoners saw to it that everyone received their fair share and that the inmates did not rob and cheat one another of their due. At mealtimes, they made sure that the soup was well mixed so that its contents would be evenly distributed among everybody. That was quite something.

'I was moved from Barrack 66 and joined Barrack 54, a children's barrack. Although I was now sixteen I looked a lot younger. Opposite the children's barrack, across the thin wire fence, was the compound of women prisoners who had been selected to serve the pleasure of the German officers. Men went in and out all day, adjusting their clothing as they left. The young women sat on chairs outside the door, on parade.'

[6] Michael Etkind, ' "Youth" Remembered', manuscript, sent to the author, 1995.
[7] A Garden of Eden (Hebrew).

As more prisoners arrived at Buchenwald, Salek Orenstein recalled how 'room was made to accommodate the steady influx by removing the dead and half dead. I could see with my own eyes that some of the people being carted away among the heaps of bodies were still alive. Whether they were conscious enough to say what was happening to them, I cannot say.' On one particular night, Salek Orenstein failed – 'I will never know why' – to go out of his barrack for the night shift in the factory. That night Allied bombers struck, 'wiping out the industrial compound; most of the workers of my shift were destroyed that night, very few came out. There was nowhere to run, nowhere to hide. All industrial enterprise ceased. Then the clearing began, machines on one pile, scrap metal on another.'[8]

The Allied air raid on Buchenwald took place on 24 August 1944. Almost four hundred inmates, and eighty SS men, were killed, including the wife and daughter of the commandant. Among the camp's installations that were destroyed were the camp laundry, the disinfection rooms, the tailor's shop and the shoe repair shop; and a totally incongruous historical feature of the camp, Goethe's Oak.[9]

Sevek Finkelstein, from Piotrkow, was just thirteen when he was deported to Buchenwald from the Czestochowianka slave labour camp. He had been at this camp in Czestochowa for only a month when the rapid advance of the Red Army in January 1945 brought the prospect of liberation to the very outskirts of the city. But the Germans did not want to relinquish their victims, who were sent by train to Buchenwald. 'In Buchenwald there were quite a few boys from my home town,' he recalled. 'I was able to move freely around the camp as long as I was back for roll-call which took place in the morning and evening. One day while walking around the camp my father spotted me and called out for me. I looked at him and came towards him and he was so happy to see me. He embraced me and began to cry, he had a piece of bread which he gave to me.

'My father looked terrible. This powerful man, to whom I had so looked up, was a skeleton of his former self. He appeared beaten and powerless, and I was very uncomfortable being with him. I made excuses to him that I had to go back, and quickly left him standing there looking at me as I left. I could not allow myself to feel any love, concern or care for my father whom I had so loved. He was a burden that I did not want to take on. He was no longer of any possible use to me.

[8] Salek Orenstein, 'Beyond Belief, A Survivor's Story', manuscript, sent to the author, 1995.

[9] David A. Hackett (editor), *The Buchenwald Report*, Westview Press, Boulder, Colorado, 1995 (prepared Albert G. Rosenberg, April–May 1945), pages 95–6.

'This episode has been haunting me all my life. How could I leave my father? Others would not abandon their families and would rather choose death. I have forgiven myself for abandoning my father, though not entirely. Many rational explanations have been given to me for my action but none are really satisfactory. Talking about it, and telling the world, has made me able to forgive myself somewhat. I know that my father would forgive me because uppermost in his mind was to save me, I just wish that I could have done it in a more humane way. The effect of seeing Father and abandoning him left me more depressed, and I ceased to show my emotions to anything.'[10]

Jack Aizenberg also arrived at Buchenwald from the slave labour camp at Czestochowianka. He was sixteen years old. 'We were so worn out,' he recalled, 'that to go somewhere else was something we were looking forward to. One thing stands out in my mind. Somehow I managed to keep some family photos. In Buchenwald they were taken away from me. For this I can never forgive them. Some time after the war I managed to get a picture of my father and mother from someone in Israel, but sadly not of my younger brother. He was nine years old. The Nazi thugs sentenced him to death. He was innocent. His "crime" was that he was a Jew.

'One day in Buchenwald I was taken to work in the quarry. It was a dangerous place to work. People carried big and heavy stones to be loaded on to small trucks. Many, because they were undernourished, used to drop the stones, and people at the bottom of the quarry as a result got hit, and many injuries took place. This was disastrous. I said to myself then that I must not go to work in the quarry again. Being a young small boy, with luck I managed to stay away. However, hunger was taking its toll. I was getting weaker.'[11]

When the first large-scale evacuations from Auschwitz began in November 1944, as Soviet forces advanced westward through Galicia, tens of thousands of Jewish slave labourers were evacuated from the barracks at Birkenau, and from the factories in the region, and sent to Germany, many of them to Buchenwald. Perec Zylberberg, who had earlier been deported from the Lodz ghetto to the Warta munitions factory in Czestochowa, reached Buchenwald on 17 January 1945. 'Almost shoeless, and dressed in tattered trousers, with no underwear or overcoats,' he later noted, 'we endured terrible frosts. I had also the misfortune to have a very painful hand which kept freezing up at the very place of injury. There were no fresh dressings available at first. One just had to endure agony, which sometimes used to cause me fainting

[10] Sidney Finkel (Finkelstein), 'My Story', manuscript, sent to the author, 12 September 1995.
[11] Jack Aizenberg, recollections, manuscript, sent to the author, April 1995.

spells. The inside of the barracks was also very cold. The barrack elder used to have a little wood stove. It hardly ever gave us much warmth. It looked then to me like a place close to the end of endurance. But as so often before, the will to see this living hell through gave me the stamina that I found at the lowest point in my camps and ghetto sojourns. I saw other horizons. To go through that winter in Buchenwald was for me sheer hell.'[12]

Perec Zylberberg recalled many facets of the conditions and activities inside Buchenwald. 'New groups of prisoners kept on arriving daily,' he recalled. 'From all directions came news and hints as to the already desperate situation for all German armies. There was another invasion of France, through the south.[13] The Russian and Allied armies were capturing big chunks of Germany proper. There was German withdrawal from the Balkans. Poland was already liberated. According to the news dispatches that even penetrated to us in camp, German border areas were already occupied by the Allies. Buchenwald, being in the middle of Germany, was a place where the Germans kept on gathering the inmates of many other outlying camps. We felt unmistakably that the ring around the hated Nazi regime was getting tighter by the day. Unfortunately for us, they, the most despised people in the world, kept the war going.'[14]

Seeing so many non-Jewish prisoners at Buchenwald was an eye-opener for the Jews who were brought there from the slave labour camps. They had not realised that other nationalities were also being incarcerated by the Germans. Hitherto, in the ghettos and slave labour camps, it had been they, as Jews, who were the sole victims of deliberate starvation and forced labour, with the exception of Gypsies and Russian prisoners of war. In Buchenwald they saw imprisoned German and other communists; French, Dutch, Belgian and Czech civilians; Poles caught after the Warsaw uprising of August 1944; Danish university students who, it was said, had been sent there because they had refused to join the Danish SS.

Most unexpected of all for the Jewish deportees were the American soldiers in Buchenwald. They had been captured behind the German lines, wearing civilian clothing. 'I felt sorry for them,' Michael Etkind recalled. 'We were old-timers; we had been used to this kind of life. We went through so many stages, while they were thrust into it without any preparations. What had their military training to do with con-centration camp life? Who taught them how to "organise" more food?

---

[12] Perec Zylberberg, recollections, diary entry for 22 September 1993.

[13] American troops had landed in the South of France in August 1944, six weeks after the Normandy landings.

[14] Perec Zylberberg, recollections, diary entry for 23 September 1993.

How to get another bowl of soup? Where to find a half-rotten vegetable?'

There was another comforting aspect to the discovery of so many non-Jews at Buchenwald. 'The Frenchmen were quarrelling with the Germans,' Michael Etkind recalled. 'The Russians were executing their traitors. On the whole, the Jews were not behaving too badly. And we could take it so much better than so many others. No, we were not inferior to anybody. Buchenwald restored my confidence in myself.'[15]

Hunger was ever-present. Solly Irving, who was fourteen when he reached Buchenwald from the Czestochowianka slave labour camp in Czestochowa, recalled an episode when he saw two prisoners carrying a large saucepan of soup. 'A guard walked behind them. Suddenly a man ran across their path, putting his hand deep in the saucepan, in the hope of getting some solids from the bottom. He didn't seem to feel the heat of the boiling water. This incident lasted only a matter of seconds, and the man kept on running. When the guard realised what had happened, he aimed his gun and shot him.'[16]

Hunger, which is so often recalled by those who experienced its most extreme forms – and the terrible effects of hunger – forms to this day a link of shared experience between the boys, and a painful theme of their recollections. 'My father did not survive,' Moishe Nurtman later wrote of their time together at Buchenwald. 'He died of starvation. I took him in to my barrack, but he could not eat any more. Apparently he was beaten up one night when I was not with him. He told me that because they brought a lot of Poles and Hungarians together, sometimes at night one would kill the other. There was a case when one prisoner killed eight people for eight pieces of bread. He got caught. People were worse than animals. It was like dog eat dog.

'I was the only survivor in my family. I got the odd one or two beatings, but I counted myself very lucky. People became kapos by selection: if a person was strong, good-looking, he became a kapo. There was no real reason why. You were just lucky. They would all want to be kapos. The kapo distributed the bread for the others, so when he was cutting it, he always left himself a bigger portion.

'In Buchenwald we were fed twice a day. In the morning a portion of bread – this lasted till lunchtime – and soup in the evening. It was a small square of black rye bread about the size of a saucer. Water we used to drink from the taps, but that was difficult to get at times. But

---

[15] Michael Etkind, ' "Youth" Remembered', manuscript, sent to the author, 1995.

[16] Solly Irving (Shloime Zalman Judensznajder), 'Memories of a Past', manuscript, sent to the author, 5 April 1995.

we somehow managed. The worst experience was the lack of food, and fear, because every human being wants to live.'[17]

Krulik Wilder had arrived in Buchenwald, with his father Lajb, on Christmas Day 1944. He was just sixteen years old. After working for nearly two years at the Hortensja glass factory in Piotrkow, he and his father Lajb had been moved to the Czestochowianka munitions factory at Czestochowa, before they were sent westward to Buchenwald. 'We were completely stripped naked in the freezing cold,' he recalled, 'and were herded into a large shower room. We thought this was a gas chamber. Many people were screaming and crying, but we were relieved to discover that it was a shower room. Our hair was shaved and then we went through to a disinfecting chamber, and one of the inmates was brushing disinfectant on our private parts. It was very painful. When it was over we were given striped trousers and a jacket and sent to the barracks. On the first day after this I became totally paralysed out of fear. I could not move my arms or legs for twenty-four hours. Luckily I had my father with me and he was able to look after me.

'After a few days I recovered and got a job in the kitchens which enabled me to steal food for my father and myself. After a few weeks we were parted and my father was sent to a nearby concentration camp. I felt his loss greatly. At the end of March 1945, while walking in the camp, I noticed a man who resembled my father, but looked like a skeleton, lying on the Appel Platz. When I approached this man, to my horror I realised that it was my father. For the next few days I managed to get hold of some extra rations which I gave to him. It wasn't much but I hoped it would sustain him.'[18]

On 9 February 1945 an Allied air raid on the nearby city of Weimar led to heavy loss of life there, including the death of three hundred slave labourers at the Gustloff works. These slave labourers had been sent to the factory from Buchenwald, and, in an episode that caused particular anger inside the camp, the German Red Cross refused to receive any of the wounded slave labourers at the city hospital. At the same time, other slave labourers were sent to the city to help clear the rubble.[19]

'It was a pretty, medieval place with a lot of old buildings,' Perec Zylberberg recalled. 'The parties that were assembled in the morning after parade were designated to clean up Weimar after Allied bombings.

[17] Moishe Nurtman, letter to the author, March 1995.

[18] Israel (Krulik) Wilder, 'Krulik's Story', manuscript, sent to the author, 1 January 1995.

[19] David A. Hackett (editor), *The Buchenwald Report*, Westview Press, Boulder, Colorado, 1995 (prepared Albert G. Rosenberg, April–May 1945), pages 95–6.

I was drafted along with most of my barrack inmates for that kind of work. We used to be taken by freight trains to the outskirts of the city and then distributed in smaller units to various parts of the city. Each group had a kapo and a German guard. We came into contact with the civilian population.

'It was the first time that I encountered ordinary Germans. I remember not knowing how to react to the sight of people going about their concerns in an unhurried manner. There were children and old people as well as lots of women of all ages and quite a number of invalids. Sometimes our guards even used to be friendly. Most of the time they were scary. We were engaged in clearing the rubble and digging up broken water and sewage pipes. The German civilians who were directing the digging were often reasonably civil. It was such a contrast to the bestiality we had encountered up till then, except for several of the German overseers in Czestochowa. Now and again some women would give us a potato or a piece of bread. The work was arduous but not debilitating. Although sometimes a rough guard would hit someone or curse, we were generally treated not too badly, considering the circumstances.

'Buchenwald itself was a very busy place. Lots of new prisoners were arriving daily. At first some inmates were sent out to nearby working camps. This stopped about the end of February. The camp was getting overcrowded. There were lots of rumours around as to the fortunes of war. The atmosphere was already highly charged with expectations.'[20]

Salek Orenstein also recalled the effect on the inmates of Buchenwald of the Allied air raid on Weimar. 'I was cleaning the machines one day in the factory block when the doors opened and a group of us were led away. The nearby town of Weimar had been bombed and the rubble had to be cleared. We were driven off in lorries and put to work among the bombed-out houses. In the cellars we found bodies, but we also discovered food. When we did there was no hesitation, we simply grabbed it. We did not know if it was poisoned or not but we took it anyway. It sounds amazing, but in those two or three days which we spent there, we recovered our strength and energy quite considerably. The titbits of food supplemented our meagre diet and made a real difference to our bodies. I felt the benefit of it straight away.

'On another occasion, I was lifting an overturned cupboard, when a pile of linen and shirts fell out. I helped myself to those, quickly tying as many around me, pushing as many as I could into my trousers, without becoming too bulky and giving myself away. Each day I brought a few bits and pieces back to camp with me. One of these items caused me

---

[20] Perec Zylberberg, recollections, diary entry for 23 September 1993.

quite a problem. I had pinched a couple of tins of sardines, but I had no way of opening them! Eventually, at the factory, I found a sharp tool, a screwdriver or something of the sort, and prised open the lid. In my haste and with such clumsy tools most of the oil leaked out and was lost. Thinking back, that was a blessing in disguise; my body could not have absorbed the fat after so many years of starvation. It would probably have killed me.

'I derived great satisfaction from doing this job. For the first time, I could see that the Germans were being squeezed, their lives and property damaged.'[21]

Among the inmates at Buchenwald was Howard Chandler. He had been brought there from Auschwitz, and was just sixteen when he reached his new camp. 'In Buchenwald there was a similar reception routine as in Auschwitz,' he wrote, 'but not as strict, because the camp was overcrowded. I did not work in Buchenwald, except when I volunteered to clear up the rubble from the bombings in the nearby city of Weimar. While in Buchenwald I searched for and found my brother, and I managed to get him transferred to my barrack.'[22]

Alec Ward had been evacuated from one of the slave labour camps at Czestochowa to Buchenwald. Not long after he arrived he was sent to do menial work for the citizens of Weimar, whose remaining menfolk had been conscripted for the impending battles with the Russians on German soil. 'On our arrival at Weimar every day,' he recalled, 'the local German population would pick out their allotted amount of slave labourer prisoners. Occasionally we would find pieces of dirty and stale bread which we took back, at the risk of being shot at the gate, to the starving fellow prisoners in our huts.'

'In my hut,' Alec Ward recalled, 'there were mainly Hungarian-Jewish prisoners who did not understand things. The first words I learned in Hungarian were "Kitchy keniere" – a "small piece of bread" – a phrase which they repeated over and over again. They could not believe that the piece of bread we were given was so small. Unfortunately they were not very resilient to any form of hardship, disease or malnutrition, and many died every day. Every morning we carried out many dead bodies from our hut. The bodies were taken away on wooden carts.'[23]

Krulik Wilder recalled the final phase for many of the Jews at Buchenwald, some of whom had been there for more than six months, as

---

[21] Salek Orenstein, 'Beyond Belief, A Survivor's Story', manuscript, sent to the author, 1995.

[22] Howard Chandler (Chaim Wajchendler), letter to the author, 23 February 1995.

[23] Alec Ward, 'My Story', manuscript, sent to the author, 31 May 1995.

American forces approached the camp from the west. They were to be marched out, to the south and to the east, away from the chance of discovery and liberation by the advancing troops. 'I took my father by the hand,' he later wrote, 'to take him with me, but unfortunately when we reached the gates one of the guards would not let him come with me because he was very ill and could hardly walk, so I had no choice but leave him on the Appel Platz. I was very distressed that I could not save him, but I was so very helpless and utterly lost. I learned later that my father died in Buchenwald. To this day I still cannot get over it. He came so near to freedom, but it was not his fate to survive.'[24]

But even as American forces drew near, ten thousand Jewish prisoners were marched out of Buchenwald. They were not even to be liberated at the moment of liberation for thousands of others. Instead, they were forced once more to take up the burden of servitude, under the vigilant and sadistic eyes of their guards.

Almost all the boys of this book who were in Buchenwald in April 1945 were marched out on the final death marches as the American army approached the camp, but not all of them. Maurice Vegh, from the Ruthenian town of Rakhov, recalled how 'one day, the commandant, a German SS man, together with a Hungarian SS man, ordered us out of our barrack and shouted, "Jews, step forward!" We knew this was to be another death march. No one stepped out. "Don't you have any Jews there?" asked the commander. The block elder said, "No, these are Hungarians and Czechs, they don't speak German". The Hungarian SS man then went up to a young lad, he could have been no more than fourteen years old, and looked very Jewish. "Are you a Jew?" he asked, poking his finger hard in the boy's chest. "Yes", said the boy. He was made to step out. When the Hungarian SS man came to me he looked me in the face – I don't look particularly Jewish – and passed me by. I was shivering. Then the sirens sounded. We were sent back into the barracks. Within two hours we were liberated by the Americans.'[25]

[24] Israel (Krulik) Wilder, 'Krulik's Story', manuscript, sent to the author, 1 January 1995.
[25] Maurice (Moritz) Vegh, in conversation with the author, 3 May 1996.

CHAPTER 8

Surviving as Slaves

THROUGHOUT THE FIRST three months of 1945 the Allied armies pressed in upon Germany from east and west. Yet although the hopelessness of the struggle was obvious to all the German military commanders, Hitler ordered it to go on. The production of war materials was to be intensified. New factories were to be built, despite the massive Allied air raids on every corner of the diminishing Reich. From those slave labour camps that found themselves in the path of the advancing armies, and especially the slave labour camps on Polish soil on which the Russian army was rapidly approaching, the Jews were evacuated and moved deeper and deeper inside Germany, to new factories, many of them built underground, and to new slave labour camps.

Forty years later, in a letter to a British bomber pilot, Jerzy Herszberg recalled the Allied bombing raids over the German city of Braunschweig, to which he had been sent as a slave labourer. 'The sound of the sirens always filled me with joy, as it did all the other prisoners,' he wrote. 'The brave pilots of the Allied armies probably never realised how much hope and joy they gave us flying over Braunschweig.' This letter, he added, 'is my first opportunity to express my appreciation'.[1]

Jerzy Herszberg had spent more than four years in the Lodz ghetto before being deported to Auschwitz. It was after five months in Auschwitz, at the age of fifteen, that he was sent to Braunschweig. 'On our arrival there,' he later wrote, 'we were divided into two groups: those working in the assembly of heavy parts and those who were sent to Büssing Werke in town, where the work was somewhat lighter. I was in the latter group and we were marched to the factory for a twelve-hour period of work on the day shift, starting at 6 a.m., or, on nights, starting at 6 p.m. When on day shift we also worked for six hours on Sunday. I worked on the second (or possibly third) floor and the number of my section was, I think, 623 or 624. I was not allowed to adjust the machines; this work was done in alternate weeks by a Pole from Pabianice and a local German worker. The latter was not unfriendly towards me and used to call me "Piccolo". My job was to file down the edges on a kind of a toothed gearwheel and then to clean them free of

---

[1] Jerzy Herszberg, letter to Denzil Jacobs, 12 June 1985.

oil. Some of these also had to be stamped with a factory number and this I did using a hammer and metal stamps. The work was not unduly heavy and the German superior seemed to be satisfied.

'When the supply of these parts was low I sometimes had to help to clean up the factory and I was then working under a German sweeper who was somewhat crippled. He was moody and spiteful and sometimes hit me for no particular reason. We were given a bowl of thin soup at the factory; this was of better quality on night shifts. On Sundays we had nothing to eat at the factory but instead we had soup with a potato in the camp. The commandant of the camp, a stocky, rather plump SS man, indulged his sadistic impulses by keeping us waiting for the food and then throwing two potatoes into our midst for the dubious pleasure of seeing some of us fight for it. There was little for us to do outside the factory and the main object seemed to be to humiliate us. The commandant would address us as "FFF" ("faul, frech und fett")[2] and we were driven out to recite slogans like "Wir, Juden, haben den Krieg gewollt" ("We Jews wanted the war"). The bodies of those who died during the day were stacked in the lavatories.'[3]

Alec Ward was taken by train from Buchenwald to Flössberg, a slave labour camp near Leipzig, where he worked in a munitions factory producing bazookas. 'The camp was built in a forest, was very swampy, and we had to walk in deep mud to and from work,' he recalled. 'The German commandant was an absolute sadist. He derived great pleasure from beating us over our heads with a stick as we passed through the gates on the way to work. None of us believed that we would come out alive from that place. By some miracle I made friends with a boy of similar age, who helped me enormously to keep up my morale there. My friend had a most wonderful voice and very often we would sing together to while away our painfully hungry time.'[4]

That friend was Arthur Poznanski (Artek), with whom, fifty-two years later, Alec Ward was to recall how 'in Flössberg a sense of humour helped us survive'. At that low point in their travails the two young boys were able to joke about the absurdity of their situation, and to derive strength from their comradeship in humour.[5]

Michael Etkind, after two and a half weeks in Buchenwald, was sent to a slave labour camp at Sonneberg, fifty miles to the south. His work there was in an industrial machine shop, testing cogwheels. 'Air raid sirens would wail more frequently now,' he recalled. 'We could hear the droning

---

[2] Lazy, insolent and fat.
[3] Jerzy Herszberg, letter (regarding his claim for compensation), 5 December 1962.
[4] Alec Ward, 'My Story', manuscript, sent to the author, 31 May 1995.
[5] Alec Ward, in conversation with the author, 12 May 1996.

sound of bombers passing overhead, but, even when the sky was clear, could not see them. It took them two hours and longer to pass.

'Even Sonneberg was bombed. We were taken to clear the debris. A dozen of us were allocated to clear the rubble of a badly damaged two-storey house. We were warned that we would be shot if we stole anything. We found a cellar. I drank half a dozen raw eggs. (I had not seen an egg for at least two and a half years.) I ate all sorts of preserves, ignoring the broken glass inside the jars. On the way back we were searched but nothing was found on anybody.'[6]

Chill Igielman, who, after six months in a slave labour camp at Wiehagen, was transferred to Hessenthal, to a camp set at the airfield there, recalled an unusual episode. 'Whilst working on the airfield one winter's day,' he wrote, 'a civilian German and a guard came to fetch four people. He was a plumber and needed help to dig up a burst water-pipe. We had to dig through frozen ground with pickaxes and shovels, but soon we were digging in water. We took it in turns, two in the hole and two removing the earth. When it was my turn to go down again I must have been too slow, because the plumber pushed me and I fell in, twisting my leg. (Later, in England, I discovered that I had fractured my kneecap.)

'I doubt I could have survived a day working in the icy water with my leg causing me such pain. Two German aircraft pilots were passing and they asked for a boy to go with them. I was chosen and taken back to their personal barrack. Inside there was an iron stove with a fire, and they fed me with bread and margarine, and soup. I spent the day resting by the fire until it was time to go back to the camp. They asked me to do no work, but must have seen my pain and wanted to help me.'

The conditions at Hessenthal were harsh in the extreme. 'One night in January, in the heart of winter,' Chill Igielman recalled, 'we walked back through a snow blizzard to the camp. We had just finished our soup when the Germans marched us back to the airfield. When we arrived we were given shovels and told to clear the runway of ice and snow. The cold and wind were unbearable, as all I had on were my pyjama-type uniform, clogs without any socks, and a paper cement sack with holes cut out for my arms. After about an hour's work, my hands, feet and legs were totally numb with cold. I dropped my shovel but I was unable to grip it to pick it up. A German guard came over and began hitting me with his rifle, but I still could not pick it up. Eventually the German picked up the shovel for me. That night two hundred people out of one thousand Jews died.'[7]

[6] Michael Etkind, '"Youth" Remembered', manuscript, sent to the author, 4 January 1996.

[7] Chill Igielman, 'A Record of the Early Life of Hillel Chill Igielman', manuscript, sent to the author, November 1994.

Chaim Liss, from Lodz, who was an only child, was with his father at a slave labour camp near Hannover, working in a quarry. 'This was, of course, very hard labour,' he later wrote, 'and the death rate among the prisoners increased drastically and people died like flies, due also to the meagre food rations we were getting. My father was among those who did not survive.' In Lodz, before the war, Chaim Liss's father had made what his son recalled as the 'excellent cakes' which were sold by his mother in the family's little café. Unknown to him at the time of his father's death, his mother died of malnutrition at a slave labour camp in Germany at about the same time.[8]

Abraham Zwirek had been sent from the ghetto at Suchedniow – from which his mother Helena had been deported to Treblinka and killed – to Skarzysko-Kamienna, and then to a labour camp in Germany. This camp was at Schlieben, near Dresden, where several thousand Jewish slave labourers were put to work, first constructing their own barracks, and then assembling the Panzer-Faust, a hand-held weapon that could be fired at enemy tanks. Zwirek was fortunate in that he managed to find work outside the camp. 'The day after I arrived at Schlieben,' he later wrote, 'at the Appel, the commandant addressed us stating that if we tried to escape we would be executed, and at the same time he announced that workers were required for certain trades. There were about half a dozen German contractors standing by the side of him, and one of them required a qualified roofer especially for tarpaulin roofing and repairs. I volunteered as I had watched my father doing this with his workers when I was young, also he had made roofs from sheet metal. Although I had only been a bystander, I felt I could do this and wanted to work outside the camp with a civilian German rather than under the German guards.

'The contractor thought I was lying and said if I was unable to do the job properly I could be shot. He took me outside the camp and took me to the SS accommodation and left me to repair their roofs. I had to make the tar pitch and cut the tarpaulin to fit the holes. When he returned, he patted me on the back, and said in German, "Very good, little one". He took a liking to me, and now and then would bring me a sandwich. One day a German guard tried to whip me, as he accused me of not running fast enough with a roll of tarpaulin on my shoulder. The contractor saw it and came rushing down a ladder to stop the whipping. I worked for him for four months.

'I was then sent to help lay a concrete foundation approximately ten feet deep below ground-level in the camp. There were four men, I was

[8] Chaim Liss, letter to the author, 30 December 1994.

the smallest and the youngest, pushing a metal skip with four wheels along a track, for holding the wet concrete to be tipped into the foundations. When we had to tip the wet mixture, we had to lever the skip halfway over with a long pole, part of which was inserted underneath the skip and the remainder of the pole was lifted up on to our shoulders. Gripping the pole firmly down, we would stand behind each other levering the skip over to empty the mixture, while the pole, was, at the other end, raised high, with *me* gripping it firmly. Unfortunately, as it was extremely heavy the three men in front lost their grip, I was left holding on, and the pole shot up rapidly like a large spring with me still hanging on. I was flung high in the air and then down into the wet concrete foundations about three feet thick. The German civilian director, who was always immaculately dressed, and obviously important, became furious and ordered the men to get down a ladder to haul me out. I was shocked and badly bruised, and the director gave orders that I was to have two days off work, and given an extra helping of soup that evening.

'I was then transferred to the factory to produce Panzer-Faust. One night there was a big explosion and it was rumoured that the Italian prisoners had sabotaged the ammunition factory.'[9]

Chaim Ajzen, who had come to Schlieben from Buchenwald, was a witness to that explosion. 'One night as I was working the German "Meister" called me by my number,' he recalled. 'He told me to go outside and unload the boxes of powder from the cart being drawn by Belgian horses. I took down the first box and in that moment there was an explosion and I was blown a few metres, and became unconscious. On recovering consciousness I felt blood running from my head and the horses were torn to pieces and covered me. I got up and could not recognise the place. The whole factory had been blown apart. I was the only one left alive from the whole factory. Only a few prisoners were alive from other places.

'I did not know which direction to take away from this hell, and then I saw the Poles from the gate. As I walked towards them I heard somebody shouting for help underneath the ruins. I took away some blocks and boards and pulled out a German engineer. We started walking – me towards the camp and he to the village – but the SS stopped to check us. Had this man not been with me I would most probably have been shot. When I returned to the camp everyone was up and trying to escape. The explosive from the factory had hit the barracks and some inmates were injured or killed. As a result of the explosion there were about three hundred dead.

'About a week later the Germans decided to rebuild the factory. It was

[9] Abraham Zwirek, letter to the author, 12 February 1996.

hell. We worked day and night without much food and many prisoners died. Whilst doing this work we used to carry a tin plate tied to our trousers. You did not move without this, because you could not live through the day without it. You always had to be ready to get a bit of food or a drop of soup – anything that could be eaten. One day a lorry was leaving the camp kitchen with a load of potato peelings. When the lorry came past me I jumped on it. I took my plate and filled it up. As I came down from the lorry the sergeant-major saw me. He took out his stick and gave me a hell of a beating, but I did not drop one peeling, so he left me and started laughing.'[10]

Lipa Tepper, then aged seventeen, was also at Schlieben. At first, he recalled, the Jewish slave labourers 'were not shot or maltreated', but as time went on 'the food diminished and we started getting people dying of starvation, and the camp appeared to be a camp like any other camp, where people just died of hunger or died of beatings and so on and so forth. I remember in particular when the Hungarian transport arrived. Unfortunately they started dying very, very quickly, because they were not used to the hard, harsh conditions we had been enduring now for something like two or maybe three years. They found it very difficult indeed, more difficult than we did.

'One night I was on night shift and there was an air raid. There used to be air raids all the time and we used to sit with our heads on the radiators literally counting the bombs as they came down. This particular night what happened is that the bombs fell on our factory. The factory was completely bombed out. Virtually the entire night shift was wiped out. It was so intense that it threw the front axle and two wheels off a cart which was transporting the anti-tank guns from one department to another, something like a hundred yards across the factory.

'In the morning there was nothing but devastation. I remember lining up with about ten or twelve people who survived. Next to me stood Benny Newton, who is now no longer alive himself. It was a very, very harsh thing and a very difficult thing to digest. Anyway, the Germans decided that the factory would be rebuilt as speedily as possible and they brought in, I'm not sure but I think it was Estonian guards, and they were terrible. The work that went on there was unbelievable and within six weeks the factory was rebuilt, literally from the first brick.'[11]

Chaim Olmer also recalled the explosion at Schlieben. He had been sent there from Skarzysko-Kamienna after two weeks in Buchenwald, where, he recalled, 'we were given clean striped clothes and clogs, and I was free of lice for the first time in two years'. The work at Schlieben

---

[10] Chaim Ajzen, 'Chaim Ajzen's Story', manuscript, sent to the author.
[11] Lipa Tepper, letter to the author, 30 January 1996. The guards were most probably Ukrainian.

'breathing in the fumes of molten chemicals', was so dangerous, he later wrote, that an extra soup ration was provided, known to the prisoners as 'Giftsoupe' – 'poison soup'. After the explosion 'they brought over Ukrainian soldiers, and the most brutal period began, clearing the site and rebuilding the factory. From then on the night shift became easy because of the air raids and blackouts. With the bombings every night of the neighbouring cities we saw fantastic "fireworks".'[12]

Kopel Kandelcukier was likewise deported to Schlieben from Buchenwald. On the night shift, he recalled, the inmates were often called on to put out forest fires caused by the Allied bombing. On one occasion a group of Jews arrived from Piotrkow, among them Ben Helfgott. 'To our amazement we discovered that there were still other Jews alive,' Kopel recalled, 'as by then we thought we were the only ones left. Ben tells me he was shocked when he saw the condition I was in, but of course you don't see this in yourself. Also, when he saw inmates fighting over a bit of soup that had spilled on to the floor, he could not believe it.'

Although he was still only fourteen, Kopel Kandelcukier had been put to men's work filling shells for warheads. The daily shift was a twelve-hour one. 'I was getting a lot weaker by now,' he wrote, 'and my will to survive was not so strong. One morning at the Appel Platz, covered in boils, I refused to stand up. The Lager Führer happened to be a brutal young blond SS leader. He asked me, when he was about to kill me, "Why didn't you stand up?" I said I had had enough. "I was a young boy working with the older men, and I should be with the young ones in the children's workroom." On hearing this, he nearly killed the kapo and told him to immediately transfer me to work with the young inmates.

'The children's workroom was situated in a big warm barrack, in which German women were doing voluntary war work. We worked alongside them, putting detonators in little boxes. Some of the women showed kindness to us and when possible gave us a little food. My job was to take the filled boxes away in a wheelbarrow to another storeroom. Also, twice a day, it was my duty to fetch the hot coffee from the kitchen, quite a walk away. Whilst waiting to fill the containers with coffee I had a chance to see what I could find that was edible, like carrots, potatoes, onions – anything. I'm sure the ladies knew what I was doing, but they said nothing. I would bring it back and share it with some of my friends. I was getting back my strength and becoming more optimistic of surviving, hearing occasionally that the war was not going at all well for Germany, as we saw hundreds of Allied planes flying over, and heard the sirens making the Germans run for the shelters. The air raids brought

---

[12] Chaim Olmer, recollections, letter to the author, 17 September 1995.

joy to our ears, and that became quite frequent. We cheered, and our spirits were lifted.'[13]

Reflecting on the difference between Schlieben and his previous camp, Abraham Zwirek commented: 'Schlieben was not as notorious as Skarzysko, there were no selections, or executions, or crematoriums, but there was still fear from whippings, disease and starvation. There was no medication, and I had to have my thumbnail pulled off by an inmate who was a Dutch doctor, as it was infected and my arm was getting poisonous. He used ordinary pliers.'[14]

Zvi Mlynarski, a survivor of the Piotrkow ghetto, was also at Schlieben. 'It took about an hour to walk to work in the freezing cold, just a striped uniform on our backs,' he recalled. 'We tried to warm ourselves by putting paper from cement bags around our chests, but the Germans checked us with a stick, and anyone with paper had to undress in the snow and received a serious beating. I was one of those caught with the paper under his shirt and beaten without mercy.'[15]

Ben Helfgott, also a survivor of the Piotrkow ghetto, recalled how, as Russian forces drew near to Schlieben, the German newspapers brought into the camp by the German women workers reported brutal mass rapes in areas overrun by the Russian forces. 'There was a German woman who worked at the same bench as I. She turned round to me – I was only fifteen – and said to me, "What are we going to do? We hear these terrible stories of rape. One can cope with one man, with two; but ten, how can anyone cope with ten?" She wanted me to sympathise, but I thought to myself, "What have you been doing to my people all these years?"'[16]

At Rehmsdorf, Berek Obuchowski was among the slave labourers who had been brought there from Buchenwald. While working at Rehmsdorf, which he described as 'hell on earth', he broke his foot, 'and was sent to a shed that was used as a "hospital". They put a cast on my foot. The following morning, one of the inmates, Meyer Hochman, dragged me out of my bunk and made me go to work. I managed to force off my cast so I could work, and at the end of the day, I made my way back to the "hospital" shed. All the patients had gone – they had been sent to their deaths. Apparently Meyer Hochman had overheard that the hospital was to be "cleared". He saved my life.'[17]

[13] Kopel Kendall (Kandelcukier), recollections, letter to the author, 2 September 1995.

[14] Abraham Zwirek, letter to the author, 12 February 1996.

[15] Zvi Dagan (Mlynarski), letter to the author, 1 March 1996.

[16] Ben Helfgott, in conversation with the author, 11 November 1994.

[17] Bob Roberts (Berek Obuchowski), recollections, manuscript, February 1996, sent to the author, 4 March 1996. Meyer Hochman now lives in Canada.

Menachem Silberstein was also at Rehmsdorf, having earlier been a slave labourer in Skarzysko-Kamienna, Czestochowa and Buchenwald. 'This, I think, was the worst camp,' he wrote of Rehmsdorf. 'Hundreds died every week. It was real horror. Very little food, hard work. I stayed there for five months. As I look back I can't understand how I survived. I got wounded there by an SS man. He hit me with the barrel of his rifle. It happened as follows. We went out in a group of twenty men to cast a roof, and when we finished ten minutes too late, the Germans started beating us and shooting. Twelve men were shot. Eight of us were left alive. When we arrived at the gate of the camp, the guard explained that there had been an attempt to escape and that they had shot twelve men. The camp leader was pleased that they had done such a very good job.'[18]

At Nordhausen, in the very centre of Germany, several thousand Jews had been brought from Auschwitz and other camps to work at a massive underground construction site nearby, known as Dora, where German scientists and technicians were perfecting the rocket bombs and missiles being launched against England. 'As we reached the place,' David Hirszfeld, who had been brought from Buchenwald, recalled, 'we were lucky enough to be a part of a group of ten to fifteen youngsters selected to work in the kitchen.' Besides being spared from the rigours of slave labour, he and his brother Moniek could use their work to supplement the meagre ration. During their time at Nordhausen many prisoners were brought in who had originally been deported to Auschwitz from Rumania and Hungary a few months earlier. 'For many of them it was the first encounter with concentration camps, and they could not tolerate it, and died from exhaustion and various diseases.'[19]

Joshua Segal had also been taken from Buchenwald to Nordhausen. He was seventeen years old. Each day he was taken with his fellow-prisoners to Dora, where a vast underground factory was being constructed for the manufacture of V1 flying bombs, and V2 rockets. At Nordhausen, he later wrote, 'Your life hung on the whim of the German commandant, who was a sadist, and would shoot or beat prisoners to test their tolerance to pain. Very few survived his tests, and afterwards they were never seen again. One day, I became the object of his amusement. We ran out of our cell for roll call and stood in the courtyard ready to be counted. The commandant always carried a wooden chair with him during roll-call. It was not intended to be sat on. He stood in front of the prisoners, running his eyes along the rows of inmates and

---

[18] Menachem (Mendel) Silberstein, letter to the author, 29 April 1996.

[19] David Hirszfeld (Hirschfeld), 'The David Hirschfeld Story', manuscript, sent to the author, 9 February 1996.

pointed his finger at me, indicating that I was to step forward and come to him. "How are you", he asked, with a look that indicated that he really didn't care. "Fine", I said, and as soon as I spoke the commandant picked up the chair and swung it at me, striking me on the shoulder and back.

'I dropped to my knees without uttering a sound. Having witnessed this before, I knew what was expected of me. I looked at the commandant from my knees as he smiled back at me with approval. He swung the chair at me again, striking me on the shoulder. I sprawled on the ground, bruised and dizzy, but I still made no sound. He raised the chair and brought it down on my head, shattering it. A short scream of pain escaped and immediately I bit my tongue to stop myself making another sound.

'I pushed myself to my hands and knees and he picked up a piece from the chair and struck me a few more times across my back, grunting with each effort. I clenched my fists and shut my eyes as he rained more blows on to my back. Blood dripped from my mouth from where I had bitten my tongue. I knew that if I made another sound, nothing could save me. "Very good, for being strong. You shall be rewarded. Get some food. Tell them I sent you and tomorrow report to me", said the commandant. Each movement caused me pain, but I tried not to show it. The next day he again praised me for being strong, and gave me a job in the staff kitchen, where the officers and scientists ate, at the V1 and V2 rocket site. By working in the kitchen I was able to supply extra food for my brother.'[20] His brother, Wovek Segal, was nineteen years old. Both boys survived.

Also working at Dora was Jona Fuks (later John Fox), together with his brother Harry and their father, Joseph. 'As we came into Dora,' he recalled, 'there were eight people hanging by their necks at the entrance. My father and I, with a group of other people, had the job at Dora of loading dead people on to trucks. We picked up these dead bodies, which were naked, and put them on a truck. There were a hundred of them. We did that every day for three or four weeks. My brother worked in the kitchen and that was our luck. He would come out of the kitchen with things in his pockets for us to eat.'

'My father got sick at Nordhausen,' John Fox later wrote. 'He got dysentery. He knew that he was going to die. I realised how sick he was when he gave me his uniform to wear. He said that I should take it and that way we wouldn't worry about what we would be wearing the next day. He just gave up. Once you got sick you died. There were no doctors. They took him to a separate barrack and he died there. We never saw

[20] Joshua Segal (Jehoszua Cygelfarb), letter to the author, 17 February 1995.

him again. All those years my father stayed with us and then he got sick and he died. It was only a few months before we got liberated. He couldn't have survived much longer anyway, because in Nordhausen if you couldn't work they killed you. My father was in his early forties when he died. I was then fifteen and my brother was twelve.'[21]

Koppel (now Max) Dessau, whose father Grojnem had died in the Piotrkow ghetto in 1942, was another of those deported from Buchenwald to Dora. 'One day I was practically dead,' he later recalled. 'They had put me in a bag near the crematorium. Then there was bombing, and they went away. I was left alone.'[22]

Manfred Heyman, who had been born in the German city of Stettin in 1929, and had spent the war years in the ghettos and slave labour camps of German occupied Poland, was sent from the aircraft factory in Mielec back to Germany, to another aircraft factory, near Flossenbürg concentration camp, together with his father Wilhelm and his brother Eugen. 'At the beginning the food was better than we got in Poland,' he recalled, 'but it got worse as time went on. It was in this camp that my father died from malnutrition and hard labour. My brother was sent to a smaller camp and I never heard of him again.'[23]

Elsewhere in the industrial regions of Germany, especially in Saxony, Jews were brought from German-occupied Poland to factories making war materials for the ever diminishing front. Fifteen-year-old Harry Balsam, from the southern Polish town of Gorlice, had been sent to Rehmsdorf. 'This was a very big refinery,' he later recalled, 'and it was bombed by the Americans, English and Russians. We had to work very hard there with very little food. They wanted us to rebuild it as they needed the oil for the war machines. Every time we repaired the factory and they re-lit the ovens, on the following day it was smashed down again.

'One day we all ran for cover. The bombs were falling and we were hiding in a very deep ditch. Some of the bombs did not explode, so again I was lucky. The soft earth from the bombs came up and it covered me up to my neck. I could only move my head watching the planes throwing the bombs out of them. I would say on that particular raid there must have been at least two hundred planes. When the raid was finished some of the inmates dug me out. Then we found out that about one

---

[21] John Fox (Jona Fuks), recollections, Gala Recognition Dinner brochure, Hilton Hotel, Philadelphia, 8 September 1993.

[22] Max Dessau, quoted in: Melissa Hoskins, 'End of death camp nightmare', *Recorder*, Ilford, Essex, 27 April 1995.

[23] Manfred Heyman, letter to the author, 5 June 1995.

hundred were missing and were buried alive in the sand.'[24]

Harry Spiro was also at Rehmsdorf. 'One time I was taken from a work party to be shot, but the kapo called me back because I was a good worker, and another man went instead of me. Another time I was in the washroom, and a man collapsed and died next to me; he had extra rations on him which I took, and this helped me through. Once we took refuge in some bunkers from an American air raid, and there were some German troops, one of whom threw us some rations.'[25]

Also in Saxony, seventeen-year-old Roman Halter was at a slave labour camp in Dresden. In November 1944, as Soviet forces approached the Baltic, he had been brought to Dresden from the concentration camp at Stutthof, near Danzig, with five hundred other Jewish slave labourers. 'I worked in Dresden under SS supervision,' he recalled. 'We worked in the basement where the bullet-making machines were, and there was no fresh air. We slept in the same building on the second floor. Here the windows were shut and bolted and the glass was painted a white opaque colour and criss-crossed with a paper tape. The smell here was of machine oil and bodies; that is until the time of the bombing. Because during the bombing other parts of the building were burned but not our dormitories. And when the SS took a group of us to collect dead bodies, those who did this work came back smelling of rotten corpses, and we were all invaded by this stench, which at night became suffocating in the spaces where we slept.'

Roman Halter remembered many aspects of life as a slave labourer. There was a fellow-prisoner, Josef Szwajcer, who had been in Auschwitz from the end of 1942 until the summer of 1944. 'It was more than his eyes which were chastised by the smoke of the crematoria chimneys. He knew the inner hell of the place, and I was afraid of him, although without reason. He joined the group in Stutthof to replace those who died in the two months that we were there. Once, another Stutthof inmate who didn't belong to our group wanted to take my daily ration of bread away from me. Szwajcer was nearby and came to my rescue. He hit that inmate with his elbow on the neck below his ear and sent him to the ground. That inmate remained on the ground. Szwajcer took a bite from the bread as his reward for helping me, and without a word to me handed me the remainder of the bread and walked away.'

Roman Halter also recalled the German overseer, Herr Hans Braun, 'who helped me a little in the factory in Dresden, where in addition to being a machine operator I was also the *Laufer* – the messenger boy – carrying drawings from the German office to the factory's machine area,

[24] Harry Balsam, 'The Harry Balsam Story', manuscript, sent to the author, 14 November 1995.
[25] Harry Spiro, recollections, letter to the author, 21 March 1995.

and so got a little bit more food from some of the office staff. It was Herr Braun who made me a Laufer.'

Roman Halter remembered a moment of supreme danger, such as many of the boys faced, each one coming very near to death in some sudden, bizarre and cruel circumstance. 'One day twelve of us were taken out in Dresden by the SS,' Roman Halter recalled, 'and placed against the factory wall to be shot. Each of us had an SS man behind him who pointed his rifle at our head. We stood there facing the wall with our hands up. I wept because my hip hurt. Normally before an execution the SS would pick on one victim and brutalise him or her.

'As we were led out of the factory down the front steps, which were lined with SS men – and SS women, because among the twelve of us who were led out to be shot, there were ten men and two women – one SS officer pointed me out to another SS man, who turned his rifle upside down and lifted it above his head like an axe. I saw all this, and so did Abram Sztajer who was next to me, and who said in Yiddish, "Move" (actually the word means "slide" – "ritz-cech"), and in that split second, when the rifle butt was over me in the air, I turned and hopped down one step. The blow slid down the side of my body and momentarily rested on my hip. I screamed. It hurt terribly.

'There was an SS woman on the opposite side, a couple of steps down. When she saw that her colleague had failed to crush my skull, she pulled me towards her and hit me with a sharp object on the side of my head, which instantly produced a gush of blood.

'We were waiting to be shot, and Sztajer, who was on my left, could see, from the corner of his eye, the bloodstained part of my face. "Cry quietly, don't let them know that they have hurt you," he whispered. For some reason I did what he told me, and gave out intermittent and suppressed groans.'[26]

Suddenly, the prisoners who were about to be shot were ordered back to their barracks. There was to be no execution. In a few terrifying moments Roman Halter had twice escaped death.

David Kutner, from Lodz, was taken to the SS barracks at Birkenau, to work in the stables there. 'The daily routine was as follows,' he wrote. 'I was woken up at 3.30 a.m., when I had to stand, together with other inmates, in one spot, for about half an hour (the Appel), to be counted, no matter what the weather, until the SS were satisfied that the number of inmates were present and correct. Then, from 4.00 a.m. to 7.00 a.m., I had to clean the horses in the stables, with a special brush. On one occasion, the SS man was not satisfied with my work, so he punched

---

[26] Roman Halter, letter to the author, 14 November 1994.

me hard in the stomach. It has damaged my bowel, and to this day, my bowel is still not right. I have, because of that occasion, endured a lot of pain.

'At seven in the morning we at last got some food, which consisted of a stale piece of dry bread and black coffee. After that, I was put to work in the fields, doing all kinds of jobs, even ploughing, a job which was most unsuitable for a boy of my age. At twelve midday, we stopped for so-called lunch, which was a bowl of soup fit for pigs. This was the last meal we had until the next morning at seven when we got the dry bread and coffee.

'After the midday break I worked right through the day, until it got dark, when I returned to work with the horses inside the stables. (Feeding the horses, cleaning, etc.) This work went on until 11.00 p.m. when we all fell, exhausted, into the bunk, to again be woken up, the next day, at 3.30 a.m. to follow the same routine, day after day.

'Needless to say, there were many dead each day. If you became ill, then you were as good as dead. Things got really bad when the winter of 1944–45 came, as we had no proper clothing to combat the weather. All through the winter weather, my hands were exposed to the severe frost, as I had no gloves, and as a result, both my hands were severely frostbitten, and to this day, my hands are still affected. My frostbite was severely aggravated by the fact that, on one occasion, the SS man made me stand in one spot during a very cold day, 25 degrees below zero, for six hours. This was a punishment for some work that I had done, not to the SS man's liking. I have had various treatments for the condition here in England, but in the end I was told that I had to live with my condition for the rest of my life.'[27]

Meir Sosnowicz was sent from Buchenwald with his two cousins, Srul and Shmuel Chaim, to the slave labour camp at Krawinkel. They had volunteered to go there. 'The camp at Buchenwald struck me as very stern, cold, with no occupation save work in a quarry,' he recalled, 'so that was what we did. The SS stood over us; any time we slowed down (in their estimation), we were beaten; on the head and/or any other part of the body. When the opportunity arose (I do not remember how) to work in Krawinkel we volunteered to work there, just as we had volunteered at Auschwitz to work at Buna. Krawinkel consisted of man-made caves which were cold and uninviting. I think the V2 bombs were stored there. It was these caves (empty of ammunition by now) in which we slept during the period that we worked there, in order to be close to

---

[27] David Kutner, 'War Experiences of David Kutner, 1939–1945', manuscript, sent to the author, 9 May 1994.

our work. We slept in the standard wooden bunks shown in any photos of Auschwitz or Buchenwald. We were transported daily to a nearby railroad station to load and unload heavy wooden beams and similar items.

'At Krawinkel we were woken at about four o'clock in the morning, and ordered to be at the Appel Platz to be counted. Here it was even worse than in Auschwitz and Buchenwald. It was the middle of a European winter, cold and damp. Nevertheless we had to stand there for at least an hour or more, clad only in scant clothing. From there we marched or were transported to the work area supervised by Hungarian guards accompanied by German shepherd attack-dogs.

'I cannot remember what part of the day we received our meagre daily piece of bread, but it must have been some time during the morning. When we returned to our quarters we received a thin soup. We always tried to get the bottom of the soup because there were more solid pieces in the bottom than at the top.

'We were at Krawinkel for about two months, during which time we lost our cousin Srul. One morning he had an upset stomach and stayed behind to recuperate. On our return that night he was no longer there.'[28]

Moniek Goldberg, having been evacuated from Auschwitz to Buchenwald in January 1945, was also sent to Krawinkel. His time there was part of what he later called the 'living hell' of his last four months of the war. The prisoners knew the camp as Bunker Lager, because they were housed in underground bunkers. 'Almost everybody got sick,' he recalled. 'We got very little to eat. It was a very small piece of bread and a cup of ersatz coffee in the morning and later a ladle of soup that consisted of half-cooked grated potatoes. I got very sick right away. Two friends from Buna helped me walk to and from work every day. At work we unloaded supplies from wagons. Things were very disorganised. We had an old German guard in charge who didn't care too much about what went on. The guards were Hungarians. It was the only time during the three years that I gave up. I told my friends to just leave me. The way it worked was, when everyone left for work, those who couldn't go were left on the side of the road. There was no Appel Platz. Soon, a truck would come to take those that remained to Ohrdruf where they would be left to die.

'That particular day the SS officer in charge decided to make an inspection of those left behind. As he walked past me he put his riding crop under my chin and asked what camp I had come from. I told him I had come from Buna. He asked what commando I had worked in. I told him the Youth Commando. He had also been in Buna and as a

[28] Michael Novice (Meir Sosnowicz), recollections, manuscript, June 1995.

result he issued an order putting me to work in the kitchen to peel potatoes. I went to see the "doctor". He was a Hungarian Jew who told me he was no doctor, but that I was not helping my condition by not eating. He told me I must force myself to eat if I wanted to live. I had a few pieces of bread saved up so I stuffed myself and it did the trick. We didn't stay there too long but it was long enough for me to regain my strength.

'Krawinkel wasn't a camp where one was beaten or overworked. Even the guards didn't seem to care. But the lack of food and water and the minimum standard of hygienic conditions, filled the camp with walking corpses. In the kitchen, almost all the workers were Russian, and befriending them helped me for the next few weeks. It certainly made all the difference, fortifying me for the march from Krawinkel to what we called the Tent Camp, as we all lived in tents pitched in a field. The lice were as bad as a biblical plague. Here the work was hard as we dynamited tunnels into the Thuringian mountains.

'They only gave us food once a day, in the evenings. It was very common for toughs, usually the Russians, to jump on people and take away their single piece of bread. Since it was cold at night another peril was that the same gang would brazenly steal your blanket in the middle of the night. People died continuously. It was complete and utter chaos. There was no discipline inside the camp. On the way to and from work anyone stepping out of line was shot. A lot of people died because they were too weak to run and there was only a minute or so to clear the area once the dynamite was set to explode. We'd often find the victims after the blast when clearing the rubble.

'I was lucky. I stuck close to the Russians with whom I worked in Krawinkel. As a result nobody stole my bread or blanket. We weren't there too long before they marched us back to Buchenwald. On the road again, things were definitely breaking down. I remember that some of our guards were Hungarians. I managed to secure some bread and cheese after a guard pulled me out of line and ordered me to carry his rucksack. Little by little, I edged away from him. The Russians created a little diversion, enabling me to get lost in the crowd. We took out all the food and threw away the rucksack.

'We only stayed in Buchenwald one night and were marched to Weimar and put on open wagons for an infamous transport to Theresienstadt.'[29]

---

[29] Joseph (Moniek) Goldberg, 'Biographical Sketch', manuscript, July 1995, sent to the author, 14 August 1995.

CHAPTER 9

On the Death Marches

W ITH THE ADVANCE of the Russian armies deep into Poland at the end of 1944 and the beginning of 1945, those Jews who were in slave labour camps on the line of advance were moved away. Those who directed the German industrial machine hoped that if the front stabilised, these tens of thousands of slave labourers would be reconstituted into a workforce. For those German soldiers who were guarding the evacuees, keeping them alive was a prudent personal protection against having to join the military forces who were at that very moment engaged in combat with the Russians. A unit of guards without any prisoners would have been drafted at once. Armed men found avoiding service were being executed by the SS, and their bodies left hanging along the roadsides as a warning to others who might seek to desert. Guarding a column of Jews was the perfect alibi.

David Kutner, originally from Lodz, was among the Jewish slave labourers evacuated on foot from the Auschwitz region on 18 January 1945. 'Anyone who dropped out,' he recalled, 'was immediately shot by the guards. Unfortunately, many prisoners, who through lack of food were so weak, collapsed from exhaustion and were therefore shot. It seems that the SS had orders not to leave anyone behind alive. On one occasion during that walk – it was night-time – a Russian woman prisoner (we were a mass transport of mixed nationalities, men and women) collapsed, and as I was passing her, the guard aimed the rifle towards her half-dead body and fired two shots at her. As it was dark, I could see the fire coming out of the rifle and go into the woman's body. This vivid picture has been haunting me to this day, and I always wondered whether the woman felt the bullets hitting into her flesh. The sight made me gain strength, as I knew if I gave up I would be shot.'[1]

Henry Abisch, from the Ruthenian town of Rakhov, was also on a death march from Auschwitz. 'I witnessed about fifteen boys trying to run away,' he later wrote. 'They were already quite a distance when a German woman on a farm pointed them out to the SS, who were also

---

[1] David Kutner, 'War Experiences of David Kutner, 1939–1945', manuscript, sent to the author, 9 May 1994.

tired and irritable. They started shooting at them. I saw them falling in the snow.'[2]

Moritz Vegh, who was also from Rakhov, was on a death march from a slave labour camp at Jawischowitz. 'Only a quarter of us reached Buchenwald alive', he recalled. His father Zev, who had been sent to a slave labour camp at Katowice, did not survive. 'Later, when I was in Prague, a young man told me that in the camp my father had been doing fine, but that on the march, one morning, the guards said that those who did not feel that they could march any farther should stay behind – to go in a truck. My father was one of them. When the truck came there was a machine gun mounted on it, and all those who had stayed behind were killed.'[3]

Hugo Gryn had been deported from Beregszasz to Auschwitz in May 1944, and then sent with his father to a slave labour camp at Lieberose, in Germany. Their task was to work on the construction of a holiday town for German officers. When the time came for Lieberose to be evacuated, he and his father were marched with 3,500 other Jews to the concentration camp at Sachsenhausen, just north of Berlin, a journey of more than a hundred miles. On the eve of the march, all those in the camp infirmary were shot. Each night as darkness fell the marchers were ordered into a field and told to lie down. They would be marched off again at dawn. There were always some, when morning came, who were too weak to get up, or who stumbled and fell when they tried to rise. As the marchers set off, they would hear the sound of shooting.

During a moment of rest, sitting with his father by the slushy roadside, Hugo Gryn saw a lorry drive past them along the road. 'By coincidence,' he recalled, 'it had my father's name still painted on its side and back. He had been a timber merchant and somehow a part of his confiscated transport fleet and we were on the same road. It was a pathetic moment and to break the silence I said, "Just you wait – one day you'll have it back again!" "No," he said, "I think this was yours anyway!" And then he explained that whenever he acquired a forest or lorries or suchlike, he rotated the acquisitions: something for my brother, something for me, something for my mother and something for himself. It seemed that everything I thought he owned was already a quarter mine. Though it was academic, I was both touched and impressed. Finally, I asked him, "Why did you do it that way?" "Well," he said, "I made up my mind long ago that anything I have to give I want to give with a warm hand – and not wait until I have to give with a cold one".'[4]

[2] Henry Abisch, manuscript notes (1981), sent to the author, 26 October 1995.

[3] Maurice Vegh, in conversation with the author, 4 May 1996.

[4] Hugo Gryn, in conversation with the author, 1986: Martin Gilbert, *The Holocaust, The Jewish Tragedy*, London, 1986, page 764.

When the marchers from Lieberose reached Sachsenhausen, less than nine hundred of the 3,500 who had set off were alive. From Sachsenhausen, Hugo Gryn and his father were among thousands of Jews who were later moved south to Mauthausen, a notorious concentration camp in Austria. There, a victim of hunger and typhoid, his father died. He was forty-five years old.

Roman Halter was in the labour camp in Dresden when the westward evacuation was ordered. 'When the SS marched us out of Dresden,' he later wrote, 'they made us halt in an area like a small market-place. We were made to sit down on the cobblestones. Germans from nearby houses came to look at us. The SS wanted to entertain these German onlookers. So they began throwing bits of carrots and bits of turnip in amongst us, hoping that we would fight and claw for them. But we didn't. Hungry though we were, we passed the word around "to sit passively" and "behave with dignity". This angered the SS so much that they began kicking us into action.'[5]

Michael Etkind, a survivor, like Roman Halter, of the Lodz ghetto, was at the Sonneberg slave labour camp when the Russian troops drew near. He recalled how he and those with him were then evacuated. It was rumoured that they were to be taken back to Buchenwald, the camp from which they had been sent to Sonneberg, but this proved impossible, as Americans troops were approaching Buchenwald even then. The marchers were therefore marched back to Sonneberg. Then, after an additional bowl of soup, they were marched out again. 'This time we were marching east,' Michael Etkind recalled. 'We spent the night in something that looked like a village hall. At dawn, after lining up for some hot "coffee", we began to march again. 'We walked along narrow winding roads, on which there was hardly any other traffic. The SS officers would consult their maps from time to time, and some of them, riding bicycles, would go ahead of the column. Although the time was early April (the first or second day of April), the weather was cold. There was sleet, which would quickly turn into mud beneath our clogs. We passed a number of small villages in that hilly countryside. It was getting dark when we were eventually ordered to stop. We spent the night in a muddy field wrapped in our wet grey blankets.

'At dawn we began to march again. One of my friends became feverish. His face was red, and his steps became unsteady. He could not keep up the pace. Whilst we were passing a cottage in a village, he tried to enter it. The guard pushed him away. A few of us tried to support him, but we did not have the strength. He began to talk incoherently (I cannot even remember his name) and by now his temperature must have been

---

[5] Roman Halter, in conversation with the author, 5 March 1996.

very high. Before long he was at the end of the column. We heard a shot but dared not look back. The pace quickened. The guards seemed to be more on edge now.

'We arrived at a farmyard. An hour later we were queuing for soup. Having eaten it, we became ravenous; the hunger became unbearable. Knowing that some soup was still left at the bottom of the drum (the cylindrical vessel in which it was boiled), we circled around it, hoping for an extra drop. Suddenly there was a scuffle and a few men tried to scoop some soup with their pots. A shot rang out. We ran back to our lines. One man was kneeling on the ground. His pot fell out of his hand. His face was turning purple, a sort of reddish blue. He was trying to stand up. The German was holding his revolver near the man's head and shouting, "Liege!" ("Lie down!"). The man was saying, "Ich werde gehen" ("I can go – I am able to walk"). His hands were holding his stomach. Three shots were fired into his head in rapid succession.'

Michael Etkind also saw how close a unit of American tanks came to liberating his death march. 'We were approaching a bridge spanning a wide river,' he recalled. 'We heard shooting and saw some tanks firing. "American tanks", the rumour spread like lightning. We were halfway across the bridge when a couple of German motorcyclists in black leather coats came racing towards us. "Zuruck!" ("Back!") they shouted – "Turn round and go back". Our guards spoke a quick word to them. A minute later we had to run in the direction we were going. We were allowed to cross the bridge while all other traffic had to go back.

'Ten minutes later we saw a group of American soldiers being led by German militia. The Americans were laughing and waving to us. We did not wave back; we knew what was in store for them. Three elderly German civilians with swastika armbands – men who were too old to be taken into the army – led the Americans off the road towards a clump of trees. We heard rifle-shots as our column was turning round the corner.

'A few minutes later we heard a series of explosions behind us. The bridge which we had just crossed had been dynamited. The van with our sick and injured was on the other side of the river. Did they survive, or did the SS, who themselves could not walk (one of them only had one leg), kill them? We never found out the answer.

'It was late afternoon as the winding road led us into a forest. The road was going downhill, when suddenly we saw the body of a young German soldier hanging from a branch of a tree. His face was waxy yellow. There were bullet holes in his body and a board was pinned to his chest with the word "*Verräter*" ("Traitor") scribbled on it in six-inch-high letters. His feet were at the height of our heads, and only a couple of yards away from us as we passed. We dared not raise our eyes to look at our guards. During the next hour, at least half a dozen men, who could not keep up the pace, were shot.

'A thought passed through my mind: "If they kill all of us, they themselves might be taken for deserters. Some of us will survive". That night we spent in another barn or a stable. I noticed some cows eating from a trough. I sneaked close to the trough and filled my pot with their food. There were some boiled potatoes mixed with the raw ones and some grain and grass in it, but the whole mixture tasted sour and I had to leave some of it.

'One of the horses broke its leg and was shot. That evening the soup was the best we had tasted for a long time, but there was so little of it. I began to search near the place where the carcass was cut up and found a raw piece of the horse's rear ankle. It was solid muscle, white in colour, and no matter how hard I chewed I made no impression on it. The following day on the march I continued to chew it for at least twelve hours, receiving envious glances from the other men.'

The march on which Michael Etkind was being taken through the western Sudetenland continued in a zigzag pattern for several weeks. 'When it was snowing or raining we would put our grey blankets over our heads to protect them a little,' he recalled. 'The guards did not like us to do so. It must have affected their aesthetic sensibilities, and they would shout at us whenever we tried to do it. In spite of that, we would do so after dark, partly in order to dry the blanket, and also to protect ourselves from the cold evening winds. On one such evening, while my head was under my blanket, we heard a shot behind. As usual a few voices were raised, asking who was shot. It was a strange feeling when I heard the reply, "Etkind has been shot". It took me a few minutes to recover. I pinched myself, took off my blanket from my head and placed it on my shoulders, and said to my next two neighbours: "Etkind has not been shot yet". Nobody found out who was actually shot that evening.'[6]

David Hirszfeld was among several thousand slave labourers who were evacuated from Nordhausen on 3 April 1945, as American forces approached the vast underground rocket construction site. 'Many of us died on the unbearable march,' he later recalled, 'and some escaped. Only a small group lasted the entire journey and ended in Theresienstadt.'[7] From several dozen other slave labour camps, tens of thousands of slave labourers were also on the move, being evacuated by the

[6] Michael Etkind, '"Youth" Remembered', manuscript, sent to the author, 4 January 1996.

[7] David Hirszfeld (Hirschfeld), 'The David Hirschfeld Story', manuscript, sent to the author, 9 February 1996.

Germans away from the advancing Allied armies which were making deeper and deeper inroads on German soil.

Most of the Jews in Buchenwald were evacuated on 5 April 1945: three thousand in all. Unknown to them, the American forces were within a week of reaching the camp. 'On one of these chilly spring days we heard announcements for all the Jews to come out of their barracks,' Salek Orenstein wrote. 'We went outside, lined up, and marched off to the gates. Beyond them I could see a road – a proper asphalted road. Germans rode alongside on motorbikes and in jeeps, flaunting their superiority. We had to walk quite a long way until we reached the railway line. The train on which we arrived had brought us directly into the camp itself, but it was a single track only. The track leading away from Buchenwald was a long way off. It seemed so far to us, and those who could not keep up with the group were shot and kicked into the ditch. Every few yards there was another casualty. We walked four abreast, in neat formation, but the longer we walked the more gaps appeared.

'We marched for four hours. We must have lost more than a hundred people. People lay by the side of the road, blood steadily seeping out of their bodies. Towards evening, the trains arrived, dirty, filthy freight trains, with their previous cargo of rock, sand and coal still visible inside them.'

At one point on the journey, desperate for something to drink, the prisoners from Buchenwald reached the German industrial city of Chemnitz. 'Quite a number of German civilians were milling around,' Salek Orenstein recalled. 'A high-ranking officer dressed in a jacket with pink lapels appeared and announced on a loud-hailer that whoever wished to offer the prisoners a drink could do so. Not one of the Germans lifted a finger to give us a drop of water. This I shall never forget. They could see who we were, what we were, it was clear that we were not soldiers – we still wore our Buchenwald uniforms!

'I thought, "Have a little bit of compassion. Bring a little water. Put yourself in our place. Who knows what the future holds for you?" This was April 1945. We had been travelling for about two weeks and I don't know how many of us were left. At daybreak, the train moved again – backwards. It lurched along the track until it came to a standstill underneath an important bridge and there we stayed. American planes filled the skies above us, turning day into night. It was a beautiful clear day but when the planes came over they blotted out the sun completely. The idea was that when the pilots swooped close to this strategic target, they would see us in our open wagons and hold fire. Human shields, that is what we were. Some of the planes did dive down low, literally over our heads and certainly low enough to see who was on that train.

Anti-aircraft guns rattled and a few planes burst into flames. No bombs fell and the bridge was saved.

'We continued our journey, stopping from time to time so that the officers could cook themselves a meal, while we were let loose in the fields to scavenge for some piece of filth to put in our mouths. We even sucked the earth to extract some moisture. I noticed a rock glistening with dew in the early-morning sun. I went over to that rock and I licked it. I kept looking for nettles. I had eaten so many of them that they no longer had the slightest effect on me. My tongue scarcely swelled up at all. As luck would have it, I found some leftover sugar beet which the farmers had not considered worth-while gathering. It was caked in mud and decomposing. This, I must tell you, was caviar. But the outcome of this feast was dreadful diarrhoea. Where the diarrhoea came from, I'll never know, I had not had a real drink for days.'[8]

Conditions were now so appalling that the bodies of those who had died in the night were lying on the floor of the wagons in which so many prisoners had still to travel. 'I climbed back on the train,' Michael Etkind recalled, 'and, together with my fellow travellers, piled up the dead to make a bench for us to sit on.

'Beside me sat a ginger-haired boy and we talked in Yiddish. He spoke a beautiful Yiddish, in the Vilna dialect. He looked about twelve years old but he could easily have been fifteen. What did we talk about? Only about our regret at leaving Buchenwald. During one of our stops, we had heard that the day after we began this dreadful journey, Buchenwald had been liberated. You can imagine the agony (we did not know that the Americans arrived too late for most of the Jewish prisoners there. The Germans had taken them out into the forests and shot them). We talked for a while, and then I realised that he had gone all quiet. He was dead. Out like a light.'[9]

Among the Jews marched out of Buchenwald on 5 April 1945 was thirteen-year-old Sevek Finkelstein. 'About this time my father was dying in his barrack,' he recalled. 'We were marching on a paved road and around us I could see the pretty German countryside. It was a beautiful spring day and I could see the flowers in blossom and everything growing. I felt good to be outside the camp and in the country. No one seemed to care about what might happen to us. We had given up a long time ago caring much about anything. We knew that the American army was just a few miles away but as far as I was concerned they, the Americans, could be back in Washington, it had no effect on me. I think that by then I was just a robot doing the next thing to stay alive. I had

---

[8] Salek Orenstein, 'Beyond Belief, A Survivor's Story', manuscript, sent to the author, 1995.
[9] Michael Etkind, ' "Youth" Remembered', manuscript, sent to the author, 4 January 1996.

no will-power or choices of my own. Later on it was always strange to hear Americans talk of choices.

'Next to me walked a young man and his father. The boy was not much older than, maybe, eighteen, and his father in his early forties. I think that they were Hungarian, they had recently come into the war, and they were totally unprepared for the hardships. We Polish Jews were hardened veterans. The father turned to the son after we had walked half an hour and told him that he could walk no further. The son pleaded with the father to walk on, it was not much further to the railroad station in Weimar. The father walked on a little longer, leaning on the son; but, after a short while, he stopped and told his son that he could not walk another step, he was totally exhausted and just wanted to fall into the ditch at the side of the road. Again the son was pleading with his father not to fall into the ditch, as we heard shots being fired by the rear guards into the people who fell into the ditch. 'The father with all his remaining strength tore himself away from his son, and with his hand covering his face he was uttering "Shema! Israel" ("Hear! O Israel") as he threw himself into the roadside ditch. The son was frantically calling to his father to get up. The German guard was standing over the father with his rifle pointed. He patiently waited to see if the father would get up. I heard the firing of the rifle as we continued to walk.'[10]

Moniek Goldberg was not quite seventeen when he was taken to Buchenwald from the slave labour camp at Krawinkel, and then, with several Russian prisoners of war who had been with him at Krawinkel, put, after only one night at Buchenwald, on the train to Theresienstadt. 'I have difficulty in describing what I witnessed on that transport,' he later wrote. 'We were given no food or water. In the beginning we were so crowded that in some wagons they used to throw people off to make room. But the problem of overcrowding was quickly eased as people died daily. When there was an air raid they allowed us to scatter into the surrounding fields. I continued to stay close to the Russians.

'One day, as we ran into the fields in the middle of nowhere we discovered a building full of grain. A huge heap of wheat. We broke through the windows and scooped wheat into the blankets we were carrying. That saved my life. On my wagon, there were three people I knew, two of whom were from Kozienice – Shapiro and Kalb – and David Slawecki of Kielce whom I knew from the slave labour camp at Pionki.

'Kalb was shot to death during a strafing from the air. Shapiro was extremely ill and near death. Years later, in Michigan, at my son's Bar

---

[10] Sidney Finkel (Finkelstein), 'My Story', manuscript, sent to the author, 12 September 1995.

Mitzvah, David Slawecki thanked me by taking the microphone and telling those guests assembled how I had shared the wheat with him and helped him survive.'[11]

Howard Chandler, then sixteen years old, remembered the day on which he, and many thousands of other Jewish slave labourers, were marched out of Buchenwald. 'We marched to the city of Weimar,' he wrote, 'where we were given two days of rations. We were packed on to an open freight train and shuffled to and fro, depending which way the front was moving. There were about three thousand prisoners on this transport, mostly Russian prisoners of war. We shuffled like this for four weeks, on two days of rations, and it took a very heavy toll. It was the worst time ever since entering the camps and the first time I saw cannibalism take place.

'When we were near the end of the journey and the war was coming to an end, we were near Terezin[12] in Czechoslovakia and people were throwing bread and other food to us. By then I was so weak and indifferent that it hardly mattered, after having been badly beaten up for committing sabotage. Czech partisans took pictures of our transport and some of our boys can clearly be identified at the end when we got to Terezin. There were only about five to six hundred left alive out of about three thousand prisoners.'[13]

Krulik Wilder was on this same train. 'The journey was a nightmare,' he later wrote. 'The trucks were open and it was freezing cold. The guards were at the end of the train watching us, so that we would not escape. Every morning we checked who was alive or dead to make more room for us. We threw the dead out of the truck. It was a very slow journey, stopping and starting every few miles. We stopped occasionally to get off and receive some food which consisted of a soup which was so bad we thought that the Germans wanted to poison us.'[14]

Solly Irving, who was only fourteen years old in April 1945, remembered that same night when everyone on the march was given some soup. 'It had a terrible taste and was very strong. Although we were starving, many of us took one sip and left it. During the night a lot of people who had eaten the soup died. We saw trucks pull up, and the dead were just thrown out. I also saw some German soldiers looking at the dead bodies and pulling out their gold teeth. Some men weren't quite

[11] Joseph (Moniek) Goldberg, 'Biographical Sketch', manuscript, July 1995, letter to the author, 14 August 1995.

[12] The Czech form of Theresienstadt.

[13] Howard Chandler (Chaim Wajchendler), letter to the author, 23 February 1995. One of the photographs which Howard Chandler mentions is reproduced here as plate 6.

[14] Israel (Krulik) Wilder, 'Krulik's Story', manuscript, sent to the author, 1 January 1995.

dead, but they pulled out their gold teeth just the same.'[15]

Perec Zylberberg was also on the deportation train from Buchenwald to Theresienstadt. On one of the days, he recalled, 'after several hours of moving, we came to a full stop. We were told to disembark. We were taken in small parties by our guard to a nearby lake. There we were told to drink in any way we could. I crouched at the water's edge and just like an animal, slurped with my tongue the small dose of water that I could find. There was not too much that I could get that way. I helped myself with my cupped hands. The awful thirst subsided. We still had to see to our natural needs. These functions had to be done in a great hurry. As soon as one group was watered the other was taken. It did not take too long to lead all the prisoners to the water. It was already afternoon. We were packed into the carriages again. Very slowly we moved forward. It seemed that we were not going forward too far. We kept on going backward quite often. Wherever we were, we did not know.'[16]

As the journey continued, the train with the evacuees from Buchenwald made its way through the hilly farmland of Thuringia to the industrial regions of Saxony. 'We passed through bombed-out cities,' Perec Zylberberg wrote. 'The sight of Chemnitz was probably as close a picture of destruction as doomsday prophets paint. We could see from the open cars a complete city destroyed. One could see from the railway lines right across the bombed-out shells of buildings, to the other side of the city. There just were not any houses that looked like inhabited places. Just skeletons and charred ruins. It warmed our hearts. We could see the work of the Allies at firsthand. All our thoughts were on the just retribution that was coming down on the heads of the hated Nazis.

'This awesome sight did not ease our nagging hunger and thirst. But we felt an inner thrust of hopefulness. We stopped just outside this bombed-out city. We quenched our thirst and again made do with some leaves and bark from young trees. At this stop, we watched a dive-bomb attack on another train that was full of army men and women. The bombers dived one after the other, spraying bombs and shrapnel on the train next to ours. We were allowed to hide under our car. There were lots of casualties among the soldiers. We also saw one aircraft hit. I am not sure what the situation was on our transport. That scene, plus the sight of the bombed-out Chemnitz, gave us a clue as to the war and its atmosphere. The Allied bombers must have seen our train. At times we could see the pilots of the diving planes. They did not shoot at us. At

---

[15] Solly Irving (Shloime Zalman Judensznajder), 'Memories of a Past', manuscript, sent to the author, 5 April 1995.
[16] Perec Zylberberg, recollections, diary entry for 26 September 1993.

long last we could almost feel that we were not alone and abandoned. We moved on. For the first time in several days we got some crusts of bread, and some soup.

'The lot of the prisoners on our transport was getting desperate. There were already many dead from exposure, hunger and illnesses. We were, in a way, getting out of the picture. I too felt the end was coming. I could feel a numbness in my whole being. We came to the Czechoslovakian border. Somehow there were fewer German faces and the language was sounding closer to Polish. We were told that we were in Czechoslovakia. It was a relief to hear it.'[17]

Harry Spiro was on a death march from the slave labour camp at Rehmsdorf. It was a march during which, he later wrote, 'the only rule was that you couldn't be left behind; you could sit down if you wanted, but by the time the end of the column arrived, if you didn't get up you were shot'. On one occasion during the march, the whole column was forced off the road to take cover during an air raid. 'I ended up in a field, and found two white beetroots which I quickly dug up and put under my shirt. I was carefully eating slices from the beetroot, when one of the others came up to me and said, "I can see you've got some food. If you don't give me some I'll let everyone know". I knew that meant I would be crushed in the rush to get food, so I gave him some. A few minutes later he came back again and I gave him some more. When he came back for a third time I showed him my knife and said, "If you come back again I'll kill you". He stayed away after that – and to this day we are firm friends.'[18]

That other boy was Harry Balsam. He was not yet sixteen. He too has vivid recollections of that final journey. 'About late March,' he recalled, 'again we were put into little trucks, we travelled for about two to three days. We came to Marienbad station, where our train was bombed and machine-gunned by the Russian air force, about a thousand were killed. Amongst the dead I saw some German guards also dead. I ran into the station where the stationmaster lived as there was a bunker built there. There was a lot of food stored there. It was very dark as there was a blackout. The Germans were frightened because they could hear the grenades. I was stuffing myself with food and was not taking any notice of the grenades or machine-guns. I was more interested in grabbing tins of meat and beans and whatever else I could, but, when I came out with the tins stuffed in my pockets, the inmates noticed and they jumped on me and threw me to the ground. They cut my coat from the back as

[17] Perec Zylberberg, recollections, diary entry for 27 September 1993.
[18] Harry Spiro, recollections, letter to the author, 21 March 1995.

I was lying on the ground and took most of my tins away. I was lucky they did not cut my body as well. The German guards stopped them, but by then I had very few left.

'Then they rounded us up again and started marching us on foot with no food or water. All the time the prisoners were being shot, as they could not walk fast enough or had no more energy to walk. When they stopped, the guards shot them. During the nights we were packed into barns.

'From Germany we crossed over the Sudetenland mountains into Czechoslovakia. On one occasion when we stopped overnight they gave us bread. One loaf of bread to share out between eight people. While they were cutting it into eight pieces one of them took two pieces and I had none. I was not very happy about it, so I jumped on the back of the policeman and pinched a whole loaf and immediately started eating the bread. I did not get a chance to swallow a piece before he came for me and started kicking and beating me with his truncheon till it broke. Then the German guard came in and he started kicking me and beating me with his rifle butt (it wasn't until 1984 that I found out that my nose had been shattered in the attack, at which time I had it repaired).

'They left me unconscious in a pool of blood and they left me for dead. In the morning I woke up and I was soaked in blood. My friend Pomeranc helped me to stand on my feet and I carried on marching. A few days later I was on my last legs. A man approached me and asked me if I would ask the German guard to give me a piece of bread for his golden teeth. I had nothing to lose any more, so I approached him and he said yes. I gave him the man's gold teeth and he gave me four slices of bread, so I had two and I gave the man two pieces. He was very pleased with the transaction, and so was I.

'On another occasion, I suddenly noticed a boy a little bigger than me run to the verge of the road. He picked something up. I went over to him and asked for a piece. It was a beetroot. He told me to buzz off. I told him that if he did not give me a piece I would tell the others and they would take it all away from him and cut him up in pieces, because we were all starving by then, so he gave me a small piece. I ate it up in one second. When I then went back for more he reluctantly gave me another piece. This boy is today my best friend. His name is Harry Spiro.

'On another occasion I saw something lying at the edge of the road. It was a raw potato. I ran over to it and picked it up. The guard thought I was running away and took a shot at me as I was bending down. He hit the back of my hand with a bullet. He only grazed the top of it, but the mark on my hand is still visible.

'We marched for about three weeks. When we started in Rehmsdorf there were about three thousand of us. When we arrived in Theresienstadt there were only six hundred survivors.'[19]

Aron Zylberszac was also on the train from Rehmsdorf to Theresienstadt. 'Despite the fact that the trains were needed to move troops and equipment,' he later wrote, 'they were commandeered to move us. I can never understand the German mentality in wanting to hang on to us at all costs. They considered us no better than useless rubbish – bodies to kill and torture at any time – without any provocation. Yet here we were, just skin and bones, and they just could not leave us behind. We were more important than their own soldiers. They took us, including dead bodies, to Theresienstadt. I didn't know this at the time.

'Throughout the journey the train was bombed by either the American or Russian forces. During one of these raids several of us ran into the woods to escape the bombing and hopefully get away. Unfortunately we were confronted by a forester with a gun. He was a very old man and there were ten or twelve of us. Had we been strong enough we could have blown him over. But as it was, we were so mentally dehumanised and physically weak that we submitted to his orders. Again as an example of mental attitudes – he said that if he could not get us back to where we had escaped he would have to shoot us. In his mind we were just like vermin – some sort of disease that must be eliminated. Once again I was spared from death. After a mile or two we came to the train. You just could not believe the sight, there were thousands of bodies spread everywhere. Not only those from our camp but during the journey they had attached trucks from Buchenwald and other camps. We had to collect all these mangled bodies and load them on the train, arms, legs, heads – every little piece. We loaded up wagon upon wagon with all these bits of bodies to be taken away. After this task was completed we were marched on to catch up with the others and eventually arrived at Thercsienstadt.'[20]

Morris Frenkel, originally from Lodz, had been deported with his family to Auschwitz. His family had been murdered there. When, four months later, Auschwitz was evacuated, he was taken by train to the concentration camp at Gross Rosen. Fifty years later he recalled the cry of the Polish prisoners when the Jewish transport arrived: 'The dirty Jews are here'.

From Gross Rosen, Morris Frenkel's transport was taken on to Dachau. There, in the third week of April, as American forces entered Bavaria, the Germans, he later wrote, 'called all Jews to report at the main gate.

[19] Harry Balsam, letter to the author, 8 May 1995.
[20] Aron Zylberszac, recollections, transcript, Imperial War Museum Sound Archives, February 1991.

We were told that we would journey to Switzerland, and there be exchanged for German prisoners of war. This, of course, turned out not to be true. Instead we were taken to Innsbruck, from where we had to march up into the mountains to a small village. There, the SS and the mayor, with other villagers, talked all night while we were left standing outside the town hall.

'The following morning we were marched down from the mountain to the station, from where we returned to Dachau. As the railway line had been damaged by bombing, the SS took us to a forest where we stayed all day and night. During the night, however, the SS ran away. We were left on our own and decided to spread out in the forest in small groups until American soldiers arrived a few days later. Quite suddenly we were free.

'Later, we found out from the mayor of the village that the SS had intended to kill us on the mountain and dispose of our bodies. But the mayor and the villagers had not allowed this to happen because of their fear of the approaching Americans.

'This is part of my life's story, a part which still seems a miracle to me.'[21]

The last concentration camp that was not within reach of Allied troops was Theresienstadt. Once it had been much publicised by the Nazis as their 'model ghetto', but almost all its original inhabitants – who had been brought there from Germany, Austria, Bohemia and Moravia between 1941 and 1943 – had died of starvation, or been deported to death camps. In April 1945 this eighteenth-century garrison town had become the final destination of the deportation trains and death marches from Buchenwald, Rehmsdorf, Schlieben, Colditz and other camps in Germany. In the chaos of the constant movement of the front lines and battle zones, the deportation trains had often been forced to retrace their tracks, or to halt for many hours at a time, uncertain if the way ahead was clear.

Still the journeys continued. 'For all those prisoners who were already on the transport for close to two weeks,' Perec Zylberberg wrote, 'life was ebbing away, with hardly any food, and unprotected from the still chilly spring weather. I remember things as if they were filtered through a net. Nothing that comes through now or in the previous forty odd years since that time is very clear-cut. At best there is a sort of fog enveloping the days and nights of that period. I remember moving around, but not the reasons why. Grass and leaves and bark were the materials that often filled my mouth. If there is a pre-ending period, this

[21] Morris Frenkel, 'The miracle in my life', *Journal of the '45 Aid Society*, No. 18, December 1994.

must have been the time that the whole transport was either moving forward or sideways or backward or standing still. We lost count of days and nights. Life, as one knows it, is a continuous chain of interlocking events, even when one period and another don't always have a direct or rational link. There is motion in life, and there is continuity, both in thoughts and deeds. From a rational point of view, we are gathering impressions and reactions as we travel on our life's road of experiences.

'If I have managed to convey my observations of the periods of life under German occupation, then our existence in those two weeks of being nowhere in particular was actually a break in the motion of life. I vaguely remember events and even some of the people around me. One such event was the stop in the middle of a field. There were some plants growing there. They could have been potatoes or beets or carrots. There were many guards on the perimeter around us. They were behind machine-gun nests. Prisoners of war and the other prisoners were mingling aimlessly on the field. I tried to sneak away and grab a shoot of some vegetable plant. I almost got to it, when a guard yelled out to get away from the plant. I froze. I only recall some Russian prisoners trying to plead on my behalf with the guardsman. I am alive today. I don't know to this day how or why they helped me. I can't forget that incident, even though everything else that happened on the transport is all so misty.

'I don't remember getting any food in the last days of that hellish journey. Eventually we must have arrived at a town. There were yells and commands. We disembarked. I remember hearing of maybe half our number dead. I even heard words to the effect of some dead people having been cannibalised. I didn't see those things myself. I don't recall anybody whom I could identify by name or looks, that had seen it himself. But I clearly remember hearing of it then.'[22]

Another of those who made that terrible journey from Buchenwald to Theresienstadt was Arek Hersh. As the train began its journey, he later recalled, 'liberation, which had been in all our minds, now seemed far away again. I was tired, hungry, cold and miserable; I felt half-dead. I was only sixteen years old, but I had seen some of the worst horrors man had perpetrated upon man.' He too recalled the details of that journey, which so few survived. One of the wagons, he wrote, 'had been reserved especially for the dead. As our bodies were nothing but bones from malnutrition, the wagon soon filled up. Every day we watched as more and more bodies were thrown into the wagon, and when the train stopped at a quiet place they buried the bodies to make room for more.

[22] Perec Zylberberg, recollections, diary entry for 28 September 1993.

On the third afternoon we were all given a piece of bread – what joy! – and a cup of black coffee as a bonus.

'We passed towns and villages where everything was so green and healthy, saw people walking freely, well-fed cows and horses grazing in the fields. How picturesque it all looked, how glittering the rivers and lush the forests. It provided a stark contrast to our own situation – packed into a railway wagon, dying a slow death. I made a large hole in the side of the wagon with a knife so that I could look out and see where we were going. Once again the train came to a stop and everybody was ordered out. I saw two houses half a kilometre away. I said to Natek and another boy with whom we had become friendly called Yakub, "Wouldn't it be marvellous if we could make a run for it and hide until the train has left?" It was a tempting thought, but we would never have made it. We had no papers, and the roads were full of Hitler Youth and police.

'We ran into the fields to urinate, but the SS men kept a very close watch on us. They allowed us out for two hours. I decided to pick some grass and get some twigs to make a fire and try to cook it. After about ten minutes I had a good fire going, which I surrounded with stones. My friend Yakub and I started cooking the grass, but we had to keep a good eye out in case somebody tried to grab it from us. This is what hunger had reduced us to. After eating the grass we found we couldn't digest it; it just sat in our stomachs. It gave us both stomach ache, but at least we didn't feel hungry any more. Soon the guards were shouting, "Schnell! Raus!" and ordered us back on the train. We hadn't even been able to have a proper wash because there had been no facilities.

'I looked around me and saw lice crawling all over people's bodies. I was no different; I was alive with lice myself. Some people were absolutely covered from head to foot in these creatures. Lice was just one of the many horrors we suffered, though in some ways it was the worst.

'We were now able to sit down at night as several older people in our wagon had been transferred elsewhere. Each night more people died. The dew was slowly getting worse, and every morning we were wet through, cold and hungry. One morning we stopped at a small station. I hoped the SS would bring us food as I was so hungry. As soon as they let us off the train, I ran to get more grass to eat, but about half an hour later the Germans brought us some bread. I put my finger down my throat and vomited the grass up, then ate the bread ravenously. We stayed at that particular station for a few hours.

'As night fell we all had to climb back on to the wagon and stand all night. About midnight we heard the sound of guards walking outside, then our wagon door was pulled open and we were all told to climb down. We saw to our delight large containers with soup. We were all given some and like hungry vultures we devoured it quickly. The soup, however, was horribly salty. It was so bad that it burned our stomachs, and the SS would give us no water to quench our terrible thirst. The train started moving again, and next morning we stopped near a river. As soon as we were let off the train, we raced down to the river to drink. The water was not very clean, but who cared? In our condition it tasted wonderful.

'As we were drinking, the SS guards began, without warning, to open fire on us. In all they killed ten people. We never received any explanation for this sudden, murderous action. Most likely the guards were just bored and had shot at us for sport. Back we climbed on to the train and the nightmare journey continued. People were dying with more frequency now, their bodies, little more than skeletons, being thrown out of the wagon. I felt anguish for them, thinking, "If only they could have lasted out a little longer, they would have been free". I heard a noise in the sky, engines roaring overhead, and looking up I saw the sky slowly filling with bombers. Everything seemed to tremble on the ground from the sound of the planes.

'Soon the anti-aircraft guns opened up and started firing in all directions. We all knew that the bombers had not come just to rescue us, but the spectacle was uplifting nevertheless. As we watched, we saw smoke start to pour from one of the planes which had obviously been hit. Slowly the bomber separated itself from the rest of the formation and started to spiral down slowly, engulfed by fire. Suddenly the plane exploded and fell towards the ground. The crew had died, but at least they had fought as free men.

'One day one of our men brought the news that Buchenwald had been liberated by the Americans on Wednesday, 11 April 1945. This was only nine days after we had been marched out. We had been the last transport to leave. It was as if a knife had been put through our hearts. All the people who had stayed behind had been liberated. We spoke in terms of dejection at this cruel piece of luck. It was difficult, after such a twist of fate, to go on hoping. I looked around at the boys in our wagon. We were now all so thin there seemed to be no life in us. I wondered then if any of us would last out. I thought, "But who knows what will happen next? We have nothing to lose. Hope is the only thing we have left."

'Again the train stopped and again we were let out. All too soon, however, the guards were shouting to us to get back on board once more. We had now been travelling for ten days, but each day seemed like a year. After a while it started to rain. It was only light, but even so we were soon drenched. We were open to all weathers, nothing to cover ourselves with, exposed and vulnerable, cold and hungry. I looked up at the sky. There had been little opportunity for prayer or the practice of any faith since the time I had left the Lodz ghetto. Now, however, I did find myself talking to God. I said, "If you are up there in Heaven, why don't you help us?" I found myself asking God to tell me what crime I had committed in my life for which I was being punished. I was only sixteen years old when I asked God this. "I have suffered more than most people of ninety," I protested to him. "And my only sin is being born of Jewish parents." It is likely that my parents would have disapproved of my speaking to God in this way, but I was desperate and dejected. I sat in the corner of the wagon and wept.'

Then came a moment that once more gave hope. Arek Hersh was sitting next to a Hungarian SS guard, an elderly man. 'He murmured something about Hitler, but I couldn't hear properly because of the noise of the train. Ten minutes later he told me, "It won't be long. You will soon be free." I looked at him with bewilderment, not believing what he was saying. He told me Hitler was dead. Somehow I knew he wasn't lying to me. I never told anybody until we stopped at the next station, and then I told some of the boys and the news spread like wildfire.

'If Hitler was dead, the German army would not fight on and the war would soon be at an end. Thank God! We had made it! We came to a station called Neisse, in the Eger region. On the other line some women from another camp were being transported elsewhere, but they didn't know where to. I climbed up on to one of the wagons and looked in. Before my eyes was a whole wagon full of dead bodies, all women, all unclothed, just skeletons. I was sickened by the sight.'[23]

Michael Etkind also remembered the moment when it became known that Hitler was dead, the first intimation of the Führer's fate being an overheard whispered conversation between of their two armed guards. 'This news spread rapidly,' he later wrote. 'That day we did not march so far. We were lying in yet another barn. The doors were open on to a field and the guards were sitting outside. One could sense their mood from a distance. Suddenly our "joker" friend, whose repertoire was inexhaustible, jumped up and began to dance. "Ich hab ubergelebt Hitler, was mehr darf ich?" – "I have outlived Hitler, what more do I want?" he was shouting at the top of his voice, in Yiddish, as he ran out into the field. The German, who understood every word, raised his gun. The joker looked like a puppet whose string had been cut as he fell some twenty yards away from the open doors.'[24]

[23] Arek Hersh (Herszlikowicz), 'My journey from Buchenwald to Theresienstadt', manuscript, sent to the author, 1995.

[24] Michael Etkind, ' "Youth" Remembered', manuscript, sent to the author, 4 January 1996.

Although Hitler's death marked a turning-point in the final phase of the war, the killing of Jews did not end. Arek Hersh recalled how, after the news became known, the train, on which he and several thousand Jewish captives from Buchenwald were being deported, continued on its slow, painful way, wending to the east and south. Its guards were now almost the only soldiers left who were willing to shoot and kill for the Third Reich. At one of the stops, Arek Hersh's friend Meier, a Jewish boy from Vilna, was shot in the shoulder by an SS man; through lack of any medical treatment, he died.

Four days after learning that Hitler was dead, recalled Arek Hersh, 'we came to a railway station in a place called Roudnice. After about ten minutes we were ordered to get off the train. I saw that on the platform were several Czechoslovakian policemen, young fellows who came over to talk to us and ask us where we had come from. They saw our starved bodies and the horror of our conditions on the train, and seemed unable to believe that such a thing could be happening. Some of them wept in front of us. We stood and watched them silently. They asked us if we would like some food, and we begged them to give us some. One of the policemen went away to get it.

'When he returned we did not snatch it from him, but just held out our hands. I saw that on the other side of the transport another policeman was giving boys some bread and meat. One of the Ukrainian SS guards also saw this, and he turned his rifle round to get hold of the barrel to hit one of the starving boys over the head. A Czech policeman saw what was happening and drew his revolver. He pointed it at the SS guard and said, "If you touch this child, I will shoot you." I saw the SS guard immediately put his rifle down and walk away. We realised that something we had never seen before was happening: an SS guard had taken orders from someone else.

'Soon after that the Czech policemen rounded up all the SS guards and took them away. It was said later that they had shot them. Our train was slowly taken into Theresienstadt.'[25]

Zisha Schwimmer, whose seventeenth birthday took place at the very start of that terrible journey, also recalled its final days. 'After nearly a month on this transport,' he later wrote, 'the German guards were disarmed (although we did not know this at the time), and we were put on different wagons, that is, those who were still alive. For twenty hours we travelled without any food, in non-stop, pouring rain. We lost our power of speech from being exposed to the elements for so long.

'At last the train stopped one station before Theresienstadt. Sitting at

---

[25] Arek Hersh (Herszlikowicz), 'My journey from Buchenwald to Theresienstadt', manuscript, sent to the author, 1995.

one point during the second week of our journey for twenty-four hours, without moving and without food, had taken its toll. We could hardly move, but we managed to look out, and we could hardly believe our eyes at what we saw. There were lots of people with bread and plates of cakes in their hands. I tried to shout greetings to them but no words came out of my mouth. Not everybody managed to get bread or cake from these kind people. It was a sight I shall never forget in my whole life. The feeling of being liberated after more than five years of living hell. It took some time to sink in.

'Thanks to the Czechoslovakian people rising against the Germans twenty-four hours earlier, we had this marvellous reception at this station. The sight was unbelievable. Of the eight thousand people that set out on this transport, only six hundred survived. The rest perished from hunger and exposure to the elements on the way from Buchenwald.

'After a while we managed to move about. All of the people in my wagon were young, in their teens, and most of us managed to survive. Because of our age we were more resistant to disease. After a while, my friend and I decided to get off the train. We were barely able to move but we managed to do it. We had some potatoes hidden in our trousers, which, a few days earlier, we had managed to get from some Czech homes, with the help of a kindly German guard. So we decided to bake them. We found some wood, and managed to make a bonfire and bake some of those potatoes.'[26]

Henry Golde was seventeen when he was taken from the slave labour camp at Colditz – within sight of the castle in which so many British prisoners of war and escapers were being held – on a death march. He later recalled his feelings as more and more of the marchers collapsed and died on the way, or were shot. 'I couldn't believe I was still alive with people all around me dying, one after another. But still I lived. I wondered why. Many times I thought the people who were dying were better off – no more hunger, no more fear, no more struggle to survive for them, but I was still going.

'There were times when I was ready to give up and I told myself: "Who needs this stinking life? It is not even a life, it's a human misery of the worst kind. Give up, it's no use, in the end they will kill you, they will kill all of us, give up, give up". But at the last moment, a feeling would come over me and I would think: "Where there's life there's hope", and so I went on. Every morning when I awoke, I wondered if this was going to be the last one, would I make it through the day,

---

[26] Jack (Zisha) Schwimmer, 'The War Memoirs of Z. Schwimmer', manuscript, sent to the author, 6 October 1994.

what would the day hold for me? Stay alive, stay alive! What a challenge, but day after day I survived.'[27]

Among the other boys on this death march from the slave labour camp at Colditz was Natek Wald. His friend Ben Helfgott, who had last seen him less than six months earlier when they were deported from the Bugaj labour camp in Piotrkow, recalled the moment when the remnants of the Colditz marchers reached Theresienstadt. 'I thought I saw a ghost. Nat was completely emaciated and gasping for food. "Give me something to eat!" he said. "Give me something to eat!" '[28]

Ben Helfgott had been comparatively fortunate. Two separate trains had left the slave labour camp at Schlieben for Theresienstadt. The train which had left before his had taken two weeks on the journey, 'and when they arrived there were many dead'. In his train, or at least in his wagon, the German guards were not the ogres of so many camps and marches. 'We had two older SS men and they were reasonably nice,' he recalled. 'They took half the wagon to themselves, but let a few boys go on their side. When we stopped on the Czech side of the border they went to the local farmers with two prisoners and brought back some food from a farm. One of the SS men came from Berlin. He gave me his address in Berlin. He said, "When the war is over, come to visit me in Charlottenstrasse".'[29]

One of the survivors of the Rehmsdorf train deportation was Menachem Silberstein. When the bombing of the train had begun at Marienbad station, he later wrote, 'I personally had no power to leave the train. I stayed on, and then I saw that the SS men had left their bags. I looked in and found a whole loaf of bread and a sausage. I ate it all up. It gave me some energy. I left the train and headed for the village. I came to the first house – a farm. I took some chickens, tore them apart, and ate the livers. Today as I think about it, I know that it gave me the power to carry on.

'They gathered us at a point from which we started our march on foot. At that time there were no more trains. This march took about twelve to fourteen days. No food, no water. Every few minutes we heard a shot and knew that one of us was killed. So every day we were fewer and fewer. There were more guards than prisoners. On the way, everything that was green or alive was eaten by us. We ate grass. We peeled the skin off trees and ate it. I remember once I even swallowed live little frogs.'[30]

---

[27] H. Golde, 'It seems like only yesterday', *Journal of the '45 Aid Society*, No. 18, December 1994.

[28] Ben Helfgott, in conversation with the author, 16 February 1996.

[29] Ben Helfgott, in conversation with the author, 26 September 1994.

[30] Menachem (Mendel) Silberstein, letter to the author, 29 April 1996.

Arthur Poznanski, then aged seventeen, had been in slave labour camps at Schlieben and Flössberg. 'With each transfer,' he recalled, 'living and working conditions deteriorated and starvation got more acute.' From Flössberg the slave labourers were to be taken by train to Mauthausen, in Austria. 'To throw off the chains binding me to the beneficent ministrations of the German Nazis, whom I suspected of planning a magnificent funeral pyre for us all,' Poznanski later wrote, 'I jumped out of the cattle truck taking us from Flössberg to Mauthausen when the train was passing the hilly regions of Czechoslovakia. My only witness to this is Alec Ward, a member of our Society.[31] Shot and wounded while trying to escape, I found that the spoon I carried in my trouser pocket saved my leg and probably my life too. Unable to walk, I crawled to the nearest village where I had the good fortune to come across Czech partisans who saved me by hiding me in a barn while the Germans looked for escapers.'[32]

Arthur Poznanski was liberated by American troops. Alec Ward, who had witnessed his escape, recalled how, for fifteen days, the other prisoners from Flössberg had been taken by train, backward and forward, with hardly any food and water. Many of them died. 'Our wagon included thirty young boys,' he later wrote. 'After realising that we were unlikely to survive the journey, we organised an escape party. A number had jumped the train and I was supposed to be the eighteenth. However, in order to deter further escapes the SS guards put a few bodies (those of boys who had just been shot) into our wagon, together with a German guard for the rest of the journey. My friend the singer – Arthur Poznanski – was one of the boys who jumped the train and was shot by the guard who was perched between the wagons. This was an unbearable blow to me, just like the earlier loss of my little brother.

'Many more prisoners died marching up to the camp, which was built in Alpine mountains with the purpose of exposing prisoners to extremes of temperature. Undernourished people could not survive such conditions for long. How I envied my little brother and my close friend the singer. They were dead and did not have to suffer any more. Those of us who reached Mauthausen concentration camp alive went through further torture and degradation. They took our clothes away from us on arrival, and we were left naked until we were liberated by the American forces on 5 May 1945.'[33]

The death marches were the final phase of the Holocaust, a period of

---

[31] The '45 Aid Society, see Chapter 23.
[32] Arthur Poznanski, recollections, letter to the author, 24 January 1995.
[33] Alec Ward, 'My Story', manuscript, sent to the author, 31 May 1995.

suffering which the boys remember with dread. Their loved ones had been murdered, most of them two or three years earlier. Their experiences of slave labour had weakened and frightened them. It was more than five years since they had known anything they could call a home, family life, security, childhood itself. As the death marches ended, overtaken by the Allied forces, those marchers who were still alive were at the very limit of their capacity to survive.

CHAPTER 10

Theresienstadt

FOR MOST OF the boys, Theresienstadt was to be the final camp in a two- and even three-year saga that had taken them to many other camps. It was the end of a road along which every mile had been agony. In this former 'model' ghetto, which Hitler had praised as an ideal for Jewish settlement, more than 33,000 German, Austrian and Czechoslovak Jews had died between 1941 and 1944 of malnutrition and disease. A further 88,000 had been deported to death camps and murdered. The place itself was an attractive eighteenth-century garrison town. Each of its sturdy brick barracks had been named after a German town – Hamburg, Dresden, etc. For the survivors of the death marches who arrived there in 1945, Theresienstadt, one of the very few camps still under German rule, was a dumping ground. There was nowhere else in the rapidly dwindling area under German control in which anyone could be held captive. By the last day of April 1945 more than 15,000 death marchers had been deposited there.

Aron Zylberszac, who had survived the Lodz ghetto and Auschwitz with his older brother Iser, having lost his brother Velvel (Wolf) in Chelmno, recalled how, as the train which had brought them from Rehmsdorf was nearing Theresienstadt, 'my brother died in my arms from dysentery. He faded away to nothing. A man who was a giant died a skeleton. I held him in my arms when he died. There was just nothing I could do. When I think about it, I sometimes blame myself. He did so much to keep me alive. I feel that had he saved some of that energy for himself he would have had a better chance to survive. I was so low physically and mentally I felt there was just nothing to live for, and I put myself on one of the carts with the dead bodies. I must have become unconscious. It was only when they were removing the dead bodies that they discovered there was still some life left in my body. They transferred me to the hospital, and that is where I found myself when I eventually regained consciousness.'[1]

Seventeen-year-old Shimon Klin from Zdunska Wola was among those slave labourers brought to Theresienstadt by train from Schlieben. 'While we were being led through the ghetto,' he recalled, 'Czech Jews watching

[1] Aron Zylberszac, recollections, transcript, Imperial War Museum Sound Archives, February 1991.

from their windows dropped down for us lumps of sugar tied to pieces of string, and waved and called out to us. We were surprised to see how well they looked in comparison with us. They seemed well-fed and they wore suits and ties; we, on the other hand, wore the concentration camp pyjamas; our feet were swollen, our faces drawn. I was sent to live in a barrack together with other young people. Every day food was brought to us: thick soup, meat, vegetables and some bread.'[2]

Fifteen-year-old Ben Helfgott from Piotrkow, who had also been brought from Schlieben, later recalled: 'Two weeks after reaching the camp I learned that my father had been killed only a few days before, trying to run away from a death transport that was on its way to Theresienstadt by foot. He, and those who tried to run away with him, had been killed by Defenders of the Fatherland, as they were called – Germans in their fifties and sixties who had been called up in the last year of the war. Somebody from my father's march, when he reached Theresienstadt, heard the name Helfgott mentioned, and I was called for. I walked in and the man said to me: "You are a young boy, and I can't hide from you what I know. Your father and a few other people ran away and they were shot. I didn't see it personally. We heard the shots. It may be that he could be alive."

'But for some unknown reason I felt that he had not survived. I was very low at the time. Up to then I was in great spirits. In the three weeks I was in Theresienstadt we didn't go out to work. Although we didn't get enough food, we could regain our strength, as we could make up our lost sleep. We could sleep to our heart's content. My father's death was the biggest blow that ever hit me. I had been with him up to December 1944, when we were separated in Buchenwald. As long as I live, I'll never forget that meeting with the man who told me. He was from Warsaw. I've never been so devastated in my life as when I heard that my father had been killed. The war was almost over. Yet in the last minute his free spirit, his courage, cost him his life. Had he not tried to escape, had he just marched obediently like the rest of the group, we would have been reunited in Theresienstadt. When my mother and my little sister Lusia were killed two and a half years earlier, I was with my father and my sister Mala. I was shattered, but we were able to comfort each other. When I heard the circumstances of my father's death, I was alone.

'I did all my crying then. The boys came up to me and tried to console me. I just cried and cried and cried. It went on for twenty-four hours. I was devastated. My father was thirty-eight years old. What a zest for life he had. You could never hold him back. He was never afraid. I had always such great confidence in my father, he was such an enterprising

---

[2] Shimon Klin, 'Day of Liberation', manuscript, sent to the author, 9 November 1994.

and energetic man, a provider. He could always get out of dangerous situations. I had great faith and belief in him. He was fearless and resourceful. Immediately after our delousing at Buchenwald, he had disappeared, only to reappear with two loaves of bread.

'Most of us survived because of luck, like those who have been shipwrecked in a storm. For most, it was likely that a wave would wash them off the raft. My father never floated off. In spite of the unusual amount of risks that he had taken for more than five and a half years, he somehow didn't allow himself to be washed off the raft. He was lucky. Then, when freedom was so close, his luck ran out.

'Alone, in those final days at Theresienstadt, I had little to eat, but I could rest. I wasn't eaten up by lice. I had clean clothes. I could relax. I could play cards. It was a kind of preparation for normality. Like the others with me, I was anxious that we might be killed by the Germans at the last moment, but we didn't see any German soldiers or SS men.'[3]

Harry Balsam was fifteen when he reached Theresienstadt. He later wrote of how, after a few days in the camp, 'I got ill with typhoid and I was in a very bad way. I remember they gave us a small piece of bread in the morning with black coffee, but I could not eat or drink. I had a very high temperature. We were ten in one room. In three days I accumulated three pieces of bread and kept them under my head. As I could not sleep I heard some of the boys saying, "Let's steal the bread from Balsam, he will not need it any more as he is going to die any minute".

'But I had a very good friend, who was lying next to me, and he shouted out to them that if anyone dared to come near me, he would cut them up with the knife he was holding in his hands, and of course it was Pomeranc to my rescue again. I was ill until the last day of the war. The Russian army walked into the camp and liberated us and it was also the end of World War Two. Ironically I probably would not have survived much longer from the typhoid.'[4]

Pinkus Kurnedz was sixteen when he reached Theresienstadt, after a two-week death march from the Jewish slave labour camp at Colditz. When he arrived, he recalled, 'Somebody said that if you were under thirteen years old you got extra rations. I therefore gave my age as twelve and I did get extra food.'[5]

Moniek Goldberg arrived in Theresienstadt on the death train from Buchenwald. He had been fortunate during a break on that journey to

[3] Ben Helfgott, in conversation with the author, 16 February 1996.
[4] Harry Balsam, 'The Harry Balsam Story', manuscript, sent to the author, 14 November 1995.
[5] Pinkus Kurnedz, recollections, letter to the author, 5 October 1994.

have obtained some wheat from a deserted storehouse. On 5 May 1945 he reached his seventeenth birthday. He was then living in the Hamburger barrack. 'While it was an improvement, in that we were given food,' he recalled, 'it soon turned into a nightmare. People were dying like so many flies. A lot of people had dysentery and were too weak to use the toilets. We could barely distinguish the living from the dead. But the worst of all was the stench. It was unbearable. On the transport people ate grass and whatever else they could lay their hands on. Now it was taking its toll and there were very few who were not ill. I was one of the very few, thanks to the wheat and the tough Russians who protected me from having it taken away.'[6]

On May 1 it had been noted in Theresienstadt that spotted fever had begun to spread from the new arrivals to the earlier deportees. Two days later a delegate of the International Committee of the Red Cross, Paul Dunant, arrived in the camp and took over the protection of its inmates. It was clear that the typhus could soon reach epidemic proportions. On May 4, the day after Dunant's arrival, Czechoslovak health workers entered the camp to try to combat the spread of the disease. The Germans, whose troops still occupied the region around the camp, were still nominally in charge of it, but on May 5 the last SS men left, and, with them, the camp commandant, Karl Rahm, also left.

'We felt that liberation was near,' wrote Shimon Klin, 'but no one knew who our liberators were to be. Some said Americans, others the English, the French or the Russians. Not knowing who our liberators would be, we hoisted first the Stars and Stripes, then the Union Jack, then the Tricolour, and lastly the Red Flag. The flag-changing went on throughout the day. All this time people were dying of typhus.'[7]

Then came the first intimation of liberation. 'One day I was standing near the wire fence with some people,' eighteen-year-old Lipa Tepper recalled, 'when a group of Czech partisans passed and one of them called out to us that the Russians would be there the following morning. I thought it was all a load of rubbish. I did not believe it and I gave it no more thought. I went back to my barracks and went to sleep. The following morning, early on May 9, somebody said to me there was a Russian tank in the camp and I said, "Look, forget about it, you are dreaming". "No," he said. "There really is a Russian tank in camp," and I went out and there it was, a Russian tank with Russian soldiers on it.

'The whole camp started buzzing, and people came out, and the

---

[6] Joseph (Moniek) Goldberg, 'Biographical Sketch', manuscript, July 1995, sent to the author, 14 August 1995.

[7] Shimon Klin, 'Day of Liberation', manuscript, sent to the author, 9 November 1994.

Russians were throwing biscuits. After that a group of people went out to town and they came back with a horse and cart with food and provisions on it. They brought sardines, they brought salami – all sorts of things, and bread. The horse and cart were fallen upon, and people were climbing all over the cart trying to get some food. I managed to get some salami, and I went back to my bunk and sat down and ate it. There seemed to have been a lot of people who ate too many things too quickly, and then a dysentery epidemic broke out in the camp and we were quarantined by the Russians. We were not allowed out, which was a very, very bad thing, because we could not go out to the town to get some food. But people seemed to go under the wire and go out and get food and come back with all different things. We survived anyway.'[8]

Sixteen-year-old Howard Chandler recalled how, on liberation day at Theresienstadt, 'there was jubilation, but most of the prisoners were by then reduced to dazed, walking skeletons, easily falling prey to epidemics and diseases, and since we were not used to eating, we succumbed to diarrhoea after being fed by the soldiers, and that too took its toll. Most of us, however, recovered and after a while we started to search for relatives. In my case, only my brother Harry, who now lives in London, and I survived the ordeal.

'From amongst the Terezin ghetto's population the young ones were assigned to a special youth house where I think we were given special attention by the Russians and recuperated further.'[9]

Krulik Wilder and those who had been deported with him by train from Buchenwald, were still on their train when, having just reached Theresienstadt, 'we heard gunfire and bombing and we realised the war was nearly over'.[10] They were still on the train the next day when Russian soldiers liberated them. Krulik was lucky that liberation took place at that moment and in that place: he already had typhus, and was able to spend the next four weeks in hospital.

Moishe Nurtman had also been brought to Theresienstadt from Buchenwald. 'When I arrived,' he recalled, 'there were Russians all over. We came at night, and somehow in the morning there was a rumour that the war was over. I cannot recollect it precisely. I was overjoyed when I heard it. But it was not like I jumped up and down. It is hard to explain. After many years of torture your mind gets hammered down and the reaction has a different end. You are not ready to absorb it.'[11]

---

[8] Lipa Tepper, letter to the author, 30 January 1996.

[9] Howard Chandler (Chaim Wajchendler), letter to the author, 23 February 1995.

[10] Israel (Krulik) Wilder, 'Krulik's Story', manuscript, sent to the author, 1 January 1995.

[11] Moishe Nurtman, letter to the author, March 1995.

CHAPTER 11

Liberation

THE MOMENT OF liberation, when after so much agony the war was over, and freedom, however precarious, was finally secured, often came slowly to those who contributed their recollections to this book. For some, that moment was hard, even impossible to recognise, coming as it did at a time of severe illness and weakness. For others, who had been victims and slaves for as many as five and a half years, it was difficult to take in – an almost unbelievable moment.

During the final weeks of the war, Michael Etkind had been on a death march through the western Sudetenland. 'The sun was hot when we passed another village,' he recalled. 'White flags were flying from many windows. Our guards had hand-grenades suspended from their belts. "Are they going to toss them at us in the last minute?" passed through my mind.

'Some bullets flew over our heads as we crossed a main road and continued on a minor one. The pace was much slower now, as if the guards no longer knew where they were taking us. They would consult their maps much more frequently. Almost every guard had a "boy", who would carry his rucksack in return for a piece of bread. The bread was not really given in payment for carrying the load, but simply to enable the "boy" to have the strength to do so. Those "boys" were the strongest amongst us. One of the "boys", a friend of mine, turned to me and said: "Keep up your strength now, it won't be long."

'We arrived in another village. We were given nothing to eat, but we stayed there for three days. I found some rotting vegetables in the yard. The only way to find some food was to tell the guard that you needed to go to the toilet and he would reluctantly go behind the barn and turn his head while you were squatting. While doing so I found an almost empty tin of condensed milk. As I was trying to drink the sweet liquid I received a blow with the rifle barrel which I felt for months afterwards.

'We were crawling with body lice. The joke was that if you were to take off your jacket and leave it on the ground, it would slowly walk away. My wooden clogs disintegrated after about two weeks of marching and for almost a month I was barefooted. It was the night of 7 May 1945. For the third night running we were lying in the same barn. Next to me was one of the older men, about thirty-five years of age, breathing irregularly. He began to talk to me. "I know that I will not survive," he said haltingly. "I will never sleep between clean sheets. I will never feel my wife's body again, and I will never eat a piece of bread and butter!" Shortly afterwards his breathing became more irregular and then suddenly it stopped.

'There was moaning, coughing, and groaning going on constantly. We could see the guards' lit-up cigarettes glowing in the dark. They were sitting on chairs near the entrance to the barn. From time to time, when somebody's coughing got on their nerves, they would get up, walk over our bodies in the direction of the offending noise, and silence the offender with a blow from the rifle butt. This would produce the desired effect, but only for a short time.

'We had to get up at dawn. At least ten men were dead, and half that number just could not get up and were shot. We were lined up on the road and counted a number of times. I felt exceedingly weak. I knew that I could not possibly survive another day's march. I had to have some food, but how? I positioned myself near the head of the column. We were about to start marching when suddenly a group of German soldiers appeared. They had no arms and no military insignia. We at once understood what had happened. They must have been captured, or they had surrendered, and were disarmed and told to go somewhere.

'Our guards talked to them for a few minutes. In the meantime the village women and children gathered round to look at us. A boy of about ten was holding a large beetroot in his hands. I had to think fast: "Even if he manages to throw it, which seems doubtful, the chances that I will get it are very small". I stepped out of the line and grabbed the beetroot. As I was stepping back into the line, I felt a swingeing blow to my left ear. The SS man nicknamed "The Dwarf" hit me with the end of the knobbly stick he always carried. I heard ringing in my left ear, the upper part of which seemed stuck. There was sticky blood on my fingers after touching the ear.

'"Achtung, attention, forward march!" We started to march at a fast pace, and going back in the direction from which we had come three days earlier. My head began to spin, and the ringing was still there. I began to fall back, and before long was near the end of the column. The road was going downhill, so the pace quickened. Suddenly we heard a shot behind us, and a command, "Halt". Two American tanks had appeared higher up the road down which we had just come.

'I ran towards them as fast as I could, and climbed on to the first tank. I thought that the shooting was about to start, but the Americans were laughing and saying, "Germany kaput". We looked down and observed the strange scene. The "boys" – the strongest of our men who were carrying the Germans' rucksacks – threw themselves on the guards and began to wrestle with them. The Germans would not dare to shoot now, but they all managed to extricate themselves after throwing away their weapons. Some of them ran into the fields without their boots, which remained in the arms of their "boys". Turning to the Americans, I pointed my finger in the direction of the escaping SS men and said, "Boom, boom". The Americans kept on laughing, shaking their heads, and repeating, "Germany kaput" and "Hitler kaput".

'They gave me a bar of chocolate, a hard-boiled egg and packets of Camel cigarettes. As I jumped off the tank I said, "It is a long way to Tipperary", the only words I knew in English, which were greeted with loud laughter. I was running back to the village and eating the boiled egg and the chocolate. They had no taste. The others joined me. The village seemed empty. We entered a cottage. An old woman came out and looked at us nervously. She gave us milk and bread and butter. No taste again. We asked for a pot in which to boil our shirts and suits. We made a fire outside, stripped naked, and washed while our striped suits and shirts were boiling. We dried them in the sun and put them on again. For the first time in months we did not have to scratch ourselves.

'Two or three of our men were walking about with guns. We ate a rich soup that the old woman cooked for us. Slowly the villagers began to return. They were elderly men and women, and children. Apparently our guards had told them that we were dangerous criminals, and as soon as the tanks arrived they ran away, and only came back when the news reached them that we had no intention of harming anybody. That night, for the first time in twenty months, I slept in a bed.

'That night I was terribly sick with stomach pains. Each time I fell asleep, I had a nightmare in which the German guards returned. I was sleeping in a clean bed, but I could not stand being covered with the eiderdown. I was glad when the night was over. I remember lying under a tree thinking of what to do. I needed to rest, but I felt very restless. I wanted to go back to Poland as soon as possible.'[1]

Alec Ward was just eighteen when the first American troops reached Mauthausen. 'It took some time to believe that I was free,' he recalled. 'The first item of food which I received after liberation was a tin of peas from an American soldier, from his tank. I drank the liquid first and was going to leave the peas for later. The liquid turned out to be too rich for my shrunken stomach and I became ill from it. I gave the peas to a friend.'[2]

[1] Michael Etkind, '"Youth" Remembered', manuscript, sent to the author, 4 January 1996.
[2] Alec Ward, 'My Story', manuscript, sent to the author, 31 May 1995.

Manfred Heyman, who was sixteen a month earlier, was on a death march from Flossenbürg at the end of April 1945. The journey had begun by train but, as Allied bombing raids intensified, it had continued on foot. 'A lot of people could not carry on walking,' he recalled. 'They were shot by the guards. One day, after we had rested in a barn and started walking again, the SS guards disappeared just as we were entering a village. Soon after that, American troops met our column of prisoners, and we were liberated. There were many Jewish Americans among the troops. They did their best for us. We were liberated on April 29.'[3]

Jack Rubinfeld was sixteen when the Americans reached Ludwigslust, where he had been taken during an eight-day rail journey from a slave labour camp near Berlin. 'They just dropped us there like living dead,' he recalled. 'No food. Lice eating us alive. Some Russian prisoners started eating dead human corpses. Prisoners were dropping like flies. I could hardly walk any more. We were just lying on a dirt floor and dying slowly. One morning, after a week or more, we realised that the Americans had arrived. A jeep with two soldiers entered the camp and we realised we were free.'

A few days later, walking down the road near the camp, Jack Rubinfeld picked up two loaves of bread from an abandoned railway freight car. 'A German woman with two small children approached me asking for food. She said that they had not eaten for a day. I looked around, ashamed to let my friends see. I broke off half a loaf and gave it to them.' This was, he reflected fifty years later, 'a decisive moment, showing my inability to seek vengeance'.[4]

Kurt Klappholz, from Bielsko-Biala, had a similar experience. 'I remember as a little child my father used to say that revenge only leads to a vicious circle which never stops,' he recalled. 'A day or two after I was liberated, I teamed up with a Russian who had been in the same camp as I, and we were walking in the direction from which the Americans had come to liberate us, and we met an American lieutenant and two American soldiers who had picked up two SS men – I think they had been guards in the concentration camp. The American lieutenant immediately recognised us as having been concentration camp prisoners, and he pointed at the two SS men and he said that we could beat them up – they had already been beaten up by the Americans – that we could take revenge on them. I said to the American lieutenant that I was far too weak to try to beat up an SS man and, moreover, even if he were lying defenceless on the ground, I would not wish to beat him up. I got

[3] Manfred Heyman, letter to the author, 5 June 1995.
[4] Jack (Israel) Rubinfeld, 'Jack Rubinfeld', manuscript, sent to the author, undated.

the impression that the lieutenant seemed to feel ashamed of himself. I still do not feel ashamed of myself for what I did then. Quite the contrary. I was grateful that my father brought me up in this way.'

That his parents must be dead was a factor in dissuading Kurt Klappholz from returning to Poland. As he later wrote: 'I did not, even for one instant, consider returning to my home town – Bielsko-Biala – even before I had any definite evidence that my parents were dead. When I heard on the American Forces radio about the gassing of Jews, of which I'd never heard before, I concluded – this time rightly – that all my family, from whom I had heard nothing, were probably dead.'[5]

Chaim Liss was fourteen when American troops reached the slave labour camp near Hannover, where his father had died a week earlier. 'By then I myself was a "Musulman",' he later wrote, 'and very near my end. As such I was amongst the few prisoners who were left for dead when the population of the camp was evacuated to Bergen-Belsen. Most of them did not survive. On the arrival of the American troops I was rushed to hospital, where I slowly recuperated. Some time later I decided to move to Bergen-Belsen, as I had hoped maybe to trace some relatives. But nobody had survived.'[6]

Rose and Hinda Kalman were in Bergen-Belsen when British troops approached. The two girls were the only survivors of their large family. Rose was fifteen, her sister in her mid-twenties. Their first priority was to find some food. But the few German guards who remained in the camp were still shooting. 'I was very frightened at first,' Rose recalled, 'and very reluctant to leave my sister – she was so sick – she had blood coming out of her mouth. We both needed food, so I ran, and the gunshots seemed quite close. I got frightened and couldn't move. I saw a woman being pushed in a wheelbarrow with a deep stomach wound. She was badly injured. As the Germans were leaving they were shooting at random. When I got back to the barracks my sister had gone. The Red Cross had taken her. I was so weak that it took a while before I made enquiries. When I did, it was such great sadness to find she had died, and was buried in a mass grave. I felt devastated. My fantasy was that when the liberation came my sister and I would find my brother, and the three of us would be together. Now I was all alone.'[7]

Chill Igielman was just seventeen when he had been brought by train from the slave labour camp at Hessenthal to the barracks at Allach, near Munich, a sub-camp of Dachau. 'We were left in the camp to die,' he later wrote. 'There was no food at all, and no roll-calls. We just lay

[5] Kurt Klappholz, 'Testimony', transcribed tape, 1995.
[6] Chaim Liss, letter to the author, 30 December 1994.
[7] Rose Goldman (Kalman), letter to the author, July 1995.

around inside and outside the barracks too weak to do anything. People were dying all the time. One night, a few days after the able-bodied left, the artillery bombardment got heavier and the camp itself was shelled. The next morning when I awoke, people were shouting that the SS had gone, and the camp perimeter wires had been cut and people were returning with food.

'At lunchtime the Americans arrived outside the camp in tanks, but they did not enter until later in the afternoon. They threw biscuits and chocolates to us out of their own personal supplies. They sealed off the camp but I was able to sneak out and returned with some potato peelings, and these I cooked in the camp on a fire between two bricks. By the evening the US soldiers managed to cook us a meal of pork and macaroni from the German supplies. No one I knew refused to eat it because pork was not kosher.

'We were fed on the pork and macaroni for several days. However, this turned out to be a killer as almost everyone in the camp got dysentery. People were dying in large numbers. By the third day a team of US army doctors and paramedics arrived, including the first black people I had ever seen. We were sprayed with DDT to delouse us and the barracks were cleaned and disinfected. Everyone in the camp was put on a diet of porridge and also black coal-dust tablets to stop diarrhoea. Even so I was so weak with the diarrhoea I was unable to walk, and so I was taken in an army ambulance to the main Dachau camp. I spent six weeks in the former SS hospital there recovering from malnutrition and exhaustion.

'When I left the hospital I stayed in Dachau, in a barrack which had been used by the SS. There were four of us in a room, and it was quite comfortable. I shared with a Pole from the Warsaw uprising, a Yugoslav and an Italian. There were not many ex-prisoners left in the camp. By that time I was able to go to the canteen for meals, and had been given a jacket and pair of trousers which had been for the Hitler Youth but with the insignia removed.'[8]

Also liberated at Allach was Steven Kanitz, from the Hungarian town of Kispest. He had been deported to Auschwitz on 9 July 1944, at the age of sixteen, on one of the very last trains before the Hungarian deportations were halted. His last slave labour camp had been at Spaichingen, only fifty miles from the German-Swiss border. From there he had been taken to Dachau, and then marched to Allach. 'I was pushed and prodded by an elderly SS with his gun,' he recalled, 'because I was a few hundred metres (or so it seemed to me) behind the main

---

[8] Chill Igielman, 'A Record of the Early Life of Hillel Chill Igielman', manuscript, sent to the author, November 1994.

body of the marchers. Why he never shot me on the spot, I shall never know. Maybe he did not have any bullets!'[9]

Another of those liberated at Allach was Betty Weiss. She was just fifteen when she and her family were deported from the Ruthenian town of Rakhov to Auschwitz. She and her sister survived the war. Her elder brother Philip died at Mauthausen five days before liberation. 'A cousin saw him lying in the straw,' she recalled. 'He had typhoid fever. He begged for food. Next day my cousin found some food and took it to him. He wasn't there any more.' Her father had died on a death march. 'He was starving. They had pulled his gold teeth out.'[10]

Pinkus Kurnedz, originally from Piotrkow, had been on the two-week death march from the slave labour camp at Colditz to Theresienstadt. Of the six hundred who set out, under guard, only sixty survived the march. 'I remember well the day of my liberation,' he later wrote, 'I think I was one of the first people who saw the Russian tanks, and I remember my first bowl of Russian soup, which I was given by a member of a tank crew; and then I remember falling asleep, and missing the opportunity of looting, because on that day we could do anything with the Germans, civilian as well as military.'[11]

Jack Aizenberg, who had been with Pinkus Kurnedz as a slave labourer, first in Czestochowianka and then in Colditz, and like Pinkus Kurnedz was a survivor of the death march from Colditz to Theresienstadt, also recalled that moment when life and hope returned. 'One heard rumours that the war was coming to an end,' he wrote. 'At this time I was so weak and getting weaker – that I am sure I was dying. Miraculously, on May 8, as I was lying on the boards which were my bed, I heard a lot of noise, and Russian music coming from accordions. Luckily I still had the faculties to realise that the Russians had arrived and that I might be free. With my last bit of energy I managed to get downstairs. Upstairs would have been impossible for me. I got outside the gates, and saw the Russian tanks rolling on towards the capital, Prague.'[12]

'Some survivors, I imagine, were strong enough to be around to see the Germans run for their lives, or saw them surrender,' Henry Green, from Strzemieszyce Wielkie, in the Zaglebie region of Poland, wrote thirty years later of the moment of liberation, when he himself was in Theresienstadt. 'It must have been a sight to see, an emotion of a lifetime to experience. I was flat on my back, ill, pretty well on my way out, and certainly past caring. Instead, I woke up one day to find myself in a

[9] S. Kanitz, 'In Spaichingen 45 Years Ago', manuscript, April 1990.

[10] Betty Weiss (Bertha Fischer), in conversation with the author, August 1995.

[11] Pinkus Kurnedz, recollections, letter to the author, 5 October 1994.

[12] Jack Aizenberg, recollections, manuscript, sent to the author, April 1994.

hospital bed. A bed with linen – clean linen, I might add – and people caring for me. Caring for ME!'[13]

Many of those liberated at Theresienstadt were at the very end of their strength and physical ability to survive. As soon as the Russians were in control of the camp, they imposed a quarantine, in order to prevent the typhus epidemic in the camp from spreading to the nearby towns, and even to Prague. They also put a considerable effort into emergency medical and nursing care. This help came just in time. In the words of Abraham Goldstein, who had been a prisoner and slave labourer in Majdanek, Skarzysko-Kamienna, Buchenwald and Schlieben: 'Were it not for the fact that I was liberated by the Russians just in time, I would have shared the fate of all those millions of Jews who perished in the Holocaust.'[14]

Michael Novice, who had been a slave labourer at Sosnowiec, Buna and Krawinkel, later recalled: 'Unfortunately I was too sick to be able to get up and see the German guards being taken prisoner. The liberation was my salvation. Had the war lasted another week, I would not have survived. Once liberated, I was placed in a sick-bay. There, Russian army doctors and nurses nursed me. My health was so poor then that there was a period when the staff gave up on me, thinking that I would not make it.'[15]

Also liberated at Theresienstadt was Pinchas Gutter, who had been deported three weeks after the Warsaw ghetto revolt to Majdanek, where his father, brother and sister had been murdered. At the age of twelve he had ended up in the slave labour camp at Colditz, and like Pinkus Kurnedz had survived the death march from there. After the liberation of Theresienstadt, Pinchas Gutter recalled, 'we all rushed out and found ourselves on the main highway where a multitude of German refugees were being expelled, or fleeing to Germany. Families with children, *peklach*,[16] with hand wheelbarrows, horse-drawn wagons, bicycles, were making their way, and were being assaulted mainly by Czechs, some by Russian soldiers, and by very few survivors. I was with a band of children, and I remember very clearly my own sentiments of pity and commiseration towards these people, because they reminded me of my own suffering. I remember similar sentiments were expressed by my companions. After all these years I still find it intriguing that instead of an intense hatred which I should have felt for these people because they

---

[13] Henry Green, recollections, The '45 Aid Society, *30th Anniversary of Our Liberation*, 11 May 1975.

[14] Abraham Goldstein, letter to the author, 12 December 1994.

[15] Michael Novice (Meir Sosnowicz), recollections, manuscript, June 1995.

[16] Packages.

were Germans, all I felt was pity and commiseration.'[17]

David Kutner, originally from Lodz, was among those who reached Theresienstadt from Buchenwald. In the open wagon in which he travelled, often sleeping without realising it on the bodies of those who had died during the night, he recalled how one day 'we came to a stop in a siding, we were there for a few hours, and all of a sudden we realised that all the German guards had disappeared. By this time, I realised that my life, what was left in me, was ebbing away. I was delirious, and very feverish. I can vaguely remember being in some kind of makeshift hospital, where I was thoroughly bathed (my body had not been washed for months) and put into bed. I passed out, and when I came to, I was told that I was lucky to be alive, as I had survived a high temperature which is peculiar to typhus.'

Those liberated after the death-train journeys were so weak that they could hardly eat. Great discipline was needed to avoid foods which the body could not absorb. After such long deprivation, not everyone could restrain themselves. 'As a result,' David Kutner recalled, 'it was very distressing to see many of my friends die from simply eating – having survived the six years of terrible experiences, concentration camps etc.'[18]

Arek Hersh was sixteen when the Russian troops reached Theresienstadt. Like many of the boys, he had arrived there only a few days earlier from Buchenwald, after a four-week ordeal. 'We all looked alike, our bodies just skeletons,' he later recalled. 'The six of us who shared the room – Jankl, Natek, Yacob, Moshe, Berek and myself – went to bed that evening utterly exhausted, but it was not long before I was woken by a commotion coming from the streets. I heard people shouting and I went to the window to see what was going on. The sight that met my eyes was of people trying to climb on to a tank, several jeeps nearby filled with Russian soldiers, and hundreds of people running towards them. I saw a soldier playing an accordion while others danced.

'I watched this scene for a few moments, unable to comprehend what was happening; people were actually embracing the soldiers! I thought it was all a dream and shouted to the boys to wake up and come to the window. Slowly the realisation dawned: this was not a dream; it was the moment we had all been praying for. Our joy was indescribable. At that moment I felt I was being born again. We all got dressed as quickly as possible. We just had to go and join the rest of the crowds.

'The streets were full of hundreds of people, many of them like us, very weak, hardly able to walk, but wanting to join in this supreme

---

[17] Pinchas Gutter, letter to the author, 12 September 1994: Martin Gilbert, *The Day the War Ended*, London, 1995, pages 285–6.

[18] David Kutner, 'War Experiences of David Kutner, 1939–1945', manuscript, sent to the author, 9 May 1994.

moment of happiness. The smell of fresh air, being able to walk once again without having a gun in our backs, eating proper food – oh, how I was looking forward to all these things! Maybe some of my family had survived after all, and I would soon be meeting them again. I felt so choked with emotion I could hardly talk.

'Natek went off and returned an hour later with his arms laden down with provisions – smoked meat, cheese, butter and chocolate. He told us that the Germans had left a warehouse intact full of food and people were just helping themselves. Imagine how we felt at seeing this kind of food for the first time in five years. To us it was indescribable. We hid the food in our room, putting some of it under our mattresses, not really believing that we would be allowed to keep it. I ate a piece of chocolate, the first in five years; it tasted so, so good. Some of the boys started eating meat, cheese, butter, everything they could lay their hands on and it was not long before they started feeling ill. Their stomachs had been empty for so long, they could not take the rich, fatty foods.

'The next morning I decided that I must see the defeated German army being rounded up. Weak as I was, I wanted to take revenge for all the suffering they had caused to me, my parents, my brother and sisters, all my relatives and all the rest of the Jewish people, and the prisoners of war who had not lived to see this day. I asked my friend, Moshe, to accompany me to Leitmeritz, a town only a few kilometres from Theresienstadt. We wanted to watch the columns of German soldiers walking towards the assembly point where they were to be directed to prisoner-of-war camps. I dragged myself along as best I could to watch this spectacle, to see this invincible army now in defeat.

'We walked for a while, then managed to hitch a lift from a farmer with a horse and cart who was going our way. Suddenly I spotted the Germans, so we thanked the farmer for his kindness, disembarked and stood by the roadside, watching the rabble of this once so mighty army pass by in twos and threes. A young Russian soldier came over to us with his machine-gun and asked us what we wanted. We told him of how we had suffered at the hands of these barbarians. He said he had no love for them either, as the Germans had also committed many atrocities against the Russian people – burning down their villages, plundering their homes and murdering millions. We told him that we had lost everybody in the war. The roads were now full of Russian soldiers who were smiling at us. "We are looking at the victors", we thought.

'We stood and watched the defeated Wehrmacht army pass. I noticed two SS men and I thought, "At last my luck has changed". We told them to stop; one was a sergeant and one a captain. They looked at us in astonishment. The sergeant had a rucksack on his back. "Take it off,"

I said. He complained that it contained his food and all his belongings. "We have been starved by you for five years", I told him. At that he said he was not a German, but a Frenchman. He had joined the SS, but had never done anything wrong. This was a phrase we were to hear again and again after the war. The captain began to argue with us, his tone arrogant, but he was silenced by the Russian soldier who held up his gun and pointed it at him. "You Germans are not the masters any more," he said.

'We told the SS men that we had only to give the Russian soldier the word and he would shoot both of them. We could see that they were afraid. There was something satisfying about their frightened eyes and trembling bodies. I let them sweat for a moment and then I said, "But we are not murderers like you". We took their food off them and told them to go. We watched as they walked away.

'I saw many boys of about my own age in German uniforms, walking towards the assembly camp. At the end of the war the Germans in desperation had been making boys of fifteen into soldiers. Watching the Germans pass by, it was hard to believe that this dishevelled rabble were the soldiers of whom we had been so terrified. They must have been wondering what the Russians would do to them. Everybody knew how the Germans had treated the Russian people when they invaded Russia. I thought, "Surely the Germans can't expect any mercy?" I thought of the millions of Jewish people they had tortured and slaughtered, and I wondered what punishments would be meted out.

'As we watched, a young German boy of about my age stopped in front of us, took a knife out of his pocket and silently handed it to me. It was a Hitler Youth knife with a swastika on it. We looked at each other, neither saying a word, then he turned and walked away. Even then that moment seemed poignant to me, and I turned to Moshe and said how happy I was that we had lived to see this day. Clutching the knife and the food we had taken from the SS officers, we made our way back to the camp at Theresienstadt.

'The Russians gave us twenty-four hours to do whatever we wanted to the Germans, but being human beings we did nothing. On arriving back at Theresienstadt we noticed two cauldrons of rice pudding. I brought out the knife the German boy had handed to me and ate my share of rice pudding ravenously. I thought of my beloved parents, of my dear brothers and sisters, and of the many relations and friends who had lost their lives. I prayed for their souls and I prayed for myself.'[19]

Chaskiel Rosenblum, who was liberated at Theresienstadt, having earlier

[19] Arek Hersh (Herszlikowicz), 'The Liberation – 8th May, 1945', manuscript.

been a slave labourer at Skarzysko-Kamienna and Schlieben, remembered how 'one day, walking by myself in my striped uniform outside the camp, I met a German officer. He had a very nice pair of boots. I ordered him – in German – to take them off, and I took them into the camp. I wanted to keep them. I was not sure he would give them to me, and he was not sure whether he should escape or not, but he decided to give the boots to me. The only thing he told me, was that his legs were swollen. This was a general phrase: all the Nazis went around complaining about their swollen legs.

'In five and a half years we had never complained about our swollen legs, and they did within five weeks. Everyone who is forced to submit to starvation has swollen legs. The officer started running. His boots were the sum of the loot I made from the Germans. The itinerary of the boots was as follows: Theresienstadt – Prague – Amsterdam – England – Scotland – (Cardross, Dumbartonshire) – Liverpool – the steamship *Drotningholm* (Swedish-American Line) – New York, where my uncle and aunt were waiting to fly with me to La Paz in Bolivia. There, in New York, my war trophy had to be left behind because it was too heavy, and over-weight on the plane would be very expensive.

'We very much enjoyed bringing a different Nazi into the barrack every day, and making him clean the barrack. Then he had to clean under the bed without moving it at all, where we left him for quite a while. This was our kick. We couldn't kill. I don't feel specially good or proud about not having been able to kill the assassins of my baby sisters, the assassins of my beaten brother, the assassins of my helpless mother and sister, the assassins of my sick father, and the assassins of the six million. But I just couldn't. However, there was a ten-year-old boy who had seen his parents being killed, and he was killing one Nazi after another.'[20]

Sixteen-year-old Salek Orenstein had been on the train of Jews and Soviet prisoners of war which had left Buchenwald on April 10, in the direction of Theresienstadt. 'It must have been at the beginning of May,' he later wrote, 'when we arrived at a place that was in ruins. When I saw this my heart leapt for joy; let them have it! That's what I thought. As we passed a station, I saw a big sign which said "Sudetengebiet".[21] It was very dark when we passed another small station with a notice saying Marienschien.

'We were rumbling along much more slowly now, until we reached

---

[20] Chaskiel Rosenblum, 'Testimony', manuscript, sent to the author, April 1995.

[21] The former Sudeten region of Czechoslovakia, which had been incorporated into Germany, as the Sudetengebiet, in October 1938, after the Munich Agreement.

some open fields where a dozen or so men stood about wearing red armbands. These were the Czech freedom fighters. One of these partisans stepped forward with a white flag and opened the door to the officers' wagon. No one stepped out. They had all absconded along the way. Only a few Hungarian guards remained. One of them produced a piece of paper with printed orders that this consignment of prisoners must be delivered to Theresienstadt.

'It was two days after the war had ended. We, of course, were the last to know. I personally was in no fit state to disembark. I was too weak. If I had attempted to jump down, I would have broken every bone in my body. There was nothing left of me. About twenty men and women wearing white coats gathered round the trains, lifting people off and wheeling them away into Theresienstadt on trolleys which they had prepared by the side of the track. They unloaded the Russian prisoners of war as well; there was one compartment full of them at the rear, next to the wagon carrying the dead. I heard that they were the only ones who ate human flesh, cutting off bits from the dead bodies.

'They lifted me off the wagon but they could not put me down anywhere because I had no flesh. Some young ladies of sixteen and seventeen in blue overalls, German girls, stood on hand to help out. These were the girls who had pleased the German officers, danced with them, slept with them. They had all been dragged out of their villages, arrested by the Czech freedom fighters, and brought into Theresienstadt to help look after the survivors. We could hardly have looked after ourselves. Each of these girls was wearing a white headscarf. I found out later that the Czechs had shaved their heads as a mark of shame, and also to stop them slipping away in civilian disguise. Now they were completely bald.

'I was put into a blanket and carried gently inside the camp. As they washed me down, although my hearing was almost gone, I overheard one telling the other that I would have to be sent to "Lazaret". This turned out to be the hospital or infirmary. I could not walk so they lowered me into a blanket and four of those girls carried me, each one holding a corner of the blanket. When we reached the Lazaret they found some string and tied up my blanket to make a type of improvised hammock.

'I lay suspended in a soft cocoon. All I wanted was to be left alone. I wasn't hungry, I wasn't thirsty, I wasn't sleepy, I was just a mass of emotions. The only faculty I possessed was my eyes, and I gazed up to the ceiling all the time. Nothing else existed for me. Not survival, not the end of the war, the beginning of the war, parents, family, what I was going to do next. Nothing.

'A Jewish woman doctor approached me. She shouted to the girls to lower the hammock. They obeyed. She ordered the girls to support my head and then, using a wooden spoon, she poured some liquid into my mouth. My lips were so fragile that if she had used a metal spoon she might easily have cut me. The spoon felt big and bulky against my lips, and as the liquid flowed into my mouth I realised that I was a human being after all.

'A day or so later, I was taken to another ward with a white ceiling and placed near the end of the ward. They told me that I had a Red Cross parcel waiting for me. They left it sitting there untouched. I had no strength to open it. They fed me my first piece of bread. I couldn't swallow it so I just chewed and chewed. I couldn't taste the bread at all, but I felt its texture. They removed my clothing and washed my body down with some lukewarm water.

'The young Jewish doctor came back and spoke to me from time to time. She spoke many languages, she was educated and highly intelligent. She told me that the Red Cross had arranged for survivors to be sent to Switzerland. I didn't take much notice.

'In the midst of all my misery, my hearing came back. Perhaps it was because physically I had lost everything else that, perversely, this bit corrected itself. Who knows? After about a week or ten days, I stood up on my own feet for the first time. I couldn't walk. Two girls supported me and I limped into a big hall filled with chairs. It looked like a theatre, there was a stage and a collection of musical instruments. I noticed a violin and asked if I could touch it. They said I could. I picked it up and played a note. They could see right away that I knew how to handle a bow.

'Gradually, I began to walk unaided. When I felt strong enough, I was free to walk out of the camp and into the nearby town of Leitmeritz. Many of the prisoners had already been out, entering abandoned German homes and helping themselves to anything of value. Clocks, watches all sorts of things. I was terribly jealous. As soon as I recovered – which I did very quickly – somehow, unbelievably – I went out too.'[22]

It was units of the Red Army who were the first to enter Theresienstadt, which was already under Red Cross supervision. Soviet military personnel administered as best they could to the tens of thousands of emaciated slave labourers who had been dumped in the camp during the final days of the war. Among these was Perec Zylberberg, originally from Lodz, one of those who had arrived by train in an open wagon from Buchenwald. On reaching Theresienstadt, he, like so many of the others who came on this transport, was in a state of almost total collapse.

'I wasn't in the freight car any more,' Perec Zylberberg recalled. 'I

---

[22] Salek Orenstein, 'Beyond Belief, A Survivor's Story', manuscript, sent to the author, 1995.

was in a building that had bunks. At the time when it all happened, I don't remember whether I was in German or Red Cross hands. There was a registration the following day. We were given some identification cards. With those cards we received some food. Still in a state of almost total mental fatigue, I remember going to the ambulatory room and being told that I have to be hospitalised. The only thing that I worried about was my piece of bread. I was allowed to take that with me. There were quite a few nurses – that, I could make out. I was undressed and, of all things, I remember being in a bed.'[23]

Of the next few days, and even weeks, Perec Zylberberg has no clear recollection. Although he would never again be without food, the prisoner's instinctive battle for every piece of bread still animated him. 'I remember raising myself out of bed in a violent swing to make sure that my bread was next to my bed,' he later wrote, 'remember being calmed down by people, who showed me the bread. I don't know if I could, or did, eat at all during that suspension-from-life period. I remember noises. I remember human figures. I know now that this was a "no life, no death" period.

'I was told by the nurse, when I could muster enough energy to ask the only question that was on my mind then – where am I and what is going on? – that I was still down with typhus and that I was in a clinic. I remember that talk. It did not stir me to any reaction. The next time that I could take in any impression that made sense was the vague outline of people atop a huge tank. There was jubilation. I saw this through the window-panes. I remember the thought that shot through my mind: the Allies are here. I don't recall any jubilation on my part, only an inner sigh of relief.

'As if spurred on by this inner spark, I turned around and saw a very small woman in a military uniform. She told me in a language that had some familiar undertones – it must have been Ukrainian or Polish – that the war was over and that we would be getting medical treatment and food. I even think that she also spoke some Yiddish. It did seem strange to my mind then. I was told to make an effort and get up. I did it instinctively and I also remember standing stark naked in front of that small woman doctor. After that encounter I found I was strong enough to look around me.

'There were quite a number of other men in the room. One or two came over and told me that I had been in a delirium for most of my stay in the clinic. They confirmed that the war was already over. The attention that was bestowed on us was friendly and healing. I don't know where they were from, but there were lots of young women

---

[23] Perec Zylberberg, recollections, diary entry for 28 September 1993.

ministering to our needs. They were probably from the women's barracks
in Theresienstadt. They spoke Polish and Czech and German. I began to
make out what they were saying. They told of the dramatic rescue by
the Russian army.

'Soldiers kept coming. They were not only Russians but from other
Allied units as well. There were Americans and Polish soldiers. The sick
and the recuperating people were given titbits the likes of which had
not been seen for the last five years: chocolates, biscuits, cheese, white
bread and many other delights. This warmth, more than anything else
around us, inspired the growth of energy and desires. Even fruit, unseen
all the war years, was seen among the staff and visitors. I didn't have
anybody, at any time, to whom I could talk, such as a friend, acquaintance, or even a person from any of the places that I had been incarcerated
in. However, there were friendly people around me. Language didn't
seem to be a barrier. Somehow, we each knew some of the languages
of the people around us. Even when we spoke in a very badly structured,
ungrammatical way, we were nevertheless able to communicate with
one another. The period of coming back to life had begun.'[24]

Harry Spiro, a survivor of the death march from Rehmsdorf, who was
also liberated in Theresienstadt, recalled how the Russian soldiers told
him that he and his fellow survivors had twenty-four hours 'to do
whatever we wanted, even kill Germans. I don't think any of us actually
did that, I'm not sure why. We were too busy looking for food, and so
relieved to have survived, but I also don't think it is in our nature to do
that. However I was with a friend, and we stopped two Germans. I took
some chocolate from one. My friend took the other's rucksack and then
spotted a tobacco pouch which he also took. The German pleaded with
him to let him keep the pouch. Then we realised why he wanted to keep
it so much, we discovered diamonds in it. We were a bit naive and told
everyone what had happened, and my friend put them under his
mattress. The next day he discovered the diamonds had gone. A man
and his two sons had taken them. We later heard that they had gone
back to Poland with the diamonds, and had been killed by the local
Poles on their return.'

At that time, Harry Spiro reflected, 'I don't remember having any
plans, and I certainly didn't feel elated at having survived, since all my
family were dead.' When, while still in Theresienstadt, he heard that
permits were available for those under sixteen to go to England, he put
his name down for the journey.[25]

Minia Munter had survived ten days in a death train before reaching

[24] Perec Zylberberg, recollections, diary entry for 29 September 1993.
[25] Harry Spiro, recollections, letter to the author, 21 March 1995.

THE BOYS
FROM THE
CONCENTRATIO
CAMPS

17. The boys join in a demonstration in Trafalgar Square, in protest against a British army raid on Jewish settlements in Palestine, and the continuing British restrictions on Jewish immigration to Palestine. Holding the placard is Alec Ward, from Parysow, who now lives in London. At the very top of the picture, next to the placard, is Zvi Dagan (formerly Mlynarski), from Piotrkow, who now lives in Israel. Below him is Moniek Buki, from Piotrkow, who now lives in the United States.

18. (above) Yogi Mayer (born in 1912), a pre-war refugee from Germany, and a member of the wartime British Special Operations Executive, who became the club leader of the Primrose Club, devoted to the boys and their rehabilitation.

19. (below) Heini Goldberg, known as the 'homely counsellor', a pre-war refugee from Breslau who went from Windermere to the hostel at Loughton. He later emigrated to Israel.

20. (above) Dr 'Ginger' Friedmann, also a pre-war refugee from Germany, who looked after the boys at the Southampton hostel.

21. (below) Zisha Schwimmer, from Gorlice (now living in London), and Sister Maria, a pre-war refugee from Germany, who looked after the boys with tuberculosis at Quare Mead.

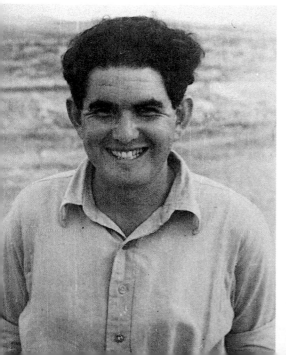

22. (above) On holiday near Ryde, on the Isle of Wight. Atop the left-hand pyramid, Ben Helfgott. At the base, Moniek Goldberg (left) and Roman Halter, from Chodecz, now living in England (right). Atop the right-hand pyramid, Zvi Dagan. Immediately below him, Jan Goldberger, from Bielsko-Biala (now living in London). The left base, Paul Gast (formerly Gastfreund) from Lodz, now in Florida. On the right, Szlomo Kuszerman, from Kielce, now living in Tel Aviv.

23. (below) Picnicing on the Isle of Wight. The three boys in the sunlight are Paul Gast (left), Szlomo Kuszerman, and Moniek Goldberg.

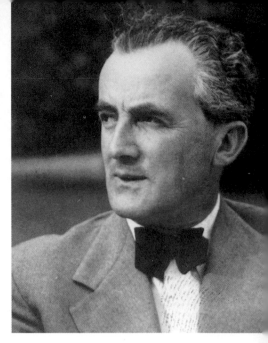

24. (above) Leonard Montefiore, one of the triumvirate of British Jews – the others were Elaine Blond and Lola Hahn-Warburg – who organised the arrival and rehabilitation of the 732 boys from the concentration camps.

25. (below) Counsellors and helpers at the Loughton hostel. In the centre, Heini Goldberg. On his right, Fay Nachmani, a pre-war refugee. On Heini Goldberg's left, Hilda Salomon; they later married, and went to live in Israel. On his far right, the matron, Malka Tattenbaum.

26. (above) Oscar Friedmann, a pre-war refugee from Germany, where he had been in charge of an orphanage in Berlin, who was responsible for the boys' needs in England.

27. (below) The Hirszfeld brothers, from Poznan. On the left, David, who became an inventor in Israel. Next to him, his brother Moniek, who served for a short period in the Royal Navy. Today he lives in Brighton.

28. (above) At the tenth reunion dinner in 1955, among those at the high table are three of the main supporters of the boys after their arrival in Britain: from left to right, Elaine Blond, Oscar Joseph (President of the '45 Aid Society until his death in 1988) and Lola Hahn-Warburg. Partly hidden by the candelabra is Ben Helfgott, the '45 Aid Society's Chairman.

29. (below) Arthur Poznanski, from Piotrkow, as Canio in Verdi's opera *I Pagliacci (The Clowns)*. He lives today in London. his brother Jerzy, who was also one of the boys, died in London in 1995.

30. (below) Perec Zylberberg (from Lodz, now living in Montreal) outside the Primrose Club, a photograph taken in 1996.

31. (above) The boys at the wedding reception of Aron and Evelyn Zylberszac's son. Centre front, in cummerbund, Krulik Wilder (Piotrkow and London). Two to his right, Aron Zylberszac (Lodz and London). Far right, front row, Victor Greenberg (Ruthenia and London). To his right, feet forward, Zigi Shipper (Lodz and London). Just above him, chin obscured but smile intact, Harry Spiro (Piotrkow and London). Just above Krulik Wilder is Kopel Kandelcukier (Bialobzegi and London) who took his new surname, Kendall, from Kendal near Windermere. On his left, Moniek Goldberg, who came from Florida for the wedding.

32. (below) The wives of the boys above, including Evelyn Zylberszac (centre, white dress). In the front row, fifth from the left, with necklace, is Minia Jay, formerly Minia Munter, from the Polish town of Warta, one of the Windermere 'boys'.

33. (above) Josh Segal (Piotrkow and Toronto) returns to the synagogue in Piotrkow and stands next to a painting of the ten commandments in the synagogue annex, the Bet Midrash (Study House). The painting still shows, after fifty years, the bullet holes made when the Germans killed a number Jews who had been incarcerated in the synagogue in December 1942. Today the Study House is a public library. The bullet holes are normally covered by a curtain.

34. (below) In 1983, on the 40th anniversary of the Warsaw ghetto uprising, some of the boys visited Birkenau. On the far left, Sam Freiman (originally from Konstancin-Jeziorna, near Warsaw, now a Londoner). Next to him, Krulik Wilder and Ben Helfgott (both from Piotrkow and London). Far right, Harry Balsam (Gorlice and London). With them are three members of the Board of Deputies of British Jews, Hayim Pinner, Dr Lionel Kopelowitz (then President of the Board) and Martin Savitt.

35. (above) Reuma Weizman, who in 1946 was a helper at the Loughton hostel. With her is one of the Loughton boys, Ben Helfgott. The photograph was taken on 29 February 1996, when Mrs Weizman, then the wife of the President of Israel, gave tea to her Loughton charges.

36 – 39. In clockwise order, four Londoners: Abraham Zwirek (originally from Plock, Poland); Kopel Kendall (Bialobrzegi, Poland); Harry Spiro (Piotrkow, Poland) and Victor Greenberg (Majdan, Ruthenia).

Theresienstadt from a slave labour camp at Oderan, near Chemnitz. Shortly after liberation, she recalled, 'as we were lining up for the daily soup, after a couple of spoonfuls I collapsed, bleeding terribly from my lungs. No one thought I could survive. I was put in a wooden bunk and given lumps of salt and calcium, which looked like lumps of chalk. I wasn't sent to the hospital because there were no beds available.

'When I was eventually moved to the hospital, a doctor took pity on me. He asked me my name and where I was from and he said I could never travel anywhere in the condition I was in. He tried to get me up twice a day for an hour for a walk and made the kitchen send me a little extra food, and then the miracle – he suggested that I should be put on a list to go to England. When he mentioned England I thought I was dreaming. I couldn't believe that this was happening to me. They didn't accept me straight away, but with the doctor's help, I was sent to a hostel nearby.'[26] This was the Kinderheim (Children's Home) established after liberation in one of the barracks at Theresienstadt.

Moniek Goldberg, who was liberated in Theresienstadt three days after his seventeenth birthday, was a survivor of the slave labour camps of Pionki, Buna and Krawinkel. He recalled how, two days after liberation, 'two other boys and myself managed to get out from the Hamburger barrack into other parts of Theresienstadt. People were dancing in the street. I don't remember having any feelings of elation. I just felt I had to get away from there. We took to the road and it was a sight to behold. There were abandoned wagons and trucks all over the countryside. It was as if a tornado had swept through. There were people on the move. There were dead horses and some dead Germans. We rummaged through the abandoned caravans looking for food and some decent clothing. We found cigarettes, which were as good as money.

'We arrived in Prague after hitching rides with the Russians. I cannot find words adequate to praise the Czech people of Prague. We went to a hotel hoping to find a place to stay, prepared to pay with the cigarettes. They wouldn't hear of it. We sold some cigarettes for currency to be able to pay our way around. But wherever we went, to a restaurant, or to the cinema, or a concert, they refused our money. All they said was "Z Koncentraku" ("From a concentration camp") and refused to accept any payment. A family invited me into their home. I met a man who was from Libochovice and he invited me to come there to stay with his family.

'In Prague at that time they started to repatriate people as the city was getting very crowded and there was a scarcity of everything. I was

[26] Minia Jay (Munter), 'My Story', manuscript, sent to the author, undated (1995).

also starting to feel ill, and when the police stopped me in the street and asked me where I was from, I said "Libochovice" and was sent there by train. By the time I arrived I was already very sick and in a daze. But I had the man's name written down and showed it to a man at the station. I don't remember what followed, but I woke up in a clean bed in a very nice room with a family named Zeman. I stayed there for about six weeks and was very well cared for, bringing me to complete recovery. One day, I was going with my benefactor on a visit to Prague and met a man on the train who told me about the Kinderheim in Theresienstadt. He said we were all going to Palestine. I said goodbye to the nice people that I had been staying with, and headed for Theresienstadt.'[27]

Among those at the Children's Home in Theresienstadt was Henry Green. 'I shared a room with four or five other boys,' he recalled. 'This of course was heaven, when you consider the crowded conditions that I had been used to until then. Erna, our matron, had two girls to help her, and soon we became one small family. Some of us were more energetic than others, but we were all getting gradually used to being individuals again. I began to discover that I was a person in my own right – quite a revelation after years of propaganda about "vermin" and "parasites", etc.

'One could not leave Theresienstadt without a permit. Add to that, that it was a garrison town, life was somewhat restricted – a good thing in a way, as it introduced us to normal life in a city in a gradual way.'[28]

Most of the boys who were liberated in Theresienstadt were extremely ill, some were in comas, others hovered between life and death for many days and weeks. 'In hospital,' Mayer Hersh recalled, 'every patient (dead or alive) received a hard-boiled egg. I was eventually able to eat my egg and also the egg from my dead neighbour. I was gradually gaining more strength and was walking about the ward trying to find any friends who had survived. I was very happy to see alive a friend of mine called Pietrushka. We knew each other at home; he was a shoemaker, a man in his twenties, married with two children. We had been taken together to our first slave camp.

'At the very beginning, in the labour camp, we had been able to receive letters from home. My elder sister would write such things as, "I came to make your bed, but there is no bed to make". I was choking with emotion when reading her letter and had difficulty answering, so

---

[27] Joseph (Moniek) Goldberg, 'Biographical Sketch', manuscript, July 1995, sent to the author, 14 August 1995.

[28] Henry Green, recollections, The '45 Aid Society, *30th Anniversary of Our Liberation*, 11 May 1975.

my friend Pietrushka came to my rescue. He would read and answer letters for me. In addition, he would try to give me hope and build up my morale by saying that "the war will soon be over and we will all be going home to our families".

'I don't think he believed a word of it himself, but it was wonderful for me to hear that and it gave me hope. In this total darkness of despair, hope was one of the vital ingredients to keep up your spirits, and so perhaps help you to survive. Finding my dear friend Pietrushka very ill with typhoid in the hospital in Theresienstadt, I tried to repay the good things he had done for me, telling him, "Pietrushka, the war is over and we are free people; you must eat something to build up your strength. Very soon we shall be going back to our families at home".

'Without lifting his head, he said, "There is nobody alive at home, there is no wife or children any more". There was nothing I could do or say that would convince him otherwise, and unfortunately he slipped away. I was devastated by his death; he was a dear friend who did so much for me and yet I failed to save his life. A few weeks later we registered with the Czech authorities our desire to go to Palestine, but the British Mandate Authority refused. We were asked if we wished to go to England. Of course we gladly accepted. We wanted to get away as quickly as possible from those places of suffering and tragedy.'[29]

The British government had in fact allocated a thousand certificates for Jews in Theresienstadt and Bergen-Belsen to go to Palestine. These were distributed early in August by the United Nations Relief and Rehabilitation Administration. On August 21, eight days after the first three hundred boys and girls had flown to Britain, the UNRRA office in Berne reported to its office in London: '706 Theresienstadters and Bergen-Belseners left for Italy en route to Palestine.'[30]

Those survivors who left Theresienstadt and Bergen-Belsen for Palestine did so with official Palestine Certificates; these were restricted to people, mostly adults, who had close relatives already living there. Only one or two boys were later to discover such relatives.

While Mayer Kochen was in Theresienstadt he learned that in order to go to England one had to be under sixteen years of age. 'I was advised to apply to the Czech government for an identity card,' he recalled, 'stating date of birth 10 March 1930 – I was in fact born on 10 March 1927 – destination Palestine. I registered to go to England with the idea of going to Palestine from there.'[31]

[29] Mayer Hersh (Herszkowicz), letter to the author, 21 November 1994.

[30] Public Record Office, London, Foreign Office papers, 371/51122.

[31] Mayer Cornell (Kochen), letter to the author, 9 February 1995. Mayer Cornell went to England, and remained there. Today he lives in Harrow, Middlesex.

Those boys who wanted to go to directly to Palestine had been unlucky. There was also another direction taken by a few of those who might have gone to England. During the terrible years in the Lodz ghetto, there were a number of teenage Jews of socialist beliefs who talked about living in a post-war Poland in a better world; a world which they would help create. At the time of the deportations from the ghetto they promised each other that if they survived they would meet again in Lodz after the war, to build a new world with their fellow-Poles. One of these idealists, Lucjan Dobroszycki, who had been together with Aron Zylberszac in Rehmsdorf, was also in Theresienstadt, but returned to Lodz before the boys left for Britain. In Poland he studied, and worked hard to build the ideal world of his youthful dreams. Twenty-five years later, disillusioned by communism and an upsurge in anti-Semitism in Poland, he left for the United States, where he pursued a distinguished academic career. When his volume of documents on the Lodz ghetto was published, the boys whom he had known in the camps launched it in Britain. It was then that he discovered that many of 'the boys' were the same boys with whom he had been liberated in Theresienstadt nearly forty years earlier.[32]

The search had begun for knowledge of the fate of parents, brothers and sisters who had disappeared. 'The first thing people did,' Zvi Dagan later wrote, 'was to gather information about surviving family from relatives, from the Red Cross, from inmates from other camps etc. I discovered that my father was killed in Austria about two weeks before liberation. He was marching, and when he couldn't take it any more, and stopped marching, he was killed. I later discovered that my brother was killed in Skarzysko-Kamienna in 1943; he contracted dysentery and was shot dead by the commandant.'[33]

On 21 May 1945, thirteen days after the liberation of Theresienstadt, Perec Zylberberg was twenty-one years old. After more than five years as a captive, prisoner and slave of the Third Reich, he had now to contemplate his future. 'Just experiencing the jubilation of being free after more than five and a half years of terrible calamities,' he later wrote, 'I felt like a 21-year-old new-born person. I did not know the extent of the destruction in all its horrible details. I certainly could not focus on what my place was in this old-new set-up. Where was my

---

[32] I had hoped to discuss this phase of his life with Lucjan Dobroszycki, who was a good friend of mine, but he died (in July 1995) before I could do so. His book, *The Chronicle of the Lodz Ghetto, 1941–1944*, was published by Yale University Press in 1984. The '45 Aid Society gave the launch for it in London in September that year.

[33] Zvi Dagan (Mlynarski), letter to the author, 1 March 1996.

place? What had become of the whole world that I knew and felt part of? I had never moved out of my home nest for any length of time, except for vacations and visits to the place of birth of my mother and surrounding localities. "Where is my family? What kind of life is there, where we lived before? Where is one to go? Could one go wherever one wanted? Who is caring for the survivors? Are there other survivors?" If there was a new thing that was directing life, what was its guiding light?'[34]

Perec Zylberberg recuperated in the Magdeburg barracks at Theresienstadt. The Red Cross provided food and clothing. 'At that time,' he later recalled, 'we saw an influx of Zionist emissaries from Palestine. There were soldiers from the Jewish Brigade and some with just "Palestine" written on their epaulettes. There were people ready to persuade you to go to Palestine for settlement. Quite a few local Jewish ex-prisoners were joining the campaign to direct us to the Middle East. How was one to choose? There were not many open avenues to take, except to go back to your country of origin. Almost all other routes outward were fraught with danger, prohibitions and real hassle.

'There were very few chances to seek advice from trustworthy people. Because we were comparatively young, we were prone to be persuaded by those who could talk glibly. We were hard pressed to make a move somewhere. As these thoughts took deeper root, I got into a state of anxious anticipation of new things to come. Somehow the air became heavy with all kinds of suppositions. It was by now quite obvious that they had wiped out the Jewish populations of most East and Central European countries. Small remnants were scattered across the terrain that the Germans had occupied in the war. The whole lifestyle of the pre-war Jewish populations had ceased to exist. There just were not any meaningful communities with a solid base.

'People were coming back from all over, to look for what was left after the Holocaust. By our own – i.e. the survivors' – reckoning, there was not much that one could expect to find. We had gone through ghettos and camps. We almost felt ourselves to have been the last ones in line. Only a lucky coincidence had helped us to survive. That kind of luck did not happen in too many places. We knew by then that those dreadful places that one had heard about during the war actually existed, and, through a well-organised murder machinery, had wiped out the vast majority of Jews that came under German occupation. We did not know all the details. In that state of terrible consciousness we had to direct our steps somewhere. What was the direction, and where?'[35]

---

[34] Perec Zylberberg, recollections, diary entry for 30 September 1993.
[35] Perec Zylberberg, recollections, diary entry for 3 October 1993.

Save for the Polish or Palestinian options, Perec Zylberberg recalled, there came 'a whispered rumour of a British option. It was half official, not too much talked about. The British government let it be known that all youngsters under the age of sixteen would be allowed into Great Britain. It was assumed that those that registered would be fairly healthy and with no parental or other supervision. This offer went from a whispered version to a fully official announcement. A new opportunity opened up.

'There were other avenues too: illegal entry into France, Belgium, Holland, even Palestine. Some ideas were even bandied around about going to Germany. This was mostly in order to be in line for a possible permit to get to the United States. Theresienstadt was full of rumours, whispers, offers, a continuous stream of newcomers from camps, and people who had already made their way to Poland and came back dejected and forlorn.'[36]

The news of a possible emigration began rapidly to gain ground. 'The rumours started that we were going to be sent away,' Pinkus Kurnedz recalled. 'Some said Switzerland, others said America. As it turned out, I came to England.'[37]

Nineteen-year-old Abraham Zwirek was one of those who had made his way from Theresienstadt to his home town in Poland. In Poland he found his father David, who had survived a succession of deportations and concentration camps. 'He urged me to go back to Theresienstadt, where a contingent of Jewish children were gathered and registered to go to England.' David Zwirek was particularly hopeful that his son could contact his aunt Esther and her family, who had emigrated to Britain before the war. Zwirek made the journey back to Theresienstadt.[38] There, the British option was being seriously canvassed.

Kopel Kandelcukier returned from Theresienstadt, where he too had been liberated, to his home town of Bialobrzegi. With him were a few other survivors from the town. 'We went back to Poland just in case there were any survivors from our families,' he wrote. 'The Poles were very hostile to us, and I was glad to get back to the safety of Theresienstadt.' There, he recalled, 'there were a large number of boys and girls without parents, with nowhere to go. A Jewish Agency representative told us we were going to go to England.'[39]

Sam Rosenblat, who was twenty-three years old at the time of liberation in Theresienstadt, had survived the Bugaj works in Piotrkow,

[36] Perec Zylberberg, recollections, diary entry for 6 October 1993.

[37] Pinkus Kurnedz, recollections, letter to the author, 5 October 1994.

[38] Abraham Zwirek, letter to the author, 30 September 1994.

[39] Kopel Kendall (Kandelcukier), recollections, letter to the author, 2 September 1995.

and slave labour at Schlieben. He was among the older survivors. 'We were free,' he later wrote, 'but we didn't know what to do or where to go. For five years the camps were our home. So we went back to "our home" – the camp!'[40] Together with his brother Isidore, Sam Rosenblat worked inside Theresienstadt to supervise the welfare of those who, eight years younger than he, were to become 'the boys'.

Together with Isaac (Issie) Finkelstein, Sam Rosenblat and his brother were asked to be in charge of the youngsters in Theresienstadt, and to oversee their journey to England. As survivors, they understood the needs and feelings of the boys under their supervision, and helped to generate a harmonious atmosphere among them.

Ben Helfgott had also gone back to Poland. On reaching Piotrkow he found two girls there who had survived in hiding: Hanka Ziegler and Jadzia Balsam. Although he did not know them personally, he was able to tell them that Hanka's brother had died and that Jadzia's brother had survived, and was even then in Theresienstadt, where he had been liberated. The two girls decided to make their way to Theresienstadt: both later went on to Britain.[41]

Ben Helfgott returned a second time to Poland. 'When I recall the nightmares of the Holocaust years,' he wrote nearly forty years later, 'there is none that fills me with a greater dread and horror than the one I experienced on my return to Poland soon after my liberation. Like so many of the flotsam and jetsam that was traversing Europe in over-crowded trains, returning to their respective homelands, I was travelling with my cousin to our home town, Piotrkow. I was fifteen years old and my cousin twelve. Both of us still looked emaciated and our hair was still conspicuously short. To the Czechs, we seemed more like an apparition than real people and they showered us with food, warmth and sympathy. We were greatly encouraged by this spontaneous reaction of brotherhood and friendship. Our faith in humanity, which, strangely enough, although bruised, we never lost, was being restored in a very manifest and palpable way.

'We crossed the Polish-Czech border with bated breath, full of excitement and expectation for a brave new world. The train stopped in Czestochowa, well-known for its pilgrims to Jasna Gora, the most sacred of shrines in Poland. At the station we were waiting for the train that would take us to our home town. Hundreds of people were milling around, talking and gesticulating excitedly, when suddenly two Polish

---

[40] Sam Rosenblat, 'My Other Life in Another Time', manuscript, sent to the author, 24 January 1995.

[41] Ben Helfgott, in conversation with the author, 14 March 1996.

officers accosted us: "Who are you? What are you doing here?" Somewhat taken aback and surprised we replied, "Can't you see? We are survivors from the concentration camp and we are returning to our home town." To our amazement, they asked for some proof, which we immediately produced in the form of an identity card which had been issued to us in Theresienstadt, the place of our liberation. They were still not satisfied and ordered us to come with them to the police station for a routine check. It seemed rather strange to us, but we had nothing to fear. Fortified by our experience in Czechoslovakia and believing in a better world, now that the monster that had tried to destroy the people of Europe was vanquished, we walked along with the two officers chatting animatedly about the great future that was in store for the people of Poland.

'The streets were deserted in the prevailing darkness, as there was still a curfew after midnight, and street lighting had not been restored yet. My cousin and I were getting tired, as we carried our cases which contained clothing we had received from the Red Cross. Casually I asked, "Where is the police station? It seems so far." The reply was devastating and shattering, "Shut your f.... mouth you f.... Jew!!!!!!"

'I was stunned, hardly believing what I had just heard. How could I have been so naive, so gullible? The Nazi cancer was removed but its tentacles were widespread and deeply rooted. How I had lulled myself into a false sense of security. I believed what I wanted to believe. I had experienced and witnessed so much cruelty and bestiality, yet I refused to accept that man can be wicked. I was grown up in so many ways, yet I was still a child dreaming of a beautiful world. I was suddenly brought back to reality and began to fear the worst. Here I was in the middle of nowhere, with no one to turn to for help. My thoughts were racing, my heart was throbbing faster and faster. On the one hand, I was castigating myself for allowing myself to be lured into this seemingly hopeless situation, on the other hand, I was scheming about how to extricate ourselves from a clearly dangerous situation. The Russians were still well in control and I was hoping against hope that if I were to see a Russian sentry, I would shout for help. Alas! there was no Russian to be seen!

'At last we stopped at a house where one of the officers knocked at a gate which was opened by a young Polish woman. We entered a room which was dimly lit by a paraffin lamp, and we were ordered to open our suitcases. They took most of the clothing and announced that they would now take us to the police station. It seemed inconceivable to me that this was their real intention, but we had no choice and we had to follow events as they unfolded. As we walked in the dark, deserted streets, I tried desperately to renew conversation so as to restore the personal and human touch, but it was to no avail. I tried hard to conceal and ignore my true feelings and innermost thoughts, pretending to believe that they were acting in the name of the law, but they became strangely uncommunicative. After what seemed an eternity, we arrived at a place which looked frightening and full of foreboding. The buildings were derelict and abandoned; there was no sign of human habitation; all one could hear was the howling of the wind, the barking of the dogs and the mating calls of the cats.

'The two officers menacingly extracted the pistols from their holsters, and ordered us to walk to the nearest wall. Both my cousin and I felt rooted to the ground, unable to move. When at last I recovered my composure, I emitted a torrent of desperate appeals and entreaties. I pleaded with them: "Haven't we suffered enough? Haven't the Nazis caused enough destruction and devastation to all of us? Our common enemy is destroyed and the future is ours. We have survived against all odds and why are you intent on promoting the heinous crimes that the Nazis have unleashed? Don't we speak the same language as you?"

'I went on in the same vein, speaking agitatedly for some time. Eventually one of the officers succumbed to my pleas and said, "Let's leave them. They are, after all, still young boys." As they put away their pistols, they made a remark which still rings loud in my ears. "You can consider yourselves very lucky. We have killed many of your kind. You are the first ones we have left alive." With this comment they disappeared into the night.

'My cousin and I looked at each other, unable to comprehend what had transpired. We were trembling and completely shattered by this experience. Racing through our minds was the realisation that we had been nearer death in a free and liberated Poland than at any time during the ordeals of more than five and a half years under Nazi tyranny.'

Ben Helfgott often reflected on this terrifying moment of his life when, after being so close to death at every turn for so many years, he came face to face with death again. 'We were indeed fortunate to have escaped this fate at the hands of the Poles,' he later wrote. 'However, I cannot help thinking of the many survivors who returned to Poland after the war and who were killed by the Poles. Since my liberation it has been my abiding preoccupation and a tremendous source of joy and pleasure to renew contact with all those with whom I shared similar experiences. I am fortunate in having had the opportunity of travelling all over the world, thus being able to renew and maintain contact with them. There are some, however, with whom I was liberated and who, like me, had returned to Poland after the war, and of whom there is no trace. I often wonder what happened to them. Were they the unlucky ones whose appeal to the misguided Poles went unheeded and whose bodies lie strewn like dogs, in unknown and forsaken places?'[42]

Shattered by his experience at Czestochowa, Ben Helfgott returned to Theresienstadt. There, his survivor friends told him, 'Do you know, we're going to England.' Ben later recalled, 'When I heard "Going to England", I couldn't think of anything else'.

Like Ben Helfgott, and like many other boys, Roman Halter also made his way back to Poland, from the farm near Dresden where he had been living under a Polish name (Roman Podlawski) with a German couple, Kurt and Hertha Fuchs, together with two other Jews who had escaped a death march, Josef Szwajcer and Abram Sztajer. 'Liberation came in the form of a Russian soldier reaching the farm and demanding watches,' Roman Halter later recalled. 'That night, my grandfather, who died of hunger in the Lodz ghetto, came into my dreams. He urged me to get up and to go back to Chodecz. It was such a vivid dream that I got up and began to dress and then realised that it was all a dream.

'Next morning, on May 5, I thought about the dream a lot, because I wanted to understand what it meant. Why did my grandfather, who was also my best friend, ask me to go back to the town of my birth? Would I meet up there with my brother Itzhak (Iccio) who might have come back from Russia already? My sister Zisa (Zosia), six and a half years my senior, might have escaped from the Warsaw ghetto and hidden with a Polish family. Now she too might have returned to our family house in Chodecz. Who knows, my other brother Pessach (Pecio) who had been a manager in a textile factory in Lodz before the war, and who together with his wife and small son had escaped to southern Poland when the ghetto was set up in the spring of 1940, might also have returned. He, with wife and child, perhaps they were making their way to Chodecz, where we would all meet up. Thinking about them made me long for my family. Perhaps then, for the first time, I realised all my beloved ones were dead and gone – dead for ever and ever.'

His companions Abramek Sztajer and Josef Szwajcer thought Roman Halter was 'impetuous to leave so quickly' but he was determined to do so. During his return journey, while still in Germany, he found a few glass jars of preserved meat in a deserted farmstead. 'As I sat there resting,' he wrote, 'I heard the sound of a motorbike in the distance, coming towards me along the road from the left. A Russian soldier drove up and stopped in front of me. I stood up. I was pleased to see him. Disliking the SS and the Nazis, I thought of the Russians as friends,

---

[42] Ben Helfgott, 'My welcome to Poland after the war', *Journal of the '45 Aid Society*, No. 10, April 1983.

liberators and good people. My mother and my father spoke Russian as well as German. My father had served in the Tsar's army. He was twenty years older than my mother. As a child I learned a few words of Russian and German from them.

'My German now was fair, but I still remembered the Russian words which I had learned from my parents. "Ruski, ja cie lublu!" I said. ("Russian, I love you") and then added, "Zdrastvite towarisz" ("Hello friend"). He looked at me strangely and began speaking Russian very fast. I smiled and said in Polish that I was unable to understand him. He looked me up and down. Then he looked at my bike and said, "Dawaj czasy" ("Give me watches"). I understood that. He pulled up his shirt sleeves and showed me his forearms full of watches and then repeated the two words again. "Dawaj czasy."

'I glanced at his eyes, they were stern and cold. I began speaking to him in Polish. I said that I hadn't got watches and showed him both my thin forearms. He pointed to the bulging blanket fixed to my bike's crossbar and said something in Russian. I went up and took out one jar and handed it to him. "Mieso," I said. "Towarisz, mieso" ("Comrade, meat"). The meat was visible through the glass. He looked at it and then at me. "Towarisz, you have it, please take it and enjoy it."

'He lifted the glass jar and held it above his head for a second or so and then smashed it on to the ground. The glass and the meat spattered in all directions. I looked at the Russian soldier and fear entered my heart. What could I say to make him leave me alone? I felt momentarily numb. "Lower your trousers," he said in his language. I stood there shaken and didn't quite know what he meant. He repeated his command and by gestures showed me what he wanted me to do.

'Though at first the bike was on the ground, now I was holding it. I must have lifted it when I went to get the glass jar of meat for him. In my thoughts I begged my grandfather to come to my aid. I put my bike carefully on the ground so as not to break the glass jars in the pouch and began lowering my trousers. "Why is he making me do this?" I thought. Perhaps he thinks that I carry a belt with watches around my waist. I must tell him that I am not a German who just speaks Polish. So, as I was lowering my trousers and showing him that I am without belt or watches around my waist, I slowly told him in Polish that I am a Jew. I knew the word "Ivrei". "Ja Ivrei," I repeated. "Ja Ivrei, ja towarisz" ("I am a Jew, I am a comrade").

'I stood before him now naked from my waist down, although my instinct told me not to take off my good lace-up boots in case he took them and left me bare-footed. I could not reach Chodecz bare-footed. So I let my trousers and pants hang over my socks and boots. I glanced at his eyes again. There was a look of contempt in them as he was viewing the exposed part of my body. I saw in them a killer's void.

'He took out his revolver from his holster, pointed at my head and pulled the trigger. There was a loud click. Without a word to me he kick-started his motorbike and drove off. I stood there for a time with my trousers and pants down and looked at him disappearing into the distance, and then I looked at the ground where fragments of glass were embedded in the precious meat that lay pancaked in one area – and spattered all around it were bits, like farmhouses surrounding my town of Chodecz.

'I thought of picking up the bigger and cleaner pieces of meat and carefully checking them for bits of glass. But I decided not to. I must value myself, I will behave with dignity. I am not a dog, I told myself. The Russians have liberated me. I am free. But why did this Russian soldier do this to me? I stood there baffled and shaken and kept on staring at the meat on the ground on which flies were now settling and heard myself saying out aloud, "Such lovely meat ... what a waste ... what a terrible waste!"

'It was quite a time before I made a move from the spot where the Russian soldier had wanted to shoot me. I must have sat there next to my bike for at least half an hour. Perhaps, I thought, he emptied his revolver on the people from whom he took the watches which he had on his forearms. Or the revolver may have jammed. All the way to Bautzen I kept on thinking of this incident. I knew that the Nazis and the SS hated us, the Jews, and wanted to murder us all. But the Russians were the liberators. They fought and defeated the Nazis, Hitler and the SS. I, a Jew, ought to be treated like a friend by the Russian soldiers.'[43]

Roman Halter reached Chodecz, which he had last seen five years earlier, at the time when his parents had been deported to their deaths at Chelmno, and he had been sent to the Lodz ghetto. On reaching his town he went straight to his former home, in which a Polish family were living. 'I had the feeling they were going to kill me,' he later recalled. 'They didn't want to give up part of the house.'[44]

Leaving Chodecz, Roman Halter made his way from Poland to Czechoslovakia, and then, about seven weeks later, 'I travelled – mostly on the tops of trains – from Czechoslovakia back to the family Fuchs, together with gifts of soap, coffee, sugar, and smoked meat, the profits from my black-market transactions. I thought I would surprise them with this gift of a few items of appreciation and thanks for having taken me in and hidden me during March and April 1945.'[45]

---

[43] Roman Halter, letter to the author, 14 November 1994.

[44] Roman Halter, in conversation with the author, 21 April 1996.

[45] Roman Halter, 'How I was helped ...', *Journal of the '45 Aid Society*, No. 16, April 1994, page 7.

Roman Halter's generous impulse was to come up against yet another harsh reality of the war years. 'When I arrived,' he later wrote, 'I found Mrs Fuchs all in black. Her face had aged by years in those few weeks since my departure from them. She screamed when she saw me and refused to speak. Her neighbour told me that a few days after I had left, the Nazis in the village had found out that the Fuchses had sheltered Jews in their home. They then went to the house and took out Mr Fuchs, Szwajcer and Sztajer. Mr Fuchs and Szwajcer were shot. Sztajer managed to talk himself out of it. Mrs Fuchs dragged her husband's body back to the garden and buried him under a walnut tree. When I heard this, I left the provisions I had brought for Mrs Fuchs with a neighbour and returned immediately to Czechoslovakia.'[46]

Remembering that terrible day forty years later, Hertha Fuchs told Roman Halter: 'When I heard the shots, I knew that my lovely Kurt was dying. So I ran out into the field and took his head on to my lap. He tried to speak, to say something to me. Szwajcer lay dead. Those who murdered my husband and Szwajcer were just walking away. One of them said, "We can get her now, too", but they just walked away.'[47]

From Dresden, Roman Halter made his way back to Prague, and then to Theresienstadt. 'I was totally lost, I was totally alone,' he later recalled. 'I smuggled myself into the camp. Someone said to me, "There is a special place here for children, they may take you in". There, they asked me my age, and said I had to be under sixteen (I had reached my eighteenth birthday on July 7). I said, "I'll be any age you tell me to be". On the following day, I met Ben Helfgott.'[48]

Roman Halter had joined those boys who were about to fly to Britain.

Arthur Poznanski had been liberated by the Americans after escaping from a deportation train on its way to Mauthausen. Having been shot in the leg while escaping, he later wrote, 'I was taken to a hospital in Klatovy where I regained the use of my severely wounded leg, and also learned Czech and Russian. When I could limp without the aid of crutches, I travelled by train to a repatriation camp in Pilsen. I escaped from this camp and rode on the roof of a train across the border to Prague, in the Russian zone. By chance I learned that my brother, Jerzy, was in Theresienstadt. Once there, however, I was unable to enter legally because it was in quarantine. So I crossed the moat and crawled through the sewers to join him.'[49]

[46] Roman Halter, letter to the author, March 1993.
[47] Roman Halter, 'Before and after', *Journal of the '45 Aid Society*, No. 18, December 1994, page 14.
[48] Roman Halter, in conversation with the author, 21 April 1996.
[49] Arthur Poznanski, recollections, letter to the author, 24 January 1995.

Arthur Poznanski had smuggled himself into Theresienstadt. From there, with his brother, he too joined the boys as they prepared to go to England. When Joshua Segal and his brother arrived at Theresienstadt from Bratislava – where their war had ended fighting alongside Czech partisans – they too had to be smuggled into the camp: two boys whom they had known in their home town of Piotrkow, Kopel Dessau and Harry Fox, 'were able to take us through a back tunnel'.[50]

Where would the survivors go? Shimon Klin recalled the day on which the Russian military governor of Theresienstadt, Major Khurzmir, 'assembled all the Jews in the courtyard of the Dresden Armoury in Theresienstadt, and addressed us from a balcony. A Jewish delegate from the Polish government was standing at his side. He began his address: "Polish Jews and Jewesses! Return to your homeland, to your own soil, to your houses, to your property." The Polish delegation continued in much the same vein. I felt that I had no reason to go back. There was already a strong Zionist movement in Germany, preparing groups for Hachshara[51] in Germany to be followed by emigration to Palestine. Children's houses were formed at Theresienstadt where we were taught a little Hebrew. We were left undisturbed by the Russians.

'At first there were rumours that the youth groups were going to Switzerland, but after a while it became quite clear that we were going to England. On hearing this, the Polish Jewish delegate raced round on his motorbike, and warned us that anyone caught wandering outside the camp gates would be sent back to Poland. Major Khurzmir took us to see an anti-capitalist film demonstrating the exploitation of workers in America. Czech soldiers, meeting us in the street, asked whether it was true we were going to England, telling us, "Russia is much better".'[52]

'In July and August 1945,' Howard Chandler recalled, 'we went before a Red Cross Commission and were destined to go to England. Those who were still ill and did not pass the health test had to stay behind.'[53]

'I was liberated in Theresienstadt,' Michael Perlmutter recalled, 'and the promise of England was a dream beyond expectation. But it happened, and how we embraced each other as our new-found family. Several hundred boys and girls became human again, and formed attachments and friendships that would never die.'[54]

Harry Balsam was nearly sixteen. 'About four weeks after the war,'

[50] Josh Segal (Jehoszua Cygelfarb), letter to the author, 17 February 1995.

[51] Agricultural training: preparation, in every European country, for life in Palestine, a central feature of pre-war Zionism.

[52] Shimon Klin, 'Day of Liberation', manuscript, sent to the author, 9 November 1994.

[53] Howard Chandler (Chaim Wajchendler), letter to the author, 23 February 1995.

[54] Michael Perlmutter, letter to the author, 4 March 1995.

he recalled, 'my friend Pomeranc and I decided to go back to Poland to look for some living relatives, and at the same time to find the treasure that I had hidden when I was in Plaszow camp. When we arrived in Prague we had a whole day to spend because the train for Poland was not leaving till 10 p.m., and whilst we were there we met up with a lot of other survivors who were also looking around the town and waiting to go back to Poland.

'At about seven o'clock my friend Pomeranc and I went to the station, because we heard that the trains were getting packed with survivors wanting to return to Poland. While at the other station we met some Jews who had just returned from Poland. We told them that we were waiting to go back home. They said that we must be mad to want to go back as they were still killing Jews in Poland. We could not believe it and asked who was killing the Jews now. They told us the Poles were doing what the Germans could not manage, and that they had been lucky to come out alive from Poland. We got frightened. We were only fifteen years old at the time. So we returned to Theresienstadt and warned the other boys not to go back because it was dangerous in Poland. I stayed in Theresienstadt until August 14.'[55]

Lipa Tepper, from the southern Polish town of Dukla, recalled how, in Theresienstadt, 'one day somebody said to me that there was a group of young people going to England, why don't I go and register. I cannot honestly remember who the man was who told me that, but I think he was a man from my home town. I think we were together in Schlieben. Anyway, I went along and registered. I was accepted and I prepared to go to England. We were then gathered together. We lived in big houses, all together, and then one day we were taken to Prague and we went to a restaurant – for the first time in so many years – and then we were taken to Prague airport and from there we flew to England.'[56]

After being liberated at Theresienstadt, Chaim Ajzen had returned to Poland, to his home town of Bialobrzegi, together with a friend, to search for any relatives who might have survived. 'When we arrived in Bialobrzegi,' he recalled, 'I did not feel well. I acquired a room for us and went out to look at the town where all my family perished. I met an old friend with whom I had gone to school. He was one of the "good Poles", and the first question he asked me was, "What – you are still alive?" I was very angry when I left him, and when I returned to our accommodation I told David that if he felt better, the next day we would leave Poland and return to Theresienstadt. On the way back we were

[55] Harry Balsam, letter to the author, 8 May 1995.
[56] Lipa Tepper, letter to the author, 30 January 1996.

arrested at the Polish/Czech border by the Poles and put into gaol together with German prisoners of war because we had no identification. However, we were lucky enough to have some cigarettes which we gave to a Polish officer and he let us go.

'We managed to catch a train back to Theresienstadt, where I met my dear, good friend Kopel[57] again. He informed me that a group of children were going to England and he took us to the appropriate agency. The manager told us that there were no more places available, but that two boys on the list had left for Poland and had not returned. It was suggested that we go to England on their names and change back to our own names once we reached England. From Theresienstadt we went to Prague, but there my luck ran out. The day before we were leaving for England, one of the boys came back; his name was Lieberman. He then travelled under the name of Ajzen and I became Lieberman. We changed back when we arrived at Windermere.'[58]

Meir Sosnowicz was among the many boys who had been so weak at the time of liberation to have been thought most likely to die. 'When I had somewhat recovered,' he later wrote, 'I joined a group in a house reserved for young people who did not know where to go or what to do with themselves. Soon we learned that the younger people (officially orphans) would be allowed to go to England. We stayed at this house until all the arrangements were completed. I spent about three months in Theresienstadt, a time of which I do not have much recollection because I was so sick.'[59]

Jona Fuks, from the small Polish town of Tuszyn, had been separated from his brother Harry after their time together at Buchenwald. Jona had been liberated near the Austrian town of Linz. He made his way to Theresienstadt in search of his brother. 'Eventually I found him,' he later wrote. 'You can imagine what that was like. He thought that I was dead and I had no idea what had happened to him. I told him that I thought that we should go back to our home in Poland. He said that he was on a list to go to England. He explained that there were three hundred children who had already passed a physical examination and were signed up to go to England.'[60]

On his way back to his home town of Bircza, Jack Rubinfeld had also gone back to Przemysl. He was sixteen years old. He recalled how, in Przemysl, the Jewish Committee provided him with food and shelter.

---

[57] Kopel Kandelcukier (later Kendall), one of the boys.

[58] Chaim Ajzen, 'Chaim Ajzen's Story', manuscript, sent to the author.

[59] Michael Novice (Meir Sosnowicz), recollections, manuscript, June 1995.

[60] John Fox (Jona Fuks), recollections, Gala Recognition Dinner brochure, Hilton Hotel, Philadelphia, 8 September 1993.

'They warned me not to go to Bircza or any other village. Survivors were getting killed by Ukrainian nationalists and Polish nationalists. I also learned that approximately forty men, who had escaped in 1944 from our camp in Rzeszow, had been killed by Polish nationalists. Obviously we had to get the hell out of there.'[61]

Jack Rubinfeld made his way to Prague, then to Munich, and finally to Feldafing refugee camp, where he learned that papers were being processed to send a group to England. He was sent to join the group at a convent, Kloster Indersdorf, in Bavaria. Their destination was not to be Windermere, but Southampton.

Mojsze Besserman was also among those boys who, after liberation, were gathered together at Kloster Indersdorf, before being flown to England. Of the Southampton group, he 'will always be remembered', Kurt Klappholz later wrote, 'for his famous reply to an UNRRA[62] worker who had chided him for (allegedly) spending too much time with one of the Polish girls who were also among the residents at Kloster Indersdorf. With an unforgettably innocent expression on his face, Mojsze issued this rejoinder, "If she loves me and I love her, surely everything is all right". After thirty-six years it is difficult to remember that this memorable phrase was not uttered in English, but it is still easy to remember that it had the desired effect: the UNRRA worker left the room, apparently at a loss for words.'[63]

Alec Ward was among those boys liberated by American forces at Mauthausen. With twelve other survivors he lived for some while with German families near Regensburg. 'Some of us worked for the American forces in return for food which we shared with the German families,' he later recalled. 'When I was leaving for England the German lady of the house cried bitterly.'[64]

Not everyone who hoped to go to Britain was able to do so. One of the unlucky ones was Rudy Karmeinsky, who was born in the Upper Silesian town of Rosenberg in 1927 and had been deported to Auschwitz in 1943, where he became a slave labourer at Buna. He had been liberated by the British at Belsen. 'I and others failed to get to England,' he later wrote. 'We missed the '45 group because somebody decided that we should go to Palestine or the United States, but certainly not to England. There were about fifty of us, and a plane had been arranged.' It was to be a year before Rudy Kennedy, as he later became, was able to make his way to Britain. Later he joined the boys in the '45 Aid

[61] Jack (Israel) Rubinfeld, 'Jack Rubinfeld', manuscript, sent to the author, undated (1995).

[62] United Nations Relief and Rehabilitation Administration.

[63] Kurt Klappholz, 'Morris (Mojsze) Besserman' (obituary), *Journal of the '45 Aid Society*, No. 9, December 1981.

[64] Alec Ward, letter to the author, 12 June 1995.

Society.[65] Fifty years after liberation, in the society's commemorative brochure, he dedicated a page to the memory of his father Ewald, his mother Adele, his sister Kate 'and all others who were murdered by the Germans during the Holocaust'.[66]

Sala Kaye's mother survived the war. Mother and daughter had been together throughout the war, first at the slave labour camp at Blizyn and then at Auschwitz. After liberation they went back together to their home town, Wolanow, near Radom. 'We arrived home, to our house,' the sixteen-year-old girl recalled, 'and found Polish people living in it. They turned on us threateningly, "You had better go back where you came from; it is very dangerous here for Jews". We were afraid, and stayed there only a very short time, but we found out that Joseph, my oldest brother, had been killed one day before liberation. He was not yet thirty. The Poles denounced him to the Germans. His wife and baby had perished in Treblinka.'[67]

Sala made her way back to Prague, where she was put on the list of those waiting to begin the journey to England.

As soon as the Russian quarantine was lifted at Theresienstadt, and the typhus epidemic declared at an end, those who were well enough to leave did so. Many of the boys went to Prague. Others, who had been liberated elsewhere, also went there in search of food and shelter. Henry Golde, from the Polish town of Plock, recalled many 'memorable' days in the Czech capital. 'This was the first time we were out of the camps, and for the first time I realised that I was finally free. How could I not love this place after what I had been through?'[68]

Michael Etkind, who had been liberated while on the death march from Sonneberg, was brought to the Russian military hospital in Prague in the Russian military uniform which his liberators had given him. Not wanting to remain under Russian control, he managed to walk out and transfer to a temporary civilian hospital, housed in a school. 'The building was very crowded,' he recalled. 'I took off my uniform and was given a pair of pyjamas. I was surrounded by men of different nationalities. When I closed my eyes, it reminded me of the times before the war when I would turn the knobs on the radio and hear different languages. People were speaking Hungarian, Dutch, Polish, Yiddish, Rumanian and other dialects I could not place.

[65] Rudy Kennedy (Karmeinsky), 'Remember Bloomsbury', manuscript, sent to the author, 18 December 1995.

[66] '45 Aid Society Commemorative Brochure, May 1995.

[67] Sala Kaye (Bernholz), 'Sala Kaye Remembers', *Holocaust Testimony 1*, published by Roman Halter and Michael Etkind, London, 1983.

[68] Henry Golde, letter to the author, 16 March 1995.

'I became feverish and called a nurse. A young nurse came to me and took my pulse. I told her that I could hear my sister's voice outside. She called two other girls. I heard very clearly my sister's voice saying "Let me in, my brother is in there!" I yelled at the top of my voice, "Henka!", and immediately realised that it was a hallucination. The young girls looked alarmed and tried to calm me down. "I am Henka," said one of them. I smiled and shook my head. I felt ashamed. They called a young Hungarian Jew, who was praying in the next room. We both felt awkward. He asked me whether I wanted to join them in a prayer. I shook my head. When I fell asleep I dreamed that they were saying "Kaddish" over me (the prayer for the dead). I woke up in a sweat.'

Transferred to yet another hospital, Michael Etkind doubted if he would ever regain his health. One day he decided to leave hospital altogether, and try to live as normal a life as possible in the city. 'The day was sunny and the streets of Prague were beautiful,' he recalled. 'Cheerful crowds were milling around. Everyone was smiling, People would come up to me and insist on giving me money. Tramcar conductors would not accept my fare. Restaurants would not accept any payment from me. I started to go to a place called "Charity". It was a convent where hundreds of people from the camps would gather to eat and to meet one another. I recognised people from Lodz. "Whatever you do, don't go back to Poland", was the advice. "The Poles are killing all the Jews returning from the camps" was the constant story. "Your sister did not survive," I was told by a woman I knew in the ghetto. "She died of TB before the final evacuation." I ran away from that woman. I did not want to hear any more. I did not want to believe her. "Maybe she is lying," I thought. "How does she know anyway? She could be mistaken." And yet I knew that if I went back to Poland, something terrible would happen to me. I had never known such fear. Not even in the camps.

'There was a place where clothing was being issued to people from camps. Since none of us had any identification papers, some would queue a number of times giving different names on each occasion. I found this practice repulsive. The Czech people were so kind to us, and yet some people found it necessary to cheat, and of course everybody's reputation was tarnished by the behaviour of a few.'

For a while Michael Etkind left Prague, to work on a farm run by two elderly sisters not far from the city. His strength began to come back. Returning to Prague, he would sleep each night in a different school, 'eat mainly at the "Charity" and meet hundreds of people from all over the world. Here we knew what was going on. Prague was the centre of the world. Each night we would go to another cinema. The place was milling with people from all over Europe. Everybody was talking to everybody else. A girl from Rumania approached me and my friend

Szlamek. "Why don't you come with me to Rumania?" she said. "My family have a farm and a vineyard there, it's a good life."

'A man of over forty sat down beside us, and we immediately began to talk. He was from Lvov, and he had managed to survive the war by pretending not to be Jewish. "Once I was caught," he said, "and taken to the police station. I insisted that I was not Jewish, and so they wanted to see whether I was not circumcised. The guard took me outside, and we went behind a shed. I managed to knock him down and to run away." I was impressed. Not many Jews had the courage to do that.'

One day Michael Etkind and his survivor friend Szlamek met two girls, one of whom was Szlamek's cousin. 'The girls were smartly dressed and they invited us to their hotel. There were about six or eight girls in that hotel apartment. They were all very pretty and their ages varied from seventeen to twenty. "Why don't you go to Terezin?" they said to us, while we were eating cakes and drinking tea. They told us all about Terezin. "There are hundreds of boys like you and they will be going abroad, why don't you join them?" We immediately liked that idea. "Come with us," I said as we were about to say goodbye. "What are you doing here?" I immediately regretted the question, which I sensed had made them embarrassed. They took us down in the lift to the foyer of the hotel. I noticed that the Russian officers we passed were on familiar terms with the girls.'

Michael Etkind took the girls' advice and went to Theresienstadt. There, some boys took them to the administration building. 'They led us into a room,' Michael Etkind later wrote. 'A big man with a moustache was sitting in the middle with a pencil. "What is your name? How old are you?" "Twenty." He looked at me incredulously. "You were born in 1930", he said. "Go and find a bunk to sleep".'[69]

Sixteen was the upper age-limit for the journey to Britain. Many boys who, like Michael Etkind, were older, took the advice he was given and reduced their ages, in his case by five years.

Michael Etkind now qualified for the journey to Britain. When the day of his departure arrived, he gave what Czech money he had to a girl who was going to Palestine with her mother.

Chaim Olmer had been evacuated from Schlieben to Theresienstadt. There, immediately after liberation, he had been in a coma for six weeks. As he recovered, the nurse in charge of the hospital told him that she had been in a camp with his sister Sarah until about six weeks before the end of the war. Then, while walking in the street in Prague, 'an open-topped lorry went by and somebody shouted to me that he had

---

[69] Michael Etkind, '"Youth" Remembered', manuscript, sent to the author, 4 January 1996.

seen my sister in Poland'. It was also in Prague, Chaim Olmer recalled poignantly, 'that I saw a small child for the first time since 1942'.[70]

Misa Honigwachs (Michael Honey) was not a Polish-born but a Czech-born Jew. He had been among the original Czech deportees to Theresienstadt in 1942, and had later been deported to Birkenau. His father had gone to England before the war, intending that his family would join him, 'but due to delays in the issuing of visas', his son later wrote, 'we were unable to leave Czechoslovakia and so became stuck in the mire which became the Holocaust'.

In July 1945 Michael Honey returned to Czechoslovakia. Shortly after he reached Prague, he learned that a transport of children whose parents had been murdered was about to leave for England. Determined to link up with his father, 'I quickly concluded that the best thing would be to join such a transport. I could always worry afterwards about establishing my father's address in England. Eventually someone told me to ask at the Ministry of the Interior in Prague. The Ministry occupied a large building on Karlovo Namesti, where I enquired in almost every room if anyone knew who was organising a transport of children to England. At that time the whole building was in a hopeless muddle, and people in adjacent rooms did not even know what the officials in the room next to them were doing. 'It was a Kafkaesque situation writ large. I worked my way round the top floor and was halfway around the floor below when I walked into the room of Victor Fischl. He is now the writer Avigdor Dagan. When I told him what I wanted, he asked who I was, and I told him my name, Misa Honigwachs. To my delight, he said that he knew my father in London and that he himself had just returned to Prague, together with the Czech government which had returned to Czechoslovakia from its wartime exile in London. He told me that it was his wife Stella who really knew my father well from before the war. He said that somewhere on his desk he had a letter from my father.

'His desk was a heap of papers in terrible disorder. He looked for about ten minutes, but eventually gave up. He took my Prague address, and said that he would write to his wife in London who could then tell my father about me. Most importantly, he said he knew about the transport of children to England, and that he would see to it that I joined these children. I went to see him about twice every week and learned that the transport had to wait because the planes which would bring the Czech air force back to Prague from England would then take the children on their return journey.'[71]

---

[70] Chaim Olmer, recollections, letter to the author, 17 September 1995.

[71] Michael Honey (Misa Honigwachs), 'Bilong Notbilong' ('Belong, Not belong'), *Journal of the '45 Aid Society*, No. 18, December 1994.

Michael Honey waited in Prague for another month, and then joined the boys at Ruzyne airport, to board one of the Lancaster bombers that were to take them, and him, to England.

Solly Irving had, like so many of the boys, returned to Poland after the Buchenwald death train had deposited him in Theresienstadt. Returning by train to his home town of Ryki, he found that wherever he went in the town, people threw stones at him. 'The police, and Polish soldiers, stood around and laughed as stones were being thrown at me,' he later wrote. 'Some Poles said: "Look. There's still a Jew alive." So I went back to the station.'[72]

Returning to Theresienstadt, Solly Irving also joined those who were going to England.

On 11 August 1945, three months after the end of the war in Europe, the boys in Theresienstadt who were to be flown to England were taken to Prague by train. They travelled along the main Dresden-Prague railway line, along which some of the death trains had travelled a few months earlier. From the railway station in Prague the boys were taken on foot to a hostel. 'Suddenly,' recalled Pinkus Kurnedz, 'one of the boys saw his father, and he left the column and ran up to him, and they embraced.'[73]

In Prague, the boys were taken to the Belgitska Street Hostel, where they were looked after for the next three days. Bad weather had held up the Lancaster bombers that were to come from Britain for them. The boys now awaited one of the more unusual missions of mercy of the post-war months. It had its origins three months earlier, in May 1945, when a British Jewish philanthropist, Leonard Montefiore, had gone to Paris. While he was there, he saw some of the very first concentration camp survivors, who had been liberated from camps overrun by the British and Americans a few weeks earlier. These survivors had been flown to Paris direct from the camps. 'I had never seen anything so ghastly in my life,' Montefiore later commented. 'The people I saw were like corpses who walked. I shall never quite forget the impression they made.'

The question that concerned Leonard Montefiore – as it had concerned his famous kinsman, Sir Moses Montefiore, a hundred years earlier – was how to help Jews in need. 'When we got down to considering what could be done,' he said, 'there were immense difficulties. No money could

---

[72] Solly Irving (Shloime Zalman Judensznajder), 'Memories of a Past', manuscript, sent to the author, 5 April 1995.

[73] Pinkus Kurnedz, recollections, letter to the author, 5 October 1994.

be sent out of the country, and if money had been sent, there was nothing to buy. But if we could bring the people we wanted to help to this country, then the currency difficulties were cleared out of the way.

'In June 1945 the Home Office gave permission for a thousand orphans under the age of sixteen to be brought over for recuperation and ultimate re-emigration overseas. We pointed out immediately that it was unlikely that any documents would be available giving proof of age, and that children rescued from the concentration camps would most probably have no identity papers of any kind.

'Then we went back to the army and enquired if they had found any children still alive in the camps. At first we were told there were no children left alive at all, and it seemed as if our plans had been made in vain. But in August, relief workers for UNRRA told us there was a group of three hundred children from Theresienstadt who could be evacuated. This group had been collected at Prague and had been passed fit to travel by a local doctor approved by the British Embassy.'[74]

The documents giving permission for the youngsters to enter Britain stipulated that they could remain there for two years. Theirs was not the right of permanent residence, but a *permit de séjour*, permission to visit. They were to be rehabilitated, and then sent on.

On 14 August 1945, in the centre of Prague, the three hundred boys and girls were lined up and photographed. Behind them was the statue of Jan Hus, the Czech national hero who was burned at the stake in 1415 for his religious reforming zeal. The boys then boarded buses for the journey to the airport. On the way to the airport, Henry Golde recalled, 'I was feeling sad to leave this country, and the Czech people who treated us so well. But, on the other hand, I wanted to get away, as far as possible, from all the places and things that I had experienced – hell on earth.'

The boys and girls were taken by bus to Ruzyne airfield, just to the west of the city. The ten Lancaster bombers waiting on the tarmac were symbols of British air power, and of the systematic wartime destruction of German industry. That August morning their task was a mission of mercy. Led out to the runway towards them were 260 boys and forty girls, as well as thirty younger children between the ages of three and twelve, who, though they had not been through the slave labour camps, were, like the boys, to be rehabilitated in Britain.

'When I first looked at the planes, they looked gigantic,' Henry Golde recalled. 'Nothing like I remembered them during the bombing of

---

[74] Leonard G. Montefiore, *Address given to the Cambridge University Jewish Society on 18th October, 1946.*

Germany. At that time they were flying high and looked so very small. I remember how glad I was to see them raid Germany, even though the danger was to get killed by the bombing. I felt at that time, however, that it would be better to get killed by the Allied bombing than to be killed by the Nazis.'[75]

Jack Aizenberg remembered a Russian officer coming over to him at the airport, just as the boys were about to board the Lancaster bombers, and saying: 'Look, my boy, you are going to England. When you join the army or the air force, and when you are asked to bomb Moscow, I hope you will refuse. Don't forget we have liberated you.'[76]

[75] Henry Golde, letter to the author, 16 March 1995.
[76] Jack Aizenberg, recollections, manuscript, sent to the author, April 1995.

CHAPTER 12

Crosby-on-Eden: a 'precious cargo'

O N 14 AUGUST 1945 a dozen Lancaster bombers flew with their three hundred young passengers from Prague. 'We sat on the floor in the plane,' Howard Chandler later wrote. 'I found a spot in the nose of the plane just below the navigator and had a good view. I tried to talk to the crew, but only in sign language. They gave us white square slices of bread. Never having seen white bread, I thought it was cake or *challah*.'[1] The bombers stopped in Holland to refuel, where refreshments were provided for the youngsters on the tarmac. They then flew on to Crosby-on-Eden, a wartime bomber airfield just outside Lancaster.

Pinkus Kurnedz recalled 'lying in the nose, and above was sitting the navigator. I remember him eating sandwiches of white bread – we all thought that as they were crewmen they got special rations of white bread.'[2] 'I shall never forget that flight,' Sala Newton-Kaye recalled. 'So many were sick. We were sitting on the floor of the plane, with blankets, being ill. But what excitement! What joy!'[3]

Among those who accompanied the boys was Isidore Rosenblat, himself a survivor, who was some fifteen years older than the boys. He had looked after them in Theresienstadt, as had the two other leaders on the flight, Issie Finkelstein, and Rosenblat's brother, 23-year-old Sam, who had been in Buchenwald and Schlieben. All three were survivors of the Piotrkow ghetto. 'The flight was my first flying experience,' Sam Rosenblat later wrote. 'I was actually sitting in the centre of the plane in a gun turret on the floor – the belly of the plane. All the children were around me; I could look through the Plexiglas bubble of the turret to see the countryside beneath us. I was nervous, excited, frightened and joyful all at once. Since we were in a war plane (not a plane constructed for passenger flights) the flight was very rough. The children were frightened, but happy too! I had those same feelings.'[4]

One of those youngsters was Henry Golde. He was just sixteen. 'We

---

[1] Howard Chandler (Chaim Wajchendler), letter to the author, 26 February 1996.
[2] Pinkus Kurnedz, recollections, sent to the author, 5 October 1994.
[3] Sala Newton-Kaye (Hochspiegel), recollections, letter to the author, 10 December 1995.
[4] Sam Rosenblat, 'My Other Life in Another Time', manuscript, sent to the author, 24 January 1995.

were sitting very still throughout the flight,' he recalled. 'I, for one, was afraid that if I moved I might tip the plane and make it crash. This was my first time on a plane and I was scared to death. Throughout the flight I had mixed emotions. Was I doing the right thing going to England? A strange new country, a language which I didn't know. Will I be able to learn? Maybe I should have gone back to Poland, to my home town. No, there is nothing left there for me but bad memories. There are three hundred of us survivors. It is like a family, so I am not alone. If we stay together, we will all be fine.'[5]

Waiting for the boys on the tarmac at Crosby-on-Eden was a small welcoming party. Among them were two members of the Carlisle Women's Voluntary Services, Mrs Mark Fraser and Mrs Honeyman, as well as customs officials from Liverpool, and two officials from the Ministry of Health, Mr J. E. Etchells and Miss E. S. Thompson.

Those who had come to welcome the boys were headed by Leonard Montefiore, in his capacity as chairman of the specially created Committee for the Care of Children from the Concentration Camps, and Joan Stiebel, executive director of the Central British Fund, the two main organisations helping Jewish refugees when they reached Britain. 'When they arrived,' Joan Stiebel recalled, 'the children were not in very good shape. The plane had come down en route and the travellers had been plied with chocolate and oranges – not a good combination in rather choppy flying conditions!'[6]

That chocolate had made its impact on the boys. 'This was the first time in years that I had tasted chocolate,' Zvi Mlynarski recalled, 'after completely forgetting what it tasted like.'[7]

The place chosen for the immediate reception of the first three hundred youngsters was an unused wartime hostel near Windermere, in the Lake District. Detailed plans to receive the boys had begun many weeks before their arrival. Among those waiting to welcome them was Berish Lerner, himself a refugee who had come to England from Germany just before the war. He had reached Windermere on 6 July 1945, where, he later wrote, he helped prepare the accommodation and awaited the arrival 'of the children of the Theresienstadt transport'.

'On "D"-Day, August 14, when at long last we were informed that the Theresienstadt children would be arriving that evening, at the airport in Carlisle, there was great excitement and anticipation amongst the

[5] Henry Golde, letter to the author, 16 March 1995.
[6] Joan Stiebel, 'Children from the Camps', *Journal of the '45 Aid Society*, No. 19, December 1995.
[7] Zvi Dagan (Mlynarski), letter to the author, 1 March 1996.

staff. During the waiting period, we had many discussions and numerous questions were raised; how would we be able to cope with these traumatised youngsters who had been subjected to almost five years of persecution and witnessed wholesale murder, most of whom had lost parents and families? We asked ourselves whether we could succeed at all in bringing back to them some semblance of what was considered "normal".

'To me in particular, as well as to other religious *madrichim* – counsellors – there were additional questions which we discussed amongst ourselves.[8] How would the survivors react to our attempts at reintroducing Jewish traditions, which they were forced to leave behind when leaving their homes, which, in most cases, had been of a traditional Jewish background with observance of Kashrut, Shabbat and festivals? What feeling would a Siddur, Chumash and Tallit evoke?[9] Would the boys, without being pressured, join a Minyan for Tefillah?[10] Or would they resent being influenced to lead a traditional Jewish life once again which, for most of them, ceased in the ghettos and concentration camps? These and many other problems occupied our minds when the first buses, with their precious cargo, arrived.'[11]

Joan Stiebel was awaiting that 'precious cargo' at Crosby-on-Eden. 'Immigration officers and MI5 representatives were there, as were the Press', she recalled.[12] One of those members of the press was eighteen-year-old Joseph Finkelstone, a junior reporter working for the local newspaper, the *Carlisle Journal*. He had been living in Newcastle, and crossing the Pennines to Carlisle had been, for him, 'a chance to be trained'.[13] In his report, which was published three days later, headed 'They find refuge in the Lake District', he wrote of how the three hundred boys and girls had slowly emerged from the bombers: 'They looked pale, bewildered. Some seemed sick and weak. A tall, thin, austere white-haired man, wearing a light, well-tailored suit, welcomed them. As he did so, extending his hands and smiling, one youngster became sick and bespattered the front of the suit. The man appeared not to notice the incident, but kept on patting the heads of the boys and girls.'[14]

---

[8] *Madrich* (feminine *madricha*; masculine plural, *madrichim*; feminine plural, *madrichot*): the Hebrew word most frequently used by the boys for those who were their leaders and counsellors in Britain.

[9] Siddur: a prayer book. Chumash: the five books of Moses. Tallit: a prayer garment with fringes worn under the shirt.

[10] Minyan: ten people gathered to make a quorum for prayers. Tefillah: prayers.

[11] Berish Lerner, 'Windermere '45', *Journal of the '45 Aid Society*, No. 19, December 1995.

[12] Joan Stiebel, 'Children from the Camps', *Journal of the '45 Aid Society*, No 19, December 1995.

[13] Joseph Finkelstone, in conversation with the author, 6 May 1996.

[14] *Carlisle Journal*, 17 August 1945. The article was published anonymously; Joseph Finkelstone later became a distinguished journalist, serving for many years as Foreign Editor of the *Jewish Chronicle*.

Many years later, Joseph Finkelstone recalled: 'As a teenage junior reporter of the *Carlisle Journal* I had been ordered to "cover the arrival of some young people from Europe". It was not explained to me who they were. Only when I saw the boys and girls, in their ill-fitting clothes, tense as they entered a new world, did I suddenly realise with a pang that they had experienced the greatest human-made hell in history. They had seen their parents, sisters and brothers shot, starved and gassed by the Nazis. Seeing these youngsters, brought out from the horrors of Nazi Europe, had a profound effect on me. By that time, I already knew that most of my own close relatives, including cousins of the same age as the youngsters at the airport, had been murdered. As I sat down in front of the typewriter in the office to write the report for the paper, I was suddenly overwhelmed by emotion. Putting my head down on the typewriter, I wept.'

Two stories had struck Joseph Finkelstone with particular force. One concerned the stowaway. 'Precautions were taken to prevent any unauthorised person from joining the party,' he wrote, 'but the daring and resource of a Polish boy of thirteen and a half, Icek Korotnicki, overcame all obstacles. While working in the Polish town of Czestochowa he heard a rumour that there was going to be an evacuation of children to Britain from Prague, and arrived there four days before the children were due to leave. He was told that he could not be taken, and officials heard nothing more of him until, on the plane's arrival at Crosby, it was discovered that he was amongst the passengers. The boy was immediately put in a room by himself. When seen by a *Journal* reporter he was apparently oblivious of the stir he had caused and was quietly munching a piece of cake.'

The second story which Finkelstone reported – 'one that fascinated all those present' – was of a boy of fifteen who was dressed in a miniature United States Army uniform. 'He explained in hesitating English, that he was in Buchenwald when the Third American Army arrived and became attached to a tank destroyer company. An American captain became so interested in him that he took him to other fronts and the boy actually fought in several battles and was awarded a medal. When the two, now close friends, had to separate, the officer gave the boy a letter addressed to the American authorities. In it he stated that when conditions permitted and the boy could go to the States he would guarantee his schooling and work.'[15]

'The camps had been overrun by Allied troops in April and May,' Leonard

[15] Joseph Finkelstone, 'Fifty-year victory for waifs of war; how we gave life and love to death camp orphans', *Evening Standard*, 14 August 1995.

Montefiore later remembered, 'and it was now August. But I still had in mind the walking skeletons, with sunken eyes and yellow parchment skins, I had seen in Paris a few months earlier. It was a shock and a pleasant surprise to see the first batch get out of the planes, looking much fitter and stronger than anything we had expected.'[16]

Joan Stiebel waited in the airport building. 'Some time during that hectic afternoon,' she recalled, 'there was a call from one of the MI5 men: "Miss Stiebel, come – we've got a stowaway." This was Icek Korotnicki. 'He was clearly not a spy,' Joan Stiebel commented fifty years later.[17]

Another of those waiting that afternoon at the airfield was Alice Goldberger. It was her forty-eighth birthday. A pre-war refugee from Germany, her task was to look after the few young children who were believed to be on the flight. 'Plane after plane of youths arrived, mostly boys, but very few girls,' she later recalled. 'They had a grey, aged look which made it difficult to tell how old they were. We were relieved by their happiness on arrival. They joked, they laughed, they asked us whether they would be able to go to school. We welcomed each and when asked their age, most said they were between thirteen and fifteen, but it was hard to tell. (Later, we realised that even those who were over sixteen would not admit to it because they would not have been allowed to enter the country as part of this special children's airlift if they were older.) We began to worry after so many planes of youths arrived that there would be no small children. I thought about the dolls and bears in each of the beds and what a joke that would be to these adolescents when they got to their beds in Windermere. Finally, the last two planes arrived with less than twenty young children in them.'[18]

There were seventeen youngsters, each under the age of twelve, on that final flight. The six youngest – they were only three and four years old – were taken to Bulldog Banks, a cottage at West Hoathly donated for the purpose by Lady Clark, the wife of a Member of Parliament. There, they were looked after by two sisters, both of whom were pre-war refugees from Germany, Sophie Dann, a nursing sister, and Gertrude Dann, a teacher, and by Maureen Livingstone, a Scottish nursery school teacher. The eleven older children – those aged between four and eleven – were taken to Weir Courteney, a country house at Lingfield, Surrey, made available by Sir Benjamin Drage. Eleven other small children, most of whom had survived the war in hiding, were brought to Britain, and

---

[16] Leonard G. Montefiore, *Address given to the Cambridge University Jewish Society on 18th October, 1946.*

[17] Joan Stiebel, 'Children from the Camps', *Journal of the '45 Aid Society*, No. 19, December 1995.

[18] Alice Goldberger, quoted in Sarah Moskovitz, *Love Despite Hate, Child Survivors of the Holocaust and Their Adult Lives*, Schocken Books, New York, 1983, pages 5–6.

to Lingfield, eight months later. In all, twenty-four little ones were looked after by Alice Goldberger and her team of helpers at Lingfield.[19]

Maureen Livingstone, who was in charge of the six youngest of those who arrived at Crosby-on-Eden on August 14, later remembered her shock when 'I saw those six little children with shaved heads'. She became devoted to them. One, a boy named Jona, later became a taxi driver. Joanne, one of the girls, became a Justice of the Peace. Another, 'a little Hungarian girl – who seemed to be untouched by the whole thing – married a dentist in the Midlands.' Another girl was found by an aunt who had come to Britain before the war. The little children had one curious feature in common, Maureen Livingstone recalled. 'They were absolutely petrified by feathers. This was their big fear. They had a pillow fight – the feathers came out – they clung together in terror.'[20]

It was late in the evening before all the formalities had been dealt with. Then the boys were driven southward towards Windermere by bus and truck. Pinkus Kurnedz recalled looking out of the window of the bus and reading the advertising signs. 'A lot of the signs were "Wills Cigarettes". I did not know that "Wills Cigarettes" was a company. I thought that "Wills" meant "wants" a cigarette.'[21]

It was during that drive that a man on a bicycle called out that the Japanese had surrendered: the Second World War was over. For the boys the war in the Far East had been remote from their consciousness. Their war had ended three months earlier.

The last convoy reached Windermere in the early hours of the morning. 'The children were in amazingly good spirits,' Joan Stiebel recalled, 'and Mr Montefiore used to tell a story which indicated their joy at being in a free country. The truck he was in broke down en route and he apologised to his group for the delay. One boy said: "Don't apologise. It is an honour to break down on a British road". Surely that said it all.'

'The next day must have been a strange one for them all,' Joan Stiebel later wrote. 'There was so much that had to be done. Medical examinations, clothing distribution, acclimatisation to such a new environment and much more. One thing that stands out in my mind is the first main meal which the children had. Some of them emerged from it, their new jerseys bulging. Believing that there might not always be food, they had taken bread as a stand-by.'[22]

---

[19] The story of the Lingfield children has been fully and movingly told by Sarah Moskovitz, *Love Despite Hate, Child Survivors of the Holocaust and Their Adult Lives*, Schocken Books, New York, 1983.

[20] Maureen Livingstone, in conversation with the author, 3 May 1996.

[21] Pinkus Kurnedz, recollections, letter to the author, 5 October 1994.

[22] Joan Stiebel, 'Children from the Camps', *Journal of the '45 Aid Society*, No. 19, December 1995.

Harry Balsam recalled: 'We got a welcome reception. Everybody was very nice to us. They had prepared a single room for each of us. In the room was a bed, wardrobe, dressing table, pyjamas, a toothbrush, soap, towel and some slippers.'[23] Krulik Wilder later wrote: 'After arriving in Windermere, I was given a room to myself with a single bed, and blankets, and other bits and pieces that we had been deprived of for so long. The three months I spent in Windermere I was given food and some basic education in English. I used to go a lot to the cinema, walking, sightseeing and boating on Lake Windermere. It was sheer heaven, never in my life until then had I known such luxuries. I only have beautiful memories of this place.'[24]

'We were absolutely overjoyed!' recalled Mayer Hersh. 'It was paradise! On arrival, we were given trifle, and each one a bed with clean white sheets; it was heavenly!'[25]

'I remember our lorry broke down,' Mayer Cornell recalled of the drive from Crosby-on-Eden, 'and we arrived in Windermere in the early hours of the morning, to be greeted by a saintly looking gentleman with a full grey beard – Rabbi Dr Weiss.'[26]

Berish Lerner had been waiting at Crosby-on-Eden when what he had called his 'precious cargo' arrived. As he wrote fifty years later: 'The arrivals were mostly boys and, together with a few girls, they were led into the large centre hall. After receiving food and drinks, some preliminary personal details were recorded, followed by a medical examination by a team of doctors and nurses. I was put in charge of some forty boys and led them to a block, one of many low buildings. Each building was divided into many single cubicles into which the boys took their meagre belongings.

'In a sense, both the location near the village of Windermere, and, in particular, the layout of the individual cubicles, were really ideal for our purpose, because, for the first time in years, these young people had some privacy. During the war, the site and its buildings had been used by the Ministry of Aircraft Production as a hostel to accommodate workers in the aircraft industry. Windermere itself, with its adjoining large lake, gave one a feeling of a miniature Switzerland. It was in such beautiful surroundings that we were to spend many months together; but on this evening of the group's arrival, my thoughts were far removed from the idyllic countryside, for it took the staff many hours of making appropriate arrangements for the boys to settle down.

[23] Harry Balsam, letter to the author, 14 November 1995.
[24] Israel (Krulik) Wilder, letter to the author, 1 January 1995.
[25] Mayer Hersh (Herszkowicz), letter to the author, 21 November 1994.
[26] Mayer Cornell (Kochen), letter to the author, 9 February 1995.

'It must have been close to three in the morning of August 15, after the boys had gone to bed in their little rooms, when I went to each one in order to have a little chat and wish them a good night. I spoke to them in Yiddish, which was the only language we had in common. I realised then that by my speaking to them in fluent Yiddish, a bond was forged and I subsequently became known amongst them as "Berish der heimisher Madrich" – "Berish, one of our own".[27]

'Even during that little encounter at their bedside, I realised what a deep emotional contact was made between us, because I felt that I could identify with these boys, having had a similar background during my childhood, and it was as though we had known each other before this encounter. When asked what their place of birth was, I heard names that I recall from my childhood such as Cracow, Zmigrod, Piotrkow, Rymanow and other places. It gave me a feeling of nostalgia, because I left Poland as a young child in 1929, but still retained vague memories of these names of places from which my own parents and families came: and, except for one brother, all had perished during the war. I looked upon these boys as the *She'erit Hapleta* – "the remnant of those who survived" – the remnant of my own family. I felt great warmth and tenderness towards them.'[28]

Abraham Zwirek was one of the last to reach Windermere on that first night. He shared the wonderment of all the boys. 'When I woke in the morning and looked around,' he recalled, 'I thought I was in Heaven, there were white sheets on the bed and there was white bread to eat.'[29]

An official report prepared by the Westmorland County Council in 1946 described how 'as the children arrived, they were given cocoa and biscuits in the open air. They were then admitted to the first room, where their names were recorded. There was no nominal roll of the children and some of them did not know what their names were, as they had not seen their parents for up to six years; information had to be given by their comrades. Next the children were completely stripped, their clothes made into bundles and labelled, and each was handed a blanket. They then went into the next room where they were carefully inspected for cleanliness and vermin by a staff of nurses, and passed on for a final check by the doctor. Finally they entered a third room where they received fresh clothing and were sent to bed. The younger children

[27] Literally: 'Berish, our homely counsellor'.

[28] Berish Lerner, 'Windermere '45', *Journal of the '45 Aid Society*, No. 19, December 1995. The Hebrew phrase *She'erit Hapleta* is also used to describe those survivors who returned to Palestine, mostly, between 1945 and 1948, as illegal immigrants.

[29] Abraham Zwirek, letter to the author, 2 December 1994.

especially were unspeakably pathetic and very tired, and all of them were most thankful to get to bed.

'This cursory inspection was sufficient to reveal that their general state of cleanliness was excellent and not a single case of vermin was found. After working through the night, the inspection finished at 3.30 in the early hours of August 15, and hardly were the children safely disposed in bed when a detachment of infantry from a neighbouring camp marched by celebrating VJ-Day. After seeing and hearing all we had that night our feeling at being expected to celebrate a moment of victory and rejoicing can be imagined.'

During the next few days, the Westmorland County Council report noted, 'a complete examination was made of all the children and it proved that their condition was not as satisfactory as first appeared. Many of them were obviously above the age of sixteen (which was supposed to be the upper age-limit) and, indeed, they openly confessed that they had understated their ages so as to be allowed to come. Subsequently it was found that many were seventeen or eighteen, and one was even over this age.

'They appeared on the surface stout and well nourished, but this proved to be surplus fat which had apparently accumulated since they were properly fed and had been released from heavy work. In many cases superficial scars due to septic sores were visible on their limbs and bodies, and in some cases the sores were still discharging. A number of them had tattooed on the left arm the initial letter of the camp they had been in and their number.'

Four classes of 'defect' in the boys were identified by those who examined them in the first few days. The first was nutritional, resulting in some obesity and pulse-rate abnormalities: 'On exertion it was found that they easily became breathless and could take part in games for only a short time.' The second 'defect' was the post-typhus condition, seen particularly in those boys who had caught typhus in the epidemic at Theresienstadt the previous May; several of them were found to have 'a sallow complexion, an anxious expression, slight jaundice of the eyes and hair which was very thin and was commencing to grow again.... These children were definitely below weight, nervous, irritable and, in some cases, showed cardiac dilation.'

The third most frequently found 'defect' was that related to slave labour. 'Some of the children showed effects of the hard work which they had been made to do; there were several boys who showed a marked degree of varicose veins in the legs, one boy had a large scarred area over the shoulders caused by carrying damp bags of cement, whilst a girl showed marked lateral spinal curvature from the effects of carrying bricks when building bridges. There was considerable evidence of ill treatment including three cases of gunshot wounds, teeth knocked out and missing, and a very severe case of frostbite in which the stumps of the toes were still discharging; the boy had been compelled to walk with his feet in that condition.'

The fourth health 'defect' listed by the report was tuberculosis. 'Of the three hundred children,' the Windermere Tuberculosis Officer reported, 'eleven were open cases with Tubercular Bacilli in the spit which required hospital treatment. There were fifty-one others who showed signs of past infection and required supervision.'

The conditions under which the children had lived and worked 'must have made infection universal', the officer reported. His examination showed that they could be divided into three groups: '1, Those who in spite of everything had managed to develop and maintain a resistance. 2, Those in whom resistance had either not developed or had broken down, and who showed active breaking-down lesions, some with cavitation. A rather small group who probably represented those who had managed to "hang on" till rescue came without reporting sick (to go sick apparently meant a quickly fatal "termination"). 3, An in-between group with infection in which there were definite signs of healing and fibrosis – cases which one feels were "in the balance" and would probably have developed into TB if they had not been rescued at the time they were.'

The Tuberculosis Officer concluded that his remarks emphasised 'the toughness of these children' and gave 'some idea of the numbers who must have succumbed to this disease'.

As well as the physical problems, the psychological problems confronting the boys were also the subject of enquiry in the early days at Windermere. This aspect of their care was in the hands of Oscar Friedmann. A pre-war refugee from Germany, Friedmann had been sent to an orphanage in Berlin at the age of ten. He knew from firsthand experience a child's frustration and misery in an unsympathetic institution. Friedmann had been born in Germany in 1903. After training as a teacher and social worker, he became director of a Borstal near Berlin in 1932; when the Nazis came to power a year later, he and his charges were all sent to Sachsenhausen concentration camp for several months. As a result of a physical assault by one of the guards there, Friedmann suffered a permanent partial paralysis of the face, and some unsteadiness in one hand. He remained in Berlin after his release, and of his own free will returned to work with the boys in the Borstal. In 1938 he brought a large number of German Jewish children to Britain. He had intended returning to Germany, but was prevailed upon to stay in Britain, making his base Bloomsbury House, the London headquarters of the Central

British Fund. The main focus of his concern at that time was the mental health of the pre-war refugees.

Oscar Friedmann was forty-two years old when the boys came to Windermere. He became their devoted counsellor from the first days. The boys, a report on his work noted, 'came from a class of Jewish craftsmen who had a pride in the appearance of their children and a very strong family life'. One of the most noticeable features of the pattern of development of the boys in Britain, and in their other eventual destinations, was how this 'very strong family life' to which Friedmann had referred was to re-emerge as a central factor in their own lives.

In dealing with those at Windermere, Oscar Friedmann's policy had been 'a marked success', the report noted, 'and has shown his great wisdom. His principle was to allow all the social freedom possible, freedom to do anything which did not oppose ordinary social life; he made no rules that could not be reasonably explained, and as few as possible. The education of the children had been abandoned for as long as six years in some cases, and had literally to recommence; the children showed the utmost eagerness to learn all they could, and it is interesting to note that though there has been a certain amount of truancy from some classes there has always been a hundred per cent attendance at the English lessons; they were inquisitive to learn about the world in general and what was happening, and to try and ascertain what security they had in the future.

'A few showed marked nervous symptoms, sleeplessness and bad dreams, and there were two cases of somnambulism. These symptoms, however, have steadily improved, and there is only one case in the camp which still gives rise to anxiety.'

The Westmorland County Council Report revealed that 'from the time of their arrival from Prague there was a delay before the camp could be adequately organised, food for a few days was definitely poor in supply and cooking, and although this was recognised by the children, there was no complaint. It was explained to them that people here were being rationed, and that there was not an unlimited supply, and this caused them considerable surprise, as they were under the impression that England was a land of plenty.

'Clothing had to be supplied to them and only came through in gradual issues, and the chief difficulty was to deal with those who were awaiting clothing and could not understand the delay. Indeed they seemed to attach more importance to being clothed decently than to anything else, feeling that this was a certain proof that they were to be cared for and looked after. Their general mental attitude has proved rather different from what one normally might have expected. There was no marked depression, and they were eager to take up life more fully than their strength and opportunities permitted. They were exceedingly grateful for the kindness shown them and became genuinely attached to the staff.

'There was no deficiency in personal courage, indeed the quarrels which arose, as they were bound to do among all young folk, were often fought with exceeding ferocity. An interesting feature was the damage done to crockery, and it seemed that a boy would sometimes break an article deliberately as an expression of his aggression and independence, and not from carelessness. Similarly, if a chair moved it would not be put down quietly but firmly banged on the floor.'

In one of its sections the Westmorland Report revealed a basic inability, on the part of those who had only a casual acquaintance with the boys, to appreciate the full nature of what they had been through. In the years to come there would always be those who would characterise as exaggeration even the relatively mild descriptions which the boys gave of the terror of the camps. This lack of comprehension of what the boys had experienced between 1939 and 1945 was revealed in the report in the sentence: 'The tendency to exaggerate their adventures is dying down.'[30]

'Some "adventures"!' commented Ben Helfgott on reading that sentence.[31]

The report went on to say that the boys were 'now constantly thinking of the future and want to learn crafts; if any of their relations can be found they wish to join them and go wherever they go, but if such a prospect is not attainable they wish to go to Palestine. As a group, therefore' – the report concluded – 'there is remarkably little evidence of the effects of the strain they have been through; they are forming friendships in the camp, and while there is a very definite feeling of *esprit de corps* among them there is no formation of gangs. Although they are allowed complete freedom to go where they like, attend picture houses, etc., there has not been one single complaint of juvenile delinquency from the local police. They have also lived in the midst of the local population, and have been pestered by young English girls, but no complaints of any kind have been made about their behaviour in this respect.'[32]

Thorough dental examinations were also made soon after the boys arrived at Windermere. In his own report, the Senior Dental Officer of

[30] J. W. Dow, MD and Marjorie A. Brown, MA, *Evacuation to Westmorland, from Home and Europe, 1939–1945*, Westmorland Gazette Ltd, Kendal, 1946, pages 50–9.

[31] Ben Helfgott, in conversation with the author, 8 May 1996.

[32] J. W. Dow, MD and Marjorie A. Brown, MA, *Evacuation to Westmorland, from Home and Europe, 1939–1945*, Westmorland Gazette Ltd, Kendal, 1946, pages 50–9.

the county noted that 'examination of the mouths of the Jewish children revealed much gross caries and sepsis. 87% of the children inspected required some form of treatment – the remainder, mainly the youngest age groups, having been treated in Theresienstadt either during the war or since regaining their freedom. Examination of the sound teeth showed that these children had, naturally, well calcified dentitions, and but for this, would have been in a much worse state as the result of the abnormal conditions which they had experienced.'

The 'unsound teeth' fell into two main classifications – '(1) Those that were carious or septic as the result of neglect, lack of hygiene, bad feeding and absence of vitamins from the diet; (2) Those that were fractured by blows from SS guards. Many incisor teeth were missing for this reason.'[33]

As the boys settled down in Britain, there was another aspect of their hopes that was, for the moment at least, submerged in the struggle for recovery. 'The majority of us had arrived in England as a way to reach Palestine,' Ben Helfgott recalled forty years later. 'It never entered our minds to settle in England. After liberation we had been provided with passes as an identity, and on these we had to put down what our destination was, which in most cases was Palestine. But the British White Paper made it impossible to go straight to Palestine.'[34]

In the event, more than half of the 732 boys who were to reach Britain by the spring of 1946 remained in Britain. About a hundred made their way to Palestine after the declaration of the State of Israel in 1948. Two hundred went to the United States. About forty found their way to Canada, a few others to Australia, Brazil, Argentina and Switzerland. But as the first three hundred boarded the buses and trucks from Crosby-on-Eden to Windermere that evening, what mattered most to them was where they would sleep that night, and what they would eat in the morning.

[33] Senior Dental Officer, 'Dental Report on the Jewish Refugee Children', J.W. Dow, MD and Marjorie A. Brown, MA, *Evacuation to Westmorland, from Home and Europe, 1939–1945*, Westmorland Gazette Ltd, Kendal, 1946, pages 59–62.

[34] Ben Helfgott, speech to the Oxford University Jewish Society, Hilary Term, 1985.

CHAPTER 13

Windermere

'CHILDREN, CHILDREN, A cup of cocoa, a cup of cocoa.' These were the words with which Shimon Klin recalled being welcomed at Windermere. The person speaking them was Rabbi Dr Weiss, of the Ultra-Orthodox Gateshead Jewish community, who was then seen 'stretching out his hand and giving us a cup of cocoa, which was very refreshing and satisfying after our long, tiring journey'.[1]

The wooden barracks were decorated with blue-and-white posters with the Star of David on them. Among the three hundred boys who reached Windermere that August night in 1945 was Chaim Olmer, originally from Sosnowiec. 'The return to humanity began,' he has written. 'Clean clothes, a normal bed and bedding, and kind people to talk to.'[2] 'I was reborn,' Mayer Kochen, from Kielce, recalled, 'and started to feel like a human being again.'[3]

'On arrival,' Henry Green recalled, 'I was shown into a tiny room with a bed, chest of drawers and wardrobe. A room all to myself! Has anyone ever lived so luxuriously? It was a particular time of my life when there could have been no gift more precious. For the first time in years, in my short life, I would have the luxury of a room ALL TO MYSELF. I could have danced in the street for joy. I could, and would have, except for a small "technicality" – the clothes in which we arrived were suspect from a cleanliness point of view, and so it had been planned to have new clothes waiting for us. There was a hitch. We arrived first. No clothes, except for underwear. Well, we were issued these and naught else. Since we could not wear our old clothes, underwear was all we had. I just danced, metaphorically speaking, in my room.'[4]

Sam Freiman, from the Polish town of Konstancin-Jeziorna, later wrote of his arrival at Windermere: 'I went to sleep. I woke up in the morning to a new life. I did not know the language of the people around me, but all the people round me were friendly and kind.'[5]

Jack Aizenberg, from Staszow, likewise recalled the problem of clothing

[1] Shimon Klin, 'Day of Liberation', manuscript, sent to the author, 9 November 1994.
[2] Chaim Olmer, recollections, letter to the author, 17 September 1995.
[3] Mayer Cornell (Kochen), letter to the author, 25 December 1994.
[4] Henry Green, recollections, The '45 Aid Society, *30th Anniversary of Our Liberation*, 11 May 1975.
[5] Sam Freiman, recollections, letter to the author, June 1995.

on the first day at Windermere, when underwear was all that had been issued to them, the suits not yet having arrived. 'So we were stuck in the chalets. After a few hours we got impatient and restless, we decided to go outside and slowly go down to town. On top of it, it started to drizzle, and I can remember people looking at us in amazement. Really we did not realise that it is not suitable attire for an afternoon stroll in town. Some boys even took bicycles which were parked in front of houses and started riding them, and all this in their underwear. Fifteen years later I read in the letters page of the *Manchester Evening News* that a lady from Stockport wrote: "I would like to know what happened to the boys in underwear and if some of them would get in touch with me, I would like to see the difference and talk about the past". I thought this was a typically sweet English lady who has always thought about us.'[6]

There were counsellors waiting at Windermere from various Zionist organisations, including Habonim and Hashomer Hatzair, and the religious Zionist Bachad movement.[7] 'A disciple of Freud,' commented Leonard Montefiore, 'is linked in a not-too-happy union with an ultra-Conservative rabbi.'[8] But the immediate well-being of all their charges was the overriding concern of every helper.

'I remember the food, oh the food!' Pinkus Kurnedz later enthused of his time at Windermere. 'White bread, milk, and cakes twice a day. I remember going to the cinema for the first time, and I can still remember the first film I saw. It was called *The Seahawk*.[9] The local people were very kind and tolerant, getting off the local bus so we could get on. I can also remember running round in my underwear the first day we came to Windermere, as they took all our old clothes away, and we were given just a vest and underpants. However, the weather was good.'[10]

Howard Chandler also remembered those first days: 'We were given very good care by very dedicated and caring staff mainly made up of former Jewish refugees who had come to England before the war. We

---

[6] Jack Aizenberg, recollections, manuscript sent to the author, April 1995.

[7] Habonim: a Labour Zionist youth movement, the British branch of which had been founded in 1928 for young people between the ages of twelve and sixteen; it avoided ties to any political or religious group and encouraged adherence to Jewish values and traditions. Hashomer Hatzair: a Zionist Socialist pioneer youth movement whose aim was to educate Jewish youth for kibbutz life in Palestine; founded in Vienna in 1916 by refugees from Poland and Central Europe, between the wars its Warsaw headquarters published two Hebrew-language periodicals; the British branch had been founded in the late 1930s. Bachad: 'the League of Religious Pioneers' had been founded in Germany in 1928.

[8] L. G. Montefiore, memorandum, 15 October 1945. Archives of the Central British Fund.

[9] A 1940 American adventure film about buccaneer pirates, starring Errol Flynn and Flora Robson.

[10] Pinkus Kurnedz, recollections, letter to the author, 5 October 1994.

were given everything we needed including lessons, medical and dental attention, and new friendships were forged. I think we terrified the local population by behaving in such an un-British way. We all have fond memories of Windermere.'[11]

Michael Perlmutter recalled: 'I was reborn in Windermere in 1945. The promise of England was a dream to a teenage boy who no longer believed that he could believe in dreams. But it happened.'[12] David Hirszfeld, who was six days short of his sixteenth birthday when he reached Windermere, later expressed his feelings in four words: 'It felt like heaven'.[13]

Chaim Liss, from Lodz, did not stay long at Windermere. 'I shall never forget those first wonderful experiences,' he recalled, 'when each one of us children felt that we were brought back from hell to a new and civilised existence. A couple of days later I was told that due to a touch of tuberculosis I was being sent to a sanatorium for recuperation.'[14]

Roman Halter, from Chodecz, was also at Windermere. 'I went to see the doctor,' he recalled, 'and asked him how I could put some meat and muscle on my bones. He said, "Take up swimming in the lake". So I swam morning and afternoon, and became quite a good swimmer, so much so that by 1950 I took part in the Maccabiah – the Jewish Olympics.'[15]

Among the first visitors to see the boys at Windermere was Elaine Blond, a daughter of the founder of Marks and Spencer, and a driving force in the Central British Fund. She remembered that the accommodation at Windermere was 'fairly spartan by most standards', but that the boys were 'ecstatic. Clean sheets were a novelty; so was a toothbrush. As the dentist was soon to confirm, there were boys at Windermere who had not cleaned their teeth in five years.'[16]

The immediate transition to life in Britain was difficult. 'I remember that some of our habits acquired in the camps were hard to break,' Harry Spiro recalled. 'We would sit at long tables to eat, and the bread would be given to the top of the table. The first round of bread never

[11] Howard Chandler (Chaim Wajchendler), letter to the author, 23 February 1995.

[12] Michael (Meier) Perlmutter, 'Here and now, the bonds of Windermere', *Journal of the '45 Aid Society*, No. 18, December 1994.

[13] David Hirszfeld (Hirschfeld), 'The David Hirschfeld Story', manuscript, sent to the author, 9 February 1996.

[14] Chaim Liss (Lis), letter to the author, 29 April 1996.

[15] Roman Halter, filmed interview, 5 May 1996.

[16] Elaine Blond (with Barry Turner), *Marks of Distinction, the Memoirs of Elaine Blond*, Vallentine, Mitchell, London, 1988, page 92.

reached the bottom of the table, because "the boys" would always take extra bread to hide for later.'[17]

'My main concern, after all the hunger I had suffered, was with food,' Zvi Dagan, originally from Piotrkow, wrote. 'I was always worried as to whether there would be something to eat. There was always enough food on the table, and what we didn't finish we took to put under our beds, just in case we weren't fed the next day.'[18]

Jona Fuks, from Tuszyn, who had come to Windermere with his younger brother Harry, later recalled: 'The first two or three days that they served us food we didn't know how to eat with a knife and fork. We knew how to eat with a spoon but not with a knife and a fork. They taught us how to eat the English way. Those first few days they brought in the food and it all disappeared. Most of us didn't eat. We put the plates on our laps. We wanted to make sure we would get enough and that they were not going to take anything away from us.'[19]

Abraham Zwirek, from Plock, also recalled those early days. 'The scenery was magnificent,' he wrote, 'and all the people were so kind. I found it difficult to learn to eat with a knife and fork, we used only spoons in the camps, or ate with our fingers. We were quite wild and needed taming, the staff were very patient with us and we learned that food, which was so important to us, would always be available.' Commenting on that wildness, Zwirek wrote: 'We were not used to society and the behaviour required, and of course, we were unruly where food was concerned. We would pass the food along the tables, usually underneath, so that the plates were hidden, and pile the food on to one plate so that there were three to four helpings on one plate, and then say that some of us had not had any food, and we needed more for those who had not received any; and hide the empty plates underneath the tables. Also we preferred to shovel the food into our mouths with spoons, as it was much faster.

'We also used to go to the local cinema, and only one or two of us would pay, while the others sneaked in, while the cashier was distracted. We were quite demanding and wanted more pocket money later, and things like bicycles, and we were loud and unruly if we did not get these things immediately, like "wild" children.

'We were treated with great patience and realised later that we had to learn to negotiate and to conform to the new society we were to live in. In the camps we were treated like animals, and now we had to be rehabilitated, as we had begun to behave like animals. It had been a

---

[17] Harry Spiro, recollections, letter to the author, 21 March 1995.

[18] Zvi Dagan (Mlynarski), letter to the author, 1 March 1996.

[19] John Fox (Jona Fuks), recollections, *Gala Recognition Dinner Brochure*, Hilton Hotel, Philadelphia, 8 September 1993.

matter of the survival of the fittest. We soon learned however to have respect for the doctors and carers in charge of us, and they did a wonderful job. Looking back I would say that on the whole we behaved quite well, considering the traumas and horrendous acts we had endured and witnessed. We could have turned into criminals or psychopaths, so, with hindsight, the "wildness" was quite trivial.'[20]

For Sam Laskier, who had been born in Warsaw and survived the Warsaw ghetto, the impact of Windermere was considerable. 'I walked on the streets without fear,' he recalled.[21] Perec Zylberberg, a survivor of the Lodz ghetto, later reflected on those who were their first helpers and guardians. 'The German Jews who managed to get to Great Britain before the outbreak of the war were the natural element for this kind of effort,' he wrote. 'There were many young people among those refugees. Quite a number of them became our group leaders and teachers. I remember clearly the words of some of those people who took charge of us. They spoke to us, of course, in German. In their references to the doings of the vandals and barbarians they were continually designated as the Nazis and not the Germans. To us, this was a little strange. Previously, we all used to call the beasts just Germans. It became clear, though, as time went by, that there was a deeply ingrained sentiment by the German refugees for their former land, and also for some of their neighbours who had shown them sympathy before they left their country. For us, this was strange behaviour. Didn't those Jews know what befell us? That sort of question came up often when we talked about our immediate past experiences. It probably would never be answered totally one way or another.'[22]

One subject which concerned the former German refugees, and all those who looked after the boys, was the religious aspect. 'The more thinking and the more intelligent among the boys,' commented Leonard Montefiore, 'have obviously received a great mental and spiritual shock.' One boy had said to him: 'If you have seen your father and mother shot before your eyes, would you still believe in an omnipotent and merciful God?' On the other hand, Montefiore noted, 'many boys are clearly happy in reverting to traditional Jewish observances and customs'.[23] These observances and customs would be catered for, and Friday night and the main Jewish festivals would be observed.

The work that was done to set up and maintain Windermere, to try to appreciate and attend to the needs of so many orphaned refugees, and to prepare them within a few months for life in hostels throughout

[20] Abraham Zwirek, letter to the author, 2 December 1994.
[21] Sam Laskier, letter to the author, 14 September 1995.
[22] Perec Zylberberg, recollections, diary entry for 12 October 1993.
[23] L. G. Montefiore, memorandum, 15 October 1945. Archives of the Central British Fund.

Britain, was the responsibility of the Jewish Refugees Committee. This Committee, recalled one of its most active members, Carmel Gradenwitz, was the 'caseworking arm' of the Central British Fund. The resources of the Fund made it possible for the committee to do its work. The Committee's inspiration was Leonard Montefiore. Under him were 'some remarkable men and women', Carmel Gradenwitz wrote, 'who helped the youngsters to rebuild their shattered lives.'[24]

Ben Helfgott later reflected on the problems that confronted the boys in those early days in Britain. 'We had to come to terms with ourselves,' he said, 'to realise that we were alone, that we had lost our parents. So there was both joy and despair at the same time.'[25]

A few weeks after the boys reached Windermere there was what Howard Chandler described as an 'unexpected and excited reunion'.[26] The fortunate boy was Salek Falinower, a survivor of the Warsaw ghetto, Majdanek, Skarzysko-Kamienna, Buchenwald and the death marches. While still in Prague in the summer of 1945, Salek had managed to make contact, through the Red Cross, with his brother Gerald, who in 1937 had gone from Warsaw to England to study engineering. On reaching Britain he sent him a telegram. 'At the time of the telegram,' Salek recalled, 'my brother was stationed at Morecambe, Lancashire, awaiting demobilisation. He was granted immediate compassionate leave and arrived at Windermere with his commanding officer, on a motor-cycle. His arrival created a bit of a sensation. There were three hundred of us, none of whom had any family, and here one of our number not only produces a brother, but a brother in uniform as a member of the Allied armed services. Up to then the only uniforms seen were SS, Wehrmacht, Gestapo, etc., so this was really something different, and I am always remembered because of this!

'When I last saw my brother he was thirteen and I was seven. He had his Bar Mitzvah, and the whole family turned out at Warsaw railway station to say goodbye on his departure for England. I remember my mother, and others, crying. Now, after eight years, I meet a 21-year-old and I am sixteen and we have both changed. We spent many hours walking and talking, and he asked me very detailed questions about every member of the family, and I remember telling him everything in chronological order. I shall never forget seeing him – my brother, an airman in uniform – breaking down and crying uncontrollably.

'There and then I vowed to myself that if what I had seen and

[24] Carmel Gradenwitz, letter to the author, 27 August 1995.
[25] Ben Helfgott, filmed interview, 5 May 1996.
[26] Howard Chandler (Chaim Wajchendler), letter to the author, 26 February 1996.

experienced could upset my own brother, then I would not discuss my experiences with people outside our own '45 group, because those experiences were too horrific and almost unbelievable. I have therefore managed to block this horror out of my mind and do not wish to visit Warsaw – despite Ben Helfgott and my son's attempts to persuade me to go – since I feel that should I go and visit my home town it would be like walking on the graves of my family.'[27]

Salek Falinower was sent to boarding school. He had a brother and several cousins with whom to spend the school holidays. 'Later,' he recalled, 'I joined the family metal business in England.'[28]

Perec Zylberberg later described the problems that beset those at Windermere even when they were both liberated and safe. 'The quest for a safe haven seemed to have come to a reasonable solution. What remained now was the realisation of the immensity of our personal tragedies. When we touched down in the United Kingdom we became painfully aware of having gone away from the continent of Europe. Very few of the crowd around me had one or more siblings. Mostly we were alone. Together with the lectures given to us by our supervisors and teachers, we were forever making enquiries from whoever crossed our path regarding family and relatives. I too tried to find out all I could, where to look for avenues leading to possible clues. When the news of our arrival in Great Britain spread amongst Jews and Gentiles alike, all kinds of people started coming to visit us. There were journalists from London and from the United States. There were religious lay leaders and rabbis. Zionists came in droves.

'Among all those constant visitors came a group of Yiddish-speaking journalists. For very many of the youngsters crowding around those journalists, this was a heart-warming affair. To hear Yiddish spoken loud and clear was for me too a real joy. Of course we wanted to know where these newspaper people were from. They in turn wanted to know how we felt and where we were from. At that stage, there were not too many questions about the wartime experiences. The token assertion that we came from the concentration camps sufficed.'[29]

Chaskiel Rosenblum has written of Windermere: 'Fifty years have passed and I still remember the human warmth towards us. Then, and only then, I had a complete awareness of the end of the war. I was too busy being alive, I had no time to cry for my lost family. Crying came about twenty years later.'[30]

[27] Stanley Faull (Salek Falinower), letter to the author, 1 November 1995.

[28] Stanley Faull (Salek Falinower), letter to the author, 12 October 1995.

[29] Perec Zylberberg, recollections, diary entry for 13 October 1993.

[30] Chaskiel Rosenblum, 'Testimony', manuscript, sent to the author, April 1995.

Among the counsellors at Windermere from the earliest days was Wolfgang David Gordon, himself a refugee from pre-war Nazi Germany, who had been asked to organise the camp school. In a report which he wrote about his work, he commented that 'when preparing ourselves for the reception we expected to meet frightened and intimidated youngsters who would approach us with distrust and scepticism. Reality proved us wrong and we were soon face to face with a lively crowd of children who seemed completely uninhibited and active.

'Far from being reserved they talked freely about their sufferings, and showed themselves very eager indeed to relate their experiences. It was not long before a very good relationship of trust and confidence between staff and children was established. The reason for this success lies, in my opinion, in the fact that most of the workers were young and experienced youth leaders. That they were also Jewish, and the fact that all that had happened to the children could have happened to them, undoubtedly made it easier for them to gain their confidence.

'The children's genuine respect for almost all the educational staff was remarkable. They would repeatedly express their gratitude for the help extended to them, and for the fact that they were treated as normal and equal. Soon regarding us as real friends, they frequently told us of their wish to become the normal human beings they saw us as, insisting that they themselves were in many ways inferior, having been robbed of a normal, healthy and secure development. Consequently, their main concern was to make up speedily for all they had missed, to acquire knowledge and generally to become "a human being like you". Although it can be seen from this that a very healthy attitude to life was the basic characteristic of those youngsters, which was expressed in a strong urge to build their own future, it was, of course, natural that their experiences did affect their behaviour.

'Aggressiveness was one of the results of those past experiences. It found an outlet in the rather destructive treatment of furniture and, especially in the initial period, in the many quarrels and fights between the boys. These fights were often of a serious nature, and the highly excited state of the boys made intervention very difficult. Much tact as well as calmness were needed in the handling of such situations. So frequent were these conflicts during the first few weeks that it was inadvisable to leave the boys to themselves, even for a short while.

'As a consequence of starvation, and because they had usually had to fight for food, the children were extremely greedy and would ask for larger helpings than they could manage. However, when they discovered that food was plentiful, this greediness receded after some weeks.

'The distribution of clothes created a fairly serious administrative problem, and was found to have a direct bearing on the relationship between staff and children, touching as it did on one of the most important problems of the individual girl and boy. Whilst being sincerely grateful for our educational endeavours, the children showed an altogether different attitude towards material possessions. Having been stripped of all their belongings, they came to this country full of hopeful assumptions and illusions, and presuming that they would be generously equipped. These confident expectations were reinforced by a very deep-rooted conception on their part that they, the victims of a cruel fate, had every right to demand material help from those who were spared the horrors of German persecution.

'Due mainly to an acute shortage of clothing coupons and general supply difficulties, only a few items of clothes were available for distribution. There were therefore from the beginning not enough suits, shoes, shirts, etc., to satisfy everybody at the *same time*. This aroused suspicion and distrust, provoking many of the children to resort to dishonesty, when often they would claim not to have received their due share. They would frequently complain that one or other of their comrades had been given more. Rather than wait for further supplies, many would take shoes, etc., which did not fit them, in order to exchange them later.

'The importance of clothing cannot be overstated. The problem of clothing caused the only real disturbance in the children's relationship towards us, and proved to be a disruptive element in the life of our otherwise very happy community. This anxiety to secure one's share of clothing not only signified the children's wish to be well dressed, but was a material expression of their desire to regain their individual personality. They wanted to have things which they could call their own, and about the use of which they alone could decide. This was borne out by the fact that after receiving their share, both boys and girls would often, and without regret, give some of their belongings away to others. After discussing the distribution of clothing, and the problems arising from it, the staff agreed that it would have been better not to give out any item before a sufficient quantity had accumulated for all the children to have their share at the same time.'[31]

The contrast between life in Britain and the horrors and privations of Europe did not prevent the boys from plunging into their new lives with enthusiasm, indeed, it rather acted as a spur. Arek Hersh remembered his first adventure. 'I borrowed a bicycle from a girl whom I could not understand,' he later wrote, 'as I couldn't speak English but we

---

[31] Wolfgang David Gordon, 'Some Notes on the Work with Continental Youth from the Concentration Camps, May 1946': *Journal of the '45 Aid Society*, No. 9, December 1981.

communicated with each other through sign language. Dressed in my combinations I started to cycle on the main road to Ambleside. I didn't realise that in England you had to cycle on the left-hand side. I was on the right creating chaos with the oncoming traffic on these winding narrow roads. One driver got out of his car and started waving his fist at me and I realised he was very cross with me about something. I decided to return to the camp still cycling on the right-hand side of the road. What a sight I must have looked, the local people must have thought I was some kind of nutcase.'

Life rapidly settled down to a pleasing and restorative pattern. 'After several days our clothes came,' Arek Hersh continued, 'and we all got fitted out in the proper-sized suits. With all the good food, plenty of fresh milk and physical exercise, I was soon aware that I was growing taller. I used to love to swim in the lake but the water was ice-cold. We even had a football team and our rabbi was "in goal". I would go for long walks exploring the local countryside which was so beautiful, and we were taken on coach rides to the seaside.'

There could also be moments when things did not seem to be going quite so smoothly. 'On one occasion,' Arek Hersh recalled, 'coming out of the dining hall after breakfast, I noticed a coach waiting to pick up some of the children. Without asking where it was going I joined the coach, which was only half full. The driver took us in the direction of Windermere. Eventually we arrived in Kendal. We were told to leave the coach, walking in twos towards a large house. We were told to sit down in the hall and wait, still not knowing where we were. Two of the boys were told to go through this door, then my turn came. Walking into the room I saw there were two dentists' chairs. I was told to sit in one of them. By now I was terrified. One of the dentists examined my mouth. Then I felt a mask being put over my face. I was paralysed with fear. When I came round, I realised he had extracted two of my teeth. After this episode I never volunteered again for any of the trips, until I knew for certain where they were going.'[32]

Kopel Kandelcukier recalled a visit to the boys at Windermere by Polish airmen whose base was near them, and also many outings to different parts of the Lake District. 'We were taken into Kendal to be fitted out with clothes donated by Burtons (who later became my competitor). I took my new surname from Kendal. We had a marvellous time in Windermere; we played football, table tennis, and all other sports.'[33]

Perec Zylberberg remembered several facets of the early months at

[32] Arek Hersh (Herszlikowicz), 'Departure for England – August 1945', manuscript, page 144.

[33] Kopel Kendall (Kandelcukier), recollections, letter to the author, 2 September 1995.

Windermere: 'Sporting events were arranged. We were taken to local theatre shows. They were the light entertainment kind, where the language barrier was partly overcome with the use of odd German phrases and hand movements. We ventured on our own outside the hostel. We paid visits to Bowness and other spots in the beautiful Lake District. The state of our health was generally not too bad. There was a doctor in the hostel to supervise the care still needed for some youngsters. I remember fondly an outing that was offered to me with a group chosen by Dr Ernst, our doctor.

'Our doctor's husband, who was himself a doctor, came visiting one day. He took great interest in our welfare. One day he asked for permission to take a group out into the nearby mountains. It was exciting and, for me, a new experience. I had never been in a mountainous region before. The day was warm. The doctor spoke to us in German. He and his wife had emigrated to Great Britain from Germany some time before the war. Both were wonderful people. Compassionate and caring. That excursion was really great. We talked with Dr Ernst about all sorts of things. Very little was mentioned about the war's atrocities and the personal experiences of those who were in that group. We had seen this phenomenon many times before. Hardly ever was this the topic of conversation. But we spent a nice afternoon in the mountains around Windermere.'[34]

Mayer Hersh recalled that, at Windermere, 'the staff in charge of us were wonderful. We were given the opportunity to take part in lots of social activities, and all sorts of outdoor games; also religion was reawakened in us. All this was excellent therapy, and positively helped us to integrate and rehabilitate, and take our minds off the terrible loss of our dear ones.' Mayer Hersh's mother Riwka Rachel and his three younger brothers, Hershel (eleven years old in 1939), Chaim (eight) and Tovie (seven) had been deported from the Sieradz ghetto to Chelmno, and murdered there. His father Ajzyk Leib had been deported from Sieradz to the Lodz ghetto in 1942 and gassed at Auschwitz two years later, when he was forty-eight. His sister Kaila was likewise deported to Lodz and Auschwitz, then taken to Stutthof, and murdered in December 1944 when she and hundreds of other Jewish prisoners were put into a boat in the Baltic Sea which was then deliberately sunk. Only his brother Yakov, who was seventeen in 1939, survived the war.

English lessons were a main feature of the Windermere calendar. 'We were encouraged to learn English,' Mayer Hersh recalled. 'I thought that as the indigenous population was not prepared to learn Polish, it was a very good idea! I spent a lot of time engrossed in a dictionary, which

---

[34] Perec Zylberberg, recollections, diary entry for 15 October 1993.

certainly helped me immensely. As a result, my friends nicknamed me the "Professor".'[35]

The English language was a major feature of life at Windermere. Every day there was a compulsory lesson. There were also lessons on current affairs, arithmetic and history; and, as Berish Lerner recalled, 'at an early stage we tried to introduce certain English customs and generally tell them about life in England. We, the religious counsellors, laid great stress on teaching Jewish history and included in our lessons and socials a sprinkling of *Divrei Torah*.[36] I was astonished and delighted to find that most of the boys had such a lively interest in many subjects; they seemed to have an insatiable thirst for knowledge. It was obvious that, having missed most of their formal schooling throughout much of the war, they were eagerly mopping up any knowledge that might come their way.'

Berish Lerner also remembered both the entertainment, and the warm atmosphere among the boys, at Windermere. 'The large dining hall which seated many hundreds,' he wrote, 'also served as an assembly hall with its own stage and large cinema screen. I had been instructed in the use of a cinema-type projector and had also been given the address of the British Council Film Library, from where I ordered (at a cost of twelve to fifteen shillings) main feature films such as Charles Laughton's *The Hunchback of Notre Dame*, and *Henry the Eighth*.[37] I particularly remember *The Battle of Tobruk*, a documentary in English, showing General Montgomery's Eighth Army's victory in that famous North African campaign. The hilarious part in all this was that I gave, or at least, tried to give, a simultaneous running translation in Yiddish.

'I remember, with pleasure, the time when I organised our choir, which was an easy task because many of the boys were blessed with lovely voices. They could still remember the many songs, mainly in Hebrew, such as the popular *Shomer Yisrael*,[38] and Hebrew marching songs, as well as some Russian ones.

'There was a thrilling atmosphere in the dining room on Friday nights when we sat down to our Shabbat meal during which the hall was filled with the harmonious singing of zemirot.[39] It was then that I heard, for the first time, the stirring tune of *Tzur Mishelo Achalnu*[40] brought over

---

[35] Mayer Hersh (Herszkowicz), letter to the author, 12 December 1994.

[36] The sayings of the Torah.

[37] *The Hunchback of Notre Dame* was produced in 1939; as well as Charles Laughton it starred Maureen O'Hara. *The Private Lives of Henry VIII*, 1933, was produced and directed by Alexander Korda; it became known as 'the first British film to conquer the world'.

[38] The guardian of Israel.

[39] Hebrew songs sung after the Sabbath (Shabbat) meal, following Grace After Meals. (Zemirot means 'songs' in Hebrew.)

[40] One of the songs, dating back to late medieval times, that are sung, to different tunes, following Grace After Meals, or, in the case of this particular song, often to introduce Grace After Meals. The

by some of the boys. Incidentally, that tune subsequently became so popular all over the world that it is now sung as part of zemirot in thousands of Jewish homes.'[41]

Not only English, current affairs, films and Sabbath songs, but also sport, were part of the intensive rehabilitation work at Windermere. The job of games master was advertised, and a local man, George Lawrence, who lived at Troutbeck Bridge, only a few miles from the hostel, applied and was taken on. 'I do not know what language they spoke,' he remarked fifty years later, 'whether it was Polish, Yiddish, German, but we got on famously. The boys loved sport and competed with immense enthusiasm.'[42]

None of the boys had any pre-war photographs. At Windermere snapshots were taken soon after they arrived, on the lawn leading down to the lake. Many of the boys signed copies of them for George Lawrence. Most of them wrote their messages to him in Polish. 'I was even learning a bit of the Polish idiom,' Lawrence later wrote, 'which I enjoyed at the end of the day, when some of the "Boys" came to my house after the day's fun was over. I say "fun" because for me that's what it was, and I think the "Boys" enjoyed it as much as I did.'[43]

Later, the boys were to sign their messages for their games master in English. Looking at the photographs after fifty years, Ben Helfgott commented: 'Although now enjoying the beautiful and serene surroundings of Lake Windermere, the scars of their terrible experiences in the Nazi death camps are still visible on their faces and in their stance. Their eyes look out as if from a different, harsher world.'[44]

After a few weeks at Windermere, as many as forty of the new arrivals were diagnosed as carriers of tuberculosis, and required isolation. 'But where?' commented Elaine Blond in retrospect. 'The Home Office had stipulated that infectious illness was a disqualification for entry to the country, so we were not to expect any help from that quarter. But the game was not lost. With typical enterprise Lola Hahn-Warburg chased off to a sanatorium near Ashford, where she persuaded the doctor in charge to let her borrow an empty ward. All we had to provide were the nurses.'[45]

title is from the first words of the song, which begins: 'The Rock of Whose bounty we have eaten, bless Him, my faithful.'

[41] Berish Lerner, 'Windermere '45', *Journal of the '45 Aid Society*, No. 19, December 1995, pages 12–13.

[42] 'The Games Master – George Lawrence', *Journal of the '45 Aid Society*, No. 19, December 1995.

[43] George Lawrence, letter to the '45 Aid Society, 21 September 1995.

[44] 'The Games Master – George Lawrence', *Journal of the '45 Aid Society*, No. 19, December 1995.

[45] Elaine Blond (with Barry Turner), *Marks of Distinction, the Memoirs of Elaine Blond*, Vallentine, Mitchell, London, 1988, pages 91–2.

Before the war Lola Hahn-Warburg had been a leading figure in the Official Representation of German Jewry. A member of the German-Jewish banking family, the Warburgs, she was a close relation of Otto Hahn, the founder of Gordonstoun school, and was deeply involved with him in the Atlantic Colleges after the war. For the boys, she was an elegant figure, herself a refugee; 'a formidable woman', Ben Helfgott later recalled, 'with a tremendous sense of purpose – with a devotion to young people – who played a tremendous part for those whose health was worst affected'.[46]

Those who were suffering most acutely from tuberculosis were sent immediately to the Westmorland Sanatorium, before joining the others at the Grosvenor Sanatorium at Ashford in Kent. Minia Munter, one of the few girls among the boys, had the incredible good fortune, while she was recuperating at Ashford, to discover that her sister, from whom she had been separated at Birkenau, was still alive. 'That was the greatest joy of my life,' she recalled. 'But we could not be reunited, as I had to be in the sanatorium to be cured of the tuberculosis. When my sister heard that one of the Munters was alive, she never believed it was me, and thought it must be a cousin. When she found out it was me, we were both overwhelmed with joy.' Minia stayed at Ashford for nearly a year. Then she was transferred to a hospital at King's Langley in Hertfordshire. 'There I convalesced and recovered my health.'[47]

Lipa Tepper was less happy than many at Windermere. He had come from an Orthodox Jewish home in Dukla, his small, somewhat isolated town in southern Poland. 'I, in particular, found it extremely hard to adjust,' he later wrote. 'I had found that my entire world had fallen to pieces. You would need to understand that before the war I was primitive and believed implicitly in a God who is all-powerful and who does not allow wrongdoing. I now found that this God, whom I had considered all-powerful, who did not allow wrongdoing, had allowed five years of wrongdoing. I found it terribly traumatic, terribly difficult to understand, and terribly difficult to accept.

'I started doing something then which I had never done before, that was to question my belief, and my reasons for believing. I found that there were insufficient answers to justify a continuation of my former life. I found that everything was destroyed and there was nothing in its place. I looked scornfully at synagogues. I looked scornfully at rabbis, then I looked scornfully at religion in general. I walked away from it because I refused to believe. More than that, I was terribly, terribly annoyed with God, with religion and with everything that it stood for.

---

[46] Ben Helfgott, in conversation with the author, 4 May 1996.
[47] Minia Jay (Munter), 'My Story', manuscript, sent to the author, undated (1995).

'Life carried on and we left Windermere, which was a very, very good place. We had time to relax and I had time to think, although I realise that emotionally I had not grown up. I found that a lot of the boys were more advanced in their thinking than I was. I had simply not grown up.'[48]

Abraham Zwirek was among the few boys who had a relative in England, his aunt Esther, who had left Poland when he was four years old, and whose departure from the railway station at Plock was his first childhood memory. 'The authorities began searching for my aunt Esther and her family, and found her, through the British Army,' he recalled. 'Her husband was serving in Belgium and made contact through them with the authorities in London, where she had been living. In November 1945 I arrived at Euston Station with some of my friends who were going on to Ashford in Kent, and I was to meet my aunt at Euston. I cannot to this day speak about my emotions – when I saw my aunt running towards me on the platform – but I will never forget it. After staying with my relatives a couple of months, I began to miss my friends and wanted to be with them.

'I could not speak English and was desperate to learn the language. I persuaded the Jewish Refugees Committee to move me to Nightingale Road hostel to be with my friends and to have tuition in English, and also to be able to visit my aunt. I always felt very relaxed in England and was not looking over my shoulder for fear of either verbal or physical abuse as I did in Poland as a child, or fear of death or beatings as a teenager in the camps of Poland or Germany. For the first time I felt free and unafraid. I had two obsessions – food – and to learn English.'[49]

Abraham Zwirek was also unusual among the boys in that both his father David and his sister Gerdi had survived the war. In 1946 he received a letter from Germany telling him that his sister had been liberated in Dachau. She was living in Germany with their father, while waiting to emigrate to the United States, her chosen destination. 'Unfortunately my father was killed in a car crash in 1948 in Munich,' Abraham Zwirek wrote. 'He was waiting to come to England.'[50]

Each boy has different memories of Windermere, which are brought back by events in later life. During a visit to Israel in 1995, as he was watching some young Israeli soldiers, Sidney Finkel remembered how, 'when I was in Windermere, we were shown a movie of Tel Aviv, and

---

[48] Lipa Tepper, letter to the author, 30 January 1996.
[49] Avram Zwirek, letter to the author, 12 December 1994.
[50] Avram Zwirek, letter to the author, 30 September 1994.

all of a sudden we saw a Star of David flag on the screen. There was a spontaneous cry from all of us watching.'[51]

One boy, the Czech-born Michael Honey, had joined the boys in order to get to England and link up with his father. Despite the extraordinary good fortune of having a father alive, he was not happy with the way in which he and his father were reunited. On reaching Windermere, Michael Honey had been taken straight to a hospital. 'I had sores full of pus on my earlobes, and my neck, and most uncomfortably on my behind,' he recalled. 'I only spent one night there, because the next morning I was called to a head nurse. She tried to impress me with her kindness and started asking all kinds of involved – and what I considered to be silly – questions. I perceived her kindness to be quite false.

'After a while, I had to ask the purpose of her questioning. She then continued about my family and those who had been lost, and that she had some news for me. Eventually, I had to ask her to be more direct. I explained that for more than a year I had been alone in quite difficult and traumatic circumstances, that she could not possibly have any news that could upset or be a worry to me, and could she stop pussyfooting and get to the point. She then told me that my father was waiting for me in the next room.

'That silly interrogation lengthened by half an hour the separation of five and a half years already endured by my father and myself. At that time, the fact that I had a family link to a living person – that I belonged – was even more important to me than all the sores I was then burdened with. Because of her own ideas of fear, trauma and psychology, the nurse had subjected my father and his son to yet another period of waiting, when we had both been desperately looking forward to being reunited with each other. She did it because of her goodness.'[52]

Such an attitude was a source of pain to Michael Honey. For most boys, however, there was more often a memory of affection and helpfulness in the attitude of those who helped them. The contrast between what they had been through, and how they were now being treated at Windermere, made a deep impression on their minds, even though the weight of the war years was pressing heavily upon them. 'My experiences in England, being one of the youngest "boys", were certainly negligible in comparison with those of the war years,' Joseph Ribo, from the 'end-of-the-track' Polish village of Cecylowka, has written. 'I can only generalise and say that my coming to England brought me back to civilisation. It gave me

---

[51] Sidney Finkel (Sevek Finkelstein), recollections, *Journal of the '45 Aid Society*, No. 19, December 1995.

[52] Michael Honey (Misa Honigwachs), 'Bilong Notbilong' ('Belong, Not belong'), *Journal of the '45 Aid Society*, No. 18, December 1994, pages 18–19.

the desire to want to learn, and catch up with the studies I was deprived of during the war years. It made me believe again that people were also humane, and not only beasts.'[53]

Sam Rosenblat, who, at the age of twenty-three, as a liberated prisoner at Theresienstadt, had helped with his brother Isidore and Isaac Finkelstein to bring the boys to England, was impressed by how warmly the youngsters were welcomed at Windermere. 'The Jewish Refugees Committee assumed control of, and responsibility for, these children,' he later wrote. 'We felt our task was completed. We were free to leave. We took a train to London. We went to a boarding-house that the committee had arranged for us to stay in temporarily. Also, we were given clothing and pocket money. Through some friends, we were able to find employment, and then we moved into an apartment. It was a good feeling, getting used to being independent.'[54]

[53] Joseph Ribo (Yosek Rotbaum), letter to the author, 18 April 1995.

[54] Sam Rosenblat, 'My Other Life in Another Time', manuscript, sent to the author, 24 January 1995.

CHAPTER 14

Southampton

THE SECOND FLIGHT of boys from Europe came, not from Prague
but from Munich. These were likewise orphaned boys, but they
had ended the war not in Theresienstadt but in Bavaria, mostly
in Dachau, where they had been liberated by the Americans. Among
them was Witold Gutt, from Przemysl, who was sixteen at the time of
liberation. From a Polish Displaced Persons camp near Munich, he had
been transferred to the DP camp for Jews which had been established at
Feldafing. There, he helped the United Nations Relief and Rehabilitation
Administration (UNRRA) 'to organise the transport of people up to
sixteen to England'.[1]

Chill Igielman, who had been liberated at Allach, a sub-camp of
Dachau, had spent time at Dachau itself recuperating, with other
survivors. He had also been taken to Feldafing, which during the war
had been a Hitler Youth camp. 'While at Feldafing,' he recalled, 'we did
nothing but swim in the nearby lake and eat in the canteen. It was
summer. Sometimes we used to hop on a train to Munich. We had no
money to buy a ticket but no one asked us for our fare. Once in Munich
we used to wander about in the bombed streets. The thought of strolling
around in a German city did not bother us.

'UNRRA started registering people for repatriation or immigration. I
did not want to return to Poland as I knew I had no family left there.
The remaining choice was for the United States, England or Palestine,
and I put my name down for all three. Whichever came up first was
where I would go. A couple of months later, as autumn approached, I
was told I could go on a transport to England. England was allowing a
certain number of refugees under the age of sixteen to enter. The
organisers of Aliyah Bet[2] said that the British and American authorities
were allowing mainly the younger refugees to enter their countries,
hence their opposition; they wanted us to go to Palestine. The Americans
took all of us who were destined for England out of Feldafing to

---

[1] Witold Gutt, 'Biographical Notes of Dr Witold Henryk Gutt', manuscript, sent to the author, 17
September 1994.
[2] Organised illegal immigration to Palestine.

another Displaced Persons camp, at Föhrenwald, because Aliyah Bet had threatened to block the road to our departure.

'A few weeks later, it being the beginning of December 1945, some American lorries arrived to take us to the airport. We waited for three hours at Munich airport, but were then told it was foggy in England. They took all two hundred of us, all Jewish, to a convent, where we stayed for a few days. Each morning, after the nuns gave us breakfast, the Americans used to take us on trips in lorries to famous Alpine beauty spots such as Garmisch Partenkirchen. Whilst on one such trip, a motorcycle arrived and we were told to go straight to Munich airport where RAF planes were waiting. At the airport we were given as many doughnuts as we could fit in our pockets instead of lunch. We sat on the floor of the plane as it had no seats. Three planes took off but because of fog each landed at a different airport. We landed in London.'[3]

Manfred Heyman was also on the flight from Munich. He had been born in the German Baltic port of Stettin. In February 1940 all the Jews of Stettin had been deported by train to the small town of Belzyce, in the Lublin district. 'It was one of the coldest journeys I have ever experienced,' he later wrote. 'A lot of people suffered from frostbite, including me. I have disfigured fingers to this day.'

The last phase of Manfred Heyman's war had been a death march from the concentration camp at Flossenbürg, on the Czech border, to Bavaria, where he was liberated by the Americans. 'Not many people survived that march,' he recalled, 'and I was at the end of my strength when I was liberated.' [4]

Alec Ward was another of the boys who had been liberated by the Americans in Bavaria. While in the city of Regensburg he met a woman official of the UNRRA whom he asked to help him 'to emigrate to any other western country'.[5] She had taken him by jeep to a Displaced Persons transit camp in Kloster Indersdorf, near Dachau, where he was looked after for some months by German nuns. Manfred Heyman had also been brought to Indersdorf. 'We celebrated the Jewish holidays in that convent with some American Jewish soldiers,' he recalled. From there, he wrote, 'we were taken to Munich airport and put on Royal Air Force bombers'.[6]

Arieh Czeret had survived the war masquerading as a Ukrainian in Eastern Galicia. Later he had made his way westward. While in Lodz with a number of other young survivors, he recalled, 'we heard of a

---

[3] Chill Igielman, 'A Record of the Early Life of Hillel Chill Igielman', manuscript, sent to the author, November 1994.

[4] Manfred Heyman, letter to the author, 21 December 1994.

[5] Alec Ward, letter to the author, 21 February 1996.

[6] Manfred Heyman, letter to the author, 21 December 1994.

pogrom in Cracow and other towns. We decided, most of the group, to leave Poland and set off towards Palestine. In Katowice we bought forged papers to go west. I was supposed to be an Austrian Jew from Salzburg going back from the concentration camps. The papers had signatures from the Red Cross and transit visas to Czechoslovakia. And so we arrived in Prague. We made our way towards the American Zone, to Pilsen. After crossing the German border by train, we arrived in Bayreuth, Bavaria. There we got a Displaced Person's card from the American authorities, forbidding us to use the trains. So four of us started hiking toward Munich. In Ingoldstadt, about seventy kilometres from Munich, we were stopped by the American Military Police and interrogated. After that, they arrested us and put us in prison.

'In the prison were convicts on lifetime imprisonment. It was managed by the German authorities. As nobody bothered about us, we started a hunger strike, but that did not help much. One of the boys had an idea. He started grinding his teeth and spitting blood. We started shouting that he had TB. The prison governor got scared and sent him under guard to a doctor. Luckily, the doctor had been an inmate in Auschwitz, as a political prisoner. He worked for the American authorities, and obtained our release. We reached Munich. There the Jewish Refugees Committee sent us to the Children's Home in the camp of Feldafing. After several weeks we were sent to the United Kingdom.'[7]

Another of those who was preparing to fly to Britain from Bavaria was Arthur Isaaksohn. He had been born sixteen years earlier in Richnow, in East Prussia. His father died when he was a baby. When war came he was living with his mother, Cecilia, in Berlin. With several thousand other Berlin Jews, they were deported to the Riga ghetto at the end of 1941. 'I saved her twice,' Arthur Isaaksohn later recalled, but in the end he was unable to protect her from deportation from Riga to Auschwitz. From Riga, Arthur had been taken to the Baltic port of Libau, and then by ship to Hamburg. From Hamburg he was taken to Belsen, where he was liberated by the British.[8]

The refugee flights from Munich on 5 November 1945 went, not to Windermere, but to Southampton. As at Windermere twelve weeks earlier, Leonard Montefiore and Joan Stiebel were at the airport to greet them. 'We arrived in Southampton,' Alec Ward recalled, 'and the staff of the RAF airport laid on the most wonderful tea for us, with cakes and oranges.'

Whereas the boys at Windermere were housed in wartime accom-

---

[7] Arieh Czeret, letter to the author, 22 March 1995.
[8] Arthur Isaaksohn, in conversation with the author, 11 May 1996.

modation erected by the Ministry of Aircraft Production, those who went
to Southampton were taken to a beautiful old house, Wintershill Hall,
lent for the purpose by its owner. 'I was intoxicated with the freedom in
England,' Alec Ward recalled. 'I could walk freely wherever I wanted. I
could ride a bicycle, and everyone was so extremely kind and helpful to
me.'[9]

Among those reaching Southampton was Abraham Broch, who had
lost a leg during the war, and yet managed to survive. 'Despite his
serious disability,' Kurt Klappholz later recalled, 'Abraham always seemed
cheerful, and I still remember his charming gentle smile, which was so
indicative of his character.'[10]

Also on that flight were Rose Dajch and her friend Edzia Warszawska.
They had first met in the barracks at Birkenau, and were later together
in the slave labour camp at Oderan, near Chemnitz. 'In England we
arrived in Southampton and subsequently many more hostels – always
"together",' Rose Dajch recalled. 'We noticed that the other girls in the
hostels did the same thing. Each of us found a "best friend". It was Rela
and Minia, Maryla and Stefa, Mala and Adela, Nelly, Dolly and Silvia,
and so on. It was more than just friendship. We shared a common past,
lived together in the hostels, and dreamed of a bright future, vowing to
stay friends for life.'[11]

Jack Rubinfeld, who had been in the Przemysl ghetto, recalled fifty
years later those first months of rehabilitation. 'Almost every aspect was
new and fascinating,' he wrote, 'including getting to know the large
group, discovering a new way of life with beds, bathtubs, food and
movies. The people taking care of us were the nicest people I had yet
met. They cared for us with love and respect, yet without intrusion into
my individuality. This was at a time when the only love I could
comprehend was that of my family, which was now gone.'[12]

From time to time the boys at Southampton would go up to London.
It was on one of his very first visits to the capital that Alec Ward noticed
a boy in the street who resembled his friend the singer, the young man
who had sustained him while at Flössberg slave labour camp, and had
been killed when trying to escape from the train that was taking them
to Mauthausen. 'When we got nearer we instinctively embraced, had
tears in our eyes, and for a while found it very difficult to talk. He had
not been killed after all when he was shot in the leg while jumping off
the train. He had managed to crawl into a forest and somehow survived

[9] Alec Ward, 'My Story', manuscript, sent to the author, 31 May 1995.
[10] Kurt Klappholz, 'Obituary', *Journal of the '45 Aid Society*, No. 4, March 1978.
[11] Rose Fogel (Dajch), 'A friend in need is a friend indeed', manuscript, sent to the author, 10
November 1994.
[12] Jack I. Rubinfeld, letter to the author, 26 March 1996.

the rest of the war. His name is Arthur Poznanski.'[13] He had been with the Windermere boys.

At Southampton, as at Windermere, recuperation and rehabilitation went hand in hand, with English lessons high on the syllabus. 'We were very well looked after by volunteers of the Central British Fund,' Alec Ward recalled, 'and there was one outstanding personality at Wintershill Hall who was our mentor, guardian and dear friend. His name was Dr (Ginger) Friedmann. I shall cherish his memory for the rest of my life. There, we started learning English and I particularly enjoyed riding a bicycle in the open countryside. It was the first time in five years that I felt a free person in a free country.'[14]

The impact of Dr Friedmann was considerable. He had been born Fridolin Moritz Max Friedmann in Burgkunstadt, Bavaria, in 1897. In the First World War he fought in the trenches and was slightly wounded. After receiving his doctorate in 1925, he taught at various schools, becoming headmaster of a Jewish co-educational school at Caputh, near Potsdam. From 1937 to 1939 he taught in Berlin: the interior of the school was destroyed on 9 November 1938, during the Kristallnacht. In 1939 he emigrated to England, teaching first at a Zionist farm camp whose pupils were training to go in due course to Palestine, and then at Warwick School, where he taught German. In October 1945 he was asked to take charge of the boys at Wintershill Hall. Later he went on to another hostel that had been set up for boys who arrived early in 1946, at Millisle, near Donaghadee, in Northern Ireland. From 1949 until his retirement in 1961 he was the History Master at Carmel College, the Jewish boarding school in southern England.

Although Dr Friedmann's work for the Wintershill and Millisle boys lasted only from October 1945 to August 1946, its impact was considerable. Kurt Klappholz, from Bielsko-Biala, later wrote: 'When I first met him, I naturally had no idea that Dr Friedmann already had a distinguished educational career behind him (this I was to learn only much later). Yet I soon became aware of his quite unusual gifts as a devoted teacher who knew how to guide his charges with understanding kindliness. At the time, and even more in retrospect, he seemed to me a *Menschenkenner*[15] of remarkable perspicacity, who accepted people as he saw them. Perhaps because of this he was able, at Wintershill Hall, to establish close contact with people who not only had very diverse backgrounds but also very different interests, attitudes and views.

'I don't think that, in order to be accessible to all, he needed in any

---

[13] Alec Ward, 'My Story', manuscript, sent to the author, 31 May 1995.
[14] Alec Ward, letter to the author, 21 February 1996.
[15] Someone who understands people.

way to disguise his own interests and preferences, and I do not think he did. For example, I had the impression that he felt more personal affinity with those who showed some intellectual interests, yet this in no way detracted from his easy intercourse with all.

'Similarly, although he never (at least as far as I can remember) let slip any remarks that might be thought derogatory of religion, I had the clear impression that his personal sympathies lay rather with the non-religious members of our group; yet it was equally clear to me that this in no way impeded his relationship with our more religious members. His perspicacious *Menschenkenntnis*, allied to an almost boundless tolerance, made him at once the ideal father-confessor and adviser, but at the same time the highly respected "Herr Doktor Friedmann". It was by that title that we knew Friedmann at Wintershill Hall.'[16]

On 2 March 1946 the *New Yorker* magazine published an article, in its Reporter at Large series, under the title 'A quiet life in Hampshire'. The author was Mollie Panter-Downes, who provided an insight into the life of the boys and their helpers, in particular Dr Friedmann. 'One morning recently,' she wrote, 'I went down to visit the hostel at Durley, a tiny hamlet in a part of Hampshire where you see nothing much but quiet, brown fields, an occasional thatched cottage, and a lot of windy sky. Wintershill Hall, where this particular hostel has been set up, is a large, rather gloomy-looking Georgian mansion whose conventional pattern of park, formal gardens, and greenhouses has been somewhat altered by a block of army huts.

'I entered a hall decorated only with multicoloured paper-chains – I just had time to notice a lot of children milling about in the background – and a boy led me into the office of Dr Friedmann, the head of the hostel, and his organising secretary, Mrs Katz. Dr Friedmann is an eager, thickset, red-headed man with humorous eyes and the vitality of the successful youth leader. He got out of Germany himself four months before the war started, and has since been a professor of languages and history at a university in the Midlands. He speaks excellent, lively English, and his first group of children had arrived at Wintershill Hall five weeks earlier, he said; there were a hundred and fifty-two, the majority of them Polish. Now there were just half that number. Most of the others had been sent to other hostels or to hospitals for medical treatment, and a few were living with recently discovered relatives.

'Ever since it had been announced that the children were coming, Bloomsbury House had been besieged by anxious callers, come to scan

[16] Kurt Klappholz, recollections, published in George Mandel (editor), *In Memory of F. M. Friedmann*, privately printed, London, 1978, pages 16–17. Dr Friedmann died in London on 15 October 1976.

the lists of each fresh party of arrivals for the name of the Polish niece, the German grandson, the Czech cousin who had disappeared behind the Iron Curtain in 1939. Sixteen children had been reunited with relatives in the London area, and a few fathers who had gone to America before the Nazis took over in their home towns had turned up, wearing American uniforms, to collect what was left of their families. Usually it wasn't much. Dr Friedmann said that the children were mostly eleven or older, and there were far fewer girls than boys, only twenty-eight girls out of the hundred and fifty-two children at Wintershill Hall. "The young ones and the girls died more easily", said Dr Friedmann simply.

'I asked what would happen to the children who did not find relatives or were not adopted, and Dr Friedmann said that at the moment this was hard to answer. The British authorities had let them all in on a two-year-visit permit, provided they would agree not to take any jobs. The older ones would, however, be permitted to receive some sort of vocational training. The Australian Jewish community was willing to take a large number of children, but transportation for them was not yet obtainable. It was hoped that eventually most of the homeless children would be allowed to go in a group to Palestine, a hope which the present difficulties of that troubled land have not exactly simplified. "It is what the children themselves wish, naturally," Dr Friedmann said. "While they were in Germany, Palestine appeared indeed a promised land. Some of them feel very bitter towards the British about it, though they will possibly change their minds when they have been here a while and have heard all sides of the question. But what appeals to them most is the idea that in Palestine they would all be together. They dread being parted from each other. Children who have been together in Belsen and Buchenwald, who have lost parents and relatives, cling pathetically to the shared experience because it is all the background they possess in the world."

'Dr Friedmann's face brightened. "But in spite of all they have gone through," he went on, "these children have managed to retain their will to survive. They are anxious to succeed, they are hungry to learn. And they have no sense of being under obligation to anyone. No, the very reverse! They feel that it is up to society to make the best deal it can for them. People say to me, "But in this house, in this lovely country – for these children to come here from Belsen and Terezin and so on – must be heaven!"'

'Dr Friedmann flung up his hands and laughed delightedly. "Not in the least! They are highly critical! When we give them a coat, they will touch the cloth and say, 'Terribly poor quality', or they may criticise the cut. It is not lack of gratitude, it is that they worry about their futures, you understand. How they look is extremely important to them. They are anxious to look well. The boys carry little combs in their pockets and comb their hair all the time. They do not want to be set apart from the rest of the world by what they have gone through. No, already they feel that they are individuals. You can understand why it is our aim to encourage that feeling."

'The health of the children, Dr Friedmann said, has been on the whole surprisingly good. The months of proper food since their liberation have worked a considerable change. There is no delinquency among them. Their terrible sufferings have not made them vicious, as might have happened. At first they couldn't get used to the idea that there would always be enough food for all at regular hours. It was one of the Nazis' ideas of humour to break up bits of stale bread occasionally and throw them among these starving little wolves just to see them fight for it. So when our meal bell rang there was a rush, a mad stampede.

' "I have seen boys jump clean over tables in their anxiety to get there first and grab the food before the others. When they understood, after a few days, that each had his *own* chair, his *own* share of food, which was to be respected by the others, they were perfectly reasonable. But their emotions are still strong. They are up in the air one moment, down the next. Suddenly it will come over a child: I have no father or mother, I am alone, I do not know what will happen to me. And of course they are terribly restless. They would like a cinema each night, each day something new to happen. Imagine the life of violent, terrible happenings to which they were accustomed!" '

Mollie Panter-Downes asked Dr Friedmann if those in the hostel – she referred to them as 'children' – were allowed to go outside the hostel grounds. 'He said that they certainly were. They go down to the village when they want to do a bit of shopping or see a movie. Each child is given three shillings a week pocket money, which he can spend as he wants; many, said the doctor proudly, had started little savings-bank accounts. Twice a week the village boys come up and there are what Dr Friedmann called "the sport" – football games on the muddy playing field, between the Durley lads, and the lads of Belsen, Buchenwald and places east. Both sides apparently enjoy themselves.'

Dr Friedmann continued: 'In the afternoons there are handicrafts, too. Such work is valuable for calming the mind. Or we may have an informal discussion group on current affairs. You might hear one later. But our real work is in the morning. We have three periods: one English, one Hebrew and the third on Palestinography – history and government, civic affairs, and so on. No boy or girl is forced to attend classes, but they are encouraged and persuaded by us to do so. And most of them have a thirst for learning; they wish to soak it up as fast as we can give it to them. Some find that they cannot keep up with the brighter ones, and then they have a tendency to stop trying, to give up all hope immediately. The habit of hope is still so new to them. In these cases, we have to coax them until their confidence in themselves slowly, slowly emerges.'

Mrs Katz also commented on the state of mind of the boys. Lack of confidence 'in anything or anybody' was, she felt, 'the chief mark left by the concentration camps. Even though they like us now – perhaps they even love us – they still don't trust us completely. If you tell one to do something, you see him wondering what your motive is in telling him to do that. They don't trust humanity yet, and they have no idea of sharing or of the communal spirit, either. When it came to handing out clothing outfits, a boy would immediately be bitterly jealous and resentful if another boy got a pullover or boots of a better quality. Even if it was his best friend, it made no difference. Because we guessed this would happen, we were very anxious to get all the children outfits exactly alike. But this turned out to be impossible; with clothing terribly short, we had to take what we could get. Even our determination not to give them any second-hand things failed. All their lives they had worn old, cast-off rags, and it would have been so wonderful psychologically to start them out with a brand-new outfit that was theirs alone. Sad to say, we just couldn't manage it.'

As they continued their conversation, Dr Friedmann told Mollie Panter-Downes: 'They all smoke. Girls and boys, even the little ones. How can one stop them? After they were liberated the soldiers paid them in cigarettes for doing odd jobs.' The two of them then went into lunch with the boys. 'After the soup,' she reported, 'came a hearty helping of boiled beef and carrots and then some highly spiced pudding. When the children had finished, a young woman passed along the tables carrying a bowl of vitamin pills (the children are required to take them), and then the young man who had opened the door for me began to chant grace in a loud, high voice. This took some time, but the children loudly and with great gusto sang the responses. When grace was over, they got up and cheerfully clattered out of the room. "They have kept their religion," said Dr Friedmann. "In the camps, the Nazis would make them do all sorts of forbidden jobs on the Sabbath day, but when the work was over, they would immediately say their prayers." He pointed out two posters bearing Hebrew inscriptions in red, on the walls. He translated one as "From slavery to liberty," and the other as "A new light will shine upon Zion."

'Dr Friedmann and I went into a big, bare classroom where about twenty boys and three or four girls were sitting on chairs they had dragged up in a semicircle around a sofa, on which he and I sat. The children looked bright and expectant. "I say everything in German and then repeat it in English. They are supposed to reply in English," Dr Friedmann said to me. He began by holding up a newspaper and calling out, "What is this in my hand?"'

'"A newspaper!" the children shouted.

'"What is contained in the newspaper?" Dr Friedmann asked in German, and then repeated it in English.

'"*Politik!*" the children called out, and one boy, who was wearing American battledress, got up and began a rambling political speech which made everybody laugh. "They're all ardent politicians," Dr Friedmann said to me, and then added encouragingly to the speaker, "Good. But what else is in the paper?"

'"News of the world," some of the children said. "Economic news," said a dark, handsome, intelligent-looking boy named Witold, who, Dr Friedmann told me, was the son of a Polish municipal engineer shot by the Nazis in 1939.[17]

'"Can you remember one piece of recent news that especially concerned us here in this hostel?" asked Dr. Friedmann.

'"Belsen children arrive in England!" cried someone, and there was laughter.

'"Less food for everybody in England!" cried another boy.

'"Less food for everybody in England," said Dr Friedmann. "Now, is that political news or economic news?"

'"Both," said Witold.

'The discussion touched on British traditions and characteristics. "What I like best about England," one boy said, "is that each man is free to speak what he thinks. Also, he can read what he likes. That is the democratic life, and it is good."'[18]

Dr Friedmann then mentioned the Nuremberg trials, which were then taking place, and Mollie Panter-Downes noted that when he did so 'the group began to thaw out. They all started talking at once, and Dr Friedmann had to hold up a hand to slow them down. "The English are too soft," shouted Arthur.[19] Kurt jumped to his feet, energetically protesting, but was stopped by Dr Friedmann, who calmly said, "Didn't we say that free speech was the best part of a democracy? Each can say what he will?"

'"All know the Nazis are murdering, bad men,' said Arthur passionately. "Why have the English give them trial and try to save them? All the Germans laugh at the English and the Americans because they so soft. Is true," he added, glancing defiantly at Kurt.

[17] This was Witold Gutt, from Przemysl.
[18] This was Kurt Klappholz, from Bielsko-Biala.
[19] This was Arthur Isaaksohn.

'Nearly all his companions nodded. "Kill every Nazi twice", someone shouted. Kurt looked distressed. Keeping his eyes cast down on the pencil he held in one hand, he said earnestly, "If the English kill them without trial, all the other Germans have felt that the English are no better than Nazis themselves. Then they have given up hope, and maybe another Hitler finds it a good time to come into power."'

Dr Friedmann told his visitor: 'These children find it impossible to believe that people in England want to feed the starving Germans. I have told them that there is a movement in this country, headed by Victor Gollancz, an English publisher who is a Jew, like themselves, to send food to Germany, but it is incomprehensible to them.'

At the end of the discussion, Dr Friedmann asked the children what they wanted to be when they grew up. 'Lots of the boys, including Witold, said, "Technician". "Cook and pastry-cook!" cried Arthur, smacking his lips pleasurably, as he saw a lifetime of apple strudel before him. Several others said that they wanted to be cooks; possibly because they felt they didn't want to take any chances in the future. One boy said that he wanted to be a gravedigger, and a boy with dimples got up and said shyly that he wanted to be a leatherworker. "Mein Vater," he explained, "was a tanner". "I go to America!" shouted a merry-looking boy, and Dr Friedmann murmured, "He has a father there, last heard of fighting in the Pacific. Who knows?" "Atlantic City!" the boy cried, looking knowledgeable and laughing.

'Dr Friedmann said that before I left I must take a look at the sick bay. Invalids are put in what was formerly the chauffeur's flat – several sunny, warm rooms, now in the charge of a bright-faced nurse. One patient, a boy, was sitting up in bed playing with a chemistry set. "He's one of the few children who have found relatives among other refugees in this country," the nurse said. "One of the workers from the Windermere Reception Centre, where the first lot of Belsen children went, was here helping me get ready for a group. We had all the children's tooth mugs lined up, with each child's name on his own, and when this girl saw this boy's mug, she said, 'Why, that's the same name as two boys in our camp!' They turned out to be his brothers, who had been parted from him for years – the parents disappeared somewhere in the usual concentration camp way – and now they're down here with him. He's just escaped pneumonia, but he's getting on fine. Thank goodness, we haven't had a ghost of an epidemic since the children arrived. We keep a careful lookout, naturally."

'There were two other children in the sick-bay – a girl who reared a startled head from a nest of blankets as we entered her room, and a dark-complexioned boy, dressed in American army shirt, pants, and overseas cap, by the fire in the nurse's sitting-room, laboriously tackling the critical first row of a newly cast-on bit of knitting. "There's nothing the matter with him any more, but he likes to drop back and see me," said the nurse. "All the children like it over here. It's cosy and more home-like, I suppose. I've been showing one of the girls how to knit, and he had to try too." The boy had run into a snarl, and he confidingly handed his knitting over to her to straighten out, as though he were a much younger child. His occupation and his soldierly kit made an odd contrast. When she had straightened out the snarl, the nurse passed the knitting back to him and said to me, "That little girl Margaret you saw lying down upstairs – she'll be down to tea in a moment. She was very ill with typhoid, but she's quite all right now. But she slips back to me whenever she can." She smiled warmly. "What Margaret needs is what they all need and have never had in their lives. A little mothering, that's all."'

In fact, it was the mothering they had received when they were children, and the warm family life of their first ten years, that was a shared memory for almost all the boys, and one that gave them much of the strength they needed to face the world alone.

Education was the next topic of discussion. 'The more advanced ones have private lessons,' Dr Friedmann told Mollie Panter-Downes. 'They're quick linguists, most of them. Many of the children can speak Polish and Russian, and maybe Hungarian or Rumanian, as well as German of a kind, and now some English. As I have told you they are eager to learn, not only from books but from the world. They know that they have missed so much and they are starving for experience of all kinds.

'The other evening a children's ballet from Southampton came to dance for them. They were entranced; they sat spellbound. No rude noises from the bigger boys. Nothing. We arrange similar little treats for them – trips to London to see a few sights, and so on. There is tremendous competition for these trips, but I take the children strictly in turn, and when I say to a boy, "It will be your turn next time," he goes away with a dark face, and I know that he does not believe me. They have no faith, no belief at all in a next time."

'Dr Friedmann sighed and ran his hands over his hair. "That is perhaps the worst thing Belsen and Buchenwald have done to these children," he said. "But they will learn. I do not believe that it will ever leave their minds completely, but they will learn to be men and women who take pride in themselves, who can hope, who can look forward to tomorrow and know that it will come."'[20]

Dr Friedmann's hopes were not to be disappointed. Twenty years after

[20] Mollie Panter-Downes, 'A quiet life in Hampshire', *New Yorker*, New York, 2 March 1946.

his death, Kurt Klappholz expressed the great warmth that he felt towards his former mentor. 'He was universally admired by the then residents of Wintershill Hall,' he noted with affection. 'He was a liberal man, the kind of person I greatly admired.'[21]

---

[21] Kurt Klappholz, recollections, letter to the author, November 1995.

CHAPTER 15

Further Flights

THERE WAS A certain unease in British government circles at the number of Jewish refugees reaching Britain. At a Cabinet meeting on 6 November 1945 the Home Secretary, J. Chuter Ede, told his colleagues that the problem of young people between the ages of eighteen and twenty-one being admitted was that their arrival would involve 'a permanent addition to the foreign population competing in the employment market with British subjects'. Later in the discussion the Foreign Secretary, Ernest Bevin, suggested that those refugees who were admitted should be trained in agriculture, in order to spread them 'more widely' and prevent too many of them seeking what he described as 'openings in commerce'.[1]

In February 1946, three months after this Cabinet discussion, a third group of teenage boys were flown from Prague to England. Most of them were originally from Ruthenia, the Czechoslovak province which had been annexed by Hungary in 1938. After the German occupation of Hungary in March 1944, the Jews of Ruthenia, as of the rest of Hungary, had been incarcerated in ghettos and then deported to Auschwitz. The 'Hungarian' boys awaited their flight from Prague, as the earlier group had done, at the Belgitska Street hostel. 'We knew that the British were insisting that we should be under sixteen,' Hugo Gryn, one of the boys at Belgitska Street, recalled. 'So I said, "Right, everyone shave. Girls, no make-up. We are all children". The British Ambassador came to see us off.'[2]

Some of the boys were flown from Prague to Prestwick, in south-west Scotland, and some to Northern Ireland. One of the pilots who brought them over, Denzil Jacobs, later recalled the two flights which he made, the first on 15 February 1946. On the way out 'there was a stop at Shepherd's Grove. This was the airfield near Oakington in Cambridgeshire. We were instructed to proceed there on February 15 for briefing by the Intelligence Officer regarding our dealings with the Russians in Prague. Also the signal from the Air Ministry told us to pick up "two Jewesses" who were to come with us to Prague, and one of these ladies

---

[1] Cabinet minutes for 6 November 1945: Cabinet papers, 128/2, Public Record Office, Kew.
[2] Hugo Gryn, in conversation with the author, 11 March 1996.

would accompany the youngsters back to Great Britain.' One of these ladies was Ruth Fellner, then working at Woburn House: by chance she was the sister of Denzil Jacobs' best friend.

'We proceeded to Prague without any problems,' Denzil Jacobs added, 'and stayed there for three days. On the 19th the youngsters were put on board the aircraft and I seem to recollect that most of them sat on the floor. The first leg of the flight, to Brussels, was uneventful.'[3]

Hugo Gryn recalled how, at Brussels airport, they were taken into the terminal. 'Some local Jewish ladies were there. They had arranged some refreshment for us. To our horror, they poured out tea with milk. In our experience, you only gave milk to sick people. We were afraid the British would not want to take in sick people. I said to the boys, "Don't drink this stuff", and to the ladies, "We are healthy". But we were thirsty. So people went to the bathroom to drink the water there. I was not that popular with the crew, or with our hosts.'[4]

From the start of the second leg of the journey, from Brussels, Denzil Jacobs recalled that the flight 'was extremely bumpy and I believe many children were sick. What they didn't know is that at one time I thought we were in serious trouble. I had been given the wrong weather information from Brussels and the wind forecast was correct in direction (a head wind from the north-west) but incorrect in velocity, as it was much stronger than the forecast.

'We had no radar on the aircraft, and from about Cambridge to Prestwick we had no visual or wireless aids because of bad weather. In fact, just before we were fortunate enough to pick up Prestwick by voice contact, I had almost decided that the pilot should turn west for, say, twenty minutes' flying, and then come right down, as I thought we would be over the sea, and then try to find my way back inland again. However, fortunately, we contacted Prestwick by radio-telephone and I can still remember the voice from the ground asking our position and my pilot saying, "We have no idea where we are and we have not known where we have been for the last four hours". With hindsight, I think we were very lucky.'[5]

At immigration that night, the boys from Prague were the only arrivals. Hugo Gryn remembered the difficulty the immigration officer had with the spelling of their names. 'When I said I was "Gryn" he wrote "Green", so I said, "No! No! No! Ypsilon". He did not know that this was the continental form of the letter "y". So he made no change in the word "Green". I insisted, "Ypsilon! Ypsilon! Ypsilon!" at which

---

[3] Denzil Jacobs, letter to Ben Helfgott, 4 June 1985.
[4] Hugo Gryn, in conversation with the author, 11 March 1996.
[5] Denzil Jacobs, letter to Ben Helfgott, 4 June 1985.

point he took me by the hand and led me to the toilet.'

Having landed at Prestwick and gone through immigration, the boys were taken by bus to Polton House, Midlothian, a large farmstead. The manor house was to be their hostel. It had been used during the war for Jewish refugees from Germany. Some of those refugees returned in 1946 to act as counsellors; one of them, a young man called Marcus, was killed two years later in the Israeli War of Independence.

'It was a farm school,' Hugo Gryn recalled, 'with chickens and vegetables and cows. The boys were mad at me. We were outside a Scottish village. Where were the bright lights, the girls, the paradise that I had promised them in Prague, when I had been certain we were going to be sent to London?'[6]

'We were all assigned duties on the farm,' Maurice Vegh, a boy from the Ruthenian town of Rakhov, recalled. 'Each week you found your name on a different list. Sometimes I worked in the vegetable garden, sometimes in the clothing store. We had really fierce fights with the local boys over the local girls – these girls just clung to us, they loved us. We played soccer with the local boys. They never won one game. Every time they lost a game they would start a fight. They couldn't beat us on the soccer field, they couldn't beat us with the girls. They just gave up. After what we had been through, we had to excel. We just had to excel.'

Looking back fifty years later, Maurice Vegh reflected on those who had been brought with him to Polton House from Prague: 'We were like family. We had each other. We had no one else. We had no mothers or fathers. We only had each other.'[7]

Another of those who was taken to Polton House was Betty Weiss, who was from Rakhov, like Maurice Vegh. 'It was in its own grounds,' she recalled, 'with a beautiful garden. We were there in that hostel, all of us, it was the best thing that they could have done for us. There were some German Jewish boys and girls who had been there from 1939, some of them worked on the farm. The purpose of our being there was to learn English. We went to the village school. We were also taught mathematics, and all the rudimentaries which we needed to know for living in England. After lessons we all of us had a job to do looking after the house.'[8]

Scotland was an unexpected start to a new life and new learning. To this day, Hugo Gryn enjoys mimicking the Scottish accent with which he first spoke English.

[6] Hugo Gryn, in conversation with the author, 11 March 1996.
[7] Maurice (Moritz) Vegh, in conversation with the author, 3 May 1996.
[8] Betty Weiss (Bertha Fischer), in conversation with the author, August 1995.

Denzil Jacobs' second flight to Prague was on February 25. 'We went one day and returned the next. This time we flew to Belfast, and I can still remember being greeted by the local Jewish community, who had somehow got to the airport and put on a very good tea, which was appreciated not only by our young passengers, but by members of the crew as well. In fact, quite undeservedly, it did my ego a lot of good because all the ladies of the community treated us like conquering heroes!!'[9]

Among the boys on the February flights was David Herman, from the Ruthenian town of Mukacevo. His first home in Britain was Montfort Hall in Lancashire. Another of the February flights went to Northern Ireland. The Central British Fund had rented a farm, Millisle, near the small port town of Donaghadee. At their first meal the boys asked how much bread they could take. The reply was, 'As much as you want', which resulted, Victor Greenberg recalled, 'in some of us taking bread to hide in our bunk beds, thinking that this was an opportunity not to be missed.' There was much else that was memorable. 'One luxurious incident I will never forget, when all of the lads were granted a tailored suit by Burtons,' he later wrote. 'We were taken to their store in Belfast and given the choice of cloth. I remember spending at least an hour before deciding which to order. This was really one of the most exciting gifts that I have ever received. Even though I used to receive a nice little outfit for Pessach[10] when I was a kid, to be given the opportunity to choose from so many patterns, made an enormous impression on me.

'Our routine was to have prayers for the boys each morning, followed by a hearty breakfast. We had English tuition in the mornings by the staff. They were not professional teachers, but it certainly helped us enormously. Afternoons, we had recreation and games in the playing fields, and some of us did gardening. The good food and exercise helped to develop our bodies, which we desperately needed. We were given half-a-crown pocket money a week.[11] We used this for going to Donaghadee to the cinema at a reduced entry fee and the amusement arcade. We were often visited by some members of the Jewish community, occasionally by the Rabbi of Belfast. During the summer, we were invited by the Dublin Jewish community for two weeks' holiday, when we were split up and taken in, usually two to a family. That was also a wonderful luxurious revelation. I still have embedded in my mind the experience of when, at dinner, we were served multicoloured jelly for dessert. It looked and tasted outstandingly beautiful.

---

[9] Denzil Jacobs, letter to Ben Helfgott, 4 June 1985.
[10] Passover.
[11] Half-a-crown was one-eighth of a pound. In today's money values it is about £12 ($18).

'While we were in Dublin we performed a play for the Jewish community about Pharaoh and Joseph which was written and produced by Dr "Ginger" Friedmann, with the help of one of the boys called Isaac Brandstein. It was very successful and was most appreciated by the community. That was when I was given the name of Kushy (meaning black person in Hebrew) because I was Pharaoh's servant and my face was blackened. I am still called Kushy by some of the '45 members.

'Overall, it was a splendid spring and summer which gave us back some dignity and we are indebted to a number of people for their efforts on our behalf. In the main they succeeded in showing us the good side of humanity which we desperately needed.'[12]

'Ginger' Friedmann, of whom Victor Greenberg wrote, had come to Millisle from Wintershill Hall in February 1946.

In the spring of 1946 there were three more journeys to England, made by a group of survivors specially brought out from Europe. They came by boat, sailing from the Polish port of Gdynia to London's Tilbury Docks. The first of the three boats arrived on 29 March 1946. These were not the orphaned teenagers gathered in Prague or Bavaria, but a group of children, most of whom had been hidden during the war and thus saved from deportation and slave labour. They had been gathered together by Rabbi Dr Solomon Schonfeld, the senior member of the Chief Rabbi's Religious Emergency Council, who had received permission from the Home Office to bring over sixty children; in fact, he brought 150 youngsters back with him on the first boat.[13]

Rabbi Schonfeld had been active in rescuing youngsters from Germany before the war; among those whom he had brought out then was a future Chief Rabbi, Immanuel Jakobovits. In 1945 he had returned to Europe in British military uniform, as an army chaplain. 'People were not quite sure of his rank,' Chaim Bermant has written, 'but he acted as if he were Chief of the Imperial General Staff. He gave orders right and left, set up soup kitchens, synagogues and study rooms, and commandeered whole transport fleets.'[14]

The 'Schonfeld' children remain deeply devoted to their rescuer's memory.[15] When the Windermere and Southampton boys had settled down to life in England, they were to make contact with them, and help to entertain and encourage them. Later still, some, but not all, of these youngsters were to join the boys in the '45 Aid Society, and to participate

[12] Victor Greenberg, recollections, letter to the author, 8 December 1994.

[13] Helen Jacobus, 'We are eternally grateful', *Jewish Chronicle*, 26 April 1996.

[14] Chaim Bermant, 'One of God's Cossacks', *Jewish Chronicle*, 19 February 1982.

[15] On Rabbi Schonfeld's seventieth birthday a set of tributes was published, *Solomon Schonfeld: His Page in History*, edited by David Kranzler and Gertrude Hirschler (Judaica Press).

in its events. Some, like Lucy Hyman from Lodz, were only three or four years younger than the boys when war broke out: she was six years old in September 1939.

Escaping from a ghetto in the small town of Ilza, near Radom, Lucy Hyman and her mother lived on false papers, under assumed names, posing as Catholics, in the town of Busko Zdroj. 'In 1944,' she recalled, 'we were denounced, ran away, were caught, and miraculously released. We were finally liberated by the Russians and returned to Lodz.'[16] There she found that her father had been killed while fighting with the partisans. Rabbi Schonfeld brought her to Britain.

Lili Stern had been liberated in Lvov, the city of her birth, with her mother Cecylia, who came to Britain soon after her. They were the only survivors of a large family, and owed their survival to the help of the head of the Uniate Church there, Metropolitan Andreas Szeptycky, who, together with his brother Klemens, the head of the Studite monastic order, had saved more than a hundred Jews in Lvov. It was the Chief Rabbi of the Polish forces, Rabbi David Kahane, who had searched in southern Poland on behalf of Rabbi Schonfeld for children to be brought to Britain. Lvov having been annexed from Poland by the Soviet Union, Lili and her mother had made their way to Cracow.

Lili Stern was seven days short of her sixteenth birthday when the boat docked. Because she spoke German, she served, both on the boat and afterwards, as Rabbi Schonfeld's interpreter. For his part, she recalled, 'he taught us many an English song and poem as part of the introduction to our life in England'.[17] Also from Lvov, among Rabbi Schonfeld's children, was Nathan Lewin, another of those who had been saved by Metropolitan Szeptycky. He had not yet reached his ninth birthday when the German army entered Lvov.[18]

Another of Rabbi Schonfeld's children, Charles Ettinger, was a survivor of the Warsaw ghetto, where his father had been killed. He was fifteen when brought to Britain. Later active in local government, in work for the homeless, and in the cause of penal reform, he died in 1992. 'He never forgot his Polish origins,' commented his obituary, 'and was held in great esteem and affection by London's Polish community, many of whom were present at his last birthday party.'[19]

---

[16] Lucy Hyman, letter to the author, 18 July 1995.

[17] Lili Pohlmann (Stern), letter to the author, 7 February 1996.

[18] Nathan Lewin, letter to the author, 8 April 1996. Lewin's elder brother Kurt had also survived in Lvov, disguised as a monk, thanks to Sheptytsky. He later published an article, 'Andreas Count Sheptytsky, Archbishop of Lviv, Metropolitan of Halych, and the Jewish Community in Galicia during the Second World War' in *The Annals of the Ukrainian Academy of Arts and Sciences in the United States*, volume VII, 1959. (Lviv is the Ukrainian form of Lvov; the Polish form is Lwów.)

[19] Gladys Dimson, 'Refugee who became a tireless defender of the defenceless', *Guardian*, February 1992.

Bronislawa Medrzycki was not quite eleven when war broke out. She had survived in and around Warsaw, together with her father, both of them masquerading as Poles. 'Several times, Poles threatened to deport us if we did not pay a ransom,' she recalled, 'and we often had to move.' Both her mother and her brother were betrayed while in hiding. Both were murdered. When, in 1946, Bronislawa's father heard about Rabbi Schonfeld, he sent her to London. There, she lived with a widowed aunt who had gone to Britain before the war. Her father later made his life in Munich. After thirty-three years of happily married life in London, Bronislawa writes: 'I still live out the traumas of my childhood every day, from which my family suffers'.[20]

There was one final gathering together of teenage survivors in Prague. This took place in April 1946. Most of them were fifteen-year-olds from Ruthenia. They were taken by train to Paris, where for six weeks they stayed in a hostel in Taverny. In June they went by train and ship to Dover, and on to London. There were a hundred in all. 'Why did we come over?' one of them, Israel Taub, from Mukacevo, asked. 'Because there was this choice. We wanted to get away from the communists.'

Israel Taub had been deported to Auschwitz with his family; only he and his older brother Hershel survived. Hershel had been blinded by a blow to the head by an SS man, but his younger brother managed to stay with him and to look after him. They were among a few hundred boys who were spared during a massive selection by Dr Mengele in which five thousand were taken to the gas chamber. Liberated at Gunskirchen, they returned to Ruthenia, and finally went to Prague for the journey to Britain. In London, they were taken to the Jews' Temporary Shelter. They, and about twenty others in this last group, were Orthodox Jews. 'We were very Hassidic,' Israel Taub recalled. 'We weren't satisfied with the *kashrut*[21] in the shelter. We started a revolution. They arranged for us to have a separate hostel, at 75 Highbury New Park.'[22]

The full quota of a thousand children, as permitted by the Home Office in the summer of 1945, was never met. This was despite the two separate flights in August and November 1945, two the following February, three groups of children sent by boat (the work of Rabbi Schonfeld), and a final boat journey in June. 'It is important to realise

---

[20] Bronka Gordon (Bronislawa Medrzycki), letter to the author, 28 September 1995.
[21] The kosher nature of the food.
[22] Israel Taub (and Hershel Taub), in conversation with the author, 16 March 1996.

what the devastation of the Holocaust really meant,' Ben Helfgott has commented. 'Despite all the efforts that were made, not a thousand children could be found.'[23]

[23] Ben Helfgott, lecture, Oxford University Jewish Society, Hilary Term, 1985.

CHAPTER 16

Life in the Hostels

F ROM WINDERMERE THE three hundred boys were dispersed to hostels throughout Britain. On 7 January 1946 the last five left Windermere: they were those with tuberculosis who had been in the local sanatorium throughout their three and a half months in Westmorland. 'They are now leaving in groups to go to various parts of the country,' the Westmorland County Council Report noted in December 1945, of the three hundred. 'Great care is being taken to make the groups as happy as possible, friends and those of similar interests being kept together. In the small units to which they go they will receive training in crafts. It is hoped that the majority will be fully restored to health.'[1]

There were twenty-four hostels in all. Here the boys were to continue with their recuperation, and to be taught the skills needed to be able to enter British society. Pinkus Kurnedz, from Piotrkow, remembers to this day 'my first decision. "Where am I to live?" I chose Manchester. I believe I chose well. I always feel at home in Manchester, and whenever I go away, be it on holiday or business, I am always glad to be back in rainy Manchester.'[2] Mayer Hersh was also happy in the hostel at Manchester, where he recalled 'the love and devotion of the staff', among them Rabbi Hans Heinemann; Eva, who became the rabbi's wife; and Benno Penner and his wife. 'We had a great time in the hostel, receiving religious as well as secular education.'[3]

Friendship was also a crucial factor for those who had seen evils perpetrated for so many years; who had seen friendship itself distorted by the destructive power of the need for survival. The friendships made at Manchester, Sam Laskier recalled, 'remain to this day'.[4] Sala Hochspiegel went to a girls' hostel in Moss Side, Manchester. 'At the beginning,' she recalled, 'lots of people came to see us and to ask us questions. I hated it. Some were people in authority – the Jewish Refugees

---

[1] J. W. Dow, MD and Marjorie A. Brown, MA, *Evacuation to Westmorland, from Home and Europe, 1939–1945*, Westmorland Gazette Ltd, Kendal, 1946, page 59.

[2] Pinkus Kurnedz, recollections, letter to the author, 5 October 1994.

[3] Mayer Hersh (Herszkowicz), letter to the author, 21 November 1994.

[4] Sam Laskier, letter to the author, 26 October 1995.

Committee. But some were just curious, hangers-on.'[5] After eighteen months, Sala was fluent enough in English to begin training as a student nurse at Manchester Jewish Hospital. Later she married another of the boys, Ben Newton (Najszteter).

Kitty Rosen, then sixteen years old, also went from Windermere to Manchester. She was one of the very few Windermere 'boys' who had been born in Czechoslovakia, as opposed to Poland. 'My first contact with English people,' she later recalled, 'was through a girl who offered to teach us some English, and took a few of us to her home. We were invited frequently, mostly in twos and threes to make us feel more at ease in the strange surroundings. I gained the impression there that English people were always encouraging and not given to sneering when one made a blunder, whether in the language, in sports or even in the rules of courtesy and etiquette. At first, I remember, I was rather taken aback by the apparent coolness of everybody, but I soon learned that behind this superficial indifference lingered in most cases a warm heart and a real desire to help.'

There were also lessons inside the hostel, not only in English but in mathematics, history and geography. 'These lessons only brought home to me the vast gaps we all had in our education,' she wrote. 'I was made even more aware of this when I was taking my matriculation course and was sometimes completely ignorant of things which were as familiar to my class-mates as the ABC.'

There was much to be amazed by. On a visit to London, Kitty Rosen went to Hyde Park Corner to hear the soap-box orators. 'When I heard them denounce the Government and the various Ministers in the most abusive terms, I realised for the first time that "freedom of speech" was not merely a figure of speech, but something to which the English really adhered.'[6]

The Committee for Care of Children from the Concentration Camps had its headquarters in London, at Bloomsbury House, known to the boys as 'the' Bloomsbury House. The senior social worker was Shoshannah Gale, who had gone to Europe at the time of the liberation of the camps. Among those working there was Susan Medas, born in Germany, who came to Britain from Prague, as a refugee, before the war. She remembered the boys coming up to Bloomsbury House for clothing. 'The Jewish Refugees Committee was not exactly affluent,' she recalled. 'In

---

[5] Sala Newton-Kaye (Hochspiegel), recollections, letter to the author, 10 December 1995.
[6] Kitty Rosen, *CBF News*, The Bulletin of the Central British Fund for Relief and Rehabilitation, No. 14, September–October 1949.

Bloomsbury House we had a clothing department; the boys could get second-hand clothing from there.'[7]

There were five women working at Bloomsbury House with special responsibility for refugees. One of them, Celia Rose Eisenberg, recalled 'the inspiring direction of Oscar Friedmann. My main job,' she later wrote, 'was "Billeting Officer". Our young people had come from Jewish homes of varying degrees of orthodoxy. When they were old enough or ready to leave the hostels and live a more independent life, we would find homes for them all over London. We were not looking for foster parents. We were looking for an appropriate sympathetic environment. I do not remember what the Committee paid for each individual housed or what contribution, if any, was expected from the young working person. We advertised in the *Jewish Chronicle* and I would look at the home offered in terms of accommodation, spirit and Jewish culture. "Very orthodox" and "Kosher but not orthodox" were two of the most frequently used categories at the end of my reports. Then I would confer with Shoshannah Gale and the caseworkers to match the individual with the home.'

Of Leonard Montefiore's visits to Bloomsbury House, Celia Eisenberg wrote: 'He was a charming man, elegant in spirit and looks. Conferring his blessing on our work helped to give us a spirit of camaraderie and devotion.'[8] Another of those who formed, with Leonard Montefiore and Lola Hahn-Warburg, the triumvirate responsible for the boys, was Elaine Blond. At the time of her death in 1985, Ben Helfgott recalled: 'She played an important part in our rehabilitation. She helped to create the conditions in which our faith in humanity was slowly and imperceptibly restored. Not only did she take an interest in the hostels, which she frequently visited to ensure that our needs were satisfied, but she also took a personal interest on an individual basis. She never tired of enquiring about our personal well-being, proffering advice and encouragement, but was never shy to admonish and to remonstrate whenever we relapsed into the habits that we acquired in the concentration camps.'[9]

The religious question was often in the minds of the helpers. 'There was a competition to win souls,' Joan Stiebel recalled. 'To the credit of the Jewish Refugees Committee, Oscar Friedmann dictated the policy as to where the children were placed.'[10] There were ultra-Orthodox, Orthodox,

[7] Susan Medas, in conversation with the author, 5 May 1996.

[8] Celia Rose Eisenberg, letter to the author, 24 November 1995.

[9] Ben Helfgott, speech to the Women's International Zionist Organisation (of which Elaine Blond was the President), 1985.

[10] Joan Stiebel, in conversation with the author, 7 March 1995.

religious Zionist and secular Zionist-oriented hostels. Every effort was made to fit the boys where they would feel most at ease spiritually. 'The decision,' Ben Helfgott recalled, 'was entirely up to each and every one of us. Since I belonged to the Zionist group, that wanted to go to Palestine, I finished up in Loughton.'[11] As to the direction the boys' activities should take, 'there was no pressure on us', he said. 'We were offered choices and options – we could see the wardens any time. The hostels worked out very harmoniously. They provided for us a period for transition, a return to normality.' Several organisations, Ben Helfgott added, 'vied to offer us care – like missionaries. Some were really very disappointed that not more attached themselves to them.'[12]

Among the Hungarian boys who went to Manchester was Steven Kanitz. He had already learned from other survivors of the fate of his parents. His father, sent to a slave labour camp shortly after they were separated at Birkenau, had later been sent back to Birkenau and gassed. His mother had died in Bergen-Belsen of typhoid after the war was over. 'I never cried at either time when I heard the above news,' he later wrote. 'Crying came when I had already been living for some months in Manchester with the "Boys", when one morning the post brought me a letter from a cousin in Slovakia, in which there was a 1943 photograph of my brother and myself. Then I cried and cried all day.'

Steven Kanitz's brother Gyuri (George) was two years older than he. Shortly after the German occupation of Hungary he had been called up to serve in a labour battalion attached to the Hungarian army. 'I walked with him, and carried his backpack to the tram stop, where he met his friends from Kispest who were also going to the same unit,' Steven Kanitz recalled. 'That was the last time I ever saw him.'

Gyuri Kanitz later escaped from the labour battalion and made his way back to Budapest, acquiring false papers. 'One day in January 1945, only a few days before the Russians entered Budapest, a "Nyilas"[13] patrol on the way home from work stopped him on Szondi utca, and although his papers were all right, he was ordered to drop his trousers. As soon as the thugs saw he was circumcised he was shot dead on the spot.'[14]

To this day, the murder of his brother has troubled Steven Kanitz, who has been pressing the authorities in Kispest to indicate on their war memorial that the Jews of the town were murdered not only by the

---

[11] Ben Helfgott, in conversation with the author, 7 March 1995.

[12] Ben Helfgott, speech to the Oxford University Jewish Society, Hilary Term, 1985.

[13] Hungarian Fascists.

[14] Steven (Istvan) Kanitz, 'Recollections by S. Kanitz', manuscript, sent to the author, 19 December 1994.

Germans but also by Hungarian Fascists. Half a century later, he reflected on 'the feelings of futility which at times engulf me when I think of my brother. Ironically, I do not feel the same about my parents' death in the war. I have been where they have been, and I knew what to expect when the war was to be over. But I was not ready for Gyuri's death. That is why the memorial in Kispest is bothering me so much, when I know that Hungarians killed him!'[15]

Sam Laskier, originally from Warsaw, also went, like Steven Kanitz, to Manchester. His life in Britain had begun at Windermere. 'After the Lakes,' he wrote, 'Manchester was quite a shock, foggy and cold. We were taken to a hostel at 3 Middleton Road run by the Jewish Refugees Committee. There were about thirty of us, and tutors were provided to help us with English and other subjects. These were very happy times, and friendships made then remain to this day.' Those at Middleton Road later moved to another hostel, in a building which also housed two Jewish youth movements, Bachad and Bnei Akiva, both Orthodox. 'Consequently many boys and girls from the local community came to the hostel,' Laskier recalled. 'We learned to socialise, and very soon some sort of normality entered our lives. We began to feel like normal young men.'[16]

Also at Manchester was another Windermere boy, Arek Hersh, who joined the Bnei Akiva youth group. He recalled the local Jewish boys and girls with whom friendships were made, and also the different speakers who came 'and told us about the life in Palestine'. Among the speakers at that time was Amos Ben-Gurion, the son of the leader of Palestine Jewry. Arek Hersh was one of the boys who were interested in the possibility of making their way to Palestine. First he went to a farm at St Asaph, in Wales, and then to a farm in Essex, where 'at each place we learned about farming as a preparation for work in Palestine'.[17]

Chill Igielman was at Southampton when the question of moving to a hostel arose. 'A few of us decided we would go to Manchester,' he recalled, 'although we knew nothing about it. We were accompanied on a train to Manchester and taken to a newly opened hostel for about thirty Jewish refugees at 25 Northumberland Street, Salford. We were given lessons in English and arithmetic each morning, and for a while they even tried to teach us French but this did not work out. The afternoons were free. After one year the lessons stopped. I could make

---

[15] Steven (Istvan) Kanitz, letter to the author, 29 April 1996.

[16] Sam Laskier, letter to the author, 26 October 1995.

[17] Arek Hersh (Herszlikowicz), 'Departure for England – August 1945', manuscript, sent to the author, 1995.

myself understood in English, and could read and write quite well although my spelling was poor.

'We were told that we would have to look for jobs. I got a job working nights in a bakery on Cheetham Hill Road, Manchester, but one week of night work was all I could stand after the camps. I then got a job as an apprentice upholsterer. The hostel was to close down and so we all had to find lodgings. Once in rented accommodation I had to move frequently, as the landladies usually got greedy, wanting more rent or by providing little food. At about the time the Northumberland Street hostel was closing, I started going to Laski House, which was a young Jewish social club which also had some rooms for Jewish refugees from the war. There I met Edna Epstein, who was fifteen years old at the time, and who was to be my future wife. We did not start going out until she was nineteen, and we were married when she was twenty years old.'[18]

Edna Igielman's parents had been born in Manchester. Her father's parents had come from Lithuania, and her mother's parents from Warsaw, at the turn of the century, escaping Tsarist persecution.

Rose Dajch, from Lodz, was among the few girls who had come to Britain. With her friend Esther Warszawska, she was unhappy, first at Southampton and then in the hostels. The matron of her first hostel, she recalled, 'imposed very strict orthodox rules and regulations. We were not permitted to leave the hostel after curfew or on Saturdays. Boys were not allowed to visit us. In a sense it was good for us girls to be together, because of our common past experiences. But I think we would have been better off living with a family and going to school. We would have learned the language and the English way of life faster and better. Some of us might even have gone on to further education.

'As it was, we were moved around from one city to another living in hostels. We had no contact with the outside world. Most of us were depressed. Some of the girls decided to become independent. They took jobs and moved out of the hostel. We were told that we could no longer depend on Bloomsbury House for support. An opportunity came to emigrate to Canada. Esther and I registered. Unfortunately they found a scar on her lungs and she was kept back. With a heavy heart I went on to Canada, she went back to Germany.'[19]

Esther Warszawska died young, after a long illness. It was a blow to Rose Dajch. The two girls had been together since the dark days of

[18] Chill Igielman, 'A Record of the Early Life of Hillel Chill Igielman', manuscript, sent to the author, November 1994.

[19] Rose Fogel (Dajch), letter to the author, 18 January 1995.

Auschwitz. 'I will always remember her,' Rose wrote, 'and what she meant to me when I needed her most.'[20]

Another girl who had reached Britain with the Southampton group was Greta Dawidowicz. She had been born in Czestochowa. In London she lived at the Cazanove Road hostel. 'Among her friends,' wrote one of them, 'she was known for her dry humour and forthrightness, which she never lost.'[21]

In the King's Langley hostel, Rela Jakobowicz, originally from Sieradz, wrote a poem in Polish with her friend Edzia. It was addressed to her dead mother. The final stanza reads:

> I have written a letter though I cannot send it
> What way shall I find to get it to you?
> Maybe the wind will carry to you my feelings, yearnings
> O mother, how I long to see you![22]

Jack Rubinfeld was sent to a hostel in Northampton. 'We settled in a nice house fronting a beautiful park,' he recalled. 'The staff there took care of us fully and lovingly. Despite this, a group of us did get a little rebellious when Mr Marx tried to insist on attendance at the daily morning services. It is something that I am not proud of, since we could easily have accommodated him. It does also demonstrate how easily we got spoiled with all the attention and care we received. The rabbi from town taught us Hebrew, and his daughter taught us English. Their superior knowledge of the subject and their friendly approach challenged us and we respected them very much. We also mingled well with the English teenagers that used to wait for us in the park.

'In all, the attention and care we received during our stay in Northampton as well as in Winchester was exemplary, and many times I have wondered whether regular parents would have had the capacity and patience to emulate it.'[23]

Lipa Tepper was among twenty-five boys who went to a hostel in the south of England, Overbury Court, near the Hampshire town of Alton. It was a large house with a tennis court. 'During the morning we would have English lessons after breakfast,' he later wrote, 'and then we would ride into town. Funnily enough, the owner of the local cinema was Jewish. He allowed us to visit the cinema free of charge, and so we used

[20] Rose Fogel (Dajch), 'A friend in need is a friend indeed', manuscript, sent to the author, 10 November 1994.

[21] Charlotte Benedikt, 'Greta Levent (Dawidowicz)', *Journal of the '45 Aid Society*, No. 12, March 1985.

[22] Edzia and Rela, 'Dear Mother', *Journal of the '45 Aid Society*, No. 2, September 1976.

[23] Jack I. Rubinfeld, letter to the author, 26 March 1996.

to go – and continually go – and see the same film, because it was free, and we had nothing very much better to do.

'I think it must have been six or nine months after we arrived in Alton that movement started taking place, i.e. some boys started leaving and some arriving. We were never informed of any of these movements, except that all of a sudden a new person would arrive, or suddenly one of the boys who was at our hostel would no longer be there. We completely accepted that as a natural phenomenon.'[24]

Also at Alton was Joshua Segal, originally from Piotrkow. There, he recalled, was an instructor, Heinz Reidel, 'who taught us to work with wrought iron. We made coffee tables, candlesticks and other art items. We later had an exhibition of our work in London.'[25] Perec Zylberberg was also sent to the Hampshire hostel. 'We were located in an old farmhouse about three miles from Alton,' he later recalled. 'Again, we went out exploring the neighbourhood. Of all things to be close to our house was a real country pub. It promised to be exciting. Overbury Court was a real retreat into country living.'

The group at Overbury Court came to be known as the Alton Boys. 'I think I was the oldest of them all,' Perec Zylberberg reflected. He was then twenty-one. 'I had a fair-sized group around me at all times, eager to learn about all kinds of things. They were mostly from traditional homes. Their education was very minimal. The world was moving forward. They were mostly very adept at fending for themselves. They came from many parts of Poland and two brothers were from Germany and one came from Hungary. We had several supervisors who were the administrators and teachers and counsellors to the thirty boys. Most, if not all, of the staff was made up of German Jews. They were pleasant and understanding. The food was reasonable in quality and quantity. Great Britain was still strictly rationed in most staples and meats. But we were never hungry. We started getting a small amount of pocket money for personal needs.

'There was a younger couple among the supervisors who were ardent Zionists. They organised a group of followers of the left-wing Zionist Hashomer Hazair youth movement. Not being a Zionist, I resented the division that was created amongst us. It prompted me to start organising a small group of Bundist-oriented boys. We had debates and tried to persuade each other as to the importance of our respective outlooks. Although I was not able to get current literature about the ongoing debates among other Jewish survivors and amongst Jews in general, I

---

[24] Lipa Tepper, letter to the author, 30 January 1996.
[25] Josh Segal (Jehoszua Cygelfarb), letter to the author, 17 February 1995.

had a certain knowledge from my contacts with the representatives of the Bund in the United Kingdom.

'When we had settled down in Alton, we were once taken on a trip to London. The trip included a visit to the Yiddish Theatre in the East End of London. It was a heart-warming experience. Not only were we allowed in free of charge; a reception was laid on for us after the show. Of course it was all in Yiddish. The show and the speeches by the director and administrator of the theatre, and a few actors, were a real balmy experience. Of course everybody stressed the happiness of seeing such a nice group of Jewish boys enjoying the light entertainment that they provided for us. Also present at the theatre were some of the London-based boys. We were a fair-sized group.

'After tea and cakes and general socialising, I was invited to acknowledge the welcome that we received. I was not told in advance, so it was an impromptu speech. It must have sounded not too bad, because I got applause, and a rejoinder from the director. He said that to hear a young survivor speak about Yiddish theatre and Jewish writers was pleasant music for all those Yiddish speakers who were in Great Britain during the war. I got the impression that those who supported the Yiddish-speaking cultural and linguistic side of Jewish life in London were genuinely happy with our arrival in the United Kingdom.

'That event opened the way for many of our boys to get close to the Yiddish-speaking Jews of London. I was one of those people. Our tour of London included some sightseeing and a visit to the offices of the Jewish Refugees Committee. We stayed overnight at a Jewish youth club that arranged our sleeping quarters.'

During that visit to London, Perec Zylberberg made contact with Lucjan Blit, a journalist 'from the only Yiddish daily newspaper in the United Kingdom. I enquired if it could be arranged to have some names inserted in their "search for relatives" column. The journalist asked me to send him a list of those who wanted such a service. I availed myself of this opportunity. I was looking for news about my mother's oldest brother and his family. I was hoping that they were still in the United Kingdom. I also enquired about the brother of a friend of mine who had left Lodz before the war and was living in Great Britain at the beginning of the war. Filled with lots of impressions and glad to have seen London and part of the Jewish cultural life, and some of the boys whom we knew from Windermere, we returned to Overbury Court in good spirits.'[26]

A particular friendship was formed between three boys who had not known one another before coming to England, even though each had been a slave labourer in one of the slave labour camps in Czestochowa:

[26] Perec Zylberberg, recollections, diary entry for 16 October 1993.

they were Perec Zylberberg from Lodz, Lipa Tepper from Dukla, and Bronek Nisenbaum from Warsaw. They were joined by another boy from Lodz, Icek Jakubowicz (now Ray Jackson). 'In Overbury Court we became almost inseparable,' Perec Zylberberg recalled. 'We went for long walks together. When we got second-hand bicycles, we went on rides in the surrounding countryside. The four of us formed the nucleus for that larger Bundist group later on. We heard that the second group that had arrived in Great Britain was housed in a hostel not far from us. The four of us, plus a few others, decided on a trip by train. The bicycles were stored in the baggage compartment of the train.'[27]

At the nearby hostel, Perec Zylberberg found Rose Dajch, a girl whose family had given his own family shelter in the Lodz ghetto, when they were escaping from a deportation. Her parents had not survived, nor had her sisters and brother.

At the Jews' Temporary Shelter in Mansell Street, East London, Barbara Pinto and Richard Barnett – he was then Assistant Keeper (later Keeper) of Western Asiatic Antiquities at the British Museum – were asked to make friends with the boys, mostly from Windermere, who had been allocated the Shelter as their hostel. There were two dormitories, one for boys and one for girls. 'Walking slowly round the girls' dormitory, a huge square room measured by beds separated by lockers,' Barbara Pinto later wrote, 'it was strangely quiet. We were told there was no common language. There were certainly many languages. Absence of trust at that early stage was a far more likely explanation. They had only had a short experience of living together.

'From here everyone was attending classes in English and their progress was rapid. Then assessments were made, and everyone was assisted in making a plan for further education or training – and to finding landladies and jobs. It seemed a brief time before all were scattered across London, with quite ordinary living conditions, or went to join relatives in Australia, the United States, Canada or Palestine.

'Of these forty girls, one stood out, Magda Herstkowitz (later Rosenberg). A strong, large-limbed young woman, who looked you straight in the eye, a forearm missing – it had been blown off in an Allied bombing raid – she has never accepted an artificial replacement and today leaves the stump bare for all to see. There are striking facts to tell of her adaptation to life in London in the first few years, then in New York, married, with four children.

'Magda has evolved a system of exercise for the elderly and handi-

---

[27] Perec Zylberberg, recollections, diary entry for 17 October 1993.

capped, written about it, appeared on television, and published a book.[28] She used to ride a specially equipped tricycle to travel around Long Island, where she lives. Her personality is markedly extrovert. This has made it possible for her to face her situation squarely.

'We noticed that if someone started to hum a tune, they would all join in. We started inviting people to Richard's uncle's flat, for supper, and to painting sessions, and to listen to music on gramophone records. They preferred rhythmic and romantic music, not Bach. Invitations were accepted, but often they didn't turn up. It took some time to develop any trust and friendship – friendships which have survived until today.'[29]

Richard Barnett is remembered with affection to this day by those whom he nurtured. Fifty years after reaching London, Betty Weiss, from the Ruthenian town of Rakhov, and a survivor of Auschwitz, commented: 'He taught us music appreciation; he opened a world to me.'[30]

Fifty years later, Barbara Barnett remembered the difficulties which it was thought would confront those who looked after the boys. 'Leonard Montefiore said to us, "These people are going to be delinquents".' But this proved not to be the case. 'They loved the lift at the Shelter,' she remembered. 'They used to go up and down in it. The warden locked it. They took a key and picked the lock. That was the only act of delinquency. I remember the girls choosing clothes. They chose the gaudiest things imaginable. But they were soon adapting. That was the secret of their success. A fellow-helper, Helen Bamber, and I, discussed whether we should encourage them to open up. They talked about their childhood – they talked warmly about their childhood – but not about their wartime experiences. We always had a traditional Friday night. They loved that.'[31]

Moshe Rosenberg, from Cracow, who less than two years earlier had been among the thousand and more slave labourers protected by Oscar Schindler, was among the religious boys at Windermere. The hostel to which he was sent was in Gateshead, one of the centres of Jewish Orthodoxy in Britain. But he was not happy there, as the Orthodox community was far from Zionist 'and my aim was to go to Palestine'. He therefore moved to a hostel in Liverpool – 'a religious place but not fanatical' – and then to a farm at Thaxted, in Essex, where he spent a year in agricultural training for Palestine.[32] But he could not go immediately: the British government was continuing to refuse to relax the tight

[28] Magda Rosenberg, *Sixty-Plus, Fit Again, Exercises for Older Men and Women*, M. Evans and Company, New York, 1977.

[29] Barbara Barnett, 'Memories and impressions', manuscript, sent to the author, 1996.

[30] Betty Weiss (Bertha Fischer), in conversation with the author, August 1995.

[31] Barbara Barnett, conversation with the author, 4 August 1995.

[32] Mike Ridley (Moshe Rosenberg), letter to the author, 13 December 1994.

pre-war immigration restrictions, even in favour of concentration camp survivors.

Berek Obuchowski, from Ozorkow, also went from Windermere to Gateshead. 'I had lost five years of my life when I decided I would go to Gateshead to learn about Judaism,' he wrote. 'I spent two years in a hostel at Gateshead, and then moved to London, where I chose to live with a Jewish Orthodox family in Stoke Newington, London. Since I came from a small town in Poland, I found life in London very exciting, with many people and a new busy way of living, and another language to learn. It was suggested to me at that time that I could either be apprenticed to a tailor or an upholsterer – I chose the latter, and went to work for a large furniture company. I learned the upholstery trade for a number of years, and in 1953 I opened my own business.'[33]

Shimon Klin, from Zdunska Wola, also went to Gateshead, 'although I was disappointed afterwards,' he wrote, 'because it was too Orthodox for me. I attended the yeshiva in Gateshead for a short time, because I had some yeshiva background, having studied in a small Hassidic yeshiva in the Polish shtetl where I was born. But I dreamed of the Land of Israel and my goal was to get there as soon as possible. I became active in the Zionist Religious Movement, but the leaders in the Gateshead hostel did not like it, so I had to leave Gateshead, and consequently I moved to London. In 1948, when the Jewish State was proclaimed, I left England, and arrived in Israel in July 1948.'[34]

Like so many of the boys, Shimon Klin had lost his whole family in the Holocaust. 'I got messages from friends,' he wrote, 'that my brother Lipman was alive until 1944 in Birkenau. I do not know what happened to my sister Raisel and her family. My sister Doba was sent to Treblinka.' Also murdered were his father Yehuda Shaul, his step-mother Henja, and his brother Lipman's wife and children. Of his family, he has written, 'I am the only survivor!'[35]

A hostel had also been made ready in Scotland for the boys from Windermere, at Darleith House, Cardross, a former monastery thirty miles from Glasgow. It was organised by two Glasgow Jewish women, Dora Woolfson and Elsie Heilbronn, who had earlier set up the Garnethill Refugee Hostel in Glasgow for young pre-war refugees from Germany and Austria: more than two hundred refugees had already been the beneficiaries of their work and care. Maureen Livingstone, who went every week from Glasgow to teach English to the Windermere boys at

[33] Bob Roberts (Berek Obuchowski), recollections, manuscript, February 1996, sent to the author, 4 March 1996.

[34] Shimon Klin, 'Day of Liberation', manuscript, sent to the author, 9 November 1994.

[35] Shimon Klin, letter to the author, 16 January 1995.

Cardross, recalled how they 'were supposed to be at risk from tuberculosis; they didn't want to send them out into the world for a while.'[36]

Among the Windermere boys who made the journey northward to Cardross was Chaskiel Rosenblum. 'We all had something wrong,' he recalled. 'I had one lung split. After a bombing in Schlieben, we were discharging a wagon of cement. The Germans were like dogs, barking all the time. I carried two cement bags on my back. The doctor at Cardross told me that physically I was all right, except for the lung, which needed time to heal. It healed completely over the years.'[37]

Steven Pearl, from Cuhea in Transylvania, who was among those sent to Cardross from Southampton, recalled the problem which had earlier beset the boys at Windermere, of having to learn 'to behave normally at the dinner table, because when food was put on the table we would all grab for it, as much as one could get, and stuff it in our pockets – especially the white bread.'[38]

Mayer Kochen, from Kielce in Poland, was also among those who went to Cardross. 'Darleith House was a large beautiful mansion,' he recalled, 'set in its own grounds, with outhouses, gardens, and fields, surrounded by mountains. This was an ideal place to continue our recuperation. The matron in charge of the house was a very kind Scots lady, who helped us in every way possible. She approached the director of education in Dumbartonshire to send his teachers for all the essential subjects. Like most of us I was very keen to learn and I started to catch up with some education that I missed in the last six years.'[39]

Catching up had its problems. 'A group of us decided to go to Dumbarton and enrol for evening classes,' Mayer Kochen later wrote. 'We had difficulty in communicating properly with the people there, and in turn the administration had no idea where to place us, so they sent us back. The following day our matron contacted the director of education again, and in no time got a host of teachers to teach us all subjects under the sun, from English, maths and science to woodwork. These teachers realised that we were very hungry to learn, and responded accordingly. They gave up a lot of their spare time in order to teach us. Some of the teachers became very interested in us, and we were invited to their homes for Sunday tea, and play-reading. The Glasgow Jewish Community also sent us a teacher to teach us classical and modern Hebrew.'[40]

Krulik Wilder was also among the boys sent to Cardross. 'It was a

---

[36] Maureen Livingstone, in conversation with the author, 3 May 1996.

[37] Chaskiel Rosenblum, 'Testimony', manuscript, sent to the author, April 1995.

[38] Steven Pearl, letter to the author, 3 February 1996.

[39] Mayer Cornell (Kochen), letter to the author, 25 December 1994.

[40] Mayer Cornell (Kochen), letter to the author, 9 February 1995.

beautiful building set in the middle of the countryside,' he recalled. 'The nearest village was three miles away. We were sent there to recuperate, as most of us still had something wrong, and also for us to learn English and other subjects. A few months later other boys of various nationalities joined us, from Poland, Hungary and Rumania. The hostel became very lively and exciting. The following year I had a fantastic life in the hostel, trying to learn English, which was not very easy, and to begin a new life and try to put the sad and bad memories behind me as best I could.

'We settled into a daily routine and life began to return to normal. Many people came to visit us both out of compassion and curiosity to see what Holocaust children looked like. Life continued in a similar fashion for the next twelve months until the time came for us once again to move on. We settled in another hostel in Glasgow, where I was apprenticed to a watchmaker in the Gorbals, where my salary was the grand sum of £1 per week. I made such good progress that after a year my boss, who was very pleased with me, increased my salary to £5 per week. I felt like a king, in those days it was a fortune.'[41]

Chaim Olmer was also sent to Cardross, where he recalled the 'intensive tuition' initiated by the local education authority.[42] 'It was a most delightful place,' he commented. 'The drive from the main road to the house was about five hundred yards long and lined with magnificent rhododendrons. The house was a beautiful manor in its own grounds, with tennis courts, and a view of the Clyde Estuary which was filled with the ships of the Home Fleet. A walk of about two miles brought us to Balloch at the head of Loch Lomond. Life was very pleasant in the hostel. The bedrooms were large – we were four boys to a room – and the common rooms were large and pleasant. Miss Mahrer was the cook and she made sure that we were well fed.

'The Dumbartonshire education department sent teachers to the hostel for our secular education, and the Glasgow Jewish Community provided teachers in Jewish Studies and religious education. That community was also very supportive and most of us made very good friends with families in Glasgow.'[43]

Julie Mahrer, the cook, recalled fifty years later: 'It was a pleasure to feed them, because they used to eat!'[44]

Roza Gross, one of those who had been deported from Ruthenia to

---

[41] Israel (Krulik) Wilder, 'Krulik's Story', manuscript, sent to the author, 1 January 1995. In the money values of 1996, Krulik Wilder's salary had been increased from about £20 ($30) a week to £100 ($150) a week.

[42] Chaim Olmer, recollections, letter to the author, 17 September 1995.

[43] Chaim Olmer, letter to the author, 30 September 1995.

[44] Julie Mahrer, in conversation with the author, 30 April 1995.

Auschwitz in May 1944, was at the Montford Hall hostel in Lancashire. 'My memories of England after the war are ones of great cameraderie among our boys and girls,' she later wrote. 'We all needed each other desperately.'[45]

From Scotland, many of the boys moved to London. But twenty-five of those at Cardross were transferred to another hostel, in the heart of Glasgow. 'I was in a room with six other boys,' Chaim Olmer recalled, 'with only a chair between each bed. We were advised to learn a trade, and we all did. I chose to learn dental mechanics. At the same time I went to evening classes every night of the week, where I studied English, maths, German and Polish seriously, and also some geography, physics, chemistry and Hebrew.'[46]

Another of those who went from Cardross to Glasgow was Mayer Kochen. There, he started work in mechanical engineering by day, and went to evening classes at night. 'However,' he recalled, 'I had a disappointment. I was taken ill, and was diagnosed with TB. In April 1947 I was sent to Quare Mead Convalescent Home. There I stayed until 1950, with a short spell in Broomfield Hospital, near Chelmsford. Quare Mead was not a happy place for me. The place was very nice and the people kind and understanding, but I was not able to settle there. Most of the time I was restless and eager to get back to normal life. I had too much time to think about the past, which did not help me medically.'

Mayer Kochen was fortunate, however, in that he met his future wife, Tauba Tenenbaum, while he was recuperating at Quare Mead, which the Jewish Refugees Committee was able to take over for the boys with tuberculosis. It was located in the village of Ugley, near Bishop's Stortford. Tauba was a survivor of the Lodz ghetto, Auschwitz, Ravensbrück, a slave labour camp at Mühlhausen, and Bergen-Belsen. Suffering from TB, and taken by the Red Cross to Sweden, she had been in various hospitals in Sweden for four years. Having recovered her health, she came to England in 1949, but there she had a relapse, and was taken to Quare Mead. 'We were married in 1953,' Mayer Kochen recalled, 'and are very happy to this day, although our doctors advised against it for medical reasons. In due course we had two daughters and are a very happy family. Both our daughters are happily married with children of their own, and we are very happy grandparents.'[47]

Chaim Liss, a Southampton boy, having recuperated from TB at the sanatorium in Ashford, went to the hostel at Ascot. The warden there

---

[45] Rosalyn Gross-Haber (Roza Gross), 'A personal report', *Journal of the '45 Aid Society*, No. 16, Passover 5753/1993.

[46] Chaim Olmer, letter to the author, 30 September 1995.

[47] Mayer Kochen (Cornell), letter to the author, 25 December 1994.

was Manuel (Manny) Menachem Silver, a 22-year-old Jew from Leeds who had begun working as a youth counsellor with Jewish evacuees at Ascot during the war. 'Twenty-five teenagers from Buchenwald and Theresienstadt,' he later wrote, 'descended on Woodcote, a large country house directly facing Ascot racecourse. What greater contrast could there be between their previous life and this corner of England. Shelter, food, clothing, security – all that they had tenaciously fought for – were now theirs. But there was a serious problem adjusting to a new way of life. In the camps, survival meant breaking the rules. "Me first" was the only rule. But despite all this, there were countless examples of altruism.

'Now, in Ascot, they were required to accept the control of staff who had to learn the hard way how to care for their wards. Boarding-school discipline could not apply. After the Nazis, what punishment could there be for someone who stole food, refused to get up in the morning, did not come to class, disrupted others, stayed out late at night? We devised a co-operative way of life, based on mutual respect and understanding of the different responsibilities of staff and young people, and how best we could prepare them for future life.

'Although we were not qualified teachers, we taught them English, mathematics, geography, in preparation for when they might be able to attend regular schools. Of course we taught Hebrew – for many of them wanted to go to Palestine – and Jewish studies, and celebrated Shabbat and the festivals. All of them needed medical and dental help. Listed as orphans, they all cherished the hope that parents would be found alive. Gradually they accepted their new way of life and adjusted to the regimen.'[48]

Ben Helfgott later reflected: 'One always hoped, "Maybe, maybe". I knew that my mother had been killed. But my father, his death was hearsay; it was just what a man had said to me in Theresienstadt. I thought, "Perhaps I will get a letter". It preyed on my mind. "Maybe he is somewhere." On the other hand, I thought that after a few months, if he were alive, he would have made every effort to find me. There was that lingering hope, but only for a very short time. A few parents had turned up a few months later; like my friend Nat's father. So some kept hoping and thinking, "If only, if only, perhaps...."'[49]

Three of the staff at Ascot were Jews in their early twenties who had come as teenagers from Germany just before the outbreak of war. Later they were joined by a fourth German Jewish refugee, Heinz Samuel, who had been a youth worker in Germany before 1939. Manuel Silver later

[48] Dr Manny Menachem Silver, 'How CBF Changed My Life', *Update* (Newsletter of the Central British Fund, World Jewish Relief), No. 20, London, January 1995.
[49] Ben Helfgott, in conversation with the author, 4 May 1996.

recalled other aspects of Ascot days. 'They loved outings. Whenever possible, we would take the bus to a local place of interest and explore. Windsor and the Thames were great attractions. Of course the Ascot races were a novelty, and there was plenty of space to play games. I recall buying used bicycles. There was not enough money for new ones, and every boy wanted his own. I do not remember how many we obtained, but they spent a lot of time fixing them up. Visits to doctors and dentists were plentiful, and onerous for the staff who had to be there, both to help and to translate. Shopping was always an adventure. They arrived with only basic clothing, and though we had a limited budget, we went shopping with them from time to time.

'The "Jewish Hostel" was well known in Ascot due to our prior work with evacuees. Before the youngsters came, I met with the police and other officials to enlist their help in rehabilitating them. The horrors of the Shoah[50] were well known, and the locals overcame their usual British reserve with numerous acts of kindness.

'To this day I well remember a song I learned from them. Most came from Theresienstadt, and they often sang the theme song of the camp with its name as part of the refrain.[51] For my part, I taught them many English folksongs as part of my English as a second language lesson. Our weekly staff meetings, often with invited professionals, enabled us to cope with the myriad problems that inevitably developed. Policy and practice decisions were arrived at via consensus.

'In retrospect, I remember that year as a successful effort by a handful of idealistic, devoted but untrained young workers to act *in loco parentis* and help our wards forge the basis of a new life. Thinking back on my own long professional training and work, I am amazed that we had the chutzpah to think that we could do the job (I was only twenty-two years old). But no one else was trained for it – and who would accept the minimal pay and working conditions? As the Talmud says, "In a place where there is no man, try to be a man".

Unfortunately, the circumstances of my leaving have left a bitter taste in my mouth, even now after half a century. In the summer of 1946 I was informed that my services were no longer needed because my approach to supervision was "too liberal and easy going". A professional, experienced social worker was evidently hired before I was dismissed. He would be "strict", as his background was Borstal schools for difficult youngsters. When I informed the staff and youngsters, they were dis-

---

[50] The Hebrew word for Holocaust, meaning Catastrophe (in Yiddish, the word Churban is used, meaning Destruction).

[51] The boys I have spoken to cannot remember this song. 'I remember we used to sing the partisan song – "Don't ever say this is my last road" – and various Polish ditties,' Krulik Wilder recalled (in conversation with the author, 22 April 1996).

mayed. A few of them travelled to London early one morning (at their own cost, and without permission) and complained to Leonard Montefiore, but to no avail.'[52]

The brothers David and Moniek Hirszfeld were among those sent to the hostel at Loughton. 'I attended the ORT High School and learned metalwork,' David Hirszfeld recalled. 'Moniek studied to become a tailor. In the end, he became a cook.'[53] Izzie Light was another Loughton boy who studied at ORT. While at Loughton, he recalled, 'we used to go to plays, and we used to dance. We often went to the Yiddish Theatre in Whitechapel. We were in several shows there. One of them was *King Lear* in Yiddish.'[54] There was also a bicycle excursion to the Isle of Wight.

Moniek Goldberg was another of the boys at Loughton. 'Can any of us at Loughton forget Heini or Anita or Ruth?' he asked, fifty years later. 'Or Mrs Tattenbaum, or Sonia, our first matron? Can any of us from Loughton forget Dr Cohen who took an interest in us? Or Reverend Einhorn? Of course the best thing that happened to us was that we developed friendships that have lasted fifty years.'[55]

Another of those who taught at Loughton was Mr Harrison. He had come from Germany before the war. 'He took us for lessons, and we also went out with him to the theatre,' Ben Helfgott recalled. 'He helped us in many ways. When we saw an advert for sixteen-year-old boys to join the RAF, he wrote away for us for the applications – only to receive the answer that as we were not born in England, we could not join. We were very keen to join!'[56]

The leadership of Heini Goldberg at Loughton made an impact on all the boys there. He had been born in Breslau and came to Britain, with his parents, before the war. He was a keen Zionist. 'Although most of us were Zionists in the sense that we ardently believed in a Jewish State,' Ben Helfgott has written, 'we knew very little about the history and ideology of Zionism. It was he who filled this vacuum. He did this with subtlety and sensitivity. He was a clear thinker, and whenever he spoke we devoured his words voraciously.' Among those whom Heini Goldberg brought to Loughton to speak to the boys was the head of the foreign department of the Jewish Agency, Moshe Shertok (later Foreign Minister of Israel), and the head of the Jewish Agency London office, Berl Locker

[52] Dr Manuel Silver, letter to the author, 17 April 1995.

[53] David Hirzfeld (Hirschfeld), 'The David Hirschfeld Story', manuscript, sent to the author, 9 February 1996. For a note on ORT, see page 416, footnote 19.

[54] Izzie Light (Licht), in conversation with the author, 7 May 1996. The Yiddish King Lear had a happy ending.

[55] Joseph (Moniek) Goldberg, 'Biographical Sketch', manuscript, July 1995, sent to the author, 14 August 1995.

[56] Ben Helfgott, in conversation with the author, 11 May 1996.

(later Chairman of the Jewish Agency in Jerusalem). 'Heini not only encouraged us to attend Zionist meetings, which were then very frequent,' Ben Helfgott added, 'but he also stimulated our interest in music and theatre. It was indeed a very exciting period of our lives.'[57]

Another Loughton boy, Kopel Kendall, recalled of Heini Goldberg (who emigrated to Israel in 1948 and settled on a kibbutz): 'He was a great Zionist whose idea was for us to go to Israel'. Young English Jewish boys and girls from the Habonim movement came to Loughton every Friday night, 'and we had a lot of fun learning Hebrew songs, talking about Palestine, and about life in general'.[58] Among those who taught the boys those Hebrew songs at Loughton was Reuma Schwartz, a twenty-year-old Palestinian Jewish girl who was in London for a year studying to be a teacher. Wanting to earn some pocket money, she had applied for a job at Loughton. 'You have to be an assistant cook', she was told. 'I don't cook,' she replied. 'You don't have to cook', came the answer, 'only to be an assistant cook, to wash dishes, to clean vegetables.'

Reuma Schwartz was quickly drawn to the boys at Loughton, and they to her. 'They were so rough in the yard,' she later recalled. 'The only way to get them quiet was to say "food, food".'[59] 'When, each afternoon, the boys came back from their studies,' she remembered, 'I had to be prepared with a hot meal for them. They were hungry, and wild. I thought to myself, "If I can show them I can hit a ball, then they will take to me". Within a week they were under my command.'[60] To the boys, Reuma was a lively and attractive young woman who brought with her the flavour of the spirit that pervaded the Jewish community in Palestine, which so many of them still hoped to be a part of. 'We wanted to learn from her as much as possible about Jewish life in Palestine,' Ben Helfgott recalled, 'especially as we could not go there then, because of the White Paper restrictions.'[61]

Malka Tattenbaum also recalled her time as a helper at Loughton. 'The building, once a private mansion, was by then rather dilapidated,' she later wrote, 'but its situation in the countryside was beautiful. Thanks to the efforts of the boys and the staff it was turned into a very pleasant home. One of the first things I did was to replace the bunks with proper beds, to give a home-like atmosphere, as different as possible from the camps. I also had curtains put up, and changed the china and

---

[57] Ben Helfgott, 'Heini Goldberg – Chaim Golan' (obituary), *Journal of the '45 Aid Society*, No. 16, Passover 5753/1993.

[58] Kopel Kendall (Kandelcukier), recollections, letter to the author, 2 September 1995.

[59] Reuma Weizman, in conversation with the author, London, 29 February 1996. In 1950 she married Ezer Weizman, who in 1993 became President of the State of Israel.

[60] Reuma Weizman, in conversation with the author, 29 December 1994.

[61] Ben Helfgott, in conversation with the author, 16 March 1996.

cutlery to make the atmosphere less like that of an institution.

'I collected together a group of people to act as friends of the hostel and they helped in various ways; for example, traders in the East End of London generously contributed food to supplement the rations which were still rather meagre. Our cook was a young woman called Fay and she had to provide fifty meals a day. For Friday night we always had a special meal, with a white tablecloth, wine and candles. The boys always appreciated this, even if they had arrived very tired after a day in town.

'We held many discussions, giving the boys an opportunity to unburden themselves, and I used to tell them about life in Palestine. I noticed that in the dining-room a photograph of Stalin had been put up. I understood the reason for this – the Red Army had liberated some of the camps – but after discussion the warden and I persuaded them to substitute a photograph of Herzl, explaining the importance of the Zionist vision of a homeland for the Jews.

'A committee at Bloomsbury House interviewed each boy, to find out his interests and aptitudes and guide him into suitable training or further education. I recollect a debate which took the form of a play where five boys took the parts of English diplomats (complete with top hats), five were dressed as *chaluzim*[62] and five as Arabs – whom I dressed in traditional Arab costume. We had a lively discussion on how the Jewish State was to be achieved.'[63]

The boys' interest in Zionism was heightened in the autumn of 1946, when, in a surprise dawn raid, British security forces entered a large number of Jewish settlements in Palestine and seized weapons that were being hidden there. In London, the Zionist organisations called for a mass protest demonstration in Trafalgar Square. Many boys left their hostels to participate, under their own banner. 'We played a part,' Ben Helfgott later reflected, with pride.[64] It was their first public involvement in post-war politics.

Among those who looked after the boys who were suffering from tuberculosis, first at the Ashford sanatorium and later at Quare Mead, was Maria Simon, known to the boys as Sister Maria. She had been born in Berlin in 1903. Immediately after the First World War she trained as a nurse in one of Berlin's leading hospitals. Her speciality was as a children's nurse. When Hitler came to power in Germany she left for Italy, resuming her nursing work in Naples. When Hitler visited Italy a year later to meet Mussolini, all German refugees were interned in

[62] Zionist pioneers.
[63] Mrs M. Tattenbaum, 'A few recollections', *Journal of the '45 Aid Society*, No. 7, April 1980.
[64] Ben Helfgott, in conversation with the author, 2 May 1996.

prison for the duration of the visit, Maria Simon among them. When Mussolini introduced anti-Jewish laws, she emigrated to Britain, and during the Second World War worked at the Hampstead Hospital for Children. After working with the boys at the Ashford sanatorium, Sister Maria became matron at Quare Mead.[65]

'She was more than a nursing sister to us,' recalled Shmuel Dresner – one of the many boys who was found to be suffering from TB when he reached Windermere – 'as we realised soon enough when she had to leave and other matrons took her place. She fulfilled many roles in Quare Mead, from that of a caring mother and confidante to friend and adviser.'[66]

Among the other Windermere boys at Quare Mead was Zisha Schwimmer. He was one of the few boys whose father had also survived the war. After his father's death in 1984, at the age of ninety, his son recorded Mayer Schwimmer's unusual story. Throughout the First World War he had served in the Austrian army, fighting on both the Russian and the Italian fronts. He was twice wounded. He was a guard of honour at the funeral of the Emperor Franz Joseph in Vienna in 1916. In 1918, while he was on his way home from the front, he was stopped at a station in Poland by Polish Legionnaires, conscripted into the Polish Legion, and fought in the Russian-Polish War of 1920 against the Bolsheviks.

During the Second World War, at the Jeruzolimska camp in Cracow, Mayer Schwimmer managed, his son recalled, 'to slip away from a firing squad, thus escaping death'.[67] Father and son were together in Czestochowa and Buchenwald, but in Buchenwald they were separated. Meier Schwimmer was sent first to Dachau and then to Mauthausen, where he helped to save the life of a fellow-prisoner by giving him some food. He was liberated by the Americans and taken to the Displaced Persons camp in Landsberg, from where he returned to his home town, Gorlice, to look for his son. Not finding him there, he went to Prague, where somebody told him that his son had survived, and was in England.

By now Mayer Schwimmer was hoping to travel to the Argentine, to join a sister-in-law who had emigrated to Buenos Aires before the war. She sent the necessary papers to enable both father and son to join her there. But the Argentinian authorities in Paris, where Mayer Schwimmer stayed for eleven months in the hope of finalising the documents, refused

[65] A note in the *Journal of the '45 Aid Society* of April 1983 states: 'Maria died on the 5th of July 1983 and was cremated in Golders Green. Unfortunately only very few people knew of her sudden death and could attend the cremation.' *Journal of the '45 Aid Society*, No. 11, April 1984.

[66] Shmuel (Sam) Dresner, 'Sister Maria', obituary, *Journal of the '45 Aid Society*, No. 11, April 1984.

[67] 'Obituaries', *Journal of the '45 Aid Society*, No. 11, April 1984, page 42. Further information in Jack (Zisha) Schwimmer, letter to the author, 21 February 1995.

to issue a visa without a Polish passport. The Polish consulate in Paris refused to issue a passport without a birth certificate. No such documents had survived the war. Zisha Schwimmer thereupon persuaded the Jewish Refugees Committee in London to find an employer who would guarantee his father a job in the shoe trade, and he came to London, where father and son were reunited.

Michael Perlmutter was one of the boys who had to go to the sanatorium at Ashford. Shortly after being liberated in Theresienstadt he had learned that his brother had survived, and was in a Displaced Persons camp in Bavaria. Recovery at Ashford was the essential pre-liminary to being able to see his brother again. They were the only survivors of their family. 'Medical doctors visited us almost daily,' he recalled of his time at Ashford, 'and the nursing staff made sure that we followed all the doctors' orders to the letter. Life at Ashford was routine, and for the most part, uneventful. Those who were very seriously ill with TB were confined to total bedrest, fortunately that was the minority. Most of us were required to have four to five hours of bedrest daily, and the rest of the time we were free to move about, go for short walks on warm days, or simply sit around and reminisce about our home life, or the many miracles that had finally brought us to this safe haven. Books were made available and we taught ourselves the English language, with a great deal of help from the nurses. They were all more like angels! I remember especially Sister Maria, who was one of the most dedicated human beings I had ever met. She cared for us all lovingly, and with a tenderness usually reserved for a mother towards her children.

'I recall that period with a great deal of fondness and warmth. Having come from a background of horror, that time spent in Ashford seemed like a paradise.'[68]

As soon as he was discharged from Ashford, Michael Perlmutter made his way to Germany, where he was reunited with his brother Moishe for the first time since they had been separated in the slave labour camp at Skarzysko-Kamienna three years earlier.

Another of the boys whose early years in Britain were spent recovering from tuberculosis was Meir Sosnowicz, who had been sent while at Windermere, to the Westmorland sanatorium, and then to Ashford. At the Ashford sanatorium, he recalled, 'we, the survivors, had a wing to ourselves. The doctor was Dr Pine, from the regular sanatorium staff. Professional nurses and lay people attended us. All were relief workers hired by the Jewish Refugees Committee. Those of us who were allowed out of bed were able to play ping-pong, or cards, or learn English from

[68] Michael Perlmutter, letter to the author, 8 March 1996.

the resident teacher, Mr Engelhart (I believe), or go for walks.

'Some of the staff were themselves survivors, but were paid for their services. Some had accompanied us from Windermere, and a few even from Theresienstadt. One of those who came with us from there became my special friend, Erna Regent (now Kohn). She is now married and lives in New York. I am still in contact with her. Such friendships last! As we recovered, we went on outings, led by Mr Engelhard, to some of the neighbouring places of interest. The places we visited included Dover and Folkestone, on the English Channel, very beautiful places.

'As we recovered, one by one, the doctor gave us permission to lead a more normal life, to study, learn a trade, and so on, allowing some of us to leave the sanatorium for other hostels, or various living arrangements, to work and become independent. Some of us needed continued medical supervision, however, and so one day, in the autumn of 1946, those still at Ashford were transferred to the convalescent home at Quare Mead.'[69]

Three years after they had arrived in Britain, there were still several boys suffering from tuberculosis. In January 1949 Lola Hahn-Warburg asked one of the nurses who had worked in Belsen immediately after the war, Eva Kahn-Minden, to take over at Quare Mead from Sister Maria. Eva Kahn-Minden had come from Germany as a refugee just before the war. When she went to Quare Mead she was twenty-six years old. Within two weeks she was writing to a friend (who, like herself, had come from Germany, and was in charge of the hostel at Gateshead): 'Morris, one of the boys, has gone down, which means that he is not allowed to wash alone at present. Tommy, his room-mate, has been promoted, which means he may wash himself now. Chaskiel got out of bed when we were not looking, and I am afraid that it will be bad for him as he is quite ill; and Meir, the thin one, is aggressive sometimes and I have to quieten him.'

The boys, Eva Kahn-Minden added, 'are not badly sick, just comfortably sick in bed, no pain, no cough, but too weak and too damaged after two years to get up. They put on a happy front all the time but I guess they are not so happy inwardly. They play chess and write and read. The teacher comes three times a week and very enthusiastically teaches them Jewish subjects and English, and some even dream of matriculation. Miss Rothschild, the teacher, helps them all in turn, and then she comes down to our room and sighs, and says how sorry she is for them. But when she goes upstairs she smiles and tries again. She says that they know very little yet and she has not much time for each one.'[70]

[69] Michael Novice (Meir Sosnowicz), recollections, manuscript, June 1995.

[70] Eva Kahn-Minden, letter of 11 February 1949, quoted in Eva Kahn-Minden, *The Road Back, Quare Mead*, Gefen Publishing House, Jerusalem, 1991.

On the following day Eva Kahn-Minden wrote: 'One has to tread carefully here. Everyone is so easily hurt and everyone has such a sad story behind them. I do not ask questions, as we did not ask in Belsen, but at least I have an idea of what goes on in their minds. It needs some experience not to be shocked at their talk, and to take them as they are because of their past. Sam, who is up and about, tried to repair an electric lamp, but did it all wrong, and I said carelessly and in fun, "You should know how to put the wires straight", when I saw how I had hurt him. He cannot get anything straight, he cannot concentrate enough to learn, he is not strong enough to earn, he cannot marry because he is sick – what a life! And he has not even a mother to give him moral support. Actually, he paints and has a room of his own so that he can spread out his paintbrushes. He paints pictures, he is quite artistic. Everyone likes Sammy because he likes to help, and, as he is up for two hours in the morning and two hours in the afternoon, he does a lot for others.'[71]

Eva Kahn-Minden wrote again nine days later: 'I cannot tell the friends and neighbours much, because somehow I feel that the boys trust me to keep their home as their castle and I could not possibly admit all the strangers. They have no other place to call "home". We are a closed community in Quare Mead, but being so varied it is not much of a home, when you come to think of it. Staff versus patient, medical personnel versus house personnel, the Polish group versus the Hungarian crowd, two of Austrian origin, two religious ones, the others non-religious. A few boys do have some relatives somewhere, the others have none, and all these live together under one roof as one family! I am glad I have not got a crowd of girls, I fear they would be harder to handle. Boys are friendly and co-operative – they are gentlemen.'[72]

One of the most welcome visitors to Quare Mead was Lola Hahn-Warburg. Her visit was particularly appreciated because she was not in good health. 'She is a very sick person,' Eva Kahn-Minden wrote, 'but makes the effort to come out here every few months because she loves the crowd here, and her heart melts for them with sympathy. On her last visit she was so happy to see them up and about, really active by Quare Mead standards.'[73] Another frequent visitor was Oscar Friedmann. 'He explained a few things about the boys,' Eva Kahn-Minden noted after one of his visits. 'He instilled into me more hope and more patience with their restlessness and their attitude of "I couldn't care less" which is so worrying. Here in this limited life in England the boys try to behave

---

[71] Eva Kahn-Minden, letter of 12 February 1949. The characteristic of helping others has remained with this particular Sammy throughout the years since.

[72] Eva Kahn-Minden, letter of 21 February 1949.

[73] Eva Kahn-Minden, letter of 26 October 1950.

like English gentlemen with decency, fair play and politeness, but all the time there is the undercurrent of "What does it matter?"'[74]

The third frequent visitor was Leonard Montefiore. 'Monty has been to pay one of his flying visits,' Eva Kahn-Minden wrote in June 1950. 'Taxi arrives; coat thrown into some corner, he greets me, asks how things are; the boys meet him, shake hands, talk, jest; up the stairs two at a time into Nathan's to deliver "a few highbrow magazines" and to discuss the latest on science, politics and art; down to inspect garden, cowshed; a word to Mrs Binder and Herr Gemahl in German; shakes hands with Max, with the gardener and with anyone else around; sits down to rest a minute with all the boys around, exchanging a word with each about his special field of interest; a parting remark to me and he is off again.

'When he has left, everyone has the feeling that he has come just for him or her – a remarkable man! Intelligence, compassion and financial freedom – which is the strongest? Love, concern and a certain shyness coupled with some extrovert abilities – perhaps that would describe him even better. He was sixty-one this year. Till 120!'[75]

The search for relatives continued. One of Ben Helfgott's sisters, Mala, had survived and was in Sweden; his father, mother and youngest sister, Lusia, had been murdered. Perec Zylberberg found that his sister Esther had survived, and that an uncle and aunt who had emigrated to Britain before the war, another uncle in Argentina, and a great-uncle in Jerusalem, were also alive. But when his sister wrote to him, it was with the news that their mother had been killed. 'She did not make it through the selection in Auschwitz. They had stood in line together. Only Esther survived.'[76]

Several boys found that they had relatives who had escaped the war altogether. Howard Chandler was among these lucky ones. 'While in England we searched and found an uncle, my father's brother Mottel (Mordechai) Wajchendler, who had left for Palestine before the war,' he recalled. 'In his first and most welcome letter he informed us that we had two aunts in London with whom we immediately got in touch, and that we also had two aunts in Canada.'[77] The two aunts in London were his father's sisters. They had lived in London since before the war.

Howard Chandler later recalled: 'As time passed, groups were formed and assigned houses or hostels in different parts of Britain which were

[74] Eva Kahn-Minden, letter of 23 February 1949.

[75] Eva Kahn-Minden, letter of 28 June 1950. 'May you live to 120' is the Jewish way of wishing a person long life. Leonard Montefiore died in 1961, at the age of seventy-one.

[76] Perec Zylberberg, recollections, diary entry for 18 October 1993.

[77] Howard Chandler (Chaim Wajchendler), letter to the author, 29 March 1995.

properly staffed. These groups were determined mainly by friends, or religious leanings. My brother and I chose a group that was sent to a hostel at 32 Princess Road, Liverpool, where we stayed until we found out that we had two aunts in London who were willing to take us in. After going to London we still kept in touch with those boys who lived in hostels in the London area, particularly the ones in Stamford Hill and at Loughton. Our relatives treated us very well and also welcomed all our friends for meals and lengthy visits. All this was supervised and funded by the Jewish Refugees Committee operating out of the Bloomsbury House. We were reverting more or less to a normal existence, and had to acquire new skills in order to cope with daily living. We were afforded opportunities to go to school and learn English and to be apprenticed in certain trades.

'Not wanting to be charitable cases, my brother and I chose to go to night school to learn English, and go to work during the day. My brother was able to obtain a position in a diamond factory and learn diamond polishing. I was apprenticed for a very short time as a cabinet-maker, but later changed and joined my brother after he pleaded with the owner, a Mr Morgenstern, of the Paramount Diamond Cutting Company, of 11 Hatton Gardens. I was liked by my teacher, Harry Saperstein, an expert diamond cutter. I was very eager to learn and was making very good progress. How good the progress was, I was only to find out after a year and a half, when the chance came for me to join a group to go to Canada. When I started to work I was earning ten shillings weekly. Occasionally I got a little bonus, and at the end of one to one and a half years I was earning £1 a week.

'One day I received a letter from Bloomsbury House informing me that I did not qualify for a scheme to go to Canada. But quite soon I was able to be included in the group, and was assured that if I settled in Canada and liked it, my brother would be able to follow. Prior to leaving, I made an appointment with my governor to give my notice of leaving and to express my appreciation for giving me a chance to learn a trade. Apparently he had followed my progress at the factory and was very satisfied with my work. He tried to to talk me out of leaving and offered me £5 a week instead of £1 if I would stay on. However, I had set my mind on leaving, and since he could not change my mind, he wished me well. Since I had only worked for a year and a half, yet had completely mastered my trade, he gave me an excellent letter of reference. I still found it odd that I was only getting £1 a week, if I was worth £5.'[78]

*   *   *

[78] Howard Chandler (Chaim Wajchendler), letter to the author, 23 February 1995.

After spending almost two years in the sanatorium at Ashford, Michael Perlmutter was placed in a hostel in London, at 833 Finchley Road.[79] 'That,' he later wrote, 'is where I started turning my life towards normality. I got a job and I also attended evening classes to complete my basic education. My social life took on a new meaning. I had this urgent need to make more and more friends, to fill the void the loss of my family created within me. To this day my friends have never let me down.'[80]

Also at 833 Finchley Road was Kurt Klappholz. 'Our matron in the hostel, Mrs Leo Feuchtwanger, was a relative of the famous German Jewish novelist,' he later wrote. 'She certainly ran the hostel in a very good way, and we were also very lucky in our madrich, whose name was Herbert Luster. He met his death when he flew back from Israel in an El Al plane which was shot down over Bulgaria.[81] It was a very tragic death. He was a very able young man who would have been very successful in life. What else can one say? This was a bitter blow. I only heard about it long after I had left the hostel.

'I still remember walking up and down Finchley Road and around the clock tower in Golders Green and finding it quite incredible that I should be in London. As a child, my father often talked to me about the western countries, namely England, France, perhaps also Holland – countries whose political set-up he admired – and I am sure he wished that that particular set-up had also prevailed in Poland. But unfortunately at the time it did not. And, remembering that I came to London straight from Germany, it was really quite incredible that I should have ended up in London. So I can only repeat what I said before; that I was extremely lucky. Extremely lucky.'

In one respect, Kurt Klappholz was unhappy at the Finchley Road hostel. This was the attempt made to encourage greater religious worship. 'On the first Friday in the hostel,' he recalled, 'a madrich announced that since it was Friday we would soon be going to synagogue. Some of our residents objected strenuously since they had no wish or intention to go to synagogue. I did not object. I simply went to my bedroom and waited to see what would happen. There were approximately fifteen residents at 833 Finchley Road. Out of the fifteen of us, about four were orthodox. I would not have wished to live in a different sort of hostel, but approximately half of the residents were not orthodox but were quite prepared to go with the wind.

'Some of us were not prepared to do that, however, and those people

---

[79] By chance, many years later this building was bought by one of the boys as an investment.

[80] Michael Perlmutter, letter to the author, 4 March 1995.

[81] In August 1955 an El Al passenger plane crossed the Bulgarian frontier in error. It was shot down by a Bulgarian Air Force fighter, and all fifty-eight passengers and crew were killed.

were in due course to find that considerable pressure was put on them to make them go to synagogue. In the end such people were asked to leave the hostel. Before they left they found the situation most uncongenial. It was not expected that people of our age – who after their recent experiences regarded themselves as adults – would welcome having the details of their lives dictated to them. In my own case, my stay at 833 Finchley Road led to my becoming more anti-religious and quite explicitly so, more than I had ever been in my life. Admittedly, previously my father was an atheist and certainly did not expect me to behave in a religious way.'[82]

Harry Balsam was sent to the hostel in Loughton, Essex. 'Our hostel became the most popular of all,' he later wrote. 'The housekeepers who looked after us became very proud of what they had achieved. They wanted us to grow up to be good citizens. In 1947 most of us wanted to go to Palestine to fight for independence. Most of my friends were accepted, they passed the medical. However I did not pass because I had a bad foot and had to have an operation, which I had in St Mary's Hospital, Paddington. Most of my friends came back after nine months.

'I had been living in England for two years when I discovered that I had cousins living in London. They were very excited too, because, from their entire family, only I had survived in the Nazi camps. My father and brother had survived in Russia. These cousins were very good to me and after a while they persuaded me to come and work for them in their trouser factory.'[83]

Having taught first at Wintershill Hall and then at Millisle, Dr 'Ginger' Friedmann had gone on to teach at Bunce Court School, at Otterden Place in Kent, taking with him a few boys from Millisle whose education he hoped to advance. One of those boys was Wilem Frischmann, who was then sixteen. In the summer of 1944 he had been deported to Auschwitz, together with his mother Nelly and eleven-year-old sister Bösyi, who had perished there, and with his father Lajos, a former Czechoslovak civil servant, who died of malnutrition.

Recalling after fifty years his teacher's love of Greek history and mythology, Wilem Frischmann remarked: 'That was his speciality. He was a lovely man. When I listened to him telling the story of the Odyssey I realised that there was other history besides Jewish history, and that was very exciting. He would also tell us all about European history, from the French Revolution up to 1930, the period we were studying for

[82] Kurt Klappholz, letter to the author, November 1995.
[83] Harry Balsam, 'The Harry Balsam Story', manuscript, sent to the author, 14 November 1995.

matriculation. He allowed us to come into his room to listen to the nine o'clock news. We had to go to bed straight after that.'[84]

At Easter 1949, 'Ginger' Friedmann's namesake, Oscar Friedmann, asked two of the boys, Jerzy Herszberg and Ben Helfgott, to visit the home at Lingfield run by Alice Goldberger, 'with a view to giving a helping hand'. Under Alice Goldberger's care, assisted by Sophie Wutsch, were the twenty-four very young children who had survived the Holocaust, mostly in Theresienstadt, and who had been brought to Britain at the same time as the boys. That visit was highly significant in the story of the boys, for it showed their ability to care for others; in this case, for those who were even younger than themselves. Over several years, Jerzy Herszberg and Ben Helfgott, and at different times Hugo Gryn, Henry Green, and Wolf Blomfield – who had come to Britain as a refugee from Germany in 1939 – would spend time with Alice Goldberger's young charges, and help out at their summer camps. 'Alice called them "Our Boys",' her biographer has written, 'and they provided welcome older male companionship for the young children.'[85]

Alice Goldberger's story was recounted in an episode of the television programme, *This is Your Life*, transmitted on 25 October 1978. Jerzy Herszberg, who was present at the party afterwards, later recalled: 'There were some very emotional scenes. People who had not seen each other for over thirty years, and could not even speak the same language, embraced each other and seemed to have a mutual understanding.'[86]

David Gordon and his wife Bianca had come to England from Germany before the war. He was twenty-five years old when he took over the Nightingale Road hostel in Stamford Hill. He and Bianca had married in September 1945, just after the International Red Cross had confirmed that her parents had died in the war. 'My father, a pious scholar, perished in Buchenwald; my mother, and a large section of my family in Auschwitz,' Bianca later wrote.[87] It was only a few days after their wedding that the Gordons arrived at the Stamford Hill hostel. In a report about how he saw his work in the hostel, David Gordon commented: 'At Windermere, great freedom was given to the children, because they needed a period of rest, and were not yet in a position to adjust to the reality of a regular, disciplined life. In the hostel this adjustment must be aimed at, and the daily life should, as nearly as possible, take the form of that of normal adolescents.

[84] Wilem Frischmann, in conversation with the author, 12 May 1996.

[85] Sarah Moskovitz, *Love Despite Hate, Child Survivors of the Holocaust and Their Adult Lives*, Schocken Books, New York, 1983, page 15.

[86] Jerzy Herszberg, 'This is Your Life', *Journal of the '45 Aid Society*, No. 6, May 1979.

[87] Bianca Gordon, letter to the author, 4 May 1995.

'Of equal importance to educational work with our children is the creation of a feeling of confidence in the future. Only this confidence in their future will effectively counteract their inner restlessness, anxieties and tensions. Educators must discuss with the children their ideas and plans and then help them to adjust their present life and work to future plans.

'In conclusion, I would like to say how greatly moved I was by the way in which these boys and girls proved able to regain self-respect and to achieve a positive attitude to life, and without forgetting their terrible experiences during the war years.'[88]

In October 1946, Leonard Montefiore twice publicly expressed his thoughts and feelings about the boys. His first forum was in an article he wrote for the magazine *Jewish Outlook*, the second was a talk to the Cambridge University Jewish Society. His magazine article contained a sentence that was to mean a great deal to the boys themselves over the years. 'If we lavish care on the few survivors,' he wrote, 'we are, at the same time, paying tribute to the dead.'

The aim of Montefiore's magazine article was to stimulate charitable donations. Voluntary funds, he pointed out, not State funds, had been used to house, clothe, feed and train the newcomers. The problem with regard to education, he stressed, was money: £125,000 had been already been spent on the boys since the arrival of the first group in August 1945.[89] More funds were needed. 'They want things more difficult and more expensive to provide,' Montefiore noted. 'They want opportunities to learn, regular schooling, sometimes of the academic type. We must have forty boys or more who want to study for the London matriculation. How far should we meet their wishes?

'They have suffered and endured so much, it seems hard to say that, in all cases, the cheapest course must be adopted and the earliest moment must be taken to free the Anglo-Jewish community from this burden. Moreover, it is a long job. To complete the task will take a long time, several years at least, before the last of these boys and girls has been given a real solid chance in life. And as time goes by, enthusiasm wanes, pity grows cold and the public, even the Jewish public, begins to want something fresh to think about. "Time hath, my Lord, a wallet on his back, wherein he puts alms for oblivion."[90] Oblivion, forgetfulness.

---

[88] Wolfgang David Gordon, 'Some Notes on the Work with Continental Youth from the Concentration Camps', May 1946: published in the *Journal of the '45 Aid Society*, No. 9, December 1981.

[89] In the money values of 1996, more than £2 million ($3 million).

[90] Shakespeare, *Troilus and Cressida*, III, iii, 145. The next lines read: 'A great-siz'd monster of ingratitudes / Those scraps are good deeds past; which are devour'd / As fast as they are made, forgot as soon / As done.' The boys do not, in the main, subscribe to such a negative philosophy.

Dachau and Buchenwald will soon be forgotten, except by those who escaped thence with their lives.'[91]

In his address to the Cambridge University Jewish Society on 18 October 1946 Leonard Montefiore spoke of 'an experiment in education or rehabilitation that before so many months or years will be concluded'. The boys were in England, he said, 'for a period of rest, re-training and rehabilitation in mind and body before leaving for their permanent homes, wherever those permanent homes can be found, in Palestine, in America, or the British Commonwealth'. He made no mention of Britain. As he explained to his audience: 'When we asked these children what they wanted to do, and occasionally were told they would like to spend seven years in this country studying to be a doctor, or a professional pianist, or to become a portrait painter, we had to say "Think of something else". Somehow we had assumed that the answer Palestine or the USA, the reply given in most cases, would be given in all cases. We had assumed, too easily perhaps, that an answer would be given after five years spent in prison, and those five years from thirteen to eighteen. They had gone to prison, children, and they came out in some ways mature beyond their years and in other ways just as when they had been separated from their parents for the last time.'

Montefiore gave his listeners an account of what he saw as a flaw in the character of the boys. 'Nearly a year after their arrival in this country,' he said, 'I suggested to one of these boys that it would be a useful piece of work to help in the harvest fields. After all, he was a guest in this country and food was short. I used the stock arguments that would have been accepted with resignation, if not with enthusiasm, by any sixth-former. Not so the ex-inmate of Buchenwald. He merely said that he was not interested in the British harvest. His work among the sheaves was unlikely to increase his bread ration and that was the only thing that interested him. The reply was unexpected, but when you come to think of it not unnatural. The only work that boy had ever done in his life was forced labour for the Nazis. Work *pro bono publico* was unknown.[92]

'Or again, a boy was found tucked up in bed about eleven o'clock in the morning. To suggestions that it was about time to get up, he merely replied, "For the past three years I worked sixteen hours a day for the Nazis. If you imagine that I am going to do another hand's turn for the next three years, you are greatly mistaken." Yet, in other cases, boys will make considerable sacrifices in order to acquire learning, and have

[91] Leonard G. Montefiore, 'Thou art the helper of the fatherless', *Jewish Outlook*, October 1946.

[92] In their later years, in Britain and elsewhere, many of the boys were, and still are, involved in considerable charitable work.

had to be restrained from sitting up till the small hours of the morning over their books.'

Later in his address, Montefiore commented: 'We take so many things for granted. The home that always has been and always will be open to us, under all circumstances, whatever we do or leave undone. I contrast my own boyhood with that of the boy I visited a few days ago. He had spinal tuberculosis and is semi-paralysed. He is having every care and attention but the clinic is in the country and some distance from London. On Sunday afternoon, visitors come and there is a cheerful buzz of conversation in the ward. But the Jewish boy lies alone staring into vacancy. Yes – Hitler has passed this way.'

Montefiore had originally been asked to speak to the Cambridge University Jewish Society, not about the boys, but about Reform Judaism, of which he was a pillar. He had decided to speak about the boys instead, but he ended his remarks with a reference to his original topic. 'By no stretch of the imagination,' he said, 'is it conceivable that any one of these children will become a member of the Reform Synagogue. So I can, at least, say that I am not seeking recruits for my own particular tabernacle.'[93]

Montefiore was convinced that the boys would eventually leave Britain, some to Palestine, some to the United States. 'I hope when they leave this country,' he said, 'there will be the same diversity of outlook among these children as when they arrived. That diversity has made them a very interesting group. I hope they will have gained insight into, and appreciation of, the essential virtues of this country, its kindly tolerance, its profound sympathy with suffering, its willingness to help if given the opportunity. And, just here and there, perhaps, there may be a few people who would otherwise have remained ignorant, who will have learned the virtues of the Polish Jew, his courage and patience, his humour and gaiety, his many engaging characteristics which have survived undimmed the years of persecution and cruelty.'[94]

How long the hostel system would last, and the boys remain together, was a question much on Leonard Montefiore's mind. 'When they leave this country' was a phrase he had used several times in his talk. Yet within two years there was a change which gladdened him. 'Boys who, on their arrival, would have flown out in a passion at any rebuke,' he wrote in a magazine article in July 1947, 'now accept a telling-off with an engaging grin. They have become less fanatical, more balanced, more

[93] In fact, one of the boys, Hugo Gryn, originally from Beregszasz, was to become Senior Rabbi of the Upper Berkeley Street Synagogue (in 1964), and later President of the Reform Synagogues of Great Britain (in 1990).

[94] Leonard G. Montefiore, *Address given to the Cambridge University Jewish Society on 18th October, 1946.*

reasonable as it would seem to me. But one cannot say how long this mood of patience will persist. Many of them have relatives, near or more distant, in many parts of the world.[95] They would like, in theory at least, to be reunited. Others without kith or kin would be well content to remain in this country if they were permitted, and thus provide a small additional quantity of manpower in British industry.'[96]

Those boys who wanted to do so, were permitted to stay in Britain, the temporary nature of their original visitors' permits being in due course rescinded by the authorities. Leonard Montefiore had underestimated the desire of many of the boys to stay in England, and their determination to become Englishmen. As the years went by, those who did stay in England, the majority, adopted the customs, and adapted to the way of life, of the country that had taken them in. Many took English names. Although in most cases they retained their central European accents – and, when they arrived, did not imagine that they would stay on – they made a full commitment to Britain. 'I have always felt a sense of gratitude to this country for letting me come here and settle down,' Zisha Schwimmer wrote. 'I have therefore always felt patriotic to this country.'[97]

The thoughts of another boy, on Britain and the British attitude towards them, were expressed in verse by Michael Etkind:

> The rugged coastline of your lands
> surrounded by the restless seas.
> Your mist at night;
> The steady drizzle overhead –
> Your rolling fields with hedgerows
> interspersed, divided into varying shades
> of green.
>
> The clumps of trees.
> Your brooding past.
> The feeble sun of your indifferent clime.
>
> You made so few demands upon my
> cunning and skill.
> You never cared if I succeeded/failed,
> loved you or not.
>
> England, you took me in your stride.[98]

---

[95] In fact, only a few of the boys had any surviving relatives.

[96] L. G. Montefiore OBE, 'Our Children', *Jewish Monthly*, July 1947.

[97] Jack (Zisha) Schwimmer, letter to the author, 1 January 1995.

[98] 'England': Michael Etkind, 'The Unfinished Notes of a Holocaust Survivor', manuscript.

CHAPTER 17

The Search

URING THEIR FIRST months, and even years, in Britain, almost every boy still lived in the hope of finding some member of his family still alive. Almost all of them were to be disappointed. Some wondered if their mothers and fathers, who had mostly been in their forties at the time of the deportations, might not, by some miracle, have survived. Others hoped that a brother or a sister might somehow have evaded death, and be alive somewhere in Europe. The search for relatives was a desperate, and usually a hopeless quest. But sometimes it was successful.

Mayer Bomsztyk, from Staszow, later wrote: 'Photographs of survivors from the camps were taken and published all over the world, so that people could trace their families. An uncle who lived in Buenos Aires recognised my name, and wrote to me in Windermere to tell me that my sister Hela had survived, and had been liberated in Bergen-Belsen. She now lives in America. I visit her every year.'[1]

'I was still in Sweden,' Ben Helfgott's sister Mala recalled, 'not knowing who had survived, but not really expecting anyone to be alive when, one day, I received a letter from my brother Ben.' She added: 'Ben, who no doubt takes after our father, was always very resourceful, a keen sportsman with an interest in people and particularly the family. He started making enquiries immediately after the war. He even returned to Piotrkow to enquire if anybody survived. He made the journey from Theresienstadt where he was liberated. To have travelled on the Continent at that time was no mean achievement, there was absolute chaos.'[2]

In March 1947 Mala Helfgott was brought to Britain by the Central British Fund. She was met at Tilbury Docks by her brother. She was sixteen years old. Having lost all opportunity for schooling and studying in the war, she became a shorthand typist within a year, working for the London office of the *Cape Times*. Twenty-five years later, having in the meantime brought up a family, she took an external degree in sociology as a student at London University.

[1] Mayer Bomsztyk, recollections, sent to the author, 6 May 1996.
[2] Mala Tribich (née Helfgott), recollections, letter to the author, 14 March 1996.

David Herman, one of the boys from Ruthenia, was fortunate in that several of his brothers, and also a sister, survived. One of his younger brothers, Abraham, known as Abie, joined him in Britain in 1947, going to Bunce Court School, near Ashford in Kent, where they were under the tutelage of Dr Friedmann, 'the Ginger One'. Abraham Herman later recalled his schooldays in Mukacevo, with fighting 'all the time' between the Jewish and non-Jewish boys. In the ghetto established after the German occupation in March 1944 he remembered women handing over their diamond rings 'for a piece of bread'. Deported to Auschwitz, where his mother was killed, he was sent to work in the nearby SS barracks and farm. He remembered a German overseer who 'must have murdered one a week there – beating him to death – giving him twelve lashes – and they didn't last long after that.' Later, on a death march in the Sudetenland, a Czech woman ran across the road and tried to hand him a piece of bread. 'She was hit over the head with the butt of a gun for it by a German soldier.'[3]

After schooling at Plaistow Grammar School, Abie Herman studied architecture, later putting his studies to good use by becoming a property developer. 'His greatest love was music,' Ben Helfgott recalled, 'and he became an accomplished pianist, having played at the Wigmore and Toynbee Halls. Those who knew him well thought that, had he been able simply to follow his inclinations, he would have devoted himself to the pursuit of music.'[4]

Hugo Gryn, from Beregszasz, was fortunate that his mother, Bella, had survived. On New Year's Eve, 1945, two months before he joined the last flight of boys to leave from Prague to Britain, he smuggled his mother over the new Soviet border, so that she could rejoin her two surviving brothers. In 1947 he made the journey from Britain to Karlovy Vary to see her. But a year later Communist rule was imposed on Czechoslovakia, and he was unable to return until many years later.[5]

Jack Rubinfeld's oldest brother Izzy had left Poland for the United States before the outbreak of war. Fortunately, after all his trials and tribulations, in the Przemysl ghetto and a succession of slave labour camps, Jack was able to remember his brother's pre-war address. Using this information, the staff at his hostel, at Winchester, wrote to the American Joint Jewish Distribution Committee – 'the Joint' – 'who then found him'.[6]

Harry Balsam, from the Galician town of Gorlice, was another of the

[3] Abraham Herman, in conversation with Ben Helfgott, 15 March 1989; transcript. Abraham Herman died a month after this interview.

[4] Ben Helfgott, 'Abie Herman', obituary, *Journal of the '45 Aid Society*, No. 14, May 1990.

[5] Hugo Gryn, in conversation with the author, 15 April 1996.

[6] Jack I. Rubinfeld, letter to the author, 26 March 1996.

fortunate ones. His brother and father had travelled to Russia immediately after the German invasion. The train that was to have taken the whole family to the relative safety of Russia had drawn out of the platform before Harry and his mother could board it. They were at that very moment unloading their baggage from a truck. 'There was no whistle, and no one waved a green flag. We heard some planes overhead, there was an air-raid going on, and the driver must have panicked.'[7]

Harry Balsam's brother and father had been put to work in Siberia, in the gold mines there, and in the forests cutting down trees. 'They did not return to Germany until 1946,' he wrote, 'by which time I was already in England. After a while in Germany they found out through the Red Cross that I was living in England and had survived the war. I was the only one from the rest of my family to survive the Nazi murders. When I say family I mean my uncles, aunties, cousins and so on. I could easily reckon well over one hundred of my immediate family perished.'[8]

Harry Balsam's father and brother settled in Israel. 'My father died there in 1972. He was eighty years old. I was at his funeral.'[9] Harry Balsam was one of the very few boys whose father survived. Manfred Heyman's father and brother had died in the last months of the war. His mother Herta, who had been deported from a slave labour camp in Poland to Auschwitz, and from there to Belsen, was among those at Belsen who were liberated by the British. She was suffering from tuberculosis, and taken by the Swedish Red Cross to hospital in Sweden. It was while he was in the hostel in Glasgow that Manfred Heyman received a letter from the Red Cross, to whom he had written while he was at Ascot, sending him his mother's address. 'In the winter of 1946 to 1947,' he recalled, 'I went to visit my mother in Sweden. I travelled by boat to Gothenburg and from there by train to Stockholm. My mother had TB and so was in a hospital near Stockholm. The journey to Sweden was very cold but I enjoyed the food on board ship.'[10] Not long afterwards, Manfred Heyman's mother died.

Alfred Huberman, from Pulawy, had gone to the hostel in Ashford. 'Whilst in Ashford,' he later wrote, 'I came across a Yiddish newspaper, which was published in Paris. I noticed a column in which people were searching for lost relatives. Since I knew that I had relatives in France before the war, I wrote to the newspaper, mentioning the names of aunts, uncles and cousins. At this time my uncle happened to be

---

[7] Harry Balsam, 'Harry Balsam Remembers', *Holocaust Testimony 2*, published by Roman Halter and Michael Etkind, London, 1983.

[8] Harry Balsam, letter to the author, 8 May 1995.

[9] Harry Balsam, 'Harry Balsam Remembers', *Holocaust Testimony 2*, published by Roman Halter and Michael Etkind, London, 1983.

[10] Manfred Heyman, letter to the author, 7 March 1996.

attending a funeral for a person who originated from my town in Poland. Another mourner casually mentioned that "some people are lucky to find relatives in England". My uncle looked at the paper and realised the announcement had been written by me. He informed the surviving members of our family.

'Thus it was that, during an English lesson, given by Mr Englehart, I received a telegram from my eldest sister Irene: "Your sister is alive, living in Paris". This was how I first learnt that one of my sisters had managed to survive the camps, and had entered France under an assumed name (she had lived in France for two years before the war and was able to speak French perfectly). She was married to a Frenchman only six weeks before we found one another.

'As a result of this miraculous find, I discovered some distant relatives in Brighton. It was because of this that I ended up living in Brighton. My Brighton relatives were in tailoring and I became a tailor.'[11]

Pinchas Gutter, the Hassidic boy from Lodz who had survived the Warsaw ghetto, Majdanek, Skarzysko-Kamienna and Buchenwald, lost his whole family, including his twin sister Sabina. When, after the war, lists of survivors were published, to enable families to find each other, he found the name of his cousin Anja, who was then living in Paris with her husband and daughter. 'They persuaded me to come and live with them,' he recalled.[12] For several years he stayed in Paris, working in his cousin's textile factory. Later he emigrated to Canada.

Aron Zylberszac had hoped that one of his nephews, Yossel, might have survived. 'But when queried, the Red Cross stated that he was last seen in Bergen-Belsen, and that is all I know.' Aron's parents had been murdered in Birkenau. His elder brother Velvel had died in his arms in Theresienstadt, shortly before liberation. His younger brother Iser and his three sisters, Zlato, Rifka and Chana, had all been killed. All his nephews had been murdered. 'All my family were killed by the Germans. The only person to survive was one of my nieces who escaped to Russia.'[13]

Meir Sosnowicz, from Warsaw, was fortunate while in England to be able to make contact both with his elder brother Charles, who had left Warsaw for Paris nine years before the outbreak of war, and also with his sister Hela, who had survived the Warsaw ghetto. 'In the summer of 1946,' he recalled, 'my brother Charles came to visit me at Ashford Sanatorium from Paris. The last time I had seen him was in 1930 in

---

[11] Alfred (Abram) Huberman, recollections, letter to the author, 7 May 1996.

[12] Pinchas Gutter, recollections, letter to the author, 23 March 1996.

[13] Aron Zylberszac, recollections, transcript, Imperial War Museum Sound Archives, February 1991.

Warsaw, when I was about three years old. By the time Charles came my health must have improved considerably, because I remember going to Croydon airport by myself to meet him on his arrival.'

Finding his brother had come about as follows. 'After our liberation, while still in Theresienstadt, a Russian soldier asked us if we had any names and/or addresses of relatives who might have survived the war. He gave us postcards, and it so happened that, despite the fact that I had forgotten much of my pre-war years, for some reason I remembered my brother's Paris business address. The soldier sent the card off for me. The postcard merely said that I was alive, but mentioned no return address, because I did not have one. My brother himself had to hide all over France during the German occupation, but was now back in his old business, and received my card! Soon after we arrived in England, the Jewish Refugees Committee encouraged and helped us to search for relatives. So, in due course, I wrote to Charles once again, this time giving him a return address. Soon we started a correspondence, and it is therefore obvious that his visit in 1946 was a particular thrill for both of us.

'My sister too had to hide, as a Christian, in Poland, after the liquidation of the Warsaw ghetto. Toward the end of the war she was arrested and sent to Bergen-Belsen, as a Christian. She was liberated there by the British. She too remembered Charles's address in Paris, and so, gradually, we all corresponded with each other. We met in Marseilles in 1948, when she boarded a boat to Israel together with her husband Yecheskel, also a survivor.'[14]

Chaim Olmer was another boy for whom the news from Europe brought great joy amid the sadness. In February 1946, while he was still at Cardross, he managed to contact his one surviving sister, Sarah, in Poland. She was already on her way to Israel. Perec Zylberberg was also lucky. Soon after he began corresponding with some friends of his family who had emigrated to the United States before the war, in what seemed a vain hope of finding any surviving relative, he received an enquiry from his sister Esther, who was in Sweden. She had survived Bergen-Belsen. 'The news was stunning,' he wrote. 'Could it be that my little sister was among the lucky ones? I could not quite believe it. It was too good to be true. How did such a miracle take place?

'I must have acted like a possessed individual. It just could not enter my conscious mind for a while. But before long I settled down to the knowledge of indeed not being alone. Everything seemed different now. I soon received an answer from my sister. Her state of mind was similar to mine. She told me a bit about her miraculous survival in the typhus-

---

[14] Michael Novice (Meir Sosnowicz), recollections, manuscript, June 1995.

ridden camp of Bergen-Belsen. She also told me that a number of mutual friends were with her in Sweden. We exchanged knowledge about the search for other members of the family and relatives. Each of us started looking for clues. My sister was not too well. She was very exhausted. The Swedish government was very helpful in caring for the refugees. It was however, very heartening to get her long letters. Life became filled with mutual care and concern.'[15]

Like most of the boys, Perec Zylberberg also waited, as did his sister in Sweden, for any indication that other close relatives might, somehow, still be alive. In so many cases there was no absolute certainty, in 1946, that those deported to the death camps had been murdered. At three of the death camps – Chelmno, Belzec and Treblinka – to which the families of most of the boys had been sent, the deportees had been murdered on their arrival. The camp authorities had not even compiled lists of those whom they murdered.

Meanwhile, throughout 1946 and 1947, Jews who had fled from Poland to Russia in 1939 were returning to Poland. 'People kept on arriving by trainloads from every corner of the Soviet Union,' Perec Zylberberg recalled. 'My sister's and my own hopes were rising with each new development. Maybe some of our family and relatives would be among those arriving. The people who survived the camps, and those hidden by Polish people, had in most cases become known to other survivors. Now, when this last chance to see your dear ones presented itself, and when hopes were raised, the tensions were hard to bear. I enquired of all the people I could think of, as to the whereabouts of others who had not shown up yet.

'My city, Lodz, became an important centre of activity for the new-comers. Lodz had managed to get through the war without being destroyed by bombs or shrapnel. The Central Committee of Polish Jewry was operating there. The Bund was again a fairly large organisation. Except for some very distant relations, however, nobody from our family or close relatives arrived in Poland from the East. We were still hoping for more arrivals. Maybe they would be there. As time went on, hope diminished. It was already one and a half years since the end of the war.

'The full extent of our losses as a people was staggering. It was hard to comprehend the total catastrophe. Our father did not survive. He was probably a victim of Treblinka extermination camp. Mother did not make it at Auschwitz. All the numerous uncles, aunts, cousins and second cousins did not show up anywhere. Our brother in the Soviet Union did

[15] Perec Zylberberg, recollections, diary entry for 14 October 1993.

not show any signs of life. It was only the hope of some new information, and the concern to get back your own health, that kept us going.'[16]

These hopes were, in almost every case, chimeras. Slowly the full truth became unassailable. Those who had been brought from Prague to Britain were in almost every case the sole survivors of their immediate families. The few reunions that did take place were dramatic. On 7 April 1947 Esther Zylberberg arrived at Tilbury Docks from Gothenburg. 'I spotted my brother while I was still on the boat,' she later recalled.[17]

Perec Zylberberg also recalled the day when his sister Esther reached Tilbury Docks from Sweden. 'The ship arrived in good time. There on the deck stood my little sister, the same expression that I remembered so well on her smiling and tearful face. We went straight from the port to the family in Romford where she had been accepted as a domestic help. A new chapter opened up for both of us. At last, after all the travails and desperation and almost lost hope, we faced each other. Although a far cry from our numerous family, we felt the poignancy of this reunion.'[18]

Chaskiel Rosenblum, from Konskie, was able to make contact with an uncle who had emigrated to Bolivia before the war. In 1946 he wrote him a letter, addressed care of the Chief of Police, La Paz, and received an answer direct from his uncle: a telegram saying that a visa for Bolivia was waiting for him in London, 'and that I should go to Bolivia'. A few months later Chaskiel Rosenblum was on his way. The decision to make the journey, he later wrote, had 'deep psychological roots. In my home town, my father talked day and night about going to Bolivia where my uncle lived. Before the war, during the war, and on his deathbed, my father was invoking Uncle Salomon. Thus, my uncle was not a real human being, but a character who represented life and well-being.

'Since my father couldn't accomplish his most longed-for desire, who else but me could do it for him? This I understand now, but, at that time, I didn't have the slightest doubt. I just knew I had to do it. It was stronger than everything, and in spite of everything, that was my mission, and my trip was the completion of my mission. I was deeply conscious of the fact that my father had died without being able to go. When in Cardross they organised a small farewell party for me, we all sang "Arum dem feuer" ("Around the fire"). And instead of singing "Israel is my aim", the *madricha* sang "Bolivia is my aim". This disturbed me a little, but not to the extent of changing my aim, whatsoever.'

Chaskiel Rosenblum made his life in South America. In 1956 he

---

[16] Perec Zylberberg, recollections, diary entry for 24 October 1993.
[17] Esther Brunstein (Zylberberg), in conversation with the author, 7 May 1996.
[18] Perec Zylberberg, recollections, diary entry for 25 October 1993.

married. He and his wife had two children, Pepe and Monica. From Bolivia they emigrated to Argentina, where they sent their children to an English primary school, and then to an Argentinian secondary school, where Pepe received two gold medals, one for English and one for Spanish. Then came the years of the military dictatorship, and Pepe, who was active in student politics, went into hiding for six months. 'But six months became nine years,' Chaskiel Rosenblum later wrote, 'and things got far from calm: Pepe became one of the "disappeared". Our mourning was long, silent, terrible. It still goes on.'

A month before setting down his memories of the war years in Europe, Chaskiel Rosenblum, like all the parents of the 'disappeared', read the account of a retired Argentinian naval captain who described how the 'disappeared' were given injections, taken on naval planes, and thrown, asleep and alive, into the ocean. The pilot confessed that he had nightmares about what he had done. 'Now I am confused,' Chaskiel Rosenblum wrote, 'squeezing my brain to elucidate how this man's nightmares have entered my life's testimony and become a part of it.'

The only reason for writing his own testimony, Chaskiel Rosenblum added, 'is my deep love for "The Boys of the '45 Aid Society", who are the rest of my family. I have always felt that I owed them the story of my life after I left England. I have always felt that my silence and the geographical distance were unfair towards them and myself. I have always felt, and will always feel, one of "The Boys".'[19]

Jacob Hecht, one of the Southampton boys, had three brothers and two sisters. Two of his brothers, Schmuel Avrum and Israel, had been with him throughout the war, and were with him still on one of the death marches. 'We were just outside Munich,' he later recalled, 'when it was decided that as they could walk no further, they should follow the call to climb on to the trucks. They were never seen again. Other prisoners said that everyone had been shot – but had they? I fantasised. Maybe they had pretended to be dead – perhaps they ran into the forests and had even found a hideout.

'Anything but death.

'Eventually, after liberation, I came to England. Like my friends, I too was asked if I had any relations, anywhere, no matter how remote. The months passed and someone in New York believed me to be his cousin. It took several letters to convince him otherwise. Another "cousin" wrote from Palestine, but to no avail.

'Meanwhile, I was endeavouring to find my brother Moshe and sister Batya in Palestine. At last we made contact, almost at the same time as

[19] Chaskiel Rosenblum, 'Testimony', manuscript, sent to the author, April 1995.

my name was given out on the radio bulletins. To receive a letter from my brother was wonderful, but he wanted to know if Schmuel Avrum and Israel were alive. I told him my account of events and we both agreed that where there is hope there is life.

'Then, one day, my brother received a telephone call from Jerusalem. A man spoke of two young boys in his care. Their parents had been called Joseph and Hannah, just like ours. My brother held his breath – the boys' names were Schmuel Avrum and Israel. A meeting was arranged, and Moshe and Batya packed food for the journey from Rehovot, and of course for the boys.

'They set off on their horse and cart from the farm where they were staying. At last, they reached their destination and their host gestured them to wait in a room. The door then opened and two very young boys appeared. They had big brown eyes – they were religious boys, just like our family. They stepped towards Moshe – he hugged them, but could only say, "They are not my brothers". The boys were far too young and bore little resemblance to them. They eagerly accepted the gifts of food and there was a sad farewell.

'To this day, it is a mystery as to how they could have the exact names of my brothers and, uncannily, those of my parents. Perhaps they had been given new identities? Who knows? One thing is for sure, that they were the epitome of life and hope.'[20]

In the years following the war, Roman Halter had searched in vain for news of the farmer's wife, Hertha Fuchs, with whom he had sheltered in the last weeks of the war, and of his fellow-survivor Abraham Sztajer, thirteen years his senior, whom he had last seen when he left the Fuchs' farm in 1945. During the Communist years his enquiries in East Germany, even a visit to Dresden, proved futile. Then, in 1992, after the fall of the Berlin Wall, Hertha Fuchs began to search for him, and found his address. In May 1993 he made his way to Dresden. 'After forty-seven years, Mrs Fuchs and I found each other,' he wrote. 'She is eighty-five years of age, still clear in mind but weak in body. We talked about her life all alone, how she managed under the Communists, and about the many things which had happened during the past forty-seven years.'

Hertha Fuchs had one request: 'Please, Roman, try to find Sztajer. I have a feeling that he is alive.' He promised to do so, but it proved a difficult task. 'I began making telephone calls to many cities in America and Canada. I spoke to Sztajers and Steers and Stairs, but to no avail. None of them was the person I was looking for. When I was almost on

[20] Jack (Jacob) Hecht, 'Where there is life there is hope', *Journal of the '45 Aid Society*, No. 18, December 1994, pages 7–8.

the point of giving up, a contact through Yad Vashem[21] in Jerusalem put me in touch with Benjamin Lasman who lives in Jerusalem. We were together in the Lodz ghetto, Auschwitz, Stutthof, and Dresden. Benjamin and his wife were coming to London for a holiday, so we met and talked again, mainly about the past. Did he, I asked, remember Abramek Sztajer? Yes, he did. Abraham Sztajer, he told me, is his second cousin. 'No, no', he corrected himself, 'a cousin twice removed.'

In 1993 Roman Halter had written to me, 'I never found out what happened to Abramek Sztajer, who would now be 78 years of age.' A year later he sent me a triumphant note: 'I searched for him for a long time and now I have found him!'[22] The two men met, embraced, and, during two intense hours, remembered the days when their lives were so closely linked, and endangered.

The boys can never forget that the fate of so many of those nearest and dearest to them has never been formally or officially ascertained. For most of their families who were taken to their deaths in 1942, 1943 and 1944, or shot on death marches in 1945, there is not the smallest documentary trace of their actual murder. Only the ashes which can be found in abundance at every camp bear witness to the scale and enormity of the destruction of the lives of the deportees.

Roman Halter later wrote: 'One of my sisters, her name was Zosia (in Yiddish "Zeese"), who was six years my senior – in 1939 she was eighteen – ended up in the Warsaw ghetto. At first, in 1939, we still managed to send parcels to her from Chodecz.' After that, all contact with her was broken.

When a group of photographs taken in the Warsaw ghetto by a German soldier in 1941 was exhibited in Britain in 1993, fifty years after the Warsaw ghetto revolt, Roman Halter asked to see all one hundred and twenty of the photographs (only fifty were displayed). He was still looking for some trace of his beloved Zosia. 'I spent a couple of hours with a magnifying glass searching for her face,' he wrote.[23] But his search was again in vain.

The search for those who had sheltered the boys could also be a vain one. Fifty years after her wanderings and rescue, and her years in England, Hanka Ziegler, who had spent two years being kept by a Polish woman in a village near Piotrkow, went back to Poland with her brother. They wanted so much to revisit the village where they had been sheltered, but they could not remember its name, and, hard as they

---

[21] The main Holocaust museum and memorial in Israel.
[22] Roman Halter, letter to the author, 1 May 1993.
[23] Roman Halter, letter to the author, 2 April 1991.

searched throughout the region, they could not find it. 'I remember my name,' Hanka reflected, 'but I can't remember the name of the village.'[24]

For some boys, even the passage of half a century cannot obliterate the hope that some relative might still be alive. While I was talking to Sam Weizenbluth in Toronto in 1994, he suddenly asked: 'Help me to find my brother.' His brother, Berek Wajcenblit, was, he recalled, 'about fourteen' when war came to Poland in 1939, and they were living in Warsaw.[25] At that point Berek had left for Russia. He has not been heard of since. He would now be over seventy. Had he reached Russia? Had he survived there? Perhaps no one will ever know. Perhaps a brother's search will never end.

Sam Weizenbluth's agonising request reflects the deep cry of so many survivors, the boys included, who always cherish the thought that perhaps, somewhere, some day, someone of their destroyed family might still reappear.

---

[24] Anna Smith (Hanka Ziegler), in conversation with the author, 16 March 1996.
[25] Sam Weizenbluth, in conversation with the author, 20 September 1994.

CHAPTER 18

The Primrose Club

BY 1947 THE BOYS were scattered, some in hostels, some beginning to earn a living on their own. Yet after less than two years in Britain, their need to maintain the intense companionship which had been created in the camps and during their first months in Britain was strong. The establishment of a club in London was to serve that need. Perec Zylberberg recalled: 'A club was created to serve as a focal point for all the individuals who were by now on their own. I also participated in the effort. It looked promising as a meeting place. It was not easy to gather people from right across the huge city of London. But it was pleasant to come there and meet old buddies.'[1]

'It was so urgently necessary that they should meet,' Barbara Barnett, one of those who worked closely with the boys, later recalled. 'They were family; they were their own – and only – family. Once they left the hostels, most of them were solitary. They needed a meeting place.'[2]

The person chosen to lead the new club was Paul Yogi Mayer, a pre-war refugee youth leader from Germany, who had served in Special Operations Executive in the war, and who had been working as an instructor in sports and arts at the Brady Boys' Club in the East End, one of London's longest-established Jewish youth clubs. He later recalled being summoned to an interview with Oscar Joseph, Elaine Blond, Lola Hahn-Warburg, Leonard Montefiore and Oscar Friedmann: the leading figures of the Jewish Refugees Committee. 'When I outlined my ideas,' he later wrote, 'I was told that the funds available should only be spent for the benefit of those young people rescued from the camps. This I could not accept. I believed in what we called "social groupwork", an interaction between young people, groups with varied interests, pursuing activities of their own choice. If the club was leading those boys and girls away from the horror of the camps into a personal development and realisation of their potential, then the club had to be "open", i.e., encouraging local Jewish boys and especially girls to become members as well. If that was not acceptable to the Committee, then there was no incentive for me to give up working with young people in the East End.

---

[1] Perec Zylberberg, recollections, diary entry for 21 October 1993.
[2] Barbara Barnett, in conversation with the author, 4 August 1995.

'It was Leonard Montefiore who accepted that there was a need to merge with other boys and especially girls. Only a very small number of girls had survived the camps. Meeting girls would be an important step for these boys, now growing up in this country. As it happened, some of those girls who were proudly invited as supporters after a football match were mainly those who had come to this country with the "Kindertransporte" six years earlier.'[3]

The opening meeting of the Primrose Club was held on Sunday, 6 July 1947. Oscar Friedmann was in the chair. It was he who had stressed to Yogi Mayer during the planning stage that contact with those who were not survivors was 'essential' for the boys.[4] He opened the proceedings with a few words about the need for a central club 'for our boys and girls in London'. He then introduced Yogi Mayer, and also the matron, Miss F. Haftka, who had come to Britain from Poland before the war. The new club was located in two adjacent buildings in northwest London, 26 and 27 Belsize Park. Yogi Mayer explained that, as one part of the building was still occupied by a hostel, and the other building was still partly occupied by the Hot Pot Restaurant, the new club would not be able to start its full programme before September. 'In spite of all handicaps', however, some activities would start at once, and the restaurant would serve the boys from the outset. Set up during the war to be a place where those whose husbands were away could gather, talk, and make use of shared cooking facilities, this 'British' restaurant, as the chain was known, was run by Mrs Glucksmann, the former director of a Jewish youth training centre at Lehnitz, near Berlin – a village only two miles from Sachsenhausen concentration camp.

'When the excitement of the first club night calmed down,' Yogi Mayer recalled, 'we sat in the new coffee bar and discussed what we should call the club. "The Freedom Club" was the first suggestion.'

'No. What about "The Friendship Club"?'

'Wait a moment, I have a better idea, let's call it "The Churchill Jewish Youth Club".'

'Surely we will not get permission to use his name, and it may take some time to get an answer.'

There was a suggestion, from some of the Zionist boys, that the club be called 'The Herzl Society', after the founder of political Zionism.[5]

'I suggested calling it Klepfish Club,' Perec Zylberberg recalled. 'It was meant to honour the memory of one of the heroes of the Warsaw ghetto

---

[3] P. H. Y. Mayer, 'The Primrose Story', manuscript, 1995. The Kindertransporte was the rescue of 10,000 young Jewish refugees brought to Britain from Germany and Austria in 1938 and 1939.

[4] Yogi Mayer, in conversation with the author, 6 July 1995.

[5] Yogi Mayer, in conversation with the author, 3 May 1995.

uprising. But the leader of the club warned of people who would make fun of the name, and maybe even ask "what kind of fish" a klepfish was.'[6]

'You are talking about a kind of fish, while I am talking about a great Jewish leader,' Perec Zylberberg told them angrily. Michal Klepfish, he explained to the sceptical, was a Bundist leader, an engineer by profession, who had been one of the organisers of the Warsaw ghetto revolt. 'He served as a kind of engineer to the resistance, creating a kind of Molotov Cocktail, as weapons were in such short supply. At one moment he was in charge of a group of fighters who were holding up a column of German soldiers; he died at his post. In recognition of his valour, he was awarded the Virtuti Militari Cross by the Polish Government in exile.'[7]

'And so the discussion went to and fro,' Yogi Mayer recalled, 'one suggestion following another until Natek Wald, who had been born in the Polish-corridor town of Grudziadz, and was later in the Piotrkow ghetto, pitched in. "You lot will never agree. It's getting late. We could just as well call it the Primrose Club after our telephone exchange. At least to start with".'[8]

Another of the boys, Moniek Buki, from Piotrkow, had the same idea. The name was accepted, and it stuck.

As a Jewish youth leader in the early years of Nazi Germany, Yogi Mayer had been berated by the Gestapo for his wish to help German Jewish youth. He now devoted himself not only to the boys' physical renewal, but also to their cultural and spiritual well-being. Three groups were created: boys under nineteen, known as the Seniors; boys over nineteen, known as Old Boys; and girls, for whom a special girls' room was set aside. A Club Cabinet was then announced; its work was intended as a continuous exercise in self-government: to discuss the club's programme, to find ways of being involved with the local community, and to decide on membership criteria beyond the original Windermere and Southampton boys.

In the club newsletter reporting the opening event, Yogi Mayer noted that 'the canteen was well provided with cakes, buns, sandwiches, hot and soft drinks, served by voluntary helpers'. The tea was followed by a dance, attended by 150 boys and girls, who also made what Yogi Mayer called 'good use' of the library and the table-tennis room.[9]

Despite the problems with the readiness of the building, the Primrose Club – known formally as the Primrose Jewish Youth Club – continued

[6] Perec Zylberberg, recollections, diary entry for 21 October 1993.

[7] Perec Zylberberg, in conversation with the author, 10 May 1996.

[8] Yogi Mayer, in conversation with the author, 3 May 1995.

[9] P. Y. Mayer, 'Dear boys and girls', *Club Letter*, No. 1, July 1947.

to operate throughout the summer of 1947, at first on Tuesdays, Thursdays and Sundays only. On the second Sunday, July 13, there was a chess tournament, volleyball (for which club members were asked to bring PT kit), and a talk on current affairs, followed by a dance. By the middle of September the club was opening five days a week. Guests were welcome. The Hot Pot Restaurant, which remained at No. 26 Belsize Park, offered a three-course kosher supper for one shilling and three pence.[10]

Julie Mahrer, originally from Vienna, who had cooked for the boys in the hostel in Glasgow, came down to London and cooked at the Primrose Club. 'The restaurant was a great attraction for the boys,' Ben Helfgott recalled. 'It was one of the ways to entice them into the club.'[11] 'Miss Mahrer was a great influence on the boys,' Yogi Mayer commented. 'She was a very buxom woman. A bit of their mother's cooking came through to them. It was terribly important.'[12]

One of those who came in contact with the boys at the Primrose Club was London-born Clinton Silver, a university graduate who was the same age as the boys, indeed younger than some. Fifty years later he recalled how special funds were set aside for those who would be unable to cope with life. 'We assumed there would be many, but there were very, very few – only one or two – who became welfare cases.'[13]

Richard Barnett, who had first volunteered to help the boys at the Jews' Temporary Shelter hostel in London, started a music appreciation group at the Primrose Club. For the boys, who had been deprived of music for so many years, it was a marvellous innovation. Barbara Pinto, later Richard Barnett's wife, started a drama group. 'I was only a couple of years older than they were,' she recalled.[14] The boys would read plays together; they performed a few of them on stage at the church hall opposite the club. One of the plays was Emlyn Williams' *Night Must Fall*, in which Chaim Liss, a boy from Lodz, played the leading role.

Only later did Barbara Pinto, who was then training as a social worker, realise the part that drama therapy can play in assisting people, through role-playing, to work through dilemmas in their lives. 'One of the debates among the volunteers,' she recalled, 'was whether we should encourage the boys to talk about the years of incarceration. In fact, they talked very readily, but only about their earlier lives, the happy times, and their liberation – and that fully. There was complete silence about the years in the camps. They put every ounce of their energy into the

---

[10] In the money values of 1996, £2 ($3).
[11] Ben Helfgott, in conversation with the author, 30 April 1995.
[12] Yogi Mayer, in conversation with the author, 13 June 1995.
[13] Clinton Silver, in conversation with the author, 30 April 1995.
[14] Barbara Barnett, in conversation with the author, 4 August 1995.

present and the future.'[15] And in a note written some years later, she commented: 'Astounding determination to succeed dominates the lives of those I still know.'[16]

During the course of a few years the Primrose Club became one of the most competitive clubs in the Association of Jewish Youth, winning many trophies. Yogi Mayer understood the torment which 'his' boys had been through. Once, when he rebuked a boy for fighting after a football match, the boy replied: 'I've lost so much that I cannot keep on losing.'

Within a short time, a number of former refugees who had come to Britain just before the war joined the club. One of them was Edith Buxbaum, who had been born in Germany in 1925. Aron Zylberszac's wife Evelyn recalled: 'I stood in awe of this lovely girl who acquitted herself so marvellously, and who was greatly admired by all for her sporting prowess. I often thought of her as one of "the boys" as she could outrun and outperform many of them.' At the club, Edith Buxbaum met and fell in love with one of the boys, Jeff Frydman, originally from Lodz. They emigrated to the United States, married in New York, and later moved to Florida. 'She was honest and truthful,' Evelyn Zylberszac wrote in Edith Frydman's obituary in 1989, 'and was never scared to speak her mind.'[17]

Yogi Mayer was insistent that the boys should be allowed to bring girls to the club; local Jewish girls who were known as the 'English' girls. A number of other boys met their future wives at the Primrose Club. Most of these girls had been born in Britain, of parents who had come to Britain at the turn of the century, as refugees from Russian Poland, or had themselves come to Britain as refugees just before the war. This influx of girls accelerated the integration of the boys into British society. Among the boys whose story is told in these pages, Aron Zylberszac met his wife Evelyn (Edith Buxbaum's friend), and Krulik Wilder met his wife Gloria, at the Primrose Club. Two of the Hungarian boys, Frank Farkas and Maurice Vegh, also met their wives, Carol and Phyllis, at the club.

The club dances were remembered many years later. One of those who recalled them was Margaret Acher, who had come to Britain as one of the Schonfeld children. She had survived as a child, first in the Warsaw ghetto, and then hidden by Christian friends and in a convent.[18]

Among those who came to help at the Primrose Club was Lou Hoffman,

---

[15] Barbara Barnett, in conversation with the author, 21 March 1996.

[16] Barbara Barnett, manuscript notes (undated).

[17] Evelyn Zylberszac, 'Edith Frydman', *Journal of the '45 Aid Society*, No.13, May 1989.

[18] Margaret Acher, letter to Ben Helfgott, 20 March 1996.

a young man from the East End of London, who taught ballroom dancing to prize medal standard, as well as coaching a number of table tennis teams. 'We also fielded four football teams in the various Association of Jewish Youth leagues,' Yogi Mayer recalled, and, 'based on a weekly swimming class at the Finchley Road pool, participated in the swimming championships of the London Federation of Boys' Clubs, where Roman Halter gained the winner's medal. When I found a large unused hall at the Haverstock Hill Estate, we formed a basketball team.' Football was played on Hampstead Heath.

There was one unexpected problem to be overcome. 'When affiliating our four football teams,' Yogi Mayer wrote, 'I was asked by the Football Association to produce their birth certificates. This I was obviously unable to do. I just had to plead that their special circumstances should be taken into consideration. After all, they had been robbed of playing games at a time when boys in this country played on its pastures green. And so the Football Association, to their credit, accepted my word.'

Among the footballers were David Herman and William Rosenberg, both from the Ruthenian town of Mukacevo. Fifty years later, at the wedding of David Herman's daughter in London, William Rosenberg, who had flown from New York to be at the celebration, was vividly to recall those footballing days. He had gone from the Primrose Club to the United States, where he was able to finish high school, graduate from New York University, and pursue a career in dentistry.[19]

Cricket was also embarked upon at the Primrose Club. With the help of some of his pupils at the Hasmonean Grammar School, where Yogi Mayer taught physical education part-time, he was able to arrange for the Primrose Club to field a cricket team. Moniek Reichkind, a Primrose boy, opened the batting.

Even as the boys started apprenticeships, or went to the ORT school, or took a job in order to earn just enough money to stay in digs, the Primrose Club continued to cater for them. 'They came to the club for their meals,' Yogi Mayer recalled, 'enjoying Miss Mahrer's *Wiener Küche*.[20] I was amazed to see the enormous portions they were able to manage. Maybe their past had taught them not to leave any food on their plate. A special treat was Miss Mahrer's pastries on a Sunday, after football and before the discussion session started, in which many dozens of members participated, quite unique for any youth club. The day ended with a social, which also attracted so many local Jewish girls.

'To me it was important to develop self-programming, and so I followed Ben Helfgott's suggestion to start a weightlifting group and to get our

[19] William Rosenberg, in conversation with the author, 12 May 1996.
[20] Viennese cooking.

own equipment. He and Roman Halter had seen some men weightlifting at the Hampstead Heath "men-only" swimming pond. Ben had asked to lift up the weights, and had done so.'

The Primrose Club also embarked on its own holiday activities. 'Instead of joining another Brady Camp with a few boys,' Yogi Mayer recalled, 'the Cabinet suggested that we should have our own holiday. And so we went twice to Jersey.' For many it was the first time that they had been on a ship, having arrived in Britain by plane. There were many other activities. 'We published our own printed paper, called the *Primrose Leaves*, with our own "letters from America", as some boys had gone to join relatives in the United States.

'Those staying at the hostel on the first and top floors loved to have a game of cards. When I confiscated the kitty for a donation to charity, they replaced the cash with matches. So I watched for a while, then just pinched a card. That was the end of their games evening. There was of course a loud protest, and it took me some time until I discovered them having their "spiel" down in the boiler room. When, for the first time, we caught a card player replenishing his missing fare-money to work from the pocket of another boy, they accepted my reasoning. But cards they play still, fifty years later.

'It must have been somewhat strange for those boys, who had learned to hate the sound of German, to have a club leader who had this German accent. For them, I must have been what they call in Israel a "Yeke". For me, they were "ekes", those boys whose names were Beniek, Romek, Bolek, Mietek, Natek – and now have had their names cut short to Ben, Roman, Paul, Michael, Nat.'

Yogi Mayer's pride in the achievements of his boys is ever-present. 'When a German Jewish film producer asked me to assist him to produce a film he called *Antwort auf Auschwitz* (Answer to Auschwitz),' he later wrote, 'there was Roman, now a qualified architect; Kurt Klappholz, a Reader at the London School of Economics; Rabbi Hugo Gryn, by then a well-known radio personality; and Ben Helfgott, who represented Britain not only in the Commonwealth Games, but also at the Olympic Games: they all spoke about their past and present life. Of course, the commentary was in German, and apart from my wife and myself, as well as Kurt Klappholz, all the others insisted on speaking English with the accent of their mother tongue. The film was not only shown on German television, but also in Austria and Switzerland.[21]

'Listening to *Antwort auf Auschwitz* I became aware of how much we had achieved at the Primrose Club. The boys were free of hate and of a

---

[21] The producer of *Antwort auf Auschwitz* was a German Jew, Gunther B. Ginzel, born after 1945. His parents had survived the war in hiding in the Austrian mountains.

longing for revenge. They did not speak of a collective guilt of the German people, but expressed the hope that they, with their own lives, could demonstrate the way to a better world – for themselves and their children. Leonard Montefiore, the great humanitarian, would have listened with deep satisfaction.

'The club was a substitute for a lost family. Attending the annual reunions, I am aware how many marriages were based on the life in the club. Of course, after years of segregation in those camps, it took some time for the boys to be at ease in the presence of girls. Even in Jersey, there was a sudden demand for "men only". But increasingly, girls gained their place in the club, in the Cabinet, at various sports and games, or contributed to the club's journal *Primrose Leaves*. Girls were a vital element in the system of social groupwork.

'Intentionally, I never spoke with any of the club members about their immediate past, those years in which they were robbed of their youth. I had to leave it to Oscar Friedmann to try, as a psychologist, to relieve the pressure of the past. Some hated those sessions like the dentist's chair. Others found the sessions a great relief. For me, it was important to evaluate the place of individual members within a grouping, to create positive relationships through participation, and to achieve an increasing amount of self-programming. Probably the most valuable work I ever did was that I refused to look back and to talk about the past.'[22]

Today, at the age of eighty-four,[23] Yogi Mayer is full of affection for those who, like himself, were only in Britain because of the Nazi madness; and who had been uprooted from their very different, and very vibrant worlds and traditions. He strove to make the boys an accepted and accepting part of the society in which they found themselves. 'How they lost their temper if they were beaten,' he recalled. 'How proud they were if they got a certificate.' And he went on to reflect on aspects of their life at the club: 'They loved Leonard Montefiore, the modesty of this man who could have come in a Rolls Royce but came in a taxi, it impressed them enormously.

'The club was their home. They came after work. There was a bit of a garden behind where they played volleyball. They developed a very positive approach to life. They were very forward looking. I was very proud afterwards of what they achieved. Quite a number of marriages stem from friendships at Primrose, and as far as one can say, there are very few divorces.

'As to religion, this group of survivors are not perhaps great believers

[22] P. H. Y. Mayer, 'The Primrose Story', manuscript, 1995.

[23] Yogi Mayer was born on 8 September 1912 at Bad Kreuznach, later the headquarters of the German Army. He recalls as a schoolboy having to present flowers 'to the giant Field Marshal' – von Hindenburg.

in the commandments of the Torah and Talmud, but they are very strong in their involvement in living Judaism. Those terrible years, which were part of their youth, have not strengthened the religious belief of many, and religion for them has not been their "comfort" or their "rod" on the way into a new life. But all of them are part of a warm and close Jewish family – before and after Primrose.

'When they came here, their Judaism was sentimental. They were much more interested in Israel and Zionism. Of course there was Friday evening, but very few went to synagogue on Saturday. On marriage they rejoined the community.'[24]

Yogi Mayer is as devoted to the boys today as he was five decades ago. 'As a group,' he says, 'they are unique. The group is a substitute for the family they lost.'[25]

This was true not only for the boys who had been brought to Britain by the Central British Fund in 1945 and 1946, but for other survivors who had reached Britain by themselves, and who, hearing about the Primrose Club, turned to it in expectation. Zigi Shipper, originally from Lodz, had come to England to be reunited with his mother, who had left his father and their home in Poland before the war. Zigi was seventeen when he reached Britain. 'For the first six months,' he later wrote, 'all I did was to go to the cinema, eat, drink and sleep. My mother wanted me to go to school and study, but I had other ideas. I did learn English, and then found a job in tailoring, which I hated. I had still made no new friends, and felt quite lonely. Then one day I met someone who mentioned that there was a youth club in Belsize Park, where young survivors like myself met. One Saturday evening, I decided to go along to a dance organised by the club. As I walked in, I recognised boys whom I had been with, both in the ghetto and also in the camps. From then on, everything in my life changed. I felt as though I had found my family again. After a few months, I met Jeannette, a French girl, at the club, and started going out with her. Eventually we got married.'[26]

After a few years the Central British Fund felt it could no longer finance the Primrose Club. Its priority was helping refugees when they arrived in Britain, not maintaining them beyond a certain point. Richard Barnett pressed the Fund hard, urging it to allow the club to continue. 'It was an awful fight,' Barbara Barnett recalled. 'The CBF said, "It's a luxury; they've got to fend for themselves now". Richard said, "The club is all they've got".'[27]

[24] Yogi Mayer, in conversation with the author, 13 June 1995.
[25] Yogi Mayer, in conversation with the author, 9 March 1996.
[26] Zygmunt (Zigi) Shipper, recollections, letter to the author, 16 April 1996.
[27] Barbara Barnett, in conversation with the author, 4 August 1995.

The crisis came to a head in 1949, when the landlord at Belsize Park refused to renew the lease and the Primrose Club lost its home. But, recalled Yogi Mayer, 'the understanding vicar of St Peter's Church opposite offered us the use of their church hall, at least until we had found a new home. In the meantime, Brady had approached me with an offer to become their club leader. I felt my task had been completed. Those boys and girls were adults and should be able to stand on their own feet. They had gained maturity and – so I thought – independence, like other young people at the end of their teens. I was mistaken.'[28]

The influence of Yogi Mayer in the work of the Primrose Club cannot be exaggerated. 'He was a true leader with imagination, drive, commitment and dedication,' Ben Helfgott wrote in celebration of his mentor's eightieth birthday. 'Above all he had a great sensitivity and understanding of the needs of young people and ours in particular. It was his vision that created the conditions that encouraged local Jewish youth to become Primrose members, thus helping to hasten the process of our integration. Yogi led by example, he knew how to motivate us and bring out the best in our competitive and enthusiastic spirit. He constantly extended the scope of our activities and introduced wide-ranging activities that enriched our lives.'[29]

'He encouraged all sports, and also ballroom dancing which I loved,' Kopel Kendall recalled. 'We had the finest instructors for everything. We also had current affairs, music and drama. I fancied myself as a great actor.' In the event, Kopel Kendall became a tailor, working for a firm in Baker Street which gave him one day off a week to go to evening classes to learn cutting and design. In the evenings he went to classes at the Regent Street Polytechnic and St Martin's School of Art. In 1956, nine years after reaching the shores of Britain, he started his own business, Zenith Tailors, in Finchley Road, London. After forty years in business 'making clothes for the rich and famous', he plans to retire in 1996. He is also an active member of the Council for Christians and Jews.[30]

In place of Yogi Mayer, Solly Marcus and his wife Thelma were appointed club leaders. Local Jews formed a management committee, chaired by the local rabbi, the Reverend Harry Isaac Levy, who was also the senior Jewish chaplain of His Majesty's Forces. Rabbi Levy had entered Belsen shortly after liberation. His warm personality endeared itself to the boys, in whose company he himself felt very much at ease. 'By the time I met

---

[28] P. H. Y. Mayer, 'The Primrose Story', manuscript, 1995.

[29] Ben Helfgott, 'Yogi Mayer', *Journal of the '45 Aid Society*, No. 15, Jewish New Year 5753/1992.

[30] Kopel Kendall (Kandelcukier), recollections, letter to the author, 2 September 1995.

them,' he recalled, 'they could speak English quite well. Ben Helfgott made a great impression on me with his weightlifting.'[31]

Because the boys could no longer use the two houses in Belsize Park, the club met in the church hall in nearby Buckland Crescent. 'One of my overriding memories,' Thelma Marcus recalled, 'was how close they were, the way they supported each other. The club would meet two or three evenings a week. We had to get to know them, they were such a closely-knit group. They could be suspicious of anyone who came within their circle. Their shared experiences were totally beyond us. We had to work hard to gain their confidence. It was a learning process.'

From the church hall in Buckland Crescent the club moved into new premises at 523 Finchley Road. The building was purchased thanks to the help of Ernest Joseph, a leading architect, who was also the chairman of the Jewish Youth Fund. The Fund, which had been created after the First World War as a memorial to British Jewish soldiers killed in action, had long assisted with the formation of Jewish youth clubs and helped maintain them. The Fund was later headed by the British-born banker Oscar Joseph, a member of the Jewish Refugees Committee, and the treasurer of the Central British Fund, whose father had come from Germany at the turn of the century.

It was a time when the boys, already in their early twenties, were beginning to fall in love; and when some of the parents of those they wished to marry were reluctant to see their daughters married to concentration camp survivors. Thelma and Solly Marcus did their utmost to act as facilitators, and were present at several of the weddings that eventually took place. They also saw a change come over the boys. 'Gradually they began to speak about the past,' Thelma Marcus recalled. 'They started diffidently, not easily, and we never pushed. I remember when Ben Helfgott told us the story of how he left Theresienstadt with a sack of sugar. We were quite overwhelmed at times by their experiences.

'We had a flat upstairs. The boys would come up. They would just drop in. It was a very exciting period for them and for us, and a very humbling one for us, trying to help them to acclimatise further. They loved the idea of the club. They were already completely in command of themselves. They played a lot of football. We did Israeli folk-dancing. A whole group of our girls went and danced at County Hall. We had very good club refreshments. We had a library, snooker and table tennis. We did theatre trips. Clinton Silver led a drama group at one time. Richard Barnett gave the club a lot of his time. We had very interesting discussion groups. One year we went on a camping holiday to La Napoule in the South of France. We loved the work, we loved being with the group. It

---

[31] Harry Levy, in conversation with the author, 6 May 1996.

was demanding, but we always wanted to give more. You can never stop giving. We tried to maintain their already great cohesiveness; not to intrude, but to be there if they wanted us.

'The atmosphere in that club was so vibrant, it was so homely. Most of the boys were in lodgings by then. They didn't have homes to go to. The club filled that gap. We used to celebrate all the Jewish festivals. We had a Seder every year; they always helped with the Passover preparations, and always presented me with a small gift afterwards. Then, as the boys themselves grew older, we opened the club to English boys and girls from a younger age-group. "Our" boys and girls were getting married.'

The boys were slowly outgrowing the purposes of the Primrose Club. They were no longer teenagers, but still they wanted somewhere to congregate. When, in 1955, Solly Marcus returned to his work with the Jewish Blind Society, the club was taken over by Thelma Marcus's cousin Della Saltiel and her husband Ralph. In the flat above the club, Arnold Wesker, Della's brother, took up residence for a while. A young man of twenty-three, yet to embark upon his distinguished career as a playwright and director, he was at that time struggling to make his way as a plumber's mate, farm labourer, seed sorter and pastry-cook. 'To earn myself some pennies,' he recalled, 'I became the "drama instructor" and wrote a musical specially for the group. It was called *Life is Where You Live* (God help me). The music was composed by a young woman called Fiona Castiglione, niece of the English opera composer Rutland Broughton. I have little memory of the men and women whom I tried to pull together in a production which, needless to say, never took place. Either I wasn't inspirational enough, or they were more interested in each other, or making their way in life.'[32]

Being with the boys led Arnold Wesker, who had been born in London, to a personal reflection. 'Had my mother remained in Transylvania,' he wrote in his autobiography, 'Della and I – or a variant of us – could have been among them. Many of us feel, "There but for the grace of God ... ".'[33]

During the period when Della and Ralph Saltiel ran the club, more and more local Jewish youngsters joined it. The boys who had been teenagers when they reached Britain in 1945 and 1946 were then in their twenties, intent on pursuing their careers, and with less and less time to participate. But the importance of the club in their lives had been considerable. Reflecting on its place in the rehabilitation of the boys, Thelma Marcus commented: 'The club was a life-saver. The Central

[32] Arnold Wesker, letter to the author, 30 March 1996.
[33] Arnold Wesker, *As Much As I Dare*, Century Publishing, London, 1994, pages 471–2.

British Fund could not have done anything better for these people – giving them a base, an introduction to the new life that was to sustain them.'[34]

The impact of the Primrose Club was to be long-lasting. 'From the start, we kept together,' Ben Helfgott noted more than thirty years later. 'Twenty married within the group. And we have gone from strength to strength. Today we are not only concerned with helping each other – the few in long-term psychiatric hospitals are visited every week and we take hell out of anyone who fails to take their turn! – but we give financial and moral help wherever required.'[35]

Three of the boys, but no more, were confined to psychiatric hospitals for long periods; in 1996 there was only one, Maurice Diamond (Moishe Kadzidlo). He had been born in Radomsko in 1927. Originally a Windermere boy, for the past twenty years he has been at the Shenley Hospital near Borehamwood.

Among those boys who married, in Ben Helfgott's phrase, 'within the group', were Sala Bernholz from Wolanow, who married Henry Kaye from Konin; Sala Hochspiegel from Lodz, who married Bennie Newton from Skarzysko; Mayer Cornell from Kielce, who married Toby from Lask; and Morris Frenkel from Lodz, who married Esther from Wloclawek.

The Primrose Club not only provided the boys with a chance to meet old friends who had been dispersed. It also introduced them at the club, as Yogi Mayer had insisted from the outset – and as Thelma and Solly Marcus ensured – to young people from the wider Jewish and non-Jewish community. One of these was a London-born schoolgirl, Phyllis Fleischer. Her first contact with the boys had been through some of the girls among them. 'I met a number of the girls at school – the John Howard School for Girls, Laura Place, Clapton,' she remembered. 'Girls like Gita Weinberger and Marta Gruber, who took me along to the Primrose Club where I felt more than "at home" amongst the wonderful Eastern European youth who were determined to "live for today and tomorrow", not forgetting the past, but trying to find a way to prevent a recurrence of the atrocities of the past. Our home was always open to the friends I made at the club, as so many with whom we are still friendly in the United States remember. I even got myself married to one of the guys – Maurice Vegh.'[36]

Arthur Poznanski, who had been lonely in the hostels, later wrote that his loneliness persisted until the Primrose Club was formed, 'and I could again mix with people from my own background'. There were

---

[34] Thelma Marcus, in conversation with the author, 15 April 1996.

[35] Ben Helfgott, lecture, Oxford University Jewish Society, Hilary Term, 1985.

[36] Phyllis Vegh, 'Dear Editor', *Journal of the '45 Aid Society*, No. 6, May 1979.

problems, however, leading to a renewal of loneliness. 'The Anglo-Jewish community,' he later recalled, 'so ready to help our group or any individual in many ways, was far from happy to accept us socially or welcome us into their homes. Their daughters could socialise or dance with us but, when it came to proposals of marriage, quite a few of us were rejected by a girl's parents. As well as the heartaches of broken romances, we suffered from injured pride and a resentment that we barely dared discuss amongst ourselves.

'And although I had begun to succeed in my musical endeavours, I was too proud to face a rejection of this kind, so I avoided dating or getting involved with an Anglo-Jewish girl. I was very lonely, and as I struggled to forge a future for myself my music remained my only consolation or means of escape, lifting me out of my humdrum reality to a spiritual level where ordinary material values did not apply. For a time this bohemian way of life suited me.

'All the time, however, irrespective of my daytime and evening activities, I suffered recurring nightmares of scenes from the Holocaust in which I was chased, caught, tortured when trying to escape, shot at, and in terror of hiding in unsafe places. I also saw other members of my family in the hands of the Nazis. I was used to waking with a headache that could last all day, sometimes for much longer.

'Trying to analyse my recurring feelings of depression and unhappiness, I came to the conclusion that I was in a rut, realised the limitations of living on a very low income, and felt exploited, with little prospect of a better career. I concluded, for instance, that to become a solicitor I would have to study for several years to get a degree, then be articled for two or three years, working for no money, which would undoubtedly mean giving up my singing. I could not even consider giving up the music that meant so much to me but the question remained as to how I could earn a living. Moishe, a friend from the Primrose Club, approached me with a proposal to manage his small textile business. He offered me an immediate increase of forty per cent of my current earnings plus driving tuition and I accepted with little hesitation. Now I could afford to buy better clothes, go to clubs, meet girls, go to operas, concerts, and drive the firm's van, which made me independent of public transport late at night – in a word, I could have a social life. I would have more money for my tuition and my singing engagements in various clubs and concerts didn't seem to interfere with this new job.'

One evening in 1959, Yogi Mayer invited Arthur Poznanski to play the guitar and sing at a social evening at the Brady Street Club. 'It was there that I met Renée, who would later become my wife,' he recalled. 'I shall never forget our meeting and all it meant to me. We were married in May 1960. Unfortunately her mother died from cancer on the morning of our wedding day. On a rabbi's advice, the ceremony took place but the celebrations had to be cancelled and we had to stay separated for the week of the mourning period. But from here my life changed.

'It is difficult to build an ordinary life from the ashes of tragedy. I had lost my family at such a young age and had no opportunity for goodbyes. Love and stability meant so much to me, and my wife gave me the support and tenderness that I had missed for so long. And the birth of our daughter, and later the birth of our son, completed the joy I felt in our family life.'[37]

Several of the boys made their first steps into the world of work and family life from the portals of the Primrose Club. 'While I was there,' Gary (Salamon) Winogrodzki recalled, 'the Committee decided that I should be taught a profession. I was taken by one of the club leaders to a tailor's factory, to find out if he would teach me the profession. He agreed to take me on, but he expected me to pay him for the privilege of teaching me. When the club leader explained that I was a Holocaust survivor and living in the Primrose Club he then agreed to take me on and pay me £2 a week. I progressed quite well as a tailor's cutter, and in time he increased my wages. By the time my wages reached £3 10s I had to leave the Primrose Club and move into lodgings, and pay for everything myself.

'At the same time I was trying to live as normal a life as possible, by going to Jewish youth clubs and social events, and in 1951 I met a beautiful young girl of seventeen years whose name is Sheila. I liked her very much and we met socially. After a little while she asked me to meet her family. They made me very welcome and treated me like one of their children. They had three children already and I made the fourth child. After about a year I proposed marriage and she accepted me, and we were married in 1954. We lived in the East End of London and we had three rooms which we were renting, and things were very, very hard. After a few years we managed to buy the house in which we are still living. And in 1963 our beautiful daughter Karen was born. Karen got married in 1988 and in 1992 she presented us with a beautiful granddaughter.'[38]

The competitive spirit among the boys, which the Primrose Club fostered, and their gradual mastery of English, was evident in 1949 when an English essay competition was organised. The winner was Kitty Rosen. Then aged nineteen, and already registered for emigration to the

[37] Arthur Poznanski, recollections, letter to the author, 24 January 1995.
[38] Salamon Winogrodzki, letter to the author, 20 March 1995.

United States, she wrote of her impressions of her first full year at school. 'I was of course infected by the enthusiasm for sports prevalent throughout the school, and when Denis Compton hit a century against the Australians, or Don Bradman was out for a "duck", I was quite beside myself with excitement.'[39]

One of the runners-up was nineteen-year-old Hugo Gryn, born in Beregszasz, and subsequently deported to Auschwitz, Lieberose, Sachsenhausen and Gunskirchen. At the time of writing the essay he was a theological student based at the West London Synagogue. Like Kitty Rosen he had also registered for emigration to the United States, to continue his rabbinical training at the Hebrew Union College in Cincinnati. In his essay, commenting on 'England, the land of sports!', Hugo Gryn wrote: 'From the moment a baby catches a ball in his cot until his last round of golf or cricket (at whatever age that may be) sport becomes an essential part of his everyday life. The expression "sportsman" does not merely denote excellence on the field, but a sense of "fair play" in matters of utmost importance.'[40]

The Primrose Club served as a home not only for the 732 boys who had been brought to Britain by the Central British Fund in 1945 and 1946, but also for other survivors who came individually to join their families both then and later. They felt comfortable in the club with those with whom they had shared experiences. They drew sustenance and support from each other, finding in the club a deep well of encouragement at this crucial time of readjustment. Perhaps the most powerful testimony to that is the reflection of Zigi Shipper, originally from Lodz, who recalled how, when he entered the Primrose Club on that first evening, a dance evening, 'I felt I was at home again. I found my family and I found the boys – and after fifty years we are still together.'[41]

[39] Kitty Rosen, *CBF News*, The Bulletin of the Central British Fund for Relief and Rehabilitation, No. 14, September–October 1949.

[40] Hugo Green (Gryn), *CBF News*, The Bulletin of the Central British Fund for Relief and Rehabilitation, No. 14, September–October 1949.

[41] Zigi Shipper, filmed interview, 5 May 1996.

CHAPTER 19

Soldiers

IN MAY 1948 THE State of Israel proclaimed its independence. Within a few hours the armies of five Arab States had attacked, crossing its borders and seeking to destroy the new State altogether. From the very first days of the war, volunteers reached Israel to join the struggle. They were given the collective name Mahal.[1] In Britain the boys, who were then still in their hostels, or beginning work as apprentices, felt a particular stirring. Many had been members of Zionist families before the war. Many had hoped that they would make their way to Palestine, and not to Britain, after the war. The fighting in Israel, and the dangers facing the new State, made many of them long to participate in the struggle.

'There were about forty of our boys who served in the Israeli defence forces,' Arek Hersh, who was one of them, recalled. He himself served in the Israeli army for sixteen months.[2] Another of the volunteers, Victor Greenberg, a Millisle boy, recalled that 'the nearest thing to being killed or wounded was when I left the armoured car to relieve myself and a bullet went through my sleeve'.[3]

It was a remarkable episode, when those who had suffered so much, and were still under the impact, physical and emotional, of five and a half years of torment, set aside the relative comfort of their new lives, and their gradual rehabilitation into the world of schooling and commerce and community, to risk their lives for a distant country. But most of them had, in their childhood, been brought up with a strong sense of Jewish national identity, as part both of the Jewish Nation in Poland, and of the Jewish people, and the historic Jewish yearning for a homeland had affected them, making them willing to take the sort of risks they might reasonably have been expected to have put behind them for ever.

Among those who made the journey across Europe and the Mediterranean to Israel was Chaim Liss, from Lodz, one of the Southampton

---

[1] An acronym for the Hebrew words for 'foreign volunteers', '*Mitnaddevei Huz la-Arez*'. Most, but not all, of the volunteers were Jews. In all, there were about 5,000, of whom 1,000 came from Britain.

[2] Arek Hersh (Herszlikowicz), letter to the author, 22 February 1995.

[3] Victor Greenberg, recollections, letter to the author, 8 December 1994.

boys. He had studied electrical engineering at the ORT school in South Kensington before going on, he later wrote, 'to another trade – of all things, in the manufacture of chocolates'.[4] 'I left England in August 1948,' he recalled, 'after I had volunteered to join the Israeli army. Earlier I was furnished with a travel permit, a *titre de voyage*, with a visa through France. I crossed the Channel from Dover to Calais. I remember the customs official in Dover asking whether the clothing I was taking with me wasn't a bit light for Switzerland. It seems that although we attempted to disguise our true destination, the British knew where we were heading.

'I was not alone on the trip. Travelling with me were a few of the "boys" such as Menachem Silberstein, Sam Freiman, Jimmy (Zelig) Rosenblatt, Zvi Brand and David Turek.[5] From Calais we took the train for Paris where we reported to an office in the Boulevard Hausmann. We spent only a few hours in Paris and went on by train to Marseilles where we arrived some twelve hours later. In Marseilles we stayed in Camp St Jerome, which served as a transit camp for volunteers for the Israeli forces. For some reason we had to stay there for nearly two months, when we were flown to Haifa. During our stay we had some sort of semi-military training, which was to prepare us for the military service which lay ahead in Israel.

'We arrived in Haifa on 6 October 1948, and were sent on to Tel Litvinsky camp and inducted into the Israeli army as Mahal volunteers. Together with the "boys" I had travelled with, I joined the 72nd Infantry Battalion of the newly established 7th Brigade. Our company was composed almost entirely of volunteers from Anglo-Saxon countries, many of them veterans of British, Canadian, American, South African and Australian armies.

'After a few days in Tel Litvinsky we moved north to Camp Samaria, near the coastal town of Nahariya. This was to become our base for a while. We were issued brand new rifles which had just arrived from Czechoslovakia and began basic training. A few days later we got right into the fight by getting attached temporarily to a unit which was fighting the Arabs high up in the hills of western Galilee. Our job was to carry mortar bombs in our backpacks and bring them up to the forces fighting near Kibbutz Eylon.

'When we came back to base we realised that this was not going to be some sort of picnic. This was war. Later on we took part in the battles of Operation Hiram, the conquest of the western and Upper Galilee. We

---

[4] Chaim Liss (Lis), letter to the author, 30 December 1994.

[5] David Turek was from Warsaw, born in 1927. Before setting off for Israel he was at the Stamford Hill hostel.

fought in the battle for Meron and a number of Arab villages. Then the war in the north seemed to come to an end. After a week or ten days we came back to Camp Samaria and celebrated the end of the war in the area by getting drunk. We were then given four days' leave and went to Tel Aviv to see relatives and celebrate.'[6]

Chaim Liss remained in Israel, where he made his career in the Israel Aircraft Industries, and where he lives to this day.

Like Chaim Liss, Arieh Czeret had also studied at the ORT school in South Kensington. Having first studied in the electrical department, he transferred to the radio department to study electronics. While there he volunteered to take part in the War of Independence. When the war was over, he recalled, 'I got discharged and started working as an electronics technician in the Israeli Post Office, constructing radio stations for the international telephone communications of the country. After forty-five years I finished as a department manager. I have a family of two; a boy and girl. The boy has three children and the girl one child.'[7]

Sam Kuczer, one of the Southampton boys, was another who made his way to Israel to fight. One of the few survivors of the Hrubieszow ghetto, he was something of a legendary figure among the boys (as well as a noted optimist) in that, in the last days of the Second World War, he had saved not only his own life, but those of about thirty others, by having the presence of mind to tell the SS that they were not Jewish.[8]

Krulik Wilder was also one of the boys determined to take part in the defence of Israel. Reaching London from Glasgow, where he was earning the princely sum of £5 a week as an apprentice watchmaker, he spent several weeks at the Primrose Club, discussing with his friends what they should do. 'We left the country clandestinely,' he later wrote, 'and we made our way to Marseille. While there we received one week's training, after which we boarded a boat and sailed for Israel. On the boat there were hundreds of people from all over the world, with the same ideals as mine. The journey itself was dreadful. For four days the sea was very rough, most of us were seasick, and we could hardly leave our bunks.

'On our arrival in Haifa, I was very ill, and was kept in the infirmary for two days. After I recovered I was sent to a training camp, and received three weeks' training and was sent to the front. For nearly six months we were moved to different parts of the country but fought in the south. One particular action stands out in my mind. Approximately

---

[6] Chaim Liss (Lis), letter to the author, 29 April 1996.
[7] Arieh Czeret, letter to the author, 22 March 1995.
[8] 'Sam Cooper (Kuczer)', 'Obituary', *Journal of the '45 Aid Society*, No. 4, March 1978. Sam Cooper was forty-six when he died.

ten of our men were ambushed and it took us some time to find them. To our horror when we did find them the bodies were mutilated. I had seen dead bodies before, those shot by the Nazis, and those dying from starvation, but never before could I have imagined that the Arabs would resort to dismembering our fellow soldiers after they had killed them. It showed another gruelling aspect of the terror of war.

'When a cease-fire was arranged I decided to return to England as my travel document was expiring and I wanted to become a British subject. Looking back I am very proud to have participated in the War of Israeli Independence and to have belonged to the select group of what is known as Mahal. When I was shunted around for four weeks from Buchenwald to Theresienstadt, and was literally gasping for life, the last thought that would have been in my mind was that I would one day play my part in fighting for a Jewish State, an aspiration for which our ancestors had been striving for two thousand years.'[9]

Another of the boys who wanted to fight for Israeli independence was Solly Irving. He was eighteen years old when the State was declared in May 1948. He had previously been involved, near his hostel in Stamford Hill, in fights with groups of Mosleyite Fascists. 'I managed to obtain a travel document from the Home Office, and a visa,' he later wrote, 'and booked a holiday in Europe. I was given an address in Paris from where I obtained tickets and papers to travel to Marseille. Once there, I reported to the Hagana,[10] and was given very limited army training, using a stick in place of a gun.

'I jumped for joy when I met up with an old friend by the name of Shamai Fuks, with whom I had spent some years in different concentration camps (we were separated before the end of the war). Shamai had arrived from a Displaced Persons camp in Germany. Within a few days we left Marseille, bound for Israel.

'In the army we received very little training and my first experience was when a platoon of us were sent out on patrol. We were each given a gun with only ten bullets. The gun I carried was manufactured in Czechoslovakia, and was bigger than me. I also remember a time when we were on guard duty up a hill. Below us was a field full of watermelons. It was a hot day, and I decided to go down and bring some back. I was attacked by a group of Egyptian soldiers and had to lie in the field for some time until help arrived.

'Our brigade was the first to enter Beersheba. The name means seven wells, but we did not find any water. All we found were metal tins of

---

[9] Israel (Krulik) Wilder, 'Krulik's Story', manuscript, sent to the author, 1 January 1995.

[10] The pre-State army of the Jews of Palestine. After independence it became an integral part of the Israel Defence Forces (IDF).

halva. Most of the Arab population had vanished from the town before we entered. There wasn't much food about, nevertheless there were loads of cats, as well as a few chickens running around. After a few days in Beersheba we were sent to Bet Gubrin, near Hebron, high up on a hill. We had to keep watch on that area. We were ambushed a number of times and suffered many dead. It seems I was destined to survive, as my father had entreated me to many years earlier.

'The army camp I was in received an order that the majority of us were to be sent to Latrun to fight the Jordanian army. My friend Shamai Fuks and I looked at each other and decided that this was not for us, and we did not report for transportation. We were eventually found and arrested by the Military Police and put in prison. The sergeant in charge of the prison had been together with us in different concentration camps. Also he and his family had spent the ghetto days in my parents' house. So he released us from prison and sent us on to a different army camp. Tragically, most of the soldiers who were sent to Latrun did not survive.

'In April 1949, just before Passover, we were surrounded and attacked. Quite a few of my group were killed, but the rest of us managed to hold the strategic hill until there was another cease-fire. We were relieved by another group and sent to an army camp at Kfar Bilu for a rest. The cease-fire was holding, and things were quite relaxed. We started going into Tel Aviv and meeting up with our friends from England, as well as visiting the Saxon Club in Yarkon Street.

'Some of the boys started returning to England, because those that came from England were volunteers and belonged to Mahal. We did not come under the same jurisdiction as all the other recruits, although we were all given citizenship. My army number was 58252. In the spring of 1949 we started getting ready for the first Independence Day parade. We were taught how to march and how to smarten ourselves up. The march was to take place in Tel Aviv, but it turned into a fiasco. It was later known as the parade that never happened.

'After a month I requested a discharge from the army, as I intended returning to England. When I arrived back in England I was questioned for many hours by the immigration authorities at Newhaven. They wanted to know how I had got to Israel without a visa, and – as my travel documents showed an exit visa from Israel but did not show that I had officially arrived in Palestine – what I had been doing in Palestine for all that time. My alibis were convincing, and I was allowed to remain in England for three months. When the three months were up I got my stay extended several times, and then for an indefinite period.'[11]

[11] Solly Irving (Shloime Zalman Judensznajder), 'Memories of a Past', manuscript, sent to the author, 5 April 1995.

Sam Freiman found work in London with various fur companies; by 1948 he was earning £6 a week. 'I worked there for a while,' he recalled, 'and heard that some boys were going to Israel to join the Hagana. I joined. My employers tried to dissuade me, as I was the only one left of my family, of my whole town, and should not risk my life, as there would be no one left to bear witness. I felt that I had an obligation to fight for a Jewish State as my father had been a staunch Zionist. I felt he would have wanted me to fight and would have been proud of me.

'I joined a group of boys and we went to France. There was a training camp near Marseilles. We trained for four weeks. Then we were taken by plane to Israel. We landed in Haifa. From there we were sent to a military camp, Sarafand. We received some sort of uniform, a rifle, twenty rounds of ammunition, and two hand-grenades, for which we were responsible. At the same time we were given three days' leave in Tel Aviv, to see if we could find any relatives. Some of the boys found family. I did not. After the three days' leave we came back to camp. The following night we were sent out to the trenches near Lydda airport. This was the front line at that time. We had hardly had any training with arms. Had we been attacked that night I do not know what would have happened.

'A few days later we were taken to another camp near Nahariya and given two weeks' training with arms, and then sent to the front in the Galilee. We slept in a cemetery in Safed. We started an attack at night and by early morning we had taken Meron. Then I fell asleep near a tree. I slept so well (never have I slept so well in my life). When we woke up we started walking up a mountain. We came to the top, where we dug in and made trenches. We sat there for a few hours. Then the Syrians started to shell us and for a while it was very frightening, until the shelling stopped. I was a runner to Captain Appell.[12] He sent me down the mountain to bring up other soldiers who would be taking over our positions. I remember the soldiers were older men who had come from the German camps. They were carrying mattresses and tins of food, and while I was taking them up they were very noisy. I was scared that the Syrians would hear us and start shelling again.

'We got up to the trenches. As I was sitting in the trench, a Canadian

---

[12] Captain Tom Derek Bowden, known as Captain Appell (his *nom de guerre*). A British, non-Jewish, army officer, he had enlisted in the cavalry in 1938, and had fought against the Vichy French forces in Syria in 1941, when he was badly wounded (Moshe Dayan, his guide in that campaign, lost an eye in the fighting). Joining the Parachute Regiment, Captain Bowden was captured at Arnhem, escaped, and was captured again. As he was carrying some letters from his girlfriend in Haifa (a Palestinian Jewess, Hannah Appell) he was sent to Belsen, where he was later liberated by the British. Returning to Palestine before the establishment of the State of Israel, he fought at the Battle of Latrun, and later served as a company commander in the Galilee. After the war he founded the Israeli parachute regiment.

soldier was sitting next to me. Suddenly he collapsed. A sniper got him in the head. He was wearing a helmet but it did not help. The man was dead. Then we were taken away from the front and back to barracks for more training and soldiering. There were more attacks and cease-fires and it went on and on. I spent approximately ten months to one year in the army. Then I was discharged.

'I tried to find a job in Israel but it was impossible. I did not have anywhere to live, so I decided to return to England. Then I got a ticket to London on a Czechoslovakian plane. On the way the plane engine caught fire and I looked out of the window and saw the flames. Fortunately for me the pilot managed to land in Malta. We went out of the airport and made our way to Valletta, where we walked about for a few hours. We were told then that the plane had been repaired and we went on to Zurich, where I managed to get on a plane going to London. I landed at Northolt military airport and was arrested because my documents had run out by three days. The immigration officer would not let me into London. I contacted the Jewish Refugees Committee and they arranged for me to stay in England for three months. In the meantime the immigration authority sent me a bill for the time I spent under arrest. Apparently the Jewish Refugees Committee paid this for me and got permission for me to stay in England. I found a job in the fur trade and started earning £8 a week.'[13]

Reflecting almost half a century later on his part in the fighting, and on his father's Zionism, Sam Freiman commented: 'If he could have seen me fighting to defend the Jewish State – he would have gone to heaven.'[14]

One boy who hoped to go to fight in Israel was Ben Helfgott. He was then studying at Plaistow Grammar School. His fellow schoolboy John Harris later recalled: 'In May 1948, when the State of Israel was declared, Ben decided to leave for Israel to fight in the War of Independence. His teacher, Helen Wilks, heard about this and spent many hours trying to persuade him not to go, because this was just before his Higher Schools examination and he would have been throwing away all the work of the previous two years.'[15]

Miss Wilks asked Ben Helfgott to join her after school for a cup of tea in a nearby café. There, for two hours, she tried to talk him out of going to the war. She herself was a pacifist, and when he told her that he was determined to go, she asked that at least he serve in an ambulance unit. He returned to the hostel in Belsize Park, where the Primrose Club was

---

[13] Sam Freiman, recollections, sent to the author, June 1995.

[14] Sam Freiman, in conversation with the author, 12 May 1996.

[15] John Harris, letter to the author, 6 February 1996.

located, to have supper, and then went by bus, changing twice, to the recruiting office. By the time he reached the office, however, it was closed. The last of the volunteers was just leaving.

Ben Helfgott returned to school the following day and told his teacher about his unsuccessful efforts. She said it was 'providential', and that he should take this as 'a sign not to proceed'.[16]

Among the other boys who did reach Israel, and who participated in the War of Independence, was Eli Pfefferkorn, who had arrived in Britain with the Southampton group, and was living in the Freshwater Hostel in the Finchley Road. One of the Loughton boys, Issy Pomerantz, who had been born in Dzialoszyce, and had survived in, among other camps, Plaszow and Skarzysko-Kamienna, joined the fledgeling Israeli air force. His 'decency and reticence' were recalled after his death in 1983. 'He was a loyal friend,' wrote Ben Helfgott, 'whose charm will be sadly missed.'[17]

Hugo Gryn, from the Ruthenian town of Beregszasz, was also among the boys who went to defend Israel in its hour of need. On arrival he was trained as a night sniper, and sent to the Beersheba front. 'One day a machine-gun arrived in a wooden crate,' he recalled. 'It was from Czechoslovakia, and the instructions were in Czech. "Who knows Czech?" we were asked. I said I did, was made a corporal, and was told to assemble the gun. I called for two volunteers. They did not know a word of Czech. But they knew about machine-guns. They could put it together with their eyes closed. But then someone more important came along, and the gun was given to them.'

From Beersheba, Hugo Gryn was sent to the northern front, to Rosh Pina in the Galilee. On arrival there, he contracted jaundice and was sent to hospital – at Degania, the pre-First World War farming settlement which was the first kibbutz. One day a medical orderly said to him, 'You're not dying. You're just sick. You're taking up the bed of somebody who is seriously wounded. Go home'. 'I don't have a home', was Hugo Gryn's truthful reply. He was sent away nevertheless. His close friend Jonathan Balter, a London Jewish boy and medical student, who had often gone with him to visit the younger survivor children at Lingfield House, served with the Israeli army on the northern front and was killed by a mine. In a letter which was found on his body, he asked Hugo Gryn to collect his belongings and books, and to give them to Lingfield House. On his return to England, Hugo Gryn carried out this sad mission.[18]

---

[16] Ben Helfgott, in conversation with the author, 22 March 1996.
[17] Ben Helfgott, 'Issy Pomerantz', *Journal of the '45 Aid Society*, No. 10, April 1983.
[18] Hugo Gryn, in conversation with the author, 15 April 1996.

Among the boys who stayed on in Israel was Menachem Waksztok, from the small Polish town of Klodawa. He was to fight in all Israel's subsequent wars. He made his home in the seaside town of Ashkelon, where he became a travel agent.

Menachem Silberstein, originally from Lodz, who had gone from Windermere to the Stamford Hill hostel, and studied Talmud there, and then studied dental mechanics, likewise stayed on in Israel, where he married an Israeli girl. He named his son Shlomo after his father, who died at Skarzysko-Kamienna; and his daughter Esther after his mother, who was deported to Treblinka. He now has five grandchildren. Like Menachem Waksztok, he also fought in each of the Arab-Israeli wars, serving as a medical officer, with the rank of sergeant. A dental technician since his early training in England, he established a dental laboratory in Tel Aviv.[19]

Another of the boys who stayed in Israel once the war was over was Moshe Rosenberg, who had been born in Cracow. He was just twenty when the War of Independence began. Today he is a production manager of a leading manufacturing firm in Tel Aviv. To this day he recalls with bitterness how a Jewish kapo at Plaszow camp had demanded gold as the price for putting his name and his father's name on Schindler's list. Father and son had no gold. Later, at another camp, his father had died in his arms of typhus.[20]

David Hirszfeld, who had been born in the tiny village of Biesna, in southern Poland, and who was later incarcerated in Plaszow, Skarzysko-Kamienna, Czestochowa, Buchenwald and Nordhausen, also decided to make his way to Israel during the War of Independence. 'It might be difficult to understand,' he later wrote, 'why people like us who were just barely saved from extermination would volunteer to go to a country they had never seen before, that was in a state of war, and would risk their lives again. But, for many of us, there was a sense that it was essential for the Jewish people to have a place of their own, where they could protect themselves and have their own armed forces.

'I volunteered, without telling my brother Moniek about my plan. It was an illegal activity, and in addition, I didn't want to influence him to take a similar risk. I was sent with other volunteers to France, and from there on the ship *Kedma* to Israel. When I arrived, I joined the forces, and due to my training in metalwork, I was assigned to work in a mechanics shop for armoured vehicles. Our job was to fix the vehicles that participated in the fierce fight.'

One of those who had helped the boys in the Loughton hostel, Malka

---

[19] Menachem (Mendel) Silberstein, letter to the author, 29 April 1996.
[20] Newspaper interview, *The Sun*, London, 18 February 1994.

Tattenbaum, had given David Hirszfeld the address of her relatives for him to contact in Israel. He did so, and there met Pnina, whom he married in 1951. They made their home in Israel, where David worked until his retirement for the Egged Bus Co-operative. In 1976 he was nominated as the Israeli Worker of the Year. His wife Pnina died of cancer at the age of fifty. He dedicated his recollections to her, 'who died before she had the opportunity to enjoy any of her grandchildren', and to 'all my family members who did not survive the atrocities embedded in the history of our people'.[21]

In 1976 an Israeli newspaper reported that, after David Hirszfeld's daily work at the bus co-operative was done, he devoted his time 'to designing and constructing mechanical inventions. One is an engine-removing device, a kind of lifting machine which enables one person to remove a bus engine, hold it well above the ground while it is being repaired, and then place it back into the bus'.[22] David's older brother Moniek, to whom he had said nothing in 1948 of his decision to fight in the War of Independence, had remained in England, where he worked as a hotel chef, and then as a telephone technician in Stratford-on-Avon, before retiring to Brighton.

The attraction of Israel was great for many of the boys. They had come to Britain because the way to Palestine was closed, and the way to Britain unexpectedly open. While in the hostels, many of them still hoped to make the journey to Palestine, and many, while in Britain, learned Hebrew for this very purpose. After the establishment of the State of Israel in 1948, all the previously strict immigration controls imposed by the British were swept away, and a new law – the Law of Return – established the right of any Jew to enter the new State. Several boys were among the earliest people to avail themselves of this open door. Zvi Brand was from the small southern Polish village of Ulucz. Of his seven brothers and sisters, only two survived the war. He himself had been a slave labourer at Plaszow, Skarzysko-Kamienna, Czestochowa and Colditz. He had also been at Buchenwald and Theresienstadt.

After Windermere and the hostels, Zvi Brand later wrote, 'I enrolled in the London ORT school in South Kensington and took a course in electrical engineering which I completed. Later I continued my studies at the Hackney Technical School. In the middle of my studies I felt that it was my obligation and duty to go to Israel and make my life there. I have been living in Israel ever since. Until my recent retirement I

---

[21] David Hirschfeld (Hirszfeld), 'The David Hirshfeld Story', manuscript, sent to the author, 9 February 1996.

[22] *Ma'ariv*, Tel Aviv, 28 December 1976.

have been employed as an electrical technician and subsequently as a department manager in the Tel-Aviv Municipality.'[23]

Of the forty boys who went to Israel and fought in the War of Independence, about half stayed on and made their lives in Israel. Three years after liberation almost to the day, a challenge had presented itself whereby they could take their place in the defence of a national ideal; an ideal which had first attracted many of them a decade earlier as youngsters in Poland and Czechoslovakia. Each of those who stayed on in Israel, as well as those who subsequently joined them there, made their contributions to the young State.

[23] Zvi Brand, letter to the author, 26 October 1994.

CHAPTER 20

New Paths

LEAVING THE HOSTELS, the boys slowly made their way in the world. At first life was difficult, particularly in Britain, which had not yet fully recovered from the war; these were the years of austerity. Lipa Tepper, aged twenty, recalled going into lodgings in north-west London 'with a little old Austrian lady', a pre-war refugee from Nazism. The Jewish Refugees Committee still helped them with rent and offered other financial support, but that was soon to change. 'Very few of us went to school or college or anything like that,' he wrote. 'We went to work. We were put into jobs which for one reason or another were picked by the Committee. I was taken to a place in Paddington which was a handbag factory. In actual fact it was not making handbags at the time, it was making writing-cases, and one other of our boys was working there when I started work. I got on reasonably well with my employer, his wife and his daughter and all the people who worked there. But after a time my employer called me into his office and informed me that my hands were too heavy to do the work which we had to do in that factory, and that I was not suitable for the work.

'As I went home, I remembered that during the war I had worked for a short time in a bakery. I was staying in lodgings with one other of the boys – and discussed it with him. We decided to approach a baker whom we both knew and he gave me a job in a bakery. I used to go to work every morning by bike and come home every night the same way. In the evening I would go to one of the hostels to see some of the boys there, and talk and socialise.'

Tepper continued to work as a baker for some while. Two incidents remained lodged in his memory from that time. 'One day we were standing at the table working and the manager, Mr Reynolds, was standing next to me – he was working as well – and he suddenly said to me, "Do you know what a front-wheel skid is?" I looked at him, my English was very poor at the time, and I said, "No". "Oh," he said, "It doesn't matter."

'Then, another day, the foreman said to me, "Why should there be a separate Jewish bakers' union when we already have a bakers' union?" and I just said casually that they probably wouldn't feel very welcome in the general union so they formed a union of their own. We never discussed anything of that nature ever again, but years later, when I learned slang properly, I found that the rhyming cockney slang for "Yid" is "front-wheel skid". That was my first encounter with anti-Semitism in England.'

While working as a baker, Tepper, in common with all the boys, maintained close contact with the Jewish Refugees Committee. 'When we first came to London they supported us completely, and paid our lodgings and everything,' he recalled. 'When we started working they reduced it as we earned more money up to the point when they considered that we were self-sufficient and then they stopped supporting us. But we were still in touch with the Committee, and we used to go up periodically to Bloomsbury House and request permission to go to Burtons to have our suits made.

'I started developing as an independent and ordinary human being, although at night I used to suffer terribly from nightmares. They used to plague me terribly. It seemed that the happier I became during the day the more I suffered at night.'[1]

Sam Dresner, one of many boys who had been in the slave labour camp at Skarzysko-Kamienna, spent his first four years in England recovering from TB in various hospitals, and at Quare Mead. 'After leaving the convalescent home,' he later wrote, 'and trying different jobs, I decided to be a painter. I studied in various art schools while working in the evening as a stage-hand. I have had some exhibitions, but my main motivation for painting, which was to paint the images that haunt me, has escaped me so far, but not for lack of trying. It just seems impossible to convey those feelings. Or maybe I have not got enough talent. It is a struggle, but it gives me a justification for being alive.'[2]

Settling down was a struggle for every boy. Mick (Abraham) Zwirek recalled how, after life in the hostel, 'I became unsettled, as I could not adapt myself to a job that I cared for, until I became apprenticed to the fur trade, which I enjoyed. I became a furrier with a survivor friend, Jack Bajer (who had been in the Lodz ghetto) and we had our own business for thirty-two years until we retired.'[3]

Chaim Olmer moved into lodgings from his Glasgow hostel in July 1947, began work in a dental laboratory for £1 a week, and received a further £4 a week from the Central British Fund. 'I bought a second-

[1] Lipa Tepper, letter to the author, 30 January 1996.
[2] Sam Dresner, letter to the author, 28 January 1995.
[3] Abraham Zwirek, letter to the author, 30 September 1994.

hand bicycle for ten shillings, which I used for transport until I left Glasgow in 1953, when I sold it for ten shillings,' Chaim Olmer recalled. He was one of the few boys who went on to university. The first year, 1948, 'was a difficult one', he wrote. 'I had to adjust to laboratory work and the language was also something of a problem, especially the spelling! I also tried to earn a little extra money in the dental laboratory during the weekends and holidays. By the second year I had no more difficulties and got distinctions in physiology and pathology. The third, fourth and fifth years continued to a satisfactory conclusion.

'I left Glasgow on 4 July 1953 to go to my first job, in Reading, as a dental surgeon. By September the same year I had saved enough money for a trip to Israel to meet my sister for the first time since 1942. My brother was by then living in the USA but we did not meet again until 1962.'[4] This was Chaim Olmer's older brother Joseph. Unusually, two of his five brothers and sisters had survived.

From the hostels, most boys went to one or other of the big cities, to earn their living. Perec Zylberberg left Overbury Court hostel for London. 'At that time I could not bring out more than a few very basic words in English,' he recalled. 'But armed with determination, I considered it a great challenge. Through the efforts of the Committee, I was able to rent a room in Tottenham, a low-income neighbourhood. The people spoke English – only with a few odd Yiddish words. It was not very enticing, but for my needs then, it was sufficient. I got an apprentice-type job with the man who had helped install the workshop in Overbury Court. I was put in the electrical maintenance section to learn the craft of electrician. For me it was interesting and a challenge. I already wanted to be in the electrical field in my last year at school. It was all new and fairly exciting. I got to know a number of pleasant people there. The Committee helped with the rent and board. I did not earn much money, just enough to pay for transportation and for some cigarettes. But it was a start.'[5]

The boys frequently had to face up to the problems posed by outside attitudes to their experiences. There was such a wide gap between what they had experienced, and what was understood of their experiences by those who met them after the war, even by those who tried to be understanding. Not only disbelief, but even hostility, could confront them during their early years in Britain. This hostility was difficult to respond to. Moniek Goldberg, who went from Windermere to Loughton, and

---

[4] Chaim Olmer, letter to the author, 30 September 1995.
[5] Perec Zylberberg, recollections, diary entry for 20 October 1993.

then to Belsize Park, recalled how people would broach the subject of the Holocaust. 'Invariably they would say, "If it is too painful to talk about ...", or, "I imagine you would rather forget about the past ..." Many questions have been asked of me, such as the one which my former British employer, Mr Levy, posed in 1946: "Was it all true? Or was it just war propaganda to make us hate the Germans more?"

'How was that for empathy? Another question often asked was, "How could you, a mere youngster, have survived, if it was so tough?" Or, "Why didn't you do something? Why did you let yourselves be slaughtered like sheep?" I answered Mr Levy, "It was propaganda". As a rule I have avoided such discussions.

'At first I felt hurt, but as I grew older I came to realise that I could not expect people to understand; or to comprehend the incomprehensible; to believe the unbelievable. The tragedy that befell our people was so great, so complete, that one cannot imagine it. Six million people – the mind boggles – and so it becomes a statistic, along with other statistics; a symbol rather than a reality.

'To me and to others like me, the tragedy is not a statistic. It is not a six and six zeros, that is so often used at fund-raisings and communal *yizkors*.[6] I can see the faces of my mother and father; of my sisters – not a six and six zeros. I can see the faces of my aunts and uncles, and close to fifty cousins whom I knew, and many others whom I never had a chance to know. I can see the faces of neighbours and playmates who are no more. If I want to indulge in statistics, I think of all the children with whom, at the age of seven, I started primary school. Then I take from that number my gentile schoolmates who are still alive, and estimate the number of children and grandchildren they have. Then I think of my Jewish schoolmates of that year, and I know that beside myself only Andzia is still alive today. She was lucky because her parents left Poland before 1939. I do not know how many children or grandchildren she had. I have four children. So much for statistics.

'Our tragedy is so great, the places of death are so numerous, that it is no wonder that people have a hard time remembering any except the few most infamous ones: Buchenwald, Auschwitz, Majdanek, and Treblinka. Whoever heard of Kruszyn? It is never mentioned, yet I lost six cousins and many more friends and *landsleit*[7] there. Nor does it ever come up that in Kruszyn a group of Jews threw themselves at their guards near the pits, and with their bare hands grabbed a few of their murderers to die with them.'[8]

[6] Holocaust memorial meetings. Yizkor is the prayer for the dead.

[7] People from the same town.

[8] Joseph (Moniek) Goldberg, 'We and the Holocaust – Today', *Journal of the '45 Aid Society*, No. 6, May 1979.

The trades which the boys had been taught, and the adjustments to British society they had mastered, enabled them to survive, not always without struggle, in the world of commerce. A few felt the need to try to obtain a higher education, even if it meant putting back the time when they could go out and earn their living. A British schoolboy at Plaistow Grammar School in East London, John Harris, recalled the day in September 1946 when his headmaster, Dr Harold Priestley, summoned him and a friend to his study and explained 'that four boys, refugees from the concentration camps, would arrive later that day. He had decided to place them in our class (there were two other lower-fifth forms) because we were the only Jewish boys and he asked that we should make them feel welcome and look after them in any way we could. The four who arrived were Beniek (Ben) Helfgott, Natek Wald, Paul Gastfreund and Moniek Reichkind (now Michael Preston). Paul, whose Polish name was Bolek, had to make a quick name-change because it caused great hilarity. He now lives in Florida.

'Moniek and Paul stayed only a few months and then left, to do accountancy. Ben and Nat were to stay for two years during which time they completed the equivalent of four years' studies, passing their School Certificate and Higher Schools examinations in the process. Nat was quiet and studious, even introverted. His English, considering the short time that he had lived here, was excellent, but he was always somewhat withdrawn. We thought this was due to his experiences in the camps and didn't question him about it. He took no part in sports or PT, we thought for the same reason. Ben, on the other hand, was extrovert, spoke fractured English, and became extremely popular, being known to everyone as Bennie; he only became Ben in later life.

'My most vivid memory is of Ben's first day in the gymnasium. His first action was not only to stand on his hands but to walk with his legs in the air across the floor of the gymnasium. None of the rest of us could do anything like that. It was the sort of action that endeared him to the fourteen-year-old boys that we were.

'One teacher who took a particular interest in the two boys was the English mistress, Helen Wilks. She not only appreciated that Nat and Ben needed special tuition to bring their English up to the standard needed both to pass examinations and live a successful life in England, but she also took a personal interest in their lives. I can remember a number of theatre trips which I also attended: *Romeo and Juliet* (with a young Paul Schofield as Mercutio), *Saint Joan* with Alec Guinness as the Dauphin and a number of other outings, all of which she funded from her own resources. She had a nice garden at her home in Wanstead and some of us would go during the summer for play-readings in her garden. She was a most dedicated teacher, and I believe Ben in particular owes her a great deal.

'Our form master was a Mr Ironmonger, known to all of us as Ted, an affable, easygoing man, but this was typical of most of the teachers at Plaistow Grammar School. Ben, I know, particularly remembers a Mr Prothero, who doubled in art and economics. He coached Ben in economics in just six months to a standard whereby he was able to obtain a credit in School Certificate.

'The strange thing about the time Nat and Ben were at school with us was that I cannot recall anyone, including me, asking them about their wartime experiences. When I meet Ben now we do talk about it but then we concentrated on the sort of things that young people talk about. The contrast between their experiences between 1940 and 1945 and during their time at Plaistow Grammar School from 1946 to 1948 must have been as extreme as you can get. The choice of school may have been lucky or inspired, but I'm sure that it was the best adjustment to normal life that they could have received.

'Nat Wald emigrated to the United States and I gather was very successful in the financial world. Unfortunately he died at the age of forty-one, of a brain haemorrhage.'[9]

Some boys felt that they had been deprived of the opportunity to make up for lost education. 'The Committee did not encourage anybody to take up studies,' Perec Zylberberg recalled. 'They forever complained of lack of funds. Before too long the hostel shut down. So did other hostels all around the country. With very few exceptions everybody was directed to some sort of occupation. Only a few got to some school or another. I do not know even now what merited that kind of support.'[10]

A few boys were fortunate. Wilem Frischmann, from the Ruthenian border town of Uzhgorod, who had begun life in Britain at the hostel at Millisle in Northern Ireland, later studied under 'Ginger' Friedmann at Bunce Court School. He became a structural engineer, obtained his doctorate at City University, and was involved in the construction of several of London's most impressive structures, among them Centre Point and the National Westminster Tower. In 1990 Wilem Frischmann was awarded the CBE, one of only two boys to be so honoured. His award was 'for services to engineering and industry'. The other boy who is a Commander of the Order of the British Empire – 'for services to inter-faith relations' – is Hugo Gryn, from Beregszasz, less than forty miles from Wilem Frischmann's home town.

---

[9] John Harris, letter to the author, 6 February 1996.
[10] Perec Zylberberg, recollections, diary entry for 21 October 1993.

It was while he was at the Freshwater Hostel in the Finchley Road that Witold Gutt prepared for and obtained his London University matriculation. He then studied chemistry at Birkbeck College, after which he spent thirty years in the Scientific Civil Service. The only one of the boys to become a senior civil servant, he reached the grade of Senior Principal Scientific Officer, as head of the Materials Division. His special interest was the safe utilisation of industrial by-products in building materials, thereby reducing water pollution and land dereliction in industrial areas. Later he became consultant to the World Bank in relation to the manufacture of cement in developing countries. Some eighty research papers were published from his work. Looking back fifty years after the war, he was particularly proud of his family's past achievements in Poland, where he could trace his mother's ancestry back to 1757. During the inter-war years, his mother's brother, Dr Stanislaw Peiper, was a judge in Sambor. His cousin Tadeusz Peiper was a famous Polish poet. And his grandfather, Dr Leon Peiper, wrote the standard Polish pre-war reference works interpreting legislation. 'His books are still in use in Poland', writes Witold Gutt with pride.'[11]

Despite the notable contribution his family had made to Poland before the war, Witold Gutt has never returned. 'I have not been able to face returning to Przemysl,' he wrote, 'and it is improbable that I shall ever see it again.'[12]

In addition to Witold Gutt, two other boys, Jerzy Herszberg and Meir Sosnowicz, decided to pursue academic careers to the level of a doctorate. Before proceeding to his doctorate, Jerszy Herszberg obtained a first-class degree in mathematics at King's College, London, and was awarded the prize for having obtained the highest mark in that examination. Meir Sosnowicz started his academic life while still a patient at Quare Mead, during the slow process of recovering from TB. 'Since I was not well enough to leave Quare Mead to attend school,' he later wrote, 'I took a correspondence course to prepare me for my London University matriculation examination. I passed this in January 1948. After passing the matriculation, the Jewish Refugees Committee gave me permission (and the funds) to continue with my studies, and the doctor allowed me to leave Quare Mead. These studies had to be in a regular school, and so it was necessary for me to transfer to an institution that would accept me. I spent the summer of 1948 in Cambridge to get some practical experience in chemistry, which was also not possible through a cor-

---

[11] Witold Gutt, 'Biographical Notes of Dr Witold Henryk Gutt', manuscript, sent to the author, 17 September 1994.

[12] Witold Gutt, letter to the author, 7 December 1994.

respondence course. This was in preparation for my intermediate studies starting in September 1948.

'To attend courses in Cambridge as a non-regular student, which I was, it had to be by special arrangement. My situation was brought to the attention of the Cambridge Jewish Student Association by Leonard Montefiore, and it was they who made these arrangements for me. At Quare Mead we became acquainted with a number of the people in the Cambridge Jewish Student Association because from time to time they visited us, to perk up our spirits. To appreciate the efforts of their visits one must realise that the distance between Cambridge and Ugley was about thirty miles. The students came to us on bicycles, the main means of transport for students in those days. It must have taken them several hours each way. The names of certain students stand out for me, since it was they who helped me the most that summer in Cambridge. In particular I remember Hannah and Oliver French (medical students) and Ernest Rabinowicz, a physicist who became a well-known professor at MIT.[13]

'The Jewish Refugees Committee was particularly generous to me in relation to my studies. Only very few of us "Boys" undertook a university study leading to a profession. For the boys it was a hard thing to do, the studies were difficult, and it took a clear mind to prepare for and pass the exams. Most of us were still too full of our recent experiences, and for the Committee it was a financial burden and a responsibility which they were reluctant to undertake. In my case they carried the burden for seven years, that is from August 1945 to August 1952. This included the five years of study, and I am forever indebted to the Committee for their kindness in supporting me for so long a period.

'Today I still have recollections of my first exam in London for the matriculation. To boost my courage, the teacher from Quare Mead accompanied me to London. We stayed the week at the Primrose Club, the social meeting-place for the boys. The club was supervised by Paul (Yogi) Mayer and was an important institution because it gave the boys somewhere to go, something to do and a place to meet friends. Our stay there was by special arrangement, so that I could present myself at Imperial College in good time every morning for my exams. Sleep more or less escaped me that night, and in the morning I had to take public transportation by myself to get to the college. Once I arrived at my destination, I had the usual butterflies in my stomach. The hardest subject for me was English, one of the two compulsory subjects (the other was maths). We had to write a half-hour essay in a language with

[13] The Massachusetts Institute of Technology, Cambridge, Massachusetts.

which I was still not very familiar. The other subjects were not all that hard for me, and I did pass the whole exam.

'When the four-day matriculation exams were finally over, Sister Maria treated the teacher, and herself, and me, to a celebration. We went to a concert at the Royal Albert Hall, the Brahms Violin Concerto, which has been a favourite of mine ever since.'

In September 1948 Meir Sosnowicz moved to Chelmsford, Essex, to attend Mid-Essex Technical School. 'This was the first time that I left the group, a scary feeling,' he recalled. 'It was also where I opened my first bank account, a proud feeling, since I now had to manage other people's money – responsibly. Of course, money was tight, and so I had to be very careful with the funds allocated to me. I received a second-hand bicycle for transportation. In Chelmsford I lived as a lodger.' In 1949 Meir Sosnowicz was awarded his Intermediate degree, and in 1951 he passed the B.Sc. General degree in maths and physics. 'This degree alone would have qualified me for a job in the outside world,' he wrote. 'However, I felt that one more year of study for a B.Sc. Special degree in physics would give me necessary qualification to aim higher in the future. Once again the Jewish Refugees Committee permitted me to continue. In June 1952 I graduated with the desired B.Sc. Special. Then, with the best wishes of the Committee, and their congratulations, I launched out on a search for my first job.'

That first job was in an electronics company in the East End of London, at a weekly salary of £7. 'This was a very proud time for me,' Meir Sosnowicz recalled, 'especially when, after a probation of three months, my salary was increased to £10 a week. I was now independent.'[14]

As well as the three boys who pursued their academic careers to doctorate level, there was a fourth, Kurt Klappholz, who obtained a first-class degree at the London School of Economics. For more than forty years he taught and researched there, lecturing as a Reader in Economics until his retirement. 'I must say that my time at the LSE was perhaps my most exciting period,' Kurt Klappholz recalled of his student days. 'After all, we did not have any education of any kind in the camps, and before the war I was much too young to have had any proper education. I never went to high school since I was too young, and when the war broke out all education for Jews stopped as soon as the Germans marched in. I found my period of study at the LSE intellectually most stimulating. At LSE I associated with people who were interested in intellectual matters and this was extremely exciting for me.'[15]

---

[14] Michael Novice (Meir Sosnowicz), recollections, manuscript, June 1995.
[15] Kurt Klappholz, 'Testimony', transcribed tape, 1995.

The Jewish Refugees Committee took one step that was specifically intended to help the boys face the many problems of life away from the hostels. This was the establishment of a small group of counsellors, under the guidance of Oscar Friedmann, whose task was to talk to the boys, their landladies (and landlords) and employers, and to try to narrow the gap in perceptions between the two groups. One of these counsellors was Helen Bamber, who throughout 1946 and 1947 had worked with survivors in Belsen. She felt an immediate bond of sympathy and understanding with the boys, as they began to work for employers who were not always willing – or able – to recognise what their new employees had been through. She also helped the boys take their first steps towards living alone. 'My job was to be responsible for their boarding,' she recalled. 'We paid a number of Jewish landladies and landlords to take them in. A number were either at school, or learning a craft of some kind. They had just begun to find employment. Not all the landladies and landlords had any deep understanding of trauma and its effects, and they found in their midst young people with whom they couldn't really communicate.

'It was a bleak period for them. They had come out of the hostels. They lost their group identity. They had to take another step forward. They did it by functioning – by taking work – but they were very unhappy. At work, they felt terribly exploited, because they had been a commodity before – a dispensable commodity. They weren't treated well, just like every other employee at the time. It was just after the war and conditions in the workplace were hard. Employers had choices, they didn't have to take on those children. I spent my days and nights feeling very angry indeed.

'On one occasion, with a boy who wanted to go to school, I went before a panel of headmasters who met in London to look at special cases. I put the boy's case. I spoke quite eloquently, about his past, about the deprivations, about his total lack of schooling between the age of ten and fifteen. The chairman then said, "Are you telling me that they didn't give them books to read in the camps?" Fortunately, the boy got his place.'

Helen Bamber understood the problems confronting the boys as they embarked on their new paths. 'This was the first time since arriving in Britain that they had dispersed. It was quite a difficult period for them and for us. There were some stormy periods. There was a lack of understanding, not only by the individual landlords and landladies, but by society as a whole – a lack of understanding as to what really had happened to these young people. One did one's best, but it was a struggle. I had the same trouble with the employers. I think that, for the boys, the betrayal by people from whom one had expected better was worse than ill-treatment by the enemy. They were not exploited as they had been before, but it was exploitation nevertheless, and for them it was a repetition. It recalled the memories of the past. It smacked of past deprivations and cruelty. When there were ordinary disagreements, when things didn't work out well with the employer, for our young people it was magnified beyond imagination. They had reason to be angry. It is what we call "triggering memories". Someone shouting, a child crying – it may be irritating to us – for them it recalled the most appalling memories, of children being killed, of the shouting of the enemy.

'I pleaded, and spent hours with landlords and employers, explaining what the young people had really suffered. Many Jews were suffering a sense of guilt at that time. The rather aggressive appearance of the boys, their assertive, strong countenance – they stood there like some kind of accusation – employers couldn't take that.

'Oscar Friedmann was in charge of our work. He was quite remote in some ways. He didn't exude warmth. But he did have enormous experience in containing the impossible. I found it very difficult sometimes to bear the stories I heard. He trained me over the years. He taught me a great deal about the psychology of violence, and the effects that people have to live with afterwards. Many of the boys respected him, but they did not love him. They never felt we did enough. We could never make up what they had lost. All we could produce for them was very mediocre from their point of view. The young people did not feel that we could give them what they needed – and how could we?

'Oscar Friedmann fought for them; he fought for their future in a very profound way. He was an ethical man who really fought internally (about funding, for example – we had considerable lack of resources) and externally. He would fight very hard for them, but they never realised it.

'They didn't – couldn't – talk about their childhood. Their experience was so overwhelming. Hugo Gryn said to me many years later that when you face annihilation every morning – you get lined up either to live another day or to be killed that day – something quite terrible happens to the human psyche. All their energies, everything they have available to them, is aimed at surviving another day. Morality disappeared. It stripped them for a long time of any feelings of guilt about how they survived.

'I remained with Oscar Friedmann until the end. The end was very disturbing; the unit was closed in 1947 or 1948. We both felt that some provision should have been made for continual attention and follow-up for this extraordinary group of young people. I feel very sad about that. I don't think that we offered them sufficient support – it never could be sufficient – I feel guilty about that, that we could not help them achieve something better for themselves in their lives. They survive, yes, and they function – by normality, we mean the capacity to function – but I feel we could have done more for them.'[16]

The boys could sometimes find themselves caught up in a bureaucratic tangle. One of them, Arthur Poznanski, was caught in a particularly unfortunate trap. He had gone first to a hostel in Manchester but had been unhappy there and, after what he later described as 'a few clashes with the management', was transferred to the Jews' Temporary Shelter in east London. From there he had gone to the hostel in Nightingale Road. 'What I felt I needed most, and never really got at this stage,' he later wrote, 'was an assessment of my abilities and advice or guidance as to my future. So I pondered what I should do and what work would make me happy. I had always loved music, had grown up surrounded by music. My mother taught the violin and played and sang to us as children. She had a lovely mezzo voice, soft and warm, and just the thought of it took me back to the peaceful days of my childhood. My aunt Regina was a solo soprano with the Silesiana Opera Company and often performed for us. In the ghettos of Wielun and Piotrkow I became quite proficient on the harmonica. In the camp of Bugaj I composed the lyrics of the camp song. And I showed an ability to sing. It allowed me to transcend the loneliness, cold, and indecision, took me to a more spiritual plane, kept me linked to my family, and let me give of myself in the only way I knew how.

'I decided to study singing in the hope of making it a career. I studied first under Professor Ivor Warren at Trinity College of Music and later, when he died, with Mrs R. Bell of the same college. I progressed well, but found the actual learning of voice production and technique a very slow process. It became obvious, however, that I would have to get a job to keep myself. My first full-time employment was manufacturing spectacle frames where the other workers were not at all friendly. At least I could continue to study singing and to practise in the evenings. The hostel was closing down and I had to find lodgings – and I was looking for a place that included the use of a piano. From then on I was on my own and my loneliness increased.

'My wages in those days were very low, but I struggled from one job to another, seeing little improvement in material circumstances. I fought a mounting depression with the help of my music and singing and then suddenly a better future seemed in sight because I received an offer to sing with a travelling troupe calling themselves the Viennese Opera

[16] Helen Bamber, in conversation with the author, 29 March 1996.

Singers. They offered me the solo part – the role of the Italian tenor – in their production of *Die Fledermaus*. I learned the part, confidently attended the evening rehearsals and was thrilled when they offered me a contract. But it was subject to a permit from the Ministry of Labour and my dreams began to crumble as the Ministry refused the permit because I was an alien and not a member of either the Musicians' Union or Equity. I applied for membership but I was rejected by both unions because I did not have a valid permit from the Ministry. I tried to explain the position at the Ministry but it seemed a "Catch 22" situation. I did not know how to obtain legal advice or whom to ask for help. The group could not wait for me indefinitely and cancelled the contract. And, in despair, I turned yet again to the optical industry for another job.

'But I refused to give up my dream of a musical career. I didn't have the money for extra tuition so I joined amateur operatic societies to widen my knowledge of singing, especially opera, and sang principal parts such as Turiddu in *Cavalleria Rusticana*, Canio in *I Pagliacci*, and Cavaradossi in *Tosca* in public performances. I took part in many concerts that gave me the stage experience I so needed and much spiritual satisfaction. It helped me to tolerate my daytime jobs; but unfortunately it offered no financial rewards.

'Matters came to a head when my singing got me sacked from a job. In retrospect, I suppose, it was quite funny. While drilling little holes in the sides of the spectacle frames, I was submerged in the monotony of the hum of the machinery, that, to me, sounded like the background music to an aria. So, accompanying the oompah-pah of the machinery, I started to sing "La donna è mobile". Suddenly I felt a tap on my shoulder. Without stopping my work I asked: "Yes?" It was the manager, who asked me to follow him to his office and fired me as we got there. When I asked why, he told me it was because of my singing. Thinking it was a joke I said, "But I did not stop working." "No", he said, "but everyone else did." Apparently the entire workforce had stood there agape, listening to my song. I was too proud and angry to ask for another chance, so I just collected my papers and pay to date and left, vowing never to return to such a working atmosphere. But now I was unemployed and had very little savings. And, if nothing else, my rent had to be paid. Once again I was in need of a job.'

At this point, Arthur Poznanski was helped by Richard Barnett, who found a job for the unhappy twenty-year-old in a solicitor's office. Then Poznanski was asked by the Polish community in London to sing at some of their social and theatre functions, 'my first paid engagements'.[17] Today, it is Arthur Poznanski whom the boys ask, at each of their

---

[17] Arthur Poznanski, recollections, letter to the author, 20 January 1995.

annual reunions, to sing Grace After Meals. At their fiftieth anniversary dinner, in the summer of 1995, as he began to sing the first melody in his beautiful voice, one of the boys exclaimed, 'Pavarotti, eat your heart out!'[18]

While they were in the hostels, and particularly at Loughton, so close to London, 'quite a number of the boys', recalled Ben Helfgott, 'had an opportunity to go to school. But the majority could not cope. They just fell out. It was at the ORT school for rehabilitation and training in South Kensington that they found their niche.[19] At the ORT school it was a question of learning the basics of education, and then learning a trade. At this they excelled. The ORT school really was their salvation.'[20]

Many of the boys who had suffered so much, academically, as a result of the irrecoverable loss of six years' education, went to the ORT school. There, they were able to build on their natural technical skills, and to learn a trade. Izzie Light, from Lodz, remembered studying maths, algebra and trigonometry in the mornings, and mechanical drafting and welding in the afternoons, under the encouraging eye of the head of the school, Mr Levinek. 'We were very fortunate to be able to go to that school,' he reflected; later he was to emigrate to Canada.[21]

From their arrival in Britain, the goal of many of the boys was Palestine – which in May 1948 became the State of Israel. Bibi Gross, who had flown to England with the Southampton group, finally moved to Israel in 1960, fifteen years after reaching Britain. 'My pre-school education was at Auschwitz and Mauthausen,' he later wrote.

In Britain, aged eleven, Bibi Gross went to school in Oxford, at the St Philip and St James's Primary School (known as St Pip and St Jim). In 1959 he qualified as an agricultural engineer, and left for Israel the following year. On arrival, he joined the Israeli government's soil conservation department, 'then worked as an irrigation engineer in the Upper Galilee, where my work included flood control and small dam construction; I also spent a year as construction engineer in the civilian airfield at Saint Catherine's Monastery at the foot of Mount Sinai. The last six years have been the most satisfying for me as I have been involved in the restoration of the destroyed Jewish Quarter of the Old

---

[18] This was Krulik Wilder, humorist extraordinary.

[19] ORT was founded in St Petersburg in 1889 to provide technical training for Jewish teenagers in Tsarist Russia. Its initials are an acronym for the Russian words 'Society to Promote Trades and Agriculture'. After the Bolshevik Revolution its headquarters moved to Berlin, in 1933 to Paris, and after the fall of France in 1940 to London, where International ORT (which is now particularly active in Russia) has its centre today.

[20] Ben Helfgott, in conversation with the author, 12 May 1996.

[21] Izzie Light (Licht), in conversation with the author, 11 May 1996.

City of Jerusalem, where I have reconstructed one of the old houses to make a home for my family.'[22]

Abraham Goldstein, who, like so many of the boys, had gone to London after being in hostels at Ascot and Bedford, recalled being summoned to Bloomsbury House by Oscar Friedmann and asked, 'How long shall we have to feed you?'[23] He was eighteen years old. Eventually he learned welding at the ORT school. He then emigrated to Israel.

Another of those at the ORT school was Zvi Dagan, from Piotrkow. He later became a leading manufacturer in Israel. Also at ORT was David Hirszfeld, from Bruznik. He was later a successful inventor. Many other boys built on their ORT training for their careers.

Meir Stern, from the small Ruthenian town of Svalava, a survivor of Auschwitz, had spent his first two years in Britain recovering from tuberculosis, first at Ashford and then at Quare Mead. Coming to London, he went to art school at Borough Polytechnic, but, having been told that there was 'no future in art', transferred to the study of dental mechanics. Art remained his goal, however, and he eventually became a picture restorer, a craft which he practises in Israel to this day.[24]

When the hostels were dissolved, the boys dispersed, except for most of those who were in the hostel in Manchester. There, they learned trades, took jobs, established themselves, and became an integral part of the local Jewish community. They were to play, and continue to play, an important part in the activities of Manchester Jewry. At the same time, they retained their distinctive identity as boys. One of them, David Sommer, became the chairman of their group within the '45 Aid Society, highly regarded as a man of integrity, and highlighting what could be achieved, both in business and in the wider community, by those who had begun their careers with great disadvantages.

---

[22] Zev Kedem (Bibi Gross), 'My Testament', *Journal of the '45 Aid Society*, No. 4, March 1978.
[23] Abraham Goldstein, letter to the author, 17 February 1995.
[24] Meir Stern, in conversation with the author, 11 May 1996.

CHAPTER 21

New Worlds

AFTER WORKING AS apprentices in London, some of the boys went far afield. Jake Fersztand, one of the younger members of the Windermere group, who after his time in the hostel at Cardross had gone to London to study structural engineering, made his subsequent career in Switzerland. Shamo Frajman, originally from Piotrkow, went to the United States, fighting with the American forces in the Korean War, and being wounded. On returning from Korea he lived in New York until, one day, he disappeared without trace.

Yasha Kurtz (John Carlisle) also served in Korea; he later became a taxi driver in New York, where he was noted for what Arthur Poznanski has called his 'chivalrous behaviour, great wit and physical toughness'.[1] An accomplished chess player, Kurtz was unique among the boys in that, shortly after he came to London from his hostel in Manchester, he learned that his mother was alive and well in Berlin.

In the 1950s Simon Gilbert, originally from the Galician town of Rymanow, served with the American army in Germany, in military intelligence. A Windermere boy, he was a survivor of the Rzeszow ghetto, slave labour camps at Huta Komorowska and Pustkow, deportation to Birkenau – 'where I got my tattoo' – slave labour at Laurahutte, Mauthausen and Gusen, and a death march from Dresden to Theresienstadt. In America he became a watchmaker and jeweller, first in New York and then in Fort Lauderdale, Florida.[2] He had gone to America to join his brother Sidney, nine years his senior, who had left Poland for America 'on the last ship before war broke out'.[3]

Sam Rosenblat, who together with his brother Isidore and Izzy Finkelstein had helped to gather the boys together in Theresienstadt for the journey to Britain, also made his way to the United States. 'The joy and happiness of my present life,' he wrote, 'has helped me to erase some of the memories of the past.'[4] David Borgenicht, a Windermere boy who

[1] Arthur Poznanski, 'John Carlisle (Jasiek Kurtz)', obituary, *Journal of the '45 Aid Society*, No. 10, April 1983.

[2] Simon Gilbert (Lecker), letter to the author, July 1995.

[3] Simon Gilbert (Lecker), letter to the author, 2 October 1995.

[4] Sam Rosenblat, 'My Other Life in Another Time', manuscript, sent to the author, 24 January 1995.

had spent seven months at Quare Mead convalescent home, and then completed an electrical course at the ORT school in South Kensington, left for the United States in 1949. First in Buffalo, and then in Los Angeles, he struggled for many years to build a business career. In 1991, aged sixty-three, he retired to Florida. His pride is his 'large family portrait: our three children, their spouses, and seven grandchildren'.[5]

Perec Zylberberg, from Lodz, was among several dozen boys who decided to go to Canada. Reaching Montreal in 1958, he began work in the clothing business, the trade he had learned in London. Moniek Goldberg, from Glowaczow and Kozienice, also went to Canada, in 1948, for it was there that he traced his mother's brother's family; they had emigrated from Poland to Canada as long ago as 1912. A year later he married Fay, a local London girl whom he had met at the Primrose Club, and moved to the United States. Today he has four children and ten grandchildren. He has been in the clothing business for more than four decades, like his parents in Poland before him. In 1976 he moved to Miami and subsequently opened a factory in Costa Rica. 'My boys, after graduating from college, decided to join the family business,' he wrote. 'It was a new adventure. I had to learn Spanish, and found the whole venture quite a challenge. At the age of sixty-seven I am slowing down a bit, but I am still active.'[6]

Howard Chandler, originally from the small Polish town of Wierzbnik, left Britain to join his mother's two sisters in Canada. They had emigrated from Poland before 1939. On reaching Toronto in December 1947, 'I was most warmly welcomed', he recalled, 'and made to feel part of my aunt and uncle's family in Toronto, Mrs Fayga and Lois Hochberg, with whom I lived until I got married in 1951. I feel very close to the whole family. My other aunt was Mrs Yeutel Obsbaum. My mother's two other sisters and their families perished in the Holocaust.'[7]

Life in Canada was, for Howard Chandler, a true New World. 'In Canada I immediately found a job as a diamond cutter,' he wrote, 'and later changed to become a self-employed jeweller and diamond setter, from which I recently retired. In 1951 I got married to Elsa who was also a Holocaust survivor, and who had come to Canada in 1948 and was able to go to school here. Elsa is a school board Trustee with the North York Board of Education, an elected position, and she has been continuously re-elected for the past fifteen years. We have four children, three daughters and one son. All are married and independent and they have given us four grandsons.

[5] 'Here and Now', *Journal of the '45 Aid Society*, No. 15, Rosh Hashana 5753/1992.

[6] Joseph (Moniek) Goldberg, 'Biographical Sketch', manuscript, July 1995, sent to the author, 14 August 1995.

[7] Howard Chandler (Chaim Wajchendler), letter to the author, 29 March 1995.

'We belong to a Conservative synagogue, Adath Israel. Also, we are active members of various Jewish and non-Jewish organisations. We own our home and also have a summer cottage by the lake, a great gathering-place for the whole family.'[8]

Another of the boys who lives in Canada today is Joshua Segal, originally from Lodz. From Overbury Court hostel at Alton he had gone to another hostel in Bedford, where he worked as an apprentice mechanic on Rolls-Royce and Daimler cars. 'In Bedford,' he recalled, 'an uncle found me. He was residing in Nottingham and was looking for survivors of the family. He gave me addresses of my uncles, aunts and cousins in Canada. I learned of another aunt who was living in Paris. After contacting her and telling her who I was, she told me she had been trying to find me for two years, and that my brother Wowek was living at her place.

'My Uncle Joe and Aunt Lily applied for permission to bring me to Canada as a landed immigrant. It was a hard battle because Canada had restrictions. But with the help of Senator Croll he succeeded and I was one of the first boys to arrive in Toronto. I arrived at Halifax on the *Ascania* on 27 December 1947 with seven hundred war brides. I lived with my uncle and aunt and my cousins for the next seven years. They treated me like their own children. The Hebrew Aid Society established a temporary home in Toronto for Jewish Holocaust survivors on Markham Street, so I became the "greeter" for our boys from England. After three years, I brought my brother and his wife to Canada.'

Joshua Segal married in 1953. He and his wife Malka have four children, all of them married, and, as of February 1995, six grandchildren 'and one on the way'. His brother, with whom he had shared so many torments, died in 1993. 'We are fortunate that our children and grandchildren live near us, and we are a very close-knit family.'[9]

Another of those who went to Canada was Rose Dajch. Like Josh Segal she was originally from Lodz, and she arrived in Canada on the same ship as he. In Canada, she recalled, 'We were housed in a hostel for a short time. Subsequently Jewish families took each of us to live with them. I was taken in by a Canadian Jewish couple who had two daughters. They sent me to high school with their children, and treated me like their own. They even wanted to adopt me. In spite of it all I felt like an outsider. Those were people who lived normal happy lives, knew nothing of hardship and suffering, hunger, and war. I missed my friends in England. School was hard, I missed the first half of the school year, I

---

[8] Howard Chandler (Chaim Wajchendler), letter to the author, 23 February 1995.

[9] Joshua Segal (Jehoszua Cygelfarb), letter to the author, 17 February 1995. Joshua Segal's seventh grandchild, Nicole Segal, was born on 19 April 1995.

had to do subjects I had never learned before. I only finished six grades of elementary school. But I managed to finish high school.

'Soon after leaving school, I took a summer job, and met some people like myself who had survived the war in concentration camps. We were all lonely and had a common background. Pretty soon I started dating boys. For the first time in my life I was enjoying myself. My husband and I met when he was visiting relatives in Toronto. He was living in the United States. He too is a survivor. We had the same interests and a similar background. We fell in love and got married in November 1949, when he brought me to the United States. In 1952 I gave birth to our son George, named after my father. In 1960 I gave birth to our daughter Debbie, named after my husband's mother. We tried to keep the memory of them alive.'

Fifty years after her liberation, Rose Fogel reflected on the half century that has passed since the war. 'We never forgot our lost family,' she wrote, 'and speak about them often. Even though I forgot what they looked like.'[10]

While he was in England, Michael Perlmutter, originally from the Polish town of Opatow, learned that his elder brother Moishe had also survived the slave labour camps and the death marches, and had gone to live in the United States. He decided to join him there, leaving England in 1951. He was twenty-two years old. 'Life was very difficult for both my brother and I, those first years in the United States,' he later wrote, 'but we had very good training in perseverance. My brother became successful in the house-building business, and I was involved in retailing.' It was in his first store that Michael Perlmutter met his future wife, Caroline. They were married in 1956. 'We have a son and a daughter, and a set of twins for grandchildren. They are our pride and joy!'[11]

It was in 1947 that Jack Rubinfeld, from Bircza, made contact with his brother Izzy, who had left their small town three years before the war and emigrated to the United States. Two years later Jack joined him there, and in 1951, at the age of twenty-three, as an American soldier, was posted to Germany, where he served in military intelligence. 'It was a great promotion,' he wrote, 'from being a despised prisoner without right or value, to being an American soldier, at that time, an elite. I had what was considered a prestigious job. I was in military intelligence because of my language skills and having scored high on my aptitude tests. With the exception of the first months spent in Nuremberg in

---

[10] Rose Fogel (Dajch), letter to the author, 12 March 1995.
[11] Michael Perlmutter, letter to the author, 4 March 1995.

processing, I spent about ten months in Bavaria as a member of an intelligence team.

'Our job was as liaison with the German border police, interrogating border-crossers from the east about the Russian military presence. We covered an eighty-four-kilometre border section with sixteen border police stations. My job naturally elevated my stature and self-esteem. I was the envy of my American military comrades, and was treated respectfully and enviously by the German population. My social life bloomed and I enjoyed the appetites of youth to the full. I felt no need for vengeance, nor did I have any bad feelings toward the regular civilian population.

'I was amazed when the Russian and East German police started tightening the border, installing towers and ten-metre ploughed strips with barbed wire. A flood of East German refugees streamed across the border and I spent all night in a schoolhouse to which they were brought. I did not bother interrogating them, and had the same feelings of compassion and hurt as when the Jewish refugees from Austria were streaming through my little town in Bircza after Hitler's occupation of Austria in 1938. I must admit I totally failed the hate and vengeance test. My father just failed to teach me that lesson.

'As for myself, the army service both in Germany and in America was a great and beneficial experience for me. It hastened tremendously my integration into the American lifestyle. It also wiped out any doubts I might have had about my inferiority of character and intellect. For the first time I started realising and appreciating the treasures of my father's teachings: the most important being to always be a *Mensch* – which includes being just, compassionate, and caring. That feeling has prevailed until today, and it has made my life free, rich and very enjoyable.'[12]

Returning from his military service in Germany to the United States, Jack Rubinfeld was 'blessed', he writes, 'with what I believe to be a very successful life, socially, economically, professionally and emotionally'.[13]

Maurice Vegh, from the Ruthenian town of Rakhov, also went from Britain to the United States, where he was drafted into the army. After training at Fort Dix he was posted to Salzburg, serving as an interpreter. While in Europe he made contact with Phyllis Fleischer, whom he had first met at the Primrose Club. Later he took her back to the United States, where they were married. 'She had a family, she had a country,' he later recalled. 'I finally had a feeling of belonging somewhere.' Today, on Long Island, Maurice and Phyllis Vegh are active in their local synagogue, where he is the only Holocaust survivor. One of their three

[12] Jack I. Rubinfeld, letter to the author, 26 March 1996.
[13] Jack I. Rubinfeld, 'Jack Rubinfeld', manuscript, sent to the author, undated (1995).

sons, Zev, is named after Maurice's father, who was killed on a death march. Another son, Draze, is named after Maurice's mother, Raizel, who was murdered at Auschwitz. The Veghs have six grandchildren, all boys. 'Mine is a happy ending', Maurice Vegh reflected. 'Others were not so lucky.'[14]

Zvi Mlynarski, from Piotrkow, who had been at the Loughton and Belsize Park hostels before going to the ORT school in London, discovered an uncle in the United States who had emigrated from Poland before the war, and also an aunt in Palestine. 'My uncle sent me papers to come to the United States,' he recalled. But it was not to the United States that he went. 'I was very indecisive, and after hearing that Israel had declared its independence, I decided to go there. The Jewish Agency advised me to finish my studies and then emigrate. I did so, and on 12 September 1949 I reached Israel, and started to learn Hebrew.'[15] Within two decades, Zvi Dagan (as he became) was the director of a large machine-tool factory in the Israeli coastal town of Ashkelon. Since 1973 he has managed his own company, employing more than a hundred people; almost half of them are new immigrants from the former Soviet Union.

Icek Jakubowicz, from Lodz, had been on the terrible journey from Rehmsdorf to Theresienstadt as the war drew to a close, and had survived the Allied bombing raid when the train reached Marienbad. After Windermere and Alton – where Perec Zylberberg tried in vain to convert him to Bundist socialism – he studied optics at the London Polytechnic, becoming a Fellow of the British Optical Association. Then he went to work for a British optical company, first in India, then in Burma, and later still in Malaysia and Singapore. 'My only surviving relations, as far as I knew, lived in Israel – an aunt and two cousins who had gone there from Poland before the war,' he remarked. 'But my background was not Zionist, and I wasn't a Zionist either. Then, one day, on my way to the Far East, the plane stopped at Beirut airport. Someone said, "On the other side of those hills is Israel". I thought to myself, "What a bloody fool I am to be here". It was 1969. Not long afterwards I emigrated to Israel.'[16] He was forty-two years old.

In 1964, Warsaw-born Meir Sosnowicz (who had become Michael Novice), having built up a successful career in electronics in Britain, and with a Ph.D. in Physics, emigrated to the United States. He crossed the Atlantic on the Queen Mary from Southampton to New York. 'Now, great excitement,' he recalled. 'For Shabbat came a very special visitor –

[14] Maurice (Moritz) Vegh, in conversation with the author, 3 May 1996.
[15] Zvi Dagan (Mlynarski), letter to the author, 10 March 1996.
[16] Ray Jackson (Icek Jakubowicz), in conversation with the author, 11 May 1996.

Shmuel Chaim made a special trip from Toronto to New York to welcome us to the American continent! Sam Novice (Shmuel Chaim Sosnowicz) was the cousin with whom I spent the war years from Ostrowiec onwards.'[17]

Roza Gross, whose hostel had been Montford Hall, near Edinburgh, emigrated to the United States in 1948. She was fortunate that her brothers Alex and Sam had also survived the war. But tragedy struck the Gross family in the New World. Alex Gross's only son died in an accident when he was fourteen. Nine years later his wife was murdered in Atlanta. 'Despite this double tragedy,' Ben Helfgott has written, 'Alex has continued to be resilient, his zest for life remains undiminished, and his commitment to the community has never faltered. We salute his indomitable spirit.'[18]

Henry Golde, originally from Plock, was another of the boys who made his way to the United States. 'New York!' he later wrote. 'I was told I would find gold in the streets. Ha! I would hate to tell you what you find in the streets of New York. I became an entrepreneur. I did everything from working in the sweatshops of the garment district to driving a cab, to selling prefabricated homes and selling land in Florida, owning a tavern in Wisconsin, where I now live, to politics. I have worked and travelled all over this beautiful land and have seen a lot. I am retired now.'[19]

For many years Henry Golde has been one of those boys who has shared his wartime experiences with young and old, speaking, he explains, 'to grade schools up to college campuses, to service clubs and other organisations, in fact to anyone who will listen. Above all, it is most gratifying to talk to the kids, especially with the message I tell about prejudice, bigotry and love versus hate. Every one of us should tell his or her story over and over again to the children. They are the new generation. They are our future leaders and soon they will go into the world. If they remember only a part of our story, especially the part about hate and prejudice, then they will never allow it to happen again. But if people do not remember, I feel another Holocaust could happen at any time to anybody in this world.'[20]

Howard Chandler is another of the boys who talks about his experiences in the Holocaust to schools in and around Toronto. 'We've been studying it for two weeks,' one student, Lisa Dove, told the *Oshawa Times*.

---

[17] Michael Novice (Meir Sosnowicz), recollections, manuscript, June 1995.

[18] *Journal of the '45 Aid Society*, No. 16, Pessach 5753/1993.

[19] H. Golde, 'It seems like only yesterday', *Journal of the '45 Aid Society*, No. 18, December 1994, page 10.

[20] H. Golde, 'It seems like only yesterday', *Journal of the '45 Aid Society*, No. 18, December 1994, page 11.

'But it doesn't hit home until you actually talk to someone. I'm really glad I got to talk to Mr Chandler. I learned a lot about courage and human perseverance and man's inhumanity to man.'

'It makes you wonder if there's a cruel person in everyone, and what it takes to bring that out,' added Cindy Mennel.

'Why didn't people stop it?' asked Paula Atansio.

Howard Chandler tried to answer this question, one with which he, and other survivors, are often confronted. 'So many people could have stopped it and didn't,' he replied. 'In Poland and other occupied territories, if a Jew hid from the Nazis the townspeople revealed them. Even priests turned their backs on the Jews. The occupied populations gave their passive consent to atrocity. They just closed their eyes to it. Maybe they were terrified themselves, for the system was terrible. This must never recur. There's no room for hatred of one another. What I told you is what it can lead to. It happened before and it has happened since. If you see a person mistreating another and you just stand by, you are just as guilty.'

The newspaper account continued: 'The father of four has overcome the nightmares he used to have when he first began speaking to class groups. He does it with the conviction that he must share his experience with as many people as possible. It is painful enough to live through it, but to hear people try to deny that the Holocaust happened, is ludicrous, he said. "I can't understand their motives for denying it. And there are a diminishing number of individuals who can personally refute those who deny it took place." '[21]

An increasing number of boys have begun to lecture and speak about their experiences. As early as October 1978 John Fox chaired a pioneering conference on Teaching the Lessons of the Holocaust in Philadelphia. He did so as President of the Philadelphia Jewish Labour Committee, a position which he had held for the previous three years. In April 1990 Perec Zylberberg, who had made his home in Montreal, gave his first public talk, at the age of sixty-seven. The audience had gathered to commemorate the Warsaw ghetto revolt. 'A large crowd,' he recorded in his diary two years later, 'tense atmosphere, emotions run high. I am satisfied I spoke to the point. I felt within me that it made an impression. Since then I have spoken to many audiences. Both in Yiddish and English, on the Holocaust and other topics. But the speech described above is very meaningful to me. It was an appearance that made me at one with my past and present.'[22]

[21] Kay Fisher, 'A true story of abject horror', *Oshawa Times*, 6 April 1989.
[22] Perec Zylberberg, diary entry for 6 May 1992.

In Atlanta, Alex Gross, one of the boys from Ruthenia, who became a property developer, has been active on behalf of a group of concentration camp survivors, and has written several articles in local newspapers. He has also established a small Holocaust museum in Atlanta.[23] Sidney Finkel, originally from Piotrkow, belongs to an American organisation called Facing History and Ourselves which trains teachers about prejudice and discrimination. 'As part of that,' he wrote in the summer of 1995, 'they will be sending me into many schools to tell my story to the students. I feel very fortunate that I have the opportunity to do this work, even though it often wipes me out for a few days. I feel that I have experienced a lot of healing as a result of telling my story.'[24]

In September 1995 Sidney Finkel wrote to me from his home in Park Forest, Illinois: 'So far this year alone I have given thirteen talks and have a heavy Fall schedule. I am totally amazed by the interest shown in the Holocaust story by a cross-section of the population, including minorities like Spanish Americans and African Americans. The Holocaust story seems to have universal appeal. I feel myself very fortunate that I have the opportunity of doing this work, and the ability to come across to my audience.'[25]

The response of their listeners is heartening to those among the boys who speak about the past in public, particularly to schools. In 1993 the *Journal of the '45 Aid Society* published two letters received from schoolgirls, one in Britain and one in the United States. The British schoolgirl, Rebecca Cresswell, had heard Aron Zylberszac, originally from Lodz, and Abraham Zwirek, who had been born in Plock, speak together about the Holocaust. 'Although we will never be able fully to comprehend the suffering that these men both witnessed and endured,' she wrote, 'their talk was both enlightening and incredibly emotive. They answered all questions with lucid recollection.'[26] The second letter was sent to Alec Ward from Janelle Johnston, a sixth-former at Claremont High School in California. 'I cannot pretend to understand what you went through during the war,' she wrote, 'although I am sure that coming to us to talk about your experiences was quite distressing, and I thank you for your sacrifice. The discussion particularly brought home to me the reality of the events which took place during the war. Up to that time, the events of the war were, for me, like a bad dream. Speaking to you and listening to your story, as one who was actually there, made me realise

---

[23] 'Members' News', *Journal of the '45 Aid Society*, No. 4, March 1978.
[24] Sidney Finkel (Sevek Finkelstein), letter of 8 July 1995, *Journal of the '45 Aid Society*, No. 19, December 1995.
[25] Sidney Finkel (Sevek Finkelstein), letter to the author, 12 September 1995.
[26] Rebecca Cresswell, *Journal of the '45 Aid Society*, No. 16, Pessach 5753/1993.

that these things happened to real people with real families.'[27]

Some boys feel more strongly than others about the wisdom, and the purpose, of conveying the story of what they went through. Moniek Goldberg, who became a clothing manufacturer in Florida, commented in 1979: 'We are told that we have an obligation to talk about the Holocaust. That we must tell our children. But what do I tell them? Do I take them by the hand and say, "Come, I'll guide you through a wilderness, a devastation, I shall recount to you a litany of deaths, suffering, and annihilation in all its gory detail?" Shall I do that? I do not think I can. After all, it isn't quite like our rabbis telling of the Exodus; they were relating a miracle not a bitter tragedy.

'What do I tell them then? What is the miracle of the Holocaust? Who delivered the Jews? The Poles? The Germans? The Ukrainians? The Latvians? The Hungarians? The Pope? Franklin Roosevelt? The British government? They all delivered the Jews. But to whom? Or to what? Some a greater number, some a lesser number, some by acts of commission, some by acts of omission – but a total of six million were delivered to their deaths. There is no doubt about Eichmann's guilt, but had he refused (as he should have) there were others eagerly waiting to do his murderous job; which would have resulted in the same tragedy. Had Mr Roosevelt given haven to the Jews on the ship (as he should have) they would have been saved.[28]

'Finally, I can tell them, and perhaps this is the miracle of the Holocaust, that the Jews are a people with whom I was during their darkest hour of a long history of suffering, and never did our enemies succeed in bringing us down to their sub-human level. I can tell them that Jewish heroism stands out as a beacon of light in a dark sea of collaboration of the non-Jewish populations, whether it was in Warsaw, Vilna, Kruszyn or in many other places. I can tell them that Jewish resistance in the Warsaw ghetto took longer for the Germans to conquer than did the whole of Poland.[29] And I can tell them about a man named Chaim who gave us encouraging words from the gallows in Buna. Yes, we have paid a terrible price, but when I look at my children and the

[27] Janelle Johnston, *Journal of the '45 Aid Society*, No. 16, Pessach 5753/1993.

[28] A reference to the German liner *St Louis*, which set out from Hamburg on 13 May 1939 with 930 German Jewish refugees on board. Of these, 734 held United States quota numbers, permitting entry within three years. All held Cuban landing certificates. Only twenty-two were allowed to enter Cuba. None were permitted to enter the United States. Colombia, Chile, Paraguay and Argentina also refused entry, and the refugees had to sail back to Europe. They were taken in by Britain (287), Holland, Belgium and France. Those who were taken in by Holland, Belgium and France were to come under German rule within twelve months of their return.

[29] The Germans occupied Warsaw three weeks after invading Poland. It took them four weeks to destroy the Warsaw Jewish insurgents.

children of my friends I realise more than ever that the victory is ours. We are able and useful citizens of society, with families who give us a lot to be proud of.'[30]

What can be conveyed? This question troubles the boys as much as it troubles many other survivors. One of the boys, Michael Perlmutter, from Opatow, has tried to convey the terrible nature of hunger in the slave labour camps by telling an audience in his home town in New Jersey: 'We have all known the pangs of hunger at one time or another – missing breakfast to catch a train or bus, giving up lunch to lose a few pounds, Yom Kippur, a long and arduous day of fasting. These are examples of hunger; and they all have one thing in common, they end quickly. If we miss breakfast, we make up for it during lunch. Yom Kippur becomes bearable, because we know it will end at sundown with bagels and lox.

'I am not, however, referring to the temporary type of hunger. I am talking about the non-stop hunger in the concentration camps of Skarzysko-Kamienna, Czestochowa, Buchenwald, Treglitz and Theresienstadt. Those were the places where I started learning about hunger when I was thirteen years old. It was the kind of hunger that did not end with bagels, or for that matter with any kind of food. Hunger that was like an entrance to a tunnel, leading to another and another without any glimmer of light. Hunger is a relentless assault on the body and mind; hunger that does not stop bringing pain, that eats away at your body piece by piece, until it infects your mind. You become animalistic, and your days and nights consist of images; of a piece of bread, that you could put in your mouth and chew. That hunger caused many of us to wish not to wake up in the morning, rather than face another day of pain and despair. I have seen the inexplicable cruelties of man to man, but nothing is as devastating as hunger. Not one of us would have ever hesitated to put our life on the line, just to get a little food.'

Such stories, Perlmutter commented in his speech, 'have been told many times much better than I tell it here, so why do I tell it again?' Then he answered his own question: 'I am telling it for my mother, for my father, for my sister, for all the other members of my family too numerous to mention, and for all the other victims of that infamous era. I believe and I feel that they are watching and observing. And I would like to assure them that they are not forgotten by any one of us. For there are, strangely, some out there who deny the history of the Holocaust. They are basically anti-Semitic attacks on the truth, but still

[30] Joseph (Moniek) Goldberg, 'We and the Holocaust – Today', *Journal of the '45 Aid Society*, No. 6, May 1979, pages 7–8.

they grow. I therefore ask you, and beseech you, not to forget. Don't let your children's children forget. Because if we forget, who will remember?'[31]

Michael Perlmutter lives today in a retirement community in New Jersey, 'where I play a lot of bridge, a little golf, and have a lot of good conversation', he writes. 'There are two thousand people in this community. Whenever possible I speak to them of the agony of the Holocaust, and plead with them not to forget!'[32]

[31] Michael Perlmutter, speech to the Yiddish Club, Toms River, New Jersey, 7 November 1994.
[32] Michael Perlmutter, letter to the author, 4 March 1995.

CHAPTER 22

'Laying a Foundation for the Future'

ACH BOY SET out with tenacity to earn a living. There were so many problems: language, lack of any formal education for as many as six crucial years, the constant anxiety of being a stranger and a newcomer. Yet the will to succeed was strong, and the struggles, though hard, were remarkable. Krulik Wilder later recalled his own early efforts, after his return from the Israeli War of Independence, when he took up residence at the Primrose Club. 'I lived in the club quite a while,' he later wrote, 'because I was completely broke. Eventually I found a job as a watchmaker. I was earning £4 per week. After a few months I changed jobs to work for another firm in Hatton Garden, London. My salary increased to £6 per week. I worked there for twelve months, and in 1951 I left my job and started my own business with a partner, repairing watches. It was very hard to make a living, but we persevered and eventually things improved.

'In 1952 I met my darling wife Gloria in the Primrose Club, we got married in June 1953. The first eighteen months of our married life we lived with my wife's parents. Life was not easy, we worked very hard and saved every penny, and in 1955 we bought our first house, just six months before our eldest son Paul was born. I was happy that it was a boy, as I had lost all my family and relatives, and it was gratifying to know that the Wilder name would be carried forward. By that time I had a shop in Hatton Garden, and financially life was a little easier, even though I still had to work very long hours, which I did not mind as I was laying a foundation for the future of my family.

'In 1958 our second son Simon was born, more joy and happiness, and again, in 1960, our third son Martin was born, more jollification. At that time my partner decided to go to the United States. I bought his share. I made improvements and introduced new jewellery lines to the business. I was making steady progress and continued to work very hard and long hours to achieve success. In 1963 we moved to a larger house as the old one was too small for the five of us. We were very happy in our new house, the boys were growing up, they became Bar Mitzvah boys and in time married. Now they have families of their own.' Paul and Martin Wilder work with their father. Simon Wilder chose another career as a graphic designer. 'I am very proud of my three sons, they are very fine men,' Krulik Wilder writes. Nor, he adds, could he have achieved everything without the support of his wife, 'who was always there to encourage and support me in whatever business venture I chose'.[1]

Pride in the achievements of their children is a constant factor among the boys, whose own education had been so terribly disrupted. In 1951, when he was twenty-six, Abraham Zwirek married his cousin Ida, the one-year-old girl whom he could remember having seen off at Plock railway station when he was four years old. They had two children, David, named after Abraham Zwirek's father, and Helen named after his mother. 'I am now retired and have no regrets about coming to England,' he wrote fifty years after liberation. 'I was given the opportunity to have a family and make a successful contribution to this country. My son and daughter received a good English education with my son graduating from Oxford University in 1981.'[2]

Many of the boys' children have already achieved success in the professions, working as doctors, solicitors, architects, business executives and management consultants. Other children are at the start of their careers: Abraham Zwirek's son David began work in October 1995 as a trainee press and public relations officer with the Royal Navy.

Alec Ward was not so fortunate. In 1981, after thirty years of marriage, and having worked first as a tailor and then as a quality controller in the ladies' garment industry, he lost his 23-year-old son Mark, a victim of cancer. 'During the war I knew who my enemy was,' he wrote. 'In 1981 I did not know.' While a student at Exeter University, Mark Ward had become president of the Jewish Society. 'He was a sincere, loyal Jew,' his rabbi wrote in an obituary notice, 'and showed great promise for the future. Anglo-Jewry lost a potential leader.'[3]

Solly Irving, having returned to England after his time in the Israeli army, worked first as an apprentice electrical engineer, then in the handbag trade. In 1962 he married a British Jewish girl, Sandra Silver. Tragically, she died nine years later. 'I have never recovered from that tragedy,' he wrote. He is proud of his two daughters: 'They have grown up to love and respect our Jewish heritage'. His 'biggest disappointment', as he described it, 'is that I have no close family left, nor do I have pictures of my parents. I wonder if I would recognise them.'[4] Solly is now sixty-five years old. He was twelve when his parents and three of

[1] Israel (Krulik) Wilder, letter to the author, 1 January 1995.

[2] Abraham Zwirek, letter to the author, 30 September 1994.

[3] Alec Ward, 'My Story', manuscript, sent to the author, 31 May 1995.

[4] Solly Irving (Shloime Zalman Judensznajder), 'Memories of a Past', manuscript, sent to the author, 5 April 1995.

his sisters (Rivka, Leah and Hendil) were deported to their deaths.

Harry Balsam's early steps towards earning a living were taken in partnership with two other Windermere boys, Harry Spiro and Johnny Fox. 'We were making suits to measure,' Harry Balsam recalled, 'and selling ready-made ones as well. After about one year Johnny got married and decided to go to live in America. So we paid him off his share. After a while Harry got married and then I got married, and it was not enough for two families to live on, so we decided to go our separate ways. Harry paid me out and kept the business for himself, he is still there today.

'I opened a menswear shop in Watford. After a while I opened another one. Then I branched out and bought more shops, two in the Edgware Road, one in Hammersmith, three in Oxford Street, one in Regent Street, one in Thayer Street, one in Kilburn and one in Kensington. I had my sons with me in the business. Today, as I am writing my life story, I have only one shop left in Kilburn which is enough for me. My sons now work in different businesses. Stephen is in advertising and Colin is in the music business.

'I am happily married to Pauline. My sons are very happily married too. My oldest son Stephen's wife is Rochelle; they have three lovely children, one girl and two boys. Natalie is twelve years old, Jason is ten years old, and Adam is six years old. Colin my youngest son has been married to Amanda for six months and they are expecting their first child in January 1996.'[5]

Harry Balsam, like all the boys, cannot and does not forget the past. His account of his past life ended with the sentence: 'This story is dedicated to my mother Adele, my sister Gitel and my brothers Sanek and Joseph who perished at the hands of the Nazis.'[6]

Lola Hahn-Warburg, whose concern to help the boys dated from the summer of 1945, when preparations were being made to receive them in Britain, remained in touch with them, and with their needs both while they were in hostels, and beyond. Ben Helfgott later wrote: 'I heard about her from other boys, although my first encounter with her did not take place until 1953 – long after the hostels had been disbanded. A very close friend of mine (I shared my accommodation with him) had suffered a brain haemorrhage and was taken to hospital. I immediately informed the committee of his critical state. A few hours later Lola and Stella Epstein (the then secretary of the Jewish Refugees Committee) turned up at the hospital.

'There was very little that we could do, but I do remember the anxiety

[5] Jack Balsam was born on 10 January 1996.
[6] Harry Balsam, 'The Harry Balsam Story', manuscript, sent to the author, 14 November 1995.

and anguish on her face and her request to me to keep in touch with her. Miraculously, after some time my friend recovered.'[7]

At their annual gatherings, the boys enjoy recounting what one or another of them has achieved. The *Journal of the '45 Aid Society* reflects this pride. The 1995 issue of the journal, after noting that Mick Jagger had just been elected an honorary fellow of the London School of Economics, pointed out that one of the boys, Kurt Klappholz, had been the singer's tutor at the LSE. When Mick Jagger found the accounting and finance course not to his taste, he consulted his tutor, suggesting that he would like to take up music. Kurt Klappholz encouraged him, recommending him to take a year off to try out a career in music, while warning that 'he would never make any money at it'.[8]

Obituary notices are also a feature of the journal. They are affectionate notices by friends of those whose original families were mourned long ago. Each notice recalls a facet of the pattern of life of the boys. When Michael Flasz died in Manchester in May 1995 his friend and former business partner Mayer Bomsztyk recalled how, for part of the war years, 'he fought in the woods, with the Polish partisans, and also went as a volunteer to Israel in 1948'.[9] Michael Flasz, a handbag manufacturer in Manchester, was a quiet, well-liked member of the Manchester '45s.

The death of Jerzy Poznanski, also in May 1995, was widely mourned. After their parents had been deported from the Piotrkow ghetto and murdered in 1942, he and his brother Arthur had tried to stay together. But, as Arthur recalled, 'within a year I was sent to another slave labour camp and we were separated. From that time on he was left completely on his own in the bitter struggle for survival.' Jerzy Poznanski was then thirteen years old. 'By sheer chance,' Arthur wrote, 'I found him in Theresienstadt, pitifully emaciated and weak, some weeks after liberation.'

Living in Gateshead, Jerzy Poznanski combined the pursuit of Talmudic studies with a career as a watch repairer. Although never rich, his help for those in need in the local Jewish community was unstinting. 'Jerzy was not only observant,' his brother wrote of him, 'he "walked in the ways of Torah". He understood that rituals, mainly symbolic, are insufficient, and that deeds and behaviour towards fellow men are of the utmost importance. He applied the precepts of honesty, tolerance and charity in everyday life, and never complained of hardships. Small wonder that the whole town, including many gentiles, who liked and

---

[7] Ben Helfgott, 'An Appreciation', manuscript, sent to the author, 9 May 1996.
[8] *Journal of the '45 Aid Society*, No. 19, December 1995, page 62.
[9] *Journal of the '45 Aid Society*, No. 19, December 1995, page 56.

respected him for his honesty, skills and friendliness, came to pay their last respects when we, his family, sat in mourning. Literally hundreds turned up; many from Manchester, Newcastle, Sunderland and London. They will all miss him. However, his children, their spouses, his grand-children and I miss him most of all.'[10]

Arthur Poznanski managed, after his wedding in 1960, to become a professional singer. He obtained engagements all over Britain. But after three years he had to take on work in the textile business to supplement his income as a singer. Later, he became the choirmaster of his local synagogue. 'I teach and rehearse the choir and the cantor,' he wrote in 1995, 'and have composed several settings to psalms and prayers for them to sing.' He is proud of his children. 'My daughter Angela has a BA from Hull in French and Politics and a postgraduate diploma in publishing from Oxford. She lives in California with her husband and son, where she works as an editor for a textbook publishing company. My son Victor has a B.Sc. in computer science and electronics from Manchester and a Ph.D. in artificial intelligence from Cambridge. He works as a senior research scientist in Oxford. He also has a love for music and plays the piano and organ. And I hope to be able to teach my grandson, Joseph, the joys and comfort to be found in music.

'My wife and I are both proud of having been able to give our children the education that I missed. And I am happy and proud when I think that from being a helpless Jewish child left alone in Nazi Germany I was able to survive, live as normal and comfortable a life as I could have wished for myself, bring up a flourishing family in freedom and continue to learn and pursue the subjects that command my attention.'

As to the Holocaust, Arthur Poznanski wrote, 'I remain deeply troubled by my past and all I witnessed, and need to know if there are any answers as to the ways of the world, and why things happen, or, for that matter, do not happen.'[11]

Harry Spiro had first taken work in London using the skill he had learned in the glass-making slave labour factory in Piotrkow. But, not yet twenty-one, he fell foul of British trade union rules when an engineer failed to turn up for work, and he changed a mould himself. 'They wouldn't give me a full union card until I was twenty-one,' he recalled, 'so they said I had to work at apprentice rates even though I already knew how to do the job. The union told the company that they had to pay me much less. I carried on for a few weeks, but it was so unfair I gave the job up.'

After considerable difficulties, Harry Spiro managed to find work as a

---

[10] *Journal of the '45 Aid Society*, No. 19, December 1995, pages 57–8.
[11] Arthur Poznanski, recollections, letter to the author, 24 January 1995.

tailor with Harry Balsam and Johnny Fox. Eventually he set up in business by himself. At the height of his business he employed five hundred people in three factories. 'We had a German au pair girl in the sixties,' he later recalled. 'A neighbour said how could I do that, after what the Germans had done. My answer was that whilst some of the Germans genuinely hated Jews, most just went along with it, accepting the lies. So the most important thing is to show them that Jews are normal people, who live normal lives and look after their families.

'Our family is our greatest achievement. When I look at my three children, all happily married, and seven (soon to be eight) grandchildren, I think about my mother and her last words, that at least one member of the family should survive.

'For so many years, if someone heard my surname and then asked, "Are you related to so and so?" I always answered, "No", since all my family were dead. Now, with three children happily married, and my grandchildren, I always need to check who they mean. And so I think of my mother's foresight in throwing me out of the house, when the majority of the Jews of my town, Piotrkow, were deported to the gas chambers of Treblinka, so that "one of the family should survive", and I look on my family as her victory – and my victory over what the Nazis failed to do.'[12]

Pinkus Kurnedz, who had gone from Windermere to a hostel in Manchester at the age of eighteen, remained in Manchester to work, and then opened a very successful luggage business in nearby Oldham, in partnership with two other boys, David Sommer and Jack Aizenberg. 'I have been married to a local girl for thirty-two years,' Pinkus Kurnedz wrote in 1994, 'and we have three children and five grandchildren who live in Israel. We go to visit them at least three times a year, but somehow I always want to come home to Manchester – is it not strange?'[13]

After his life of hunger, brutality, fear and uncertainty in the ghetto, in the slave labour camps, and on the death marches, Pinkus Kurnedz found true security in Manchester. That city also provided in later years an example of the link between the boys and their children – the 'Second Generation' as they call themselves. Mendel Beale, a survivor of the Lodz ghetto and Auschwitz, who came to England after the boys, but became

---

[12] Harry Spiro, recollections, letter to the author, 21 March 1995. With the birth of his eighth and ninth grandchildren, Harry Spiro reflected: 'I'm continuing to see my mother's words coming to fruition. She had foresight.' (Harry Spiro, in conversation with the author, 21 April 1996). Harry Spiro's eighth grandchild, Daniel Saul Moses, was born on 4 September 1995; his ninth grandchild, Hannah Gita Spiro, on 14 February 1996.

[13] Pinkus Kurnedz, recollections, letter to the author, 5 October 1994.

an active member of the '45 Aid Society – and co-founder with David Sommer of its Manchester branch – was one of those who inspired the Second Generation to meet, and to form their own group. In that group, his daughter Tania Nelson was particularly active from the outset. Much of the work of the Second Generation is educational. Those in Manchester speak at Jewish schools throughout the Manchester area, have published a teachers' training pack, and take part in radio discussions about the Holocaust, with which the life and fate of their parents was so bound up, and of which their parents were eyewitnesses.

The families, which most of the boys started in the 1960s, gave them a sense of renewal that cannot fully be understood by those who have not lost their whole family, or almost all their loved ones, at an early age. Among those who had come to Britain under their own devices, and joined the Primrose Club soon after his arrival, was Zigi Shipper. Shortly after getting married, he and his wife opened a delicatessen. It did not work out, and after about two years he joined his father-in-law in the stationery trade. Later he started up on his own, and today he has a successful printing and stationery business. 'In 1956 my first daughter, Michelle, was born. In 1961, my second daughter, Lorraine, was born. At last I felt I had a family of my own,' he reflected.

'Today, both my daughters are happily married, and I have four grandsons and one granddaughter. You cannot imagine how I felt when my oldest grandson had his Bar Mitzvah recently, and when, in his speech, he said he would like to share it with me – as I was never able to have one of my own (I was in the Lodz ghetto on my thirteenth birthday, on 18 January 1943) – I was able to share this joyous occasion with my closest friends, survivors like me, with whom I have been together for the last fifty or so years. Having no brothers or sisters, they are my brothers and sisters.'[14]

As each boy saw his own family grow, he retained, as Zigi Shipper had done, a sense of family with his fellow-survivors, who were always welcome and much-loved participants at the Bar Mitzvahs and weddings – and, increasingly in recent years, the silver wedding anniversaries – which continue to link the new post-war family with the ever-flourishing family of the boys.

[14] Zygmunt (Zigi) Shipper, recollections, letter to the author, 16 April 1996.

CHAPTER 23

The '45 Aid Society

THE PRIMROSE CLUB had been for teenagers; by the middle of the 1960s those teenagers were grown up. It was then, after a few years without a club, that Issie Finkelstein – one of the three older survivors who had accompanied the boys from Theresienstadt to Windermere in August 1945 – suggested it was time for the boys to form their own society. Yogi Mayor, who had become club leader at the Brady Club, offered his club's premises for the first meeting.

Calling itself 'the '45 Aid Society' – a reference to 1945, the year of their liberation, and of their first journeys to Britain – the new enterprise was intended by the boys from the outset to help any member of the society who might fall on hard times, and also to make charitable donations of its own. Equally important, it would serve as a gathering point for those who, since the days of the Primrose Club, had gone their various and varied ways.

The family that had been dispersed would be brought together again. Oscar Joseph, then chairman of the Central British Fund, was asked to be President and accepted. Ben Helfgott was elected chairman. Also closely associated with the society from its inauguration was Leonard Montefiore's widow Muriel. Muriel Montefiore and Oscar Joseph shared, Hugo Gryn has written, 'the roles of mother – and father – figures which we thrust upon them'.[1]

Since 1965 the '45 Aid Society has held an annual dinner. It has also established an annual lectureship in memory of Leonard Montefiore: these lectures have included a fifty-year retrospective on the Nuremberg Trials given by John Tusa, and a survey of wartime Paris by David Pryce-Jones. At other meetings of the society during the course of the year, old friendships are renewed; members meet in London and Manchester, Toronto and Tel Aviv. 'Many a Friday night,' Felix Berger has written, 'have I left the table of a close relative to be with our "boys". Those meetings have always held a certain magic for me. I don't know about the Savage or the Athenaeum, but I belong to a damn good club.'[2]

[1] Hugo Gryn, 'Mrs Muriel Montefiore', obituary, *Journal of the '45 Aid Society*, No. 13, May 1989. Muriel Montefiore died in 1989, at the age of ninety-seven.

[2] Felix Berger, 'Tel-Aviv Diary', *Journal of the '45 Aid Society*, No. 4, March 1978. A survivor of the Lodz ghetto, Felix Berger was at Windermere and Cardross; he later became a veterinary surgeon.

On 11 May 1975 the boys held their thirtieth anniversary reunion. Among those who crossed the Atlantic to be at the London event with their former companions were a number who had settled in Canada. On their return they decided to form their own branch of the society. The boy most active in setting up the branch was Izzie Light, originally from Lodz. In all, there were twenty-five boys and six girls living in Canada, fifteen of them in Toronto. Almost all of them had been among the boys liberated in Theresienstadt. 'Among the survivors of the camp,' the *Canadian Jewish News* reported, 'are Maurice and Edith Kaufman of Dundas, Ontario. They speak of the intensity of the bond between them and their fellows, such that wherever they travel, they seek each other out like lost relatives.'[3]

Edith (Jadzia) Kaufman, from Piotrkow, was one of the two girls whom Ben Helfgott had met immediately after the war when he returned to Poland. On hearing from Ben that her brother, Marshall Balsam, was alive, and in Theresienstadt, Jadzia had travelled with her friend to Theresienstadt, and later flown with her brother to Crosby-on-Eden.

After the 1976 reunion, held at the Piccadilly Hotel in London, Kitty Dessau, the wife of a Windermere Boy, Kopel Dessau, who was later in the Alton and Bedford hostels, wrote: 'I'm sure other groups would have drifted apart and gone their own separate ways after all these years. But then the "Boys" have (sadly) been through so much, they are bound together with memories of mutual suffering and loss.'[4]

Kopel Dessau, originally from Piotrkow, had been at the Dora slave labour camp. 'I lost an eye in Dora,' he later recalled. 'I was hit by a club.'[5] Among those at the Piccadilly Hotel that night was Bernard Kaufmann, a boy from the Ruthenian town of Slatinske Dole, who had settled in Australia. He had travelled all the way to London for the dinner.

In his chairman's speech at the 1976 reunion, Ben Helfgott gave voice to feelings that others felt, even if they did not have his gift of expression. 'We have shown,' he said, 'that the misery, cruelty, despair and injustice that were inflicted on us did not break our indomitable will. It did not consume us with hatred to the point of destroying our own and other peoples' lives. Instead we set out to create a new life.'[6]

---

[3] Ellie Tesher, 'Survivors of Theresienstadt prison camp plan formation of Canada '45 Aid Society', *Canadian Jewish News*, 16 May 1975. I am grateful to Marylyn Light for sending me this cutting. Her husband, Izzie Light (formerly Licht), is one of the boys. He is at present (1996) preparing a book of recollections of his childhood, entitled 'Light at the end of the tunnel, a childhood relived'.

[4] Kitty Dessau, 'In Praise of the '76 Reunion', *Journal of the '45 Aid Society*, No. 3, April 1977, page 22.

[5] Max (Kopel) Dessau, in conversation with the author, 30 April 1995.

[6] Ben Helfgott, speech notes, May 1976.

Michael Etkind, the boy from Lodz who had become the boys' poet, set out his thoughts on the 1976 reunion in verse:

Hello! How are you? Yes, I know your face
You are from Manchester Do I know the place?
You were in Windermere, Block 'D' What's your name?
O yes, I remember, your face's still the same

So much emotion, so much more to say
Yet so much expressed in this artless way

So full of life – anxious to succeed
Eager to satisfy all material need

So normal, so fit, so healthy a crowd,
I wonder, should I mention,
That each and every one of us deserves his
                bloody pension

So loud-mouthed, pushing, ambitious, greedy,
And yet so generous, and anxious to help the needy

So cynically sarcastic, and critical of one another
                and yet
Their devotion greater than that of brother
                for brother

Silence! The prayers are soon to begin,
Be quiet, stop talking. I know what you mean

The speeches will follow as they did last year,
    and food fit for kings and music that the deaf can hear

And money donated will exceed expectations and
Other contributions will follow donations

Suddenly it's over, this brief reunion of souls
Linked together in a strange communion
Linked by a past that none could foretell,
And none understand,
      unless he'd seen Hell.[7]

The first issue of the *Journal of the '45 Aid Society* was published in April 1976. The journal was to serve as a means of contact, enabling members to exchange addresses, and publishing articles by the boys about their wartime experiences, and reports of visits made to Europe, and of

---

[7] Michael Etkind, 'The Reunion', *Journal of the '45 Aid Society*, No. 3, April 1977, page 23.

ceremonies attended in Israel and elsewhere. One of the first of these ceremonies to be reported in the journal was the formal opening in December 1976 of the gateway to Yad Vashem, the Holocaust memorial in Jerusalem. The artist of this impressive gateway – through which in due course many Heads of State and Prime Ministers were to pass, including, in 1977, President Sadat of Egypt – was one of the boys, Roman Halter. As a slave labourer in Dresden in early 1945 he had been worked almost to death. On two occasions he had come within a few inches of being killed, once while a slave labourer, and once immediately after liberation. Now his art was to be seen by hundreds of thousands of people every year.

The opening ceremony of the Yad Vashem gates was reported in the boys' journal by one of their number who had gone from Britain to live in Israel, Menachem Waksztok. He had been born in the small Polish town of Klodawa, a mere twenty kilometres from Roman Halter's home town of Chodecz. 'On the morning of December 20,' he reported to the journal, 'my three children were very excited. Today we were taking them to see the work of Romek, whom they know. We arrived to be greeted by most of our Israel Boys and Girls, some of them having come from as far away as Beersheba. It was a most loyal turnout. We greeted one another in the French kiss-on-both-cheeks style, now the accepted thing amongst our group (someone, seeing Brezhnev on TV, asked whether he is also one of our group). With the noise of our "Hellos" – "Ma Shlomech" – "Ma Shlomcha"[8] – and our numbers, we quickly began to dominate the proceedings.' When Roman Halter was asked to participate in the service of dedication 'we, all in the family of Boys and Girls who were there, were overwhelmed with pride for him'.[9]

Roman Halter had worked in Britain as an architect, focusing his work on buildings which had a social importance. He later developed the creation of stained-glass windows, using a laser technique for cutting the metal frames for the glass. His stained-glass work, the main motifs of which are flowers and children, has graced several synagogues and public buildings in Britain. His wife Susie, who had survived the war in Budapest, was living in Britain in 1948 when the Hungarian Olympic Games team co-opted her as a swimmer. She was later the outstanding champion swimmer in the 1950 Maccabiah Games in Israel.

The boys who went to Israel to fight in the War of Independence, and who stayed in Israel after the war, or who emigrated there later, formed their own branch of the '45 Aid Society. One of them, Meir Stern, from Svalava, later reflected: 'Having been like a family in England, I myself

[8] The Hebrew for 'How are you?' (in its masculine and feminine forms).
[9] Menachem Waksztok, 'Letter from Israel', *Journal of the '45 Aid Society*, No. 3, April 1977'.

felt that we should organise ourselves to take care of each other. I had a dream that one day we should have a home – that as we grew older we should relive our Primrose period. We feel very comfortable. Among ourselves we can talk about the past without emotion.'[10]

Moshe Rosenberg, from Cracow, whose father had died on a death march to Theresienstadt less than three weeks before the end of the war, is another of the boys who live in Israel. 'We are together at every wedding and Bar Mitzvah,' he reflected. 'Wherever we meet, "boys will be boys". We're all alike. Wherever we are in the world, we're all the same.'[11]

The comradeship of the present can never eliminate the burden of the past. Icchak Raizman, from Lodz, a Windermere boy who lives today in Israel, would speak only in the most general terms of 'a lot of bad memories'.[12] Behind those five words lay an eternity of suffering.

Sometimes those who did not experience the Holocaust are brought into the circle of the '45 Aid Society. An early honorary member was Shamai Davidson, originally from Scotland, whose psychiatric counselling was of immense importance to the boys, not least because of his sympathetic understanding of their past torments. As the director of the psychiatric centre of the Tel Aviv University medical school, 'he is truly amazed', one boy reported in the journal, 'how normal we all are'.[13]

The question of the 'normality' of the boys was one which much concerned Shamai Davidson and those who worked with him in rehabilitating the survivors of the Holocaust. Barbara Barnett has commented, in a reflection encompassing their whole period of rehabilitation: 'As far as I know, no other survivors on arrival in a host community were treated as a group as these were or offered such a carefully mapped process to assist their rehabilitation and integration. Leonard Montefiore's Committee for the Care of Children from the Concentration Camps and their advisers made an inspired plan; they seem to have based it on a clear philosophy. It was sensitive, realistic and very practical.

'The process: this began in Britain with the Windermere experience, then periods spent scattered across the country in hostels to learn English and be introduced to the British social and cultural scene. There followed individual counselling for The Boys, and their easing into independent living, study and work, with the Primrose Club – in itself a unique

---

[10] Meir Stern, in conversation with the author, 30 December 1994. Meir Stern's son David, who lives in London, is married to a great-granddaughter of Camille Pissarro.

[11] Moshe Rosenberg, in conversation with the author, 30 December 1994.

[12] Icchak Raizman, in conversation with the author, 30 December 1994.

[13] Felix Berger, 'Tel-Aviv Diary', *Journal of the '45 Aid Society*, No. 4, 1978. Shamai Davidson died in 1986, much mourned by the boys, and by those of the Second Generation whom he had helped.

phenomenon – serving as a support system in London after their dispersion from the hostels. Unexpectedly its members demonstrated exceptional prowess at sports events and it became rapidly recognised as a centre of excellence among the existing Jewish youth clubs. This was a quite extraordinary achievement – under the able leadership of Yogi Mayer. Thus was spelt out The Boys' absolute determination to succeed at whatever they did – the mark of the successful survivor.

'The group dynamics: strong "bonding" quickly developed and has stayed steady amongst the majority of the original group – relationships that emerge in times of stress as much as in times of celebration. As in any family, tensions and disagreements wax and wane; there is a sort of "sibling rivalry" – especially among the larger number in relation to those who have widely-known success stories.

'Those of us who became involved with the group had no comparative example, no prior experience to guide us. But it became evident that once opportunities arose, and tools were put in their hands, these "war-damaged" children (to quote Margot Hicklin, who had been involved with The Boys at Windermere) just dashed ahead into full-blown adolescence – rapidly making up for those years of horror when they were literally starved – physically and intellectually, socially and emotionally.

'They wanted only to rediscover normal life and be treated like others who had never known incarceration. Most told us of an early childhood based on a secure foundation, with a settled pattern whatever their social or economic standing. The child, initially protected by the family from the increasingly hostile external world, was suddenly propelled from all that was safe and familiar and incarcerated in unspeakable conditions; yet the memory and experience of those secure early years I believe was a crucial component of that will to survive – at all costs.

'This was unlike survivors who were already young adults in 1940. One I know, for example, shows all the strengths of survival but still wants to be recognised as different, and respected by us for the damage done to her and hers; but almost all The Boys chose not to even mention their camp experiences till they were reaching retirement and their children became independent; by that time they had shown the world that they were Survivors, and had won.'[14]

In his chairman's address at the annual reunion of the '45 Aid Society in 1978, Ben Helfgott expressed the feelings of many of the boys when he declared: 'I have revelled at the thought that despite our experiences, and the early loss of our parents, we are a happily integrated group, our

---

[14] Barbara Barnett, 'Some further thoughts about The Boys', manuscript, sent to the author, 7 April 1996.

family ties are deep and strong in the true Jewish ethical tradition, and above all, our children have been reaching high academic standards.'[15]

The closeness of the boys made a strong impact on those who knew them and had worked with them. Barbara Barnett later reflected: 'One member of the group told me that fifty per cent of his social life was spent with one or other of The Boys and their families. This is true of happy or sad occasions – a Bar Mitzvah, or a tombstone setting. When one member was receiving severely threatening telephone calls from a Fascist group, threatening to burn his shop down, and "send him back home", a whole lot of The Boys came to protect him.'[16]

In May 1978 those boys who had gone to New York from Britain held their own first reunion, a dinner dance like the reunions in London. Many had not been in touch with each other since the days of the hostels and the Primrose Club. Phyllis Vegh, the London-born Jewish girl who had been one of the Primrose Club's frequent visitors, and who had herself moved to New York to marry Maurice Vegh, originally from Rakhov, was among the guests. As she wrote to the Journal in London, the boys were exuberant at meeting again: 'It was great to learn of their achievements in the business world, to hear of their marriages and the families they were raising.'[17]

From the outset, charity had an important place in the work of the '45 Aid Society. Among those to whom money has been sent are Cystic Fibrosis Research and the Tottenham Home for the Incurably Sick. Funds have also been raised for, among other causes, two children's hospitals in Israel: the Micha Society for pre-school deaf and dumb children, and the Alyn Hospital for children with severe disabilities. A former helper at the Loughton hostel, Reuma Weizman, recalled how, immediately after the Six Day War of 1967, when her husband was Deputy Chief of Staff of the Israel Defence Forces, she received a telephone call from Ben Helfgott, who had come out to Israel. 'I was one of the boys in Epping Forest', he told her. 'We're here. We have a small delegation. We have some money we want to give. We hear you have done some voluntary work for deaf children.'

'Why me?' Reuma Weizman asked.

'We want to repay you', was Ben Helfgott's reply. 'We feel we want to repay.'[18]

This element of wishing to repay, and to help others less fortunate

---

[15] 'Chairman's Address', *Journal of the '45 Aid Society*, No. 5, November 1978.

[16] Barbara Barnett, in conversation with the author, 21 March 1996.

[17] Phyllis Vegh (née Fleischer), 'Dear Editor', *Journal of the '45 Aid Society*, No. 6, May 1979, page 22.

[18] Reuma Weizman, recollections, in conversation with the boys (and with the author), London, 5 May 1996.

than themselves, has been an integral part of the character of the society since its foundation. When Elaine Blond, who had done so much to help bring the boys over in 1945, died in 1989, the society donated £5,000 to a charitable cause in Israel that had been dear to her heart. To honour Oscar Joseph, who over the years was their father-figure, the boys donated £5,000 to establish an audiovisual centre at the Wiener Library in London. Another project was to finance a Holocaust research fellowship for a year at the Oxford Centre for Postgraduate Hebrew and Jewish Studies. Help has also been given to the Jerusalem Holocaust memorial – Yad Vashem – for various educational projects.

The charitable donations of the '45 Aid Society are more than a casual aspect of their work. As Ben Helfgott explained, in his speech at the 1977 reunion: 'Originally we only raised funds to help members of our society who for different reasons found themselves in financial difficulties, but as time went on we felt that it would be fitting if we, who were once recipients, were also to become donors in a collective way. I say "collective", as most of us are individually involved in supporting many worthy causes. So, in addition to aiding our needy members, we have, over the years, donated to hospitals in Israel, many charities in England and to the Central British Fund.[19] We have chosen the CBF for it was they who were responsible for bringing us over to this country and since the CBF – unfortunately – continues to be called upon to support Jewish victims of persecution, we are happy to identify ourselves with their work.

'I know that I express a platitude when I say that fund-raising is not a palatable occupation, albeit very necessary. I am pleased to say that we are well supported by our members. I appeal to you all to be even more active in fund-raising and take a collective pride in our society. Remember, your action is a reflection on our society.'[20]

The charitable work which the boys have done, collectively, through the '45 Aid Society, prompted Thelma Marcus, who had seen them at close quarters in the Primrose Club, to comment: 'To give back to other causes – to other refugees – they are to be really applauded.'[21]

In 1985 the boys celebrated the fortieth anniversary of their liberation. Among those who came from afar for the celebratory dinner was Michael Perlmutter, one of the boys who had gone from Windermere to the Ashford Sanatorium, to recover from pneumonia, and who had then lived at the Finchley Road hostel. 'Because of my need to touch someone

---

[19] Later called World Jewish Relief.
[20] Ben Helfgott, 'Chairman's Address', 1977 Reunion.
[21] Thelma Marcus, in conversation with the author, 15 April 1995.

in my family,' he later wrote, 'I left England for America, where my brother waited.' But he was determined to return across the Atlantic for the reunion. 'What a glorious experience that was, stirring and tearful,' he recalled. 'That event again solidified our bonds. It was as though we had never left each other, my friends of Windermere and I.'[22] After that reunion dinner, 110 of the boys travelled to Israel, where a gathering of more than 300 survivors from Britain celebrated the fortieth anniversary of their liberation. 'We were the second largest contingent,' their annual minutes noted with some pride, 'and no other group was as cohesive or close.'[23]

That year, many members of the '45 Aid Society also participated in activities connected with the fortieth anniversary of the ending of the Second World War. Victor Greenberg and Minia Jay were interviewed on television with regard to the liberation of Auschwitz. Mala Tribich was taken to Bergen-Belsen to be filmed there. Roman Halter was active in helping to mount an anniversary exhibition at the Wiener Library, and in designing a memorial at Waltham Abbey to the murdered six million. Also that year, in a symbolic act, the society donated £732 to the Central British Fund, 'representing £1 for each of us who came here to England under the auspices of the Fund'.[24]

For many years, it has been to the Central British Fund that the main charitable donations of the society have gone. The members of the society are tenacious in remembering those to whom they owe their foundations in England. Of particular pride to the boys was that one of their number, their chairman Ben Helfgott, became treasurer of the Fund, a post held earlier by two of those whom the boys most admired, Leonard Montefiore and Oscar Joseph.

Over the years, the '45 Aid Society welcomed to its gatherings, and into its ranks, those survivors who were not part of the original group of 732 boys, but who reached Britain afterwards, in different ways. Most of them had made their way to England in 1946 or later. They found comfort in the society, and, some, salvation. Here was a welcoming group of people, many of their own age, a few younger, with whom they had many shared experiences, so difficult – if not impossible – for those who had not been through them to understand.

Joseph Kiersz was born in the small Polish town of Uniejow. His father died young, three years after his marriage, leaving three tiny children, Rachel, Joseph, and Yehuda. An uncle, Charlie Lando, who lived in

[22] Michael (Meier) Perlmutter, 'Here and Now', *Journal of the '45 Aid Society*, No. 18, May 1979, page 9.
[23] Minutes of the 22nd Annual General Meeting of the '45 Aid Society, London, 7 July 1985.
[24] Minutes of the 22nd Annual General Meeting of the '45 Aid Society, London, 7 July 1985.

Cricklewood, London, having emigrated to Britain at the age of thirteen, sent the family £1 a week in the 1930s – 'we all lived very comfortably off it,' Joseph Kiersz recalled. During the terrible years of the Holocaust, his mother, brother and sister perished. Joseph never forgot the word 'Cricklewood'. Soon after being liberated by the British, he was able to use the Forces Mail to make contact with his uncle, whom he joined in London in 1947. Later he linked up with the boys, at whose meetings and reunions he is a frequent attender.[25]

Sam Pivnik had been born in the Polish town of Bedzin and deported to Auschwitz: of his parents, grandparents, five brothers and two sisters, only he and his brother Nat survived. They came to Britain in 1946. After fighting in Israel's War of Independence, Sam Pivnik returned to London. 'I had no hostel or family to go to,' he recalled. 'I was not protected by Montefiore or Dr Schonfeld. There were times in London when my brother and I went hungry as we had no family or friends to advise us on anything.'[26] For Sam and Nat Pivnik, the '45 Aid Society became a source of comfort and a haven of friendship.

Some of those who joined the '45 Aid Society had survived, like Lea Goodman, because they were hidden by Christian families; in her case, first in Poland and then in Slovakia. She was only four when the war began. Her father was killed by the Germans. After being liberated by the Russians in Slovakia, she and her mother moved first to France and then, in 1952, to England. 'I joined the '45s by asking if they would have me. It was as simple as that,' she later wrote.[27]

Also coming to England independently was Ken Roman, from the southern Polish town of Gorlice. It was on 14 August 1942 that the inhabitants of the Gorlice ghetto had been assembled in the market square. The majority, seven hundred, were then deported to Belzec and to their immediate death. Sixty were selected to remain in Gorlice, to work in the sawmill. Ken Roman was one of them. Later he was sent to the slave labour camp at Mielec, working in the aircraft factory there. After the war he reached Italy, from where, having joined the Polish army as a cadet, and without divulging that he was Jewish, he made his way to Britain in the summer of 1946. His first job was as a bicycle delivery boy for a delicatessen shop. A year later one of the customers to whom he delivered invited him to breakfast, quizzed him about his experiences, and offered him a job in his engineering establishment. Ken Roman worked there for seventeen years.[28]

It was in 1947 that Laib Rosenstrauch reached England, where he

[25] Joseph Kiersz, in conversation with the author, 12 May 1996.
[26] Sam Pivnik, letter to the author, July 1995.
[27] Lea Goodman, letter to the author, 20 March 1995.
[28] Ken Roman, 'Recollections by Ken Roman', manuscript, sent to the author, 23 February 1995.

took the name Leo Robeson. Most of his family, including his father, had been killed in Lodz soon after the German army entered the city. 'We met at a Primrose Club dance,' recalled Salek Benedikt, his childhood friend from before the war. 'It was he who recognised me at once, and our mutual joy knew no bounds. Since I was separated from my family before the establishment of the ghetto, Leo was able to tell me how my family fared during this period, as he used to see them quite often. We never tired of exchanging childhood experiences and reminiscences of life in Lodz before the war.'[29]

Morris Frenkel was nineteen when the war ended. He had an uncle living in Britain, and, coming to London on 23 June 1947, was met by him at Victoria Station. 'He came over to me and said, "Are you Moniek Frenkel?" and I said, "Yes". This was the end of the journey.'[30] Later that year Morris Frenkel joined the Primrose Club. He has been a member of the '45 Aid Society since its foundation. 'I am the only other survivor of my family,' he wrote. 'My mother had six sisters, and families; my father had two brothers, and families: they all perished.' His mother, sister and brother had been taken straight to the gas chambers after they had been deported, with him, from the Lodz ghetto to Auschwitz. 'I was selected to work with the men. I survived the hard work, the beatings, the selections.'[31]

Michael Lee also reached Britain in 1947, after the Red Cross had managed to trace two uncles and an aunt who had emigrated to Britain between the wars. Born in Lodz in 1924, he had survived the Lodz ghetto, deportation to Auschwitz (where he was given the tattoo number B8405), slave labour at Gleiwitz, the death marches from there to Gross Rosen, Buchenwald, and Allach – a sub-camp of Dachau. Liberated by the Americans, he had spent two years at the Displaced Persons camp at Feldafing before coming to Britain to join his family at the age of twenty-three. 'Having no skills, I started work at a handbag factory where I learned the trade, earning £4 a week. After several years I opened my own factory.'[32]

Another of those who later became members of the society, and who came to Britain in 1947, was Toby Trompeter. Born in the Polish town of Mielec, she had been an eyewitness of both the first German atrocities there and the day of deportation. Sent from Mielec to Plaszow, she later wrote of how, in July 1943, 'my sister Sarah and I were deported from Plaszow to Auschwitz. My Auschwitz number was A-17537. From

[29] Salek Benedikt, 'Leo Robeson (Laib Rosenstrauch)', obituary, *Journal of the '45 Aid Society*, No. 18, December 1994.

[30] Morris (Moniek) Frenkel, letter to the author, 18 September 1995.

[31] Morris (Moniek) Frenkel, letter to the author, 3 September 1995.

[32] Michael Lee, letter to the author, July 1995.

Auschwitz, in the autumn of 1944, we were deported to Bergen-Belsen. My dear sister and I were liberated on 15 April 1945. Unfortunately she died eight days after liberation. I had to stay on at Belsen.'[33]

Toby Trompeter remained in Belsen as a Displaced Person for more than two years. 'Nobody wanted us,' she recalled. Then she met a Jewish soldier in the Polish army, himself originally from the Polish town of Zamosc. 'In 1946 I met my husband Max who was serving with the Polish army under the British command. We married in Belsen on 7 August 1946.' Later they travelled together to Britain. 'When I arrived,' she later recalled, 'I went to a Polish army camp in Wiltshire.'[34] She had lost her four sisters, her parents and her grandparents in the Holocaust. Of her immediate family, only her two brothers survived.

Joe Perl was born in the small Ruthenian town of Bochkov. In 1940 his family was deported to Poland, where he witnessed the shooting of his mother Freida and four of his eight sisters: Frimid, Rivka, Leah and Priva. 'We were a religious family,' he reflected. 'All the hopes my parents had for their children came to an end.' His father survived the war, living after it behind the Iron Curtain; father and son only discovered each other's existence nineteen years after liberation. Two of his surviving sisters made their way to Israel. After reaching Britain on his own, he was briefly at the Jews' Temporary Shelter, but then spent four years in hospital. It was only in later years that he made contact with the boys; today he is a regular attender at the meetings of their Society. 'I came back into the fold', he commented.[35]

Eve Oppenheimer was liberated by the Russians on the Elbe. In 1936, her mother, who had lived in Berlin before the war, had gone to London for her daughter's birth. Eve Oppenheimer was therefore a British subject. But her mother returned to Europe after her birth, and when war came, she and her parents were in Holland, which the Germans overran in May 1940. Her four grandparents, also from Germany, had joined them in Holland; they were deported to Sobibor and murdered there in July 1943. Later Eve and her mother and father were sent to Belsen, where her parents died. She herself was liberated in Belsen at the age of eight. An uncle of hers was then serving in the British army. He took her back to Britain in September 1945 – a month after the boys, whose society she was later to join, had been flown to Carlisle. For two years she lived with her uncle and aunt in London; then she went to Lingfield House to be looked after by Alice Goldberger and 'Gertrude, Sophie and Susie. They were the greatest help to us all.'[36]

[33] Toby Biber (née Trompeter), recollections, sent to the author, 7 May 1996.

[34] Toby Biber (née Trompeter), in conversation with the author, 12 March 1996.

[35] Joe Perl, in conversation with the author, 12 May 1996.

[36] Eve Oppenheimer, 'A Briton in Belsen', manuscript, sent to the author, 15 August 1995.

Liberated in Buchenwald by the Americans, Mark Goldfinger went from there to France. While in France he discovered that his father was in England, with the Polish-Jewish ex-servicemen. His father brought him to Britain. With his terrible experiences of slave labour at Biezanow, Prokocim, Plaszow and Skarzysko-Kamienna, Mark had much in common with the boys, and soon became a part of their meetings and reunions. As a youngster he had lived in the resort town of Rabka Zdroj, in the hill country south of Cracow, the town in which Arthur Poznanski had spent his summer holidays before the war.

From the age of nine, Mark Goldfinger could remember the terrors perpetrated by the Nazis in Rabka. In what had been the Roman Catholic High School for Girls, the SS set up a training school for SS and Ukrainian units, usually brought there five hundred at a time, in preparation for the murder of Jews in occupied Russia. The SS training was not theoretical. 'Jews were snatched off the streets,' he recalled. 'They were then subjected to terrifying humiliations and torture before being killed. Often they were buried in pits while still alive.' His own grandmother was murdered there. 'Our house was situated only a few hundred yards from that school complex, so that the firing of guns – or sometimes, depending on the wind direction, the screaming of people – could clearly be heard in our apartment.' On a single day, 26 May 1942, the commander of the training school, Wilhelm Rosenbaum, 'personally shot approximately seventy people. Whilst the executions were in progress, he was seen to laugh continuously.'[37]

Mark Goldfinger feels, as do many of those in the '45 Aid Society, that the terrible events of a particular town or camp – in his case Rabka Zdroj – are not sufficiently widely known. One reason is that in almost every such case there were no – or almost no – survivors, and few witnesses. He has done everything possible to set the record straight.

Although most of the boys are positive in their outlook on the past, a few remain to this day bitter and angry with the Germans. 'The scars of my past experience can never leave my subconscious mind,' Barbara Stimler – who had been deported from the Lodz ghetto to Auschwitz, and both of whose parents, Jacob and Sarah Krakowski, had perished – wrote fifty years later. 'If ever a cataclysm were to befall this world, and I was to be the victim, I would be happy in the knowledge that the German nation has been wiped off the face of this earth.'[38]

Edyta Smith was born and brought up in Warsaw. At the time of the deportations in 1942, when she was thirteen years old, she was able to

---

[37] Mark Goldfinger, 'Historical Information on Rabka Zdroj (Spa), Poland, 1939–1945', manuscript, sent to the author, September 1995.

[38] Barbara Stimler (Krakowski), 'The Holocaust Experience and Autobiography of Barbara Stimler', manuscript, sent to the author, 27 August 1995.

leave the ghetto with her mother, some months before the uprising. 'We lived in fear as Christians,' she later wrote, 'and watched the ghetto burning.' Her father was deported from a slave labour camp in Warsaw to Poniatowa, and murdered there during the 'Harvest Festival', seven months after the ghetto uprising was crushed. In the years before the uprising, half a million Jews had been trapped in the Warsaw ghetto. Edyta Smith was among the few hundred who survived. She was liberated by the Russians. Reaching Britain some years later, she recalled how impressed she was by the members of the '45 Aid Society – 'their togetherness, trying to be a family, with the '45s as the roots'.[39]

Another survivor of the Warsaw ghetto who joined the '45s was Rena Zabielak. Like Edyta Smith, she had managed to find sanctuary in Christian Warsaw. She too had seen from afar the ghetto in flames at the time of the uprising. 'Often I contacted my father, begging him to escape,' she recalled, 'but the same reply always returned, that he was like the captain of a ship, and until everything was prepared and every man was saved, he would not leave.'[40] Her father, Yechiel Channoch Litwak, was killed after throwing a grenade on a German military vehicle from the top of a building in the ghetto that was about to be blown up.

Brought to Britain by someone from his home town who had arrived just before the war, Heniek Kawalek (Henry Kaye) from Konin had lost both his parents and his only brother. He too found comfort among the ranks of the '45 Aid Society. He also helped Theo Richmond, the historian of Konin Jewry, with recollections of life in Konin before the war. But both he and his wife Sala, herself a survivor and a member of the society, were unable to leave out their wartime experiences when talking to the historian. 'It's a shadow hanging over our lives,' she reflected. 'After talking about this today, I shall have nightmares for weeks. We have been marked for life.'[41]

Most of those in the '45 Aid Society had lost all their relatives in the war. One of these was Harry Braffman, the only member of the society from Vilna. 'He was the only survivor of his family,' Ben Helfgott has written, 'and had no relatives of any kind anywhere in the world. His only family substitutes were members of our society, and it was only to be expected that they would be the largest contingent of mourners at his funeral.'[42]

Among those who joined the '45 Aid Society, and who soon became

---

[39] Edyta Smith (née Klein), letter to the author, 28 April 1995.

[40] Rena Zabielak (née Litwak), 'Resistance', manuscript, sent to the author, 4 September 1995.

[41] Sala Kaye, quoted in Theo Richmond, *Konin, A Quest*, Jonathan Cape, London, 1995, page 35.

[42] Ben Helfgott, 'Harry Braffman', obituary, *Journal of the '45 Aid Society*, No. 16, Pessach 5754/1994.

one of its leading supporters, was Jack Kagan. He was born the furthest east of any of the boys, at Novogrudek, in what was then eastern Poland, was later the Soviet Union, and is today Belarus. Novogrudek had first been annexed by the Soviet Union in October 1939, as a result of the Nazi-Soviet Pact, when Jack was ten years old. It was later overrun by the German army immediately after the German invasion of the Soviet Union in June 1941.

Many of the Jews of Novogrudek were murdered by a special SS killing squad on 8 December 1941. By chance, this was the first day on which the Jews of the Lodz region were murdered in the gas vans of Chelmno. By early 1944 Jack Kagan's mother, father, sister and grandmother had all been killed, in a series of murder actions in which the local German SS would take Jews out of the ghetto and shoot them down. In the east, there were few deportations to distant death camps: the killing was done in woods or ditches on the outskirts of the town.

At one moment, in the freezing winter, Jack Kagan's frostbitten toes had to be amputated. 'There was no doctor, no medicine, no bandages, nothing,' he wrote. Four people held him down while a dentist performed the amputation. 'It was not so painful when he cut the flesh, but when he used tooth pliers for the bones, it was agony.'

After the war Jack Kagan wanted to go to Palestine. Many of his survivor friends did so, travelling on the immigrant ship *Exodus*. 'I was rejected because of my feet. So I made my decision to go to England and try from there.' A cousin of his, from the town of Karelicze, near Novogrudek, had lived in England since 1938, when she had come to study; he obtained permission to join her, arriving in London on 23 June 1947, and has lived in England ever since. One of his sons did go to live in Israel, as Jack Kagan had himself hoped to do, 'and so', he wrote, 'my wife and I have four Israeli grandchildren'.[43]

Following the collapse of Communist rule in 1991, and the break-up of the Soviet Union, Jack Kagan made a tremendous and successful effort to persuade his home town to put up a memorial to the murdered Jews. He also has a film of pre-war Jewish life in Novogrudek, which he shows at memorial and educational gatherings. In the '45 Aid Society's fiftieth anniversary brochure, he took a whole page to list his eighteen closest relatives murdered in Novogrudek between 1941 and 1943, among them his grandmother Gitl Gurevitz, his forty-year-old mother Dvorah Kagan, and his seventeen-year-old sister Nachama. Also murdered was his fourteen-year-old cousin and best friend, Leizer Kagan.

Jack Kagan's father, Jankiel Kagan, had been killed in February 1944, while escaping from the nearby slave labour camp at Koldichevo. He

---

[43] Jack Kagan, 'Lucky to be alive', manuscript, sent to the author, 1995.

was then forty-three years old. Underneath the list of his murdered relatives – on which the youngest person was his eight-year-old cousin Nochim Kapushevski – Jack Kagan added the words: 'Not to forgive and not to forget.'[44]

The members of the '45 Aid Society are vigilant in preserving the memory of their murdered loved ones. At all their reunions, those memories are revived, and a sense of common purpose prevails: 'Not to forget'.

Reunions are an important part of the life and fellowship of the boys, who had celebrated the first anniversary of their liberation at the Stern Hall in London in 1946, and the fifth anniversary at the Refectory in Golders Green four years later. Their tenth anniversary reunion was held in a hall off Leicester Square in 1955, and their twentieth in a hall in Kilburn in 1965. At their twenty-fifth anniversary reunion in 1970, many of the boys, now with their wives, came from many lands. At each of these reunions, men and women who were embarking on their careers, and then slowly building them, came together to recall the miracle of their own survival, and the tragedy of the murder of so many of their loved ones. 'What happened to us cannot be buried,' one of the boys, Joshua Segal from Toronto, has written, 'and I realise that it is important to remember, so that others should not forget. No one should ever forget.'[45]

In 1975 the boys celebrated the thirtieth anniversary of their liberation. One of those who had helped them from their earliest moments in Britain, Lola Hahn-Warburg, wrote the next morning, in her letter of thanks: 'I was moved by the spirit of brotherhood. I feel deeply your dedication and your deep gratitude that a miracle saved you all. Coming home last night, I looked through your brochure, and read all the tributes, and feel that when I cast my mind back over those thirty years, it was that noble personality of Leonard Montefiore, and Oscar Friedmann, with whom I worked so closely, who guided you all. I feel so often in life, when you give you receive. Last night, the few of us who were there thirty years ago received in abundance.'[46]

In a '45 Aid Society newsletter, specially prepared for the thirtieth anniversary gathering, Ben Helfgott wrote of the successes of the members of the society over the previous thirty years, 'extending from a trade union leader to a millionaire'. However, he added, 'our greatest

[44] ''45 Society (Holocaust Survivors) 50th Annual Dinner and Ball', *Souvenir Brochure*, 30 April 1995.

[45] Joshua Segal (Jehoszua Cygelfarb), letter to the author, 17 February 1995.

[46] Lola Hahn-Warburg, letter, quoted in her obituary notice, *Journal of the '45 Aid Society*, No. 14, May 1990. Lola Hahn-Warburg was eighty-eight when she died.

achievement and tremendous source of pride is that we can boast of having no delinquents, criminals, revenge-seekers and above all, none of us is consumed with hatred and venom. On the contrary, most of us are imbued with a deep sense of purpose, compassion and responsibility to our fellow citizens. Our children, having been permeated with these values and growing up in an atmosphere of love and serenity, are well on the road to success – some have gained scholarships to universities and others have already attained their degrees.'[47]

One of the boys who had been able to pursue an academic career, Kurt Klappholz, commented in this same newsletter: 'For us, the anniversary of our liberation is literally a second birthday anniversary. The liberation not only snatched us from certain death, it also ended a period during which, though physiologically alive, it could hardly be said that we had lived. Thus our celebration commemorates a communal resurrection, which is one of the bonds that has united us hitherto, and will continue to unite us until not one of us is left to celebrate another anniversary.'

In this article Kurt Klappholz also grappled with a problem that troubles all the boys, and all survivors: that of attitudes towards the murderers of their families and friends. 'We have no alternative,' he wrote, 'but to live with the memory of lives gratuitously and wickedly destroyed. Each one of us has to decide for himself how to cope with these memories, for which time does not seem to be the proverbial healer.' These memories, he believes, 'do not lead us to bear grudges against, or feel hatred towards, individual people merely because they are members of a particular group (e.g. Germans). Had we succumbed to such feelings we would have provided our erstwhile persecutors with an entirely gratuitous victory, for we would have adopted *their* attitudes. Our own history testifies to the fact that we did not succumb in this way. This is one of the victories our erstwhile persecutors did not achieve.

'There is no escaping the fact that our celebration is not only a celebration; it is also, always was and will be, an occasion for reliving the most painful memories and for saying a uniquely bitter Kaddish.'[48]

Wherever the boys went to live, they made their contributions to their new land. None went back to live in Eastern Europe. In their early years after liberation, almost none of them wanted to visit the scenes of their youth and torment. As time passed, however, opportunities arose which were tempting, despite the pain of returning. Krulik Wilder recalled how, in 1983, he and his wife Gloria, together with a few other boys, and

[47] Ben Helfgott, 'Yesterday's Recipients, Today's Donors', *News Letter*, Autumn 1974.
[48] Kurt Klappholz, 'On celebrating the 30th anniversary of our liberation', *News Letter*, Autumn 1974.

with several senior members of the Board of Deputies of British Jews – of which Ben Helfgott was a member – went to Warsaw for a special service of commemoration on the fortieth anniversary of the Warsaw ghetto revolt. 'This was the first time I had returned to Poland since the end of the war,' Krulik Wilder wrote. 'Poland was still under the control of the Communists and the atmosphere was very tense. The ceremony itself was very impressive in front of the monument dedicated to the fighters of the Warsaw ghetto uprising.

'The next day a few of us – including my wife and two other "boys" – went back to my town, Piotrkow, and returned to my apartment. My feelings were traumatic and electric, to say the least. There it was, exactly as I remembered, with very little change. The young man who now lived there was very excited after I told him that I and my family had lived there forty-two years ago. He invited us in, and the memories and sounds all came back to me. We walked all around the town, and saw on the door-posts the holes where the *mezzuzahs* once were.[49] The town looked more shabby and the houses unpainted and derelict, and I am very pleased I don't live there any more.

'We all went to visit the synagogue, which is now a public library, and a lady showed us a wall hidden by a curtain with the Ten Commandments painted on it. The bullet holes were still there where the Germans had lined up the people against this wall and shot them. That brought back the most dreadful memories. All I could picture was my mother and sister standing there. I could hear the people screaming and crying, and I tried to describe to my wife and friends just what it had been like, but I could not. I just broke down crying.

'We went to visit Auschwitz. This was the first time I had been to that camp. Walking around the camp was horrendous. I could see the corpses lying around. The guide was telling us as we were walking that we were walking on human ashes. On our return to Warsaw we were drained, and I am sure everyone was ready to leave Poland. I know I was.'[50]

The two other boys who were with Krulik Wilder on his journey back to Piotrkow were Ben Helfgott and Moishe Malenicky, who had become a successful caterer and property owner in London; in Piotrkow his father had been a baker and pastry-cook.

'The houses and streets are still the same,' Ben Helfgott wrote, 'except that they are older and look more shabby and drab. It was a strange

---

[49] The *mezzuzah* is a small ornamental wooden or metal box, containing a prayer written on a small piece of paper or parchment, which Jews affix to their front door, and to the door posts of other rooms in the house, as instructed in the Torah: 'These my words ... And thou shalt write them upon the door posts of thine house, and upon thy gates' (Deuteronomy 11:20).

[50] Israel (Krulik) Wilder, 'Krulik's Story,' manuscript, sent to the author, 1 January 1995.

sensation to walk in familiar places with memories and thoughts flooding back in torrents. The hustle and bustle, that ubiquitous hallmark of the prevailing pre-war scene, was conspicuously absent, but every nook, every cranny reminded us of a life that had ceased to exist long ago. There were people walking in the streets, but to us they seemed strange and faceless. We seemed surrounded by shadows and a sea of voices which returned to us for a few precious moments. Entire families, who disappeared without a trace and for whom there is no one to say Kaddish, vividly stood before our eyes. Sad as it may seem, it was nevertheless an exhilarating experience, as we realised that they have not been forgotten, that in our thoughts they were still there.

'As we walked along we kept on remarking to one another, Krulik, Malenicky and I, "Do you remember Cederbaum's bookshop and his printing works renowned for printing Jewish prayer books, the Yesodah Hatorah cheder, the Maria Konopnicka Jewish elementary school, the Gomolinski family, the Ajzensztejns?" and so on. Of course, we went to our famous synagogue which has, indeed, a special and most horrifying tale to tell.'[51]

In a talk at Oxford in 1985, when the boys celebrated the fortieth anniversary of their liberation, Ben Helfgott reflected on their state of mind, their aspirations, and their links to the past. 'I have lived a full life,' he told a university audience, 'and taken part in everything available to me in the way of sport, culture, and socially. I think of myself as an all-round, integrated person. But the time I went through between the ages of ten and fifteen I do not want to forget. If I did forget it, I would not consider myself worthy of being a survivor. Of the thirty-two boys and girls in my class at school I am the only one alive today – apart from one girl who is utterly broken by those experiences. So, as I was fortunate enough to survive, the least I can do is to inform the world of what happened to my family and my friends. This is how most of us feel about it. This is what is important now.

'We are interested in building a new life. Just as soldiers, after fighting a war, want to build a new life, so we consider this our duty and responsibility. The majority of us have led our lives with the past example of our parents in mind. Our children, for instance, are brought up in homes where they hardly realise what their parents have been through in concentration camps. They are developing as healthy and well-integrated young people. I am very pleased to say that at least sixty to seventy per cent of children of survivors have gone to university or into

[51] Ben Helfgott, 'The Commemoration of the Warsaw Ghetto Rising in Warsaw', *Journal of the '45 Aid Society*, No. 11, April 1984, page 9. Moishe Malenicky, a boy from Piotrkow, became a successful caterer and property owner in London.

higher education, a far higher percentage than in any other group. Now they are on the road to making their own way, building on what their parents have established.'[52]

In 1988 the boys were deeply saddened by the death of the President of the '45 Aid Society, Oscar Joseph. He was eighty-seven years old, and had been associated with the boys from their very first years in Britain. As President of their society he had been particularly supportive. 'He was the very paragon of good manners, unobtrusive, easily approachable, and ready to proffer wise and practical counsel,' Ben Helfgott wrote in the obituary notice in the journal. 'He took immense pride in our achievements and derived great pleasure from attending all our functions.'[53]

It was my good fortune to have been asked to succeed Oscar Joseph as the society's President, and to have been their guest at all their subsequent annual reunions, each of which has proved to be an exceptionally lively event in my calendar.

Jona Fuks, who had emigrated to the United States in 1953, and had became a trade union leader in Philadelphia, returned to Poland for the first time in 1989, fifty years after war and destruction had come to his home town of Tuszyn, and its Jewish inhabitants. He made the journey with his wife, two of his daughters, and his son-in-law. 'I took them to see the house where we lived,' he later wrote, 'but it was no longer there. The entire block where all the Jews of the town had lived had been erased. All the buildings were gone. The synagogue and the Bet Hamidrash[54] where we prayed were gone. They had even changed the names of the streets in the section of the town where we Jews lived.

'We went to the school which I had attended when I was a young boy. It's still there. We went into the classroom where I had been a student and we saw the bench where I had sat more than fifty years ago. I wrote my name and a message in Polish on the blackboard for the students, who were on their summer vacation at the time.

'I showed my family the pump that I had used to get water for my mother, since we didn't have running water in the house. I showed them the type of outhouse toilet that we had where a farmer would come twice a year to empty it and use what he got for fertiliser. It was very difficult for them to believe that I had been brought up in those conditions. It was hard for me to believe it too.

[52] Ben Helfgott, 'The Story of the '45 Aid Society', lecture, Oxford University Jewish Society, Oxford, Hilary Term, 1985.

[53] Ben Helfgott, 'Henry Oscar Joseph, OBE', *Journal of the '45 Aid Society*, No. 13, May 1989.

[54] Study house.

'I walked through the town looking for someone who would remember me or my family. I thought that I might find an old school friend or someone who knew my family or my uncles. I found only one person in the entire town who remembered the Fuks family. This man had known my father and my uncles, and in fact he lived in the house which had belonged to one of my uncles. He didn't admit that the house had belonged to my uncle, and I didn't want to argue with him because I didn't want him to think that I had come to take the property from him.

'We went to visit the place where we had a summer home and a general store. There used to be a dancehall and music and a lake where I learned how to swim. It's all gone. There is nothing there today but a swamp. Today there is a group of squatters living on that land. No one takes care of the place. These squatters are too preoccupied with getting food to feed themselves and their families to worry about how the area looks.

'Walking through the town was like being in a dream. It was very eerie. It's impossible to describe exactly how I felt. My family could not quite believe that we were actually in the places where I had been raised, and neither could I. There were ghosts in that town for me. I could see the field where we played football. I could see all of the friends I had grown up with. I saw all of my family. I saw my father and my mother and all of my aunts and uncles. Each of these families had a house of their own and a factory where they worked. I had dozens of cousins in that town back in the 1930s. We all knew each other and loved each other. The school, the town hall and the police station are still there, but the Jews are all gone. The town is the same, but all of the Jews are gone and my remembrance of them has been all but erased. Even the Jewish cemetery, where generations of Jews were buried, is gone. The gravestones have been used in the town for doorsteps. The last vestige of any existence of Jew in that town has been removed.'[55]

In 1990 Chaim Olmer returned for the first time to his home town of Sosnowiec. There he met a Polish woman who remembered his family. As they talked, she told him that she recalled, during the war years, seeing an SS man 'eating an apple, shoot one of our neighbours, and continue eating the apple as if nothing had happened'.[56]

In 1991 Maurice Vegh returned for the first time to his home town of Rakhov, in the Carpathians. 'For forty years I didn't want to talk about the Holocaust,' he reflected. 'Then I took my wife with me. I wanted to show her that I am not just a "Holocaust survivor". I came

---

[55] John Fox (Jona Fuks), recollections, Gala Recognition Dinner brochure, Hilton Hotel, Philadelphia, 8 September 1993.
[56] Chaim Olmer, letter to the author, 1 November 1995.

from somewhere. I was somebody before I was a Holocaust survivor. I once had a home, a family, a mother, a father, a sister, uncles and aunts, friends, religion; I was somebody. We were happy in our home town. We were excelling. I am not just a "survivor". We spoke Yiddish. The non-Jewish boys in the town learned Yiddish to play with us.'

Returning to Rakhov, Maurice Vegh quickly found his former house. 'But it was not my house. They had pulled it down and built another in its place. This is where I had lived until I went to the railroad track. There was not one Jew left in Rakhov, not one. As I looked at where my house had been, the people in the houses next to it were hiding. They thought I was coming back to claim their property. Then a neighbour came out and took us in for tea and biscuits. She took out some pictures. One was of her daughter with whom I used to play as a young boy. There had been very little progress in the town. The houses still had outside toilets. I went to the synagogue where I had celebrated my Bar Mitzvah. It was still standing – it was a warehouse. I cried my eyes out.'[57]

Maurice Vegh was only thirteen when, a few months after his Bar Mitzvah, he and his family were deported to Auschwitz. Two years after his return visit to Rakhov the synagogue building was pulled down. The municipality wanted to build a church, and needed the bricks.

Many of the boys went back to Poland in 1993 for the fiftieth anniversary of the Warsaw ghetto revolt. For Jack Rubinfeld, as for most of those on that journey, it was the first time they had been in Poland since the war. 'Until I read in the journal of this upcoming trip,' he wrote, 'I had no intentions of ever setting foot in Poland again. Only the lure of spending time with the "boys" prompted my agreeing to make this trip.' There were some bad moments. 'In Warsaw and Lublin I encountered a fair amount of unfriendly faces; both silent and vocal. That sobered me up in a hurry. I hope they were a minority.' Returning to his home town of Bircza, and recognising his house, his school and his neighbourhood ('everything was much smaller than I remembered'), Jack Rubinfeld recalled the irony that when the Catholic children called out 'Christ killer', 'Judas', and 'mangy yid' at the Jewish children, neither group of children was aware that Jesus and Judas were both Jews.[58]

For Krulik Wilder, the 1993 journey was his second visit to Poland. 'This time the atmosphere was different,' he wrote. 'No more Communist rule, and there were many people from all over the world. Particularly exciting was to see a contingent of three thousand teenagers from Israel

[57] Maurice (Moritz) Vegh, in conversation with the author, 3 May 1996.
[58] Jack Rubinfeld, letter to the author, 26 March 1996.

all waving the Israeli flag. This time instead of going to Auschwitz I went to Treblinka concentration camp, which in a way is even more horrific than Auschwitz. While I was standing near the railway tracks I could only visualise trains arriving daily loaded with Jews for extermination. Treblinka has no houses or barracks, just stones, all shapes and sizes, each one representing a town or village wherever Jews lived. It was disturbing to me to stand among all those stones and rocks, and I was relieved to return to Warsaw.

'The day after that we went back to Piotrkow. We visited the Hortensja glass factory. One of the ladies who showed us around in the factory told us that there is a register with the names of all the people who worked there during the war, and she very kindly allowed us to look through it.

'The date was 20th April 1993. I remembered my father was born in 1900, but I had no idea of the day or the month. On opening the register I noticed that my father's date of birth was 20th April. I was very excited to find out his birthday, but I was even more overwhelmed at the thought that the date of my visit to the Huta Hortensja coincided with that of my father's date of birth.

'We walked around the town remembering every cobble, every stone where we played as children. I could not return to our old apartment as they were renovating it and no one was living there. There was a happy occasion on this visit to Piotrkow, as we joined up with our American friends from Piotrkow; they had come to put a plaque in the synagogue in memory of the people who were murdered in the synagogue. As I was one of the survivors from the synagogue, I was honoured to unveil the plaque. After the ceremony we were entertained for lunch by the local dignitaries. They made us very welcome and in the evening a dinner and reception was given in our honour.

'Among the guests was a Pole who was invited to meet us. During the war he had saved two Jews, but he did not wish to have any publicity about this, as this would make him unpopular amongst the Poles. It was a painful reminder to me that even without Jews there is still anti-Semitism in Poland. During dinner in the evening our friend Ben Giladi from New York played the piano, entertaining us with Yiddish, Israeli and Polish songs. It was a very joyous occasion as the Poles also joined in the chorus. I am sure they enjoyed the humorous atmosphere as much as we did.'[59] Like Krulik Wilder, and like forty other of the boys, Ben Giladi was from Piotrkow; he is the editor of a journal of recollections of his home town.[60]

---

[59] Israel (Krulik) Wilder, 'Krulik's Story', manuscript, sent to author, 1 January 1995.

[60] *New Bulletin*, published by the Piotrkow Trubunalski Relief Association (established for First World War refugees in 1914), New York. The forty-third issue was published in May–June 1996.

Also returning to Poland in April 1993, and doing so for the first time since the war, was Bernard Dreihorn, originally from Lodz. His father had died in the Lodz ghetto, his mother and sister had perished after the deportation from Lodz to Auschwitz, and both his brothers had died shortly before liberation. He had come to Britain in 1948, to join an aunt who had lived in London since before the war, and he had quickly become a member of the circle of boys. On that 1993 visit to Poland he and his wife Ruby – who was born in Manchester – travelled to Lodz. 'For me,' Ruby Dreihorn recalled, 'it brought back to reality all the stories I had listened to over the years.' As for her husband, 'I think that although he was fine whilst he was in Poland, the trip made a very deep impression on him, and reawakened a lot of unpleasant memories which he had previously let lie dormant.'

Bernard Dreihorn died ten months later. 'His ties with the "boys" grew stronger as the years went by,' his wife wrote, 'and for me they were a tower of strength when he passed away in February 1994.'[61]

For more than ten years, Ruby Dreihorn has been the secretary of the '45 Aid Society, indispensable for the smooth functioning of the organisation, its events and its reunions.

Memorial meetings, anniversaries and reunions are often painful. Perec Zylberberg, the boy from Lodz who lives in Montreal, noted in his diary his thoughts during a visit to Miami in January 1993, with his sister Esther, herself one of the British 'boys'. 'We both managed to see a lot of old friends and acquaintances. Some of those encounters were highly emotional. Esther saw friends and distant relatives that she hadn't seen since the end of the war. Some since even before the war. In each case it was close to half a century. What an encounter. She must surely have felt very elevated and excited. I felt good for her. I also got emotional and sentimental. All in all, it was "some happening".

'A recurrent theme in all those highly charged conversations was of course the war, the ghetto, camps and the war's end. It can't be helped. It crops up almost imperceptibly, whenever people meet. We, the generation of survivors of this most cruel war, can't shake off its impact. Sometimes I try to stay clear of conversations, where details of horrible events are brought out. Consciously, I want to think of the beauty of reunions. One has to rub hands or touch one's forehead. It springs forth. It envelops you. It is probably stronger than we know. I think times are coming when I would want to pour out all that I walk around with. It seems like the paths are leading that way.'[62]

[61] Ruby Dreihorn, letter to the author, 18 March 1996.
[62] Perec Zylberberg, reflections, diary entry for 21 January 1993.

Even with the outpouring of published reminiscences, many boys were reluctant to contribute to the growing mass of Holocaust memoirs. It was as if their experiences were too personal, they had been too young, they did not want to disturb their lost parents and brothers and sisters. 'When I came to Israel,' Zvi Dagan, originally from Piotrkow, recalled, 'I decided to put the Holocaust behind me and only kept my thoughts occupied with providing for my family and being successful at business. The Holocaust only came back to me when my grandchildren (we have six) started to ask me questions and then I began to tell my story. Even today, my closest friends and business associates in Israel and abroad do not know my true story and all that I lived through.'[63]

Hugo Gryn confronted his past when he returned for two weeks in 1989 to his home town of Beregszasz to make a television film. He did not go alone; the director and producer of the film was his daughter Naomi, the associate producer was his daughter Rachelle. 'For me,' Naomi Gryn recalled, 'the peak moment was when we were standing in the derelict Jewish cemetery in the village of Vary, on the border with Hungary, where my father's father, Geza, was from, and we were saying Kaddish at the grave of a great-great-grandmother, Esther. The crew were packing up their gear. My father said to me: "Picture this, once there were hundreds of villages just like this all over the Carpathians". And I could picture it – his grandfather Jacob, with his white beard, who studied Torah and milked his cows; and his uncle who played the violin with the Gypsies on moonlit nights. I could picture villages full of laughter and life, where Jews had lived side by side with their non-Jewish neighbours for centuries. And at the same time I could picture his grandfather with my uncle Gaby – then only ten years old – forced to strip naked and walking hand in hand towards the gas chambers of Auschwitz. The next day we were filming in my grandfather's former vineyards. My father went off. I found him by a tree. He was crying. "It was so beautiful," he said, "I had such a beautiful childhood".'

In her search for photographs, Naomi Gryn asked all remaining thirty-five Jews of Beregszasz to bring whatever pictures they had to the Shabbat service at Beregszasz's last functioning synagogue. 'One woman brought this one picture. My father looked at it and paled. It was as if he had seen a ghost. There was my uncle Gaby in the back row with his class. It was as if Gaby had found a way to get into the film as well, and brought his schoolmates too.'

The film, *Chasing Shadows*, was a sensitive portrayal of a lost world. It was first transmitted on Channel 4 in April 1991. It had been during Passover 1944 that the Jews of Beregszasz had been rounded up and

---

[63] Zvi Dagan (Mlynarski), letter to the author, 10 March 1996.

sent to the ghetto to await deportation; for that reason, the film was
transmitted during Passover. 'So much of the difficulty faced by the
boys,' Naomi Gryn reflected, 'has been trying to process their traumatic
past. Going back has been an essential part of that. As for me, I needed
to fill in the murky edges of my father's shadow, because it is part of
my shadow too, and I wanted to seek out and slay the Nazi monster
that has always haunted me – that's why I went.'[64]

In the summer of 1995 the boys celebrated the fiftieth anniversary of
their liberation, and their journey to Britain. They travelled to London
from many countries, and were welcomed at a reception given by Hugo
Gryn at the Seymour Hall of the West London Synagogue. On the
following night they held a dinner and dance in a London hotel. Sidney
Finkel, who had left Britain for the United States in 1951, flew in from
Illinois. 'This would be the first time I would see my old group again,'
he wrote. 'I was worried that they would not remember me. That they
might remember my most difficult days of adjustment after the war and
think badly of me.'

'We met in the social hall of a synagogue in the West End of London,'
Sidney Finkel continued. 'The place was crowded and I was very nervous.
I asked myself again, "Would they remember me?" If they didn't I could
tell them I was Issie's younger brother. They would surely remember
him. He was one of our leaders when we first came to England. His wife
was with us that evening. He had died in 1992.

'I threw myself into the crowd and began to feel excited. I now wanted
to meet up with the people who had shared my experiences in the
Piotrkow ghetto, with those who were with me in the work camps and
in Buchenwald, and on the train journey from Buchenwald to Theresienstadt. I had experienced so many lapses of memory when it came to my
past, I hoped this would be my chance to fill in some of the empty spaces.

'Once again I feared no one would remember me. This kept going
through my mind. To my amazement and delight many of the "guys",
fifty years later, not only remembered me but called out to me in my
Polish name, "Sevek"!! There was a lot of laughter, some tears at the
painful memories and much hugging. We shared a lot that day and it
was a VERY emotional and satisfying time. We shared joy and sadness.
Most overwhelming to me was that after being separated from them for
so long, I was once more reconnected and accepted as one of the "Boys".
It was easy to see that night that the "Boys" cared for and loved each
other. Our common suffering and experiences had bonded us together.
I left that party feeling happy that I had been accepted as one of the

---

[64] Naomi Gryn, in conversation with the author, 16 April 1996.

"Boys". I also realised that some good can come out of even the worst experiences.'

Of the fiftieth anniversary dinner on the following evening, Sidney Finkel wrote: 'It was not only a celebration of our fifty years of liberation, but even more. The evening demonstrated to me that we were here to celebrate life. These survivors who, fifty years ago, wore the torn clothes of their camps, and had not been able to have a bath for years at a time, were now resplendent in their fancy suits and accompanied by brilliantly attired wives in the best that the world could provide.

'The most miraculous happening of the evening was my finding a long-lost friend. I had a photograph with me that was taken in the Bedford hostel in 1945. I showed this picture to some of the "Boys". Krulik said, "That is Harry Suskin, he is sitting right over there." He pointed to a far-off table. Harry, or Herschel as I knew him, was also from Piotrkow. We went through the entire war together in the ghetto and later at Bugaj and Buchenwald. In Buchenwald he and I escaped from a building where Jews were placed and later exterminated.

'Harry and I were both on the infamous train journey to Terezin. We of course came to Windermere together. We lost track of each other when I was sent to school and Harry was studying to be a mechanic. Among the many with whom I went through the war, I was closest to Harry. When I arrived at his table he looked at me for a minute and very slowly exclaimed: "Sevek! I cannot believe it. I have been thinking about you."

'We had a great chat and arranged to see each other with our wives the next day. For me to have found my childhood friend was a real wonderment.'[65]

The boys also find delight in remembering those who helped them after their arrival in Britain, and with whom they try to maintain contact. Sometimes news of a figure from the past emerges unexpectedly and the very thought gives them pleasure. On such person is Fay Nachmani, who lives today in Israel, and with whom they had lost contact since the days when she was a helper at the Loughton hostel. Reuma Weizman, who had herself been helping at Loughton in Fay Nachmani's time, told the boys of Fay's whereabouts. Shortly after that, Fay herself wrote to Ben Helfgott from her home in Jerusalem: 'I have a photo, where you, with a group, went to the seaside. On it – you, Roman Halter, Moniek Goldberg, Bolek Gastfreund, Zvi Mlynarsky and Janek. What happened to Janek? At the time he had no relatives.[66]

[65] Sidney Finkel (Sevek Finkelstein), *Journal of the '45 Aid Society*, No. 19, December 1995.

[66] Janek (Jan Goldberger) did not find any surviving relatives. He lives today in London. The photograph mentioned by Fay Nachmani is reproduced here as plate 22.

'There was Bergmann, Kuszerman, Kutner.[67] And Jona and his brother.'

The 'Jona' (now John Fox) about whom Fay Nachmani asked now lives in Philadelphia. His brother Harry Fox lives in London; on 27 August 1995 his wife Annie gave birth to their daughter, Lucy Janet Rhoda Fox. The name Rhoda was chosen because it was that of her father's sister, Rhoda Fuks, who was murdered at Treblinka at the age of ten.

Fay Nachmani continued: 'There were two who played at the Yiddish Theatre.' One of the two boys whom she remembered from the days when he played at the Yiddish Theatre was Selig Rosenblatt, from Warsaw. He later fought in the Israeli War of Independence, and, returning to Britain, became a businessman in London, where he died in 1976. The second boy was Joe Rentz (formerly Ratz) from Rzeszow; today he is a businessman living in Brighton. Two other boys from the Loughton hostel who also played in the Yiddish Theatre were Izzie Light, from Lodz (now living in Toronto) and Benny Newton (Neustatter), originally from the town of Skarzysko, a Londoner, who died in 1992.

Fay Nachmani went on to ask Ben Helfgott: 'How is Roman doing, haven't heard from him in a long time, hope he is okay and successful in his artistic occupation. How are you yourself doing?'[68]

Ben was able to reply that Roman Halter continues to do magnificent works of art in stained glass, painting and metalwork; and I was able to write to Fay that Ben remains the active chairman of the '45 Aid Society, masterminding its meetings and reunions, and ensuring that the boys' charitable work is unstinting: and that he is also an active adviser to the Imperial War Museum, London, where a Holocaust museum is being built.[69]

The fiftieth anniversary reunion served as a moment when all the boys recalled their murdered loved ones. In the reunion brochure several pages recall and honour murdered families. Krulik Wilder dedicated a page to his mother Chaja, his father Lajb and his sister Basia: 'We shall never forget them'. Pinchas Gutter dedicated a page to his parents Menachem Mendel and Helena Chaja Gutter, his sister Sabina, his grandparents Shimshom and Mirel Silberstein, and Itzhak Meir Gutter, and his cousin Noah Gutter. 'Let's hope,' he added, 'that there will be an end to suffering for all the oppressed people of our world.'[70]

---

[67] Herszel (Harry) Bergmann lives today in New York. Szlama Kuszerman lives in Israel. Icek Kutner, from Lodz, went to Canada, where he died in 1989.

[68] Fay Nachmani, letter to Ben Helfgott, 20 April 1996.

[69] The author to Fay Nachmani, 12 May 1996.

[70] ''45 Aid Society (Holocaust Survivors) 50th Annual Dinner and Ball', *Souvenir Brochure*, 30 April 1995.

Krulik Wilder and Pinchas Gutter were among the boys who were even then writing accounts of their wartime experiences. It was not easy for any of those who did so to describe, even after fifty years, the full extent of their personal, family suffering. 'It was too distressing to put it down,' Salamon Winogrodzki told me at the reunion. 'I didn't do it for fifty years. But I'm glad I did it – for my daughter.'[71]

Alec Ward was likewise hesitant to set anything down. 'As requested, I enclose my story, which I found very stressful to write,' he commented in response to my appeal for material. His own story, like so many, encompassed life in the ghetto, the murder of those closest to him, slave labour, and a terrible final death march. 'I am not able to watch any form of violence on the television,' he commented.[72]

'This is the first time I have truly recorded my thoughts,' John Fox wrote to me, enclosing his recollections. 'Yet I realise, with each passing year, the importance of these recollections for future generations. You will forgive me if my memory of fifty years ago is not 100% accurate. My intentions are sincere regardless.'[73]

John Fox's caveat is a salutary one; but when the same event is described by two or more boys who witnessed it, the remarkable thing is how similar the accounts usually are. Memory, which can so often play false, seems to be particularly sharp when events of such horror are recalled. A greater problem is the nature of the horror. 'During this entire period,' Jack Rubinfeld wrote, 'I witnessed the most bestial, gory, and cruel behaviour of man against man. I am still not able fully to write about this.'[74]

After their London reunion in 1995, two hundred members of the '45 Aid Society travelled to Israel, just as a hundred of them had done ten years earlier, for 'a very emotional gathering with our boys there', Howard Chandler, from Toronto, recalled.[75] While the boys were in Israel, Alec Ward was asked to lay their wreath on the memorial in Jerusalem to the six million murdered Jews, including one and a half million children. Many of those children would have been the same age as the boys who were commemorating them. The boys are so few, and those of their contemporaries who were murdered were so many; so many lives cut short before they could finish their schooling, or earn their living, or marry, or have children, or become, as so many of the boys have become, grandparents. The boys, as they gather at their

[71] Salamon Winogrodzki, in conversation with the author, 30 April 1995.
[72] Alec Ward, 'My Story', manuscript, sent to the author, 31 May 1995.
[73] John Fox (Jona Fuks), letter to the author, 3 October 1994.
[74] Jack Rubinfeld, 'Jack Rubinfeld', manuscript, sent to the author, undated.
[75] Howard Chandler (Chaim Wajchendler), letter to the author, 26 February 1996.

reunions, are a powerful reminder of just how much was destroyed.

Alec Ward wrote, after his return from Israel, in response to my request for recollections: 'I shall never forget or forgive what the Nazis did to six million Jewish people during 1939–1945, including almost my entire family. I decided after the war not to hate anyone. To have lived with hatred in my heart for the last fifty years would have been self-destructive, which was what the Nazis would have wanted. It was very painful for me to write this story, but the fact that I succeeded in outwitting the ingenuity of the Nazi plan to destroy me is giving me a great amount of satisfaction.'[76]

Each boy reflects on his experiences in different ways, returning again and again to the theme of responsibility. 'While my behaviour towards individual Germans and Poles is very forgiving,' Jack Rubinfeld wrote, 'I am fully aware of the enthusiastic participation by the majority of Germans, Poles, and Ukrainians in the hatred and gross mistreatment of the Jews. As a group, I have not forgiven them. For me, the main responsibility lies within Catholic, Eastern Orthodox and Protestant clergy and churches, that planted and nourished the seeds of this hatred. After so many generations of calculated cultivation, it became part of their genes or cultural landscape. Unfortunately for the believers, even hell is an absolute truth.'[77]

More than half a century after liberation, Ben Helfgott reflected: 'On the one hand we have recovered. On the other hand we have been damaged, a damage that is not outwardly visible. We have integrated so well that even our families are not aware of our trauma. There is not a day that goes by that does not evoke some painful memory of the past. Germans should see that the damage is still there. Nothing, but nothing, has eased the suffering. We are human beings who understand, but we cannot forgive. As I get older it haunts me more. It preys on my mind. What went through my mother's mind when she was taken to be shot? I keep thinking about it. It doesn't affect my getting on with my life, but it keeps coming back to me. In the end there is no one-hundred-per-cent recovery. Every time I read of some atrocity, whether it is in Ireland, Africa or Bosnia, or a random killing like that of the schoolchildren at Dunblane in Scotland, I feel for those who are left to grieve. And at that time I cannot help recalling those nearest and dearest to me who were killed so young and were so innocent.'[78]

Two days later, Ben Helfgott returned to this theme. 'I can't get over

[76] Alec Ward, 'My Story', manuscript, sent to the author, 31 May 1995.
[77] Jack I. Rubinfeld, letter to the author, 26 March 1996.
[78] Ben Helfgott, in conversation with the author, 28 March 1996.

it. It hurts me more and more. My mother and my little sister being taken away to be shot. It hurts. It is agonising. What were they thinking? We boys of the '45 Aid Society may have led a full life. We have enjoyed the luxury of living. But we lost our parents when we were young. We did not have the pleasure of sharing our life with them – our achievements and our disappointments. There was always the missing ingredient of not being able to share with the people who brought me into this world. It is not something you can ever run away from. We have risen above it. We have attacked adversity. But the family life that could have been was denied us. We had a taste of it when we were young. That is why the memory is so painful. It gets worse. I do not talk about it, but I feel like screaming, and saying, "Why? Why? Why?" '[79]

The boys who met for their fifty-first anniversary reunion on 5 May 1996 were in both festive and reflective mood. As usual, those who could not come sent messages from afar. From the United States, Michael Perlmutter wrote to Alec Ward: 'Give our regards to Salek and Ciciek, and please tell them I miss you all!'[80]

Zvi Dagan and Menachem Silberstein had come to the reunion from Israel. 'I left England in 1948,' Menachem Silberstein mused. 'Ever since I always felt I had a little bit of England in me. I never knew what it was until tonight. Now I know – it was the boys. They are my England.'[81]

Maurice Vegh came from the United States. A boy from Rakhov in Ruthenia, and from Polton House in Scotland, for him it was the first-ever reunion. 'It was really like meeting my family all over again,' he said. 'It is like coming home – to the family.' That some of the boys whom he had known in his Polton House days had died was a source of great sadness to him. 'Some of them are not here,' he said simply. He had been worried before the dinner whether anyone would remember him. 'Some of them, I didn't recognise, they recognised me. It was very, very emotional for me, because at that time we had nobody, we only had each other, and we were like brothers and sisters, and that is why I feel so close to everybody here.'[82]

Joseph Moss, from the southern Polish hill town of Krosno, has been going to every reunion for many years. 'It is a special bond to have survived with all of them together,' he said. 'That's why I come here

[79] Ben Helfgott, in conversation with the author, 30 March 1996.

[80] Michael Perlmutter to Alec Ward, 2 May 1996. Salek and Ciciek: Salek Benedikt, from Lodz, Wintershill Hall and the Finchley Road hostel; and his wife Ciciek, a survivor from Hungary.

[81] Menachem Silberstein, in conversation with the author, 5 May 1996.

[82] Maurice Vegh, filmed interview, 5 May 1996.

every year, to join in the celebration. We kept together and we survived together – that is a special spirit.'[83]

As the celebratory evening drew to its close, Michael Etkind reflected: 'We were much younger when we came to this country, and somehow the name "boys" remained. "The boys", "the boys" – and although there were a few girls as well, we became known as "the boys". It sounds a bit silly now, because I myself am seventy-one years old, but we went through the same experiences – similar, and yet different – and that is our bond. Some of the boys I may not see for a year or six months. I would say we are like brothers. That doesn't mean we don't have our quarrels. On the contrary, we do argue and have disagreements, and yet there is a bond because of our past.'[84]

To be one of the boys 'meant more', Roman Halter commented, 'than just having a cousin that you haven't seen. When I survived I found that I had an aunt and a cousin in Switzerland. I went there, and I felt a stranger to them, because they were just cousins – in name. Here, among the boys, we shared a certain experience together, many experiences, and that really brought us very much closer. When we needed to help one another, we didn't have to discuss it, we dug into our pockets and helped one another. I think going through that hell is such a sort of depth, that we all felt that we had started life again, and that we shared something that no other human being has shared.'[85]

That sense of sharing, and of delight in each other's company, was seen again a week after the fifty-first reunion, when, on 12 May 1996, David Herman, one of the boys from the Ruthenian town of Mukacevo, and his wife Olive, invited more than thirty of the boys, and their wives, to their daughter's wedding. To see the boys together, dancing with gusto, talking with zeal, and teasing each other with merciless fun, was to catch a glimpse of the bonds that bind them and of the affection that animates them until today.

In preparing their recollections, many boys found it difficult to tell their stories. Jack Rubinfeld wrote to me, in the aftermath of Ben Helfgott's appeal for recollections on my behalf: 'I have spent the last fifty years erasing and forgetting my unpleasant experiences of the war. For the last fifty years I believe that I have done it successfully. I have a great life and, I believe, a successful life. I am grateful every day. So forgive me for ignoring for so long Ben's pleadings that I write down my memories. After giving a talk to two hundred seventh-grade students

---

[83] Joseph Moss (Moszkowicz), filmed interview, 5 May 1996.
[84] Michael Etkind, filmed interview, 5 May 1996.
[85] Roman Halter, filmed interview, 5 May 1996.

last week in a local school, I was inspired. So I prepared this in a couple of days. I am not a writer, and had to proceed quickly so that I would not give up.'[86]

Of Lipa Tepper's preparation of his story, Ben Helfgott wrote: 'He found it very hard to do it; very, very hard to do it.'[87] Tepper had spent his first years in London as a baker. Then he had gone into the wholesale haberdashery business. From the smallest, most risky of beginnings, he flourished. In 1971 he married and shortly afterwards bought his first house. By the mid-1970s he was selling at annual trade exhibitions. He is proud that his eldest son is at university and his youngest son is in the business with him, 'making excellent progress through the ranks'. But just as it was hard for him to set down his story, so there are elements of the past that always remain with him. 'Life generally is not too bad,' he wrote in 1996, at the age of sixty-nine. 'I have a loving wife and two lovely sons. Unfortunately, I still look back to the horrific times and ask "WHY?"'[88]

Aron Zylberszac, a survivor of the Lodz ghetto, Auschwitz, and the death marches, wrote, forty-seven years after his last camp experience: 'You fall asleep and you dream about it. It all comes back. You are being chased by the Germans and then you wake up covered in sweat. Everything is soaked with fear. You have to get out of bed and change your pyjamas and bedclothes.'[89]

Ben Helfgott told the boys, at their forty-fourth reunion in May 1989: 'Most of us can be proud that soon after our liberation and our arrival in England, we harnessed all our energies and concentrated all our efforts on rebuilding and revitalising our lifeline and spiritual revival. We did not allow Hitler to enjoy a posthumous triumph over us. In our early upbringing our parents inculcated in us a deep sense of purpose, compassion and responsibility to our fellow citizens and this has stood us in good stead. No matter how much we were degraded and deprived of all vestiges of human dignity, we did not succumb to corruption. The idea of revenge hardly entered our minds nor were we consumed with hatred and venom.'[90]

Through the lives of so many of the boys, the traditions of pre-war Jewry live on. The destruction of family life, that warm cocoon for Polish and Hungarian Jewry, is remembered by the boys with great sadness. Rose

---

[86] Jack (Israel) Rubinfeld, letter to the author, undated (1995).

[87] Ben Helfgott, in conversation with the author, 30 March 1996.

[88] Lipa Tepper, letter to the author, 30 January 1996.

[89] Aron Zylberszac, recollections, transcript, Imperial War Museum Sound Archives, February 1991.

[90] Ben Helfgott, 'Chairman's Address', May 1989.

Kalman was the only one of six brothers and sisters to survive. While in England, she married and had two sons. One of her sons died at the age of twelve. 'When my husband died two and a half years ago,' she wrote, 'I was left alone with my second son. I often wonder how my life would have developed had there been no Holocaust. Having had brothers and sisters, we would have been a large family with uncles, aunties, cousins. As it turned out, my children never knew what it is like to have grandparents and cousins and uncles and aunts.'[91]

Every boy tries to come to terms with what he experienced. There are many questions, but no answers. Hunger and fear left their cruel mark. 'You can never come out of it,' Moishe Nurtman reflected. 'It is a terrible turmoil to inflict on a human being. Even today I am not a normal human being who was normally brought up with love and affection. We missed out on living as normal human beings. I am sure most of us still have a chip on our shoulder. It is difficult for me. I cannot understand. To me our persecutors were a bunch of animals who were able to get power to destroy just people. They were not human beings. It is difficult for me to analyse it, because I cannot understand it. Why kill me? Was Hitler better than me? Who was he to decide who should live or die? It is just difficult for me to accept the whole structure of the human element. I cannot understand it – in this century. The world had such great people in the past, and we allowed ourselves to be so vicious to one another. That I cannot understand.'[92]

The story of the boys, from their earliest childhood days in Europe, to their life and work today, is one that displays many elements of the troubled yet aspiring human condition. Before 1939 they were part of a settled world that, for all its problems, was evolving and even flourishing, before it was deliberately and irrevocably destroyed. They are the eyewitnesses of vanished communities and vanished patterns of life which Jews had practised for many centuries. Then, while the world around them was literally consumed in violence and fire, they were subjected to the tyranny of slave labour over a prolonged period, and saw the cruellest of tortures practised by one group of human beings on another. They survived, but only just; many of them were very near to death indeed at the moment of their liberation; some were in what might well have been their final coma, had liberation been delayed even by one more day.

The generous impulse which led the Central British Fund to bring the boys over to Britain created a bond and a focus among them that were

---

[91] Rose Kalman (Goldman), letter to the author, July 1995.
[92] Moishe Nurtman, letter to the author, March 1995.

in many ways unique. Some had known each other in their home towns and in the camps, but it was when they were brought together in Britain that the strong links between them were forged. These links have persisted to this day, unbroken, and indeed strengthened as the years pass. Their cohesion as a group is unusual in the extreme. Most of them had no other family when they reached Britain: their parents, and their closest relatives, had been murdered. First the hostels, then the Primrose Club, and in more recent decades the '45 Aid Society, became their home and the centre of their creative energies. It was in these surroundings that they renewed their lives, facing a very different world to the world of their youth; educating themselves, finding work, earning a living, marrying, raising families, and becoming an integral part of the communities in which they settled.

The past is an ever-present reality for the boys, as it is for all survivors. Yet they have not allowed its pain to embitter them, or to cloud over the constructive wellsprings of daily life, in which their own achievements have been considerable. Theirs are the achievements of new family circles in which their wives, deeply aware of their wartime torments, have played a pivotal part; and the achievements of friendships, many of them born in time of adversity, and which have been maintained and enhanced during fifty years of constructive enterprise and charitable endeavour.

'Fifty years on,' wrote Moniek Goldberg fifty years after liberation, 'I reflect that I could tell my father that I have not forgotten what I learned as a boy. I helped my fellow man when I could. I am proud to be a Jew, for I have seen man behave worse than beasts, but the Jews remembered Rabbi Hillel who taught us, "If you find yourself in a place where there are no men, you must strive to be a man." We were amongst the beasts, and I am proud to declare that we upheld the dignity of man.'[93]

---

[93] Joseph (Moniek) Goldberg, 'Biographical Sketch', manuscript, July 1995, sent to the author, 14 August 1995.

MAPS

1. Birthplaces

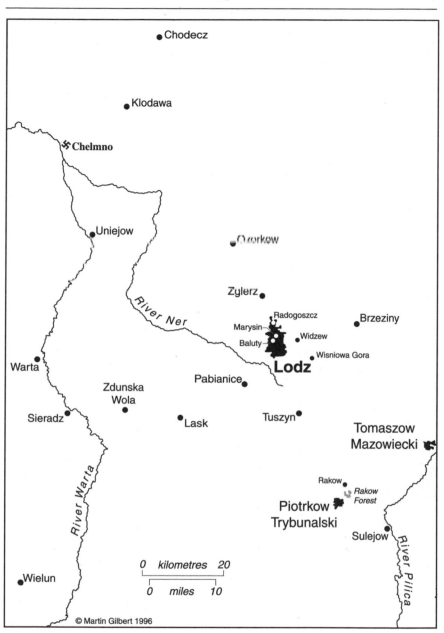

2. Birthplaces in and around Lodz

3. Birthplaces in and around Radom

The places in bold were Death Camps and places of mass murder mentioned in this book; the places in ordinary type were the locations of slave labour camps, almost all of them in German-occupied Poland, to which the people whose stories are told in this book were sent to forced labour.

GERMANY

Danzig

Stutthof

EAST PRUSSIA

0 kilometres 100
0 miles 60

River Vistula

Otoczno

Poznan

Chelmno

Treblinka

Warsaw

Lodz

POLAND

Szycki
Jedlinsk Kruszyn
Deblin

Sobibor

Rakow Bugaj
Piotrkow Hortensja
Strzalkow
Poniatowa

Breslau

Skarzysko-Kamienna

Lublin

Gross Rosen

Czestochowa
Blizyn

Majdanek
Trawniki

Czestochowianka
Warta

Budzyn

GERMANY

Laurahutte

Belzec

Gleiwitz
Strzemieszyce Wielkie
Sosnowiec

River Vistula
Huta Komorowska

CZECHOSLOVAKIA

Katowice
Auschwitz
Cracow

Mielec

Pustkow
Rzeszow

Szebnie

© Martin Gilbert 1996

Babice

Auschwitz

Buna

Birkenau Monowitz

Cracow
Jeruzolimska
Plaszow

River Vistula

Prokocim
Biezanow

Wola
Duchacka

Jawischowitz

0 kilometres 15
0 miles 10

© Martin Gilbert 1996

4. Slave labour camps on Polish soil

5. The Auschwitz region

6. Slave labour camps on German soil

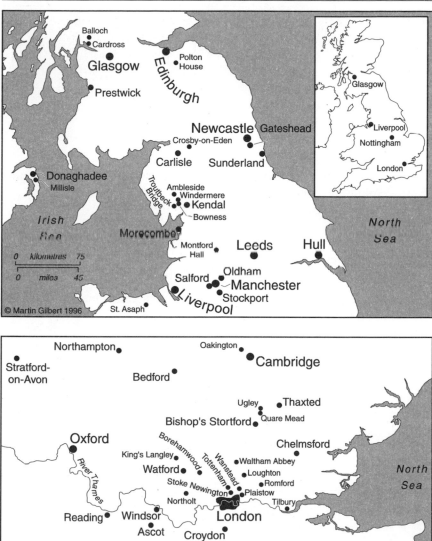

7. Havens and hostels

8. Havens and hostels in South-East England

GLOSSARY

Aleph-bet (alef-beis): the ABC
Aliyah: emigration (of Jews to the Land of Israel; the word means ascending, or going up)
Aliyah Bet: illegal immigration to Palestine (1939–48)
Appel: roll-call
Appel Platz: roll-call square; any place where a roll-call was held
Av Beth Din: head of the rabbinical court

Bachad: a Jewish youth group, the League of Religious Pioneers, founded in Germany in 1928
Bais Medrash (Bet Hamidrash): house of prayer
Bajrat (Beirat): Council of Elders (in the Lodz ghetto)
Balebusta: the woman in charge of a household
Bar Mitzvah: the ceremony for every Jewish male on reaching thirteen years of age
Bet Hamidrash: house of prayer
Bet Yakov: Jewish Orthodox school system for girls
Beth Din: rabbinical court
Block: a barrack in a concentration camp
Bnei Akiva: Orthodox Jewish youth group
Brit Milah: circumcision
BUND: Jewish socialist workers' party, and movement

CBF: Central British Fund (now World Jewish Relief)
Chaim: life (Hebrew)
Challah (chollah): plaited bread eaten on Friday night and during the Sabbath
Chaluzim: Zionist pioneers (in Palestine)
Chas ve-Challilah: Heaven forbid
Chazer: non-kosher food
Cheder: religious classes for children
Chulent: a traditional Saturday dish, prepared before the Sabbath
Chumash: the five books of Moses
Churban: the Holocaust (the word used in Yiddish; literally, Destruction)

Chutzpah: nerve, cheek
Cupke: headscarf

Davening: praying
Diaspora: the dispersal; places where Jews have lived outside the Land
    of Israel since the first and second destructions of the Temple
Divrei Torah: the sayings of the Torah
DP: Displaced Person (1945 and after)
Droshki: horse-drawn carriage

Ersatz: artificial

'Front-wheel skid': a Jew (London cockney rhyming slang for Yid)

Gan Eden: Garden of Eden
Gemara: discussions and elaborations on Biblical commentaries, par-
    ticularly of the Babylonian and Jerusalem Talmuds
Gestapo: Geheime Staatspolizei (Secret State Police), the German political
    police, headed, like the SS, by Himmler
Goy (Goyim): a non-Jew (non-Jews)
Grenz Schutz Politzei: German Border Police
Gymnasium: high school

Habonim: a Zionist socialist pioneer youth movement
Hachshara: preparation, usually in agriculture, prior to settlement in
    Palestine.
Häftling: prisoner
Hagana: Jewish defence force in Mandate Palestine, forming part of the
    Israel army from 1948
Hakenkreuz: swastika
Halva: a sweet made of sesame seed
Hashomer Hatzair: left-wing Zionist movement
Hassid: an orthodox Jew who follows the teachings of the Eastern
    European sage and religious leader, the Baal Shem Tov (died 1760),
    and his disciples and spiritual descendants. Among Hassidic centres
    in which some of The Boys lived before the war were Kozienice,
    Mukachevo, Opatow and Warka
Heimish: homely

Jewish Brigade: Jewish military formation within the British Army, est-
    ablished in 1944.
Jude: Jew

Kaddish: prayer for a dead person; recited at funerals, memorial services, synagogue services, the graveside, and on the anniversary of a death

Kapo: a prisoner put in charge of a barrack or work detail

Kapoteh: long black coat

Kashrut: the laws of the preparation and status of kosher food

Kibbutz: a Jewish communal farming settlement in Palestine (later Israel)

Kiddush: sanctification; the blessing over wine on the Sabbath

Kiddush Hashem: the sanctification of God's name; martyrdom

Kierowniczka: a woman director (of an orphanage or institution)

Kinderheim: Children's Home (in Theresienstadt)

Kindertransporte: flight of German Jewish children to Britain, 1938–9

KL: Konzentrationslager, concentration camp (also KZ)

Klapsedra: a black-edged death notice; an emaciated person near to death

Klezmer: traditional Eastern European Jewish music

Kol Nidre: the synagogue service on the first night of the Day of Atonement

Koppel (kippa): skull cap

Kosher: food acceptable to Jewish dietary laws, and cooked accordingly

Kvutzah: a small rural settlement in Palestine (Israel)

Lagerführer: male camp-director

Lagerführerin: woman camp-director

Landsleit: a person from the same town or region

Laufer: messenger boy

Lazaret: field hospital

Lockshen: noodles

Lox: smoked salmon

Ma Shlomech: the Hebrew greeting, How are you? (feminine, Ma Shlomcha)

Madrich: counsellor (feminine, madricha; plural, madrichim)

Magen David: Star of David (the five-pointed Jewish star)

MAHAL: foreign volunteers in Israel's War of Independence (1948–9)

Meister: an overseer in a labour camp

Melamed: teacher

Mensch: a decent fellow, a good person

Mezzuzah: the small ornamental box on a doorpost, containing extracts from the Old Testament. Pious Jews touch it, and say a prayer, on entering a house

Mikva (Mikveh): ritual bath

Minyan: the ten men needed to constitute a formal prayer meeting

Musulman (muzulman); a camp inmate who is near to death

Mutze: cap worn by concentration camp prisoners

Nyilas: the Hungarian Fascist organisation, active against the Jews of Hungary, and in particular Budapest, 1944–45

ORT: 'Society to Promote Trades and Agriculture', founded in Russia in 1889; today, a world-wide Jewish educational system, teaching trades to those who have left school

Palant: a children's ball game

Panzer-Faust: a hand-held anti-tank weapon

Parasha: the weekly portion of the Five Books of Moses read in synagogues on Saturday

Peklach: packages

Pessach: the festival of Passover, recalling the Exodus from Egypt

Peyot (payot): side curls worn by Orthodox Jews

Pirkey Avot : Ethics of the Fathers

Purim: the festival commemorating the rescue of the Jews of ancient Persia from Haman's determination to murder them

Rashi: the leading medieval Talmudic commentator. He was born in France in 1040 and died in 1105

Rebbe: a learned man

Rollkommando: a detachment of trucks used for deportations (Lodz ghetto)

Rosh Hashana: Jewish New Year

SS: Schutz Staffel ('protective squad'), the organisation, headed by Himmler, responsible for concentration camps and racial policy

Second Generation: children of Holocaust survivors

Seder night: the first night of Passover

Shabbas, Shabbes (in Hebrew, Shabbat): the Sabbath, starting on Friday night

She'erit Hapleta: immigrants to Palestine, many of them survivors of the Holocaust, who reached the country illegally according to British laws

Shema Israel: Hear! O Israel; the principal prayer in the daily liturgy, also the phrase traditionally said at the point of death.

Shoah: the Hebrew word for Holocaust, meaning, the Catastrophe

Shochet (shoichet): ritual slaughterer

Shtetl: a Jewish community, either a town or village
Shtiebl: a small house of prayer
Shul: synagogue
Siddur: prayer book
Simchat Torah: the festival of the Rejoicing of the Law
SKiF: the children's organisation of the Jewish socialist workers' movement (the BUND)
Sonderkommando: a special unit
Star of David: the five-pointed star, used by the Germans to identify and isolate Jews; later the centre of the flag of the State of Israel
Succoth: the harvest festival
Szpera (German, Sperre): curfew

Tahara: purification of a dead body, in preparation for burial
Tallit (taless): prayer shawl
Talmud: early and comprehensive interpretation and elaboration of the Old Testament. The Babylonian Talmud, dating from the third century, consists of some two and a half million words on 5,894 folio pages. Its Mediterranean counterpart was the Jerusalem Talmud.
Tanach: the Old Testament; a Hebrew acronym of Torah (the Five Books of Moses), Nevi'im (Prophets) and Ketuvim (Hagiographa, or Writings)
Tarbut: Hebrew-language school system, widespread in Eastern Europe before the war
TB: tuberculosis
Tefilin: phylacteries, small leather boxes containing biblical texts, worn on the forehead and arm during weekday morning prayers
Tefillah: prayers
Torah: God's teachings, as revealed to Moses on Mount Sinai; the moral, ethical and legal basis of Judaism
Toteskommander: the prisoner in charge of removing dead bodies
TOZ: a Jewish agency in Poland devoted to the health of youngsters
Treife: unkosher
Tz'doko (tzedaka): charity

Umschlagplatz: ('reloading point'), the railway siding in Warsaw used for the deportation of Jews to Treblinka
UNRRA: United Nations Relief and Rehabilitation Administration

Volksdeutsche: ethnic Germans; groups living outside the borders of Germany for several centuries, mostly in Poland, Hungary, Rumania and southern Russia, still speaking German, and feeling some affinity with Germany

Wechsel Schicht: changeover shift
Wehrmacht: the German Army
Werkschutz: Germans and Ukrainians over military age conscripted as armed guards

Yad Vashem: the Holocaust memorial and museum in Jerusalem
Yeshiva: a school for the study of Orthodox Judaism
Yiddish: the lingua franca of Polish and East European Jews, derived from medieval German, and incorporating many Hebrew words.
Yizkor: memorial prayer or service: the prayer for the dead
Yom Kippur: the Day of Atonement
Ypsilon: the letter 'y'

Zemirot (zmiros): songs of prayer for the Sabbath
Zimmerleute: construction workers

'BOYS' WHO HAVE DIED SINCE 1945

Henry Abisch
Jack Banach
John Belmont
Moshe Besserman
Harry Braffman
Avraham Broch
Jack Bulka
Sam Cooper
David Denderowicz
Ignatz Deutsch
Solly Deutsch
Bernard Dreihorn
Hersh Engel
Issy Finkelstein
Michael Flash
Menachem Freikorn
Edzia Fridel (née
   Warszawska)
Norman Friedman
Leo Frydenberger
Galka
Chaim Geller
Jack Glickson
Fredy Goldman

Leon Grossman
Majer Guterman
Abe Herman
Moishe Herszlikowicz
I. Jakob
Alek Kadasiewicz
Jack Kahan
Fiszel Kampel
Bernard Katz
S. Korman
Jack Krowicki
Jasiek Kurtz
Binem Kuszer
Icek Kutner
Guta Levine (née
   Dawidowicz)
Oscar Lister
Bruno Meier
Benny Newton
Schloimo
   Pantoffelmacher
Masza Platt (née
   Dobrowolska)
Baruch Pollack

Yitzchak Pomeranc
Jerzy Poznanski
Mietek Putermilch
Kopel Radzinski
Leo Robeson
Isidore Rosenblat
Selig (Jimmy) Rosenblatt
Joe Rubinstein
Yaacov Satz
Zenek Schwartzberg
Moniek Seligfeld
Moniek Shapiro
Chaskiel Slomovic
David Sommer
Icky Stein
Jacob Stobiecki
Sam Swimmer
Eliash Szajnberger
Lola Tarko (née
   Goldhersz)
Sam Tenenbaum
Nat Wald
David Wiernik
Julek Zylberger

INDEX

Compiled by the author